THE BEST PLAYS OF 1997–1998

THE OTIS GUERNSEY
BURNS MANTLE
THEATER YEARBOOK

THE BEST PLAYS OF
1997–1998

EDITED BY OTIS L. GUERNSEY JR.

Illustrated with photographs and
with drawings by HIRSCHFELD

LIMELIGHT EDITIONS

EDITOR'S NOTE

ON FEBRUARY 2, 1998, in New York City at the Gershwin Theater, the editor of this, the 79th volume in the *Best Plays* series of theater yearbooks, received the Theater Hall of Fame's Founders Award for contribution to the theater. The editor told those gathered for the Hall's annual awards ceremony, "*Best Plays* is a form of applause for everything the theater does, a superb means of expressing admiration for the theater and everybody in it. And as I'm sure you realize, it isn't a solo show. It takes the cooperation of the whole theater community as well as the dedicated concentration of more than a dozen people. Many of you know who they are and know that I'm speaking for them as well as myself when I thank the Hall of Fame directors for this gracious recognition of our efforts. It surely inspires us to keep on doing our best."

So that everyone may be reminded of who they are, here is the roster of today's *Best Plays* regulars who have energetically provided the comprehensive coverage, some for decades, which won this award. They have made their love for the theater manifest in yet another intimately detailed portrayal of an American theater year in this present volume. They are listed below in the order of seniority of their association with our series.

Al Hirschfeld is our senior associate both in contribution to *Best Plays* and, at 95, in age. His uniquely witty and stylish drawings characterizing the highlights of each theater year have adorned the *Best Plays* volumes since 1953, a 46-volume treasure trove of graphic artistry.

Jonathan Dodd, the former president of Dodd, Mead (publisher of the *Best Plays* series from 1920 to 1987) has been overseeing the publication of these yearbooks since long before the present editor joined the project. That he continues to do so is the major reason why the series is able to continue in full stride year after year.

Of the five critics who have edited the *Best Plays* series, Henry Hewes had the shortest tenure—three volumes, 1961–1963—but the most profound influence. He increased the size of the volume, while appropriately increasing the scope and sophistication of its whole theater coverage. He set a new standard for any editor who follows him. At present, himself a Hall of Fame Founders Award winner, he supervises our Hall of Fame listing and provides input on a wide range of matters.

Rue E. Canvin, a former member of the New York *Herald Tribune* drama department staff, has been with *Best Plays* since the present editor took over the series.

She was materially helpful in getting the new regime off the ground and has continued with several responsibilities, including the list of publications and the necrology.

The annual burden of combing the production listings for the inevitable knots of typographical and other errors is borne bravely and efficiently by Dorianne D. Guernsey, the editor's wife. But this is only the most conspicuous of the ways, in their infinity, in which she has enhanced each and every volume from 1964–65 on.

Camille Croce Dee's listing of off-off-Broadway productions—unrivaled in the breadth and accuracy of its record of onstage doings in the tributary playhouses— has adorned this volume annually since 1975. As the assistant editor of *Best Plays,* she has also taken on many other chores of collecting and editing the material for our ATCA, cross-country and Facts and Figures sections.

Thomas T. Foose began writing letters to the *Best Plays* editor in the early 1980s containing interesting historical footnotes to some of each season's productions. We have been sharing them with our readers, in the form of parenthetical inserts in our coverage of the New York season. For example, one recent Broadway production of a foreign script was nominated for a best-play Tony on the grounds that it had never been produced here before. We listed it in *Best Plays* as a revival that had been fully produced in New York under a different title. We had Mr. Foose's word on it.

All of the individuals who prepare synopses of our featured bests and prize-winning plays are themselves authors of produced plays or motion pictures. Sally Dixon Wiener, a distinguished and much-produced playwright, has been doing synopses for *Best Plays* for more than a decade. Her work has included all the August Wilson plays to date and Tina Howe's *Pride's Crossing* in this volume.

From the mid-1980s to the late 1990s Jeffrey Sweet's incomparably perceptive reviews of each New York theater season led off our coverage, and his choices of each of those season's ten Best Plays stand tall in the historical record. He is now devoting most of his time to playwriting (his *Flyovers* was a major hit in Chicago this season), but he continues to provide play synopses like that of *The Beauty Queen of Leenane* in this volume.

Mel Gussow, distinguished drama critic, selects and describes the highlights of each off-off-Broadway season. His handful of special citations of the very, very best are a valued accolade which we celebrate annually in a photo layout, to emphasize the impact and importance of the work being done in New York's smaller play-houses.

Melvyn B. Zerman's Limelight Editions, publisher of books on many theater subjects, has produced and distributed the last seven volumes of *Best Plays,* including this one, with the most conscientious and sensitive understanding of the series's editing independence and value to the theater community.

Jeffrey A. Finn took over our section on major cast replacements in 1993. He has run it with traditional *Best Plays* accuracy and scope and has expanded it to include, along with the current Broadway and off-Broadway holdovers and their road companies, the complete casting of first class road productions which are *not* spinoffs from recent New York shows.

Michael Grossberg is the most recent in the succession of chairmen of the American Theater Critics Association's playreading committee, which selects ATCA's annual awards and citations. In our experience, he is unmatched in processing this material promptly and thoroughly for the introduction to our section on new plays produced in cross-country theater.

David Lefkowitz had contributed a Best Play synopsis before he joined us, in the 1996–97 season, as the author of our report on the highlights of the Broadway and off-Broadway scene. He is an eminently qualified theater critic, reporter and enthusiast, a staff writer for *Playbill On-Line,* with a B.F.A. and M.F.A. in playwriting, film and television and with his own theater newsletter, *This Month on Stage,* now in its seventh year.

Add to the efforts of these associates the cooperation of the entire theater community from coast to coast, and with any luck you can come up with a *Best Plays* theater yearbook. It starts with the press agents, whose patient and generous distribution of information makes modern theater reporting possible. It peaks in the inspiration of playwrights whose talents make American theater activity well worth experiencing, let alone recording, and in between there are many individuals who help us in special ways. The secretary of the New York Drama Critics Circle (at present Michael Kuchwara of the AP) diligently supplies us with the complicated record of his colleagues' voting for the bests of each year, and William Schelble makes sure that our listing of the Tonys is full and correct. Reviews of each of the three major ATCA selections are an important annual feature of our coverage, this year provided by Misha Berson, Michael Grossberg and Christopher Rawson. Ralph Newman of the Drama Book Shop is annually helpful to Miss Canvin in compiling her lists of published plays. Volunteers who have gone out of their way to provide us with information on other awards include Tish Dace (American Theater Wing Design Awards), Joan M. Kaloustian (Chicago's Jefferson Awards and Citations), Edwin Wilson (Susan Smith Blackburn Prizes), David Rosenberg (Connecticut Critics) and Caldwell Titcomb (Boston's Elliot Norton Awards). Julie Taymor and the Disney staff have generously provided this volume with bounteous illustrations of Taymor designs for *The Lion King.* And we can give our readers a good idea of what the 1997–98 season looked like when house lights went out and curtains rose in New York and from coast to coast in the work of the stage photographers included in this issue: Judy Andrews, Robert Armin, Catherine Ashmore, Patrick Bennett, Michael Brosilow, Sharl Cohen, Michael Cooper, Paula Court, Marianne Courville, Michal Daniel, T. Charles Erickson, Ric Evans, Richard Feldman, Glen Frieson, Tim Fuller, Gerry Goodstein, Ken Howard, Sherman M. Howe Jr., John Johnson, Ivan Kyncl, Liz Lauren, James Leynse, Joan Marcus, Orlando Marra, Dan Rest, Carol Rosegg, Peter Rybolt, Diane Sobolewski, Marty Sohl, Paul H. Taylor, Richard Trigg, Dan Vaillancourt and Kymm Zuckert.

We offer our most sincere and admiring thanks to all of the above, whose contributions to *Best Plays* have won all of us the recognition of the Theater Hall of Fame.

OTIS L. GUERNSEY Jr.

September 1, 1998

CONTENTS

Drawings by HIRSCHFELD

THE SEASON
ON AND OFF
BROADWAY

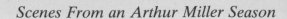

Above, Anthony LaPaglia in his Tony-winning performance in Roundabout's Tony-winning revival of Arthur Miller's *A View From the Bridge; right,* Tari Signor and Peter Falk in Signature Theater's world premiere of Miller's *Mr. Peters' Connections; below,* the author *(wearing glasses),* who was honored with 1998 Lortel, Drama Desk and PEN Awards for life-time achievement, at a rehearsal of Signature's revival of his *The American Clock* with artistic director James Houghton *(on Miller's right)* and company

BROADWAY AND OFF BROADWAY
By David Lefkowitz

CALL IT The Energizer Season. It just kept going and going and going . . .

Over the years, New York critics have learned to set their watches by the tick and tock of the theater season. There's the late-innings frenzy during Tony time, then it's basically quiet until mid-September, when major off-Broadway troupes start their seasons and Broadway lines up heavy hitters for holiday traffic. Crunchtime continues through Christmas, followed by another fallow period as productions beg for patronage in the dead of winter. Then, of course, comes springtime madness all over again. It's a silly system, really, lumping as it does so many important productions together with no time to enjoy each show's specialness. By the end of the peak weeks, bleary-eyed critics need two months to vegitate, commiserate and snoop around Theater Row for buried treasure.

1997-98 was the year vacation never came. Several of the season's biggest shows opened in mid-winter, and productions casting an eye toward Broadway—including *Chita and All That Jazz, Jane Eyre* and *Dreamgirls*—couldn't reach the starting gate because theaters were full. Only in June, after the season ended, did houses begin to open up.

I took some ribbing from my colleagues for beginning last year's *Best Plays* introduction with "Oh, happy season!", owing to an abundance of shows and of good, interesting playwriting. A year later, even the most jaded of the jaded had to admit New York theater was on a roll. Reasons for the renaissance are numerous and intertwined:

*A booming stock market—records seemingly set weekly—gave investors money to burn;

*Mayor Rudolph Giuliani, for all his unfortunate slips into Big-Brotherdom, significantly lowered the crime rate, cleaned the streets, and actually got the MTA to institute subway discounts;

*Long-running musicals brought families and prom-permed teens to the box office, as *Cats* became the longest-running show in Broadway history, 6,138 performances on June 19;

*Construction by Disney, Livent and The New 42nd Street Inc. transported Times Square from the blinking neon of a flophouse to the flashing neon of an arcade;

3

The 1997–98 Season on Broadway

PLAYS (4)

Proposals
Jackie
The Old Neighborhood
Golden Child
(revised version)

MUSICALS (10)

Side Show
Triumph of Love
The Scarlet Pimpernel
THE LION KING
MSG Productions:
  A Christmas Carol
  (return engagement)
  The Wizard of Oz
  (return engagement)
Street Corner Symphony
RAGTIME
The Capeman
High Society

FOREIGN PLAYS (5)

ART
The Herbal Bed
THE BEAUTY QUEEN
  OF LEENANE
  (transfer)
Honour
The Judas Kiss

FOREIGN MUSICALS (3)

Forever Tango
Umbatha: The Zulu
  Macbeth
The Last Empress

REVIVALS (12)

1776
The Cherry Orchard
Lincoln Center:
  Ivanov
  Ah, Wilderness!
  The Diary of Anne Frank
The Sunshine Boys
Roundabout:
  A View From the Bridge
  Cabaret
  The Deep Blue Sea
The Sound of Music
The Chairs
Wait Until Dark

SPECIALTIES (2)

Riverdance
  (return engagement)
Radio City Christmas
  Spectacular

SOLO SHOW (1)

Freak

Categorized above are all the new productions listed in the Plays Produced on Broadway section of this volume. Plays listed in CAPITAL LETTERS were major 1997–98 prizewinners or specially cited by *Best Plays*. Plays listed in *italics* were still running on June 1, 1998.

*Actress-turned-talk show host Rosie O'Donnell, building on high ratings when she hosted the 1997 Tony Awards, continued to promote Broadway on her show, motivating other morning news and late-night variety programs to do the same.

It seemed every time you turned around, League of American Theaters and Producers executive director Jed Bernstein was offering the same soundbytes: Broadway brings in more money than all the New York sports teams combined . . . The number of people who took in a Broadway production is greater than the total combined populations of the U.S.'s ten largest cities . . . For all the temptations of home technology, people still want live, "real time" entertainment.

Bernstein had reason to crow. After the record grosses of 1996-97, Broadway zoomed from riches to riches. By December 1997, receipts were up 6.4 percent over the same period in 1996, and attendance rose 2.7 percent to 5.1 million. Also, with holiday grosses exceeding $30.4 million, Broadway had its merriest Christmas/Chanukah ever.

The news only got better by the beginning of June. Broadway hit another all-time attendance high at 11.5 million (up from 10.6 million the year before and up 400,000 from the record 1980-81 season). Box office receipts exceeded spring predictions, increasing 11.7 percent over the year before to $558 million. Fewer Broadway shows actually opened (37 to the previous season's 44, by *Best Plays* count), but with *Ragtime* and *The Lion King* playing in capacious new houses, with holdovers *Chicago* and *Rent* near-sellouts all year, and with the unsinkable cash cows of the Mackintosh era, the potential for profit-taking was fairly limitless—for the lucky few. The downside of this gold rush was that, economically, most new Broadway shows failed miserably, even when they received critical huzzahs. David Henry Hwang's Tony-nominated *Golden Child* lost a producer in previews, got *another* producer (Talia Shire) before it opened and did 33 percent business until it quickly died a week before the Tonys. A smashing revival of *1776* also scored a best-revival Tony nomination, only to shutter $3 million in the red in June because it moved from the cozy Roundabout mainstage to the cavernous Gershwin Theater. Other unexpected money losers were Neil Simon's *Proposals*, the English dramas *Honour* and *The Herbal Bed,* and the new musicals *Triumph of Love* and *Side Show*.

Average paid admission went up again, to $48.58 (from $47.24), with audiences gouged even further by several shows (including *The Sound of Music* and *Ragtime*) tacking on a $1 "restoration" fee dedicated, we were told, to theater upkeep. By season's end, rumors were already swirling that top tickets on hot nights would soon hit the $80 mark. It was anti-climactic news, though, since Livent blew the lid off the pricing game earlier in the year by offering $125 "VIP Suite Service" to its expensive epic, *Ragtime*. Theatergoers with the extra bucks could enjoy a center orchestra seat, a souvenir program, complementary beverages, a light snack, access to a special lounge and, best of all, use of "private washroom facilities." Livent spokespersons defended the package deal by saying it was similar to incentives long offered at sports and concert arenas. Also, charging tippy-top dollar to those ready and willing to pay allowed the show to keep its cheap seats at a relatively affordable $31.

HONOUR—A highlight of the 1997–98 season was Jane Alexander's return to Broadway (after championing the arts with great honor as head of the NEA in Washington) in a Tony-nominated performance *(as above)* in Joanna Murray-Smith's appropriately titled play

Strong as *Ragtime* was at the box office, Livent would have had to charge $3,100 a seat to start recouping the company's losses for the past two years. Garth Drabinsky had wanted to build Livent into a theater empire, controlling everything from development to production to licensing to touring. Nice idea, but the results had the company posting a $30 million loss in 1997 and another $20 million for first quarter 1998. Trapped, Drabinsky found a savior in former "super-agent" Mike Ovitz, who invested $20 million (U.S.) in Livent—for a 12 percent share of the company. Drabinsky also surrendered his CEO title to Roy Furman, of the investment firm Furman Selz LLC. This pushed Drabinsky down to vice chairman and chief creative director for live theater.

And yet, for some, money was no object. Despite being pelted with the worst reviews of the year, and despite playing to half-empty houses, *The Scarlet Pimpernel* carried on as if it were a huge hit. The Frank Wildhorn musical opened in November 1997 and was still running at press time—incredibly—at a $10 million loss.

Musicals: The Season Starts With a Dance—And a Disaster

Auspiciously, 1997-98 began with a show that was still playing after the season ended. *Forever Tango,* yet another example of New York theatergoers' insatiable craving for Spanish dance, opened June 19 at the Walter Kerr Theater. Footwork was impeccable, as sleek as the shines on the men's brilliantined hair and as flowing as the ladies' black and silver gowns. Audiences didn't seem to mind that between every three-minute dance number came a five-minute instrumental by the tango orchestra. Fun as it was to watch sad-eyed, droopy-cheeked bandoneon player Lisandro Adrover squeeze his squeezebox as if it were a lost child, two hours of Galician elevator music was one hour too many. Nevertheless, the core audience for *Forever Tango* was so strong, when Paul Simon's *The Capeman* closed in tatters at the giant Marriott Marquis Theater, *Tango* swept in without missing a beat.

Ah, but *pobrecito Capeman!* Everything that could go wrong with a major new Broadway musical did. Or, as *Village Voice* critic Michael Feingold put it, "A titanic mishap for which Paul Simon, the H. Bruce Ismay of this disaster, should receive more blame than pity." *The New Yorker's* Nancy Franklin also waxed metaphorical: "Here, where there's smoke, there's no corresponding fire of insight, ideas, interpretation—there are only damp, sputtery logs of received non-wisdom." These logs cost $11 million and rolled, turbulently, for a mere two months, January 29 to March 28.

To be fair, the press had their knives out long before the first preview. Simon, one of pop music's most bankable commodities, made the mistake of telling interviewers he wanted to do the show his way and not fall into the glitz and fakery that, for better or worse, make most Broadway musicals go. After all, he had a Nobel prizewinning poet, Derek Walcott, for a librettist and a mostly-Hispanic cast that didn't look or act like typical Broadway hoofers. What the press saw was a pop star who had never done a musical before thumbing his nose at a tight community of legends who put their reputations on the line every opening night. Had rehearsals gone smoothly and the show gone well, all the bad press in the world couldn't have stopped Simon's fans from turning out in full force for his theatrical debut. The first preview, however, removed any illusions that Simon would take Broadway by storm. Reports filtered back that *The Capeman,* based on the life of convicted killer Salvador Agron, was three hours long, lacked any semblance of a plot structure, featured direction that had the actors standing about in a state of paralysis and, for novelty, brought in Lazarus, a white-robed, Jesus-like figure given to wandering the barrio uninvited and staying to sing and moralize.

Official denials of trouble flew out of the show's press office, but as critics' previews neared, panic set in, and the opening was delayed three weeks. As if that weren't revenge enough for the New York theater community, word soon leaked out librettist Walcott was off the project, and director and choreographer Mark Morris had been booted in favor of . . . Jerry Zaks. So much for shooting the old horses and letting the colts run the stable.

Zaks worked wonders, but not miracles. A good half hour was shaved off the show, dance numbers had more pizzazz, a story line began to emerge, Bob Crowley's sets and Wendall K. Harrington's projections received gasps of awe, and a "Songs From *The Capeman*" CD, featuring Simon and other pop artists on such tunes as "Born in Puerto Rico" and "Satin Summer Nights," climbed the charts. On the other hand, the plot was still a dramatically unmotivated mess; star Ruben Blades, though singing wonderfully, walked through his part; Lazarus was greeted with giggles; and all the performers were given to delivering Simon's lyrics as if they were one-sentence telegrams instead of interpersonal dialogues.

As if Simon and Walcott's greenness with the musical form weren't enough for the producers to contend with, the show also met with protests over its subject matter. Relatives of murder victims picketed outside the Marquis marquee, asking what was so special about this Agron character that Simon felt compelled to write a Broadway musical about him. With so many heroes in the world, why glorify a 16-year-old gang member who stabbed two innocent teenagers and showed no remorse at his trial?

A better musical might have shown why, but—leaving aside an author's prerogative to write about anything he chooses (and Broadway musicals are filled with violent protagonists, from Billy Bigelow to Sweeney Todd)—*Capeman* did give Agron an arc of committing the sin, paying the price (jail) and repenting. Also, what the critics missed in the rush to tear *Capeman* to shreds was that parts of the show were, honestly, terrific. Composer Simon may have taken his lumps for shunning the theater establishment, but by avoiding doing a typical musical in a typical way, he also came up with a show that *was* different. The non-traditional *Rent* looked like a Gap commercial by comparison. *Capeman*'s salsa-fied score, as delivered by Blades, Marc Anthony and Ednita Nazario, sounded authentic and flavorful (at least to these anglo ears). It wasn't Spanish by way of Jerry Herman or Cy Coleman; it was Spanish by way of 1950s uptown Nueva York. Opening scenes of Agron in Spanish Harlem had a thrilling insouciance, made awesome by the perspectives of Crowley and Harrington's towering, yet oddly beautiful, tenement high-rises. Agron's criminal spree, despicable as it was, was also shown to be the climax of a night of delirious male camaraderie and gang-related revenge, all fueled by Simon's bouncy music. No "Oh *dios,* I've killed someone" dirge follows the stabbings; Agron and his cohorts boogie out of the scene of the crime, the audience nearly as pumped on the senseless violence as they are.

At the end of the first act, the audience I saw *Capeman* with looked at each other with nearly one common thought: "Were the critics crazy? This is exciting stuff, musical, vibrant, and very much worthy of attention." Alas, Act II bogged down in dream sequences and Lazarus stuff and made the fatal mistake of keeping Agron's contrition internal and spiritual—and thus impossible to dramatize. No question *Capeman* was a failure, the big engine that couldn't, but reports of unmitigated disaster were both needlessly vicious and decidedly untrue.

On the opposite end of the spectrum, Disney's theatrical musicalization of their hit animated film, *The Lion King,* came to town with so much hype and rabid hosannas, even a stampede of negative reviews would barely have bruised its tail. Disney needn't have feared, however; verdicts were as ecstatic in New York as they were when the musical tried out at Minneapolis's Orpheum Theater in July. The *Times*'s Vincent Canby wrote of "an air of jubilation" and of director Julie Taymor "setting new standards" for commercial theater. Fellow *Times* scribe Ben Brantley labeled the show's opening scene "transporting magic," though he had less kind things to say about Taymor's art mixing with Disney's commerce. *New York Magazine*'s John Simon pegged it best: "The prancing giraffes and leaping antelopes, the nodding elephant and barreling warthog, keep you marveling even during the story's stodgiest galumphing."

No question, *The Lion King*'s opening scene made theater history. South African singer Tsidii Le Loka, in white makeup and looking cowerie-shell chic as a baboon, tore the lid off the newly constructed New Amsterdam Theater with her chanting. Soon she was joined by other singers, as well as long-stilted giraffes, fluttering birds on wire poles and a life-sized elephant tromping up the aisle, all this to a bouncy number aptly titled "Circle of Life." The five-minute sequence merited a standing ovation on its own, but then there was another two and a half hours of actual story to get through, and that's where director Taymor and her crew lurched in equal measure from brilliant to banal. Composers Elton John and Tim Rice did their best and bounciest work for the movie ("Hakuna Matata," "Circle of Life"), so their lesser numbers in the show sounded kitschy next to the stirring "African" melodies of Lebo M and his numerous collaborators. Dialogue scenes, by Roger Allers and Irene Mecchi, had an elementary school wit that clashed with the wizardry of the costumes, dance, and sheer zeitgeist of the piece. Early scenes of Simba the lion cub cavorting in the forest only came alive when Samuel E. Wright brought majesty and energy to his dad, Mufasa. Matters improved once evil Scar (John Vickery) moved center stage, arranging the murder of Mufasa and staging a coup backed by lazy, sloppy hyenas. (Ah, the politics of Disneyland, where the strong, good-looking lions are naturally entitled to rule over—rather than *with*—their less intelligent, less cosmetically attractive animal brethren.)

At *The Lion King*, audiences gaped in wonder at both simple effects (a grass savannah created by actors standing together while wearing sod squares on their heads) and complex ones (animals "chasing" the lions are actually carved shapes on a rolling wooden wheel, with the shapes smaller in the back and larger up front to give the appearance of a galloping herd). Indeed, the only controversy surrounding *The Lion King* had to do with the age of children parents were bringing to the show. Couples paying $150 for a pair of tickets to the theater event of the year rightfully became incensed (as did this writer) when toddlers in the audience incessantly whooped, babbled and trumpeted, "Look mommy, a hyena!" It was Disney who had the last laugh, however. Even before *The Lion King* surprised prognosticators by beating out *Ragtime* for the best-musical Tony, rumors put advance sales for the Disney show between $20–40 million.

Not that *Ragtime* went unappreciated. Terrence McNally took nearly every major award for his libretto, as did composer Stephen Flaherty and lyricist Lynn Ahrens. Indeed, Broadway pundits wondered aloud how *The Lion King* could be picked as best musical of the year without having the best book or score. (The answer, I venture, is that *Ragtime* had beauty, intelligence and tremendous craft; *Lion King* had only magic.)

After knocking them dead in Toronto with its scope and bevy of fine songs, *Ragtime* arrived at Livent's newly-built Ford Center for the Performing Arts in mid-January. From its marketing as a great American musical to its gorgeously-appointed design, *Ragtime* announced itself as a work of art. No quarrel there, though for all the abundant talent in every aspect of the show, some spark was missing. It was impossible not to admire *Ragtime,* but rather difficult to love it. So many parallel stories are interwoven, the musical carries us with its epic sweep yet fails to move us when pianist-turned-terrorist Coalhouse Walker Jr. (Brian Stokes Mitchell) meets his inevitable doom, or when Mother (Marin Mazzie) grows away from her husband and falls in love with Tateh, the Jewish immigrant (Peter Friedman). Milos Forman's underrated film version of E.L. Doctorow's novel may have had the same problem of too many stories to tell in too little time, but he managed (helped by Randy Newman's score) to find poignancy in the tragedies rather than a "this inevitably happens next" fatalism.

To be fair, those who love the two excellent cast recordings of *Ragtime* and wonder how I dare call the material cold should know the Livent's Ford Center is as impersonal as it is immense, which didn't exactly help emotion carry across the proscenium. *Ragtime* worked best when it was in high dudgeon over injustice, be it the Irish firemen who trash Coalhouse's beloved auto, or the various ways industry bosses subjugate workers and punish unionism. It is to Ford Motor Company's credit that *Ragtime* includes a scene of Henry Ford standing on a girder and caroling about progress, while dozens of proles below bend their backs and support him.

Brian Stokes Mitchell excelled as the proud, and then vengeful, Coalhouse, but it was Audra McDonald in the relatively small role of his wife, who won an acting Tony, her third (*Carousel, Master Class*). As for the score, *Ragtime*'s signature tune, "On the Wheels of a Dream" is big, anthemic and appropriate, but other numbers better show off Flaherty's lyricism, such as "The Night That Goldman Spoke at Union Square," "The Crime of the Century" and "New Music."

That Demn'd Persistent Pimpernel

If tunes alone were the measure of a musical, *The Scarlet Pimpernel* would have merited its best-musical Tony nomination. Even more than *Jekyll & Hyde,* which had a far better book, *Pimpernel* furthered Frank Wildhorn's potential as the American heir to Andrew Lloyd Webber, able to write a hummable anthem ("Into the Fire") or soaring ballad ("Storybook"). Another positive note was that unlike the effective but dour *J & H, Pimpernel* had the breeziness of an old-fashioned musical comedy. But *Pimpernel* suffered from a terminal case of the stupids, whether in the scene where noble Percy convinced his fellow lords to be less effete, or the execrable (and inaudible) climactic getaway scene in a bouncing carriage. Andrew Jackness received kudos for his lavish settings, but the feeling always lingered that the designer was given *carte blanche* to throw prettiness at the background to keep our minds off the story, the dialogue, the occasionally ungodly lyrics (all three by Nan Knighton), and the hamstrung choreography.

The show's PR machine worked overtime to turn star Douglas Sills into a matinee idol and succeeded somewhat with the matinee ladies. But anyone catching Sills being interviewed on TV or presenting a theater award had to wonder where this tall, blonde, handsome, extremely engaging person went, because he sure faded into the woodwork in *Pimpernel*. Co-star Christine Andreas sang well when not pushing her throat too hard, but Terrence Mann was the best reason to endure *Pimpernel*. He took a lot of ribbing for seeming to reincarnate Javert, but *Pimpernel*'s arch-villain Chauvelin was actually more dimensional than the monomaniac policeman in *Les Misérables*. (Most critics were rougher on *Pimpernel* than I've been, but I should add two items that put my aversion to the musical into perspective: One, unlike many of my colleagues, I quite liked *Jekyll & Hyde*. Two, I took my longtime steady to *Pimpernel* on December 9, 1997—the night I was to propose to her. The idea was to meet in the city, see the show, head back home and pop the question before midnight. Two hours and 45 minutes later, I could already imagine my girl friend divorcing me on the grounds of mental cruelty. Okay, okay, the evening had a storybook ending. Three months later we were married, six months later *Pimpernel* was still playing at the Minskoff.)

The most stupefying aspect of *Pimpernel*'s longevity was the quick failure of another musical superior in every way. *Triumph of Love* boasted a clever libretto and cleverer lyrics by Susan Birkenhead, an award-worthy turn by Betty Buckley, and a game gamine in Susan Egan. As an intellectual fop brought down a few pegs, F. Murray Abraham took swipes for his poor singing—a bit of hypocrisy, since Ron Rifkin yowled nearly as badly on *Cabaret*'s "Pineapple Song" and won the best-featured-actor Tony anyway. Still, I guess *Triumph* was missing *something* because audiences just didn't come, not even to hear Buckley sing "Serenity," one of the best, and best-delivered, show tunes in years. Pundits blamed the show's styrofoamy set design; but if audiences didn't laugh at the Marivaux madness, even left-over credenzas from *Pimpernel* couldn't have saved it.

Our consulting historian, Thomas T. Foose, informs us that this production of *The Triumph of Love* was something of a special theatrical occasion: "The first work in English translation on Broadway by Pierre de Marivaux, either in straight-play form or as a musical." The only previous Broadway staging of this particular Marivaux play was by the visiting Théâtre Nationale Populaire in their 1958 repertory, in French, as *Le Triomphe de l'Amour;* and indeed (Mr. Foose notes), "When the T.N.P. first revived this play in Paris in 1956, it was the first revival of the play there since 1732."

Another musical miss was *Side Show,* from author Bill Russell and composer Henry (*Dreamgirls*) Krieger. "Come look at the freaks!" exhorted Ken Jennings as the carnival Boss, pointing to a fat lady, bearded woman, snake girl and chicken-eating geek (all played by uncostumed, plain-looking actors). A dual love story, set in a freak show and dealing with Siamese twins falling in love with their managers, makes the mind reel with possibilities, yet Russell and Krieger could muster nothing more than a pedestrian love story. Working from the real-life story of Daisy and Violet Hilton, whose claim to lasting fame was appearing in the Tod Browning chiller *Freaks*, *Side Show* managed to be infinitely less interesting than the truth, and heaven forbid any fun creeping into the proceedings. Even a Ziegfeldian production number opening Act II looked tacky against the black backdrops, black flooring and grey bleachers that screamed, "serious musical here, no dazzle allowed."

When critics (aside from a startlingly favorable *Times* review) yawned and audiences failed to materialize in large numbers, *Side Show*'s producers had the temerity to blame the musical's imminent collapse on its "difficult" subject matter. Audiences just want fluff and won't visit a show about something unpleasant, came the whine (which must have sounded funny to the makers of *Ragtime, Jekyll & Hyde* and *The Beauty Queen of Leenane*). Once it became clear *Side Show* would fold like a tent, a small but rabid coterie of fans dubbed themselves "freaks" and waged an internet campaign to save the show. It almost worked, as the producers redoubled efforts to keep *Side Show* going long enough to build up the box office. Even after the musical called it quits, *Side Show*'s producers kept their sets and equipment in the Richard Rodgers Theater, tempted by the idea of reopening just before the Tonys. That didn't happen either, though leads Emily Skinner and Alice Ripley became something of a double celebrity. Only Ripley received a Drama Desk nomination, but the Tonys nominated the hip-linked twosome as one person, ensuring their chance to warble "I'll Never Leave You" at parties and benefits for months to come.

Two other new musicals in 1997-98 were significantly less "new." *Street Corner Symphony,* conceived and directed by Floridian newcomer Marion J. Caffey, strung together songs from the 1950s to 1970s. *Symphony* started off with a book—something about a group of friends growing up in an urban neighborhood—but later dispensed with plot entirely in favor of a second-act, "Soul Train"-style concert. Audiences laughed, in the wrong way, at the retro costumes and sat stonefaced through lengthy versions of "Midnight Train to Georgia" and other tunes more suited to a different demographic. If nothing else, *Street Corner Symphony* showcased multi-talented up-and-comer Jose Llana, and for awhile even found a groove, as when the trippiness of "Psychedelic Shack" segued into the anger of Neil Young's "Ohio."

If *Street Corner Symphony* ached to be *Smokey Joe's Cafe, High Society* would have given its last highball to be *Crazy for You*. An adaptation by lauded playwright Arthur Kopit of *The Philadelphia Story,* the musical incorporated such Cole Porter standards as "She's Got That Thing" and a weakly-staged "Who Wants To Be a Millionaire." Librettist Kopit did well crafting the romantic tangles of Tracy Lord and the three men in her life, less well with the confusing subplot of her family's background. Still, once the story was in place—Tracy is set to marry humorless George but really loves her ex-alcoholic, ex-husband, Dexter, while finding herself drawn to cynical newshound Mike—the second act could linger on some nice ballads and give each character a winning moment to hold the spotlight.

1776—Merwin Foard (Richard Henry Lee), Pat Hingle (Benjamin Franklin) and Brent Spiner (John Adams) in Roundabout's revival of the Peter Stone-Sherman Edwards musical

High Society was supposed to be the show that would launch rising starlet Melissa Errico (*My Fair Lady,* Encores! *One Touch of Venus*) into the stratosphere. But lackluster reviews and press reports that she'd been somewhat diva-ish in her career-building kept her yet again one step away from being the next Bernadette. Lovely she was, though, as the debutante, paraded in flattering outfits by costumer Jane Greenwood. Tony-nominated standouts were young Anna Kendrick, displaying solid delivery as Tracy's prepubescent sister, and John McMartin, offering his patented, bon vivant slur as drunken papa.

As for Broadway musical revivals, early in the season *1776* seemed unbeatable. In an intelligent, dramatic mounting by Scott Ellis, the still-terrific Peter Stone-Sherman Edwards musical benefitted from the intimacy of the Roundabout's mainstage. After all, the musical was known for its famously long stretch of stage time (more than 45 minutes) without a song, making it feel more like a straight play. When you consider just how split English loyalists were from the Rebels, and how colonies of the north and south were already divided over the slavery issue, the situation quivers with drama. To paraphrase *InTheater* and *Playbill On-Line* scribe Peter Filichia, the miracle of *1776* is the way it makes us throw up our hands throughout and sigh, "These people will never sign the Declaration of Independence. Damn, we'll be an English colony forever!"

Peter Stone's book, one of the best ever written for musical theater, never forgets that the delegates to the Continental Congress were men. They were hot, plagued by flies, missing their wives, stubborn, sometimes brilliant, sometimes moronic. The best of them, John Adams, is roundly disliked for his prickliness and intractability. As Adams, a proficient Brent Spiner couldn't quite expunge memories of William Daniels, especially since the *Star Trek: Next Generation* star proved more congenial than contrary. Then again, his latent niceness infused his scenes with Abigail (Linda Emond) with romance and poignancy.

Ensemble players delighted. Merwin Foard had a fine comic turn in "The Lees of Old Virginia," Lauren Ward (*Violet*) brought welcome lilt to "He Plays the Violin," and Gregg Edelman gave what may be his best performance to date as the delegate from South Carolina explaining to the Northerners just how culpable they were in the slave trade.

Ironically, the Roundabout's other major musical this season earned spectacular success in a venue that was, economically at least, frustratingly small. For months, English director Sam Mendes shopped around for a place to bring his hit revisionist revival of Kander & Ebb's *Cabaret*. After a deal with The Supper Club fell through, Mendes came to the Club Expo disco, aka the old Henry Miller Theater. Rundown and vaguely kitschy, the nightspot would provide the perfect ambience for the seedy denizens of *Cabaret*'s Kit Kat Klub. In fact, reports filtered back that during early previews, audience members would stumble over broken glass, rubbish and hypodermic needles left by junkies slumming in the seats during the theater's vacant years. Controversy—and titillation—also hit the show when people realized this *Cabaret* didn't have Liza and Joel but did have brief nudity, gay urtext, chorus girls with track-marked arms, simulated copulation (behind a screen, comically, as part of the "Two Ladies" number) and a finale that featured the emcee in concentration camp garb, shaking as electric current races through his body.

Any negativity surrounding *Cabaret* ended abruptly once critics and audiences realized they were viewing a masterwork. Unlike revisionist Shakespeares that click some of the time or illuminate one "relevant" aspect of the text while riding roughshod over the rest, this *Cabaret* brought freshness to the classic parts and even strengthened sequences that never really worked. By turning the whole show into a kind of fever dream concocted by the sly, bisexual, amoral emcee, *Cabaret* had a context in which to put scenes that were hoary even by 1960s standards. For example, though Bob Fosse wisely cut "The Pineapple Song" from his legendary film of the musical, the last two Broadway mountings reinstated the awful tune. Ten years ago, played straight, the scene between Fraulein Schneider and Herr Schultz was an embarrassment, a cutesy bit of romantic comedy in a musical form that had moved beyond such conventions. In Mendes's staging, the emcee (Alan Cumming) enters the boarding house room as Schneider and Schultz are singing, smiling coyly as pineapples descend from the ceiling and twirl to the music. Suddenly, the two old folks look like pathetic dreamers, deluding themselves into thinking their love will float past the approaching political maelstrom.

Other, even simpler touches, thrilled. To show that a brick has been tossed through the window of Schultz's shop, the emcee came out and simply dropped a cement block (with a crash sound effect) at the Jew's feet, while an empty frame swung side-to-side over the stage. When Sally Bowles finished her signature number, bellowing "and I love a cabaret!", she didn't stand there and let applause wash over her. Instead, she hurled the microphone stand to the floor, an acknowledgment that by aborting her child and breaking up with Cliff, she'd slammed the door on her last chance at a life of middle class normalcy.

Both Natasha Richardson and Alan Cumming took well-earned Tonys for their performances, though John Benjamin Hickey also deserved a nod for being the most conflicted, most persuasive Clifford in memory. Singing voices weren't always up to snuff, but that, too, contributed to the feeling of real people caught in a hopeless situation. Natasha Richardson played Sally Bowles as someone loaded with bravado and moxie but blessed with only mediocre singing talent. Not only did it make more sense that her Sally would be stuck in a dive like the Kit Kat Klub, her final number was delivered with astonishing desperation, as if she were trying to blast her way out of shell shock. (As of this writing, Jennifer Jason Leigh is set to replace Richardson in August.)

What with adulatory reviews and the marquee value of Richardson, *Cabaret* soon became the hottest ticket in town—in a Broadway theater that seated only a few hundred people. Despite charging top dollar (often for seats that, because of the theater's table and chair configuragion, offered irritatingly obstructed views), the Roundabout found itself barely able to break even on the production. As of press time, Mendes and choreographer Rob Marshall were on a serious hunt to find a bigger theater (possibly the old Studio 54 discotheque space) that wouldn't compromise the production's extraordinary esthetic.

As if to contrast the care taken to reconceive every single edgy moment of *Cabaret, The Sound of Music* was a revival of the old school—well cast, nicely appointed, able to get the job done. Not as poignant as City Opera's surprisingly fine 1990 revival (with Debby Boone no less!), Susan H. Schulman's mounting at the Martin Beck starred chipmunk-cheeked Rebecca Luker as Maria, the nun who gets von Trapped in the Alps. Predictably, critics were blase, calling Rodgers & Hammerstein's musical badly structured and too syrupy, and this staging run-of-the-mill. (Of the three criticisms, the one I'd most challenge is calling the material maudlin. Certainly *The Sound of Music* leaves eyes a lot drier than *Carousel* or *The King and I.*) It is a very nice show with a half-dozen better-than-nice songs overriding its worst failings.

If most other aspects of the New York season were booming, off-Broadway musicals were few and far between, with only two achieving any kind of far-reaching attention. Both were gay-themed and modern in approach. *The Last Session* told of a well-known singer and songwriter tired of coping with AIDS and laying down a handful of final songs at the studio on the night he intends to commit suicide. *Hedwig and the Angry Inch*—well, how *does* one describe *Hedwig and the Angry Inch* except to say John Cameron Mitchell's musical whipped elements of Ziggy Stardust, physics, German art song, Grace Jones and Marianne Faithfull into the season's most unexpected hit, moving quickly from a cult curiosity OOB to an off-Broadway must-see at the newly *de*-furbished Jane Street Theater.

The Last Session also started as an off-off-Broadway offering, at the Currican Theater, impressing viewers with its professional staging and stirring pop anthems. Credit designer Eric Lowell Renschler with his convincing recreation of a recording studio, and directors Mike Wills (OOB) and Jim Brochu (off) with the amusing byplay between Gideon, the stricken singer, and his session-mates: Vicki, his ex-wife; Tryshia, his black diva friend; Buddy, a born-again Christian songwriter bent on saving his idol's soul; and Jim, a sarcastic engineer who knows about the intended suicide but is sworn by Gideon to secrecy.

Brochu's libretto, which was surprisingly upbeat for such a dour situation, brimmed with wisecracks that nevertheless fit the characters. The score by Steve Schalchlin, on whom the story was loosely based, felt more like songs on the general theme of AIDS than theater tunes integrated into the plot, but several numbers were rousers ("The Preacher and the Nurse," "The Singer and the Song"). "Friendly Fire," a parody of wartime anthems, launched a savage attack on the inadequacy of health care and modern medicine in dealing with HIV. "Somebody's Friend," the evening's most touching tune, nicely developed a theme along the lines of, "somebody's friend read something about a cure; why is it always a friend of a friend?" An ingratiating cast led by Bob Stillman (he'd later appear in the Adam Guettel oratorio *Saturn Returns*) also helped make *The Last Session* a sleeper.

Equally contemporary and way wilder was *Hedwig and the Angry Inch* which presented John Cameron Mitchell as a cross-dressing rock-and-roll chanteuse fallen on hard times. A strikingly weird vision in platinum wig and disco heels, Hedwig told of growing up transsexual in East Germany and then meeting a man who promised to bring her to the U.S. as his wife. Alas, the "angry inch" of the title refers to Hedwig's sex organ, botched by doctors during the sex change supposed to turn him into a woman. Once in America, Hedwig became the nurturing girl friend of a brainless rocker, only to hit the usual skids when he got famous and forgot her. Add to this story some philosophical overlays about the nature of gender, an on-stage rock band featuring a female guitarist playing a bearded male, and a finale that showed Hedwig (metaphorically) bursting through the boundaries of sexuality, and you *still* don't have a sense of the show's uniqueness. In the New York *Press,* reviewer Jonathan Kalb described Mitchell as Hedwig thusly: "What linger in the mind . . . . . are the painstaking details—the precision of his phony German accent and teenage Kansan twang, for instance. And the primly placed, self-effacing Bandaid on his knee. And the way he sips Coors through a straw without disturbing his wet-wet lipstick, and high-kicks like a Rockette without mussing a blonde strand."

Yet for all the kudos greeting Mitchell's outrageous creation, it was Stephen Trask's pounding rock numbers that gave the evening puissance. Perhaps the highest compliment one could pay *Hedwig* was that songs by "Heroes"-era David Bowie, Iggy Pop and Lou Reed were played on the sound system before and after the show, but the tunes in between, including "Tear Me Down," "Angry Inch" and "Wicked Little Town," sounded just as good. Unlike other modern shows (yes, I do mean

Rent) which squeezed elements of rock and pop into the music theater idiom, *Hedwig* really, truly, rocked.

The same could not be said for the aforementioned *Saturn Returns,* a spacey collection of songs by Adam Guettel, composer of *Floyd Collins.* Guettel had a fiendish compulsion to take perfectly good melodies and put them to atonal arrangements, rendering them art-school annoying. A charming cast made some tunes palatable, while Annie Golden had the show's brightest moment with the amusing and hummable "How Can I Lose You." I hope it's not catty to suggest that the show's best (and best-received) song was an old-fashioned, pretty ballad sung to lyrical violin accompaniment.

Clue: The Musical, which took its plot from a popular board game, managed to arrive at the Players Theater despite devastating reviews for its Chicago tryout. Whatever revisions were made apparently didn't help; the critics murdered it again, and New York quickly found itself *Clue*-less. Faring even worse was *Tallulah's Party,* a rewritten version of 1983's *Tallulah* that was announced for three different theaters before opening OOB—and then closing ten days later—at the Kaufman. Tovah Feldshuh received mixed notices as the foul-mouthed star, but the show itself was roundly trashed for concentrating too much on La Bankhead's ex-husbands to the exclusion of her multi-faceted career. Another tribute, *I Will Come Back,* had cabaret favorite Tommy Femia saluting Judy Garland, but neither critics nor audiences returned the salute. *Dinah Was,* a look at the pride that wenteth before the fall of Dinah Washington (from drugs and alcohol), did well enough to transfer from the WPA theater to the brand new Gramercy Theater, for a post-season summer run. Early in the season, the regional hit *Always . . . Patsy Cline* eked out six months at the Variety Arts Theater, with Tori Lynn Palazola doing the honors as Patsy and Margo Martindale playing her brashly adulatory fan, Louise. Fingernail deep, *Patsy Cline* offered the expected hits, albeit with Palazola sounding more like Teresa Brewer than the titular warbler.

In wintertime, The York Theater Company had a low-key success with *The Show Goes On*, a career retrospective of Tom Jones and Harvey Schmidt featuring the authors themselves. With Schmidt quietly beaming and thumping at the piano, an elfin Jones introduced hits ("I Do! I Do!," "My Cup Runneth Over," "110 in the Shade," "It's Gonna Be Another Hot Day") and rarities from the boys' four-decade career. Not only did the show afford audiences an opportunity to hear good songs salvaged from unworkable shows, we were also let in on the processes of musical-making. Jones recalled penning 114 songs for *110 in the Shade,* just in case trunk material was needed. Three different versions of the song "I Do! I Do!" were also presented, each in a different style, as necessitated by a Broadway or Hollywood rewrite.

Though Schmidt and Jones obviously took as much pride in their ambitious flops as in their fluke hits, they did find room to pop in the inescapable "Try to Remember," and why not? *The Fantasticks* was still running at the Sullivan Street Playhouse after 38 years and with no closing notice in sight. That's about 36 years longer than the other "long-running" off-Broadway musicals still playing by season's end: *I Love You, You're Perfect, Now Change; When Pigs Fly, Forbidden Broadway Strikes Back* and *Secrets Every Smart Traveler Should Know,* a cabaret show that opened at the Triad in October. The latter revue compiled a bunch of generally amusing ditties on the terrors of world travel, with Michael McGrath and Kathy Fitzgerald, both of Broadway's underrated *Swinging on a Star,* leading the charge against lost luggage, brainless tourists and Montezuma's revenge. Jay Leonhart, the cabaret world's best-known bassist, scored on a couple of quirky tunes, including "Customs," wherein a passenger lists all the staggeringly illegal items he hopes a customs officer won't notice.

Off-Broadway musical revivals were nearly non-existent, with the exception of City Center's ever-lauded Encores! concert series, this year revisiting *Strike Up the Band* (with Philip Bosco and Judy Kuhn), *St. Louis Woman* (with Vanessa Williams and Charles Dutton), and *Li'l Abner* (with Dana Ivey, Alice Ripley, and Lea DeLaria as a sex-changed Marryin' Sam).

Lea who? That's what people were asking when George C. Wolfe cast an unknown, overweight comedienne as the randy cabbie in *On the Town,* a New York Shakespeare Festival summer show at Central Park's Delacorte Theater, after *Henry VIII* capped the company's Shakespeare Marathon. A star was instantly born, as reviews were high on the comic energy of Wolfe's revival and singled out DeLaria for her boisterous timing. Wrote the *Times*'s Ben Brantley, "Ms. DeLaria comes to represent the irresistible, brazen essence of the city being celebrated in this buoyant wartime offering . . . . . When she opens her mouth to sing, the notes come stomping out like a cocky all-brass band, bringing to mind an Ethel Merman with attitude. Like the town of the show's title, Ms. DeLaria makes vulgarity a highly developed art." The revival appeared certain for a Broadway transfer but for three crippling problems: Broadway houses were scarce, Wolfe was due for a kidney transplant, and the *Times* didn't cotton to Eliot Feld's choreography ("as a dance show, this *On the Town* has two left feet"). Eventually, Feld graciously bowed out for the good of the show, but Broadway plans were scuttled for at least a year.

Plays: American Masters & English Monsters

So here we are in 1998, two years before the millennium, our theaters laden with multi-media concoctions, gay fantasias, post-modern musicals and site-specific deconstructions, and who was the most omnipresent playwright? Arthur Miller. The octogenarian dramatist was as ubiquitous this season as Tennessee Williams had been a few years before, and not just because off-Broadway's Signature Theater dedicated its whole program to him. A well-received revival of *All My Sons* at the Roundabout's Laura Pels space the prior season carried over into the early summer, but bigger success awaited another Roundabout-Miller combo, *A View From the Bridge*. A stocky, earnest but volatile Anthony LaPaglia was perfectly cast as Eddie Carbone, the Brooklyn longshoreman who regrets taking two Italian immigrants into his home. LaPaglia's coup was allowing us to hope that Eddie's basic decency would conquer his growing mental illness and keep him from committing his fatal mistake.

Tension was the key to Michael Mayer's Tony-winning staging, which used sound design and supporting actors walking up the aisles to create the atmosphere of a close-knit neighborhood where everybody knows everybody else's business. Far more gripping than the 1983 Arvin Brown mounting with Tony LoBianco, this *View* also boasted notable performances by Allison Janney, as Eddie's wife, and Brittany Murphy as budding niece Catherine. Murphy turned off some critics with her precocious, very tenement-Italian approach, but her Catherine was exactly the kind of plastic-heeled, giddy, naive, bubbly but fundamentally Catholic urban high school girl you always find riding the R train, be it 1955 or 1998.

The play itself still doesn't make much sense. How can Eddie think Rodolpho's a sissy *and* be worried about the fellow's designs on his niece? And how can Alfieri say, in his eulogy for the slain longshoreman, that Eddie was "completely himself" to the end, when Eddie never came clean to the world or his conscience? Tony voters didn't look for answers when they gave the award to both LaPaglia and the play; they just went with the quickening pace and commendable performances.

None of the Miller works staged at Signature matched *Bridge*'s success, though reviews were good for *The American Clock,* a kaleidoscopic look at The Great Depression's effect on every class of citizen, from the Jewish housewife forced to give up her beloved piano, to the black owner of a diner pressured into buying a radio from the white sheriff. Scene by scene, *American Clock* could run from agit-prop to humane drama to prosaic family squabbles, but the piece as a whole had scope and the sense of something lived and truly felt by its author. Critics struggled to find the same values in Miller's new play, *Mr. Peters' Connections,* which premiered at the end of the Signature season. Delighted as audiences were to see Peter Falk onstage again, his Columbo-esque shuffle and perpetual bemusement added only peripheral interest to a play that kept asking the question, "What is the subject?" and then thought best not to answer it. Better was a revival of *The Last Yankee* on a double bill with *I Can't Remember Anything.* The former play lacked focus but created some interesting characters as it told of a woman trying to get her head together on the day she leaves a sanitarium. *Remember* couldn't decide whether it wanted to be a depressing study of two aged, difficult people with no support system beyond themselves, or a loopy sitcom about oldsters who drive each other bananas.

If Arthur Miller represented the old guard staying current through the sheer strength of dramatic situations, brash English newcomer Martin McDonagh became flavor of the month by infusing homey melodramas with ironic humor and a dollop of nastiness. Two McDonagh dramas opened within weeks of each other: *The Beauty Queen of Leenane* at the Atlantic Theater, and *The Cripple of Inishmaan* at the Public. Both boasted authentic Irish casts, both were set in impoverished Irish burgs less welcoming than even Brian Friel could imagine, both punctuated their grim comedy with moments of sadism and both had vocal enthusiasts and detractors.

Leenane, which tied for the Lortel best-play award, was the more commercially viable of the two, dealing as it did with a middle-aged frump offered a last chance at romantic happiness. Maureen's boyfriend Pato, a good sod, hopes to bring her to America. Blocking her way is her cranky, indolent mother, who cares only about her mushy bowl of "Complan" oatmeal and will not brook any threat to the continuation of her daughter's round-the-clock attention. Like an 1800s potboiler, *Leenane* hinged on a letter from Maureen's beau that mama Mag, in an act of supreme selfishness, burns.

It was in the play's final minutes that McDonagh veered from his kinsmen in approach. Brian Friel might simply have shown Mag and Maureen resigning themselves to a life stuck with each other; J.M. Synge might have sent Maureen out the door with a slam to smash Mag's Complan bowl. McDonagh, however, twists the knife differently. Not only does he endow Maureen with a homicidal impulse, he makes us reconsider the entire mother/daughter relationship. Suddenly we aren't so sure Mag was exaggerating tales of her daughter's penchant for mental illness and physical cruelty.

Leenane created a potent situation but also spent a lot of time killing time, establishing the bleakness of Mag's flat and staving off the plot's climactic moments. When ingenuity flagged, however, director Garry Hynes made sure to emphasize the play's quirky humor and create a claustrophobic sense of catastrophe in Mag and Maureen's hovel. Hynes won a Tony, as did Marie Mullen (Maureen), Anna Manahan (Mag) and Tom Murphy, as Pato's impatient brother. (The award could just as easily have gone to Brian F. O'Byrne, who was also nominated.) Much was made of the fact that this season the best-play and musical-directing Tonys both went to women (Hynes and Taymor), alongside a best-play trophy for fellow femme Yasmina Reza (*Art*).

Off Broadway, McDonagh's *The Cripple of Inishmaan* also boasted a stellar cast, including Donal Donnelly as the town gossip and Aisling O'Neill as a savage young lady who torments protagonist Cripple Billy (Ruaidhri Conroy) just a little more than she injures everyone else. A livelier work than *Leenane, Inishmaan* balanced near-farce and tragic elements in a way that recalled early Chekhov. (In fact, the play held together better than *Ivanov,* unevenly revived at Lincoln Center with Kevin Kline as its suicidal center.) When *Inishmaan* stayed put at the Public while *Leenane* moved to Broadway, it's likely because the former was more cavalier with its viciousness. *Leenane* worked up to one deliberate act of sadism (and an offstage slaying); *Inishmaan* had savage beatings, eggs smashed on faces and a finale that sent blood streaming out of tubercular Billy's mouth.

As celebrated as it was overrated, Mark Ravenhill's *Shopping etc.* (see Index) gave New York Theater Workshop's marketing department headaches but otherwise told an old story of naive kids caught in a bind and forced to raise money any way they could. In this case, the girl (Jennifer Dundas Lowe) agrees to sell drugs for a shady film producer and Ecstasy dealer, but when her boyfriend hits the nightclub scene to peddle the goods, he snorts too much blow himself, becomes overwhelmed with generosity and gives all the drugs away free. This doesn't sit well with the purveyor, who threatens torture unless the couple come up with 3,000 pounds in a week's time.

Told with energy and braced by a well-developed theme on the way people rely on each other as a support system (no matter how depraved), *Shopping* also dwelled too often on unpleasantness for its own sake. Did we really need to *see* one character

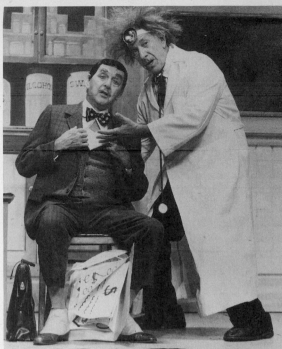

Left, Katie Finneran and Peter Rini in Simon's new comedy *Proposals; right,*
Tony Randall and Jack Klugman as old vaudevillians playing their doctor skit in
the National Actors Theater revival of the playwright's *The Sunshine Boys*

licking another's anus, stopping only when he noticed blood on the rim? And did
directors Max Stafford-Clark and Gemma Bodinetz have to end each scene with a
jolting blast of music? It was a cheap stunt, unworthy of the vivid performers and
the play's better sequences.

But not every imported play showed low-class dirtbags wallowing in greed, boredom and spite. *Art,* by French dramatist Yasmina Reza, showed three reasonably
well-to-do buddies wallowing in greed, boredom and spite. A fast-moving comedy
about the true nature of friendship, *Art* not only cleaned up at the box office, it
sneaked past *The Beauty Queen of Leenane* to take the best-play Tony Award. Reza
already had a full mantel by then, having won the 1996 Evening Standard prize and
the 1997 Olivier Award for best comedy.

Art centered on a single question: "What if your close friend spent an ungodly
sum on a piece of art that, to you, had absolutely no esthetic merit?" (If you answer
"So what?", skip the rest of this paragraph.) In the case of Serge, Marc and Yvan,
the painting in question is stark white, with a couple of etched-in striations running
diagonally. Serge crows about the work to his pals, who think he's gone 'round the
bend. Malleable Yvan can at least bring himself to judge the work as an artistic
statement. Marc can respond only with incredulity, inwardly seething that his best

pal can have such appalling taste. After all, it was Marc who taught Serge about wines, classical music and a general appreciation of culture. To Marc, Serge has become an esthetic Benedict Arnold.

An hour of arguments follows the basic setup. But *Art* doesn't nestle into some cozy, "to each his own" blather. Instead, the quarrels zero in on the way relationships change over the years. The natural flow of life changes people gradually, but severely, until sometimes we turn around and the folks we've always seen as purple have turned contentedly, but mystifyingly, orange. In a very touching moment at the end of *Art,* the three middle-aged men decide to remain friends, but they must start with a clean slate—hence the metaphor of the naked white painting. Though American audiences were deprived of seeing *Art*'s original London stars (including Albert Finney and Tom Courtenay), no one complained about Alan Alda, Victor Garber and Tony-nominated Alfred Molina. They didn't seem particularly French, but they sure knew how to keep a talky show flying.

Honour, by Joanna Murray-Smith, could have been the twin hit of *Art.* Both were English transfers to Broadway, both ran 90 minutes without intermission, both were issue/situation oriented, and both worked hard to push an audience's buttons. The difference? Murray-Smith's drama pressed the buttons with a jackhammer. Told in short, episodic scenes, *Honour* traced the quick dissipation of a marriage. Robert Foxworth played Gus, a well-off writer who has no intention of wrecking his bland but comfortable marriage to Honour (Jane Alexander) until he meets a sycophantic intern (Laura Linney). He's captivated by her passion for his work—not to mention blonde hair, long legs, and black widow's proclivity for devouring men. Unable to resist the siren call of a new life, Gus leaves Honour and their grown but emotionally stunted daughter, Sophie (Enid Graham). The rest of the play shows Honour slowly emerging from her daze to rediscover the independent woman she was before subsuming her career to her husband's.

If *Honour* sounds like a movie on Lifetime cable, well, that may have been a better place for it. Too often we could imagine author Murray-Smith congratulating herself on penning a pithy argument and following it with an even cleverer counterattack. Real people just don't talk this way, and Gerald Gutierrez's fast, ping-pongy direction only made the characters sound even more like mouthpieces. Audiences welcomed the return of Jane Alexander to the boards after years spent slaying dragons at the NEA, but it wasn't much fun watching this real-life embodiment of the gracious, astute, forthright modern woman mousing herself down into a defenseless, shell-shocked victim. Enid Graham, as daughter Sophie, had the play's only human sequence, a monologue about inadequacy that earned her a Tony nomination.

Another British play fared even worse on Broadway than *Honour: The Herbal Bed.* Peter Whelan's drama focused on William Shakespeare's daughter (Laila Robins), faced with slanderous gossip when a drunken young man espies her in the garden with a man who isn't her husband. In England, *Bed* apparently gripped audiences with its questioning of whether truth is always the best policy. Here, viewers snoozed as Susanna hurriedly set about covering her tracks and getting her housekeeper to lie for her. In the second act's central scene, a cynical Vicar questions all the semi-guilty parties, with author Whelan's point being that love and human need can be more important than bald honesty. Lacking the moral force of *The Crucible*, *Bed* didn't even use its ace in the hole—the Bard, who was kept offstage and played no part at all in the drama. That said, the play was better than its week-long run and shockingly uneven cast allowed patrons to believe, and merits reconsideration, perhaps by a solid off-Broadway repertory company.

Reviews were only slightly kinder to David Hare's *The Judas Kiss,* still another play about Oscar Wilde's legal difficulties. With Liam Neeson starring as the poet, however, the limited run speedily recouped its investment. Though o'erbrimming with lovely passages and boasting a tragically romantic hero, *Judas Kiss* had two critical dramatic strikes against it. One, *Gross Indecency,* Moisés Kaufman's less literary but more dynamic recounting of the same material, continued its smash-hit run off Broadway. Two, Hare's drama showed a main character not in crisis, but in stasis. Wilde's hangers-on debated endlessly whether he should flee his impending imprisonment—while their subject simply dawdled until the police arrived. Act II, set in Venice after the incarceration, revealed an ailing, impoverished Wilde sharing recriminations and reconciliations with a loyal friend and with Wilde's disloyal lover, Bosey. Very little actually happened in the play, and while Neeson may have been a touching and physically imposing Wilde, indolence just isn't dramatic.

Then again, decisiveness didn't help the Roundabout Theater's Broadway revival of Terence Rattigan's *The Deep Blue Sea.* Blythe Danner starred as a middle-aged woman so desperate to hang onto her dashing young lover, she takes the gas-pipe rather than suffer his abandonment. A dreary, garrulous drama, laden with accents as poor as those in *The Herbal Bed, Sea* did little to advance the cause of a Rattigan renaissance.

A bit better was *Misalliance,* one of Shaw's more prolix plays given a hyper-vigorous staging by David Warren at the Laura Pels. So hard did Warren work at keeping *Misalliance* from becoming a gabfest, he resorted to dismayingly cartoonish choices, such as making the socialist (Zak Orth), who's out for revenge against the family patriarch, a deranged character, raving with a high-pitched wheeze that barely changed throughout his lengthy time onstage. Brian Murray was the show's comic anchor.

Labored silliness also hampered Bill Irwin's Roundabout staging of Feydeau's *A Flea in Her Ear,* one that used a Jean-Marie Besset and Mark O'Donnell translation which, alas, found room for the word "asshole" and various mirthless impotence jokes. Half the actors were miscast or asked to mug without mercy. It's a truism of farce that since the opening minutes are crammed with exposition, an audience will tolerate a slow set-up because the characters' personality quirks pay off later. Disregarding this, Irwin chose to run the play at breakneck speed right from the start, sacrificing a sense of reality that would have made events so much funnier an hour later. Mark Linn-Baker proved capable but unmemorable as the businessman at the heart of the lunacy, though once he took on the second role of hapless bellhop Dodo, the comedy at last began to percolate.

Earlier at the Pels, a pared-down, thrift-shop staging of *Cyrano de Bergerac* drew thunderbolts from critics who saw it as a shameless ego trip for star Frank Langella. Of course, this wasn't the 1800s, when has-been stars would hawk their own benefit performances for food money. Quite the reverse, since the ever-handsome Langella remains as bright a luminary as he's ever been. *Cyrano* was just an obvious and generally engaging way for the Roundabout to stuff its coffers without spending too much on sets, costumes and actors. As long as this doesn't turn into a trend, no complaint here.

Whatever one thinks of Eugene Ionesco, he got his due when the Royal Court Theater and the Théâtre de Complicité brought their revival of *The Chairs* to New York, with Geraldine McEwan and Richard Briers as the leads. I've always felt the play would be a knockout at one hour's length but exhausts our patience at 90 minutes. While this revival didn't change my mind, at least Simon McBurney's staging had numerous felicities, from sound effects accompanying the old couple's creaking limbs to a lovely opening sequence of the duo looking out on the marshy water (courtesy of Paul Anderson's lighting) surrounding their barren domicile. The Tony-nominated stars never flagged in energy, with Briers, especially, giving his dissipated character equal portions of hope and lifelong frustration.

Tony Kushner's adaptation of S. Ansky's heart-rending fantasy, *A Dybbuk,* was a work of both beauty and scholarship, humanely staged by Brian Kulick. *A Dybbuk, or Between Two Worlds* managed to be a spooky ghost story and a warm look at shtetl life, all from a terribly sad, post-Holocaust perspective. Kushner also emphasized women's subjugated role in the culture and allowed his Chassidim to expound upon the war between belief and logic. Ron Leibman made a fiery exorcist, but the play belonged to its young leads: Marin Hinkle, lovely and haunted as the girl kept from her *bashert,* and Michael Stuhlbarg, the boy driven to madness by the rights denied him.

New American Plays On Broadway? No Freaking Way

The Brits lorded it over the Yanks when it came to Broadway plays. Nearly all the major American playwrights were doing their work off Broadway and regionally, while Broadway was reserved for shows already pretested in the West End. Producers couldn't be blamed for running scared from the expense of mounting new American plays, though they might've noticed half the foreign plays they brought in crashed and burned anyway.

That said, of the four new American premieres on Broadway, only a specialty solo act (John Leguizamo's *Freak*) achieved critical *and* box office success. The most surprising flop belonged to Neil Simon, who went back on his statement years ago during the off-Broadway debut of *London Suite* that he'd no longer premiere shows on Broadway. He probably regretted his reversal when *Proposals* closed to apathetic reaction after 87 total performances. (Only his 1981 *Fools* suffered a shorter run: 40). Though boasting a mix of the crowd-pleasing oneliners that made Simon a cash cow for 30 years, and the nostalgic, bittersweet themes that rightfully earned him a

Pulitzer, *Proposals* seemed like a hohum hike through familiar woods. Set in a vacation home in the Poconos on the last week of summer, Simon's play aimed for a Chekhovian mix of normal and eccentric characters reestablishing ties or declaring independence. The most enjoyable scenes featured Peter Rini as a purposefully malapropic Italian doofus who appears to have eyes for Josie, the young lady at the play's center.

Simon struck out on several fronts this season (he divorced again, and his geriatric *The Odd Couple* movie sequel, starring Walter Matthau and Jack Lemmon, flat-lined at the box office), but he did hit a smooth triple with a National Actors Theater revival of *The Sunshine Boys* at the Lyceum. Excellent reviews (and low overhead) helped push the show to a seven-month run, giving audiences a chance to savor anew one of Simon's most infallible works. Though not for a moment sentimental, the comedy received an automatic layer of nostalgia from its leads, Jack Klugman and Tony Randall. Randall, founder of the N.A.T., enjoyed quite an annum: the 78-year-old performer had his second child in two years, with his 28-year-old wife, Heather. The ever-dapper Randall still had to age, shrivel and uglify himself in order to play Al Lewis, nemesistic partner of Klugman's Willie Clark. Not lost on audiences was Randall's great mitzvah in casting his old *Odd Couple* TV cohort. Hints of their magic together peeped through in 1993's otherwise lame *Three Men on a Horse,* but that was just an exercise to push Klugman's cancer-scarred throat back to audibility. A number of *Odd Couple* benefits followed, but it was with *The Sunshine Boys* that Klugman finally repaid his benefactor. Klugman's body language hadn't changed a whit since the Oscar Madison days, and in seconds his face could go from oatmeal flat to pop-eyed rage to abject misery. He invested Clark with so much emotion, the ordinarily effusive Randall had to play Lewis close to the vest. Apart from Randall's unconvincing and unnecesssary Bronx accent, the evening was one big love-fest for both the world of Simon's comedy and the friendship of its performers.

Broadway theatergoers may have been indifferent toward Simon's new play, but he could take consolation in knowing that crowds didn't clamor for something completely different either. *Jackie,* Gip Hoppe's playful farrago on the life of Jacqueline Kennedy Onassis, came out of left field and, alas, couldn't convince ticket buyers to walk over from right and center. They missed a freewheeling, though never cruel, send-up of the Kennedy clan, complete with ingenious props and puppet designs. If, at more than two hours, this extended revue ran well past its welcome, there was always something amusing to appreciate onstage, be it a cartoon coffee cup velcroed to a one-dimensional table, or paparazzi represented by swooping puppet vultures, or Thomas Derrah (a human) as an hilariously hedonistic Ari Onassis. The funniest bit featured Gretchen Egolf's Christina envisioned as the wailing victim of a Greek tragedy. More savage attacks on power-brokers of the time would have given *Jackie* extra sizzle, but author Hoppe preferred to lampoon the era itself, as well as America's fascination with celebrity and addiction to fashion.

Golden Child was a return to form by David Henry Hwang, who was a golden child on Broadway after *M. Butterfly* but turned to lead when *Face Value* expired in previews. Critics were coolly positive about Hwang's latest (which premiered a year earlier in revised form at the Public Theater), in many ways the best Broadway play of the year. Much like the career diplomat in *Butterfly,* Eng Tieng-Bin has it all but loses everything, because he's uncomfortable in his own skin and trusts the wrong people to set him right again. Whereas the protagonist of *Butterfly* falls for a cross-dressing spy, Tieng-Bin has three wives, each of whom protects her own best interests. Wife #1 (yes, that's how the women themselves refer to each other; this was, after all, Southeast China in 1918), though an opium addict, takes the best care of her husband and their child (Tony-nominated Julyana Soelistyo). He respects her but would rather be in the bed of nubile Third Wife (Ming-Na Wen), who desperately wants to bear his child so she can rise in her household status. Stuck literally in the middle is Second Wife (Kim Miyori), neither as capable as One nor pretty as Three. Her ace in the hole is going along with Tieng-Bin's insatiable desire to Westernize his lifestyle. When he brings a Christian reverend around to discuss conversion, it is Wife Number Three who shows the most interest for, and adaptability to, modern ways.

Golden Child started as a comedy of manners, with the wives delicately insulting each other by complimenting each other (sounds odd, but it was very amusing). The play then moved convincingly to tragedy as order in the household was destroyed. A uniformly good cast aside, the most impressive aspect of *Golden Child* was the complex, sympathetic way Hwang treated assimilation. Christianity may have brought havoc into Tieng-Bin's household, but, as the golden child gratefully points out, it also unbound her gnarled feet.

Audiences were scarce for this most worthy drama but flocked to John Leguizamo's one-man marvel, *Freak.* Leguizamo actually did his sensational debut, *Mambo Mouth,* one better here, because he applied his gifts for comic mimicry and stand-up mockery to his own troubled childhood. Not only did the performer get to revel in the joys of urban Spanish culture, his material had a real and touching arc. One could quibble that by turning *everything* into broad comedy—even his father's alcohol-fueled abuse—Leguizamo the "love-me" performer cheated Leguizamo the writer. But if the author can't zip through his own disaster laden youth with elan, who can? Hilarious when dealing with young Leguizamo's gawky sexual encounters, lovely when recalling the moment dad acknowledged knowing an embarrassing secret John was gracious enough to keep to himself, *Freak* effortlessly braced its buffoonery with the underpinnings of authentic human woe.

A trilogy of David Mamet's one-acts also made it to Broadway, receiving a number of inexplicably good reviews while audiences yawned and scratched their heads. Neither a sharp Patti LuPone nor a somnolent Peter Riegert could beautify *The Old Neighborhood,* which ranged from a couple of pals reminiscing about Jewish life in 1950s Chicago, to a middle-aged man coming to terms with his sister, to the same man having a cryptic encounter with his former girl friend (played by Mamet's real-life wife, Rebecca Pidgeon). Without the harrowing danger that informed *The Cryptogram,* and missing the scorching wordplay that buoyed his early works, Mamet's latest writing mistakes asperity for profundity, paralyzing the author into becoming a third-rate Harold Pinter. In other words, there went the *Neighborhood.*

John Leguizamo in his solo show *Freak*

Revivals of American plays on Broadway did better, as evidenced by the afore-mentioned *A View From the Bridge* and *The Sunshine Boys,* and the deserved plaudits heaped on James Lapine's staging of *The Diary of Anne Frank.* Producers worked overtime convincing the press of the production's newsworthiness, since passages from Frank's diary too "provocative" to be included in the 1955 premiere were incorporated into the revival. (An example: a passage concerning Anne's budding sexuality and desire to touch another woman's breasts.) The 1997 *Diary,* newly revised by Wendy Kesselman, also went into more depth on the frustrating relationship between Anne and her mother. Otherwise, it was the story we all know—sad, claustrophobic, filled with lurking dread, but buoyed by piercing moments of hope and kindness. Wisely, director Lapine didn't posit Anne's "despite it all, I still believe in the goodness of man" speech as a Pollyana's naivete (in the book, it's actually a minor passage, written more than a year before the family's capture and shipment to the camps). One has to remember that what Anne witnessed in her attic was not the Nazi onslaught but her extended family trying to make the best of a wretched situation. For this reason, moments of joy or surprise were the production's most touching.

Natalie Portman made for a winsome young girl, pixie-ish but with a kernel of maturity that developed as the months passed. Other notables in the cast included George Hearn, Linda Lavin, Sophie Hayden and Austin Pendleton. Towering highest was Harris Yulin, who made Mr. Van Daan a chilling, hollow-eyed specimen, driven to rage by his nagging wife (Lavin) but shattered when caught stealing potatoes from the communal bin. Throughout, director Lapine steered clear of jerking tears. Only in the play's final seconds was Anne and her family's fate made truly devastating, with the credit going to lighting designer Adrianne Lobel. After Otto Frank's epilogue, one expected the lights to do a slow, sad fadeout. Instead, the words of Anne's diary, in her handwriting, were projected in sepia brown across the set, as if to say, "This is what was saved. And this is what was lost."

Two other play revivals made little stir: a capable *Ah, Wilderness!* from Daniel Sullivan, and a roundly raspberried *Wait Until Dark* from Leonard Foglia. Whereas *Wilderness* is often presented as the cheery flip side of *Long Day's Journey Into Night,* Lincoln Center's revival concentrated on the prickly conflicts under the surface of its moderately idealized New England family. Excepting Leslie Lyles's wounded Lily, the mounting was short on poetic sweetness, a deficiency compounded by the difficulty of creating a warm, expansive set on the three-sided Vivian Beaumont stage. Craig T. Nelson and Debra Monk starred, with Sam Trammell picking up the best press for his naive young pup of a Richard.

Wait Until Dark, on the other hand, had audiences screaming with terror (when the not-quite-dead killer pulls a short-lived, B-movie reincarnation)—and critics screeching with disdain. Filmmaker Quentin (*Pulp Fiction*) Tarantino, in his Broadway debut, was savaged by critics for his pedestrian, barely menacing Roat. If Marisa Tomei dumbed down heroine Suzy too much for comfort, at least she had verve, while Stephen Lang gave his henchman equal portions of decency and creepiness. Yet the show closed early, at the end of June, when advance sales didn't pan out.

Off Broadway Was Busier and Maybe Best

As usual, things were livelier for American playwrights off Broadway than on, with the season's most delightful—and arguably best—play rising from the hand of a dramatist, Douglas Carter Beane, who hadn't had a show on the New York boards since *Advice From a Caterpillar* in 1991. *As Bees in Honey Drown* buzzed along the high-toned world of art galleries, limos and ubiquitous cell phones in its tale of a naive novelist taken under the whirlwind wing of his manager, Alexa Vere de Vere. For an incredible week she transforms his life—and then vanishes just when he realizes she's raided his bank account. An immensely satisfying comedy, *Bees* boasted an impish turn by Mark Nelson as a former Vere de Vere victim, but the show lived and breathed in J. Smith-Cameron, unforgettable as madcap, melodramatic Alexa, a woman who takes life and slathers it "with great lashings of butter!" Author Beane snagged the Outer Critics Circle's John Gassner Playwriting Award for *Bees*.

Off-Broadway productions stood tall everywhere in the honors lists. Owing to a scheduling technicality, Paula Vogel's 1997 Critics Circle best-of-bests and Lortel winner, *How I Learned to Drive,* wasn't eligible for last season's Pulitzer but won this season's. In reviewing this play in my 1996-97 *Best Plays* report on The Season in New York, I recalled Vogel's "delirious classic *The Baltimore Waltz*" and noted, "We see the hand that shaped *Waltz* in *Drive*'s vignette style, its frankness about a woman's sexuality and proficiency at using almost vaudevillian laugh breaks to soften the impact of the trepidation lurking around the corner." Moisés Kaufman's *Gross Indecency: The Three Trials of Oscar Wilde,* a 1997 OOB offering that was moved to full off-Broadway status at the beginning of the 1997-98 season, tied *The Beauty Queen of Leenane* for the 1998 Lortel best-play Award. It also received a Mel Gussow citation in his *Best Plays* review of the 1997 OOB season. "Moisés Kaufman discovered a vivid new theatricality in *Gross Indecency*," Gussow observed. "As written and directed by Kaufman, this docu-drama skillfully mingled trial testimony with news events and literary commentary to create a potent play about hypocrisy and the law, art and the price of integrity. With clearsighted objectivity, the work did not overlook Wilde's own penchant for self-entrapment. Michael Emerson made an astonishing New York debut as Wilde. Although he does not bear a physical resemblance to his character, the actor conveyed an emotional and intellectual connection."

Tina Howe's *Pride's Crossing* cast Cherry Jones as 91-year-old Mabel Tidings Bigelow, determined to organize a croquet party on her birthday. Visits from her granddaughter and great-granddaughter bring up wellsprings of memories in Mabel, leading to flashbacks from her life. A stubborn, vigorous woman, Mabel endured a repressive upbringing and marriage to a wealthy, handsome, drunken bore to concentrate on her only passion: swimming. Eventually, she even made it across the English Channel. A nuanced work, willing to take time establishing mood (under Jack O'Brien's affectionate direction), *Pride's Crossing* was also conventional and episodic. Reviewers liked the play, which won the New York Drama Critics Circle best-American-play award, but saved their raves for the woman with the most twinkling eyes in all theaterdom, Cherry Jones. As the *Times*'s Ben Brantley put it, "Ms. Jones, as most Manhattan playgoers know, is a primary source of warmth in the New York theater today ... [Her] transformations are achieved without wigs or makeup, only changes of costume (usually in sight of the audience), carriage and facial expression ..... What Ms. Jones creates is a fluid, finely graded portrait that finds a continuity of self in the different ages of one personality ..... The actress is wrapping everyone, onstage and in the audience, in her insulating glow."

If Jones's presence made Tina Howe's play a must-see, another star made Jeff Baron's otherwise useless comedy, *Visiting Mr. Green,* at least a toss-up. *Green,* about a crotchety octogenarian forced to deal with, and later rely on, a good Samaritan, was the kind of lumpy TV-dinner porridge where all the hot-button issues

The 1997–98 Season Off Broadway

PLAYS (30)

GROSS INDECENCY
Manhattan Theater Club:
Seeking the Genesis
Three Days of Rain
Eyes for Consuela
Mizlansky/Zilinsky
Power Plays
Labor Day
Queens Blvd.
As Bees in Honey Drown
Mere Mortals and Others
John, His Story
Playwrights Horizons:
Baby Anger
Plunge
Mud, River, Stone
Gun-Shy
From Above
Tell-Tale
10 Naked Men
H. Finn Esq.
Two Pianos, Four Hands

FOREIGN PLAYS (4)

Virtue: Senpo Sugihara
THE BEAUTY QUEEN
  OF LEENANE
Shopping etc.
The Cripple of Inishmaan

MUSICALS (7)

Always . . . Patsy Cline
The Last Session
Clue: The Musical
Hedwig and the Angry Inch
I Will Come Back
The Wind in the Willows
Dinah Was

REVUES (3)

Secrets Every Smart
  Traveler Should Know
The Show Goes On
Hot Klezmer

SOLO SHOWS (4)

Something Blue
Alligator Tales
Mystery School
Bad Sex With Bud Kemp

REVIVALS (23)

N.Y. Shakespeare:
Henry VIII
On the Town
A Dybbuk
Macbeth
Roundabout:
Misalliance
Cyrano de Bergerac
A Flea in Her Ear
June Moon
Romeo and Juliet
BAM:
Three Sisters
Much Ado About
  Nothing
Othello
Encores!:
Strike Up the Band
Li'l Abner
St. Louis Woman
New Audience:
Richard II
Richard III
R & J

Royal Shakespeare:
Hamlet
Henry VIII
Krapp's Last Tape
Everyman
Cymbeline

SPECIALTIES (6)

Three-for-All
MindGames
Momix
Joseph Gabriel Magic
Saturn Returns
Savion Glover

Categorized above are all new productions listed (with some titles abbreviated) in the Off-Broadway section of this volume.
Plays listed in CAPITAL LETTERS were major 1997–98 prizewinners.
Plays listed in *italics* were in a continuing run June 7, 1998.

are 20 years old, and characters just about to walk out the door in a huff are always stopped by an assuaging comment or sense of guilt. A hit in Florida, *Green* had one huge draw: Eli Wallach, in his best role since a revival of Arthur Miller's *The Price* a few seasons back. He put all his scrunch-faced moxie into the most innocuous one-liners and got laughs just by the way he tossed a handful of unopened letters on a kitchen counter. Unlike Peter Falk's valiant but vain attempt to give *Mr. Peters' Connections* an emotional thru-line, Wallach actually made his negligible vehicle worth a look. Directed by Lonny Price, Jeff Baron's play became a surprise hit, with the producers so confident in the material, on Wallach's departure they decided to hire Hal Linden to keep the show going.

Ted Dykstra and Richard Greenblatt created a virtual marriage—and a virtuosic one—in *Two Pianos, Four Hands,* a play with music that wowed 'em at Toronto's Tarragon Theater in 1996 and enjoyed a healthy 1997-98 run in New York, first at the Promenade, then at the Variety Arts. Two grand pianos filled the stage, as authors/performers Dykstra and Greenblatt charted the progress of two little boys forced to take piano lessons until becoming good enough for the competition circuit. Not only did *2P4H* offer hilarious (and oh, so true) vignettes of eccentric piano teachers and familial fights about how many hours a day to devote to practice, the show managed knuckle-biting moments of drama, as when each young man suffers cruel rejection when applying for admission to a music conservatory. *2P4H* took quite a journey in two hours, one that kept a loving ear on the music from two men who lived it, were beaten down by it, and found their own charming way back in.

At the Public Theater, Philip Kan Gotanda's drama *Ballad of Yachiyo* struck some as too stylized and remote, but few disputed the production's physical beauty, with Loy Arcenas's set and Peter Maradudin's lighting earning Drama Desk nominations. Also more valued for its set than its narrative, Jane Anderson's *Defying Gravity* offered a fictionalized version of the story of Christa McAuliffe (the school-teacher who met her doom on the Space Shuttle). After picturing not only how spectators, NASA technicians and the teacher's own daughter might have felt about the debacle, Anderson concluded with a hopeful epilogue, envisioning an age when trips to the moon will be as common as weekend jaunts to the Hamptons. Typical of the play's ingenuity—and unworkability—were scenes that have painter Claude Monet (Jonathan Hadary) wandering through time and offering his impressions (pun intended) on the esthetic beauty of space. As with Wendall K. Harrington's work on *The Capeman,* Jeff Cowie's spare sets and projections created a spare yet expansive universe, in the unlikely American Place Theater space. Too bad the play rarely got off the launch pad.

Three-for-All, an import with the Spanish comedy trio "tricicle," wanted to be the next *Blue Man Group.* Alas, like the previous season's *Tokyo Shock Boys* and *The New Bozena,* tricicle couldn't make it up the hill of poor reviews and audience apathy. A shame, because Joan Gracia, Paco Mir and Carles Sans were gifted mimes, creating a comic silent movie onstage. Their simple premise had three bachelors, one a musician, one a would-be Mickey Spillane, the third a subway performance artist (well, more like an inventive panhandler) getting through a day in and out of their urban apartment. Fantasy sequences occurred when the writer (Mir) would tap out the first chapter of his latest opus on an old typewriter, his cohorts then enacting the ridiculous noirisms of Joe Ryan, private eye. Riotous bits included an indoor reenactment of the Tour de France on a stationary bicycle, a tennis match with a ball on a wire, and a trip to the moon via the living room couch. One unforgettable moment had a member of the trio taking his morning tea by opening his mouth, inserting a tea bag, following that with sugar and milk, then drinking hot water straight from the kettle. Had these gags been done on *The Kids in the Hall* or in some independent film, critics would likely have hailed tricicle's whimsy and sustained invention. Because the show tried to fill the Union Square Theater, it was three-for-all and all for none.

Though in town for a mere two-week run at the New Victory Theater *The Number 14* captivated critics enough with its masks, puppets and *commedia* techniques to bring the Axis and Touchstone Theater Company collaboration a Drama Desk nomination for unique theatrical experience. Zany in a more old-fashioned way was *Power Plays,* a trio of one-acts that marked the first time Elaine May and Alan Arkin have appeared onstage together in 30 years. Arkin told *Playbill* magazine's Harry Haun the last time they were linked was when they were featured on a bill at Chicago's Second City. Each had risen to a kind of improv stardom, yet they'd somehow never played a sketch together. Arkin recalled with chagrin that their summit resulted in "the longest, and worst, improvisation ever done." Well, 30 years and three scripts helped a lot, and each of the comedies in *Power Plays* had worthy moments of tomfoolery. May and her real-life daughter, Jeannie Berlin, starred in May's own *The Way of All Fish,* in which a hot-shot boss discovers her self-effacing secretary may be a hungrier tiger than she is. Father and son then took the stage in *Virtual Reality,* with Arkin senior and son Anthony playing henchmen waiting for a dangerous mission to commence. After a protracted opening exchange wherein the experienced foreman endlessly questions the identity of his smart-mouthed associate, the play picked up with a nod to Arkin's improv roots: both men kill time by *making believe* they're unpacking ominous goods for their assignment. Laughs were plantiful when, for example, the younger stooge would pull an invisible item out of a non-existent box, only to have the older man scrutinize an imaginary list and shake his head saying, "Oh no, that's bad. We have too many of these."

Play number three, May's *In and Out of the Light,* cast Arkin *pere* as a middle-aged dentist about to embark on his first extra-marital dalliance. He's chosen his new hygienist (May), an eye-bogglingly decrepit version of the generic sex-object nurse. Ah, but in dentistry as in comedy, timing is everything, and before Dr. Kesselman can start drilling, in comes his most neurotic patient (Berlin) with an emergency, and his son (Anthony Arkin) with an urgent "papa, I'm gay" speech. Agreeable farcical craziness ensued, capped by a final song as delightful as it was unexpected.

Eager to duplicate the success they had with *All in the Timing,* Primary Stages rounded up another batch of old and new David Ives comedies under the umbrella title, *Mere Mortals.* Though the writing on three of the six plays was first-rate, the

AS BEES IN HONEY DROWN—J. Smith-Cameron as Alexa Vere de Vere in Douglas Carter Beane's comedy, "the season's most delightful—and arguably best—play"

production as a whole had a second-drawer feeling. Blame some of the disappointment on John Rando's hyperactive direction, which created blissfully clever stage pictures but also lunged for jokey sight gags that jolted the plays out of their tone. The funny and well-directed opener, *Foreplay or: The Art of the Fugue*, followed the dating rituals of three unconnected couples on a miniature golf course. *Time Flies* took a sweetly clever look at 24 hours in the life of two mayflies—a busy day indeed, since 24 hours *is* the life of a mayfly. 1996's *Degas, C'est Moi*, a small masterpiece about a man who makes believe he's the painter Degas for a day, only to tire of the charade and then discover the wonders hidden in his own mundane existence, lacked the necessary delicate touch up until the finale, which was exquisitely staged. Among the also-rans were a spoof on David Mamet's plays that should have been sharper, a bit about reincarnated construction workers that should have been shorter, and a sketch about a desperately ill tourist visiting a mentally preoccupied nurse that should have been abandoned.

Conversely, two major off-Broadway plays impressed with their complexity and layered story-telling. Richard Greenberg enjoyed his best reviews to date with the

Pulitzer-nominated *Three Days of Rain,* which set its first act in a barren gray loft and then traveled back 35 years to the same space when it housed a budding architectural firm. Currently living in the loft (memorably lit with a gloomy slant of fluorescent light by designer Donald Holder) is Walker, itinerant son of Ned, one of the architects. Ned has recently died, leaving the family house—an architectural marvel we're told—not to Walker or to his surprisingly stable sister, Nan, but to Pip, the son of Ned's partner, Theo. Just when we've worked out the latter-day relationships, *Rain* flashes back to 1960, when Ned and Theo occupied the loft. Logical, stammering Ned served as a ballast for vivacious, ingenious Theo, though just who was the real genius is left intentionally unclear. Much of Act II finds Ned left alone with Theo's free-minded Southern girlfriend, Lina, destined after "three days of rain" to become Ned's wife, for better and mostly worse.

Plentiful funny lines aside, the great strength of Greenberg's excellent play was the way clues and cues were dropped and picked up again in a new light, such as our discovery of the reason for Ned's propensity to remain silent. There was also (as in Pinter's *Betrayal*) the poignancy of knowing a relationship will turn out badly in the end, set against our natural desire for its romantic initiation to succeed. This attention to parceling out information made *Three Days of Rain* an advancement over such entertaining but superficial Greenberg plays as *The Extra Man* and *Eastern Standard.* A cogent, empathetic work, *Rain* was neatly handled by three actors (Patricia Clarkson, John Slattery, Bradley Whitford) in six roles.

Though lacking a certain "oomph," A.R. Gurney's latest, *Labor Day,* made some very intricate playwriting *look* easy, the sign of a master playwright even when he cuts a few corners on plot. The arc of Gurney's comedy couldn't be more rudimentary: John, a veteran playwright (Josef Sommer) with several hits and more misses, has retreated to the country after a health scare. There he's learned to enjoy the company of his family, including his devoted wife (Joyce Van Patten), high-strung daugher (Veanne Cox) and preppy son (James Colby). Into this world comes a jittery young director who tells of major Broadway, and even Hollywood interest in John's latest play. The only catch? No one likes the ending except John, who doesn't think a finale embracing family life is too sentimental for the 1990s. While the director pushes John to make changes, and John's wife pushes to keep her grown children out of the play entirely, the kids struggle with their own real-life crises.

While all this is going on, Gurney also comments on the nature of playwriting, from the difference between dramatic action and mere activity, to the contrasts between rewriting a script to make it better and revising it to appeal to producers. The trade-off for all this self-reflexive material is *Labor Day*'s diagrammatical quality; it has the mechanical action of a well-thought-out conceit rather than a living story. Still, Josef Sommer could not have made his playwright more personable or more pragmatic while defending the integrity of his work.

Similar themes were explored in *Mizlansky/Zilinsky or "Schmucks,"* an early Jon Robin Baitz play expanded to become a Nathan Lane vehicle at Manhattan Theater Club. For all the familiar stuff about a hungry writer tempted by fame (handled better in Beane's *Bees*), MTC's *M/Z* was really about watching Lane play a Max

Bialystock type producer, forced to make religious records for children as a way to launder much-needed cash. Nice work, too, from Lewis J. Stadlen as Lane's former partner, sucked into the shady world of L.A. dealmaking one last time.

Mizlansky and Zilinsky were pikers in the crime game compared to Leopold and Loeb, those wealthy urchins who killed an innocent classmate for kicks and, thanks to good lawyering, escaped the electric chair. Unlike *Gross Indecency,* which organized reportage and research about Oscar Wilde into play form, John Logan's *Never the Sinner* really *was* a play, one that showed the twisted relationship between Nathan (Jason Bowcutt) and Dick (Michael Solomon) moving from smarmy intellectualism into cold-blooded murder. "Hate the sin but never the sinner," preaches their attorney, Clarence Darrow, even though "these boys" (as Darrow refers to them) are both over 18 and have absolutely no extenuating circumstances. Much like the O.J. Simpson prosecutors, opposing counsel Crowe oversells his case, while Darrow's eloquence convinces the judge (though not this viewer) to opt for mercy.

Author Logan doesn't take a stand on capital punishment, but he does examine Leopold and Loeb's sociopathy, stopping just short of blaming the duo's behavior on their inability to be homosexual in 1920s society. Fish-faced and smirking, stick-figured and furtive, Jason Bowcutt (a Drama Desk nominee) was downright iconographic as Leopold; nice work, too, from Robert Hogan's calculatedly homespun Darrow and Glen Panell's frustrated Crowe. Originally a cross-country theater production, *Sinner* transferred from the American Jewish Theater to the John Houseman, where it lost some tension but not a bit of its craftsmanship.

Not as lucky as the boys, the protagonist of *Amazing Grace* does undergo state execution, but then again this nurse poisoned more than a dozen people. Michael Cristofer's drama attempted to ask meaningful questions about forgiveness (the woman has a true religious change of heart), as well as the dual nature of a person tirelessly devoted to improving the quality of her patients' lives—until she hastens to snuff them out. Despite a convincingly sincere Marsha Mason, *Grace* plodded along without focus.

By contrast, the first act of *A Madhouse in Goa,* a 1987 Martin Sherman drama premiering in the U.S. at the Second Stage Theater, was beautifully constructed. Resembling nothing so much as a Russian short story or a less optimistic O. Henry, the playlet starts as a charming coming-of-age comedy only to turn unsettling. David (Rick Stear), an uptight and deeply miserable young man (as only a 20-something gay, Jewish artist type can be), ventures to the Greek Island of Corfu to practice photography and observe a new social landscape he can write about in his journal. At a seaside inn he meets a loquacious widow (Judith Ivey), who has vacationed there for years. When news of the Greek king's visit reaches hotel owner Nikos (Daniel Gerroll, in a performance both sexy and sinister), he imposes upon the widow, asking her to relinquish her cafe table with the best view. She refuses, leading to a heartless act of blackmail by the hotel staff that indirectly implicates David and shames him ever after. Act II tells a less convincing story that takes place in the same resort 20 years later. The only character even remotely connected to the above-mentioned tale is stroke-ridden Daniel (Russ Thacker), who recounted the table incident in a best seller. The problem? Bitter as the widow's fate was, Daniel sugar-coated the political elements and took liberties with the situation's ugliness. Along comes a brazen producer hoping to turn Daniel's fictionalization into a Hollywood musical that has even *less* to do with the truth. *A Madhouse in Goa* ended with a nasty act of betrayal that left a sour aftertaste, surely one reason the underrated play failed with critics and audiences.

Queens Blvd., a comedy by Paul Corrigan, proved so retro in its approach to gay camp, critics sat open-mouthed as one character worshiped at a shrine to Audrey Hepburn while another swanned about the kitchen in a chef's hat and apron. More stupid than funny, *Queens Blvd.* nonetheless didn't deserve the brickbats thrown at it by gay protestors, angered by what they perceived as antediluvian mockery. Sorry, but if the black community can embrace the chitlin circuit (August Wilson's term for it), and Jews can laugh uproariously at Jackie Mason, militant homosexuals can lighten up a little, too, and acknowledge that *Queens Blvd.* was nothing more than an affectionate, albeit incompetent, blast from the past.

Playwright Tom Strelich was hoping to work his way into the off-Broadway scene with his assaultive satire *BAFO* (an acronym for *Best and Final Offer*) at the American Place Theater, but his tweaking of racist issues and thumb-nosing at the U.S. military industrial complex struck reviewers as old news, shrilly announced.

Other disappointingly received plays (oddly enough, also political in nature) were Lynn Nottage's *Mud, River, Stone,* generally conceded to be a stony muddle, and *Anadarko,* Tim Blake Nelson's follow-up to his acclaimed *The Grey Zone* at Manhattan Class Company. Nottage's drama told of a black American couple having nightmarish encounters in South Africa; *Anadarko,* by all accounts a grim and ugly tale, looked at two losers guarded in an Oklahoma police station by racist hick lawmen. *H. Finn Esq.* about two modern-day Southerners, who might be the great-great-grandsons of Tom Sawyer and Huck Finn (whose traits they resemble), sounded like a clever conceit but drifted away on a raft of bad reviews. Peter Hedges's *Baby Anger,* at Playwrights Horizons, received some interest for its tale of parents raising a young boy—who's cast as a girl in a national TV commercial. Kia Corthron garnered regional success at Chicago's Goodman Studio with *Seeking the Genesis,* but New Yorkers were indifferent to her cautionary tale of giving a hyperactive child too much Ritalin.

Not that magic realism did any better than gritty realism. *Eyes for Consuela,* the latest from Sam Shepard, spent 90 minutes setting up one premise: Henry, an American hiding out in Mexico, receives a visit from Amado, a local who wants to cut out Henry's eyes and give them to his girlfriend, Consuela. The threat of physical violence allows Shepard to spill all his exposition via Amado's questioning of Henry—a pretty cheap device. At least the playwright is clear about what Henry ran from and what makes Amado and Consuela's relationship click. Less intelligible is the play's surreal windup, which has something to do with a bicycle and ribbon spooling endlessly out of a suitcase. Maybe the Octavio Paz story on which *Eyes* was based made more sense.

Tom Donaghy, fresh from the inexplicable critical success of last season's *Minutes From the Blue Route,* could have used some help from above for his *From Above,*

Above, Maryann Urbano and Jeffrey DeMunn in a scene from Richard Dresser's *Gun-Shy* at Playwrights Horizons; *right,* Rick Stear and Judith Ivey in *A Madhouse in Goa* by Martin Sherman on the program at Second Stage

a product of Playwrights Horizons' Amblin/Dreamworks commission program. Patricia Kalember, of TV's *Sisters,* starred as a woman in mourning suddenly presented with a new man in her life. Christopher Kyle, of *Monogamist* fame, also followed up a hit with a miss, though his uneven *Plunge,* about (yawn) yuppies sequestered in a weekend retreat, managed some lively exchanges. Richard Dresser's comedy *Gun-Shy* also failed to score with Horizons viewers, though the often zingy comedy found an admirer in John Simon, who called it "a *Private Lives* for our time (with) enough overarching wit to carry us past the few passages that do not sparkle, probe and illuminate." Dresser's sometimes farcical piece told of a middle-aged couple who realize they should never have gotten divorced.

Punchlines abounded in *10 Naked Men* and *Peep Show,* the latest from Ronnie *Making Porn* Larsen. When the author/director saw his core audience falter because *Peep Show* actually had women in it, he rewrote the piece, billing it as *Ronnie*

Larsen's All-Male Peep Show. Give the man credit; if Ford Motors knew its public this well, we'd all be driving Edsels.

John Leguizamo's *Freak* aside, it wasn't a big year for one-person shows. At the end of its season, Manhattan Theater Club ran three cabaret performances in repertory as *Manhattan Music,* featuring Mary Cleere Haran, James Naughton and the vocalists "Hot Mouth." Also at MTC, Anne Galjour's *Alligator Tales* offered glimpses of life on the Louisiana bayou, with authentic sounding tales of simple people bullied by nature into heroism. Alas, for all the hurricanes, sexual reawakenings and dramatic rescues that swam in Galjour's gumbo, the evening proved confusing and ponderous. Apathy also greeted Paul Selig's *Mystery School,* five monologues for women, all performed by Tyne Daly. Characters included a Christian fundamentalist, an alcoholic, a hostess of a New Age cable TV public access call-in show, an idealistic speaker at a college graduation and a widow narrating a slide show "filled with signs and symbols pointing to the end of the world and the birth of the next." The world continued, the show closed.

More eccentric solos included the return of Joseph Gabriel's *Magic* to the Lamb's Theater, with basically the same prestidigitations, the same gently amusing patter, and the same unforgettable guest artist, Romano Frediani, still bopping tennis balls across the stage and catching audience-tossed hoops around his neck. Marc Salem played *MindGames* with his audience, guessing their most recent dreams, favorite vacations and lucky numbers. His actual "tricks" were standard stuff, but the soothseeing was goosepimpling. A return engagement by card sharp-shooter Ricky Jay sold out before it even opened, an HBO special in the interim not having dampened demand for Jay's low-key wizardry. But Sandra Tsing Loh's *Bad Sex With Bud Kemp,* about dates from hell, and Michaela Murphy's *Something Blue,* about a wedding from hell, made nary a stir at Second Stage.

Moving out of Manhattan altogether, one reaches England—by way of the Brooklyn Academy of Music. The Royal Shakespeare Company came to town with a quintet of canon classics, including Alex Jennings as *Hamlet* in a controversially abridged production directed by *Art*'s Matthew Warchus. While Théâtre de Complicité's staging of Ionesco's *The Chairs* played on Broadway, two members of that company, Kathryn Hunter and Marcello Magni, staged a well-received *Everyman.* Other RSC mountings included *Cymbeline,* Edward Petherbridge in *Krapp's Last Tape,* and *Henry VIII* (under the title *All Is True, or The Famous History of the Life of King Henry VIII*) with Jane Lapotaire and Paul Jesson.

Months earlier, the New York Shakespeare Festival offered *Henry VIII* as the finale of its Shakespeare Marathon, Joseph Papp's worthy but by all accounts bumpy white elephant. Known for her acrobatic-meets-intellectual stagings (*Arabian Nights, The Notebooks of Leonardo da Vinci*), director Mary Zimmerman apparently had trouble coordinating a costume drama ensemble. It was one of those productions where an actor scorned in one critique got a glowing notice in another, though both reviews knocked the play. Nevertheless, the ubiquitous Jayne Atkinson, who scored in *Ivanov* and as a cast-replacement in *How I Learned to Drive,* won praise for her Queen Katharine.

Treated to two full productions of *Henry VIII* in the same season, our Mr. Foose was inspired to review the history of its appearance here: "It is such a rarity that talking of productions in New York one must mention television. In the BBC series *The Shakespeare Plays, Henry VIII* was shown in New York on Channel 13 on April 25, 1979. John Stride played Henry and Claire Bloom played Queen Katharine. There were only two earlier productions of this play in New York City in the 20th Century. On April 6, 1946 *Henry VIII* was the first offering of Margaret Webster's American Repertory Theater. Victor Jory was Henry. On March 14, 1916 there was a Tercentenary Production at the recently restored New Amsterdam Theater. Lyn Harding was Henry. As these things go, the play was relatively popular in New York in the 19th Century, after its New York premiere on May 13, 1799 at the Park Theater." Mr. Foose also noted that the Public's *Henry VIII* was both a first and a last—the first time New York Shakespeare Festival had ever produced this play and the last entry in its 36-play Shakespeare Marathon, begun in the 1987-88 season.

It wasn't a huge year for Shakespeare (no plays on Broadway), but the Royal National did bring an acclaimed *Othello* to BAM, with David Harewood, Simon Russell Beale (Iago) and Claire Skinner. Sam Mendes, Broadway's golden boy thanks to *Cabaret,* directed. Off-Broadway, the Acting Company stopped in with a horridly-reviewed *Romeo and Juliet* but would later redeem themselves with *Love's Fire,* an evening of one-acts by major playwrights based on Shakespeare's sonnets. Theater for a New Audience offered *Richard II* and *III* in repertory, courtesy of Portuguese-born director Ron Daniels. Explaining his conception, Daniels told the *Playbill On-Line* theater website, "Though at first, Richard II comes off as something of a tyrant, in that play all the characters are essentially moral and decent. They often act against their better natures, and they're appalled by Richard's resignation because they believe in the sanctity of the realm . . . . . By abdicating, Richard creates a void of chaos and destruction. So when we come to *Richard III,* there's not a single decent human being in it. In our set design, the beautiful church of the first play is bombed out by the second. And yet, ironically, *Richard III*'s world is much more fun and gleeful than *Richard II*'s."

Playfulness—of an almost murderous intensity—also infused the Shakespearean adaptation *R & J,* which pared the tragedy of warring families down to four characters, all of them young men in a repressive boarding school. For no given reason, the quartet decide to act out *Romeo and Juliet* for their own pleasure, taking delight in the verse and careening about the John Houseman Studio space the way growing boys would. Apart from the students' uniforms and one long red cloth, *R & J* proceeds sans costumes and props, further distancing the piece from stuffy pageantry. Fun and games quickly fade, though, when the love story kicks in. The duo playing Romeo and Juliet play for keeps, even unto kissing, which doesn't sit well with their homophobic and/or closeted comrades. Intriguing as all this sounds, especially since the Bard's works were originally acted solely by men, *R & J* still didn't have enough of a context to make it more than an earnest stunt. That didn't stop the sometimes exciting piece from becoming not only a sleeper hit, but the longest-running production of *Romeo and Juliet* in the history of New York City! (The previous champ, a 1923 mounting with Jane Cowl and Rollo Peters, ran 161 performances.) A film is planned, with adaptor/director Joe Calarco repeating his duties, and performers Sean Dugan, Danny Gurwin, Greg Shamie and Daniel J. Shore expected as well, alongside a few more actors to open the piece up a bit.

Men doing Shakespeare was nothing new for the British troupe Cheek by Jowl, which had come to town in 1993 with an acclaimed, all-male *As You Like It* but returned to BAM with a coed *Much Ado.* Much ado also greeted the news that Alec Baldwin and Angela Bassett would star in a Public Theater *Macbeth,* but by most accounts the show was a big nothing, with Baldwin too working class and Bassett too over-the-top. Director George C. Wolfe could be forgiven for being awol on this one; at the time, he was about to go under the knife for a kidney transplant.

Wolfe survived that scare, but alas, some other theater notables got cut from the earth's cast list. Dorothy Stickney, the first mother of *Life With Father,* died at 101. Theater critics Edith Oliver and Ross Wetzsteon passed, as did cabaret critic Donna Coe. We lost Jimmy Stewart, Frank Sinatra, Laurie Beechman, Stubby Kaye, literary agent Helen Merrill and Lyrics & Lyricists founder Maurice Levine. After years of flops and continuing bouts with cancer and gastroenteritis, composer/lyricist Bob Merrill, whose *Carnival* showed how people can move on despite profound misfortune, killed himself. He was 78.

Looking toward the future, the internet became an ever more powerful tool for industry communication and research. *Playbill On-Line* led the field in theater news and information (okay, I'm biased), but active websites were also maintained by *Variety, Back Stage, InTheater,* the Tony Awards and the Rodgers and Hammerstein Organization, not to mention hundreds of fan-designed homepages dedicated to stars, composers and shows. Off-Broadway theaters multiplied as well, with producer Daryl Roth opening an eponymous 499-seat space in Union Square, *Dinah Was* transferring to the Gramercy Theater, the Jane Street Theater housing *Hedwig,* and the Upper West Side's Second Stage Theater ready to break ground for a second space on 43d Street.

A final note: I might as well mention that spring 1999 is targeted for the Broadway premiere of Barry Manilow's own musical, *Harmony,* which tried out at La Jolla in late 1997. Who knows? If he gets some do's from Elton John and don'ts from Paul Simon, the kid just might make it.

A GRAPHIC GLANCE

1997–98
Drawings
By Hirschfeld

Alfred Molina, Alan Alda and Victor Garber in *Art*

Right, Anna Manahan, Tom Murphy, Marie Mullen and Brian F. O'Byrne in *The Beauty Queen of Leenane*

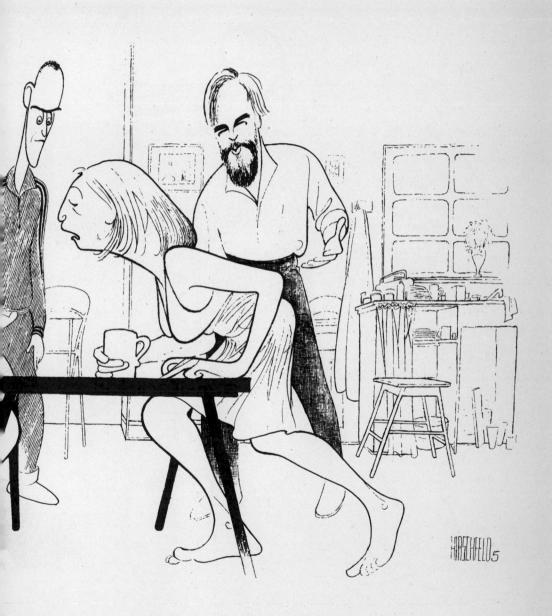

Jack Klugman and Tony Randall in *The Sunshine Boys*

Tyne Daly in *Mystery School*

Right, **John Leguizamo in *Freak***

Back row, Jim Corti *(with chain),* Lynnette Perry *(on swing)* and Judy Kaye *(hand raised); front row,* Brian Stokes Mitchell *(seated),* Audra McDonald, Mark Jacoby, Peter Friedman *(with beard)* and Marin Mazzie in *Ragtime*

Frank Langella in the title role of *Cyrano de Bergerac*

Liam Neeson as Oscar Wilde in *The Judas Kiss*

Left, Natasha Richardson and Alan Cumming with the Kit Kat Club Dancers in *Cabaret*

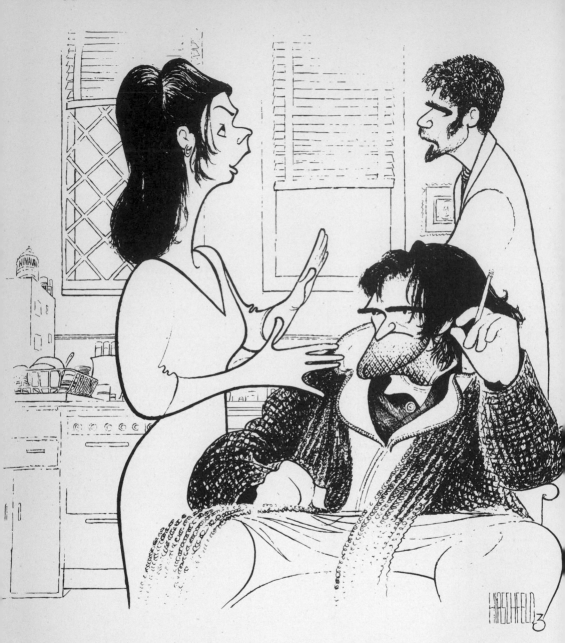

Marisa Tomei, Quentin Tarantino and Stephen Lang in *Wait Until Dark*

Debra Monk and Craig T. Nelson in *Ah, Wilderness!*

Jane Alexander in *Honour*

Left, Eli Wallach in *Visiting Mr. Green*

Margaret Colin as Jacqueline Kennedy in *Jackie*

Members of the Continental Congress including *(right foreground)* Brent Spiner as John Adams, Pat Hingle as Benjamin Franklin and Paul Michael Valley as Thomas Jefferson in Roundabout Theater's revival of the musical *1776*

Below, a Hirschfeld assembly of the von Trapp family as portrayed in *The Sound of Music: back row,* Rebecca Luker, Michael Siberry and Sara Zelle; *front row, ascending,* Ashley Rose Orr, Andrea Bowen, Tracy Alison Walsh, Matthew Ballinger, Natalie Hall and Ryan Hopkins

Ruben Blades, Marc Anthony, Ednita Nazario and Renoly Santiago in the Paul Simon-Derek Walcott musical *The Capeman*

Angela Bassett and Alec Baldwin in the Public Theater's *Macbeth*

Sophie Hayden, Missy Yager, George Hearn and Natalie Portman in Wendy Kesselman's new adaptation of the Frances Goodrich-Albert Hackett play *The Diary of Anne Frank*

Left, Douglas Sills (Percy), Christine Andreas (Marguerite) and Terrence Mann (Chauvelin) in the musical version of *The Scarlet Pimpernel*

Anthony Arkin, Alan Arkin, Jeannie Berlin and Elaine May in *Power Plays*

68

Above, Rosie O'Donnell, emcee of the Tony ceremonies celebrating the 1997–98 season characterized by Hirschfeld in a sampling *(at right)* of its acting duets: *in back row,* Patti LuPone and Peter Riegert in *The Old Neighborhood,* Anthony LaPaglia and Allison Janney in *A View From the Bridge; front row,* Geraldine McEwan and Richard Briers *(seated)* in *The Chairs,* Emily Skinner and Alice Ripley in *Side Show,* Natasha Richardson and Alan Cumming in *Cabaret,* Anna Manahan *(seated, with plate)* and Marie Mullen in *The Beauty Queen of Leenane*

HIRSCHFELD ECHOES OF THE SEASON PAST—*Above,* Julie Harris of *The Gin Game* and Christopher Plummer of *Barrymore* got together for a visit last year; *below,* Christiane Noll, Robert Cuccioli *(as Jekyll),* Linda Eder and Robert Cuccioli *(as Hyde)* in the continuing 1996–97 musical *Jekyll & Hyde*

THE
PRIZEWINNING
PLAYS

Here are the details of 1997–98's major prizewinning plays—synopses, biographical sketches of authors and other material. By permission of the playwrights, their representatives, publishers, and others who own the exclusive rights to publish these scripts in full, most of our continuities include substantial quotations from crucial/pivotal scenes in order to provide a permanent reference to style and quality as well as theme, structure and story line.

In the case of such quotations, scenes and lines of dialogue, stage directions and descriptions appear *exactly* as in the stage version or published script unless (in a very few instances, for technical reasons) an abridgement is indicated by five dots (. . . . .). The appearance of three dots (. . .) is the script's own punctuation to denote the timing of a spoken line.

1997 Critics, Lortel Awards
1998 Pulitzer Prize

○○○
○○○
○○○
○○○
○○○
○○○

HOW I LEARNED TO DRIVE

A Full Length Play in One Act

BY PAULA VOGEL

Cast and credits appear on pages 291 (off Broadway) and 334 (off off Broadway) of *The Best Plays of 1996–97*

PAULA VOGEL was born in 1951 in Washingon, D.C., where her father was in the advertising business. She graduated from Catholic University in 1974 and went on for graduate studies to Cornell, where she served for a time on the faculty of the department of theater arts. In love with the theater, she wanted to be a part of it and turned to playwriting after finding no success as an actress and believing in those days that no woman could establish herself in a career as a director.Vogel's first two plays of record in the New York theater were produced by Circle Repertory: The Baltimore Waltz *February 11, 1992 for 39 performances, winning a playwriting Obie (it was also produced in April of that year at the Alley Theater in Houston) and* And Baby Makes Seven *the following season on April 27, 1993 for 22 performances.*

Vogel's How I Learned to Drive *came onto the stage on tiptoe and took over the spotlight and the fanfare at the highest level. It was produced by the Vineyard Theater, opening as an off-off-Broadway offering March 16, 1997, moving to full off-Broadway status May 6 and soon sweeping the 1997 Lucille Lortel (best off-Broadway play), New York Drama Critics Circle (best play regardless of category) and Drama Desk (best play) Awards. According to rules governing the the Pulitzer Prize, the March opening date of* How I Learned to Drive *was a couple of weeks too late to be considered in the 1997 voting but, as a 1998 entry in the eyes of the Pulitzer committee, it was voted the prize this year.*

A new Vogel play, The Mineola Twins, *was produced this spring at Trinity Repertory in Providence, R.I., where she resides. Her plays have been produced in several regional theaters and nations, and the list of her stage works includes* Hot and Throbbing, Desdemona *and* The Oldest Profession. *Some of them have been published in an anthology entitled* The Baltimore Waltz and Other Plays. *In addition to the New York prizes, Vogel has won awards and fellowships from AT&T New Plays, the Fund for New American Plays, the McKnight, the Rockefeller Foundation's Bellagio Center and the National Endowment for the Arts. She is also a member of New Dramatists.*

As the winner of the 1997 Lortel and Critics prizes, How I Learned to Drive *was fully represented and celebrated in the Prizewinning Plays section of last season's yearbook,* The Best Plays of 1996–97. *Its synopsis with quotes from the script appears on pages 190–208 of that volume.*

Lortel Award

○○○
○○○
○○○
○○○
○○○
○○○

GROSS INDECENCY: THE THREE TRIALS OF OSCAR WILDE

A Play in Two Acts

BY MOISES KAUFMAN

Cast and credits appear on page 224

MOISES KAUFMAN was born on November 21, 1963 in Caracas, Venezuela and was educated there at the Universidad Metropolitana. He performed there as an actor with theThespis Theater Ensemble but came to the United States in 1987 and has settled here into our theater scene. From 1987 to 1990 he studied at N.Y.U.'s Experimental Theater Wing, and 1991 found him directing Women in Beckett *off off Broadway. In 1992 he founded the Tectonic Theater Project, active OOB with such offerings— directed by Kaufman—as Franz Xavier Kroetz's* The Nest *(1994, a* Village Voice *selection as one of the ten best productions of its season) and* Marlowe's Eye *by Naomi Iizuka (1996).*

Three years ago, a friend gave Kaufman a book of Oscar Wilde quotations, whose last ten pages were transcripts of Wilde's trials. "I found a fascinating event," Kaufman remembers, "an artist being asked to justify his art in a court of law!" He further explored Wilde's life and works, from which he pieced together his first work as a playwright, Gross Indecency: The Three Trials of Oscar Wilde. *Tectonic produced it OOB March 2, 1997, and in his annual* Best Plays *review of the OOB season Mel Gussow cited it as one of the year's best, calling it "a potent play about hypocrisy and the law, art and the price of integrity." It moved up to full off-Broadway status June 5, 1997, won the prestigious Lucille Lortel Award in a tie with* The Beauty Queen of Leenane *and is still running as we go to press.*

Kaufman directs for Working Classroom, an Albuquerque-based multi-ethnic arts program that produces and tours original plays. But his home base is Tectonic and

New York City, where he lives in a long-term relationship with his friend Jeff LaHoste, to whom he dedicated the published version of his play .

AUTHOR'S NOTE ON THE SOURCE MATERIAL: When the text in the play comes from a historical account, the author and name of the book from which the text comes is stated by the narrators. There are two exceptions to this:

One is when there are several texts that come from different books by the same author. When this is the case, only the first book is mentioned.

Second, as the play progresses and Oscar Wilde's world collapses, so does this formal device. Therefore, in the second act not all sources are stated.

PROLOGUE

The actors come onstage. The actor playing Oscar Wilde holds up a copy of De Profundis.

ACTOR: This is from *De Profundis* by Oscar Wilde. *(Reads.)* "Do not be afraid of the past. If people tell you it is irrevocable, do not believe them. The past, present and future are but one moment in the sight of God. Time and space are merely accidental conditions of thought. The imagination can transcend them."

ACT I

The First Trial

SYNOPSIS: The play takes place on two levels, one an elevated stage serving as a courtroom and other locations, and, below at audience level, at a long table covered with books from which the Narrators quote.

The Central Criminal Court of the Old Bailey is crowded on April 3, 1895 with spectators waiting to hear Oscar Wilde's suit against Lord Sholto Douglas, Marquess of Queensberry. Prosecuting counsel, Sir Edward Clarke, states, "The charge against him is that he published a false and malicious libel," in the form of a visiting card, left at Wilde's club by Queensberry with the message, "Oscar Wilde: posing somdomite *(sic)*." Clarke identifies his client as "a poet, a novelist, an essayist and a playwright." With that card, openly left with the club's hall porter, Queensberry has libellously insinuated that Wilde is guilty of what Clarke characterizes as "the gravest of all offenses."

Asked how he pleads, Queensberry answers, "I plead not guilty, and also that the libel is true and that it is for the public benefit that it should be published. I wrote that card with the intention of bringing matters to a head, having been unable to meet Mr. Wilde otherwise, and to save my son—" Lord Alfred Douglas "—and I abide by what I wrote."

Examined by Clarke, Wilde outlines his *curriculum vitae:* he is 39, son of a Dublin surgeon, a prizewinning scholar at Magdalen College, Oxford, married since 1884 with sons 9 and 10 years of age, living a life devoted to art and literature including international tours of lecturing on the English Renaissance of Art.

WILDE: I call it the English Renaissance of Art because it is indeed a sort of new birth of the spirit of man. Like the great Italian Renaissance of the fifteenth century, it possesses a desire for a more comely way of life, a passion for physical beauty, an exclusive attention to form. It seeks new subjects for poetry, new forms of art, new intellectual and imaginative enjoyments. In art as in politics there is but one origin to all revolutions, a desire on the part of man for a nobler form of life, for a freer method and opportunity of expression. This renaissance will create a new brotherhood among men by furnishing a universal language.

CLARKE: Mr. Wilde, you have also written several plays, two of which are currently being performed in the West End?

WILDE: Yes. *The Importance of Being Earnest* and *An Ideal Husband.*

CLARKE: When did you make the acquaintance of Lord Alfred Douglas?

WILDE: In 1891. He was brought to my house by a friend.

DOUGLAS: My first meeting with Oscar Wilde was an astonishment.

NARRATOR 3: From *The Autobiography of Alfred Douglas,* written thirty years later.

DOUGLAS: I had never heard a man talking with such perfect sentences before, as if he had written them all overnight with labor, and yet all spontaneous. He did succeed in weaving spells. It all appeared to be Wisdom and Power and Beauty and Enchantment. One sat and listened to him, enthralled.

NARRATOR 4: From a letter written in January 1893:

WILDE: "My own dear boy, your sonnet is quite lovely, and it is a marvel that those red rose lips of yours should be no less for music of song than for madness of kisses . . . "

DOUGLAS: From the moment we met, he made up to me in every possible way. He was continually asking me to dine or lunch with him. He flattered me, gave me presents and made much of me in every way. He gave me copies of all his books, with inscriptions in them.

WILDE: " . . . Your slim gilt soul walks between passion and poetry. I know Hyacinthus, whom Apollo loved so madly, was you in Greek days . . . "

DOUGLAS: I was from the first flattered that a man as distinguished as he was should pay me so much attention and attach so much importance to all my views and preferences and whims.

WILDE: " . . . Why are you alone in London, and when do you go to Salisbury? Do go there to cool your hands in the gray twilight of gothic things, then come here whenever you like. It is a lovely place—it only lacks you. Always with undying love, yours, Oscar."

DOUGLAS: I will say of him that even if he had never written a line of poetry, he would still be the most wonderful man I ever met.

But Queensberry deplored his son's friendship with Wilde as "the most loath-some and disgusting relationship" (in an 1894 letter) and threatened to disown him if it did not cease. Father and son exchanged harsh words and threats, but Douglas did not choose to break off with Wilde, who describes, for the court, an interview with Queensberry which took place in June 1894 in Wilde's library.

WILDE: I said: I do not allow anyone to talk like that to me in my house or anywhere else. I suppose you have come to apologize to me for the statements you made about me in that letter you wrote to your son. I should have the right any day I chose to prosecute you for writing such a letter.

QUEENSBERRY: The letter was privileged, as it was written to my son.

WILDE: How dare you say such things to him about us?

QUEENSBERRY: You were both kicked out of the Savoy Hotel at a moment's notice for your disgusting conduct.

WILDE: That is a lie.

QUEENSBERRY: You have taken furnished rooms for him in Piccadilly.

WILDE: Someone has been telling you an absurd set of lies. I have not done anything of the kind.

QUEENSBERRY: I hear you were thoroughly well blackmailed for a disgusting letter you wrote my son.

WILDE: That letter was a beautiful letter, and I never write except for publication. I said: Lord Queensberry, do you seriously accuse us of improper conduct? He replied:

QUEENSBERRY: I do not say that you are it, but you look it.

Laughter in the court.

JUDGE: I shall have the court cleared if I hear the slightest disturbance again.

QUEENSBERRY: You look it, and you pose as it, which is just as bad. If I catch you and my son together again in any public restaurant, I will thrash you.

Wilde then ordered Queensberry from his house and told his servants never to admit him again.

Queensberry's defense attorney, Edward Carson, tells the court that Queens-berry has acted only to try to save his son, at all risks. Douglas claims that his father's real motive is to persecute his family—his son and his divorced wife. Narrator 3 reads a comment on Queensberry by George Bernard Shaw: "His pretended solic-itude for his son and his alleged desire to save him were nothing but a hypocritical pretense. He was a Scots Marquess, Earl, Viscount and Baron, with a fourfold con-tempt for public opinion, an ungovernable temper and, after his divorce, a maniacal hatred for his family. His real objective was to ruin his son and to finally break the heart of his ex-wife."

Clarke's memoirs reveal that Douglas promised his family would pay all the costs of a suit against the Marquess. The Marquess tried to disrupt the performance of a Wilde play but was restrained by the police.

The hall porter testifies about the Marquess's leaving the card. Following this event, a letter from Wilde to his friend Robert Ross reveals that Wilde felt, "My whole life seems ruined by this man. I don't know what to do."

Frank Harris, in his *Oscar Wilde,* describes a lunch at the Cafe Royale with Shaw and Wilde, who told them that he had decided to sue Queensberry and asked Harris to testify for him in case they use any of Wilde's writings in support of their defense.

HARRIS: Yes. I am perfectly willing, and I can say more than that; I can say that you are one of the very few men I have ever known whose talk and whose writing were vowed away from grossness of any sort.

WILDE: Oh, Frank, would you?

SHAW: He was almost in tears.

WILDE: It would be most kind of you. Your evidence will win the case.

HARRIS: Anything I can do, Oscar, I shall do with pleasure. But I want you to consider the matter carefully. An English law court is all very well for two average men who are fighting an ordinary business dispute. That is what it is made for, but to judge the morality or immorality of an artist is to ask the court to do what it is wholly unfit to do.

WILDE: My solicitors tell me I shall win.

HARRIS: Solicitors live on quarrels. Let us begin by putting the law courts out of the question. Don't forget that if you lose and Queensberry goes free, everyone will hold that you have been guilty of nameless vice. The Crown could charge you with gross indecency and send you to two years hard labor. You must know that that could happen. You could go to prison for two years.

WILDE: But Frank . . .

HARRIS: You must remember that you are a standard-bearer for future generations. You are an artist and a revolutionary. If you lose you will make it harder for all writers in England. God knows it's hard enough already, but you will put back the hands of the clock by fifty years.

WILDE: What should I do?

HARRIS: You should go abroad, and as ace of trumps, you should take your wife with you.

WILDE: You are right of course, Frank. You know it's Bosie who wants me to fight his father.

HARRIS: Let Queensberry and his son fight out their own miserable quarrels, they are well matched.

Bosie (Douglas) arrived on the scene and managed to get Wilde away from the Cafe Royale before Harris could argue him out of pressing the suit. After they had departed, Harris commented to Shaw that he felt a strong similarity between Douglas and his father—"I could not get it out of my head: that little face blanched with rage and the wild, hating eyes, the shrill voice, too, was Queensberry's."

At the trial, the novel *The Picture of Dorian Gray* and a magazine called *The Chameleon* ("relating to the practices of persons of unnatural habit") have been

Michael Emerson as Oscar Wilde in *Gross Indecency:*
The Three Trials of Oscar Wilde by Moisés Kaufman

cited against Wilde in the Marquess's plea of justification for the alleged libel. Questioned by Clarke, Wilde testifies that he had nothing to do with editing that magazine, and reviews from newspapers characterize *Dorian Gray* as "a delight" and "the most moral book of the century." The defense has further attacked Wilde's character through his alleged relations with several young men, named in the plea. Wilde's testimony ends with the declaration that that there is "no truth whatever" in these accusations.

Carson's cross-examination of Wilde begins with making Wilde admit that he has understated his age by a couple of years. He is over 40, and Douglas is 24.

Carson reads the "My own dear boy" letter to Douglas previously quoted, and Wilde explains that it is a sort of poem, not an ordinary letter, and cannot be judged except as a work of art. Carson quotes another Wilde letter to Douglas describing him as "the divine thing I want, the thing of grace and beauty." Wilde calls it "a tender expression of my great admiration for Lord Alfred Douglas."

Carson brings up *The Chameleon,* an undergraduate publication to which Wilde contributed at the request of Douglas, who also contributed two poems to it. Carson proposes that a story entitled *The Priest and the Acolyte* in that magazine was immoral and even blasphemous. Wilde argues that the primary concern of literature is not morality, or even truth, but beauty. Anything that stimulates thought is good for the young, Wilde asserts, and states his position: "There is no such thing as morality or immorality in thought . . . . . I think that the realization of oneself is the prime aim in life, and to realize oneself through pleasure is surely finer than to do so through pain."

Carson proceeds to the matter of *Dorian Gray,* bringing into evidence one review saying, "The novel portrays the gilded paganism which has been staining these later years of Victorian epoch with horrors that carry us back to the worst incidents in the history of ancient Rome," and another calling it "stupid and vulgar" and "dangerous and corrupt."

WILDE: In the old days, men had the rack. Now they have the press.

CARSON: This is from your introduction to *Dorian Gray:* "There is no such thing as a moral or immoral book. Books are well written or badly written." That expresses your view?

WILDE: My view on art, yes.

CARSON: Then may I take it that no matter how immoral a book may be, if it is well written, it is, in your opinion, a good book?

WILDE: Yes, if it were well written so as to produce a sense of beauty, which is the highest sense of which a human being can be capable. If it were badly written, it would produce a sense of disgust.

CARSON: A perverted novel might be a good book?

WILDE: I don't know what you mean by a "perverted" novel.

CARSON: Then I will suggest *Dorian Gray* as open to the interpretation of being such a novel.

WILDE: That could only be to brutes and illiterates. The views of Philistines are entirely unaccountable.

CARSON: *The St. James Gazette:*

NARRATOR 4: Mr. Wilde says that his story is a moral tale, because the wicked persons in it come to a bad end.

WILDE: I never said my characters were wicked.

NARRATOR 4: In this newspaper's opinion, the work is unredeemed because it constantly hints, not obscurely, at disgusting sins and abominable crimes.

WILDE: The books that the world calls immoral are the books that show the world its own shame.

Carson reads two passages from *Dorian Gray* to support his argument: Hallward smitten by his first sight of Dorian Gray and his declaration to the youth that he adores him madly. In both these quotations, Wilde takes over the narration from Carson, so it is as though Wilde instead of his character, Hallward, were revealing his thoughts. Wilde insists that this is a work of art, a fiction, and that it doesn't reflect his own personality, nor has he ever had such feelings. There are people, Carson observes, who might consider such feelings "something wrong."

"Three strikes of the gavel" signal the end of the trial's first day.

NARRATOR 3: Thursday, 4th of April, 1895. The second day of the trial. From the *Evening News:*

NARRATOR 1: Today is the second day of the hearing of the prosecution of the Marquess of Queensberry for criminal libel by Oscar Wilde. The fame of yesterday's performance, for it was little else, has gone abroad. Newspapers around the world have front page stories on the trial. In Paris, *Le Temps:*

NARRATOR 4: This is how the English behave with their poets.

NARRATOR 1: The New York *Herald:*

NARRATOR 2: This is how English poets behave.

NARRATOR 1: Today the cross-examination intends to leave the literary plane and penetrate the dim-lit, perfumed rooms where the poet of the beautiful joined with valets and grooms in the bond of silver cigarette cases.

DOUGLAS: My father used the period right before the trial to hire two detectives to round up men who had been with Oscar.

NARRATOR 3: From *The Autobiography of Lord Alfred Douglas:*

DOUGLAS: These men were warned that unless they testified against Oscar, they themselves would be taken to court.

NARRATOR 2: The court is in session.

Three strikes of the gavel.

CARSON: Lord Queensberry learned that Wilde had been going about with young men who were not co-equal with him in social position or in age. These men, it will be proved beyond doubt, are some of the most immoral characters in London. I refer above all to the man Alfred Taylor, a most notorious character—as the police will tell the court—who occupied rooms which were nothing more or less than a shameful den. Mr. Wilde, do you know Alfred Taylor?

WILDE: Yes.

CARSON: Is he an intimate friend of yours?

WILDE: I would not call him an intimate friend. He was a friend of mine. I have been several times to his house, some seven or eight times, perhaps.

Under Carson's cross-examination, Wilde denies that he ever saw a woman's fancy dress in Taylor's rooms or that Taylor was being watched by the police under suspicion of servicing older men by introducing young men to them. In fact, Wilde himself had met a few 20-year-olds in Taylor's rooms—including Charles Parker, Sidney Mavor and Fred Atkins.

CARSON: What was there in common between these young men and yourself? What attraction had they for you?

WILDE: I delight in the society of people much younger than myself. I like those who may be called idle or careless. I recognize no social distinctions at all of any kind; and to me, youth, the mere fact of youth, is so wonderful that I would sooner talk to a young man for half an hour than be—well, cross-examined in court.

NARRATOR 2: From *Lord Alfred Douglas* by H. Montgomery Hyde: In the first interview between Sir Edward Clarke and Oscar Wilde, Clarke said:

CLARKE: Mr. Wilde, I can only accept this brief if you assure me on your honor that there is not and never has been any foundation for the charges that are made against you.

WILDE: They are absolutely groundless.

CLARKE: So you give me your word as an English gentlemen.

WILDE: I do.

NARRATOR 2: The thing that Clarke overlooked is that Wilde was an Irishman.

NARRATOR 3: This promise was made in the presence of Lord Alfred Douglas, who never thought to deny it or alert Oscar to the danger he faced if the lie was disproved in court.

NARRATOR 4: Lord Alfred Douglas was asked years later if Wilde often denied his homosexuality.

DOUGLAS: Oscar was never in the least degree ashamed of his homosexuality. Of course we didn't have that word back then. But he talked openly about his desire for men. He gloried in it. He never denied it except, as George Bernard Shaw points out, "when legal fictions were necessary in the courts of law."

Wilde testifies to having met Charles and William Parker at a birthday party for Taylor and wasn't put off in the least because one was a valet and the other a groom. They drank champagne, but Wilde denies that any "improprieties" took place. He gave Fred Atkins and Sidney Mavor cigarette cases, but again, there were no improprieties. Another youth encountered at Taylor's was Walter Grainger, a 16-year-old servant.

CARSON: Did you ever kiss him?

WILDE: Oh, dear no. He was a peculiarly plain boy. He was, unfortunately, extremely ugly. I pitied him for it.

 The court falls silent. Pause.

CARSON: Was that the reason why you did not kiss him?

WILDE: Oh, Mr. Carson, you are impertinently insolent.

CARSON: Did you say that in support of your statement that you never kissed him?

WILDE: No. It is a childish question.

CARSON: Did you ever put that forward as a reason why you never kissed the boy?

WILDE: No, not at all.

CARSON: Why, sir, did you mention that this boy was extremely ugly?

WILDE: For this reason. If I were asked why I did not kiss a doormat, I should say because I do not like to kiss doormats. I do not know why I mentioned that he was ugly, except that I was stung by the insolent question you had put to me and the way you have insulted me throughout this hearing.

CARSON: Why did you mention his ugliness?

WILDE: It is ridiculous to imagine that any such thing could have occurred under any circumstance.

CARSON: Then why did you mention his ugliness, I ask you?

WILDE: Perhaps I was insulted by an insulting question.

CARSON: Is that a reason why you should say the boy was ugly?

WILDE: No. I said it because . . .

> Wilde can't find the words to continue.

CARSON: Why?

WILDE: Because I didn't . . .

> Wilde can't find the words to continue.

CARSON: Why?

WILDE: Because . . .

CARSON: Why did you say that?

WILDE: You sting me and insult me and try to unnerve me; and at times one says things flippantly when one ought to speak more seriously. I admit that.

CARSON: Then you said it flippantly?

WILDE: Oh, yes, it was a flippant answer.

CARSON: I'm done with this witness, my lord.

WILDE: No indecencies ever took place between myself and Grainger. I went down . . .

CARSON: I'm finished with this witness, my lord!

Clarke rests the case for the prosecution without calling Douglas as a witness— he and Wilde decided it would look bad for a son to testify resentfully against his father. Douglas feels strongly that his testimony might have saved Wilde by exposing Queensberry.

In his opening speech for the defense, Carson repeats that Queensberry's only motive for his actions was the hope of saving his son from a dangerous situation, as suggested by the evidence. (Parenthetically, Douglas is quoted from *Oscar Wilde, a Summing Up,* written four decades later, "After I had known Oscar for about nine months, I did with him and allowed him to do with me just what was done among boys at Winchester and Oxford. He treated me as an older boy treats a younger one at school. He also taught me things that were new to me.") Carson promises to present as witnesses young men who will testify to Wilde's involvement in acts of the grossest indecency.

At this point, Clarke takes Wilde out of the courtroom to confer. Clarke advises Wilde that he cannot win the case and warns him that if these young men are permitted to take the stand, their testimony will inevitably lead to criminal charges against Wilde. Clarke offers to keep the case going for just enough time to allow Wilde to get out of the country before the authorities can take any action against him, but Wilde decides to stay.

Back in the courtroom, Clarke confers briefly with his rival Carson and then addresses the court: "We cannot conceal from ourselves that the evidence that has been submitted might induce the jury to say that Lord Queensberry in using the word 'posing' was using a word for which there was sufficient justification."

Under the circumstances, Clarke will accept a verdict of not guilty from the jury. Carson emphasizes that "the verdict will be that the plea of justification has been proved and that the words were published for the public benefit." Clarke indicates his agreement, and the jury proceeds to go through its motions of finding the defendant not guilty. Queensberry is discharged and the trial adjourned.

Narrators explain that Queensberry lost no time in sending the records of the trial to the Director of Public Prosecutions. The Crown issued a warrant for Wilde's arrest, charging him with a misdemeanor under the Criminal Law Amendment Act for an "act of gross indecency with another male person," punishable by two years hard labor. Shaw made a public protest against this law, which remained in force until 1954.

Wilde took refuge in the Cadogan Hotel (the Narrators continue) and wrote to *The Evening News* that he withdrew his charge rather than put Douglas into the box as a witness against his father. Everyone including his wife Constance wanted Wilde to leave for Calais at once, which the authorities were apparently willing for him to do because they did not issue the warrant until the boat train for Calais had left London at 5 p.m.. Wilde remained at the hotel, however, where he received a note from Queensberry: "If the country allows you to leave, all the better for the country! . . . . . But if you take my son with you, I will follow you wherever you may go and shoot you."

NARRATOR 4: At ten past six, two detectives came to the hotel. Wilde went gray in the face. Charles Richards:

RICHARDS: I went with Sergeant Allen to the Cadogan Hotel and saw the accused there. I said, "Mr. Wilde, we are police officers and hold a warrant for your arrest."

WILDE: Yes. Where shall I be taken?

RICHARDS: You will have to go to Scotland Yard with me and then to Bow Street.

WILDE: Can I have bail?

RICHARDS: I don't think you can. I then conveyed Mr. Wilde to Scotland Yard.

NARRATOR 1: Oscar Wilde was imprisoned on the 5th of April, and the trial was set for the 26th of April, 1895.

QUEENSBERRY *(euphoric):* You know, I have not much to do with distinguished people, but I had a very nice letter from Lord Claud Hamilton, and a kind telegram from Mr. Charles Danby, the actor, with "Hearty Congratulations," et cetera. A pile of messages wait for me at *The National Observer* and various clubs have telegraphed also.

　　　　　With a pile of messages.

Here's a message: "Every man in the city is with you. Kill the bugger!"

　　　　　Curtain.

ACT II

The Interview With Marvin Taylor

Interviewed in the present by the playwright Moisés Kaufman about the Oscar Wilde trials, Prof. Marvin Taylor, Wilde scholar at NYU and co-editor of *Reading Wilde*, states his belief that the sodomy charges were less meaningful in their time than Wilde's "subversive beliefs about art, about morality . . . . . about Victorian Society . . . . .

"See, this is what I think is important about the Wilde trials . . . . . It is *after* the Wilde trials that people began identifying themselves as a specific type of person based on their attraction to people of the same sex. See, it created the modern homosexual as a social subject. Whether Wilde himself thought he was that type of person . . . . . there's nothing in what I know of Greek and Latin literature that says that the Greeks and Romans thought of themselves as homosexuals. So there's nothing necessarily that Wilde would have read that would have made him construct his identity as a homosexual. So it's conceivable that while he loved having sex with men, and did, and promoted it through his art even, that he necessarily felt he was what we would call gay today. I'm not convinced of that. It seems more complicated to me. You know, Foucault talks about how it was impossible for men in the Victorian era to think of themselves as gay or homosexual because that construction didn't exist."

Prof. Taylor is then asked about Wilde not telling the truth on the witness stand about his relations with men. It looks as though he was lying, Taylor admits, but he believes that Wilde was less aware of and concerned with his own sexual identity than with his ideas on esthetics: "Do we want Oscar to be gay, therefore we're projecting that he's lying? . . . . . Alas," Prof. Taylor finished, "what they were trying to do, I think, was to fix homosexuality, to contain the disruption which Wilde presented, and this is a disruption of all kinds of things, of class, of gender, of . . . . . sexuality . . . . . and they did that, very successfully. But of course by that point he had released these ideas into Western culture that you know . . . are still there."

The focus then returns to Lord Alfred Douglas who takes up the narration, remembering how Wilde found himself in financial ruin after his arrest. His creditors assailed him, his royalties ceased, his house was attached and his possessions were auctioned off. Meanwhile, Wilde languished in Holloway Gaol, still refused bail by a judge who commented, "There is no worse crime than that with which the prisoner has been charged." Douglas visited Wilde there daily, "in the ghastly way that visits are arranged in prisons."

Narrator 5 observes, "On the day Oscar Wilde was arrested, six hundred gentlemen left England for the Continent on a night when usually sixty people traveled. Every train to Dover was crowded, every steamer to Calais thronged with members from the aristocratic and leisured classes."

As for Douglas, he was persuaded that his presence in England during the trial would disadvantage Wilde's defense: "His solicitors also told me that unless I left the country, Sir Edward Clarke, who was defending Oscar for no charge, would throw up his defense." So, the day before the trial, Douglas left for France, not to see Wilde again for two years.

The Second Trial

At the Old Bailey, the opening speech by Charles Gill for the prosecution of Regina vs. Wilde charged Wilde with "acts of gross indecency" with four of the young men named during the Queensberry suit. Wilde's plea was "Not guilty."

SHAW: Wilde could plead not guilty with perfect sincerity and indeed could not honestly put in any other plea. Guilty or not guilty is a question not of fact but of morals. The prisoner who pleads not guilty is not alleging that he did this or did not do that; he is affirming that what he did does not involve any guilt on his part. A man rightly accused of homosexuality is perfectly entitled to plead not guilty in the legal sense. He might admit that he was technically guilty of a breach of local law, and his own conscience might tell him that he was guilty of a sin against the moral law, but if he believes, as Wilde certainly did, that homosexuality is not a crime, he is perfectly entitled to say he is not guilty of it.

GILL: Gentlemen, the prisoner Wilde is well known as a dramatic author and generally as a literary man of unusual attainments. However, we must bear in mind the terrible risks involved in certain artistic and literary phases of the day. I will begin by reading to the jury the transcripts of the trial of Oscar Wilde vs. the Marquess of Queensberry, specifically, the cross-examination of Wilde on literature, *The Chameleon* and *Dorian Gray.*

CLARKE: My lord, I do not think it fair of Mr. Gill to insist upon reading this. It is not fair to judge a man by his books.

GILL: This is examination as to character.

JUDGE: You may proceed.

GILL: The following is from the transcripts of the first trial: Mr. Carson asked Mr. Wilde: "You are of the opinion, I believe, that there is no such thing as an immoral book?" Mr. Wilde replied, "Yes." Carson: "Am I right in saying that you do not consider the effect in creating morality or immorality?" Wilde: "In writing a play or a book, I am concerned entirely with literature, that is, with art."

WILDE: Art has a spiritual ministry. It can raise and sanctify everything it touches, and popular disapproval must not impede its progress. Art is what makes the life of each citizen a sacrament. Art is what makes the life of the whole race immortal.

Gill continues repeating some of the key cross-examination questions, while Wilde continues to elaborate his philosophy, which might be summed up in his words, "The object of art is to stir the most divine and remote chords which make music in our soul," and, "There is no such thing as morality or immorality in thought."

Douglas writes Wilde an affectionate letter from his comfortable circumstances in Paris, as Gill turns to the questioning of Wilde's young acquaintances. *("Music— 'Rule Britannia' coming from a music box. Four young men enter in Victorian underwear and set up the 'shameful den'.")* The first to be questioned is Charles Parker, who testifies that he was employed as a valet and his brother William as a groom. He first met Alfred Taylor when the latter came up to him in a bar and spoke to him about men.

GILL: In what way?

PARKER: He called attention to the prostitutes who frequent Piccadilly Circus and remarked, "I can't understand sensible men wasting their money on painted trash like that. Many do, though. But there are a few who know better. Now, you could get money in a certain way easily enough if you cared to." I understood to what Taylor alluded and made a coarse reply.

GILL: I am obliged to ask you what it was you actually said.

PARKER: I do not like to say.

GILL: You were less squeamish at the time, I dare say. I ask you for the words.

PARKER: I said that if any old gentleman with money took a fancy to me, I was agreeable.

> *The audience gasps.*

I *was* agreeable. I was terribly hard up.

> *Laughter.*

GILL: What did Taylor say?

PARKER: Taylor asked us to visit him. He said he could introduce us to a man who was good for plenty of money. If we were interested, we were to meet him (Taylor) at the St. James's Bar. We went there the next evening. We were shown upstairs to a private room in which there was a dinner table laid for four. After a while Wilde came in, and I was formally introduced. I had never seen him before, but I had heard of him. We dined about eight o'clock. We all four sat down to dinner, Wilde sitting on my left.

GILL: Who made the fourth?

PARKER: My brother, William Parker. I had promised Taylor that he should accompany me.

GILL: Was the dinner a good dinner?

PARKER: Yes. The table was lighted with red-shaded candles. We had plenty of champagne with our dinner and brandy and coffee afterwards. Wilde paid for the dinner.

GILL: What happened after dinner?

PARKER: Wilde said to me, "This is the boy for me! Will you go to the Savoy Hotel with me?" I consented, and Wilde drove me in a cab to the hotel.

GILL: More drink was offered you there?

PARKER: Yes, we had liqueurs. Wilde then asked me to go into his bedroom with him.

GILL: Let us know what occurred there.

Michael Emerson *(in dark clothing)* flanked *(standing)* by Troy Sostillio *(left)* and Andy Paris, with *(seated)* Greg Pierotti *(left)* and Greg Steinbruner, in *Gross Indecency*

PARKER: He committed the act of sodomy upon me.

  The court becomes very agitated.

PROF. MARVIN TAYLOR: From that moment on, Oscar Wilde's name would not be associated with Hellenism or Aestheticism or revolutionary artistic ideas, but with homosexuality.

Continuing to testify, Parker says Wilde gave him money that night and later a silver cigarette case and a gold ring.

In his cross-examination, Clarke leads Parker to admit that he was involved in an incident in which two other men blackmailed one of Parker's sexual partners. He also leads Parker to confess that he knew all about homosexual practices before he met Wilde, so that it was not Wilde who corrupted him.

Alfred Wood is next to testify. He was sent by Alfred Taylor to meet Wilde at the Cafe Royale and accompanied Wilde to the latter's home at 16 Tite Street where, as far as Wood knows, there was no one else in the house. "There an act of the grossest indecency occurred." Under Clarke's cross-examination, Wood admits that he took an active part in the incident of blackmail with Parker and another man.

NARRATOR 5: From *De Profundis:*

WILDE: People thought it dreadful of me to have entertained at dinner these men, and to have found pleasure in their company. But then, from my point of view, they were delightfully suggestive and stimulating. It was like feasting with panthers. They were to me like the brightest of gilded snakes, their poison was part of their perfection.

Fred Atkins, an unemployed comedian, is the next to testify. Wilde took a fancy to him and brought him along on a trip to Paris, but no indecencies occurred between them—though, Atkins testifies, he saw Wilde in bed with another man on one occasion. Clarke gets him to admit under cross-examination that he too was once involved in an incident of attempted blackmail.

The next witness is Sidney Mavor. As Mavor explains that Taylor introduced him to Wilde and that Wilde sent him a cigarette case as a token of his admiration, *The Autobiography of Lord Alfred Douglas* reports, "Before I left for Paris, I happened to see Mavor at the Bow Street Police Court while he was waiting to give evidence."

DOUGLAS: I went up to him and shook hands and said: "Sidney, surely you are not going to give evidence against Oscar?"

MAVOR: Soon after, I received a letter from Mr. Wilde making an appointment to meet him at the Albemarle Hotel. I arrived at the hotel soon after eight, and we had supper in a private room. I subsequently stayed the night.

DOUGLAS: Sidney!

MAVOR: Well, what can I do? I daren't refuse to give evidence now; they got a statament out of me.

DOUGLAS: For God's sake, Sidney, remember you are a gentleman and a public school boy. Don't put yourself on a level with Parker and Atkins. When counsel asks you questions, deny the whole thing and say you were frightened by the police. They can't do anything to you.

GILL: Did any misconduct take place that night?

MAVOR: No. No misconduct ever took place between Mr. Wilde and me.

GILL: Mr. Mavor, I repeat the question, Did any misconduct take place that night?

MAVOR: No. No misconduct ever took place between Mr. Wilde and me.
DOUGLAS: Counsel of course dropped him like a hot brick!

In his opening statement for the defense, Clarke notes that in exchange for their testimony for the Crown, the previous witnesses "have received immunity for past rogueries and indecencies, these men who ought to be the accused, not the accusers." He also argues that it is proof of Wilde's clear conscience that he remained in London to face these charges instead of fleeing to the Continent when he could.

Questioned by Clarke, Wilde testifies that he took up with these men because he is a lover of youth, and that no indecencies ever occurred with them, nor did he ever invite them to the Savoy Hotel or to Tite Street.

Gill, in his cross-examination, brings up the poems Douglas contributed to *The Chameleon* and focuses on the line, "I am the love that dare not speak its name."

GILL: There is no question as to what it means?
WILDE: Most certainly not.
GILL: Is it not clear that the love described relates to natural love and unnatural love?
WILDE: No
GILL: What is the "Love that dare not speak its name"?
WILDE: The "Love that dare not speak its name" in this century is such a great affection of an elder for a younger man as there was between David and Jonathan, such as Plato made the very basis of his philosophy, and such as you find in the sonnets of Michelangelo and Shakespeare. It is that deep, spiritual affection that is as pure as it is perfect. It dictates and pervades great works of art like those of Michelangelo and Shakespeare, and those two letters of mine, such as they are. It is in this century misunderstood, so much misunderstood that it may be described as "The love that dare not speak its name," and on account of it I am placed where I am now. It is beautiful, it is fine, it is the noblest form of affection. There is nothing unnatural about it. It is intellectual, and it repeatedly exists between an elder and a younger man when the elder man has intellect and the younger man has all the joy, hope and glamor of life before him. That it should be so the world does not understand. The world mocks at it and sometimes puts one in the pillory for it.
   Loud applause, mingled with some hisses.
JUDGE: Order! *(Three strikes of the gavel.)* . . . . . If there is the slightest manifestation of feeling I shall have the court cleared. Complete silence must be preserved.
GILL: With regard to your friendship towards the men who have given evidence, may I take it that it was, as you describe, Mr. Wilde, a deep affection of an elder man for a younger?
WILDE: Certainly not! One feels that once in one's life, and once only, toward anybody:
NARRATOR 5: From *The Autobiography of Lord Alfred Douglas:*
DOUGLAS: I am proud to have been loved by a great poet. There will always be one thousand Queensberrys for one Oscar Wilde.

After three hours of deliberation, the jury is unable to reach a verdict, so the court is adjourned pending a new trial. Clarke manages to obtain Wilde's release on bail. Wilde goes to the Midland Hotel, but after the manager finds out who he is, he is asked to leave. At another hotel on London's outskirts, he is asked to leave because a mob of toughs threatens to vandalize the place if he doesn't. At his mother's house on Oakley Street he is admitted by his drunken brother Willie, who remarks, "Thank God my vices are decent," but at least gives Wilde refuge.

Frank Harris comes to see Wilde and tell him he has a yacht waiting to take him abroad. Wilde can't bring himself to flee. He surprises Harris by informing him that he is guilty of the charges. Harris had believed him innocent, but in either case it makes no difference: "It has no effect on my friendship, none on my resolve to help you." Wilde appreciates the extent of Harris's loyalty and is also relieved for having been able to tell someone the truth, for once.

Harris continues trying to persuade Wilde to leave the country, but Wilde doesn't want those who went bail for him to lose their money. Harris would pay back half of the bail money and Wilde could earn the rest by writing, Harris insists. Both Wilde's mother and brother believe that Wilde should stay, and, as he writes to Douglas, Wilde finally decides, "It is nobler and more beautiful to stay."

In his autobiography, Douglas recalls that the Crown decided to have Frank Lockwood, the Solicitor-General, prosecute its case instead of Gill. Carson, who won the case against Queensberry but refused to prosecute the case against Wilde, asks Lockwood to let up on Wilde. Lockwood can't, because the matter now has political implications. Douglas observes, "It is a degrading coup d'etat—the sacrifice of a great poet to save a degraded band of politicians."

The Third Trial

"The sound of a heartbeat can be heard in a gradual crescendo" as Wilde, now desperate, faces a new jury at the Old Bailey. Again, Wilde is denounced by the prosecution as "the center of a circle of hideous corruption among young men," who testify much as they did previously. Other witnesses come forward with sordid details until Wilde feels sick listening to them and is convinced that the law he is accused of breaking "is a wrong and unfair law, and the system under which I'm suffering, a wrong and unjust system." Wilde finally reaches the point at which "I feel inclined to stretch out my hands and cry to them: Do what you will with me in God's name, only do it quickly. Can you not see I'm worn out? If hatred gives you pleasure, indulge it."

"Silence," as the heartbeat reaches its crescendo and ceases.

An exhausted Wilde is questioned about his relationship with Douglas, which he describes as "founded on rock." Narrators introduce lines from a letter written by Wilde from Holloway Prison to Douglas in Paris: "This is to assure you of my immortal, my eternal love for you. Tomorrow all will be over . . . . . If prison and dishonor be my destiny, think that my love for you and this idea, this still more divine belief that you love me in return, will sustain me in my unhappiness and will make me capable, I hope, of bearing my grief most patiently . . . . . Since the hope, nay rather the certainty, of meeting you again in some other world is the goal and the encouragement of my present life, I must continue to live in this world because of that . . . . . Dearest boy, sweetest of all young men, most loved and most lovable: Wait for me!"

As the case goes to the jury, Wilde reflects on himself, his life and his art. He was born with genius and a distinguished place in society. He went on to change the perceptions of the world in which he found himself: "Whatever I touched I made beautiful in a new mode of beauty." He became a legend in his own time and, finally, "I summed up all systems in a phrase and all existence in an epigram."

"Three strikes of the gavel" signal the return of the jury, whose Foreman reports that they have found Wilde guilty of acts of gross indecency. Addressing Wilde, the Judge characterizes his crime as so bad that "People who can do these things are dead to all sense of shame," so it isn't likely that any punishment could have any positive effect. But he gives Wilde the maximum sentence, two years at hard labor.

"And may I say nothing, my lord?" asks Wilde, but the Judge exits without replying. Wilde exits and the court is adjourned.

Epilogue

Narrators report the press's enthusiastically favorable reaction to the verdict. The actor playing Lord Alfred Douglas tells the audience that Wilde was injured and mistreated in prison, and while he was there his wife and two sons changed their name. He also began to feel that Bosie was to blame for this disaster. While serving out his sentence he wrote *The Ballad of Reading Gaol* including the line "For each man kills the things he love."

NARRATOR 2: After his release from prison, Wilde and Douglas lived together on and off until Wilde's death in 1900.

NARRATOR 4: After Wilde's death, Lord Alfred Douglas married and had two children. He became a Catholic and eventually a Nazi sympathizer.

NARRATOR 3: The Marquess of Queesberry died in 1899, a pathetic victim of persecution mania, convinced to the last that he was being harried to the tomb by "Oscar Wilders," as he used to describe his imaginary tormentors.

NARRATOR 4: Oscar Wilde was buried at Bagneux Cemetery on the 3rd of December, 1900. Lord Alfred Douglas was one of the twelve people who attended the burial

NARRATOR 1: By the year 1920, Oscar Wilde was, after Shakespeare, the most widely read English author in Europe.

Coda

A prose poem by Oscar Wilde written after his release from prison and entitled *The House of Judgment* imagines a conversation between God and a Man, who stands naked before God's judgment. God, reviewing the Man's life, accuses him of various forms of evildoing and considers sending him to Hell. God cannot do that, the Man protests, "Because in Hell I have always lived."

NARRATOR 5: And there was silence in the House of Judgment. And after a space God spake, and said to the Man:

NARRATOR 7: Then surely I will send thee unto Heaven. Even unto Heaven will I send thee.

NARRATOR 5: And the Man cried out:

NARRATOR 1: Thou canst not.

NARRATOR 5: And God said to the Man:

NARRATOR 6: Wherefore can I not send thee unto Heaven, and for what reason?

NARRATOR 1: Because never, in no place, have I been able to imagine it,

NARRATOR 5: Answered the Man. And there was silence in the House of Judgement.

OOO
OOO
OOO
OOO
OOO
OOO

THE LION KING

A Musical in Two Acts

BOOK BY ROGER ALLERS AND
IRENE MECCHI

MUSIC AND LYRICS BY ELTON JOHN AND
TIM RICE

ADDITIONAL MUSIC AND LYRICS BY LEBO M,
MARK MANCINA, JAY RIFKIN,
JULIE TAYMOR AND HANS ZIMMER

Cast and credits appear on pages 200–201

ROGER ALLERS and IRENE MECCHI (book) have both been associated with the Disney organization for a number of years, Allers since 1988 with Oliver and Company *and Mecchi since 1992 with the short* Recycle Rex, *which won the 1994 Environmental Media Award. Allers, devoted to the art of animated cartooning since childhood, worked on many projects—including* Sesame Street *and* The Electric Company—*before joining Disney and has been instrumental in shaping the structure and dialogue of all the Disney animated features since. He directed the movie version of* The Lion King *and now makes his Broadway debut with the stage adaptation of its book, which opened November 13th. Allers is now writing and directing a new Disney feature,* Kingdom of the Sun, *due in 1999. He lives in Venice, Calif. with his wife Leslie and two children.*

Mecchi is a San Franciscan, a graduate of the University of California at Berkeley and a former theater trainee at the American Conservatory Theater, which put on a staged reading of her play Raising Caen—*drawn from Herb Caen's 60 years of San Francisco newspaper columns—in the 1990–91 season, just before she joined the*

Disney organization. She was the co-author of the movie version of The Lion King *for which she has now co-provided its Broadway book. Mecchi's list of writing credits includes live-action movies and television productions as well as the co-authorship of* The Hunchback of Notre Dame *and* Hercules *for Disney. With her* The Lion King *collaborator, she is now working on the upcoming* Kingdom of the Sun.

ELTON JOHN and TIM RICE (music and lyrics) teamed up for the score of the Broadway The Lion King *as they had in 1994 for the film version, whose recorded score has passed the 10 million mark in sales. John is a major pop music star, world famous not only for his many songs but more recently as the adapter and performer of one of those songs in Westminster Abbey at Princess Diana's funeral. He was born in Pinner, Middlesex, England on March 25, 1947. From 1959 to 1964 he attended London's Royal Academy of Music, which awarded him an honorary membership on his 50th birthday. His newest studio album,* The Big Picture, *released late last year, marks the 30th year of his songwriting collaboration with lyricist Bernie Taupin. John was elected to the Rock and Roll Hall of fame in 1994 and, in recognition of his services to the Elton John AIDS Foundation and other activities in aid of charity and the arts, he was knighted as a Commander of the Order of the British Empire in the Queen's 1997 Honors List. John has been working with his* The Lion King *collaborator on material for a new Disney production based on the* Aida *story.*

TIM RICE has been a major contributer to the British and American musical stage for more than a quarter century. He was born in England, in Amersham, on November 10, 1944 and attended Lancing College in Sussex from 1958 to 1962. He started out as a solicitor's articled clerk but in 1966 began to study the music business, in its recording and broadcasting phases. He wrote the lyrics for Jesus Christ Superstar— *which headed the long parade of Rice musicals in London and New York, opening on Broadway October 12, 1971, playing 720 performances, and Tony-nominated for its Rice-Andrew Lloyd Webber score. The Rice parade continued with* Joseph and the Amazing Technicolor Dreamcoat *(1976 off Broadway, book and lyrics in collaboration with Webber),* Evita *(1979 on Broadway, book and lyrics with Webber music, Tony Awards for best musical, book and score);* Chess *(1988 on Broadway, conception and lyrics),* Beauty and the Beast *(1994 on Broadway, co-author with Howard Ashman of lyrics, Tony-nominated for score), the concert musical* King David *(1997 on Broadway, book and lyrics) and now* The Lion King. *Other Rice works which have not yet reached New York stages were* Blondel, Starmania/Tycoon *and* Heathcliff. *Rice has also contributed to several movies, and his published work includes 30* Guinness Books *on British pop music and 22* Heartaches Cricketers' Almanacks. *He is married, with two children, and lives in London.*

The Lion King *is a Broadway spinoff from the popular Disney animated cartoon, and its fairy-tale adventure has become familiar to a huge segment of the audience. It begins with an African lion monarch, Mufasa, presenting his newborn son and heir, Simba, to the animals of his kingdom, assembled in their multitude for the occasion.*

But the king's brother, Scar, covets the throne for himself and arranges an accident in which the king is killed—but little Simba, also an intended victim and thought to have been killed along with his father, manages to survive, flee from the Pride and join up with a pair of carefree hedonists, Timon the meerkat and Pumbaa the warthog. Simba accepts their happily irresponsible lifestyle and grows to adult lionhood in their company; but, influenced by a young lioness, Nala, who seeks him out, Simba finally comes to accept his true responsibility. Simba and his friends return to the Pride, defeat his Uncle Scar and consign him to the voracious hyenas. In their turn, Simba and Nala present their own newborn heir to their animal subjects.

The characters in The Lion King are 25 kinds of animals, birds, fish and insects, vividly imagined as costumed human beings or volatile puppets. This fantasy is most remarkable for its stagecraft, the action and appearance of its soaring winged creatures, its slavering hyenas, its balletically graceful giraffes, its 11- foot, 3- inch-high elephant and 5-inch mouse, and all the other creatures magically brought to the stage via Julie Taymor's ingenious imagination, with the seamless collaboration of Richard Hudson (scenery) and Michael Curry (co-design of puppets and masks).Under Taymor's direction, the actors wearing their symbolic costumes and/or wielding their symbolic props are visible onstage but show very little interference of the human being in their graphic representation of other species in motion.

We cannot comprehensively illustrate Taymor's direction—her lumbering elephant, her stampeding wildebeests, her frenetic meerkat—in these pages. This can only be experienced at the performance of this magical show, whose three-dimensional Taymor animals are as stylishly individualistic—in their own way—as those in the Walt Disney tradition in two dimensions. What we can offer to celebrate The Lion King, winner of the 1997–98 Tony for the season's best musical, in this volume is some insight into her remarkable achievement by tracing it to its source in a biographical sketch of her stage life and a collection of her The Lion King design sketches, with selected Joan Marcus photos of the show to suggest what some of the Taymor creatures looked like onstage.

We offer our special thanks to the Disney organization, their technical staff and their press representatives, Boneau/Bryan–Brown and Jackie Green, for making available this material illustrating the show.

JULIE TAYMOR (direction, costumes; mask & puppet co-design, additional music & lyrics) was born in Boston December 15, 1952. Her father was a gynecologist and her mother the founder of The Program for Women in Politics and Government and an activist for the Democratic National Committee. Taymor graduated from Oberlin in 1974, and her first work of record for the New York stage was the scenery, costumes, puppets and masks for Elizabeth Swados's The Haggadah, a Passover Cantata at the Public Theater March 31, 1980 (repeated at the Public the next two seasons), for which she won a prestigious Maharam Award for design. The following season found her doing the scenery, masks and puppets for Black Elk Lives off Broadway, winning a Maharam citation for Way of Snow and then working with the Baltimore Center Stage's Young People's Theater touring program and (a season later) doing the pup-

pets and masks for its production of Christopher Hampton's Savages. *Back in New York in the autumn of 1982, she designed the scenery for* Do Lord Remember Me *at American Place.*

What must have been a significant step forward in the illustrious Taymor career took place relatively inconspicuously at the Ark Theater off off Broadway, where she acted as the director—for the first time on the record—of a production May 10, 1984—her own co-adaptation (with Sidney Goldfarb) of Thomas Mann's The Transposed Heads *(produced as a musical by Lincoln Center in 1986 with Taymor direction, puppet and mask design and co-choreography).*

Her design career continued with the puppets for Bill Irwin's The Courtroom *in 1985 at Music-Theater Group (special Obie citation) and the costumes for* The King Stag *at American Repertory Theater in 1986 (cited by the Boston theater critics). Her theater direction and design careers took off in a spectacular way, in tandem, with her co-authorship, direction, puppets, masks and co-designed scenery and costumes for the Richard Rodgers Production Award-winning musical* Juan Darién, *produced by Music-Theater Group OOB March 4, 1988 and receiving a Mel Gussow citation ("Haunting folk play, tantalizing score, unearthly air of mystery"); an American Theater Wing (formerly Maharam) Design Award for concept, puppets and masks, and an Obie. Music-Theater Group took* Juan Darién *off Broadway December 26, 1989 and to Broadway (at and with Lincoln Center) Nov. 24, 1996, receiving multiple Tony nominations including those for the Taymor direction and designs. With* The Lion King, *she won both the direction and design Tonys and two American Theater Wing Design Awards.*

Taymor's theater work prior to The Lion King *has included three Shakespeare plays for Theater for a New Audience (1994) and the direction and co-design of* The Green Bird *(1996). She is also a distinguished director of opera* (The Magic Flute, Oedipus Rex, Salomé, The Flying Dutchman) *and film* (Fool's Fire *and a forthcoming feature of her adaptation of* Titus Andronicus). *In addition to all the abovementioned awards, she has received MacArthur and Guggenheim Fellowships, an Emmy and an International Classical Music Award for best opera production (for* Oedipus Rex), *and the Brandeis Creative Arts and Dorothy Chandler Performing Arts Awards.*

On opposite page: Atop Pride Rock, the baboon Rafiki (Tsidii Le Loka), flanked by the lion king of beasts, Mufasa (Samuel E. Wright, *left*), and his queen, Sarabi (Gina Breedlove), proudly displays the newborn princeling Simba to an assembly of jungle creatures

On these and succeeding pages are examples of Julie Taymor's costume designs for *The Lion King,* in some cases with photos of the characters illustrating how they were realized onstage

TAYMOR

The costume for Mufasa the Lion King as created by Taymor *(left)* and as worn by Samuel E. Wright *(above)*

Above, Scott Irby-Ranniar as Young Simba learning to fear his wicked and ambitious Uncle Scar (John Vickery), whose costume design appears in the sketch *at right*

GRA

JUNGLE CHORUS D
SPIKED LEAVES
(OPEN VIEW)

TAYMOR

JUNGLE CHORUS
LEAFY TUTU

TAYMOR

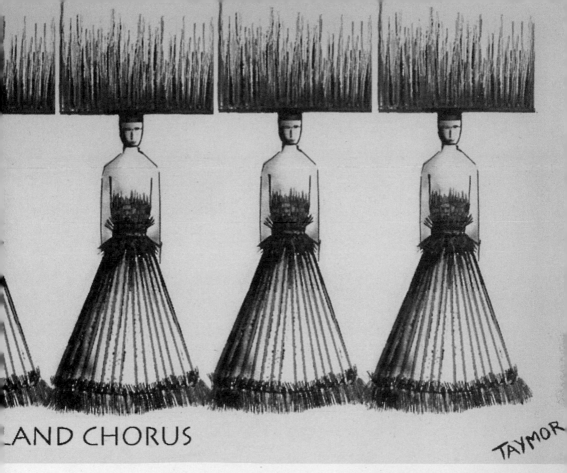

LAND CHORUS

TAYMOR

JUNGLE CHORUS G
GROUNDROW

Timothy Hunter and Ashi K. Smythe in stilted motion as giraffes

ZEBRA

TAYMOR

TAYMOR

RAFIKI

Tsidii Le Loka as Rafiki in a scene from *The Lion King*

SARABI

TAYMOR

ANT HILL LADY   TAYMOR

The lion cub Simba *(center),* having escaped Scar's murder plot and run away from the Pride, is befriended by two strange jungle creatures—Timon the meerkat (Max Casella, *left*) and Pumbaa the warthog (Tom Alan Robbins, *right*)—who teach Simba how to shrug off his worries with the slogan "Hakuna Matata"

At right, Jason Raize as Simba, no longer a cub but grown up into a lion prince; *below,* Heather Headly as Nala, Simba's future mate, who will encourage him to return to the Pride and wrest his rightful kingship from the usurper Scar

On opposite page: The Taymor costume design for one of the ever-ravenous hyenas, with whom the deposed Scar finally meets his fate

Critics Award

○○○
○○○
○○○
○○○
○○○
○○○ # PRIDE'S CROSSING

A Play in Two Acts

BY TINA HOWE

Cast and credits appear on page 243

TINA HOWE was born in New York City in 1937, the daughter of newscaster Quincy Howe. She received her B.A. at Sarah Lawrence in 1959 and pursued graduate studies in secondary education at Columbia Teachers College in New York and Chicago Teachers College. But playwriting was already in her blood after her first one-acter (Closing Time, *about the end of the world) was put on in a production directed, produced and starred in by Jane Alexander at Sarah Lawrence. Her first professional outing was the short-lived* The Nest *off Broadway in 1970. Her next major production did not take place until 1976, when her play* Museum *appeared at Los Angeles Actors Theater and then in 1977 at New York Shakespeare Festival (an OOB offering) and in 1978 for 78 off-Broadway performances. She won further acclaim with* The Art of Dining *at Kennedy Center in 1978, following a short off-Broadway run at New York Shakespeare Festival.*

Painting Churches *was produced off off Broadway by Second Stage in February 1983 for 30 performances, winning Howe a Rosamond Gilder Award for creative achievement, then moving off Broadway for 206 performances starting November 22, 1983 in this same Second Stage production and winning a Best Play citation. Three more Howe plays were produced in New York by Second Stage:* Coastal Disturbances *(OOB November 11, 1986, then to Broadway at Circle in the Square March 4, 1987 for 350 performances and a Tony nomination),* Approaching Zanzibar *(OOB April 8, 1989 for 54 performances) and* One Shoe Off *(off Broadway April 15, 1993 for 22 performances). Her* Pride's Crossing *premiered at the Old Globe Theater in San Diego January 25, 1997 and was brought to New York by Lincoln Center Theater December 7, 1997. It closed after 137 performances, but the members of the New York*

110

Drama Critics Circle remembered it enthusiastically enough to vote it the best American play of the 1997–98 season.

Other Howe plays have included Teeth *(presented in 1991 in a Reading Room Reading of the New York Public Library for the Performing Arts) and* Birth and After Birth *(produced in 1995 at the Wilma Theater, Philadelphia). She has received a Rockefeller Grant, Guggenheim and NEA Fellowships and an Academy of Arts and Letters Award in Literature. She has served as an adjunct professor at NYU since 1983, a member of the Dramatists Guild Council since 1990 and a visiting professor at Hunter College since 1990. Howe lives in New York City and is married to the novelist Norman Levy, with two children.*

The following synopsis of Pride's Crossing *was prepared by Sally Dixon Wiener.*

Time: This year

Place: Pride's Crossing, Massachusetts, and in Mabel's memory

ACT I

Scene 1: Mabel's bedroom, the end of June, the present

SYNOPSIS: The set for this memory play of a disappearing world—where mama and papa were accented on the second syllable—is minimal: *"a dreamscape of gauze panels and floating windows . . . . . a minimum of clutter . . . . . Westminster clock hung in midair,"* the author's note to the play explains. There is no actual food, and sound effects replace actual croquet balls and broken cups. There are *"images of clouds and water."* Lighting and sound indicate changes of time and place. Adding to the fluidity of the production are Mabel's almost choreographed onstage costume changes as, without benefit of makeup, she becomes her younger self at different ages.

As the play begins, Mabel Tidings Bigelow, sometimes called M.T., a redoubtable and unrepentant 90, comes shuffling onstage with her walker. The dimly-lit room (in the coach house of the former Tidings estate) has twin beds. *"One is piled high with dirty laundry, books, assorted mail and a breakfast tray."* Mabel, *"wearing a mismatched skirt and blouse,"* collapses onto the other. It's a Saturday morning. Mabel's determined to give a Fourth of July croquet party. Things ought to be passed down, and her great grandchild Minty is about to arrive from Paris for a visit. Minty's probably never seen a croquet mallet, Mabel muses.

Vita Bright, *"a hippie type woman dressed as Paul Revere, comes galloping in as if on horseback. She's in her 30s."* Mabel pretends to be alarmed. It seems Vita is going to be on horseback leading the parade on the Fourth of July. But she's a woman, Mabel demurs, and ought to be Betsy Ross or Martha Washington. Vita thinks they're boring and that men have the fun. Mabel agrees and admits she's often wished she'd been a man. She admires Vita's hat and tries it on, claiming she'd always wanted to be Charlemagne. "Soldier, emperor, scholar . . . *There* was a life." As Vita goes off with the breakfast tray, Mabel picks up a bill.

MABEL: $108? How could my phone bill be $108? I never talk to a soul. What's this? A dividend from State Street!
　　　　She kisses it.
God bless State Street and my piddling income. I shudder to think where I'd be without it. In the street, in the street.
　　　　She picks up another bill.
The Beverly Visiting Nurse Service? $833? What next?
　　　　She stuffs it at the bottom of the pile and sinks back onto the pillows, exhausted. A moment passes.
VIIIIIITAAA? Oh, VIIIIIITAAA?
　　VITA *(from off):* You called?
　　MABEL: Could I trouble you for a glass of water, please? I'm parched.
　　VITA: Coming right up.
　　MABEL: DARLING VITA . . . YOU'RE MY GUARDIAN ANGEL, MY KNIGHT IN SHINING ARMOR, MY FLORENCE . . . *(Struggling to remember.)* FLORENCE . . . *(She starts singing.)* "You are my lucky star . . . something something, my heart's desire" . . .
　　VITA *(returning with a glass of water):* Here you go.
　　MABEL: Thank you, thank you.
　　　　She drinks deeply and then makes a lurid kissing sound.
　　VITA *(picking up a bottle of pills):* Did you take your pills?
　　MABEL: Pay my bills?
　　VITA: NO, TAKE YOUR PILLS!
　　MABEL: You have such lovely skin.
　　VITA: Don't change the subject. Where's your ear?
　　MABEL: If I'd had skin like that, just think what I could have accomplished.
　　VITA: I SAID, "WHERE'S YOUR EAR?"
　　MABEL: I don't know.
　　VITA: *You don't know?*
　　MABEL: Don't scold me, I can't stand being scolded.

Vita continues haranguing Mabel about taking more responsibility for herself—Mabel *did* swim the English Channel. That only takes endurance, Mabel counters. Vita finds Mabel's hearing aid as Chandler Coffin arrives. "*He's several years older than Mabel and walks with a severe limp. He's the picture of old world elegance, dressed in a cream colored suit and jaunty Panama hat from the 20s.*" He's "a vision" Mabel declares. It seems Mabel has called Chandler to come over at once—"Something about a croquet party." Mabel stalls, not wanting Vita in on this, and peremptorily orders her out. Vita reminds her the doctor said no entertaining or she'll have another stroke. (At last year's party the fire department had to take her to the hospital.)

After Vita exits, Chandler muses about never having seen Vita wearing a pair of shoes, but Mabel feels lucky to have Vita: "Affordable live-ins are as scarce as hen's teeth." There's her "awful son" West, Chandler adds. Mabel's more tolerant than Chandler is. Mabel had children and Chandler didn't, although Mabel's daughter Emma hasn't been speaking to her for years. "Always seeking her reflection in the bottom of a glass . . . Just like her father," and it was pretty much up to Mabel to raise Emma's daughter, Julia, who is arriving the next day from Paris, staying through the Fourth. Mabel's planning a croquet party, as in the old days. She's even found some of her grandmother's lawn dresses the women can wear.

Chandler tries to talk Mabel out of the party, but she's even got a guest list, which she is fortunate enough to be able to lay hands on—Chandler, Kitty Lowell, Isobel Sargent, Gabby Ames, and "the doddering Wheelocks . . . if they're still alive." She's not to give a party, Chandler is stating flatly, as Vita's son West rushes in. *"He's around 15 and has just been in a fight. His clothes are torn and his hands and face are bleeding,"* and he's calling for his mother. He's bursting with rage, nearly in tears, and letting loose volleys of profanity. He won't let Vita touch him. He insults Chandler repeatedly and refuses to apologize. Mabel whacks her cane and orders everyone out. Chandler's treating Mabel like a child, and she will not have it! *"Fragments of their angry words dovetail into another argument Mabel witnessed some 80 years before."*

Scene 2: The Tidings dining room, summer, 1917

"The family is gathered around the table having breakfast. The room is formal and imposing . . . . . Gus Tidings, mid 40s, sits at the head of the table. He's dressed in natty sailing gear and is in a towering rage. He's flanked by his sons, Phineas, 18, and Frazier, 16. They're also dressed for sailing. Gus's wife Maud sits across from him . . . . . She's in her mid 30s and is fighting a migraine. She wears an austere high-necked long-sleeved dress. Mabel, 10, wears a starched pinafore. She sits next to Frazier, who's very red in the face."

Frazier's in trouble. He's driven his father's car—but just around the driveway. His mother is worried that someone might have been hurt. His father says Frazier knows the rules—that no one drives his car. Except Phineas, Frazier retorts. He'd allowed Phineas to drive his car when Phineas was only 13. Gus repeats that no one drives his car.

FRAZIER: You waved at him from the porch.
GUS: I waved at him from the porch?
MABEL *(trying to restrain him):* Frazier, don't . . .
FRAZIER: I remember it as clear as day.
GUS: This is getting better and better.
FRAZIER: You took off your hat and waved.

MABEL *(pulling at Frazier):* Stop it, you're making Papa angry.

FRAZIER: But I *saw* you!

GUS: It's bad enough you drove the car, now you're contradicting me!

FRAZIER: Every time he circled the driveway, you waved him on, shouting, "That's my boy!"

He stands up, miming it.

"That's *my* boy, that's my *boy* . . . "

He keeps it up.

MAUD *(passing her hands over her eyes):* Frazier, please!

GUS *(rising from his chair):* ENOUGH IS ENOUGH, GO TO YOUR ROOM!

MAUD: He's impossible.

GUS *(banging the table with his fist):* NOW!

FRAZIER *(with rising intensity):* "*That's* my boy, that's *my* boy, that's my *boy*, that's my . . . "

MAUD: Just like my father. It's in the blood.

GUS: I said GO!   •

He hurls a glass across the room. It shatters.

Frazier bows, takes his leave. His father announces Frazier will not be racing in the Commodore's Race today. Maud urges the rest to have their eggs before they're cold. When Gus insists they must leave soon—the harbor will be crowded—Mabel asks if she can come. Her parents are shocked, but Phinney claims it would be good for Mabel. It's not a place for children, especially young girls, her parents insist. She could help, Mabel pleads. Her mother is adamant—it's not done, it's not becoming. She can swim, Mabel points out. Anyone can, Maud tells her. Even the dog. Her father barks and laughs. Mabel reveals that she swam to Little Misery and back. Her father doesn't believe it, but Phinney vouches for her—"She was like a machine."

Gus observes that one of his relatives managed a "real swim" across the English Channel in 1875. Mabel is surprised that someone swam the Channel and wonders how far it is—21 miles, her father tells her, but it isn't the distance, it's the weather. He sailed those waters with his father when he was 15 and was very seasick.

GUS: How old were you when you started to dive, Phin?

MABEL: Ten.

MAUD: How would you know? You weren't even born yet.

MABEL: Yes, I was. I remember watching him dive off the rocks from the nursery.

GUS: Who would have thought our Phineas would end up an Olympic diver?

MAUD: It's not surprising in the least, look what he comes from.

MABEL: He'd stand up so straight and tall. Like an Indian Chief. Then he'd lift up on the smalls of his feet . . .

GUS: *Balls* of his feet.

MAUD: Honestly, Mabel!

MABEL: Spread out his arms and leap. I was so surprised when he dropped down, I always expected him to fly.

PHINNEY: Come on, you're embarrassing me.
MABEL: I remember one time, he arched so high I thought . . .
MAUD *(reaching for Phinney's hand):* It's true. Watching you dive is like poetry.
GUS: Accept it, Phin, you're the best there is.
MABEL: Better than the best!

Frazier reappears, covered with fake blood, wearing a loin cloth and halo and several trick arrows in his torso, a la Mantegna's Saint Sebastian. He kneels and begs his father for mercy, to let him sail. They all await Gus's reaction. He finally laughs, calling Frazier an original. Just like her father, Maud despairs. Her father, the architect, statesman, Harvard professor and symphony trustee, "Two minutes before his 45th birthday, he put on a tux, walked into the reading room of the Athenaeum, pulled out a revolver and *shot* himself through the heart!"

Gus gives permission to Frazier to sail. Before Frazier goes off he makes a formal presentation of his halo to Mabel, putting it on her head, inviting her to declare her heart's desire and it will be hers. Anything, he assures her.

Mabel is left alone with no one to hear her wish, "Someday I'm going to swim the English Channel and be famous like Phinney! *(Light emanates from her halo. It shines brighter and brighter and then snaps out.)*"

Scene 3: Mabel's living room, the next day, the present

Mabel's granddaughter, Julia Renoir, looking Parisian chic, and Julia's daughter, Minty Renoir, 10, have arrived and are facing Mabel "like soldiers on a reviewing stand." At Mabel's request, Julia kisses her, and Mabel remarks that Julia looks badly. Julia asks Minty to kiss Mabel. Minty is reluctant to do so. Mabel makes a *"lurid kissing sound,"* and Minty is told again to kiss her. She does so, quickly, on each cheek, which Mabel adores and asks her to do it again. But Mabel's coughing noises and spitting into a tissue repel the child (whose real name is Mignone). Julia speaks to her in French, and Minty does kiss Mabel again. Mabel commends her for her bravery.

Mabel gives Minty a song-and-dance about the mouse family in the upstairs bathroom with the "charming nest under the sink" made of bits of rag and toilet tissue, with a swing for the baby mice. Minty covers her ears and Mabel admits she's kidding.

Vita comes in and is introduced. Soon the women are talking about Julia's husband Jean-Paul, "still working like a Trojan," a heart specialist and handsome, to boot, and not to be trusted.

MABEL: I've had my adventures with handsome foreign men.
JULIA: The infamous David Bloom
VITA: *David Bloom?* I've never heard you mention any . . .
JULIA: The dashing Englishman who wanted to run away with her after her swim.
MABEL: All right, Julia, that's enough.

JULIA: Well, he did.

VITA: Go, Mrs. B!

JULIA: She met him over there while she was training.

MABEL (wistful): Porpoise oil!

VITA: Porpoise oil?

MABEL: He covered me with porpoise oil before I went in. He had the most beautiful hands . . .

JULIA: He was a doctor.

MABEL: Drawn from the water.

VITA: Drawn from the water?

MABEL: That's what "Moses" means.

JULIA (sotto voce to Vita): He was Jewish.

VITA (pleased): Like West's father!

JULIA: And wildly handsome. He did the swim the year before her.

VITA: So, why didn't you go off with him?

MABEL: I don't want to talk about it.

JULIA: Just think, you'd be living in London or Oxford. (Putting on an accent.) Pip pip and cheerio . . .

MABEL: I SAID I DON'T WANT TO TALK ABOUT IT!

Julia recalls that when Jean-Paul asked her to marry him she didn't think twice. Of course, she points out, he was French, and French men are sexier than English men. Mabel changes the subject, but Julia goes on. The way he looked at her . . . "It was as if his eyes had tongues." But now, she admits, he scarcely notices her.

Minty goes upstairs to see if there are mice in her room. Mabel sends Vita off to get lunch ready—shepherd's pie, corn, and apple brown Betty.

Julia wants to know how Mabel really is, but Mabel isn't about to give out much information. Julia is dismayed that Mabel's planning her Fourth of July party, but Mabel claims she loves parties. As for being frail, that's when you need parties the most. She wants to "exit with a flourish." As Vita rings the lunch bell, Minty screams and comes in with a dead mouse in a trap and drops it. Mabel releases the mouse and pops it into a nearby vase. It's dead and can't hurt you, she tells Minty.

MABEL: Chop, chop, it's time for lunch. I've never seen such a bunch of scaredy-cats! Lunch, lunch . . .

        Mabel reaches for her walker and starts to rise. She loses her balance and sways on her feet.

JULIA (rushing to her, grabbing her arm): Grand!

MABEL (whirling away from her): DON'T TOUCH ME! IF YOU TOUCH ME, I'LL FALL!

VITA (softly to Julia): Leave her alone. It's best if she does it herself.

MABEL (starts making her way across the room): "Row, row, row your boat, gently down the stream . . . "

JULIA (to Vita): She's so much worse.

MABEL: "Merrily, merrily, merrily, merrily, life is but a dream."

VITA: It's the arthritis.

JULIA: She can hardly move.

VITA: What are you talking about? This is a good day, ISN'T IT, MRS. B?

MABEL: Hmmm?

VITA: I SAID: THIS IS A GOOD DAY!

> *Mabel turns toward Vita and loses her balance again. She paddles the air.*

JULIA *(grabbing her arm):* I've got you!

MABEL *(wrenching out of her grasp, wild):* I SAID, DON'T TOUCH ME! WHAT'S THE MATTER, ARE YOU DEAF?

> *She takes several wobbly steps.*

Mmmmm, smell that sheperd's pie . . .

> *Julia can't watch and turns away.*

VITA: Atta girl, you're doing fine . . .

MABEL: Mary made the most heavenly shepherd's pie in the old days. I lived in that kitchen!

> *Mabel inches towards the dining room, recalling a summer day more than 70 years earlier.*

Scene 4: The Tidings kitchen, summer, 1922

It's an afternoon in mid-July. "*Mary, the Irish cook, is grinding chunks of cooked lamb in the meat grinder. She's in her mid 40s and wears a billowing white apron. Pru, her daughter, 18, is mashing potatoes. Mabel, 15, sits at Mary's feet shelling peas. She's at that awkward stage, wearing a fussy dress that doesn't fit right.*" Mary is telling a sad family tale.

MARY: My only sister. Seduced and abandoned at 16. *(Lowering her voice meaningfully.)* A year older than you.

MABEL: I'd die!

MARY: She almost did, poor thing.

PRU: Look on the bright side, Bridget wouldn't be here if it hadn't been for him.

MARY: He wed forty-three times before the constable finally caught up with him. Bridget has more half brothers and sisters than the daughter of an Arab sheik!

MARY and PRU *(chanting):* "Patrick McCann, Patrick McCann, forty-three rings on forty-three hands."

MABEL: Awful, awful!

MARY: I don't want you blabbing this all over town, now. My niece Bridget is a good girl. The Lowells are very happy with her.

MABEL: I won't say a word, I promise. Cross my heart and hope to die.

MARY: It's just between us. Our secret.

MABEL: My lips are sealed.

PRU *(to Mary):* Too bad your sister's weren't, back when it counted.

MARY *(swatting her with a towel):* Prudence Patricia O'Neill!

PRU *(trying to defend herself):* Help . . . help!
>   *They tussle with each other, laughing and squealing.*

Mabel reports that Mary's husband Norton is the best chauffeur they've ever had, according to her mother. Mary claims anybody could drive a car. Mabel, who keeps eating peas, admits she can't. She could if somebody would teach her, Pru points out. Pru's even driven a train. "And I've walked on water," her mother retorts. But Pru *did* drive a train, from Revere to Boston, when her friend Buddy allowed her to take the controls. Mary disapproves of Buddy, but Pru likes him. In Mary's opinion, men are devils or fools. Pru's attitude is, it's better to marry a fool than share a devil with forty-two wives.

Mary's never known a family to like shepherd's pie so much. She swats Mabel to get her to stop eating the peas. Bad enough she spends a lot of time in the kitchen. It's more fun than being upstairs, Mabel insists.

Maud calls to Mabel from off. They must leave for Phinney's polo match, the championship game. Mabel calls to go without her—she's tired of polo. Gus comes into the kitchen, angry, but formally greeting Mary and Pru. Maud follows him in and also greets them with formality. Frazier, now 21, bounces in, bows to Mary and Pru, saluting them as "sorceresses of the kitchen." Mabel begs off, claiming she doesn't feel well. Frazier teases her. Porter Bigelow (on whom he says Mabel has a crush) will be "heartbroken."

As soon as they've gone, Mabel announces she's got to get her dress off, she can't breathe.

MABEL *(heading towards the door):* I'm going to change into my bathing suit.

MARY: I should have known it was a plot to go swimming. I've never seen anyone spend so much time in the water. What on earth do you think about, hour after hour?

MABEL: Nothing, really. I count my strokes and sings songs.

MARY *(working on the brandy sauce):* Songs? What kind of songs?

MABEL: Nursery rhymes, mostly. "Row, Row, Row Your Boat," "The Farmer in the Dell." I sing each one two hundred times and then move on to another.

PRU: I'd go mad.

MABEL: It's relaxing, actually.

MARY: The girl is daft. She paddles through the freezing ocean, singing nursery rhymes.

They all sing a round. Mabel tells them she'd swim around the world if she could. Pru and Mary tease her—suppose there was a whale, or an octopus, a squid, or the Loch Ness monster! Mary's mother claims to have seen Nessie on her tenth birthday, and it was big as Buckingham Palace. Mary pretends to be the monster and chases Pru and Mabel till they fall down together. But Mabel only has a few hours and must get going. She begs them not to forget to wave to her when she swims past, it

keeps her going. Mary allows they never forget. Pru says Mabel should see herself—
no bigger than a pea, out there "bobbing up and down."

Scene 5: Mabel's living room, later that afternoon, the present

"*Mabel's sitting in her darkened living room by the phone. A light rain falls. The
fog horn moans in the distance.*" She has the guest list for the party and looks up
Kitty Lowell's number in her address book. She dials, delivers her invitation loudly,
only to realize that she's called the wrong number. She looks it up again, calls the
correct number and speaks loudly into the phone, only to discover she's got an
answering machine and has to wait through the music to give the message, which
she does in great haste. "I'M GIVING A CROQUET PARTY ON THE FOURTH
OF JULY, GOODBYE!" After hanging up and congratulating herself she remembers she didn't say who she was.

Suddenly the phone rings, and, assuming it's Kitty Lowell, she begins talking and
then finds it's the visiting nurse service. The torturous (owing to her deafness) comedy of errors phone conversation ultimately reveals that her blood tests are back,
the doctor is concerned and wants to see her, because she has too many white blood
cells. Mabel advises them to call back when Vita's there.

She slams down the receiver repeatedly, eventually hitting the cradle. It's dark,
and Vita has apparently moved the lamp. When Mabel tries to reach it, it crashes
to the floor. She calls out for help, but Vita's gone to the market, and Julia and
Minty are out, too. Nothing the matter with peace and quiet, except she can't see,
walk or hear, and her white blood cells are "out of whack." "Good old cancer," she
muses. It got Porter Bigelow, and David Bloom, too.

West comes in, and Mabel momentarily mistakes him for David. She's confused
as to where she is. She needs to catch her breath, she tells West. He hadn't meant
to scare her and asks if he can get her something.

MABEL: Would you be kind enough to hand me that shawl. I'm freezing.
WEST *(picking up a Victorian fringed shawl):* This?
MABEL: Please.
WEST *(handing it to her):* Here you go.
MABEL: Thank you, West, you're a true gentleman.
WEST: That's a first!
MABEL *(unfurling it):* God, this brings back memories! *(Whirling it around her.)*
"Blow, winds, and crack your cheeks! . . . Rage!"
        She sends a bunch of knick-knacks flying.
Take that, you stupid doctors with your tests . . .
WEST: Go, Mrs. B!
MABEL: I never saw such goings on!
WEST: You show 'em!
MABEL: Barium enemas and cat scans . . .
        More knick-knacks fly.

WEST: Yes!

MABEL: Abdominal probes and ash cans.
        And more knick-knacks.

WEST: Do it!

MABEL: Exploratory surgery and hand stands! *I can't take it any more! (Flinging the shawl to the floor.)*

WEST: Easy, easy . . .

MABEL *(trying to rise, seeing a sudden hallucination):* The horses are loose . . . They bare their teeth and rush headlong into the sea . . .

WEST *(at her side):* Easy, Easy . . .

MABEL: Look out, look out, they're coming this way!

WEST: Mrs. B?

MABEL *(clutching onto him):* Hold me, David! Hold me! Hold me! Hold me!
        West attempts to comfort her as the lights fade.

Scene 6: The Tidings living room, summer, 1927

"*A balmy August evening . . . . . The Tidingses are in the midst of a game of charades in the drawing room with Anton Gurevitch, mid 40s, the charismatic Russian conductor of the Boston Symphony Orchestra. Maud, Phinney and Gurevitch are playing against Chandler, Frazier and Mabel. Everyone's dressed to the nines.*" Gurevitch is whirling the Victorian fringed shawl and bellowing "Blow, winds, and crack your cheeks! . . . Rage!" There's the sound of breaking china, and Phinney says a goodbye to the demi-tasse cups. Chandler is upset. Gurevitch doesn't understand he's not supposed to say the phrase, he's supposed to act it out. Chandler wants the game stopped, he's given it away. Gurevitch is enjoying himself, however. Nor is he to use props, Maud chides him. Gurevitch is carried away—"You see great king lost in madness." Nor is he supposed to speak, Maud insists. Frazier comes on and takes the shawl away from Gurevitch.

        *Mabel enters carrying glasses of champagne. She's 20 and has blossomed
        into a beauty. Both Chandler and Gurevitch are smitten with her.*

GUREVITCH *(stops playing and rushes to her side):* There you are!

CHANDLER: " . . . Fairer than the evening air, clad in the beauty of a thousand stars."

MABEL: Please!

FRAZIER: What about *me*? *(Draping the shawl around himself.)* "Mirror, mirror, on the wall, who's the fairest of them all?" *(Answering as the mirror.)* "Why you, oh queen! Snow White is just a child!"

MAUD *(linking arms with Gurevitch):* Thank God Gus is off on one of his sails, he'd be appalled at our goings on.

MABEL: Poor Papa.

PHINNEY: On the contrary, he knows where he belongs.

FRAZIER: *Not* here!

MAUD: If only he weren't alone.

PRIDE'S CROSSING—Dylan Baker as Chandler Coffin and Cherry Jones as Mabel Tidings Bigelow in a scene from Tina Howe's play

FRAZIER: No one wants to go with him, given his temper.
MAUD: I worry so.
FRAZIER: He'll be all right. Only the good die young.
MAUD and MABEL: *Frazier!*
PHINNEY: If they're lucky!
MABEL: Phinney!
MAUD: Doesn't he realize he's tempting fate?
PHINNEY: That's the whole point. To risk it all.
MAUD: But why New Zealand?
PHINNEY: One perfect dive . . . and then oblivion.
CHANDLER: "Between extremities Man runs his course."

Maud has had enough of gloom and has a "killer" for the other team to act out: "Twas brllig, and the slithy toves, Did gyre and gimble in the wabe." Several energetic attempts to communicate even one word of these "Jabberwocky" lines end in failure. Finally Mabel indicates she's trying not for a single word but the whole quote with "*a fantastic rendering . . . . . complete with gyrations, soft shoe and tap. It gets increasingly lurid and violent as everyone watches, open-mouthed.*" Chandler triumphantly gets it, and Mabel throws herself at him joyously: "We did it, we did it!" Chandler explains that it was intuition, he knows what Mabel is thinking. Maud attributes this to the fact that Chandler's father is a great poet who wrote a poem about the high dive after Phinney won his Olympic medal. It was a paraphrase of Swinburne, and Chandler quotes it, embarassing Phinney: "Shot like a stone from a sling through the air, Shouting and laughing with delight, He plunged headfore-most into the approaching wave."

Mabel wants to play another round of charades, but Maud, her head resting on Gurevitch's shoulder, reminds Mabel the maestro is sailing for Vienna tomorrow.

MAUD *(to Gurevitch):* I don't know where you find the time to join us in our silly parlor games.

GUREVITCH *(drifting away from Maud and putting his arm around Mabel):* You know us Russians, we have a weakness for beautiful women.

MABEL: Maestro!

GUREVITCH *(drawing her close):* As our literature so tragically attests.
    A brief silence. The grandfather clock starts to strike eleven.

CHANDLER *(improvising):* "And so the hours of the clock parade. As we stand poised for our next charade . . . "

MAUD: Just like his father. It's in the blood.

CHANDLER: "The Maestro swoons, hearing music of the spheres, While we poor fools depend on our ears. Tis ever thus with games and art, The great ones inhabit a world apart."
    He bows, doffing an imaginary hat. Gurevitch returns the bow. Chandler
    executes a more florid one. Gurevitch tops him. Everyone laughs.

GUREVITCH: Where did you find this extraordinary young man?

MAUD: He's been a friend of the family for years. Groton, Harvard, swim-ming . . .

CHANDLER *(exaggerating his limp):* I, however, lack Phinney's grace, as you may have noticed.

PHINNEY: I merely enter the water, you travel through it.

MABEL: Last year he swam the Hellespont.

CHANDLER: Like that other famous club foot, Lord Byron!

MAUD, PHINNEY, FRAZIER and MABEL: Chandler!

CHANDLER: Come, come, it makes life so much easier if you call a spade a spade, deformed as it may be. I come from a noble, if somewhat shady line start-ing with Oedipus. Fortunately there's not much chance I'll follow in his foot-steps—pardon the pun—since my distinguished father is very much alive and gives every indication of living forever. Long live the king!

Mabel suddenly suggests a swim to Singing Beach. Maud thinks not, it being pitch black outside, but Mabel opens the curtains revealing moonlight. She has eyes in the back of her head, Maud remarks, and lovely ones, Gurevitch adds. Maud concedes Mabel has become "quite a beauty" but despairs of her taste in men. It seems Mabel has set her cap for Porter Bigelow. Maud has never seen him sober, nor any other of the Bigelows, for that matter. Phinney and Frazier defend Porter—he has style, was a great quarterback and is a great catch!

Gurevitch returns to the subject of the swim, but Singing Beach is the public beach in Manchester, and Maud disapproves. She forbids Mabel to leave the house. All the men promise to keep an eye on her, if they can keep up with her. Maud insists young ladies do not swim in the middle of the night. What about Gertrude Ederle, Mabel wonders, who swam the English Channel from France to England last year and set a new world record. Chandler's met her—"Nice girl. Strong as an ox." But Mabel's "delicate," Maud claims, with a spot on her lung. Everyone in Boston has one, Mabel pooh-poohs.

Mabel reveals to her mother that she's training to swim the Channel from England to France, which a woman hasn't done yet. Last week she swam to Eastern Point. Chandler's helping her train. Maud thinks Mabel's trying to give her a heart attack and wants to discuss it later. She has sponsors, too, Mabel tells Maud, reeling off the names of their proper and well-to-do friends. She's been getting ready for this swim for years, going out early in the morning. Her mother must have heard her but was so preoccupied with her own misery she never raised the blinds to see her. Mabel steps out of her shoes. She knows her mother heard her—she'd tossed gravel at her window. The servants had cheered her on, waving dish towels at her. She rolls down her stockings.

MAUD *(to Phinney and Frazier):* Did you know about this?

MABEL: Of course they knew. Everyone knew. Papa's been watching me for years. He'd open an eye and wink at me. Those winks propelled me all the way to Gloucester and back, but it was *your* gaze I was desperate for.
    She starts unbuttoning her dress.
I kept looking at the window, *willing* you to lift the shade and finally see me. *(Imitating her.)* "Good grief, it's Mabel! Look at her go! Past the Codmans', past the Adams's and Rantouls'." But no such luck. The shade was always drawn. The disdain . . . no, lack of interest . . . It was really quite extraordinary . . . Your "delicate" daughter, plowing through the Atlantic right under your nose . . .

CHANDLER: Off, off, take it off!

PHINNEY: Go, M.T.!

FRAZIER: Do it for all of us!

MAUD: *See here, young lady . . .*

GUREVITCH: She's magnificent!

CHANDLER: "Nymph, in they orisons, be all my sins remembered."

MABEL: I could have gotten a cramp and drowned . . . Not that you would have saved me, but at least you could have watched me go down. *(Struggling as if in the water.)* "Help . . . helllp . . . helllllp . . . "

She starts to shimmy out of her dress.

MAUD: I WON'T HAVE THIS SORT OF BEHAVIOR IN MY HOUSE!

MABEL: But drowning wasn't on my mind. I wanted you to see me swim. I imagined a pattern was involved. "She'll raise the shade after the fiftieth stroke, the seventieth, the hundredth . . . " And back and forth I'd go, swimming parallel to the house for the first hour or so. Then I thought it had to do with speed. If I go faster, she'll raise it.

Flinging her dress to the floor.

So I'd do 70 strokes a minute, 80, 90, pushing myself to the limit.

Mabel stands revealed in a bathing suit, 20s sytle.

Look at me, Mama, look at me . . . !

GUREVITCH *(whistling and applauding):* Brava, brava!

PHINNEY: Nicely done!

FRAZIER: *Brilliant!*

CHANDLER: I'm in love.

MABEL *(in tears):* Look at me!

GUREVITCH: Ah youth . . .

MAUD *(in a towering rage):* THE PARTY'S OVER! GO TO YOUR ROOM!

Mabel tells herself to give it up, and, trying to control herself, begins singing "The farmer in the dell . . . " in a voice that breaks. She can swim past islands, continents, and to other time zones, and when Maud declares Mabel won't leave the house for the rest of the summer, Mabel tells her she can't forbid her swimming. She's left Maud behind, so far she can't even see her. Maud exits. "*Everyone looks at Mabel. She raises her arms and slowly turns towards the ocean as . . . " Curtain.*

ACT II

Scene 1: Mabel's living room, four days later, the present

It's 5 in the morning and still dark. Wearing a tattered nightgown and robe, Mabel is looking for something in the hall closet. The only light comes from a dim bulb inside the closet. She probes through the wilderness of junk with her long pincers while steadying herself on her walker. The fog horn moans in the distance.

MABEL: Where *is* that damned croquet set?

Something falls with a crash.

Gently, gently . . . I don't want to wake everyone up. *(Pulling out a folding tripod chair.)* Mercy, I haven't seen this in ages! It was Mama's. She used to take it to Phinney's polo matches . . . Poor Phin, broke his neck doing a swan dive off the Rock of Gibraltar. Too much fame and too much drink . . . Gone, gone . . . they're all gone. Frazier a suicide at 31, Papa lost off the Cape of Good Hope, Mama a catastrophic stroke in the Public Gardens . . . Face down in the zinnias, kerplop! I'm the only one left, the end of the line, the sediment at the bottom of the glass . . . Who would have thought? *(She sighs.)* Oh, well, *c'est la guerre! (Pulling out a beat-*

up pair of binoculars.) Papa's binoculars! I don't believe it! *(Surveying the room through them.)* Good Lord, when did things start getting so shabby? It looks like Tobacco Road in here! The paint's peeling off the ceiling, and the slipcovers are in tatters. *(Making her way over to the chair.)* What happened to the painting that used to be in that frame? Don't tell me I sold it? I loved that painting. The broody sky and those precious sheep . . . I must have needed the money . . . *(Sitting down with a thud.)* Ugh!

   There's a crash behind the Chinese screen.
(Hand flying to her heart.) What was that? Is someone there? Hello? Hello?
   Mabel peers into the darkness. The screen starts to move towards her.
If you're a burglar, show yourself and get it over with. I can't stand shilly-shallying around!

 It's Minty behind the screen—she couldn't sleep. At Mabel's urging she comes out wearing part of the Paul Revere costume, puts on the hat and quotes "One if by land and two if by sea." It seems she plans to be an actress. Mabel mistakes actress for princess, but Minty straightens that out. Minty had the lead in her school play, *The Little Prince*, and her mother had come both nights. But not her father. She confesses she and her mother haven't seen her father in a long time, and it makes her mother cry. Minty misses him. Mabel suggests she pretend he's there. That's what she did when she swam—"I'd imagine a crowd cheering me on." Imagination is powerful. They discuss Mabel's Channel swim, and Minty asks if Mabel still swims. "God, no" Mabel demurs. Minty asks what she does all day and Mabel confesses she hasn't any idea.

 Mabel asks Minty's help in finding the croquet set in the closet. She finds a mallet and ball and then says she's found some wickets. There is a loud crash, and Minty emerges apologizing with a large silver trophy with one handle broken off. It's Mabel's Channel trophy, and she hasn't seen it in years. Mabel assures Minty it was broken a long time ago. She gets Minty to stick the wickets in between the floorboards and instructs her in playing the game.

 MABEL: I used to love croquet. We had a gala tournament every Fourth of July. Everyone came. That's where I first fell in love with your great grandfather . . . I was 14, and he was 19. He was a friend of my brother, Phinney. Talk about handsome . . . I thought I'd faint as he came striding up the lawn. He had on his tennis whites, and the sun was shining behind him, so he seemed to glow. He looked like something out of a fairy tale. He was barefoot for some reason . . . I'll never forget it. How pink his feet were against the freshly mown grass. It was as if they'd been painted, they were so bright . . . Then he smiled this smile . . . The lawn started to tilt like a falling tea tray, and everything flew upside down. Including him . . . He hovered over me like some fantastic flamingo with those blinding pink feet . . . I heard this pounding in my ears . . . The next thing I knew, I was stretched out on a lawn chair, and he was leaning over me, whispering, "May I have the next dance? May I have the next dance? May I have the next dance?" *(With a sigh.)* Porter Bigelow . . . Be wary of handsome men, Minty, they're up to no good.

MINTY: I'll try to remember.

MABEL: Beauty and virtue rarely go together.

MINTY *(preparing to make another shot):* Watch, Mou-Mou, watch!

MABEL: Particularly in men. I know . . . I learned the hard way.

By accident, Minty hits Mabel's foot with the ball. Mabel cries out in pain, then goes into a rage. Minty tries to apologize. Vita and Julia appear and want to know what's been going on. Mabel won't let Vita see her foot, and when Vita asks what she's doing with the trophy Mabel threatens to scream if Vita comes any closer. When Vita attempts to take it, Mabel, *"clutching it for dear life"*, says "It's miiiiiiiiiiine!"

Scene 2: Mabel and Porter Bigelow's living room, Boston, summer, 1942

> *Like the Tidings house, there's something oppressive about the place . . . . .*
> *An imposing staircase is visible in the hall. Mabel, 35 and Porter, 40 have*
> *just returned from a dinner party. Porter is drunk. He pours himself an-*
> *other drink as Mabel hangs up their coats offstage.*

PORTER: You think I'm blind? You think I can't see? I asked you a question! You positively threw yourself at that fellow who claimed to know your English swimmer, what's-his-name . . . David Bernstein, Brustein, Blitzstein . . . *(Imitating her.)* "You're a friend of David Blitskrieg? How *is* he? I heard he joined the RAF and flew some very dangerous missions. He was shot down over the Channel? *Our* Channel? I can't listen! . . . He survived? He had a picture of *me* next to this heart? Stop, stop, you mustn't tease!" I won't have it, I tell you! I won't!

> *Mabel enters wearing a stunning evening gown. Porter grabs her arm.*
> *They struggle.*

MABEL *(wild):* Stop it, stop it!

PORTER: You're my wife, *mine!*

EMMA'S VOICE *(from upstairs):* Mummy, is that you?

MABEL: David Bloom is married with three children! And he's a doctor! He was never a flier!

EMMA'S VOICE *(louder):* Mummy?

PORTER: Great, you woke Emma. Billy will be next.

Mabel calls up to Emma, assuring her she's all right, that she thought she'd seen a mouse. Eventually, assured her father got the mouse, Emma is told to go back to sleep.

Why did Mabel start screaming? Porter asks. He was about to hit her, Mabel states. He'd never hit her, Porter swears. "Do tell!" is Mabel's comment. Porter claims he's the one wronged. Mabel insists she didn't say "two words" to the man at the party, that she and David are history, but admits she couldn't have done her swim without him.

PORTER *(taking several gulps of his drink):* Your swim, your swim . . . you'd think you crossed the Atlantic Ocean the way everyone carries on! Mabel Tidings crossing and double crossing. To Little Misery and back, and what a misery it was. My bride to be, the pride of Pride's, the queen of tides and love that died . . . tossing and crossing with him at her side . . . How did she do it? Thirteen minutes and 42 seconds!

MABEL: Hours! Thirteen *hours* . . .

PORTER: The American girl who swam the Channel with her English lover rowing beside her. It was so brazen, so romantic . . . I wish I could have been there. *(Putting on an English accent.)* "Jolly good . . . stiff upper lip . . . keep going, old girl, and there'll be a nice fuck for you on the other side!"

MABEL: I don't have to listen to this!

PORTER: Why didn't you marry *him*? Doctor, world-class athlete, first in his class at Oxford . . . He had brains *and* brawn . . . a winning combination if ever there was one. Of course he was a Jew . . . Not that I have anything against the Jews. They're very capable people.

MABEL: You ought to hear yourself, it's frightening!

PORTER: I asked you a question. Why didn't you marry *him*?

MABEL: Porter, please . . .

But Porter doesn't let up. She had a chance to get out, to be the "belle of Europe" even though she was engaged to Porter, but she was resourceful enough to have broken the engagement. The families would have been upset, but she would have done better to have the unpleasantness then instead of "pining for him" the rest of her life. She didn't have the guts, he believes.

Emma is awake again, wondering if the mouse came back, but Porter still goes on. He thinks every time she touches her trophy it's as if she's touching David, and he throws it down, breaking off a handle, then gives it to her. "Your funerary urn, Madame, the ashes are still warm." He tells Emma he got the mouse, but she's not to come to see it, she's to go to sleep.

Mabel confesses she lacked the courage to marry David, that between Dover and Calais she lost her nerve, but she wonders what would have happened if she'd taken his hand. Porter says she would be in the middle of a war. Mabel asks what he thinks this is. She can't take any more. Porter doesn't know what came over him and apologizes. It's the same thing that comes over him every night. He must stop drinking. He gives his word, but Mabel is sick to death of his words. She's tired, she's going to bed. Porter pleads with her, but she goes to the stairway, announcing she will be in Billy's room.

Scene 3: The next day, the 4th of July, Mabel's bedroom, the present

It's about noon. "*Julia and Minty are in their slips, looking through Granny Tidings's lawn dresses. The rejects lie on Mabel's bed. Julia spies an especially elegant dress and holds it up to herself in front of the mirror.*"

David Lansbury (Pinky Wheelock), Casey Biggs ("Wheels" Wheelock), Kandis Chappell (Julia Renoir), Cherry Jones (Mabel), Julia McIlvaine (Minty Renoir) and Dylan Baker (Chandler Coffin) in *Pride's Crossing*

It's the fourth dress Julia has tried on. Minty thinks, despite the smell of what Julia explains is mothballs, that it turns her mother into a bride. Minty's having trouble finding a dress the right size, but when they hear the doorbell she hurriedly puts another on. Mabel brings in Kitty Lowell, who has on a flowered dress she's been wearing for years. Mabel orders Kitty to take off her dress and choose from the ones at hand. And if she doesn't want to? Kitty wonders. They've been friends for 80 years, but when Mabel barks, Kitty jumps, Kitty admits—"It's pathetic." But Mabel finds it "endearing." Mabel reveals that Vita's father has died, and Vita and West have gone to Florida.

The doorbell rings again. It's Chandler Coffin in a white linen suit, and the Wheelocks, both 93. "Wheels," doddering, is in white, and his wife, Pinky, is in her customary pink. Kitty and Minty squeal, caught in their slips. Chandler thinks he and Wheels ought not to be in there. Mabel tells them they're too old to be modest. Pinky shimmies out of her dress and hums a stripper's song. It seems she was not only the "fastest girl" in Miss Windsor's school, but on Beacon Hill as well!

They try on dressees and ask how they look. Mabel insists Pinky wear the one Kitty has on, and vice-versa. Wheels pops his head in, acting like some teenager.

Mabel begins to look for something for herself and comes upon a black hat with a veil, the hat she wore to Porter's funeral. And with it is the program from the service. She puts the hat on and reads, "*In memoriam*, Porter Ransom Bigelow, August 17, 1900 to April 2, 1967, King's Chapel, Boston, Massachusetts." Porter's cancer "consumed him like a threshing machine," but be bore it "like a Trojan," she recalls. And those wonderful words at his funeral—"What a chimera then is man!" "*Her voice dovetails with Dr. Peabody's as Mabel is transported back to Porter's funeral.*"

Scene 4: King's Chapel, Boston, 1967

·   "*Mabel, 60, is the only mourner who's visible, though it's clear from the sound she's not alone.*" Dr. Peabody continues with, "What a novelty, what a monster, what a chaos, what a contradiction, what a prodigy!" As the service nears its end the congregation joins him in saying the Lord's Prayer, after which Dr. Peabody raises his arms to give the blessing. A Bach organ prelude is being played over the "*sound effect of the mourners leaving.*" Mabel is still in the front row when "a woman in black tentatively approaches her." She's Pru, the former serving girl, Mary's daughter. She reminds Mabel they used to watch her when she was swimming. Mabel is surprised and amazed that Pru is "all grown up." It has to be 40 years, Pru points out. Mabel is delighted to see her and asks her to sit down, but Pru remains standing.

PRU: It was a lovely service.
MABEL: A bit long.
PRU: I've never been in a Unitarian church before.
MABEL: Well, you know the old joke: The only time you hear the name Jesus Christ in a Unitarian church is when the janitor falls down the stairs.
PRU *(bursts out laughing):* Miss, Miss . . .
MABEL: You've never heard that before?
PRU *(wiping her eyes):* No one can make me laugh like you. I'm sorry, I'm sorry.
MABEL: No, no, it's good to laugh.
PRU: But not at your husband's funeral, Miss. Mr. Bigelow was such a lovely boy. I mean, fine man.

The turnout for the service was "pathetic," Mabel remarks, only 35 at most. Pru thinks it was more like 70. From the back she had the better view. Suddenly it occurs to Mabel to ask Pru if she married Buddy, "the young man who drove the train. *(She pulls the imaginary whistle.)* Whoo oo." But Pru married a Freddy Fitzgerald.

MABEL *(with a twinkle):* And what, pray tell, does Freddy drive?
PRU *(world weary):* Me, I'm afraid.
MABEL: Men!
PRU: "They're either devils or fools."
MABEL: "Better marry a fool than share a devil with forty-two wives."

MABEL and PRU *(chanting):* "Patrick McCann, Patrick McCann, forty-three rings on forty-three hands."
> *They laugh and are suddenly quiet.*

PRU *(shifting on her feet):* Well, you'll want to be joining your family.

MABEL *(rising):* Dearest Pru, you were so good to come.

PRU: Not at all. I wanted to pay my respects.
> *They walk up the aisle together*

MABEL: And have you been happy?

PRU: *Happy?*

MABEL: Yes.

PRU: Have *you*?

MABEL *(beginning to cheer up):* When I least expect it.

PRU *(with a sigh):* Like everything elese . . . . .
> *The lights fade on their embrace.*

Scene 5: Mabel's Lawn, moments later, the present

"*Mabel's Fourth of July party is under way beneath a sparkling blue sky. The guests stand frozen in various attitudes of play—the women, elegant in Granny Tidings's lawn dresses, the men, courtly in their old linen suits. The whiteness of their clothes is brilliant against the green of the grass and overarching trees. It looks like a Sargent painting come to life.*" The guests are becoming impatient because no one is allowed to move until Mabel finds her camera. She returns triumphant (the camera was under her darning), pushed in a wheelchair by Julia. Mabel wears one of the lawn dresses, too, and the Paul Revere hat as well. Kitty complains that they look a century old in these clothes, but Mabel assures them they look "very handsome." Julia, who is to take the picture, is looking through the camera and exclaims that Mabel is right. "It's amazing!" They should see themselves. The picture-taking over, Wheels has fallen asleep in his chair.

PINKY: WHEELS, ARE YOU STILL ALIVE? *(Starts shaking him.)* Sweetheart?

KITTY: Poor Wheels.

MABEL: Poor Wheels.

CHANDLER: There but for the grace of God go I.

PINKY: Wake up!

CHANDLER: Remember Snap Sessions?

CHANDLER, MABEL, PINKY and KITTY: Dropped dead during Dr. Cummings's sermon on original sin.

CHANDLER: Pitched face forward into Tippy Loring and was gone.

MABEL: Poor thing thought he was trying to kiss her!
> *They laugh and laugh.*

KITTY: I always liked Tippy. She was a great reader, you know. She could recite entire chapters of Gibbon's *Decline and Fall of the Roman Empire* by heart.

MABEL: Gone, gone . . . We're all that's left.

CHANDLER: "Oh build your ship of death, your little ark and furnish it with food, with little cakes, and wine for the dark flight down oblivion."

MABEL, KITTY and PINKY: D. H. Lawrence.

CHANDLER: D. H. Lawrence.

Pinky is still trying to wake Wheels. She misses him! Minty is worried about him, and it's explained that he has narcolepsy.

Mabel reminds them it's a croquet party and pairs Julia and Minty to play against Chandler and Kitty. Minty points out to Mabel that she doesn't have to walk to play. She shows Mabel how she can prop herself against the walker and swing her mallet. The game is under way, and Chandler is playing well. Pinky recalls how they all used to fight over Chandler, who had eyes only for Mabel. Pinky wonders why Mabel and Chandler didn't marry each other. Chandler admits Mabel wouldn't have him.

Kitty wants to know what happened between Mabel and the English swimmer. Pinky's always wondered too. Chandler says it was love at first sight between Mabel and David Bloom. Why didn't they marry? Kitty asks. Julia feels Mabel's always elusive about him, as if she were ashamed or something. Why should she be? Mabel demands to know. "Because he was . . . you know . . . Jewish. There. I said it," Kitty blurts out.

MABEL: You're right, I *was* ashamed. Of *myself!* I wasn't up to him.

OTHERS: Up to him?

MABEL: He was a force of nature. A typhoon, a tidal wave . . . . .

JULIA: Like Jean-Paul.

MABEL: I didn't know what hit me.

JULIA: You swam the Channel, nonetheless.

MABEL: But I couldn't keep going. You, on the other hand, reached the distant shore. That's why I admire you so.

JULIA: Please . . .

MABEL: You stayed your course.

JULIA *(suddenly swamped with sadness):* I stayed my course.

MINTY *(sidling up to her):* Hi, Mommy.

JULIA: Hello, darling.

MINTY: Are you O. K.?

    Silence as Julia considers.

JULIA: Of course I'm O.K. And do you know why?

    Minty waits.

(Hugging her.) Because *you're* with me. My dearest precious Minty, I love you so! My treasure, my heart's delight! *(She kisses her.)*

Julia went the distance, but not me, Mabel mourns. No, she pulled herself together, turned back, doing the proper thing, following the rules. "Fool, fool!" She stands and takes a mallet. Julia hurries over to her, wanting to know what she's doing. What does she think she's doing, Mabel asks, hitting a ball. But it's not her turn, and not her ball, the others complain. Mabel does not care, and when Minty asks to be on her team, Mabel says there aren't teams, "It's every man for himself!"

CHANDLER: What about the rules?

MABEL: The rules, the rules ... I'm sick to death of the rules! *(Hitting a ball through a wicket.)* Come on, everyone play at once!

KITTY: Hey, that was my ball!

CHANDLER *(to Mabel):* What's come over you?

MINTY *(laying her ball at her feet):* Here's yours, Mou-Mou.

MABEL: Thank you, darling.

CHANDLER: This is a civilized game.

MABEL: And as with all civilizations, things change. It's called *progress*.

CHANDLER: But how will we know who wins?

MABEL: Who cares?

CHANDLER: I care! I was winning.

MABEL: For God's sake, Chan, we've walked out of the Dark Ages into the light of day!

Mabel demands the Wheelocks play and Pinky leads Wheels to the first wicket. He whacks the ball through, to their amazement, and then hits it through the next. Everyone is playing, a travesty, Chandler believes. Julia and Minty are singing "*Allons enfants, de la patrie, La jour de gloire est arrivé ...*" Mabel suddenly stops, hallucinating again. "The horses are massing on the shore. Look at them go!" The conversations go on around her.

MABEL *(weaving across the lawn):* Wait for me, wait for me ...

MINTY: Look out, Mommy, I'm going to get you!

> *A cacophony of voices speaking in English accents mingles with the shouts of the players. "I'll drop you off here, there's no easy access to Shakespeare Beach" ... "I know, thank you very much" ... "Good luck with your swim. An American girl did it last year, you know, but from France to England" ... "Hurry up, we only have a quarter of an hour" ... "What's your name again?" ... "Come on M.T., the world awaits," as ...*

CHANDLER *(finally noticing Mabel):* M.T., what are you doing?

> *Everyone freezes.*

MABEL *(staggers away from them, paddling her arms):* I'm coming, David. I'm coming ...

Scene 6: The Cliffs of Dover, England, 1928

"*Shakespeare Beach, off the Cliffs of Dover* ....." It's 4:30 on an August morning and not yet light. "*The cliffs are shrouded in fog. Mabel, 21, is preparing for her swim. The legendary English swimmer David Bloom, late 20s, stands beside her."* David opens a jar. It's time to grease her up, he tells Mabel. Humans were not meant to swim in 58 degree water. Maybe sea lions and polar bears, "but not scrawny young women." She's at her optimum weight, Mabel reminds him. He kisses her neck and arms, calling her his "lovely beast" and "elegant cat" as he smears her with lanolin. "It smells!" Mabel exclaims. He's added porpoise oil to help fend off the jellyfish. And he's added paraffin, too. Mabel isn't nervous, oddly enough. It's because she's in top form and could swim the Atlantic, he believes.

"The sky gradually gets lighter." Mabel wonders about the pilot boat, but it isn't 5 o'clock yet. The fog is worse than yesterday, but the weather is perfect for her swim. She couldn't ask for better winds. Mabel wishes she'd known David when he swam the Channel, breaking every record. It was luck, he reveals, a tidal stream carried him the final two miles. He didn't have to take a stroke and was actually washed onto Cap Griz Nez. "Like Moses among the bulrushes—drawn from the water. That's what 'Moses' means, in case you're interested . . . " It's like delivering babies, he muses, drawing them from the amniotic fluid.

She claims she would not be here if it weren't for David, but he knows she was very well trained by Chandler, who is in love with her. Chandler wanted to accompany Mabel, but then she'd met David. Is she heartless? "Utterly," David says. Mabel's never been as happy, and David begs her to run away with him, after the swim, when they reach France. But Mabel's engaged, to Porter Bigelow. Break it off, David urges. She made a promise! "But not a vow! There's a difference," in David's opinion. Mabel doesn't see how she could face Porter or their families.

DAVID *(taking her in his arms):* Listen to me, darling. I know I sound impulsive, but once in a while something miraculous happens. You're swimming along, and the love of your life drops down beside you. He holds out his hand . . . Or is it a wing? . . . and says, "Follow me." You have a split second to decide. Will you stay your course or take it? *(He starts kissing her.)*

MABEL: David, David . . .

DAVID: Come with me, we'll leave the sadness of the world and swim the seven seas. We'll start in the Mediterranean, travel overland to the Red Sea, round the Gulf of Aden, pick up the Arabian Sea and follow the coast of India til we hit the Bay of Bengal . . . Then it's due south to Sumatra, the South China Sea and finally the Coral Sea, ringed with doves and hummingbirds . . .

MABEL: Stop, stop . . .

DAVID: We'll live on starfish, minnows and snails. Our bodies will fuse, and we'll be absorbed into each other, like a fabulous sea anemone, phylum: *Cnidaria*, genus: *Stoichactis*, distant cousin of the passion flower . . .

MABEL: David, please . . .

DAVID: Phylum: *Passiflora,* species: *incarnata.*

MABEL: Oh God . . . Oh God . . .

DAVID: You didn't know I could speak Latin, did you? I can also throw a javelin, shear a sheep and walk on hot coals.

They see the lights of the pilot boat. David waves, calling "Over here, over here ... " "Tell it to go away," Mabel pleads. She doesn't want to go, though everything is perfect. Too late, David says, she is going to set a new world record. For a moment it doesn't seem important to Mabel, and then, *"coming back to life,"* she admits that of course she is excited. She will be brilliant, David knows, promising not to take his eyes off her even for a second. He will be right next to her.

DAVID *(kissing her):* I miss you already.

MABEL: Until France.

DAVID *(wades out to the boat and gets in):* And beyond.

PILOT'S VOICE: Come on, Miss Tidings, you'd better get started while the tide's still with you. We've timed everything down to the second.

MABEL: I'm coming, I'm coming ...

    She puts on her cap and goggles.

DAVID *(from the boat):* Good luck, M.T.

MABEL: Good luck to us all! " ... and shot like a stone from a sling through the air, shouting and laughing with delight, head foremost, *she* plunges into the approaching wave!"

    Mabel takes a deep breath, shakes out her arms and legs and dives . . . . .

"Into the water," the script directs, but in the New York staging Mabel dives into the arms of the actors playing the other characters—ironically, into the arms of her "family." *Curtain.*

Special Citation

OOO
OOO
OOO
OOO
OOO

RAGTIME

A Musical in Two Acts

BOOK BY TERRENCE McNALLY

BASED ON THE NOVEL BY E.L. DOCTOROW

MUSIC BY STEPHEN FLAHERTY

LYRICS BY LYNN AHRENS

Cast and credits appear on pages 210–213

TERRENCE McNALLY (book) was born in St. Petersburg, Fla. November 3, 1939 and grew up in Corpus Christi, Texas. He received his B.A. in English at Columbia, where in his senior year he wrote the varsity show. After graduation he was awarded the Harry Evans Travelling Fellowship in creative writing. He made his professional stage debut with The Lady of the Camellias, *an adaptation of the Dumas story produced on Broadway March 20, 1963 for 13 performances. His first original full-length play,* And Things That Go Bump in the Night, *arrived on Broadway April 26, 1965 for 16 performances, following a production at the Tyron Guthrie Theater in Minneapolis.*

McNally's short play Tour *was produced off Broadway in 1968 as part of the* Collision Course *program. In the next season, 1968–69, his one-acters were produced all over town:* Cuba Si! *off Broadway in the ANTA Matinee series;* Noon *on the Broadway program* Morning, Noon and Night *November 28 for 52 performances;* Sweet Eros *and* Witness *off Broadway that fall; and, on February 10,* Next *with Elaine May's* Adaptation *on an off-Broadway bill that ran for 707 performances and was named a Best Play of its season.*

McNally's second Best Play, Where Has Tommy Flowers Gone?, *had its world premiere at the Yale Repertory Theater before opening on Broadway October 7, 1971 for 78 performances. His third,* Bad Habits, *directed by Robert Drivas, ran the New York gamut: off off Broadway at New York Theater Strategy, off Broadway February 4, 1974 for 96 performances and Broadway May 5, 1974 for 273 performances. His fourth,* The Ritz, *played the Yale Repertory Theater as* The Tubs *before opening on Broadway January 20, 1975 for 400 performances. His fifth,* It's Only a Play, *was produced in a pre-Broadway tryout under the title* Broadway, Broadway *in 1978, then OOB by Manhattan Punch Line in 1982. It finally reached off Broadway—and Best Play designation—January 12, 1986 for 17 performances at Manhattan Theater Club, which also produced his sixth Best Play,* Lips Together, Teeth Apart, *June 25, 1991 for 406 performances, a Lucille Lortel Award winner.*

McNally's seventh Best Play, the book for the musical Kiss of the Spider Woman, *with a John Kander-Fred Ebb score, took a circuitous route to Broadway. After a 1990 tryout in the short-lived New Musicals Progam at SUNY Purchase, N.Y. and a Toronto production, it went overseas to an award-winning London staging in 1992. It finally reached Broadway May 3, 1993, just in time to win that season's New York Drama Critics Circle best-musical citation and the Tonys for book, score and show— and remained for 906 performances. His eighth Best Play,* A Perfect Ganesh, *was put on by Manhattan Theater Club June 27, 1994 for 124 performances. His ninth Best Play,* Love! Valour! Compassion!, *was produced by MTC November 1, 1994 for 72 performances, then moved to Broadway February 14 for an additional 249 performances, winning the Tony for best play and the Critics Award for best American play.*

With Master Class, *McNally joined the half-dozen illustrious playwrights whose Best Play citations have moved into double digits over the years (Maxwell Anderson 19, George S. Kaufman 18, Neil Simon 15, Eugene O'Neill 12, Moss Hart 11, Philip Barry 10).* Master Class, *which played 601 Broadway performances starting November 5, 1995, also won the best-play Tony. As the theatrical equivalent of a switch-hitting home run champion, McNally turns again to the musical stage for his 11th major citation in these volumes and second Tony award for best book of a musical with* Ragtime, *a crown jewel of the 1997–98 New York theater season, which opened on Broadway January 18 in the handsome new Ford Center for the Performing Arts for what promises to be a very long and widely-acclaimed run.*

Other notable McNally presentations in one of the most active and successful playwriting careers in this or any other generation have included Whiskey *(1973 OOB); the book for the John Kander-Fred Ebb musical* The Rink *(Broadway February 9, 1984 for 204 peformances);* The Lisbon Traviata *(1985 OOB, 1989 at MTC for 128 performances);* Frankie and Johnny in the Clair de Lune *(1987 at MTC for 533 performances); sketch material for MTC's musical revue* Urban Blight, *1988; in 1989,* Prelude and Liebestod *and* Hope *OOB and* Up in Saratoga *at the Old Globe Theater in San Diego; and in 1990 a revival of his* Bad Habits *at MTC. McNally adapted his own* The Ritz *and* Frankie and Johnny *for the movies and is the author of a number of TV plays including the 1991 Emmy award-winning* Andre's Mother. *He has been the recipient of Obies, Hull-Warriner Awards (for* Bad Habits *and* The Lisbon Traviata), *CBS and Rockefeller Fellowships, and two from Guggenheim; and a citation from the American Academy of Arts and Letters. He lives in Manhattan and has served as vice president of the Dramatists Guild, the organization of playwrights, composers, lyricists and musical book writers, since 1981.*

STEPHEN FLAHERTY (music) was born September 18, 1960 in Pittsburgh, where his father was a draftsman and his mother a teacher in the University of Pittsburgh's nursing school. He was educated in the city's Catholic school system and, having focused his life on music at an early age after learning to play the piano, went on to the Cincinnati College Conservatory of Music, from which he graduated in 1982 with a bachelor's degree in music composition.

While at college, Flaherty wrote three student shows, one of which, The Carnival of Life, *went on to other amateur productions in the Midwest. In 1983 he joined the BMI Workshop and began the collaboration with Lynn Ahrens which eventually won the Richard Rodgers Production Award for the musical* Lucky Stiff. *He places a special value on the workshop system, particularly in the development of the prize-winning Flaherty-Ahrens musical* Once on This Island *in Playwrights Horizons workshop in October and November 1989 prior to its off-Broadway production and Best Play citation May 6, 1990. He calls it "the ideal way to develop a show slowly," which the authors did together with the director and choreographer, Graciela Daniele, and the designers.*

The Flaherty-Ahrens team went on to write the score for the musical My Favorite Year *(with book by Joseph Doughterty based on the movie of the same title) at the Vivian Beaumont Theater December 10, 1992 for 37 performances, and then to the animated movie feature* Anastasia. *Now once again they take center stage as composer and lyricist for this season's* Ragtime, *which opened on Broadway January 18, has been a strong contender in every awards contest and the winner of the 1997–98 Tony Award for best score and continues to roll along in great popularity. Flaherty's other works include the incidental music for this season's Neil Simon play,* Proposals, *and the concert pieces* Suite From Ragtime *and* Anastasia Suite *which were premiered recently by the Hollywood Bowl Orchestra.*

Flaherty toured Eastern Europe in 1987 as a representative of the American musical theater under the sponsorship of the International Theater Institute, exchanging views and ideas with other theater artists. He has received grants from NEA and NMIT and is a member of the OOB group The Drama Dept. and of the Dramatists Guild.

LYNN AHRENS (lyrics) was born in New York City in 1948, her father a professional photographer with a school of photography in New Jersey. She was educated in New York schools, at a Neptune, N.J. high school and at Newhouse School of Syracuse University, where she majored in journalism and graduated with a B.A. in 1970. As long as she can remember, she's been writing songs (music as well as lyrics) and has loved the theater. Ahrens didn't approach it professionally, however, until after the decade of the 1970s when she was occupied in many other writing fields including TV commercials and children's TV. Four of the programs she created and produced were nominated for Emmys (one of them, ABC-TV's H.E.L.P., won), and her songs have been heard often on Schoolhouse Rock.

Ahrens met her Ragtime *collaborator, Stephen Flaherty, in 1983 at the BMI Workshop. By the following year, they were working on a couple of shows—*Bedazzled *and* Antler—*that never got to production. Then their Rodgers Award-winning musical* Lucky Stiff, *with book (based on Michael Butterworth's* The Man Who Broke the Bank at Monte Carlo*) as well as lyrics by Ahrens and music by Flaherty, began with a staged reading in 1987, went into off-Broadway production at Playwrights Horizons April 25, 1988 for 25 performances and moved on to the national and international stages, with six Helen Hayes Award nominations for a 1990 production in Olney, Md., and a London production. Their reputations came into full bloom with* Once on This Island—*book (based on Rosa Guy's novel) and lyrics by Ahrens, music by Flaherty—which opened off Broadway May 6, 1990 for 24 performances and a citation as a Best Play, moved up to Broadway October 18, 1990 for 469 performances and Tony nominations for book, score and best musical, and on to London to win the Laurence Olivier Award for the best musical of 1995. And now* Ragtime *is the second Flaherty-Ahrens score to be Tony-nominated and the first to win.*

After doing My Favorite Year *with Flaherty, Ahrens co-authored an adaptation of* A Christmas Carol *with Mike Ockrent and wrote its lyrics to Alan Menken's score. The show opened at Madison Square Garden December 1, 1994 and has been repeated there each Christmas season since. Ahrens has received grants from the National Institute of Music Theater and the NEA. She is a member of ASCAP and of the governing council of the Dramatists Guild. She is married and lives in Manhattan.*

In the new Best Plays *policy, beginning with the 1996–97 season, of celebrating the consensus choices of the major prizes (the New York Drama Critics Circle Awards, the Pulitzer Prize, the Tonys and the Lucille Lortel Awards) instead of the individual best-play choices of a single editor, we reserved the right, as stated in the Editor's Note in last year's volume, to make a special citation of our own whenever we feel it is demanded by both quality and circumstance. We choose to do so with* Ragtime, *close runner-up for the Critics best-musical citation and winner of many other honors. The* Best Plays *editors hereby cite it for its Tony-winning best book and score, for being one of the shows which glamorized in a very big way the outstanding 1997–98 New York musical theater season, and as an important act of artistic homage to the remarkable ethnic diversity and cultural energy of our great nation. We honor* Ragtime *for its exceptional quality and its salute to our past, eloquently expressed in the language of Broadway musical theater, an indigenous American art form.*

The agency controlling the rights to Ragtime's *script could not grant us the right to quote from it because, they informed us, exclusive publishing rights in the underlying novel had previously been granted to another publisher. We regret this limitation of our usual coverage but persist in celebrating the outstanding work of Terrence McNally and Lynn Ahrens with a brief review of the script's dialogue-and-lyrics flow, together with photographs of the show's "look"—the principal characters under*

Frank Galati's direction, costumed by Santo Loquasto, with extra attention to Eugene Lee's designs for his American Theater Wing Award-winning scenery.

The staging of Terrence McNally's book and Lynn Ahrens's lyrics begins with a prologue: a Little Boy looks through a stereopticon viewer, as the image of a large Victorian house appears on the scrims. The Little Boy explains that it is the house his father built in 1902 in New Rochelle, a suburb of New York Ciy.

People of New Rochelle sing of halcyon days of upper-middle-class pleasures, while the individual members of The Little Boy's family tell us how fortunate they are: Father (well off, the owner of a factory making fireworks and other patriotic symbols), Mother (a devoted homemaker), Mother's Younger Brother (an explosives expert who works at Father's factory) and Grandfather (a retired professor of Greek and Latin).

In Harlem, a crowd of Dancers is moving to the rhythms of a piano played by Coalhouse Walker Jr. One member of his devoted audience, Sarah, imagines that Coalhouse is playing just for her.

As the citizens of New Rochelle continue to sing in praise of their community— in which there are no blacks except those who visit daily to do the work, and no immigrants—Tateh and his Little Girl are seen as part of a group waiting to board a ship bound for America. Tateh's wife has died, and he is looking forward to making a new and better life for his daughter.

The magician and escape artist Harry Houdini, also an immigrant but now a famous one, is introduced in a succession of prominent individuals of the period: J.P. Morgan, Henry Ford, the outspoken activist Emma Goldman, Evelyn Nesbit, her lover Stanford White and her husband Harry K. Thaw.

The three factions—white, black and immigrant—mingle and rub together in a way that suggests hostility. The Prologue ends with the Company singing of a new kind of music called ragtime.

Act I begins with Father accompanying Admiral Peary on an expedition to the North Pole, leaving Mother in charge of affairs at home. On the dock to see Father off, Younger Brother notices Evelyn Nesbit in the crowd and catches a case of love at first sight. As Tateh's ship of immigrants bound for New York passes Father's ship going in the other direction, each wonders in turn what the other's purpose may be for such a journey.

Younger Brother, infatuated with Evelyn Nesbit, buys a ticket to her opening at Hammerstein's Olympia. But Chorines mingle with Sob Sisters, a Jury and a Judge. The trial of Evelyn Nesbit's husband, Harry K. Thaw, for the murder of her lover, Stanford White, takes place. Nesbit herself takes the witness stand and testifies about her love affairs. The jury finds Thaw not guilty by reason of insanity. Nesbit can now go on with a career as the scantily dressed Girl on the Velvet Swing, well publicized by the trial.

Outside the theater, Nesbit is hounded by reporters with impertinent questions. Younger Brother comes to her assistance and fends them off. She has noticed that

Above and *below* are photos of two of the models constructed by Eugene Lee for his American Theater Wing Design Award-winning *Ragtime* sets, and *at left on the opposite page* are three of his Act I scenes as they were realized on the stage: *at top,* New Rochelle; *in the middle of the page,* Ellis Island and immigrants; *at the bottom of the page,* citizens of Harlem at The Tempo Club, with Coalhouse Walker Jr. at the ragtime piano

Younger Brother attends her performance every night. As a reward, Nesbit gives him a kiss. Ecstatic, he confesses that he loves her, a love which Nesbit promptly and condescendingly rejects. She exits, leaving Younger Brother in despair.

In New Rochelle, Mother finds a newborn Negro baby boy abandoned on her property. She cradles the infant in her arms, wondering how any mother could treat her baby so cruelly. A Policeman finds and identifies Sarah, a washerwoman working in a nearby house, as the infant's mother. He is taking her to face charges, but Mother insists on assuming responsibility for both mother and child and brings them into her home, though she knows Father would probably not approve.

On Ellis Island, immigrants, including Tateh and his Little Girl, joyously sing of America, in their own languages. Tateh, enduring wretched East Side tenement living conditions, is certain that success awaits him. With a pushcart, he sets himself up as an artist with scissors making and selling silhouettes of famous people, or of the customers themselves. One day a passer-by offers to buy, not a silhouette, but The Little Girl for his pleasure. Infuriated and discouraged, Tateh decides to give up his pushcart and look for success elsewhere.

In the Tempo Club, People of Harlem sing of Coalhouse Walker Jr., a former stevedore who heard Scott Joplin's music in St. Louis, took piano lessons and has become a much-admired artist. But along with all his celebrity, Coalhouse has a broken heart because his beloved Sarah left him and disappeared. He has at last discovered where she is, and he is determined to win her back.

The scene shifts to Henry Ford's assembly line, where workers are being pressed to turn out automobiles at a faster and faster rate. Coalhouse drives off in one of the Ford cars.

Mother and The Little Boy are waiting for a trolley to take them to an appointment at the fireworks factory, when Tateh and The Little Girl—whose arm is tied to a rope fastened around Tateh's waist—appear on the other side of the tracks, carrying their belongings. Tateh shows the Conductor some coins and asks how much farther they can go on this amount of money. All the way to Boston, the Conductor believes, assuring Tateh that it's safe to let the child loose here in New Rochelle.

Mother cautions The Little Boy not to stare at the others. Tateh, annoyed at the rudeness of The Little Boy's stare, shows The Little Girl how people should behave toward each other by bowing to Mother. She joins him in polite conversation and the children exchange information about themselves. Tateh and his daughter finally board the trolley for Boston, while Mother and son take the one that goes to their factory. The Little Boy—who at times seems to be almost magically prescient—predicts that they are going to become better acquainted with these unlikely immigrants.

At the Emerald Isle Firehouse in New Rochelle, Coalhouse, searching for Sarah, asks for directions to Broadview Avenue. He is rudely rejected with racial slurs by Willie Conklin and his fellow firemen.

In the New Rochelle house, Sarah is singing to her baby about how Coalhouse could make her love him with his piano playing. He sometimes neglected her for other women and other concerns, so she left him without telling him she was pregnant. The trauma of childbirth frightened and maddened her into performing the act of abandonment for which she now asks forgiveness.

Mother takes the baby from Sarah and puts him in a crib. Coalhouse knocks on the door. It is opened by The Little Boy, who tells him he's come to the right place, both the baby and Sarah are here. Mother goes to fetch Sarah, but Sarah refuses to see him. Coalhouse comes into the house anyway and picks up the baby, as Mother comes in to send him away. Coalhouse puts his son back in the crib and declares that he'll be back next Sunday.

Coalhouse returns week after week with Sarah refusing to see him until one day Mother asks him to stay for a cup of tea. He accepts and explains to her that he is a professional pianist who now has permanent employment with an orchestra and can settle down instead of touring on the road. He plays a sample of his ragtime music on the family piano.

Months later, Father returns from the North Pole so laden with gifts that Brigit, the Irish housemaid, who has never seen him, takes him for a peddler. Mother, pencils in her hair and the baby under her arm, greets her husband with the information that the six-month audit shows the business is doing very well. Father didn't reach the Pole—only Peary and Matthew Henson managed that—but he got as far north as 72 degrees 46 minutes.

The Little Boy and the others bring Father up to date on who the baby is and why he is living in this house. Father disapproves. He hears Coalhouse playing the piano in the next room and singing—so that Sarah, can hear him—about his changed, settled lifestyle and abiding love. The music and the message reach her heart, and she comes into his arms.

Outdoors on a hillside with Sarah, Coalhouse industriously polishes his car, which he feels will carry them to a better life in which this child of theirs could follow in the footsteps of such a one as the great Booker T. Washington, awarded a degree by Harvard. His car will carry them across a country in which they will find hope, freedom and justice.

Meanwhile Tateh has found work at a mill in Lawrence, Mass., but it is affording him and his daughter nothing but misery and starvation. The labor activist Emma Goldman urges the workers to go on strike. The strike's violence is a threat to his daughter's safety, so Tateh arranges to send her on a train to friends in Philadelphia. As the train starts to leave, Tateh hears The Little Girl, fearful of being abandoned, crying out for him. He jumps onto the moving train to console her, and off they go together. To comfort her, he shows her the wonders of a book he has made especially for her amusement—a book of silhouettes of The Little Girl on skates. When the book's pages are flipped rapidly, the skater appears to be in motion.

As Tateh and his daughter get off the train in Philadelphia, the Conductor notices The Little Girl flipping the pages of her silhouette book to make the image move. He buys it for $1 as a present for his daughter. Tateh resolves to make more of them to be sold for $2.

Coalhouse, Sarah and the baby are on their way to New Rochelle in the Model T. They reach the Emerald Isle Firehouse, where Willie Conklin and his men block the car's passage. Coalhouse sends his wife and child out of harm's way and then confronts the men, who demand $25 to let Coalhouse pass. Coalhouse refuses and goes to look for a policeman. When he returns, denied help by the police, he finds his precious Model T heavily vandalized. The justice he then seeks is denied by the bureaucrats with whom he files complaints, by a white lawyer who advises him to retrieve his car and forget about the incident, and even by a black lawyer who refuses to waste his time on a case of vandalism when there are so many more serious evils with which he must contend. Coalhouse resolves that he will persist in demanding justice, he will not even go ahead with plans to marry Sarah until this wrong is righted.

In New York, J.P. Morgan and a Republican candidate are posing for photographers on the rear of a campaign train, with the recent assassination of President McKinley fresh in everyone's mind. Sarah, intending to beg publicly for justice for Coalhouse, pushes forward through the police barricade, arms outstretched. When J.P. Morgan calls out that she has a gun, the police move in with their nightsticks, clubbing Sarah. Coalhouse enters and is soon agonizing over Sarah's lifeless body.

As Sarah's funeral takes place, mourners grieve for her and express the hope that some day they will achieve universal brotherhood and pride.

An entr'acte precedes Act II. The Little Boy is asleep in bed, having a nightmare starring Harry Houdini, who is doing an escape trick for an audience of the Emerald Isle Firemen. They place a time bomb in the box from which Houdini must escape in 30 seconds. The Little Boy cries out a warning. The bomb explodes, and the box is seen to be empty.

Act II begins with The Little Boy waking from his nightmare, calling for his mother and warning her that there is going to be an explosion in which people will be killed.

Coalhouse takes the stage for a musical soliloquy in which he reveals that Sarah's death has pointed his life in a new and deadly direction. Soon, newspapers are proclaiming an act of terrorism in quiet New Rochelle: the Emerald Isle Firehouse destroyed and three firemen shot dead by a black gunman. Then Coalhouse announces publicly his demands: his car must be returned to him in mint condition and Willie Conklin must be turned over to him. Some sympathize, some disapprove. The Firemen turn against Willie Conklin for having brought this tragedy on them and force him to leave town. A group of blacks in bowler hats, carrying guns, join Coalhouse in active support. Booker T. Washington publicly and severely condemns Coalhouse's actions.

In New Rochelle Father, armed with a pistol, berates Mother for bringing trouble down on the family by taking in Coalhouse's wife and baby. Younger Brother argues bitterly with Father, pointing out the terrible wrongs that Coalhouse has suffered, with no recourse to any justice. Younger Brother leaves the house in anger.

Mother challenges Father to explain this quarrel to The Little Boy, but Father evades her challenge by inviting his son to go to a ball game where he can see well-

Ragtime:
Characters

Above, Peter Friedman as Tateh with The Little Girl (Lea Michele); *left,* Brian Stokes Mitchell as Coalhouse and Audra McDonald as Sarah; *below center,* Marin Mazzie as Mother, Alex Strange as The Little Boy and Mark Jacoby as Father, with neighbors

mannered athletes play a game in a sportsmanlike manner. The reality at the Polo Grounds, with raucous spectators hurling slangy expletives and vulgarities at the baseball umpires and players at the top of their lungs, is far from the orderly procedure Father had hoped to demonstrate to his son. The Little Boy seems to know that a ball is going to be hit into the stands near them and easily catches it when it comes.

Coalhouse announces himself publicly as the leader of a provisional American government and declares that he and his gang will keep on burning down firehouses until his demands are met. The Welfare people are trying to take the baby to one of their facilities, but Mother won't permit it.

Evelyn Nesbit and Harry Houdini make brief appearances to sing of the charms of Atlantic City. Father decides that would be a good place to take the family to live for a while, to escape the Coalhouse affair's intrusion into their lives.

In Atlantic City, elegant couples stroll the Boardwalk, where a ragtime band is playing. On the Million Dollar Pier, Nesbit sings and dances while Houdini does tricks of sleight-of-hand. It seems they are performing for a camera which is recording something called a moving picture.

Rolling in on a camera dolly are Baron Ashkenazy and his beautiful daughter. The Baron, wearing jodhpurs and carrying a glass rectangle on a chain around his neck, praises Houdini for his artistry but chides Nesbit for looking at the camera. The "Baron" is in fact Tateh, now a fledgling director of the infant art of the cinema.

Tateh dismisses the performers and, to Father's annoyance, frames Mother in his glass rectangle. Tateh apologizes and explains that he likes Mother's looks and would employ her before his camera if he could. Father states brusquely that Mother does no work. Tateh believes that his moving pictures are the dawning of a booming new entertainment form. He has just signed a contract with Pathe for a serial. He rides away with his daughter on the rolling camera dolly.

While Tateh consults his Secretary about the plot of his newest movie, The Little Boy and Girl join each other in play on the beach. Mother comes in to chat with Tateh. They both enjoy watching their children, one dark and one fair, having fun. When Mother calls him by his title of Baron, Tateh reveals to her who he really is.

In Harlem, Younger Brother is trying to arrange a meeting with Coalhouse, but he keeps getting a brushoff. Finally a man in a bowler hat lets Younger Brother follow him to a street with the sound of a ragtime piano coming from a nearby night club. Coalhouse is hiding in the shadows, thinking about the night he first met Sarah and singing to the visualized presence of his dead beloved, dancing without touching until the sound of the L train brings Coalhouse out of his reverie.

The image of Sarah disappears, as the scene changes to Coalhouse's hideout, where Younger Brother is brought in blindfold. When Coalhouse asks him what he wants, Younger Brother is so flustered he can't get the right words out. Emma Goldman appears and speaks for him—he has come to join Coalhouse in action for his cause. Finally Younger Brother manages to inform them that he is an explosives expert.

The sound of an enormous explosion is followed by the sound of thunder in Atlantic City. Father is taking his leave, preparing to board the Cannonball for New York because, he tells Mother, Coalhouse and his gang have occupied the Morgan Library and are threatening to blow it and themselves up. The authorities think Father might be helpful with negotiations on the scene because of his acquaintance with Coalhouse. This time, Father believes, Coalhouse has gone too far and is going to get what he deserves—and when Father returns, they will find a place for the baby, and their lives will return to normal. Mother asserts that she will never give up the baby to anyone but Coalhouse and suggests to Father that things will never again be as they were.

The crowd of spectators outside the Morgan Library has been cordoned off. Among the police and reporters are J.P. Morgan, Father and District Attorney Charles S. Whitman, who shouts to Coalhouse through a megaphone that Willie Conklin is being obliged to repair his car.

Father comments that there is one person whom Coalhouse respects and to whom he might listen: Booker T. Washington. But Washington merely wants to reproach Coalhouse for his recklessness in arousing the white man's fear and hatred which Washington has spent his entire life trying to ameliorate.

Outside, Whitman calls through the megaphone that the library is surrounded and its water is being cut off. J.P. Morgan is urging the others to save the library's treasures from destruction, and Emma Goldman is applauding Coalhouse's revolutionary actions.

Admitted to the library, Washington argues that Coalhouse should leave his son a memory of his father as a man who stood up for what he believed and faced the music in a court of law, even though he might suffer death, instead of recklessly leading his group of followers to their inevitable destruction. Over the protests of his men, Coalhouse accepts Washington's advice and asks for a hostage for their safe passage and a fair trial. Washington pledges his word that Coalhouse will receive both.

After Washington exits, Coalhouse's followers are furious and want to blow up the library at once, but Coalhouse stands his ground. Father enters the library to serve as the requested hostage and is surprised to see Younger Brother here. He asks Younger Brother for an explanation he can take home, but Younger Brother sends to his sister only his love and admiration.

Coalhouse doesn't believe that giving up under these circumstances means they've lost their major objectives. He tells his men to go out and raise their voices everywhere in defense of their cause and in support of justice.

Father moves to leave with Coalhouse's Men, but Coalhouse stops him, takes his hat and places it on Younger Brother's head. The men depart with Younger Brother in Father's hat, pretending to be the released hostage. Outside there is the sound of a car starting up. Father promises Coalhouse that it is safe to leave, and the District Attorney calls for Coalhouse to come out. Neatly dressed in houndstooth jacket and bowler hat, Coalhouse shakes Father's hand, thanking him for his family's kindness toward his wife and child. Coalhouse exits, and at once there is a volley of gunfire. Father cries out in dismay.

A slow rag accompanies a parade of people of the past and future, as The Little Boy operates a small manual projector.

In an epilogue, characters step out of the parade, one by one, to tell what eventually happened to them. Younger Brother joined up with Zapata's Mexican revolution. Emma Goldman was finally deported. Booker T. Washington's Tuskegee Institute became the major black American center. Grandfather went to his grave, and Evelyn Nesbit passed into obscurity. Harry Houdini did his escape act in Times Square hanging upside down. Father went down with the Lusitania. Mother mourned for a year and then married Tateh and moved to California. One day, watching the children—among them little Coalhouse Walker III—at play, Tateh got the idea for a movie about a gang of kids from all ethnic groups and walks of life getting themselves in and out of scrapes.

Coalhouse and Sarah observe this family of Tateh's and Mother's moving toward their future, as the curtain falls.

Ragtime:
Scenes

Left, Lynnette Perry as Evelyn Nesbit, "The Girl on the Red Velvet Swing"

Below, Judy Kaye as Emma Goldman *(in center, at podium)* addresses a rally in Union Square

Above, Coalhouse (Brian Stokes Mitchell) drives off in his beloved
Ford; *below,* Harry Houdini (Jim Corti) performs an escape trick

Above, The Little Girl (Leah Michele) and Tateh (Peter Friedman) with their pushcart; *below,* Sarah (Audra McDonald) and Coalhouse (Brian Stokes Mitchell) with their car

THE BEAUTY QUEEN OF LEENANE

A Play in Two Acts

BY MARTIN McDONAGH

Cast and credits appear on page 219 (Broadway) and 255 (off Broadway)

MARTIN McDONAGH was born in 1970 in the working-class neighborhood of Camberwell in South London and grew up in a house in which he still resides with his older brother John, a screen writer. Their Irish parents had immigrated to London for the father's job in construction and have since returned to their native Galway, leaving the house to their sons. Martin quit school at 16 and was unemployed for about five years, during which, partly by osmosis in London's rich performing arts environment and partly inspired by David Mamet's American Buffalo, *he began to consider trying to write and began to study up on the subject. There followed rejection after rejection of his TV, radio and film playscripts and short stories. He managed to land a job as a civil service clerk in the Department of Trade and Industry but kept on writing and as a last resort tried his hand at stage plays with Irish rural settings and themes.*

*The rest is a short history of McDonagh's rapid and phenomenal success, culminating in the simultaneous presence of four McDonagh plays in the London theater last summer and two—*The Beauty Queen of Leenane *and* The Cripple of Innishmaan*—in New York this season. His playscripts were suffering somewhat the same fate as his other works until, in 1994, Garry Hynes of the Druid Theater in Galway read* Beauty Queen, *found it perfect for her kind of theater and produced it with such resounding success that it was then put on at the Royal Court in London.* Beauty Queen *is part of a McDonagh trilogy which includes* A Skull in Connemara *and* The Lonesome West, *all three of them produced in repertory in 1996, first at the Druid*

*and then at the Royal Court. Beauty Queen was brought to off Broadway by the
Atlantic Theater Company in the Druid Theater Company/Royal Court production
February 26 and moved to Broadway April 23. It was voted the Lucille Lortel Award
for the best off-Broadway play of the season, in a tie with* Gross Indecency: The Three
Trials of Oscar Wilde.

*Meanwhile, McDonagh received a writing grant from the Royal National Theater,
which produced the first play of its author's next trilogy,* The Cripple of Inishmaan,
in 1996, while the Beauty Queen *trilogy was still running at the Royal Court.* Cripple
*appeared off Broadway on the schedule of the Joseph Papp Public Theater/New York
Shakespeare Festival April 7. The next plays in this trilogy are* The Lieutenant of
Inishmore *and* The Banshee of Innishmere. *They are set on the island of Aran, and
their final syllables, "more, maan and mere" signify "large, middle and small" island.*

The following synopsis of The Beauty Queen of Leenane *was prepared by Jeffrey
Sweet.*

Place: Leenane, a small town in Connemara,
            County Galway

ACT I

Scene 1

SYNOPSIS: As rain pours dolefully outside, Mag, a frail, heavy-set woman in her
70s, is sitting in the living-room/kitchen of the rural cottage she shares with her
daughter, Maureen. Maureen, a plain-looking woman in her 40s, enters carrying her
shopping.

We swiftly get an impression of the relationship between the two. One of Mag's
three daughters, Maureen, being unmarried, is the one who has ended up being
stuck caring for the complaining, bullying older woman. They have the radio on,
waiting for a dedication to Mag that was supposedly placed by Maureen's sisters,
Annette and Margo. But though they've been listening to the show regularly, the
dedication hasn't been played, and Maureen has her doubts if it ever will be.

Mag's latest grievance: the Complan (an over-the-counter medicinal preparation
of some sort) she tried to make for herself turned out lumpy. Maureen is sure that
Mag simply didn't follow the directions, but she'll make another batch for her soon.
She wishes her mother would try to do a little more. Mag protests ill health, but it's
more like hyponchondria, in Maureen's opinion. Mag asks her if her urine infection
is hypochondria. "I can't see how a urine infection prevents you pouring a mug of
Complan or tidying up the house a bit when I'm away. It wouldn't kill you." Mag
cites her bad back and her withered hand in her defense.

While making porridge for Mag, Maureen turns on the radio, hesitating at the
whiff of a suspicious smell coming from the sink (about which Mag protests she is

ignorant). The song on the radio is in Gaelic. Mag complains about this as well, and Maureen switches it off angrily. Mag thinks that the people on that station should stop speaking "nonsense" and speak English so they could be understood. Maureen reminds them they live in Ireland, so why shouldn't they speak the language of the country?

MAG: ..... Except where would Irish get you going for a job in England? No-where.

MAUREEN: Well, isn't that the crux of the matter?

MAG: Is it, Maureen?

MAUREEN: If it wasn't for the English stealing our language, and our land, and our God-knows-what, wouldn't it be we wouldn't need to go over there begging for jobs and for handouts?

MAG: I suppose that's the crux of the matter.

MAUREEN: It *is* the crux of the matter.

MAG *(pause):* Except America, too.

MAUREEN: What except America too?

MAG: If it was to America you had to go begging for handouts, it isn't Irish would be any good to you. It would be English!

MAUREEN: Isn't that the same crux of the same matter?

MAG: I don't know if it is or it isn't.

MAUREEN: Bringing up kids to think all they'll ever be good for is begging hand-outs from the English and the Yanks. That's the selfsame crux.

MAG: I suppose.

MAUREEN: Of course you suppose, because it's true.

MAG *(pause):* If I had to go begging for handouts anywhere, I'd rather beg for them in America than in England, because in America it does be more sunny any-ways. *(Pause.)* Or is that just something they say, that the weather is more sunny, Maureen? Or is that a lie, now?

> *Maureen slops the porridge out and hands it to Mag, speaking as she
> does so.*

MAUREEN: You're oul and you're stupid and you don't know what you're talking about. Now shut up and eat your oul porridge.

Mag complains now that Maureen forgot to make her tea. And as Maureen puts the kettle on, trying to control her exasperation, Mag rambles on. Mag thinks Maureen's trouble is that she doesn't say hello to people. Though, Mag continues, one wants to watch out who one says hello to. Strangers sometimes can be capable of murder. In a black humor, as Maureen serves her mother tea she replies she wouldn't mind if she met and brought home a murderer, wouldn't mind being murdered herself if she could be sure that the killer would go on to finish off Mag. "If he clobbered you with a big axe or something and took your oul head off and spat in your neck, I wouldn't mind going at all, going first. Oh no, I'd enjoy it, I would. No more oul Complan to get, no more oul porridge to get, and no more ... " Mag interrupts, complaining that there is no sugar in the tea. Maureen impulsively takes away the tea, dumps it in the sink and takes away and disposes of what's left of the porridge, then heads to another part of the house, leaving Mag to sit and stare *"grumpily out into space."*

Scene 2

Mag is sitting alone watching a TV show when 19-year-old neighbor Ray Dooley arrives. He has walked a mile and up the hill to the cottage to invite Mag and Maureen to a going-away party for an uncle from America. The uncle has been on holiday visiting his Irish relatives and is footing the bill for a big spread at a local hall before returning to Boston. The idea to extend the invitation came from Ray's older brother, Pato, who himself is visiting from England, where he works at a menial job on a building site. Of course, Ray comments, they know that Mag's infirmities might keep her from coming to the party, but Mag should pass the invitation along to Maureen. Mag says she will, but something in her reply (perhaps the fact that she confuses Ray with Pato) makes Ray doubt. So he writes out a message to Maureen relaying the invitation, leaves it on the table and beats a swift retreat from the old lady's annoying company.

No sooner has he gone than Mag rises, looks at the message, then sets it afire, dropping it into the stove. Hearing feet approach the front door, she returns to her seat in front of the TV just as Maureen enters.

Maureen asks if anybody phoned or stopped by while she was out, and Mag says no. Maureen shuts off the TV. Mag now remembers that Ray stopped by. Not for anything much except to say hello. Maureen nods and makes a new cup of Complan for Mag in such a way as to make sure there are lumps in it. Mag asks for a little spoon to stir it. "No," says Maureen, "I have no little spoon. There's no little spoons for liars in this house. No little spoons at all." She encountered Ray on his way from the cottage, and she knows that he left a message. So Mag will finish *"the sickly brew"* of Complan, or Maureen will dump it on Mag's head.

MAUREEN: Arsing me around, eh? Interfering with my life again? Isn't it enough I've had to be on beck and call for you every day for the past twenty year? Is it one evening out you begrudge me?

MAG: Young girls should not be out gallivanting with fellas . . . !

MAUREEN: Young girls! I'm forty years old, for feck's sake! Finish it!
    Mag drinks again.
"Young girls"! That's the best yet. And how did Annette or Margo ever get married if it wasn't first out gallivanting they were?

MAG: I don't know.

MAUREEN: Drink!

MAG: I don't like it, Maureen.

MAUREEN: Would you like it better over your head?
    Mag drinks again.

I'll tell you eh? "Young girls out gallivanting." I've heard it all now. What have I ever done but *kissed* two men the past forty year?

MAG: Two men is plenty!

MAUREEN: Finish!

MAG: I've finished!

> *Mag holds out the mug. Maureen washes it.*

Two men is two men too much!

MAUREEN: To you, maybe. To you. Not to me.

MAG: Two men too much.

MAUREEN: Do you think I like being stuck up here with you? Eh? Like a dried up oul . . .

MAG: Whore!

> *Maureen laughs*

MAUREEN: "Whore?" *(Pause.)* Do I not *wish* now? Do I not wish? *(Pause.)* Sometimes I *dream.* . . .

MAG: Of being a . . . ?

MAUREEN: Of anything! *(Pause. Quietly.)* Of anything. Other than this.

She also dreams of attending Mag's funeral and being comforted there by a nice man. Yes, the dream of Mag in a coffin brings a smile to her lips. Mag taunts her, telling her that she intends to stay alive as long as possible, till Maureen herself is old, just to make sure that Maureen never acquires the company of a man.

Maureen offers Mag a Kimberley, a kind of biscuit she knows her mother doesn't like. Mag grumbles but accepts it. She supposes that Maureen will be going to the Dooleys' party. Mag reminds Maureen that she was invited, too. Maureen makes it clear that by lying Mag has forfeited her right to attend. She thinks maybe the two of them will get into the car for a drive later. After all, Maureen should get a dress for the party. Maureen gives Mag a sharp look. It is returned sharply.

Scene 3

It is night, after the party. Maureen enters with Pato, who is in his 40s. They are both a little drunk. Maureen is wearing a black dress cut quite short. She cautions Pato not to make too much noise for fear of rousing Mag from her sleep. She notices that Mag has left the radio playing. Pato tells her to keep it on, to cover up the sounds. "What sounds?" Maureen asks. Pato replies, "The smooching sounds," and pulls her to him for a long kiss. The kettle Maureen put on when they entered now comes to a boil, and she moves to make some tea, a smile on her face. She offers him a Kimberley. Pato confesses he hates Kimberleys. Maureen says she does, too, but she gets them because Mag hates them.

Maureen comments that Pato seemed to have been interested in an American woman at the party. He tells her he wouldn't have been interested in that direction if he had realized that "the beauty queen of Leenane" would be coming to the party. Maureen wonders why, if that's what he thinks of her, he's never spoken more than a word or two to her in all the years they've known each other? Pato confesses his shyness.

PATO: . . . . . Of course, hopping across to that bastarding oul place every couple of months couldn't've helped.

MAUREEN: England? Aye. Do you not like it there so?

PATO *(pause):* It's money. *(Pause.)* And it's Tuesday I'll be back there again.

MAUREEN: Tuesday? This Tuesday?

PATO: Aye. *(Pause.)* It was only to see the Yanks off I was over. To say hello and say goodbye. No time back at all.

MAUREEN: That's Ireland, anyways. There's always someone leaving.

PATO: It's always that way.

MAUREEN: Bad, too.

PATO: What can you do?

MAUREEN: Stay?

PATO *(pause):* I do ask myself, if there was good work in Leenane, would I stay in Leenane? I mean, there never will be good work, but hypothetically, I'm saying. Or even bad work. Any work. And when I'm over there in London and working in rain and it's more or less cattle I am, and the young fellas cursing over cards and drunk and sick, and the oul digs over there, all pee-stained mattresses and nothing to do but watch the clock . . . when it's there I am, it's here I wish I was, of course. Who wouldn't? But when it's here I am . . . it isn't *there* I want to be, of course not. But I know it isn't here I want to be either.

MAUREEN: And why, Pato?

PATO: I can't put my finger on why. *(Pause.)* Of course it's beautiful here, a fool can see. The mountains and the green, and people speak. But when everybody knows everybody else's business . . . I don't know. *(Pause.)* You can't kick a cow in Leenane without some bastard holding a grudge twenty year.

MAUREEN: It's true enough.

PATO: It is. In England they don't care if you live or die, and it's funny but that isn't altogether a bad thing. Ah, sometimes it is . . . ah, I don't know.

Maureen wonders if Pato will decide to settle down in one place when he marries. Pato's embarassed reaction makes it clear that he doesn't think marriage is likely any time soon. It's not as if he has a lot of prospects. For an awkward moment or two they discuss a "creepy" old Irish song that's playing on radio. Maureen brings up the subject of the American woman at the party again, remarking that he was making free with her breasts. He insists that the woman in question was a second cousin named Delores Healey who lives in Boston, and he was simply helping her clean up something she had spilled on her blouse.

The subject of blouses and what they contain inspires him to reach for Maureen. She is more than willing to be reached for. They find themselves with her sitting on his lap, his hand inside her blouse. She asks him to stay the night. He is hesitant.

MAUREEN: Stay. Just tonight.

PATO *(pause):* Is your mother asleep?

MAUREEN: I don't care if she is or she isn't. *(Pause.)* Go lower.

> *Pato begins easing his hands down her front.*

Go lower . . . Lower . . .

> *His hands reach her crotch. She tilts her head back slightly. The song on the radio ends. Blackout.*

Scene 4

> *Morning. Maureen's black dress is lying across the table. Mag enters from the hall carrying a potty of urine, which she pours out down the sink. She exits into the hall to put the potty away and returns a moment later, wiping her empty hands on the sides of her nightie. She spots the black dress and picks it up disdainfully.*

MAG: Forty pounds just for that skimpy dress? That dress is just skimpy. And laying it around then?

> *She tosses the dress into a far corner, returns to the kitchen and switches the kettle on, speaking loudly to wake Maureen.*

I suppose I'll have to be getting me own Complan too, the hour you dragged yourself in whatever time it was with your oul dress. *(Quietly.)* That dress just looks silly. *(Loudly.)* Go the whole hog and wear no dress would be nearer the mark! *(Quietly.)* Snoring your head off you all night. Making an oul woman get her Complan, not to mention her porridge. Well, I won't be getting me own porridge, I'll tell you that now. I'd be afeard. You won't catch me getting me own porridge. Oh no. You won't be catching me out so easily.

And now, much to Mag's surprise, Pato enters the room, pulling on clothes and offering to make porridge for her. He thought of sneaking out before Mag got up, but Maureen persuaded him to stay. After all, they're adults, aren't they? Pato continues to make himself useful in the kitchen while Mag, still in a state of shock, looks at him. Pato notices how raw Mag's hand is. A scald, she explains. He replies she should be careful of scalds at her age.

And now Maureen makes her entrance, wearing only a bra and a slip. She boldly kisses Pato in front of Mag, articulating how sexually fulfilled she was by him in the night. "*Well* worth the wait," she says. She kisses him again. In a rage, Mag insists to Pato that Maureen is the one who scalded her hand, holding it down on the range and pouring chicken fat over it, and then lying to the doctor, telling him that Mag had an accident. In response, Maureen asks Pato to smell the sink. He does and is repelled by the stink of urine. Maureen explains that Mag pours her potty down the sink every morning, though she's been told time and again to use the lavatory. This is the quality of the character of the person who's accusing her, Maureen notes.

Now Mag alludes to something in Maureen's past—a place called Difford Hall in England, where Maureen was sent for a time. "A nut-house!" cries Mag. Mag

Anna Manahan as Mag, Marie Mullen as Maureen and Brian F. O'Byrne
as Pato in a scene from Martin McDonagh's *The Beauty Queen of Leenane*

signed her out and promised to keep Maureen in her care. Mag has papers handy
to prove what she says. She shuffles off to find them.

Pato insists to Maureen that he thinks it's no shame to have had a breakdown.
Lots of people do. Just means that they think about things and take them to heart.
Maureen sketches in some of the circumstances behind her troubles. She was in
England for the first time, 25 years old, cleaning offices, constantly being hit with
verbal abuse from the English. Pato gently tells her to put it behind her, it's past.

Maureen says she's trying to, but it's hard to hold onto sanity when constantly
tested by the likes of Mag. And no, she didn't scald Mag. Mag did it to herself when
Maureen was out. Maureen found her on the floor when she returned. Probably
tipped over a pan. "Only, because of Difford Hall, she thinks any accusation she
throws at me I won't be any the wiser. I won't be able to tell the differ, what's true
and what's not. Well, I *am* able to tell the differ. Well able, the smelly oul bitch."
But she supposes she has to put up with this, to live with this. The way she says this
to Pato, an unspoken question seems to be hovering—a question about how his
arrival in her life might change things.

Pato replies that it's cold and she should "be putting on some clothes."

MAUREEN *(quietly):* "Be putting on some clothes." Is it ugly you think I am now,
so, "Be putting on some clothes . . . "

PATO: No, Maureen, the cold, I'm saying. You can't go walking about . . . You'll freeze, sure.

MAUREEN: It wasn't ugly you thought I was last night, or maybe it was, now.

PATO: No, Maureen, now. What . . . ?

MAUREEN: A beauty queen you thought I was last night, or you said I was. When it's "Cover yourself," now, "You do sicken me" . . .

PATO *(approaching her):* Maureen, no, now, what are you saying that for . . . ?

MAUREEN: Maybe that was the reason so.

PATO *(stops):* The reason what?

MAUREEN: Be off with you so, if I sicken you.

PATO: You don't sicken me.

MAUREEN *(almost crying):* Be off with you, I said.

Pato's attempts to comfort and reasure her are cut off by Mag's return, carrying papers regarding Difford Hall, which she thinks will prove her complaints valid. Pato sees further conversation with Mag present isn't likely. He tells Maureen that he'll write to her from England. He repeats his promise, then takes his leave.

Mag tells Maureen that he won't write at all. And she tells her, further, that she tossed Maureen's dress into a dirty corner. Maureen runs to the dress and retrieves it. Holding it against herself, she wonders at Mag's cruelty, then quietly exits into the hall, closing the door behind her. Mag sits there dumbly, then begins to complain that her porridge is cold.

ACT II

Scene 5

Pato writes to Maureen from London. The letter begins shyly. He isn't sure that she wants to hear from him, which is why he's taken so long to write. But he's finally decided to brave it. He passes along some news about the perils of the building site where he's working, but finally works his way round to the main subject of the letter: their relationship. He wants to know how they stand.

PATO: . . . . . What I thought I thought we were getting on royally, at the goodbye to the Yanks and the part after when we did talk and went to yours. And I *did* think you were a beauty queen and I *do* think, and it wasn't anything to do with that at all or with you at all, I think you thought it was. All it was, it has happened to me a couple of times before and it has nothing to do with did I want to. I would have been honored to be the first one you chose, and flattered, and the thing that I'm saying, I was honored then and I am still honored, and just because it was not to be that night, does it mean it is not to be ever? I don't see why it should, and I don't see why you was so angry when you was so nice to me when it happened. I think you thought I looked at you differently when your breakdown business came up, when I didn't look at you differently at all, or the thing I said, "Put on your clothes, it's cold," when you seemed to think I did not want to be looking at you in your bra and slip there, when nothing could be further from the truth, because if truth be told I could have looked at you in your bra and slip until the cows came home. I could never get my fill of looking at you in your bra and slip, and some day, God-willing, I will be looking at you in your bra and slip again.

He continues. He has news: his uncle in Boston has offered him a job in the States, and he means to take it. And he hopes that she will be wanting to go there with him. He'll be back in Leenane soon to pick up his things. If she has forgiven him, he hopes to hear from her when he's back, so they can make arrangements for her to follow him to the States soon after for a life together. He knows she'll have to make some arrangement about Mag, but isn't it time for her sisters to step in? And if they don't want to, there's a home he knows where she could be seen to nicely.

"If I don't hear from you, I will understand," he continues. "Take good care of yourself, Maureen. And that night we shared, even if nothing happened, it still makes me happy just to think about it, being close to you, and even if I never hear from you again I'll always have a happy memory of that night, and that's all I wanted to say to you."

Finishing his letter to Maureen, he turns to another one to his brother Ray. He tells Ray that he's enclosing several letters and gives instructions about their delivery. The one to Maureen he is most particular about: Ray is to hand the envelope to Maureen herself. "This is important now, in her hand put it."

Scene 6

Ray has arrived at the cottage to deliver the letter to Maureen. But Maureen isn't there. Mag is. Ray has been watching TV with her for quite a while, and his patience is wearing thin. Not that he has much love for Maureen either. He remembers her being spiteful to him when he was a child; she never did return a swingball of his that Maureen confiscated when it went astray. Mag suggests he has better things to do with his time than wait to give a letter to someone who stole his swing-ball. But Ray insists that he's under strict orders to deliver the letter to Maureen personally. Mag says that if he's going to stay, then he can make himself useful and make a cup of tea for her. He declines the honor of the task, but he agrees to put some turf inside the range.

He gets up to use the poker for the job, leaving the envelope on the table. While Mag concentrates on the envelope, Ray admires the police-bashing possibilities of the poker as a weapon. He asks if she will sell it to him, but she refuses. All the while she is hoping to get her hands on the envelope on the table. Not particularly noticing her intentions, Ray puts the poker down and retrieves the letter. Mag now muses that there's a good chance that Maureen won't be home till very late at night. This gets Ray even more upset. He isn't all that pleased with the atmosphere either.

"This house does smell of pee, this house does." Mag says that cats get in and do their business in the sink. "Sure, that's mighty good of them," Ray remarks. "You do get a very considerate breed of cat up this way so."

The frustration of being stuck with Mag continues to eat at Ray. She tries to get him to make a mug of Complan for her, telling him to stir it carefully to get rid of the lumps. He replies that if he were going to get rid of a lump, his first impulse would be to go after the lump sitting in the rocking chair. He is near weeping with frustration.

RAY *(giving in sadly):* Pato, Pato, Pato. *(Pause.)* Ah what news could it be? *(Pause. Sternly.)* Were I to leave this letter here with you, Mrs., it would be straight to that one you would be giving it, isn't that right?

MAG: It is. Oh, straight to Maureen I'd be giving it.

RAY *(pauses):* And it isn't opening it you would be?

MAG: It is not. Sure, a letter is a private thing. If it isn't my name on it, what business would it be of mine?

RAY: And may God stike you dead if you do open it?

MAG: And may God stike me dead if I do open it, only He'll have no need to strike me dead because I won't be opening it.

Ray decides to leave the letter on the table. He exits from the cottage. A little time passes. He dashes in again, checking to see if Mag has moved toward the envelope. She hasn't moved at all. He is satisfied. He leaves again. Now, confident that he's really gone, Mag opens the letter and begins to read it, dropping the pages into the fire as she finishes.

Scene 7

One evening some time later, the radio plays weakly. Maureen and Mag are back at their routine. Maureen jokes about putting Mag into a home. "I'd die before I'd let meself be put in a home." "Hopefully, aye," says Maureen in reply.

Maureen apparently is in a funk because she's heard about Pato having a going-away party tonight without inviting her. Mag comments that he really only wanted one thing.

MAUREEN: Maybe he was, now. Or maybe it was me who was only after one thing. We do have equality nowadays. Not like in your day.

MAG: There was nothing wrong in my day.

MAUREEN: Allowed to go on top of a man nowadays, we are. All we have to do is ask. And nice it is on top of a man, too.

MAG: Is it nice now, Maureen?

MAUREEN *(bemused that Mag isn't offended):* It is.

Maureen continues to rhapsodize about the night of lovemaking she insists she had with Pato. But there's more to a relationship than sex. You have to have other

Tom Murphy (Ray) and Anna Manahan
(Mag) in *The Beauty Queen of Leenane*

things in common—politics, the books you read, and so forth. So, she had to tell Pato, "It was no-go, no matter how good in bed he was."

MAG: When was this you did tell him?

MAUREEN: A while ago it was I did tell him. Back . . .

MAG *(interrupting):* And I suppose he was upset at that.

MAUREEN: He *was* upset at that but I assured him it was for the best and he did seem to accept it then.

MAG: I'll bet he accepted it.

MAUREEN *(pause):* But that's why I thought it would be unfair of me to go over to his do and wish him goodbye. I thought it would be awkward for him.

MAG: It would be awkward for him, aye, I suppose. Oh aye. *(Pause.)* So all it was ye didn't have enough things in common was all that parted ye?

MAUREEN: Is all it was. And parted on amicable terms, and with no grudges on either side. *(Pause.)* No. No grudges at all. I did get what I did want out of Pato

Dooley that night, and that was good enough for him, and that was good enough for me.

MAG: Oh aye, now. I'm sure. It was good enough for the both of ye. Oh aye.

Maureen gets a shortbread finger for Mag, making a joke about how it resembles something, something Mag probably barely remembers. Mag sarcastically comments that Maureen must be an expert on the topic. Her tone alerts Maureen to the idea that Mag knows that Pato couldn't perform sexually the night they were together. She's trying to figure out how Mag would know. She begins to get an inkling of what the truth might be.

Maureen turns on the stove, puts some oil on to boil. Mag knows what is in store and tries to make her escape, but Maureen pushes her back down. She presses her how she knew. Mag insists she read it on Maureen's face. "You still do have the look of a virgin about you, you always have had. *(Without malice.)* You always will."

The oil begins to boil. Maureen turns off the gas, picks up the pan and continues the inquisition. Terrified, Mag confesses there was a letter from Pato that she read. *"Maureen slowly and deliberately takes her mother's shrivelled hand, holds it down on the burning range, and starts slowly pouring some of the hot oil over it, as Mag screams in pain and terror."*

Mag tells all. In the letter, Pato asked Maureen to go to America with him. Maureen lets her go.

MAUREEN: What?

MAG: But how could you go with him? You do still have me to look after.

MAUREEN *(in a happy daze):* He asked me to go to America with him? Pato asked me to go to America with him?

MAG *(looking up at her):* But what about me, Maureen?

> A slight pause before Maureen, in a single and almost lazy motion, throws the considerable remainder of the oil into Mag's midriff, some of it splashing up onto her face. Mag doubles up, screaming, falls to the floor, trying to pat the oil off her, and lies there convulsing, screaming and whimpering. Maureen steps out of her way to avoid her fall, still in a daze, barely noticing her.

MAUREEN *(dreamily, to herself):* He asked me to go to America with him . . . ? *(Recovering herself.)* What time is it? Oh feck, he'll be leaving! I've got to see him. Oh God . . . What will I wear? Uh . . . Me black dress! Me little black dress! It'll be a remembrance to him . . .

She rushes off and changes into the dress. Mag, still lying on the floor, cries out to her for help. Maureen refuses. Help her after what she's done? If Mag has made her miss Pato, there will be a reckoning due. She leaves. Then she comes back. Mag hopes it is to help her, but no, Maureen has forgotten her car keys. She turns off the radio and slams out of the cottage, into the car and down the hill. Mag is alone, nursing her scalded hand. "But who'll look after me, so?"

Scene 8

Later that night the room is barely illuminated. The rocking chair is moving back and forth a little. Mag is sitting in it, unresponsive, as Maureen, wearing her black dress, wanders about the room holding the poker.

MAUREEN: To Boston. To Boston I'll be going. Isn't that where them two were from, the Kennedys, or was that somewhere else, now? Robert Kennedy I did prefer over Jack Kennedy. He seemed to be nicer to women. Although I haven't read up on it. *(Pause.)* Boston. It does have a nice ring to it. Better than England it'll be, I'm sure. Although where wouldn't be better than England? No shite I'll be cleaning there anyways, and no names called, and Pato'll be there to have a say-so anyways if there was to be names called, but I'm sure there won't be. The Yanks do love the Irish. *(Pause.)* Almost begged me, Pato did. Almost on his hands and knees, he was, near enough crying. At the station I caught him, not five minutes to spare, thanks to you. Thanks to your oul interfering. But too late to be interfering you are now. Oh aye. Be far too late, although you did give it a good go, I'll say that for you. Another five minutes and you'd have had it. Poor you. Poor selfish oul bitch, oul you. *(Pause.)* Kissed the face off me, he did, when he saw me there. Them blue eyes of his. Them muscles. Them arms wrapping me. "Why did you not answer me letter?" And all for coming over and giving you a good kick he was when I told him, but "Ah no," I said, "isn't she just a feeble-minded oul feck, not worth dirtying your boots on?" I was defending you there.

She'll follow him to Boston soon. She doesn't care whether they marry or not. Just the being together will be enough. He wondered what plans she'll make for taking care of Mag. He told her that he'd understand if she felt she had to stay and take care of her mother. Maureen says she told him she'd deal with the problem. Maureen continues her account, quoting him.

MAUREEN: . . . . . "I'll leave it up to yourself so," Pato says. He was on the train be this time, we was kissing out the window, like they do in films. "I'll leave it up to yourself so, whatever you decide. If it takes a month, let it take a month. And if it's finally you decide you can't bear to be parted from her and have to stay behind, well, I can't say I would like it, but I'd understand. But if even a year it has to take for you to decide, it is a year I will be waiting, and won't be minding the wait." "It won't be a year it is you'll be waiting, Pato," I called out then, the train was pulling away. "It won't be a year nor yet nearly a year. It won't be a week!"

The rocking chair has now stopped and Mag topples over onto the floor. She is dead. Maureen has used the poker on her head. Maureen looks at her handiwork and rehearses the story she will tell—something about Mag tripping over the stile and falling down the hill.

Scene 9

On a rainy afternoon Maureen is returning from the funeral. Now she begins to pack a dusty suitcase. A knock at the door. She opens it to Ray.

From the conversation, we can glean that some time has passed since Mag's death. There was official suspicion about the circumstances. Inquests. It took a month or so for the body finally to be released to be buried. Apparently Maureen has gotten away with it.

Ray asks about the details of the funeral, and she tells him that her sisters came and are now at the post-funeral receptions. Maureen has better things to do, so she won't be seeing them before they return home.

Ray talks about his plans. He wants to get out of Ireland. Even if it means England. London. Maybe Manchester. He hears there are plenty of drugs in Manchester.

MAUREEN: Don't be getting messed up in drugs now, Ray, for yourself. Drugs are terrible dangerous.

RAY: Terrible dangerous, are they? Drugs, now?

MAUREEN: You know full well they are.

RAY: Maybe they are, maybe they are. But there are plenty of other things just as dangerous, would kill you just as easy. Maybe even easier.

MAUREEN *(wary):* Things like what, now?

RAY *(pause shrugging):* This bastarding town for one.

MAUREEN *(pause, sadly):* Is true enough.

RAY: Just that it takes seventy years. Well, it won't take me seventy years. I'll tell you that. No way, boy. *(Pause.)* How old was your mother, now, when she passed?

MAUREEN: Seventy, aye. Bang on.

RAY: She had a good innings, anyway. *(Pause.)* Or an innings, anyway.

He notices she's burning something—the porridge and Complan, the things associated with Mag. But there are still some Kimberleys, if he'd like them. He readily accepts them. He likes them fine.

As he munches on a Kimberley, he explains his visit: he's had a letter from Pato, who asked him to bring her a message—an expression of condolences. Maureen asks if the letter included any "times or details." Ray doesn't know what she's talking about.

RAY: . . . . . Oh, also he said he was sorry he didn't get to see you the night he left, there, he would've liked to've said goodbye. But if that was the way you wanted it, so be it. Although rude, too, I thought that was.

MAUREEN *(standing, confused):* I did see him the night he left. At the station, there.

RAY: What station? Be taxicab Pato left. What are you thinking of?

MAUREEN *(sitting):* I don't know now.

RAY: Be taxicab Pato left, and sad that he never got your goodbye, although why he wanted your goodbye I don't know. *(Pause.)* I'll tell you this, Maureen, not being harsh, but your house does smell an awful lot nicer now than your mother's dead. I'll say it does, now.

MAUREEN: Well, isn't that the best? With me thinking I did see him the night he left, there. The train that pulled away.

> *He looks at her as if she's mad.*

RAY: Aye, aye. *(Mumbled, sarcastic.)* Have a rest for yourself. *(Pause.)* Oh, do you know a lass called, em . . . Dolores Hooley, or Healey, now? She was over with the Yanks when they was over.

MAUREEN: I know the name, aye.

What she remembers is Dolores throwing herself at Pato at the party. Maureen thought she behaved shamelessly, "like a cheap oul whore." Ray tells his news: Pato is engaged to her. A swift courtship, yes, but they'll be married soon.

This stuns Maureen. The numbness of her reactions causes Ray to make a crack about this house being a home to loons. He turns his back on her, and she reaches for the poker. She is about to attack him when he spots the swingball she confiscated from him many years ago. *"Ray picks up a faded tennis ball with a string sticking out of it from the ledge and spins around to confront Maureen with it, so angry that he doesn't even notice the poker. Maureen stops in her tracks."* It was the best present he ever got, and she simply took it. Nor did she ever even make any use out of it, but simply kept it and let it fade. "Just out of pure spite is the only reason you kept it, and right under me fecking nose. And then you go wondering who's a fecking loon? Who's a fecking loon, she says. I'll tell you who's a fecking loon, lady. *You're* a fecking loon!" Dazed, Maureen drops the poker, saying, "I don't know why I did keep your swingball on you, Raymond. I can't remember at all, now. I think me head was in a funny oul way in them days." Ray's pointed response is, " 'In them days,' she says, as she pegs a good poker on the floor and talks about trains."

As Maureen sits in the rocking chair, Ray picks up the poker and admires it. He asks if he can buy it. She says no, it has "sentimental value" to her. Irritated, Ray says that in that case he won't forgive her for taking the ball.

As he is about to leave, Maureen asks if he'll pass along a message to Pato. That the beauty queen of Leenane says hello. Ray repeats the message to confirm it. No, she corrects: "The beauty queen of Leenane says *goodbye.*"

Ray hasn't the vaguest idea of what this means, but he'll do it. At her bidding, he turns up the radio, though he is irritated that in making the request she calls him Pato. "The exact fecking image of your mother you are, sitting there pegging orders and forgetting me name!"

With Ray gone, Maureen continues to rock in the chair as the radio plays. An announcer tells the listening audience that the next song is a dedication to a lady in Leenane ("a lovely part of the world there") named Mag from her daughters Annette and Margo on the occasion of her seventy-first birthday last month. With the announcer wishing Mag many more, the song begins to play. Maureen rises and disappears from the room. The chair stops rocking.

Critics, Tony Awards

○○○
○○○
○○○
○○○
○○○
○○○ ART

A Full Length Play in One Act

BY YASMINA REZA

TRANSLATED BY CHRISTOPHER HAMPTON

Cast and credits appear on page 215

YASMINA REZA (author) is of Iranian-Russian stock on her father's side (his family left Moscow and settled in Paris after the Russian revolution) and Hungarian on her mother's. A Parisian, she was born in 1968, studied acting and began a career in that profession, usually cast as a seductress. Acting didn't satisfy her creative instincts, however, and in 1987 she expanded into playwriting for the Paris stage with Conversations After a Burial *(Conversations Après un Enterrement), winning the Molière Award for best author. There have followed* Winter Crossing *(La Traversée de l'Hiver), winner of the Molière Award for best fringe production,* The Unexpected Man *(L'Homme du Hasard), translated by Christopher Hampton and produced in London by the Royal Shakespeare Company April 15, 1998 and now* Art, *a trans-channel and transatlantic success, winner of the Molière Award for best author in Paris, the 1996–97 Olivier and Evening Standard Awards in London and, following its opening on Broadway March 1, the 1997–98 New York Drama Critics Circle Award for this season's best play regardless of category and the Tony Award for best play.*

Reza's other writings include a translation of Kafka's Metamorphosis *for Roman Polanski, the movie* See You Tomorrow *and a novel,* Hammerklavier, *published in 1997. Reza is married, with two children, and lives in Paris.*

CHRISTOPHER HAMPTON (translator) was born in the Azores, at Fayal, on January 26, 1946 and finished his education with an M.A. in modern languages at New College, Oxford, in 1968. Before he left college his first play, When Did You Last

See My Mother?, *was put on by London's Royal Court Theater (where Hampton later served as resident dramatist, 1968–70) in June 1966, transferring to the West End and then to New York at the Sheridan Square Playhouse in January 1967. His first Best Play,* The Philanthropist, *opened in London in 1970 (winning the Evening Standard and London Theater Critics Awards) and came to Broadway March 15, 1971 for 72 performances during which its author was cited as most promising playwright in that season's Variety poll.*

Hampton's second Best Play, Les Liaisons Dangereuses *(Dangerous Liaisons), adapted from the 18th-century novel of pre-revolution French manners and mores by Choderlos de Laclos, was produced by London's Royal Shakespeare Company January 8, 1986 and won the Laurence Olivier, Evening Standard and London Theater Critics Awards. That RSC production transferred to Broadway April 30, 1987 for 148 performances, receiving the New York Drama Critics Circle Award for best foreign play, a Tony nomination for best play and—in the 1988 film version—the Academy and Writer's Guild Awards for Hampton's screen adaptation.*

Hampton received his third Best Play citation and first Tony Award (for best book) for his collaboration with Don Black on the book and lyrics of the musical Sunset Boulevard, *which played 977 performances on Broadway beginning on November 7, 1994. His translation of Yasmina Reza's* Art *now brings him his first Critics Award and second Tony in its Broadway manifestation.*

His other works produced in the U.S. through the years have included new versions of Henrik Ibsen's A Doll's House *and* Hedda Gabler *(Broadway, 1971),* Total Eclipse *(London, 1968; off Broadway at Chelsea Theater of Brooklyn, 1974),* Savages *and* Treats *(London Theater Critics Award, 1973; OOB at the Hudson Guild Theater, 1977), a translation of Odon Von Horvath's* Don Juan Comes Back From the Wars *(off Broadway at Manhattan Theater Club, 1979) and* Tales From Hollywood *(London Evening Standard Award, 1982; OOB at Cafe LaMama, 1993), not to mention the many cross-country productions of his works. In addition to the above, his plays produced in London have included* The Portage to San Cristobal of A.H. *(1982),* White Chameleon *(1990),* Alice's Adventures Under Ground *(1994), and* Faith Hope and Charity *(at the Lyric Theater in Hammersmith) and translations/adaptations of two more Ibsen plays, three Molière plays, two more Odon Von Horvath plays and Chekhov's* Uncle Vanya. *He is also the author of a long list of film and TV scripts and recently directed his own screen play of* The Moon and Sixpence. *He is married, with two children, and lives in London.*

Place: Paris; Serge's apartment, Yvan's apartment, Marc's apartment

SYNOPSIS: The main room of a flat serves for all three of the play's locations. It is *"as stripped down and neutral as possible,"* and in it *"nothing changes, except for the painting on the wall."* Marc, alone, is explaining to us, "My friend Serge has bought a painting. It's a canvas about five foot by four: white. The background is white, and if you screw up your eyes, you can make out some fine white diagonal lines."

At Serge's, the painting in question is on the floor propped up against the wall with Serge standing near it, admiring it and clearly delighted to be its owner. Serge's visitor, Marc, is also looking at it, but in a quizzical attitude. He is astonished to hear that his friend Serge paid 200,000 francs for it. Marc studies it again.

SERGE: . . . . . Look at it from this angle. Can you see the lines?

MARC: What's the name of the . . . ?

SERGE: Painter. Antrios.

MARC: Well-known?

SERGE: Very. Very!

> *Pause.*

MARC: Serge, you haven't bought this painting for two hundred thousand francs?

SERGE: You don't understand, that's what it costs. It's an Antrios.

MARC: You haven't bought this painting for two hundred thousand francs?

SERGE: I might have known you'd miss the point.

MARC: You paid two hundred thousand francs for this shit?

SERGE *(as if alone):* My friend Marc's an intelligent enough fellow, I've always valued our relationship, he has a good job, he's an aeronautical engineer, but he's one of those new-style intellectuals who are not only enemies of modernism but seem to take some sort of incomprehensible pride in running it down . . . In recent years these nostalgia-merchants have become quite breathtakingly arrogant.

> *Same pair. Same place. Same painting. Pause.*

What do you mean, "This shit?"

MARC: Serge, where's your sense of humor? Why aren't you laughing? . . . It's fantastic, you buying this painting.

> *Marc laughs. Serge's face remains stony.*

Serge maintains that Marc has no artistic expertise which would qualify him to make such a judgement, so how dare he call any painting "shit." Marc holds his ground: "Because it is. It's shit. I'm sorry."

Serge, alone, informs us that it's Marc's "know-all" attitude that particularly irritates him. Marc, alone, tells us he was so upset at hearing that Serge—comfortably off but not rich—spent 200,000 francs on this worthless painting that he had to take a large dose of soothing medicine. He decides to consult a mutual friend, Yvan, who is "very tolerant because he couldn't care less."

At Yvan's there is "*some daub*" hanging on the wall above the spot where Serge's painting was leaning against the wall in his apartment. Yvan, alone, is on the floor looking for the top of his felt-tip pen and at the same time informing us that he now has a job as a stationery salesman after having spent all of his working life in the textile business, and that he's getting married soon.

Marc comes in and proceeds to tell Yvan about Serge's painting.

MARC: ..... Imagine a canvas about five foot by four ... with a white background ... completely white in fact ... with fine white diagonal stripes ... you know ... and maybe another horizontal white line, towards the bottom ...

YVAN: How can you see them?

MARC: What?

YVAN: These white lines. If the background's white, how can you see the lines?

MARC: You just do. Because, I suppose, the lines are slightly grey, or vice versa, or anyway there are degrees of white! There's more than one kind of white!

YVAN: Don't get upset. Why are you getting upset?

MARC: You immediately start quibbling. Why can't you let me finish?

YVAN: All right. Go on.

MARC: Right. So, you have an idea of what the painting looks like.

YVAN: I think so, yes.

MARC: Now you have to guess how much Serge paid for it.

Yvan guesses nowhere near the actual amount, and when he hears what Serge paid for it he wonders, "Has he gone crazy?" But Yvan's spirit of tolerance soon shows through, as he decides that if it makes Serge happy, O.K. Marc tries to make Yvan understand that there will be serious consequences, their friend Serge will now start posing as an art connoisseur. Even this is all right with Yvan as long as it does no harm to anyone. Marc explodes: "It's doing harm to me! I'm disturbed, I'm disturbed, more than that, I'm hurt, yes, I am, I'm fond of Serge, and to see him let himself be ripped off and lose every ounce of discernment through sheer snobbery ..... What really upsets me is that you can't have a laugh with him any more." Yvan promises Marc that he can and will make Serge laugh.

At Serge's apartment, Yvan sees no sign of any painting. Yvan complains about something on his hand and shows it to Serge, who assures him it's nothing to worry about. Marc's name comes up, and they both agree that the last time they saw Marc or spoke to him on the phone he seemed all right. Serge hasn't been getting around much lately, though, because, he tells Yvan jokingly, "I'm ruined." Then he gets ready to show Yvan "something special."

> Serge exits and returns with the Antrios, which he turns round and sets down in front of Yvan. Yvan looks at the painting and, strangely enough, doesn't manage the hearty laugh he'd predicted. A long pause, while Yvan studies the painting and Serge studies Yvan.

YVAN: Oh, yes. Yes, yes.

SERGE: Antrios.

YVAN: Yes, yes.

SERGE: It's a seventies Antrios. Worth mentioning. He's going through a similar phase now, but this one's from the seventies.

YVAN: Yes, yes. Expensive?

SERGE: In absolute terms, yes. In fact, no. You like it?

YVAN: Oh, yes, yes, yes.

SERGE: Plain.

YVAN: Plain, yes . . . Yes . . . And at the same time . . .

SERGE: Magnetic.

YVAN: Mm . . . yes . . .

SERGE: You don't really get the resonance just at the moment.

YVAN: Well, a bit.

SERGE: No, you don't. You have to come back in the middle of the day. That resonance you get from something monochromatic, it doesn't really happen under artificial light.

YVAN: Mm hm.

SERGE: Not that it's actually monochromatic.

YVAN: No! . . .

Yvan does not even bat an eyelash when he hears what Serge paid for the painting, but all at once the two of them burst out into explosions of laughter, during which they are both heard to articulate the word "crazy." They have only to look at each other to burst out laughing again, but eventually they calm down enough so that Serge can tell Yvan of Marc's visit and his criticism of the painting. Yvan indicates that this comes as no surprise because "You've seen his place." Serge agrees, "Nothing to see. It's like yours, it's . . . what I mean is, you couldn't care less." What's more, Serge goes on, Marc has no sense of humor, and he is insensitive to the finer points of esthetics because he hasn't had the necessary training. At this point in time, their friendship may be fading out along with Marc.

In Marc's apartment *("On the wall, a figurative painting: a landscape seen through a window)*, Yvan has told Marc that he and Serge had a good laugh over the painting, and Marc is trying to determine exactly what kind of laughter it was. It wasn't Yvan laughing at the painting, Serge started it. It was Serge knowing that Yvan was going to laugh and joining him for friendship's sake. So Marc concludes that it wasn't genuine, spontaneous laughter, it was intended to ingratiate.

Yvan thinks over Marc's comment, then decides to tell him something which may surprise him: in Yvan's opinion, the painting isn't all that bad. There is something about it . . .

MARC: You're joking.

YVAN: I'm not as harsh as you. It's a work of art, there's a system behind it.

MARC: A system?

YVAN: A system.

MARC: What system?

YVAN: It's the completion of a journey . . .

MARC: Ha, ha, ha!

YVAN: It wasn't painted by accident, it's a work of art which stakes its claim as part of a trajectory . . .

MARC: Ha, ha, ha!

YVAN: All right, laugh.

MARC: You're parroting out all Serge's nonsense. From him it's heartbreaking, from you it's just comical!

YVAN: You know, Marc, this complacency, you want to watch out for it. You're getting bitter, it's not very attractive.

MARC: Good. The older I get, the more offensive I hope to become.

Yvan insists the painting has some sort of resonance. Marc challenges him: Yvan is marrying Catherine tomorrow, and if they received this painting as a wedding present, would it make Yvan happy?

Alone, Yvan admits that the painting wouldn't make him happy; but then he can't readily think of anything that would make him instantly happy,

Alone, Serge insists that the painting isn't all white, it includes "a whole range of greys" with even some red, and Marc's great limitation is seeing it as all white.

Alone, Marc admits that perhaps he took too aggressive a tone with his friend Serge when he criticized the painting, and he resolves to be on his best behavior from now on.

At Serge's, Marc asks for another look at the painting. Serge brings it out and suggests that it's only a painting, after all, and they don't have to get upset about it one way or the other. Marc makes no comment. Serge picks up a copy of Seneca's *De Vita Beata* and puts it in front of Marc.

SERGE: Incredibly modern. Read that, you don't need to read anything else. What with the office, the hospital, Françoise, who's now decreed that I'm to see the children every weekend—which is something new for Françoise, the notion that children need a father—I don't have time to read any more, I'm obliged to go straight for the essentials.

MARC: ... As in painting ... Where you've ingeniously eliminated form and color. Those old chestnuts.

SERGE: Yes ... Although I'm still capable of appreciating more figurative work. Like your Flemish job. Very restful.

MARC: What's Flemish about it? It's a view of Carcassonne.

SERGE: Yes, but I mean ... it's slightly Flemish in style ... the window, the view, the ... in any case, it's very pretty.

MARC: It's not worth anything, you know that.

SERGE: What difference does that make? ... Anyway, in a few years God knows if the Antrios will be worth anything! ...

MARC: ... You know, I've been thinking. I've been thinking, and I've changed my mind. The other day, driving across Paris, I was thinking about you, and I said to myself: isn't there, deep down, something really poetic about what Serge has done? ... Isn't surrendering to this incoherent urge to buy in fact an authentically poetic impulse?

SERGE: You're very conciliatory today. Unrecognizable. What's this bland, submissive tone of voice? It doesn't suit you at all, by the way.

MARC: No, no, I'm trying to explain, I'm apologizing.

SERGE: Apologizing? What for?

MARC: I'm too thin-skinned. I'm too highly strung, I overreact . . . You could say, I lack judgement.

SERGE: Read Seneca.

MARC: That's it. See, for instance, you say, "Read Seneca," and I could easily have got annoyed. I'm quite capable of being really annoyed by your saying to me, in the course of our conversation, "Read Seneca." Which is absurd!

The heart of the matter is, Marc has lost his sense of humor, Serge believes, and he lets Marc know that Yvan agrees. Marc swallows some of his calming medicine and changes the subject: Where is Serge going to put the painting? Will he have it framed? No, "the artist" has told Serge, "It mustn't be interrupted. It's already in its setting." Marc is irritated by Serge's referring to Antrios as "the artist," as though the painter is some sort of god. Serge allows that he is impressed by Antrios, who has three paintings at the Pompidou.

Serge expresses his annoyance at Yvan for being conspicuously late in joining them here for a dinner rendezvous. Marc accuses Serge of being jumpy: "The fact is, I'm getting on your nerves, and you're taking it out on poor Yvan." Serge denies this vigorously.

In an aside, Serge admits to himself that Marc's visible effort at being pleasant is getting on his nerves. Could Marc resent Serge's making the decision to buy the painting without seeking Marc's advice?

In an aside, Marc remembers that his misgivings about Serge began long before he bought the painting. It was when Serge actually, seriously, spoke the word "deconstruction," and Marc reacted flippantly. Serge asked, "You're just Marc, what makes you think you're so special?", starting Marc wondering what kind of friendship they had if his friend didn't consider him special.

At Serge's, the doorbell rings. Yvan has finally arrived, talking as he enters the room: "So, a crisis, insoluble problem, major crisis, both stepmothers want their names on the wedding invitation. Catherine adores her stepmother, who more or less brought her up, she wants her name on the invitation, she wants it and her stepmother is not anticipating, which is understandable, since the mother is dead, not appearing next to Catherine's father, whereas my stepmother, whom I detest, it's out of the question her name should appear on the invitation, but my father won't have his name on if hers isn't, unless Catherine's stepmother is left off, which is completely unacceptable . . . . . I finally agreed that my stepmother, whom I detest, who's a complete bitch, will have her name on the invitation, so I telephoned my mother to warn her, mother, I said, I've done everything I can to avoid this, but we have absolutely no choice, Yvonne's name has to be on the invitation, she said, if Yvonne's name is on the invitation, take mine off it . . . . . "

An uproar (which Yvan describes at length) ensued, resulting in a coolness between him and Catherine which wasn't resolved before he had to leave to join his friends. In his turn, Yvan is told by Serge, "Read Seneca," which leads to another caustic exchange been Marc and Serge. Yvan intervenes with the suggestion that they pick a restaurant. Serge knows of a place serving Lyonnaise food.

Alan Alda as Marc, Alfred Molina as Yvan and Victor Garber as Serge in Yasmina Reza's *Art*

SERGE *(to Yvan):* You like Lyonnaise food?

YVAN: I'll do whatever you like.

MARC: He'll do whatever you like. Whatever you like, he'll always do.

YVAN: What's the matter with you? You're both behaving very strangely.

SERGE: He's right, you might once in a while have an opinion of your own.

YVAN: Listen, if you think you're going to use me as a coconut shy, I'm out of here! I've put up with enough today.

MARC: Where's your sense of humor, Yvan?

YVAN: What?

MARC: Where's your sense of humor, old chap?

YVAN: Where's my sense of humor? I don't see anything to laugh at. Where's my sense of humor, are you trying to be funny?

MARC: I think recently you've somewhat lost your sense of humor. You want to watch out, believe me!

YVAN: What's the matter with you?

MARC: Don't you think recently I've also somewhat lost my sense of humor?

YVAN: Oh, I see!

SERGE: All right, that's enough, let's make a decision. Tell you the truth, I'm not even hungry.

YVAN: You're both really sinister this evening.

The other two offer Yvan advice about his problem with his women: of all of them, his future bride Catherine seems to be the most difficult. If Yvan can't get her under control, he faces a bleak future and had better think of cancelling the wedding. Yvan can't, he tells them, her uncle owns the stationery business where he's beginning a new career. Besides, Yvan adds, Serge's record in marriage is not one that qualifies him for giving marital advice.

They discuss the color of Serge's painting—not white, Serge asserts, and Yvan agrees: "There's yellow, there's grey, some slightly ochrish lines." This triggers Marc's anger at Yvan, calling him "an amoeba" and describing him to Serge: "He's a little arse-licker, he's obsequious, dazzled by money, dazzled by what he believes to be culture, and as you know culture is something I absolutely piss on." Yvan insists that he finds the colors touching, and Marc protests that he can't, they aren't there. Yvan decides that his best move would be to leave, but Serge stops him by pointing out that leaving would be a kind of surrender.

Serge stresses the significance of a person being "a man of his time," someone who is representative of his era, and turns on Marc when Marc belittles this concept.

SERGE: Listen, old fruit, we're not talking about you, if you can imagine such a thing! We don't give a fuck about you! A man of his time, I'm trying to explain to you, like most people you admire, is someone who makes some contribution to the human race . . . A man of his time doesn't assume the history of Art has come to an end with a pseudo-Flemish view of Cavaillon . . .

MARC: Carcassonne.

SERGE: Same thing. A man of his time plays his part in the fundamental dynamic of evolution . . .

MARC: And that's a good thing, in your view.

SERGE: It's not good or bad, why do you always have to moralize, it's just the way things are.

MARC: And you, for example, you play your part in the fundamental dynamic of evolution.

SERGE: I do.

MARC: What about Yvan? . . .

YVAN: Surely not. What sort of part can an amoeba play?

SERGE: In his way, Yvan is a man of his time.

MARC: How can you tell? Not from that daub hanging over his mantelpiece.

YVAN: That is not a daub!

SERGE: It is a daub.

YVAN: It is not!

SERGE: What's the difference? Yvan represents a certain way of life, a way of thinking which is completely modern. And so do you. I'm sorry, but you're a typical man of your time. And in fact, the harder you try not to be, the more you are.

MARC: Well, that's all right then. So what's the problem?

SERGE: There's no problem, except for you, because you take pride in your desire to shut yourself off from humanity. And you'll never manage it. It's like you're in a quicksand, the more you struggle to get out of it, the deeper you sink. Now apologize to Yvan.

MARC: Yvan is a coward.

At this point, Yvan makes his decision and exits in a rush.

Marc immediately begins to feel remorseful for attacking Yvan, who isn't capable of defending himself. Serge rubs it in by reminding Marc that the daub they so casually dismissed was painted by Yvan's father. The doorbell rings. Again it's Yvan, and again he enters talking: "Yvan returns! The lift was full, I plunged off down the stairs, clattering all the way down thinking, a coward, an amoeba, no substance, I thought I'll come back with a gun and blow his head off, then he'll see how flabby and obsequious I am, I got to the ground floor and I said to myself, listen, mate, you haven't been in therapy for six years to finish up shooting your best friend and you haven't been in therapy for six years without learning that some deep malaise must lie behind his insane aggression, so I relaunch myself, telling myself as I mount the penitential stair, this is a cry for help. I have to help Marc if it's the last thing I do . . . "

Yvan has already tried to be helpful by taking up the subject of his friends with his psychiatrist, Finkelzohn. Neither Marc nor Serge is pleased to hear this, but Serge is curious about what the psychiatrist said. It was complicated, Yvan tells them, so he wrote it down. He takes a slip of paper from his pocket and reads Finkelzohn's profundity: "If I'm who I am because I'm who I am and you're who you are because you're who you are, then I'm who I am and you're who you are. If, on the other hand, I'm who I am because you're who you are, and if you're who you are because I'm who I am, then I'm not who I am and you're not who you are . . . "

There is a short silence, and finally Marc observes sarcastically, "What a lucky man you are, to be getting the benefit of this fellow's experience." Serge echoes, "Absolutely!"

Yvan understands that his liking of Serge's painting touched off all these tensions in their friendship. Serge doesn't want to talk about his painting any more, and besides, he's getting bored with the others' company and suggests that Marc and Yvan go off and have dinner together. Impulsively, he picks up his painting and carries it out of the room, then immediately returns.

MARC: We're not worthy to look at it . . .

SERGE: Exactly.

MARC: Or are you afraid, if it stays in my presence, you'll finish up looking at it through my eyes? . . .

SERGE: No. You know what Paul Valéry says? And I'd go quite a bit further.

MARC: I don't give a fuck what Paul Valéry says.

SERGE: You've gone off Paul Valéry? . . . . .

MARC: Don't quote Paul Valéry at me. I don't give a fuck what Paul Valéry says.

SERGE: What do you give a fuck about?

MARC: I give a fuck about you buying that painting. I give a fuck about you spending two hundred grand on that piece of shit.

YVAN: Don't start again, Marc.

SERGE: I'm going to tell you what I give a fuck about—since everyone is coming clean—I give a fuck about your sniggering and insinuations, your suggestion that I also think this picture is a grotesque joke. You've denied that I could feel a genuine attachment to it. You've tried to set up some kind of loathsome complicity between us. And that's what made me feel, Marc, to repeat your expression, that we have less and less in common recently . . . . .

MARC: It's true I can't imagine you genuinely loving that painting.

YVAN: But why?

MARC: Because I love Serge, and I can't love the Serge who's capable of buying that painting.

SERGE: Why do you say, buying, why don't you say, loving.

MARC: Because I can't say loving, I can't believe loving.

SERGE: So why would I buy it, if I didn't love it?

MARC: That's the nub of the question.

Serge, hurt by Marc's lack of concern for his feelings in the blunt ridicule of his beloved painting, attacks something he knows Marc cherishes: Marc's wife Paula. Serge reminds Marc that he could have called Paula "ugly, repellent and charmless" after sitting next to her at a dinner party, but withheld his opinion out of respect for Marc's feelings. Yvan is appalled at this turn of the conversation. Marc is coldly outraged, but Serge, bolstering his opinion with an example, adds that the way Paula waves away cigarette smoke is worse than repellent. Marc can hardly believe what he's hearing.

MARC: You're speaking to me of Paula, the woman who shares my life, in these intolerable terms, because you disapprove of her method of waving away cigarette smoke? . . .

SERGE: That's right. Her method of waving away cigarette smoke condemns her out of hand.

MARC: Serge, before I completely lose control, you'd better explain yourself. This is very serious, what you're doing.

SERGE: A normal woman would say, I'm sorry, I find the smoke a bit uncomfortable, would you mind moving your ashtray, but not her, she doesn't deign to speak, she describes her contempt in the air with this calculated gesture, wearily malicious, this hand movement she imagines is imperceptible, the implication of which is to say, go on, smoke, smoke, it's pathetic but what's the point of calling attention to it, which means you can't tell if it's you or your cigarette that's getting up her nose.

YVAN: You're exaggerating!

SERGE: You notice he doesn't say I'm wrong, he says I'm exaggerating, but he doesn't say I'm wrong. Her method of waving away cigarette smoke reveals a cold,

condescending and narrow-minded nature. Just what you're in the process of ac-
quiring yourself. It's a shame, Marc, it's a real shame you've taken up with such a
life-denying woman . . .

Marc demands that Serge take it all back. When Serge doesn't, Marc *"throws
himself at Serge,"* but Yvan, who pulls them apart, is the one who takes a blow. Serge
brings Yvan a compress while Yvan declares both of the others insane. Marc reminds
Serge that Serge had once declared Paula a perfect match for Marc. "I didn't replace
you with Paula," Mark chides him, implying and then admitting that he considers
the painting a replacement for himself in Serge's affectionate admiration.

MARC *(to Serge):* There was a time you were proud to be my friend . . . You
congratulated yourself on my peculiarity, on my taste for standing apart. You enjoyed exhibiting me untamed to your circle, you, whose life was so normal. I was
your alibi. But . . . eventually, I suppose, that sort of affection dries up . . . Belatedly,
you claim your independence.
SERGE: "Belatedly" is nice.
MARC: But I detest your independence. Its violence. You've abandoned me. I've
been betrayed. As far as I'm concerned, you're a traitor.
    Silence.
SERGE *(to Yvan):* . . . If I understand correctly, he was my mentor! . . .
    Yvan doesn't respond. Marc stares at him contemptuously. Slight pause.
. . . And if I loved you as my mentor . . . what was the nature of your feelings?
MARC: You can guess.
SERGE: Yes, yes, but I want to hear you say it.
MARC: . . . I enjoyed your admiration. I was flattered. I was always grateful to
you for thinking of me as a man apart. I even thought being a man apart was a
somehow superior condition, until one day you pointed out to me that it wasn't.

Serge and Marc agree that this turn of events has become "a disaster," and Yvan,
who has been expecting sympathy for his hurt but getting none, suggests they make
up their differences. Marc accepts some of the blame for letting Serge slip away
under the influence of others until he turned into the sort of person who "goes off
and buys a white painting." It looks to both of them like the end of a 15-year
friendship.

Yvan had been looking forward to a relaxing evening with friends after the
stresses of his day, but now he wonders, "Why do we see each other?", as they all
seem to hate each other. Marc and Serge turn on Yvan and blame him for ruining
the evening by arriving late, boring them with complaints about family problems—
and, Serge adds, "Your inertia, your sheer neutral spectator's inertia has lured Marc
and me into the worst excesses." Yvan bursts into tears and into a lament about his
wedding and his new job: "What am I supposed to do? I pissed around for forty
years, I made you laugh, oh, yes, wonderful, I made all my friends laugh their heads
off playing the fool, but come the evening, who was left solitary as a rat? Who

crawled back into his hole every evening all on his own? This buffoon, dying of loneliness, who'd switch on anything that talks and who does he find on the answering machine? His mother. His mother. And his mother."

After the others calm Yvan down, Yvan feels hungry. Serge fetches a bowl of olives, which the three casually consume.

YVAN *(still eating olives):* . . . To think we've reached these extremes . . . Apocalypse because of a white square . . .

SERGE: It is not white.

YVAN: A piece of white shit!

He is seized by uncontrollable laughter.

That's what it is, a piece of white shit! . . . Let's face it, mate . . . What you've bought is insane! . . .

Marc laughs, caught up by Yvan's extravagance. Serge leaves the room. He returns immediately with the Antrios.

SERGE: Do you have one of your famous felt-tips? . . .

YVAN: What for? . . . You're not going to draw on the painting?

SERGE: Do you or don't you?

YVAN: Just a minute.

He goes through the pockets of his jacket.

Yes . . . A blue one . . .

SERGE: Give it to me.

Yvan does. Serge examines it, then tosses it to Marc. Yvan can't believe his friends will go through with what they seem to be intending. Marc looks at Serge, then approaches the painting. "*Under Yvan's horrified gaze, he draws the felt-tip along one of the diagonal scars. Serge remains impassive. Then, carefully, on this slope, Marc draws a little skier with a woolly hat. When he's finished, he straightens up and contemplates his work. Serge remains adamantine. Yvan is as if turned to stone. Silence.*"

The bone of contention at last having been well and truly buried, Serge suggests that they now go out to dinner.

Some time later, at Serge's apartment, the Antrios is hanging on the wall, as pristine white as ever. Marc is holding a basin into which Serge is dipping a cloth, and they are surrounded by a multitude of cleaning products and materials. Yvan, sitting off to the side, nods his approval that the painting is now clean. "*As though alone,*" he reflects on the ease with which he bursts into tears, recently at a touching incident at his mother-in-law's funeral the day after his wedding to Catherine, and the evening he, Serge and Marc had that quarrel over the white painting.

YVAN: After Serge, in an act of pure madness, had demonstrated to Marc that he cared more about him than he did about his painting, we went and had dinner, chez Emile. Over dinner, Serge and Marc took the decision to try to rebuild a relationship destroyed by word and deed. At a certain moment, one of them used the expression "trial period," and I burst into tears. This expression, "trial period," applied to our friendship, set off in me an uncontrollable and ridiculous convulsion. In fact, I can no longer bear any kind of rational argument, nothing formative in this world, nothing great or beautiful in the world has ever been born of rational argument.

> *Pause. Serge dries his hands. He goes to empty the basin of water, then puts away all the cleaning products, until there's no sign left of domestic activity. Once again he looks at his painting. Then he turns and advances toward the audience.*

SERGE: When Marc and I succeeded in obliterating the skier, with the aid of Swiss soap with added ox gall, recommended by Paula, I looked at the Antrios and turned to Marc: "Did you know ink from felt-tips was washable?" "No," Marc said . . . "No . . . did you?" "No," I said, very fast, lying. I came within an inch of saying, yes, I did know. But how could I have launched our trial period with such a disappointing admission? . . . On the other hand, was it right to start with a lie? . . . A lie! Let's be reasonable. Why am I so absurdly virtuous? Why does my relationship with Marc have to be so complicated?" . . .

> *Gradually the light begins to narrow down on the Antrios. Marc approaches the painting.*

MARC:
Under the white clouds, the snow is falling.
You can't see the white clouds, or the snow.
Or the cold, or the white glow of the earth.
A solitary man glides downhill on his skis.
The snow is falling.
It falls until the man disappears back into the landscape.
My friend Serge, who's one of my oldest friends, has bought a painting.
It's a canvas about five foot by four.
It represents a man who moves across a space and disappears.
> *Curtain.*

PLAYS PRODUCED
IN NEW YORK

PLAYS PRODUCED
ON BROADWAY

Figures in parentheses following a play's title give number of performances. These figures do not include previews or extra non-profit performances. In the case of a transfer, the off-Broadway run is noted but not added to the figure in parentheses.

Plays marked with an asterisk (*) were still in a projected run June 1, 1998. Their number of performances is figured through May 31, 1998.

In a listing of a show's numbers—dances, sketches, musical scenes, etc.—the titles of songs are identified wherever possible by their appearance in quotation marks (").

HOLDOVERS FROM PREVIOUS SEASONS

Broadway shows which were running on June 1, 1997 are listed below. More detailed information about them appears in previous *Best Plays* volumes of the years in which they opened. Important cast changes since opening night are recorded in the Cast Replacements section of this volume.

*Cats (6,533; longest running show in Broadway history). Musical based on *Old Possum's Book of Practical Cats* by T.S. Eliot; music by Andrew Lloyd Webber; additional lyrics by Trevor Nunn and Richard Stilgoe. Opened October 7, 1982.

*Les Misérables (4,615). Musical based on the novel by Victor Hugo; book by Alain Boublil and Claude-Michel Schönberg; lyrics by Herbert Kretzmer; original French text by Alain Boublil and Jean-Marc Natel; additional material by James Fenton. Opened March 12, 1987.

*The Phantom of the Opera (4,345). Musical adapted from the novel by Gaston Leroux; book by Richard Stilgoe and Andrew Lloyd Webber; music by Andrew Lloyd Webber; lyrics by Charles Hart; additional lyrics by Richard Stilgoe. Opened January 26, 1988.

*Miss Saigon (2,956). Musical with book by Alain Boublil and Claude-Michel Schönberg; music by Claude-Michel Schönberg; lyrics by Richard Maltby Jr. and Alain Boublil; additional material by Richard Maltby Jr. Opened April 11, 1991.

*Beauty and the Beast (1,722). Musical with book by Linda Woolverton; music by Alan Menken; lyrics by Howard Ashman and Tim Rice. Opened April 18, 1994.

Grease (1,503). Revival of the musical with book, music and lyrics by Jim Jacobs and Warren Casey. Opened May 11, 1994. (Closed January 25, 1998)

*Smokey Joe's Cafe (1,349). Musical revue with words and music by Jerry Leiber and Mike Stoller. Opened March 2, 1995.

Defending the Caveman (671). Solo performance by Rob Becker; written by Rob Becker. Opened March 26, 1995. (Closed June 21, 1997)

Victor/Victoria (734). Musical with book by Blake Edwards; music by Henry Mancini; lyrics by Leslie Bricusse; additional material by Frank Wildhorn. Opened October 25, 1995. (Closed July 27, 1997)

Master Class (601). By Terrence McNally. Opened November 5, 1995. (Closed June 28, 1997)

The King and I (807). Revival of the musical based on the novel *Anna and the King of Siam* by Margaret Landon; book and lyrics by Oscar Hammerstein II; music by Richard Rodgers. Opened April 11, 1996. (Closed February 22, 1998)

A Funny Thing Happened on the Way to the Forum (715). Revival of the musical with book by Burt Shevelove and Larry Gelbart; music and lyrics by Stephen Sondheim. Opened April 18, 1996. (Closed January 4, 1998)

***Bring in 'da Noise Bring in 'da Funk** (875). Transfer from off Broadway of the musical performance piece based on an idea by Savion Glover and George C. Wolfe; conceived by George C. Wolfe; choreography by Savion Glover; book by Reg E. Gaines; music by Daryl Waters, Zane Mark and Ann Duquesnay. Opened November 15, 1995 off Broadway where it played 85 performances through January 28, 1996; transferred to Broadway April 25, 1996.

***Rent** (873). Transfer from off Broadway of the musical with book, music and lyrics by Jonathan Larson. Opened off off Broadway January 26, 1996 and off Broadway February 13, 1996 where it played 56 performances through March 31, 1996; transferred to Broadway April 29, 1996.

***Chicago** (643). Revival of the musical based on the play by Maurine Dallas Watkins; book by Fred Ebb and Bob Fosse; music by John Kander; lyrics by Fred Ebb; original production directed and choreographed by Bob Fosse. Opened November 14, 1996.

***The Last Night of Ballyhoo** (525). By Alfred Uhry. Opened February 27, 1997.

Barrymore (238). By William Luce. Opened March 25, 1997. (Closed November 2, 1997)

Annie (238). Revival of the musical based on Harold Gray's comic strip *Little Orphan Annie;* book by Thomas Meehan; music by Charles Strouse; lyrics by Martin Charnin. Opened March 26, 1997. (Closed October 19, 1997)

The Young Man From Atlanta (88). Revival of the play by Horton Foote. Opened March 27, 1997. (Closed June 8, 1997)

A Doll's House (150). Revival of the play by Henrik Ibsen; new version by Frank McGuinness. Opened April 2, 1997. (Closed August 31, 1997)

Dream (109). Musical revue based on the lyrics of Johnny Mercer; conceived by Louise Westergaard and Jack Wrangler; music by various authors. Opened April 3, 1997. (Closed July 6, 1997)

Lincoln Center Theater. An American Daughter (88). By Wendy Wasserstein. Opened April 13, 1997. (Closed June 29, 1997) **The Little Foxes** (57). Revival of the play by Lillian Hellman. Opened April 27, 1997. (Closed June 15, 1997)

Roundabout Theater Company. London Assurance (72). Revival of the play by Dion Boucicault. Opened April 16, 1997. (Closed June 22, 1997)

The Gin Game (144). Revival of the play by D.L. Coburn. Opened April 20, 1997. (Closed August 31, 1997)

***Titanic** (460). Musical with story and book by Peter Stone; music and lyrics by Maury Yeston. Opened April 23, 1997.

Steel Pier (76). Musical conceived by Scott Ellis, Susan Stroman and David Thompson; book by David Thompson; music and lyrics by John Kander and Fred Ebb. Opened April 24, 1997. (Closed June 28, 1997)

*The Life (465). Musical based on an original idea by Ira Gasman; book by David Newman, Ira Gasman and Cy Coleman; lyrics by Ira Gasman; music by Cy Coleman. Opened April 26, 1997.

*Jekyll & Hyde (456). Musical based on the novella *The Strange Case of Dr. Jekyll and Mr. Hyde* by Robert Louis Stevenson; conceived by Steve Cuden and Frank Wildhorn; book and lyrics by Leslie Bricusse; music by Frank Wildhorn. Opened April 28, 1997.

Candide (103). Revival of the musical adapted from Voltaire; book by Hugh Wheeler; music by Leonard Bernstein; lyrics by Richard Wilbur; additional lyrics by Stephen Sondheim and John Latouche. Opened April 29, 1997. (Closed July 27, 1997)

Madison Square Garden Productions. The Wizard of Oz (42). Musical based on the story by L. Frank Baum; adapted by Robert Johanson; music by Harold Arlen, lyrics by E.Y. Harburg from the M-G-M motion picture; background music by Herbert Stothart. Opened May 15, 1997. (Closed June 8, 1997)

PLAYS PRODUCED JUNE 1, 1997–MAY 31, 1998

*Forever Tango (392). Dance musical created by Luis Bravo. Produced by Steven Baruch, Richard Frankel, Thomas Viertel, Marc Routh, Jujamcyn Theaters and Interamerica Inc. at the Walter Kerr Theater. Opened June 19, 1997.

Dancers: Miriam Larici & Diego DiFalco, Luis Castro & Claudia Mendoza, Carlos Gavito & Marcela Durán, Jorge Torres (Dance Captain) & Karina Piazza, Carlos Vera & Laura Marcarie, Guillermo Merlo & Cecilia Saia, Gabriel Ortega & Sandra Bootz, Pedro Calveyra & Nora Robles, Carolina Zokalski.
Singer: Carlos Morel.
Forever Tango Orchestra: Lisandro Adrover, Hector Del Curto, Carlos Niesi, Victor Lavallen bandoneóns; Humberto Ridolfi, Rodion Boshoer violin; Oscar Hasbun viola; Dino Quarleri cello; Silvio Acosta bass; Fernando Marzan piano; Mario Araolaza keyboard.
Directed by Luis Bravo; musical direction and arrangements, Lisandro Adrover; choreography, Dancers; costumes, Argemira Affonso; lighting, Luis Bravo; sound, Tom Craft; assistant director, Carlos Diaz; production manager, Mark Gilmore; stage manager, Jorge Gonzalez; press, Boneau/Bryan-Brown, Chris Boneau, Jackie Green.
Celebration of the music and dancing of Argentina, particularly the tango. The show was presented in two parts. A foreign production which has been presented in Europe, Canada and elsewhere in the U.S.

ACT I

Preludio del Bandoneón y la Noche .... Miriam Larici & Diego DiFalco
(conception by Luis Bravo)
Overture .... Orchestra
El Suburbio
(Time: 1880. Place: A brothel)
A Los Amigos (by A. Pontier) .... Orchestra
Derecho Viejo (by E. Arolas) .... Karina Piazza & Jorge Torres
"El Día Que Me Quieras" (by C. Gardel and A. Lepera) .... Carlos Morel
La Mariposa (by O. Pugliese) .... Laura Marcarie & Carlos Vera
Comme Il Faut (by E. Arolas) .... Sandra Bootz & Gabriel Ortega
(Time: The 1930s. Place: Paris)
Berretín .... Orchestra
La Tablada (by F. Canaro) .... Claudia Mendoza & Luis Castro

FOREVER TANGO—One of the many dancing couples in
the musical created by Luis Bravo

Milongueando En El '40 (by A. Pontier) .... Cecilia Saia & Guillermo Merlo
S.V.P. (by A. Piazzolla) .... Marcela Durán & Carlos Gavito
Responso (by A. Troilo) .... Orchestra
Azabache (by E.M. Fracini) .... Company
   (Time: Early 1900s. Place: San Telmo)

ACT II

Tanguera (by M. Mores) .... Nora Robles & Pedro Calveyra
A Evaristo Carriego (by E. Rovira) .... Marcela Durán & Carlos Gavito
Payadora (by J. Plaza) .... Orchestra
Quejas De Bandoneón (by J. de Dios Filiberto) .... Laura Marcarie & Carlos Vera
Gallo Ciego (by A. Bardi) .... Karina Piazza & Jorge Torres
"Balada Para un Loco" (by A. Piazzolla and H. Ferrer) .... Carlos Morel

La Cumparista (by G.M. Rodriguez) .... Cecilia Saia & Guillermo Merlo,
Karina Piazza & Jorge Torres, Marcela Durán & Carlos Gavito
Jealousy (by Jacob Gade) .... Orchestra
Felicia (by E. Saborido) .... Claudia Mendoza & Luis Castro
Adiós Nonino (by A. Piazzolla) .... Orchestra
Libertango (by A. Piazzolla) .... Cecilia Saia & Guillermo Merlo
Romance del Bandoneón y la Noche (by L. Androver) .... Miriam Larici & Diego DiFalco
(conception by Luis Bravo)
Finale: *Lo Que Vendrá* (by A. Piazzolla) .... Company

Umbatha: The Zulu Macbeth (6). Musical adapted from the play by William Shakespeare; written by Welcome Msomi; music by Welcome Msomi, with traditional songs. Produced by Lincoln Center Festival 97, John Rockwell director, in the Johannesburg Civic Theater production, Janice Honeyman executive and artistic director, at New York State Theater. Opened July 21, 1997. (Closed July 27, 1997)

Mabatha (Macbeth) .. Thabani Patrick Tshanini
Ka Madonsela
  (Lady Macbeth) .... Dieketseng Mnisi
Dangane (Duncan) .... Lawrence Masondo
Donebane (Donaldbain) ...... Buyani Shangase
Makhiwane (Malcolm) ....·.... Martin Jwara
Mafudu
  (Macduff) .... Qond'okwakhe Mngwengwe
Bhagane (Banquo);
  Isipoki (Spirit) .... Qed'umunyu Zungu
Folose (Fleance); Isipoki .... Shaun Dugen
Isangoma I .... S'bongile Ngqulunga
Isangoma II .... Promise S'thembile Jali
Isangoma III .... Mary-Anne Busi Mchunu
Ka Makhawulana
  (Lady Macduff) .... Philile Sibiya
Indodana; Sidakwa; King's Guard;
  Isipoki .... Skhumbuzo Nsele

Hoshweni (Ross); Isipoki ... Zam'okhule Ngiba
Linolo (Lennox); Isipoki .... Cyprian Nzama
Angano (Angus); Inceku (King's Servant);
  Umbulali III
  (Murderer) .... Thokozani Makhoba
Inceku; Dance Captain .... Mdudzi Zwane
Imbongi (King's Praise Singer);
  Isipoki .... Pa Vusi Chili
Inyanga; Isipoki .... Thol'ithemba Mthembu
Isalukazi (Nurse) .... Thokozile Gumede
Msimbithi (Messenger) .... Philani Radebe
Intombi (Maiden) .... Bulelwa Maqungo
Intombi .... Gcinile Nkosi
Inceku .... Vumisani Ncobeni
Inceku .... Xolani Ncobeni
Igosa (Warrior Captain) .... Mafika Ngwazi
Umbulali I; Ibutho (Warrior) ... Mbongwa Njilo
Umbulali II; Ibutho .... Bhekisisa Mthembu

Maidens: Thembelihe Chiliza, Bongiwe Hlophe, Nomthandaze Langa, Lady-Fair Mngadi, Thandekile Msomi, Ntombifuthi Nzama, Winile Sibuya.

Warriors: Bhekumuthi Cele, Magazine Amon Cele, Mazwi Cele, Kufakwakhe Dlamini, France Duna, Zwelibanzi Gansa, Mbokodo Mhlongo, Sipho Mngadi, Bhekuyise Mnyandu, Mkhanyiselwa Mvundla, Xolani Ngubane, Alpheus Ngwazi, Nkosibuka Qumbisa.

Drummers: William Lembede, Bernard Hlophe, Jacob Makatsanyane, David Msimango, Bong'nkosi Nxumalo.

Understudies: Miss Mnisi (Lady Macbeth)—Bulelwa Maqungo, Gcinile Nkosi; Mr. Tshanini (Macbeth)—Vumisani Ndlovu; Mr. Mngwengwe (Macduff)—Xolani Ncobeni; Others—Joseph Mnguni, Prince Gambushe, Zakufa Qwatubane.

Directed by Welcome Msomi; choreography, Thuli Dumakude, Mdudzi Zwane, Mafika Mgwazi; assitant director and vocal arrangements, Thuli Dumakude; lighting, France Mavana, Denis Hutchinson; original lighting, Mannie Manim; original sound, Emmanuel McGarth; stage manager, Mncedi Dayi; for Lincoln Center Festival 97, Carmen Kovens producer, Laura Aswad associate producer; press, Miranda Zola.

Macbeth reset among parallel conflicts of warring African factions in the 19th century, with a program note by the writer-director stating, "The Zulu traditional dancing, story-telling and music, as it was sung many centuries ago, allowed me an opportunity to take pride in the richness of our South African culture." A foreign play first produced at the University of Natal Amphitheater in 1970 and continuing on a U.S. and world tour following this presentation.

*Roundabout Theater Company. 1996–97 schedule concluded with ***1776** (317). Revival of the musical based on a concept of Sherman Edwards; book by Peter Stone; music and lyrics by Sherman Edwards. Produced by Roundabout Theater Company, Todd Haimes artistic director, Ellen Richard general manager, Gene Feist founding director, at Criterion Center Stage Right. Opened August 14, 1997. (Closed at the Roundabout November 16, 1997 after 109 performances) Reopened at the Gershwin Theater December 3, 1997.

Members of the Continental Congress

President:
John Hancock .... Richard Poe
New Hampshire:
Dr. Josiah Bartlett .... Michael X. Martin
Massachusetts:
John Adams .... Brent Spiner
Rhode Island:
Stephen Hopkins .... Tom Aldredge
Connecticut:
Roger Sherman .... John Herrera
New York:
Lewis Morris .... Tom Riis Farrell
Robert Livingston .... Daniel Marcus
New Jersey:
Rev. John Witherspoon .... Jerry Lanning
Pennsylvania:
Benjamin Franklin .... Pat Hingle
John Dickinson .... Michael Cumpsty
James Wilson .... Michael Winther
Delaware:
Caesar Rodney .... Michael McCormick

Col. Thomas McKean .... Bill Nolte
George Read .... Kevin Ligon
Maryland:
Samuel Chase .... Ric Stoneback
Virginia:
Richard Henry Lee .... Merwin Foard
Thomas Jefferson .... Paul Michael Valley
North Carolina:
Joseph Hewes .... David Lowenstein
South Carolina:
Edward Rutledge .... Gregg Edelman
Georgia:
Dr. Lyman Hall .... Robert Westenberg
Congressional Secretary:
Charles Thomson .... Guy Paul
Congressional Custodian:
Andrew McNair .... MacIntyre Dixon
Others:
A Leather Apron .... Joseph Cassidy
Courier .... Dashiell Eaves
Abigail Adams .... Linda Emond
Martha Jefferson .... Lauren Ward
Painter .... Ben Sheaffer

Orchestra: Mark Mitchell conductor, keyboard; Thad Wheeler assistant conductor, percussion; Brenda Vincent violin; Tatyana Margulis cello; Eric Weidman woodwinds; Dominic Derasse trumpets; Dean Plank bass trombone, tuba; Anthony Morris bass.

Understudies: Mr. Poe—Michael McCormick; Messrs. Martin, Aldredge, McCormick, Dixon—Rob Donohoe; Mr. Spiner—John Herrera; Messrs. Herrera, Foard, Edelman—Joseph Cassidy; Messrs. Farrell, Marcus, Stoneback, Lowenstein—Tim Fauvell; Messrs. Lanning, Nolte, Westenberg, Paul—James Hindham; Mr. Hingle—Tom Roland; Mr. Cumpsty— Michael X. Martin; Mr. Winther—David Lowenstein; Messrs. Ligon, Valley, Cassidy, Eaves—Ben Sheaffer; Misses Emond, Ward—Rebecca Eichenberger.

Directed by Scott Ellis; musical staging, Kathleen Marshall; musical direction, Paul Gemignani; scenery, Tony Walton; costumes, William Ivey Long; lighting, Brian Nason; sound, Brian Ronan; orchestrations, Brian Besterman; dance arrangements, Peter Howard; dialects, K.C. Ligon; casting, Jim Carnahan; production stage manager, Lori M. Doyle; stage manager, David Sugarman; press, Boneau/Bryan-Brown, Adrian Bryan-Brown, Erin Dunn.

1776 was originally produced on Broadway 3/16/69 for 1,217 performances and won a *Best Plays* citation and the Critics and Tony Awards. This is its first major New York revival.

Michael McCormick replaced Brent Spiner, David Huddleston replaced Pat Hingle and Carolee Carmello replaced Linda Emond 3/4/98.

ACT I

Scene 1: The chamber of the Continental Congress
"Sit Down, John" .... Adams, The Congress
"Piddle, Twiddle and Resolve" .... Adams
"Till Then" .... Adams, Abigail Adams
Scene 2: The mall
"The Lees of Virginia" .... Lee, Franklin, Adams
Scene 3: The chamber
"But Mr. Adams" .... Adams, Franklin, Jefferson, Sherman, Livingston
Scene 4: Jefferson's room and High Street
"Yours, Yours, Yours" .... Adams, Abigail Adams
"He Plays the Violin" .... Martha Jefferson, Franklin, Adams

Scene 5: The chamber
"Cool, Cool, Considerate Men" .... Dickinson, The Conservatives
"Momma Look Sharp" .... Courier, McNair, Leather Apron

ACT II

Scene 6: The Congressional anteroom
"The Egg" .... Franklin, Adams, Jefferson
Scene 7: The chamber
"Molasses to Rum" .... Rutledge
"Compliments" .... Abigail Adams
"Is Anybody There?" .... Adams

The Last Empress (12). Limited engagement of the musical with book conceived and written by Mun Yol Yi, based on his book *Fox Hunt;* adapted by Kwang Lim Kim; music by Hee Gab Kim; lyrics by In Ja Yang. Produced in the Korean language with English supertitles by Arts Communications Seoul Company at the New York State Theater. Opened August 15, 1997. (Closed August 24, 1997)

Queen	Wonjung Kim, Taewon Kim	Miura Goroh	Sung Ki Kim
Taewongun	Jae Hwan Lee	Chillyunggun; Price	Hyun Dong Kim
King Kojung	Hee Sung Yu	Court Ladies .... Young Ju Jeong, He Jung Kim	
Inoue	Hee Jung Lee	Weber	David De Witt
Itoh Hirobumi	Mu Yeol Choi	Sontag	Mary Jo Todaro
Kye Hun Hong	Min Soo Kim	Young Queen	Anne Chun

Japanese Merchants: Hak Jun Kim, Do Kyung Kim, Ho Jin Kim, Sang Hoe Park. Foreign Envoys: Tom Schmid, Eric Morgan, Claire Beckman, Samantha Camp.

Chorus, Dancers: So Youn An, Geon Ryeong Bae, Eun Jung Cho, Im Su Choi, Se Hwan Choi, Jeong Ju Doh, Soon Chul Hyun, Young Ju Jeong, Woo Jeong Jeoung, Do Hyeong Kim, Hak Muk Kim, Hakjun Kim, Ho Jin Kim, Hyun Dong Kim, Soo Jin Kim, Young Ju Kim, Young Ok Kim, Min Kyeng Kwak, He Jeong Lee, Jae Gu Lee, Ji Eun Lee, Ji Youn Lee, Kyoung Woo Lee, Sung Ho Lee, Hyo Jung Moon, Sang Hoe Park, Seung Jun Seo, Hyo In Shin, Chan Youn.

Directed by Ho Jin Yun; choreography, Byung Goo Seo; musical direction, Kolleen Park; scenery, Dong Woo Park; costumes, Hyun Sook Kim; lighting, Hyung O Choi; sound, Ki Young Kim; orchestrations and additional music, Peter Casey; executive producer, Young Hwan Kim; associate producers, Sang Ryul Lee, Su Mun Lee, Young Il Yang, Woo Jong Lee; production stage manager, Jong Il Lee; press, Tony Origlio Publicity, Maryann Lopinto.

The life and death of Queen Min (Myungsung), a matriarch of the Chosun Kingdom who influenced her society in the direction of the 20th century but was assassinated by the Japanese in 1895 at the age of 45. A foreign musical previously produced in Seoul.

MUSICAL NUMBERS—Prologue: Prelude, Japan's Choice. ACT I: Scene 1: The Day We Greet the New Queen. Scene 2: Taewongun's Regency, King & Courtesans, Your Highness Is Beautiful, Look on Me. Scene 3: Market Place, Four Japanese Merchants, Fight at the Market Place, I Am Hong Kye-Hun, A Wish for a Prince, The Shaman, Knock Knock/Song of the Soldiers. Scene 4: Grow Big and Strong, Dear Prince, You Are the King of Chosun, Until the World Needs Me Again. Scene 5: Kojong's Imperial Conference, It's All a Scheme, Seven Foreign Envoys, Four Japanese, Itoh's Ambition. Scene 6: Uprising of the Old Line Units, Military Mutiny of 1882, Back at the Seat of Power, I Miss You, My Dear Queen, We Shall Return, Wu Chang-Ching and Taewongun. Scene 7: Taewangun Is Taken to China, Inoue Threatens King Kojong, Queen Min's Return, We Shall Rise Again, Meeting on Japan's Chosun Policy.

ACT II: Scene 8: Dancing at the Grand Banquet, Come Celebrate Our Reforms, Elizabeth I of Chosun, Negotiations at the Grand Banquet, Next Morning Is Dawning in Chosun, Isn't It Strange, Snowflakes Are Falling. Scene 9: You Shall Drink Miura's Wine, Tripartite Intervention and the Atami House Conspiracy, Isn't It Strange, Snowflakes Are Falling. Scene 10: Chosun Is Tangun's Land, Miura's Audience With the King. Scene 11: The French Lesson, When the Wine Gets Cold, Welcome, Ladies, Ritual for Murder. Scene 12: Prince and Queen, Where Was It That We Met, You Are My Destiny, Take Away the Darkening Sky. Scene 13: Do Not Hurt the Queen, The Last of Hong Kye-Hun, Queen

Min Chased by the Beasts, Find the Queen, Kill the Fox, How Will I Live Now. Epilogue: Rise, People of Chosun.

Riverdance. (23) Return engagement of the dance and music revue with music and lyrics by Bill Whelan; poetry by Theo Dorgan. Produced by Radio City Productions in association with Abhann Productions, Moya Doherty producer, Julian Erskine executive producer, at Radio City Music Hall. Opened September 25, 1997. (Closed October 12, 1997).

Narrator .... John Kavanagh   Solo Singers .... Katie MacMahon,
Solo Dancers ...... Colin Dunne, Eileen Martin,   Morgan Crowley
                         Maria Pagés, Pat Roddy

Others: Tarik Winston, Eileen Ivers, Ivan Thomas, Toby Harris.

Riverdance Irish Dance Troupe: Caitlin Allen, Sarah Barry, Dearbhail Bates, Natalie Biggs, Lorna Bradley, Martin Brennan, Rachel Byrne, Suzanne Cleary, Yzanne Cloonan, Andrea Curley (assistant dance captain), Marty Dowds, Jo Ellen Forsyth, Fiona Gallagher, Susan Ginnety, Paula Goulding, Conor Hayes, Miceál Hopkins, Donnacha Howard, Kellie Hughes, Ciara Kennedy, Sorcha McCaul, Kevin McCormack (dance captain), Jonathan McMorrow, Joe Moriarty, Damien Noone, Aoibheann O'Brien, Niamh O'Brien, Cormac Ó Sé, Ursula Quigley, Joan Rafter, Pat Roddy, Sheila Ryan, Anthony Savage, Claire Usher, J.R. Vancheri, Leanda Ward.

Dance Troupe Understudies: Miss Pagés—Nuris Brisa; Principals—Conor Hayes, Joan Rafter; Others—J.R. Vancheri, Susan Ginnety, Sorcha McCaul.

Moscow Folk Ballet Company: Svetlana Kossoroukova, Ilia Streltsov, Tatiana Nedostop, Marina Taranda, Iouri Oustiougov, Serguei Iakoubov, Iouri Shishkine, Olena Krutsenko.

The Riverdance Singers: Derek Byrne, Patrick Connolly, Jennifer Curran, Tony Davoren, Maire Lang, Kay Lynch, Lorraine Nolan, Cathal Synnott (choirmaster).

Drummers: Abraham Doron, Vinny Ozborne, Andrew Reilly, Derek Tallon.

The Riverdance Orchestra: Noel Eccles musical direction, percussion; Eoghan O'Neill musical direction, bass guitar; Eileen Ivers fiddle; Brian O'Brien uilleann pipes, low whistles; Kenneth Edge soprano and alto saxophones; Nikola Parov gadulka, kaval, gaida; Éilís Egan accordion; Des Moore electric and acoustic guitars; Desi Reynolds drums, percussion; Jim Higgins bodhrán, darrabukkas, dunbeg, ouda; Pete Whinnett keyboards.

Choreography: Reel Around the Sun, Thunderstorm—Michael Flatley; Women of Ireland—Jean Butler; Shivna, Russian Dervish—Moscow Folk Ballet Company; Firedance—Maria Pagés; American Wake—Michael Flatley, Paula Nic Cionnath; Riverdance—Mavis Ascott (Irish Step Dance choreography), Michael Flatley (Lead Female Solo choreography), Jean Butler; Trading Taps—Colin Dunne, Tarik Winston; Oscail an Doras—Tara Little; Andalucia—Maria Pagés, Colin Dunne; Heartland—Michael Flatley, Colin Dunne, Jean Butler.

Directed by John McColgan; scenery and painted images, Robert Ballagh; costumes, Jen Kelly; lighting, Rupert Murray; sound, Michael O'Gorman; projection design, Chris Slingsby; orchestrations, Nick Ingman, Bill Whelan; production stage manager, James Doran; stage manager, Sara Smith; press, Merle Frimark.

Extravaganza featuring Irish step dancers as well as choral and solo songs and dances by European performers. A foreign show previously produced in Dublin and London and at the Music Hall 4/13/96 for 8 performances and 10/2/96 for 21 performances.

SCENES, DANCES AND MUSICAL NUMBERS, ACT I: Introduction. Scene l: Reel Around the Sun (Corona, The Chronos Reel, Reel Around the Sun). Scene 2: "The Heart's Cry." Scene 3: Women of Ireland (The Countess Cathleen, Women of the Sidhe). Scene 4: "Caoineadh Chú Chulainn" (Lament). Scene 5: Thunderstorm. Scene 6: "Shivna." Scene 7: Firedance. Scene 8: Slip Into Spring—The Harvest. Scene 9: Riverdance ("Cloudsong," Dance of the Riverwoman, Earthrise, Riverdance).

ACT II: Introduction. Scene 10: American Wake (Nova Scotia Set, "Lift the Wings"). Scene 11: The Harbour of the New World, I—"Heal Their Hearts," II—Trading Taps, III—Morning in Macedonia (The Russian Dervish), IV—Oscail an Doras (Open the Door), V—Heartbeat of the World (Andalucia). Scene 12: "Home and the Heartland." Scene 13: Riverdance International.

Side Show (91). Musical with book and lyrics by Bill Russell; music by Henry Krieger. Produced by Emanuel Azenberg, Joseph Nederlander, Herschel Waxman, Janice McKenna and

SIDE SHOW—Emily Skinner and Alice Ripley as Siamese twins Daisy and Violet Hilton in a scene from the Bill Russell-Henry Krieger musical

Scott Nederlander at the Richard Rodgers Theater. Opened October 16, 1997. (Closed January 3, 1998)

Reptile Man	Barry Finkel	Sheik	David Masenheimer
Bearded Lady	Andy Gale	Terry Connor	Jeff McCarthy
Snake Girl	Emily Hsu	Geek	Phillip Officer
Fortune Teller	Alicia Irving	Buddy Foster	Hugh Panaro
Fakir	Devanand N. Janki	Dolly Dimples	Verna Pierce
The Boss	Ken Jennings	Violet Hilton	Alice Ripley
Jake	Norm Lewis	Daisy Hilton	Emily Skinner
6th Exhibit	Judy Malloy		

Roustabouts: Billy Hartung, David McDonald, Jim T. Ruttman, Timothy Warmen. Harem Girls: Jenny-Lynn Suckling, Susan Taylor, Darlene Wilson. Reporters, Vaudevillians, Follies Company, Party Guests, Radio Show Singers, Hawkers: Company.

Orchestra: Lawrence Feldman, Edward Salkin, Dennis Anderson, Roger Rosenberg woodwinds; Robert Millikan, Glenn Drewes, Earl Gardner trumpet; Larry Farrell, Jack Schatz trombone; Roger Wendt, French horn; Mary Rowell, Paul Woodiel, Jonathan Kass, Nancy Reed violin; Clay Ruede,

Eileen Folson cello; Robert Renino bass; Philip Fortenberry, Lawrence Yurman keyboards; Susan Jolles harp; Gregory Utzig guitar; Raymond Grappone drums; Eric Kivnick percussion.

Standbys: Miss Ripley—Kristen Behrendt; Miss Skinner—Lauren Kennedy; Mr. Lewi—Todd Hunter. Understudies: Mr. McCarthy—David McDonald, David Masenheimer; Mr. Panaro—John Frenzer; Mr. Jennings—David Masenheimer. Swings—John Paul Almon, Kelly Cole, John Frenzer, Michelle Millerick, J. Robert Spencer.

Directed and choreographed by Robert Longbottom; musical direction, vocal and dance arrangements, David Chase; scenery, Robin Wagner; costumes, Gregg Barnes; lighting, Brian MacDevitt; sound, Tom Clark; orchestrations, Harold Wheeler; musical coordination, Seymour Red Press; associate choreographer, Tom Kosis; associate producer, Ginger Montel; casting, Johnson-Liff Associates; production stage manager, Perry Cline; stage manager, Maximo Torres; press, Bill Evans & Associates, Jim Randolph, Terry M. Lilly, Jonathan Schwartz.

The lives and show business careers of Siamese twins.

ACT I

The Midway
"Come Look at the Freaks" .... Boss, Company
"Like Everyone Else" .... Daisy, Violet
"You Deserve a Better Life" .... Terry
"Crazy, Deaf and Blind" .... Boss
"The Devil You Know" .... Jake, Attractions
"More Than We Bargained For" .... Terry, Buddy
"Feelings You've Got to Hide" .... Daisy, Violet
"When I'm By Your Side" .... Daisy, Violet
"Say Goodbye to the Freak Show" .... Company
Vaudeville
"Overnight Sensation" .... Terry, Reporters
"Leave Me Alone" .... Daisy, Violet
"We Share Everything" .... Daisy, Violet, Vaudevillians
"The Interview" .... Daisy, Violet, Reporters
"Who Will Love Me as I Am?" .... Daisy, Violet

ACT II

The Follies
"Rare Songbirds on Display" .... Company
"New Year's Day" .... Terry, Buddy, Jake, Daisy, Violet, Company
"Private Conversation" .... Terry
On the Road
"One Plus One Equals Three" .... Buddy, Daisy, Violet
"You Should Be Loved" .... Jake
The Texas Centennial
"Tunnel of Love" .... Terry, Buddy, Daisy, Violet
"Beautiful Day for a Wedding" .... Boss, Hawkers
"Marry Me, Terry" .... Daisy
"I Will Never Leave You" .... Daisy, Violet
Finale .... Company

Triumph of Love (83). Musical based on the play by Marivaux; book by James Magruder; music by Jeffrey Stock; lyrics by Susan Birkenhead. Produced by Margo Lion, Metropolitan Entertainment Group and Jujamcyn Theaters in association with PACE Theatrical Group, the Baruch-Frankel-Viertel Group, Alex Hitz, Center Stage and Yale Repertory Theater at the Royale Theater. Opened October 23, 1997. (Closed January 4, 1998)

Agis	Christopher Sieber	Hermocrates	F. Murray Abraham
Hesione	Betty Buckley	Princess Leonide	Susan Egan
Dimas	Kevin Chamberlin	Corine	Nancy Opel
Harlequin	Roger Bart		

Orchestra: Patrick S. Brady conductor, keyboard; Larry Spivak associate conductor, percussion; Rick Dolan concertmaster; Richard Brice viola; Chungsun Kim cello; William Sloat bass; Chuck Wilson, Rick Heckman, Frank Santagata woodwinds; Katie Dennis horn; Terry Szor trumpet.

Understudies: Misses Egan, Opel—Christianne Tisdale; Mr. Abraham—Paul Harman; Mr. Sieber— Tom Plotkin; Messrs. Bart, Chamberlin— Tom Plotkin, Paul Harman.

Directed by Michael Mayer; choreography, Doug Varone; musical direction, Patrick Brady; scenery, Heidi Ettinger; costumes, Catherine Zuber; lighting, Paul Gallo; sound, Brian Ronan; musical supervision and arrangements, Michael Kosarin; orchestrations, Bruce Coughlin; music coordinator, John Miller; associate producers, Charles Kelman Productions, Inc., Marc Routh; casting, Jay Binder; production stage manager, Arturo E. Porrazi; stage manager, Gary Mickelson; press, Boneau/Bryan-Brown, Chris Boneau, John Barlow.

Place: The garden retreat of the philosopher Hermocrates, an 18th century Greco-Roman topiary labyrinth.

The last New York production of the Marivaux play *(The Triumph of Love)* was a special matinee at the Criterion Theater 2/8/04. This musical version was previously produced last season in regional theater by Baltimore's Center Stage, Irene Lewis artistic director, and the Yale Repertory Theater, Stan Wojewodski Jr. artistic director.

ACT I

"This Day of Days" .... Hesione, Harlequin, Dimas, Agis, Hermocrates
"Anything" .... Princess Leonide
"The Bond That Can't Be Broken" .... Princess Leonide, Agis
"Mr. Right" .... Corine, Harlequin
"You May Call Me Phocion" .... Princess Leonide, Hesione
"Mr. Right" (Reprise) .... Corine, Dimas
"Emotions" .... Hermocrates, Princess Leonide
"The Sad and Sordid Saga of Cecile" .... Princess Leonide, Agis, Corine, Harlequin, Dimas
"Serenity" .... Hesione
"Issue in Question" .... Agis
"Teach Me Not to Love You" .... Company

ACT II

"Have a Little Faith" .... Corine, Princess Leonide, Harlequin, Dimas
"The Tree" .... Hesione, Hermocrates
"What Have I Done?" .... Princess Leonide
"Henchmen Are Forgotten" .... Harlequin, Dimas, Corine
"Love Won't Take No for an Answer" .... Hermocrates, Hesione, Agis
"This Day of Days" (Reprise) .... Princess Leonide, Agis, Corine, Harlequin, Dimas

The Cherry Orchard (16). Revival of the play by Anton Chekhov in the Russian language; simultaneous English translation provided by Erika Warmbrunn. Produced by Moscow Arts Festival on Broadway (see note) under the patronage of the Mayor of Moscow (Yuri Luzhkov) and The Russian-American Arts Foundation (Marina and Rina Kovalyov) in the Moscow Sovremennik Theater Company production, Galina Volchek artistic director, Leonid Erman managing director, at the Martin Beck Theater. Opened October 30, 1997. (Closed November 9, 1997)

Ranevska	Marina Neyolova	Epikhodov	Avangard Leontiev
Anya	Maria Anikanova	Dunyasha	Darya Frolova
Varya	Elena Yakolevna	Firs	Rogvold Sukhoverko
Gayev	Igor Kvasha	Yasha	Valery Shalnikh
Lopakhin	Sergei Garmash	Passerby	Aleksander Savostyanov
Trofimov	Aleksander Khovansky	Head of Railway Station	Vladislav Pilnikhov
Simeonov-Pishchik	Gennady Frolov	Postal Official	Vladimir Suvorov
Sharlotta Ivanovna	Galina Petrova		

Directed by Galina Volchek; scenery, Pavel Kaplevich, Peter Kirillov; costumes, Vyacheslav Zaitsev; lighting, Efim Udler, Vladimir Urazbakhtin; composer, Rafail Khozaik; arrangements, Aleksander

Aizenshtadt; assistant director, Aleksander Savostyanov; production stage manager, Olga Sultanova; press, Keith Sherman & Associates, Keith Sherman, Kevin Rehac.

Place: Ranevskaya's estate. The play was presented in two parts.

The last major New York revival of *The Cherry Orchard* was the Peter Brook staging at the Brooklyn Academy of Music 1/23/88 for 87 performances.

Note: The Moscow Arts Festival also presented the Moscow Novaya Opera Theater production of Peter Ilyich Tchaikovsky's opera *Eugene Onegin* at the Martin Beck Theater 11/19–11/30/97, conducted by Evgeny Kolobov and directed by Sergey Artsibashev.

Proposals (76). By Neil Simon. Produced by Emanuel Azenberg at the Broadhurst Theater. Opened November 6, 1997. (Closed January 11, 1998)

Clemma Diggins	L. Scott Caldwell	Annie Robbins	Kelly Bishop
Burt Hines	Dick Latessa	Vinnie Bavasi	Peter Rini
Josie Hines	Suzanne Cryer	Sammii	Katie Finneran
Ken Norman	Reg Rogers	Lewis Barnett	Mel Winkler
Ray Dolenz	Matt Letscher		

Understudies: Miss Caldwell—Brenda Denmark; Miss Bishop—Kit Flanagan; Misses Cryer, Finneran—Nina Garbiras; Mr. Rini—Rick Pasqualone; Mr. Winkler—Chuck Patterson; Mr. Rogers—Rick Pasqualone, Matthew Rauch; Mr. Letscher—Matthew Rauch; Mr. Latessa—Robert Silver.

Directed by Joe Mantello; scenery, John Lee Beatty; costumes, Jane Greenwood; lighting, Brian MacDevitt; sound, Tom Clark; incidental music, Stephen Flaherty; associate producer, Ginger Montel; casting, Jay Binder; production stage manager, William Joseph Barnes; press, Bill Evans & Associates, Jim Randolph, Terry M. Lilly.

Place: Near a resort in the Pocono Mountains, Pennsylvania. The play was presented in two parts.

The romantic adventures of a family on vacation in the Poconos.

Radio City Christmas Spectacular (196). Spectacle including *The Living Nativity* pageant; originally conceived by Robert F. Jani. Produced by Radio City Productions, Arlen Kantarian president, Howard Kolins executive producer, at Radio City Music Hall. Opened November 7, 1997. (Closed January 5, 1998)

RADIO CITY CHRISTMAS SPECTACULAR

Santa Claus; Narrator	Charles Edward Hall	Elves:	
Mrs. Claus	Deborah Bradshaw, Melanie Vaughan	Tinker	Michael J. Gilden
		Thinker	Adam Brown
Clara	Ann Brown, Pamela Elaine O'Herson	Tannenbaum	Rebekah Wood
Skaters	Laurie Welch & Randy Coyne, Karyl Kawaici & Greg Bonin	Bartholomew	Marty Klebba
		Thumbs	Leslie Stump-Vanderpool
Young Boy	Christopher Rayan Trousdale, Reed Van Dyke	Swings	Steve Babiar, Randy John Rowe Jr.

Rockettes: Abby Arauz, Leslie Barlow, Kiki Bennett, Tara Bradley, Christine Brooks, Jessica-Leigh Brown, Dani Brownlee, Elizabeth Charney, Jennifer Clippinger, Cathy Cohen, Renee Collins, Lillian Colon, Helen Conklin, Susan DeCesare, Prudence Gray Demmler, Susanne Doris, Jenny Eakes, Juliet Fisher, Anne Gaertner-Kulakowski, Ida Gilliams, Alison Court Goodman, Julie Harkness, Susan Heart, Vicki Hickerson, Ginny Hounsell, Jennifer Ivascyn, Pamela Jordan, Temple Kane, Donna Kapral, Natalie King, Debby Kole, Amy Krawcek, Christine Laydon, LuAnn Leonard, Shannon Lewis, Judy Little, Kimberly Lyon, Jean Marie, Kelly Marshall, Setsuko Maruhashi, Tabbatha Mays, Mary Frances McCatty, Patrice McConachie, Lori Mello, Dottie Belle Meyman, Beth Woods Nolan, Desiree Parkman, Kerri Pearsall, Renee Perry-Lancaster, Laureen Repp-Russell, Linda Riley-D'Alessio, Kimberly Rokosny, Marisa Rozek, Lainie Sakakura, Tamlin Shusterman, Jane Silane, Leslie Guy Simmons, Alyssa Stec, Jennifer Stetor, Leslie Stroud, Lynn Sullivan (Rockette Captain), Christine Teixeira, Tracy Terstriep, Karyn Tomzak, Kristin Tudor, Rhonda Watson, Darlene Wendy, Marilyn Westlake, Jaime Windrow, Elaine Winslow, Eileen Woods, Deborah Yates, Courtney Young.

Ensemble: Alan Bennett, Linda Bowen, Michelle Chase, Eric Clausell, Michael Clowers, David Combs, Laurie Crochet, Derek Daniels, John Dietrich, Carolyn Doherty, Madeleine Ehlert, Robert

Fowler, Ivy Fox, Darren Gibson, Cynthia Goerig, Jamie Harris, Andrew Hubbard, Susannah Israel, Lesley Jennings, Tom Kosis, Jennifer Krater, Richard Lewis, Michelle Lynch, Troy Magino, Joanne Manning, Richard Mastacusa, Marty McDonough, Corinne McFadden, Michael McGowan, Hannah Meadows, Joni Michelle, Mayumi Miguel, Mark Myers, Ginger Norman, Tina Ou, Sean Palmer, John Salvatore, Tim Santos, Stephen Seale, Michael Serapiglia, Rebecca Sherman, Sam Sinns, Dana Solimando, Scott Spahr, Michael Susko, Kathleen Swanson, Bill Szobody, Jim Testa, David Underwood.

Radio City Orchestra: Henry Aronson conductor; Grant Sturiale assistant conductor; Mary L. Rowell concertmaster; Andrea Andros, Eric De Gioia, Carmine DeLeo, Michael Gillette, Nannette Levi, Susan Lorentsen, Samuel Marder, Holly Ovenden violin; Barbara H. Vaccaro, Richard Spencer viola; Frank Levy, Sarah Carter cello; Dean Crandall bass; Kenneth Emery flute; Gerard J. Niewood, Richard Oatts, John M. Cippola, Joshua Siegel, Kenneth Arzberger reeds; Daniel Culpepper, Nancy Schallert, Lisa Pike, French horn; Richard Raffio, Hollis Burridge, Dave Rodgers trumpet; John D. Schnupp, Thomas B. Olcott, Mark Johansen trombone; Andrew Rogers tuba; Thomas J. Oldakowski drums; Mario DeCiutiis, Maya Gunji percussion; Anthony Cesarano guitar; Susanna Nason, Grant Sturiale piano; Jeanne Maier harp; George Wesner, Fred Davies organ.

Directed and choreographed by Robert Longbottom; musical direction, David Chase; lighting, Ken Billington, Jason Kantrowitz; original orchestrations, Elman Anderson, Douglas Besterman, Michael Gibson, Don Harper, Arthur Harris, Phillip J. Lang, Dick Lieb, Don Pippin, Danny Troob, Jonathan Tunick, Jim Tyler; dance music arrangements, David Chase, Peter Howard, Mark Hummel, Marvin Laird; "Silent Night" arrangement by Percy Faith; associate producer, Steve Kelley; production stage manager, John Bonanni; first assistant stage manager, Robin R. Corbett, Doug Fogel; stage managers, Tom Aberger, Kathy J. Faul, Peggy Imbrie, Carey Lawless, Joseph Onorato, Nichola Taylor; press, Steven Henderson.

Original music—"Santa's Gonna Rock and Roll" and "I Can't Wait Till Christmas Day" music by Henry Krieger, lyrics by Bill Russell, arrangements by Bryan Louiselle; "What Do You Want for Christmas" music by Larry Grossman, lyrics by Hal Hackady; "It's Christmas in New York" by Billy Butt.

65th edition of Radio City Music Hall's Christmas show, starring the Rockettes and including the traditional Nativity pageant, presented without intermission.

SCENES AND MUSICAL NUMBERS: Overture—Radio City Orchestra (arrangement, Don Pippin; film score arrangement, Bryan Louiselle).

Scene 1: Santa's Gonna Rock and Roll—Santa, Rockettes (choreography, Robert Longbottom; scenery, Michael Hotopp; costumes, Gregg Barnes; Rockette dance arrangement, Peter Howard).

Scene 2: *The Nutcracker*, A Little Girl's Dream—(choreography, Robert Longbottom; scenery, Michael Hotopp; costumes, Gregg Barnes).

Scene 3: The Parade of the Wooden Soldiers—Rockettes (choreography, Russell Markert; restaged by Violet Holmes; scenery, Charles Lisanby; costumes, Vincente Minnelli).

Scene 4: Here Comes Santa Claus—Santa (choreography, Robert Longbottom; scenery, Michael Hotopp; costumes, Gregg Barnes; dance music arrangement, David Chase).

Scene 5: Christmas in New York—Rockettes, Radio City Orchestra, Company (choreography, Marianne Selbert; Rockette choreography, Violet Holmes; scenery, Charles Lisanby; gowns and Rockette costumes, Pete Menefee; ice skating coach, Jo Jo Starbuck).

Scene 6: Ice Skating in the Plaza.

Scene 7: Santa & Mrs. Claus: In Concert—(choreography, Robert Longbottom; scenery, Michael Hotopp; costumes, Gregg Barnes; dance music arrangement, David Chase).

Scene 8: Carol of the Bells—Rockettes, Company (choreography, Scott Salmon; scenery, Charles Lisanby; costumes, Pete Menefee).

Scene 9: Santa's Toy Fantasy—Santa, Mrs. Claus, Elves (choreography, Scott Salmon, Linda Haberman; scenery, Charles Lisanby; costumes, Pete Menefee; Elves costumes, Gregg Barnes).

Scene 10: The Living Nativity With One Solitary Life—"Silent Night," "O Little Town of Bethlehem," "The First Noel," "We Three Kings," "O Come All Ye Faithful," "Hark, the Herald Angels Sing" (restaged by Linda Lemac; scenery, Charles Lisanby; costumes, Frank Spencer).

Jubilant, "Joy to the World"—Organ, Company.

*The Scarlet Pimpernel (233). Musical based on the novel by Baroness Orczy; book and lyrics by Nan Knighton; music by Frank Wildhorn. Produced by Pierre Cossette, Bill Haber, Hallmark Entertainment and Ted Forstmann with Kathleen Raitt at the Minskoff Theater. Opened November 9, 1997.

THE SCARLET PIMPERNEL—Douglas Sills as Percy with his men of the League of the Scarlet Pimpernel in the Nan Knighton-Frank Wildhorn musical

Mme. St.Cyr	Marine Jahan
St. Cyr	Tim Shew
Marie	Elizabeth Ward
Tussaud	Philip Hoffman
Dewhurst	James Judy
Chauvelin	Terrence Mann
Percy Blakeney	Douglas Sills
Marguerite St. Just	Christine Andreas
Lady Digby	Sandy Rosenberg
Lady Llewellyn	Pamela Burrell
Armand St. Just	Gilles Chiasson
Ozzy	Ed Dixon
Farleigh	Allen Fitzpatrick
Leggett	Bill Bowers
Elton	Adam Pelty
Hal	Ron Sharpe
Hastings	William Thomas Evans
Ben	Dave Clemmons
Neville	R.F. Daley
Robespierre; Prince of Wales; Fisherman	David Cromwell
Grappin	Ken Labey
Coupeau	Eric Bennyhoff
Mercier	Jeff Gardner
Jessup	James Dybas

French Mob, Soldiers, British Guests, Servants: Stephanie Bast, Nick Cavarra, Sutton Foster, Melissa Hart, Lauri Landry, Alison Lory, Don Mayo, Kevyn Morrow, Katie Nutt, Terry Richmond, Craig Rubano, Charles West.

Orchestra: Ron Melrose conductor; Wendy Bobbitt associate conductor, keyboards; Andrew Wilder assistant conductor, keyboards; Michael Roth concertmaster; Joan Kwuon, Britt Swenson, Lisa Matricardi, Laura Oatts, Ashley Horne violin; Liuh-Wen Ting, Leslie Tomkins viola; Daniel D. Miller, Sarah Hewitt cello; Richard Sarpola bass; Edward Joffe, James Roe, Andrew Sterman, Gilbert Degean woodwinds; Chris Gekker trumpet; Mike Christianson trombone; Chris Komer, Kelly Dent, French horn; Robert Gustafson keyboards; John Meyers, Benjamin Herman percussion.

Standby: Mr. Sills—George Dvorsky. Understudies: Miss Andreas—Lauri Landry; Mr. Mann—Eric Bennyhoff; Mr. Chiasson—Craig Rubano; Mr. Cromwell—James Dybas; Mr. Dixon—Ed Sala; Mr. Judy—Adam Pelty. Swings: Paul Castree, Sarah Knapp, Catherine LaValle, Ed Sala.

Directed by Peter Hunt; choreography, Adam Pelty; scenery, Andrew Jackness; musical direction and vocal arrangements, Ron Melrose; costumes, Jane Greenwood; lighting, Natasha Katz; sound, Karl Richardson; fight direction, Rick Sordelet; orchestrations, Kim Scharnberg; musical supervision, Jason Howland; music coordinator, John Miller; casting, Julie Hughes, Barry Moss; production stage manager, Steven Beckler; stage manager, Bonnie L. Becker; press, Boneau/Bryan-Brown, Adrian Bryan-Brown, Michael Hartman.

Time: May into July, 1794. Place: England and France.

An Englishman disguises himself as a fop in order to lead a band of heroic Englishmen rescuing French aristocrats from the guillotine, as in Baroness Orczy's novel and co-authored play produced on Broadway 10/24/10, a musical version produced off Broadway 1/7/64 for 3 performances and the movie starring Leslie Howard.

ACT I

"Madame Guillotine" .... French Chorus
"Believe" .... Percy, Marguerite, British Chorus
"Vivez!" .... Marguerite, Lady Digby, Lady Llewellyn, Percy, Company
"Prayer" .... Percy
"Into the Fire" .... Percy, His Men
"Falcon in the Dive" .... Chauvelin
"When I Look at You" .... Marguerite
"The Scarlet Pimpernel" .... Percy, Marguerite, Marie, Armand, Lady Digby, Lady Llewellyn, Servants
"Where's the Girl?" .... Chauvelin
"When I Look at You" (Reprise) .... Percy
"The Creation of Man" .... Percy, Prince of Wales, Percy's Men
"The Riddle" .... Chauvelin, Marguerite, Percy, Company

ACT II

"They Seek Him Here" .... Percy, Prince of Wales, Lady Digby, Lady Llewellyn, Company
"Only Love" .... Marguerite
"She Was There" .... Percy
"Storybook" .... Leontine, French Chorus
"Where's the Girl?" (Reprise) .... Chauvelin
"Lullaby" .... Helene, Chloe
"You Are My Home" .... Marguerite, Armand, French Prisoners
"Believe" (Reprise) .... Company

Jackie (128). By Gip Hoppe. Produced by Bob Cuillo, Roger Dean, Mark Schwartz and Jackie International Inc. at the Belasco Theater. Opened November 10, 1997. (Closed March 1, 1998)

CAST: Sotheby's Auctioneer, Janet Bouvier, Betty Fretz, Inga, Eunice Kennedy, Howard K. Smith, Zapruder's Secretary—Lisa Emery.
Jacqueline Kennedy—Margaret Colin.
Black Jack Bouvier, Monty, John Husted, Jean Kennedy, Frank Sinatra, Richard Nixon, Oleg Cassini, Abraham Zapruder, Chorus—Derek Smith.
Lee Bouvier, Susan, Pat Kennedy, Christina Onassis—Gretchen Egolf.
Hugh Auchincloss, Biff Hutchinson III, Bjorn, Bobby Kennedy, Chorus— Bill Camp.
Ward Johnson, Calvin, Charles Bartlett, Teddy Kennedy, Joe Kennedy, Truman Capote, Charles Collingwood, Aristotle Onassis, Mur Doch—Thomas Derrah.
Martha Bartlett, Rose Kennedy, Marilyn Monroe, Sander Vanocer—Kristine Nielsen.
John Fitzgerald Kennedy, Ron Galella—Victor Slezak.
The Rat Pack, Ron Galella, Secret Service—Sam Catlin.
Secret Service—Linda Marie Larson.

American, French Citizens, Greeks, Appliances, Furniture: Thomas Derrah, Gretchen Egolf, Lisa Emery, Linda Marie Larson, Bill Camp, Sam Catlin, Kristine Nelson, Derek Smith, Victor Slezak.
Understudies: Miss Colin—Gretchen Egolf; Messrs. Camp, Derrah—Kent Adams, Sam Catlin; Messrs. Slezak, Catlin—Kent Adams; Mr. Smith—Sam Catlin; Women—Linda Marie Larson, Maggie Moore.

Directed by Gip Hoppe; scenery, David Gallo; costumes, Susan Santoian; lighting, Peter Kaczo-rowski; sound, J. Hagenbuckle; puppets, The Big Nazo Studio; musical staging, Lynne Taylor-Corbett; associate producer, Moin Kirmani; casting, Bernard Telsey; production stage manager, James Harker; stage manager, Lindsey Ferguson; press, The Pete Sanders Group, Pete Sanders, Clint Bond Jr.

Scenes from the life of Jacqueline Bouvier Kennedy Onassis.

*The Lion King (229). Musical adapted from the screen play by Irene Mecchi, Jonathan Roberts and Linda Woolverton; book by Roger Allers and Irene Mecchi; music by Elton John; lyrics by Tim Rice; additional music and lyrics by Lebo M, Mark Mancina, Jay Rifkin, Julie Taymor and Hans Zimmer. Produced by Disney at the New Amsterdam Theater. Opened November 13, 1997.

Rafiki	Tsidii Le Loka	Shenzi	Tracy Nicole Chapman
Mufasa	Samuel E. Wright	Banzai	Stanley Wayne Mathis
Sarabi	Gina Breedlove	Ed	Kevin Cahoon
Zazu	Geoff Hoyle	Timon	Max Casella
Scar	John Vickery	Pumbaa	Tom Alan Robbins
Young Simba	Scott Irby-Ranniar	Simba	Jason Raize
Young Nala	Kajuana Shuford	Nala	Heather Headly

Ensemble Singers: Eugene Barry-Hill, Gina Breedlove, Ntomb'khona Dlamini, Sheila Gibbs, Lindiwe Hlengwa, Christopher Jackson, Vanessa A. Jones, Faca Kulu, Ron Kunene, Philip Dorian McAdoo, Sam McKelton, Lebo M, Nandi Morake.

Ensemble Dancers: Camille M. Brown, Iresol Cardona, Mark Allan Davis, Lana Gordon, Timothy Hunter, Michael Joy, Aubrey Lynch II (dance captain), Karine Plantadit-Bageot, Endalyn Taylor-Shellman, Levensky Smith, Ashi K. Smythe, Christine Yasunaga.

Orchestra: Joseph Church conductor; Karl Jurman associate conductor, keyboard synthesizer; Claudia Hafer-Tondi concertmistress; David Weiss wood flute soloist, flute, piccolo; Francisca Mendoza, Avril Brown violin; Ralph Farris violin, viola; Eliana Mendoza, Bruce Wang cello; Bob Keller flute, clarinet, bass clarinet; Dan Grabois, Kait Mahoney, Jeff Scott, French horn; Rock Ciccarone trombone; George Flynn bass trombone, tuba; Luico Hopper upright and electric basses; Tommy Igoe drums; Kevin Kuhn guitar; Valerie Dee Naranjo, Tom Brett mallets, percussion; Junior "Gabu" Wedderburn, Rolando Morales-Matos percussion; Ted Baker, Cynthia Kortman keyboard synthesizer.

Understudies: Miss Le Loka—Sheila Gibbs, Lindiwe Hlengwa; Mr. Wright—Eugene Barry-Hill, Philip Dorian McAdoo; Miss Breedlove—Camille M. Brown, Vanessa A. Jones; Mr. Hoyle—Kevin Cahoon, Danny Rutigliano; Mr. Vickery—Kevin Bailey; Mr. Irby-Ranniar—Kai Braithwaite; Miss Shuford—Jennifer Josephs; Miss Chapman—Lana Gordon, Vanessa A. Jones; Mr. Mathis—Philip Dorian McAdoo, Levensky Smith; Mr. Cahoon—Timothy Hunter, Frank Wright II; Mr. Casella—Kevin Cahoon, Danny Rutigliano; Mr. Robbins—Philip Dorian McAdoo, Danny Rutigliano; Mr. Raize—Timothy Hunter, Christopher Jackson; Miss Headley—Lindiwe Hlengwa, Sonya Leslie.

Directed by Julie Taymor; choreography, Garth Fagan; musical direction, Joseph Church; scenery, Richard Hudson; costumes, Julie Taymor; lighting, Donald Holder; mask and puppet design, Julie Taymor, Michael Curry; sound, Tony Meola; orchestrations, Robert Elhai, David Metzger, Bruce Fowler; music coordinator, Michael Keller; vocal arrangements and choral direction, Lebo M; music produced for the stage by Mark Mancina; associate musical producer, Robert Elhai; production stage manager, Jeff Lee; stage managers, Mahlon Kruse, Elizabeth Burgess, Steve Zorthian; press, Boneau/Bryan-Brown, Chris Boneau, Jackie Green.

As in the Disney film *The Lion King* on which it is based, a lion cub is robbed of his royal heritage by the murder of his father and usurpation by his uncle, then recaptures his kingdom with the help of his friends—here enacted by a cast imaginatively costumed as African animals and birds. Winner of the 1997–98 New York Drama Critics Circle and Tony Awards for best musical; see the Prizewinning Plays section of this volume.

ACT I

(New material for the Broadway musical, except as noted)
Scene 1: Pride Rock
    "Circle of Life"*** .... Rafiki, Ensemble

Scene 2: Scar's cave
Scene 3: Rafiki's tree
Scene 4: The Pridelands
"The Morning Report" .... Zazu, Young Simba, Mufasa
Scene 5: Scar's cave
Scene 6: The Pridelands
"I Just Can't Wait To Be King"*** .... Young Simba, Young Nala, Zazu, Ensemble
Scene 7: Elephant graveyard
"Chow Down"* .... Shenzi, Banzai, Ed
Scene 8: Under the Stars
"They Live in You"** .... Mufasa, Ensemble
        (music and lyrics by Mark Mancina, Jay Rifkin and Lebo M)
Scene 9: Elephant graveyard
"Be Prepared"*** .... Scar, Shenzi, Banzai, Ed, Ensemble
Scene 10: The gorge
Scene 11: Pride Rock
"Be Prepared" (Reprise) .... Scar, Ensemble
Scene 12: Rafiki's tree
Scene 13: The desert/the jungle
"Hakuna Matata"*** .... Timon, Pumbaa, Young Simba, Simba, Ensemble

ACT II

Entr'acte: "One by One"** .... Ensemble
        (music and lyrics by Lebo M)
Scene 1: Scar's cave
"The Madness of King Scar"* .... Scar, Zazu, Banzai, Shenzi, Ed, Nala
Scene 2: The Pridelands
"Shadowland"** .... Nala, Rafiki, Ensemble
        (music by Hans Zimmer and Lebo M, lyrics by Mark Mancina and Lebo M)
Scene 3: The jungle
Scene 4: Under the Stars
"Endless Night"** .... Simba, Ensemble
        (music by Lebo M, Hans Zimmer and Jay Rifkin, lyrics by Julie Taymor)
Scene 5: Rafiki's tree
Scene 6: The jungle
"Can You Feel the Love Tonight"*** .... Timon, Pumbaa, Simba, Nala, Ensemble
"He Lives in You" (Reprise) .... Rafiki, Simba, Ensemble
Scene 7: Pride Rock
"King of Pride Rock"** .... Ensemble
        (music by Hans Zimmer, lyrics by Lebo M)
"Circle of Life" .... Ensemble
*Written by Elton John and Tim Rice for the Broadway musical
**New material based on songs from the animated feature's follow-up album
***From the animated feature
Grasslands chant and Lioness chant by Lebo M; Rafiki's chants by Tsidii Le Loka.

Madison Square Garden Productions. Schedule of two return engagements. **A Christmas Carol** (96). Musical based on the story by Charles Dickens; book by Mike Ockrent and Lynn Ahrens; music by Alan Menken; lyrics by Lynn Ahrens. Opened November 18, 1997. (Closed January 4, 1998) **The Wizard of Oz** (46). Musical based on the novel by L. Frank Baum; adapted by Robert Johanson; music and lyrics of the motion picture score by Harold Arlen and E.Y. Harburg; background music by Herbert Stothart. Opened May 1, 1998. (Closed May 31, 1998) Produced by Madison Square Garden Productions, Tim Hawkins producer, at the Madison Square Garden Theater.

A CHRISTMAS CAROL

Beadle .... Del-Bourree Bach
Mr. Smythe .... Chris Vasquez
Grace Smythe .... Tavia Rivee Jefferson,
                                    Olivia Oguma
Scrooge .... Hal Linden, Roddy McDowall
Cratchit .... Todd Gross
Old Joe; Mr. Hawkins .... Kenneth McMullen
Mrs. Cratchit .... Robin Baxter
Tiny Tim ...., Christopher Cordell,
                              Patrick J.P. Duffey
Poulterer; Judge .... Roland Rusinek
Sandwichboard Man;
   Ghost of Christmas Present .... Ken Page
Jonathon .... Adam Barruch,
                          Christopher Marquette
Lamplighter; Ghost of
   Christmas Past .... Joel Blum
Blind Hag; Scrooge's Mother ... Debra Cardona

Fred .... Paul Jackel
Mrs. Mopps .... Marilyn Pasekoff
Ghost of Jacob Marley .... Paul Kandel
Scrooge at 8; Ignorance .... Anthony Blair Hall,
                          Joseph Louis Santos III
Fan at 6; Want .. Zoe Petkanas, Gemini Quintos
Scrooge's Father;
   Undertaker .... Wayne Schroder
Scrooge at 12 .... Paul Franklin Dano,
                                  Evan Silverberg
Fan at 10 ...... Elizabeth Lundberg, Jenell Slack
Fezziwig .... Ray Friedeck
Scrooge at 18 .... Tom Stuart
Young Marley; Undertaker .... Ken Barnett
Mrs. Fezziwig .... Joy Hermalyn
Emily .... Kate Dawson
Fiddler .... Brad Bradley
Sally .... Whitney Webster
Ghost of Christmas Future ... Christine Dunham

Charity Men: Roland Rusinek, Wayne Pretlow, Erik Stein.
Street Urchins: Paul Franklin Dano, Anthony Blair Hall, Zoe Petkanas, Gemini Quintos, Joseph Louis Santos III, Evan Silverberg.
Lights of Christmas Past: Matthew Baker, Christopher F. Davis, Sean Haythe, Sean Thomas Morrissey.
The Cratchit Children: Paul Franklin Dano, Elizabeth Lundberg, Sean Thomas Morrissey, Jenell Slack, Evan Silverberg.
Business Men, Gifts, Ghosts, People of London: Del-Bourree Bach, Matthew Baker, Ken Barnett, Robin Baxter, Leslie Bell, Carol Bentley, Renee Bergeron, Brad Bradley, Debra Cardona, Candy Cook, Christopher F. Davis, Kate Dawson, Ray Friedeck, Peter Gregus, James Hadley, Sean Haythe, Joy Hermalyn, Paul Jackel, Louisa Kendrick, Carrie Kenneally, Donna Lee Marshall, Kenneth McMullen, Aixa M. Rosario-Medina, Elizabeth Mills, Sean Thomas Morrissey, Christopher Nilsson, Marilyn Pasekoff, Meredith Patterson, Wayne Pretlow, Gail Pennington, Josef Reiter, Pamela Remler, Samuel Reni, Roland Rusinek, Vikki Schnurr, Erik Stein, Tom Stuart, Chris Vasquez, Whitney Webster.
Swings: Rachel Black, Alex Brumel, Dana Chechile, Alexander Dollin, Rob Donohoe, Carissa Farina, Brett Figliozzi, Matt L. Hedge, Yvonne Meyer, Rommy Sandhu, Scott Taylor, Cynthia Thole, Jeff Williams.
Angels and Children's Choirs: Park Middle School, M.S. 330, South Middle School, P.S. 95.
Red Children's Cast: Adam Baruch, Alex Brumel, Dana Chechile, Christopher Cordell, Paul Franklin Dano, Anthony Blair Hall, Matt L. Hedge, Elizabeth Lundberg, Olivia Oguma, Zoe Petkanas.
Green Children's Cast: Alexander Dollin, Patrick J.P. Duffey, Carissa Farina, Brett Figliozzi, Tavia Riveé Jefferson, Christopher Marquette, Gemini Quintos, Joseph Louis Santos III, Evan Silverberg, Jenell Slack.
Orchestra: Paul Gemignani conductor; Mark C. Mitchell associate conductor, keyboards; Karl Kawahara, Ann Labin, Sebu Serinian violin; Clay Ruede cello; Charles Bergeron bass; Les Scott, Kenneth Dybisz, Alva Hunt, Daniel Wieloszynski, John Winder woodwinds; Stu Sataloff, Phil Granger, Dominic Derasse trumpet; Ronald Sell, French horn; Phil Sasson, Dean Plank trombone; Nick Archer keyboards; Jennifer Hoult harp; Michael Berkowitz drums; Glenn Rhian percussion.
Directed by Mike Ockrent; choreography, Susan Stroman; musical direction, Paul Gemignani; scenery, Tony Walton; costumes, William Ivey Long; lighting, Jules Fisher, Peggy Eisenhauer; sound, Tony Meola; projections, Wendall K. Harrington; flying, Foy; orchestrations, Michael Starobin, Douglas Besterman; dance arrangements and incidental music, Glen Kelly; associate director, Steven Zweigbaum; associate choreographer, Chris Peterson; casting, Julie Hughes, Barry Moss; production stage manager, Steven Zweigbaum; stage manager, Rolt Smith; press, Cathy Del Priore.
Time: 1880. Place: London. The play was presented without intermission.
This is the fourth annual production of this musical version of A Christmas Carol.

SCENES AND MUSICAL NUMBERS

Scene 1: The Royal Exchange

"A Jolly Good Time" .... Charity Men, Smythe Family, Business Men, Wives, Children
"Nothing to Do With Me" .... Scrooge, Cratchit
Scene 2: The street
"You Mean More to Me" .... Cratchit, Tiny Tim
"Street Song (Nothing to Do With Me)" .... People of London, Scrooge, Fred,
                    Jonathon, Sandwichboard Man, Lamplighter, Blind Hag, Grace Smythe
Scene 3: Scrooge's house
"Link by Link" .... Marley's Ghost, Scrooge, Ghosts
Scene 4: Scrooge's bedchamber
"The Lights of Long Ago" .... Ghost of Christmas Past
Scene 5: The law courts
"God Bless Us, Everyone" .... Scrooge's Mother, Fan at 6
Scene 6: The factory
"A Place Called Home" .... Scrooge at 12, Fan at 10, Scrooge
Scene 7: Fezziwig's Banking House
"Mr. Fezziwig's Annual Christmas Ball" .... Fezziwig, Mrs. Fezziwig, Guests
"A Place Called Home" (Reprise) .... Emily, Scrooge at 18, Scrooge
Scene 8: Scrooge and Marley's
"The Lights of Long Ago" (Part II) .... Scrooge at 18, Young Marley, Emily,
                                                            People From Scrooge's Past
Scene 9: A starry night
"Abundance and Charity" .... Ghost of Christmas Present, Scrooge, Christmas Gifts
Scene 10: All over London
"Christmas Together" .... Tiny Tim, The Cratchits, Ghost of Christmas Present,
                                                    Fred, Sally, Scrooge, People of London
Scene 11: The graveyard
"Dancing on Your Grave" .... Ghost of Christmas Future, Monks, Business Men,
                                              Mrs. Mopps, Undertakers, Old Joe, Cratchit
"Yesterday, Tomorrow and Today" .... Scrooge, Angels, Children of London
Scene 12: Scrooge's bedchamber
"London Town Carol" .... Jonathon
Scene 13: The street, Christmas Day
"Nothing to Do With Me" (Reprise) .... Scrooge
"Christmas Together" (Reprise) .... People of London
"God Bless Us, Everyone" (Finale) .... Company

THE WIZARD OF OZ

In Kansas:
Dorothy Gale .... Jessica Grové
Toto .... Plenty
Aunt Em .... Judith McCauley
Uncle Henry .... Bob Dorian
Hunk .... Lara Teeter
Hickory .... Dirk Lumbard
Zeke .... Ken Page
Almira Gulch .... Eartha Kitt
Professor Marvel .... Mickey Rooney
In Oz:
Glinda .... Judith McCauley

Mayor of Munchkinland ..... Eugene Pidgeon
Barristers .... Steve Babiar, Wendy Coates
Coroner .... P.J. Terranova
Wicked Witch of the West .... Eartha Kitt
Scarecrow .... Lara Teeter
Tin Man .... Dirk Lombard
Cowardly Lion .... Ken Page
Wizard of Oz .... Mickey Rooney
Nikko .... Martin Klebba
Winkie General .... Bob Dorian

Lollipop Guild: Martin Klebba, Mark Povinelli, Deborah Wilson. Crows: Renee Bonadio, Christine
DeVito, Martin Klebba. Crow Voices: D'Ambrose Boyd, Casey Colgan, Daniel Herron, D.J. Salisbury,
Russell Warfield. Apple Trees: Casey Colgan, Daniel Herron, D.J. Salisbury. Apple Tree Voices: Gail
Cook Howell, Heidi Karol Johnson, Angela Robinson. Dance Captain: Donna Drake.

Munchkins, Poppies, Citizens of Oz, Jitterbugs, Flying Monkeys, Winkies: Steve Babiar, Renee Bon-
adio, D'Ambrose Boyd, Bill Brassea, Wendy Coates, Casey Colgan, Christine DeVito, Kassandra Marie
Hazard, Kristopher Michael Hazard, Daniel Herron, Gail Cook Howell, Heidi Karol Johnson, Martin
Klebba, Shauna Markey, Andrea McCormick, Caroline McMahon, Eugene Pidgeon, Mark Povinelli,
Angela Robinson, Mary Ruvolo, D.J. Salisbury, Kristi Sperling, Andrea Szücks, Leslie Stump-Vander-

pool, P.J. Terranova, Russell Warfield, Wendy Watts, Deborah Wilson. Swings: Lenny Daniel, Donna Drake, Ron Gibbs, Jamie Waggoner.

Orchestra: Jeff Rizzo conductor; Rick Dolan concertmaster; Heidi Modr, Peter Martin Weimar violin; Maxine Roach viola; Chungsun Kim cello; Joseph Bongiorno bass; Svjetlana Kabalan flute; Lynne Cohen oboe; Mark Thrasher, Eddie Salkin, Don McGeen woodwinds; Katie Dennis, Kelly Dent horns; Rich Raffio, Liesl Whitaker trumpet; Mike Christianson trombone; Richard Rosenzweig drums; Lou Oddo percussion; Nina Kellman harp; Don Hite, Maggie Torre, Madelyn Rubinstein keyboards.

Understudies: Mr. Lumbard—Daniel Herron, D.J. Salisbury; Mr. Teeter—Casey Colgan; Mr. Dorian—Lenny Daniel; Miss Kitt—Angela Robinson, Heidi Karol Johnson; Miss McCauley—Gail Cook Howell, Jamie Waggoner; Mr. Page—D'Ambrose Boyd, Russell Warfield; Miss Grové—Caroline McMahon, Christine DeVito; Mr. Rooney—Bob Dorian; Plenty—Ashley; Mr. Pidgeon—Steve Babiar; Mr. Terranova—Ron Gibbs.

Directed by Robert Johanson; choreography, Jamie Rocco; musical direction and additional orchestrations, Jeff Rizzo; scenery, Michael Anania; costumes, Gregg Barnes; lighting, Tim Hunter; sound, David Paterson, Mark Menard; orchestrations, Larry Wilcox; dance and vocal arrangements, Peter Howard; animals, William Berloni; special effects, Ian O'Connor; flying, Foy; associate choreographer, Donna Drake; music coordinator, John Miller; casting, Julie Hughes, Barry Moss; production stage manager, John C. McNamara.

This is the second annual Madison Square Garden Productions presentation of this musical, which was first produced by the Paper Mill Playhouse, Angelo Del Rossi executive producer. The play was presented without intermission.

MUSICAL NUMBERS

Overture .... Orchestra
Scene 1: The Gales' farm in Kansas
"Over the Rainbow" .... Dorothy
Scene 2: Professor Marvel's wagon
Scene 3: The Gales' farm
"The Cyclone"
Scene 4: Munchkinland
"Come Out, Come Out" .... Glinda, Dorothy, Lollipop Guild, Munchkins
"Ding Dong the Witch Is Dead!" .... Glinda, Mayor, Barristers, Coroner, Munchkins
"Follow the Yellow Brick Road" .... Dorothy, Munchkins
Scene 5: A cornfield
"If I Only Had a Brain" .... Scarecrow, Dorothy, Crows
"We're Off to See the Wizard" .... Dorothy, Scarecrow
Scene 6: An apple orchard
"If I Only Had a Heart" .... Tin Man, Dorothy, Scarecrow, Apple Trees
"We're Off to See the Wizard" .... Dorothy, Scarecrow, Tin Man
Scene 7: A wild forest
"Lions, Tigers and Bears" .... Dorothy, Scarecrow, Tin Man
"If I Only Had the Nerve"/"We're Off to See
the Wizard" .... Cowardly Lion, Dorothy, Tin Man, Scarecrow
Scene 8: A field of poppies
"Poppies"/"Optimistic Voices" .... Glinda, Dorothy, Scarecrow, Tin Man,
Cowardly Lion, Wicked Witch, Poppies
Scene 9: Outside the gates of the Emerald City
"Optimistic Voices" .... Female Chorus
Scene 10: Inside the Emerald City
"The Merry Old Land of Oz" .... Dorothy, Scarecrow, Tin Man, Cowardly Lion,
Guard, Citizens of Oz
"King of the Forest" .... Cowardly Lion, Dorothy, Tin Man, Scarecrow
Scene 11: The Wizard's chamber
Scene 12: The Haunted Forest
"March of the Winkies" .... Winkies
"The Jitterbug" .... Wicked Witch, Dorothy, Cowardly Lion,
Scarecrow, Tin Man, Jitterbugs
Scene 13: Inside the Witch's castle
"Ding Dong the Witch Is Dead!" (Reprise) .... Winkies, Dorothy, Cowardly Lion,
Scarecrow, Tin Man

THE OLD NEIGHBORHOOD—Patti LuPone and Peter Riegert in a scene from David Mamet's program of one-act plays

The Old Neighborhood (197). By David Mamet. Produced by Carole Shorenstein Hays and Stuart Thompson at the Booth Theater. Opened November 19, 1997. (Closed May 2, 1998)

The Disappearance of the Jews		Jolly .... Patti LuPone
Bobby .... Peter Riegert		Carl .... Jack Willis
Joey .... Vincent Guastaferro		*Deeny*
Jolly		Bobby .... Peter Riegert
Bobby .... Peter Riegert		Deeny .... Rebecca Pidgeon

Standbys: Mr. Riegert—Jordan Lage; Misses LuPone, Pidgeon—Mary McCann; Messrs. Guastaferro, Willis—Jim Frangione.

Directed by Scott Zigler; scenery, Kevin Rigdon; costumes, Harriet Voyt; lighting, John Ambrosone; casting, Laura Richin; production stage manager, Richard Hester; press, Philip Rinaldi, Barbara Carroll.

A trio of episodes in a divorced middle-aged man's emotion-generating visit to his old Chicago neighborhood. In *The Disappearance of the Jews,* he reminisces over a drink with an old friend; in *Jolly,* he spends an evening going over his family's past with his sister and her husband; in *Deeny,* he comes face to face with his ex-wife. The play was presented without intermission. Previously produced in regional theater by American Repertory Theater, Cambridge, Mass., Robert Brustein artistic director.

Mary McCann replaced Rebecca Pidgeon 1/98.

Lincoln Center Theater. Schedule of three revivals. **Ivanov** (51). Revival of the play by Anton Chekhov; adapted by David Hare. Opened November 20, 1997. (Closed January 4, 1998) **Ah, Wilderness!** (54). Revival of the play by Eugene O'Neill. Opened March 18, 1998. (Closed

May 3, 1998) And *Twelfth Night* by William Shakespeare scheduled to open 7/16/98. Produced by Lincoln Center Theater under the direction of Andre Bishop and Bernard Gersten at the Vivian Beaumont Theater.

IVANOV

Nikolai Ivanov	Kevin Kline	Avdotya Nazarovna	Lynn Cohen
Mikhail Borkin	Tom McGowan	Kosykh	Jeff Weiss
Anna Petrovna	Jayne Atkinson	Pavel Lebedev	Max Wright
Count Matvyei Shabyelski	Robert Foxworth	Sasha	Hope Davis
Yevgeni Lvov	Rob Campbell	Gavrila	William Preston
Zinaida Savishna	Marian Seldes	Pyotr	Stuart Zamsky
Marfusha Babakina	Judith Hawking		

Guests: Joan Buddenhagen, Jane Cronin, John Michael Gilbert, Lawrence Nathanson, John Newton, Thomas Schall, Evan Thompson, Susan Wilder, Stuart Zamsky.

Understudies: Mr. Kline—Thomas Schall; Messrs. McGowan, Zamsky—Lawrence Nathanson; Misses Atkinson, Hawking—Susan Wilder; Messrs. Foxworth, Preston—Evan Thompson; Mr. Campbell—John Michael Gilbert; Misses Seldes, Cohen—Jane Cronin; Messrs. Wright, Weiss—John Newton; Miss Davis—Joan Buddenhagen; Guests—Stuart Zamsky.

Directed by Gerald Gutierrez; scenery, John Lee Beatty; costumes, Catherine Zuber; lighting, James F. Ingalls; original music, Robert Waldman; sound, Aural Fixation; *"Andante Cantabile"* from String Quartet #1 in D by Peter Ilyich Tchaikovsky; casting, Daniel Swee; stage manager, Frank Hartenstein; press, Philip Rinaldi.

Time: The late 1880s. Place: A province in Central Russia. Act I: The garden of Ivanov's estate. Act II: A reception room at the Lebedevs' house. Act III: Ivanov's study. Act IV: One year later, a drawing room in the Lebedevs' house. The play was presented in two parts with the intermission following Act III.

The last major New York revival of *Ivanov* took place on Broadway 5/3/66 for 33 performances in the John Gielgud adaptation.

AH, WILDERNESS!

Essie Miller	Debra Monk	McComber	James Murtaugh
Tommy	Rufus H. Read	Norah	Siobhan Dunne
Nat Miller	Craig T. Nelson	Wint Selby	Mark Rosenthal
Mildred	Jenna Lamia	Belle	Jenn Thompson
Arthur	Dylan Chalfy	Bartender	Steven Marcus
Lily Miller	Leslie Lyles	Salesman	Jack Davidson
Sid Davis	Leo Burmester	Muriel McComber	Tracy Middendorf
Richard	Sam Trammell		

Understudies: Messrs. Nelson, Burmester—Jack Davidson; Misses Monk, Lyles—Susan Pellegrino; Messrs. Chalfy, Trammell, Rosenthal—Joshua Wade Miller; Misses Lamia, Middendorf, Thompson, Dunne—Emily Bergl; Mr. Read—Casey Klein; Messrs. Murtaugh, Marcus, Davidson—Edward James Hyland.

Directed by Daniel Sullivan; scenery, Thomas Lynch; costumes, Dunya Ramicova; lighting, Peter Kaczorowski; original music, Stanley Silverman; sound, Scott Lehrer; casting, Daniel Swee; stage manager, Roy Harris.

Time: 1906. Place: A small town in Connecticut. Act I, Scene 1: The porch of the Miller home, July the Fourth. Scene 2: That evening. Act II, Scene 1: Back room of a bar, 11 o'clock that night. Scene 2: Miller sitting-room, around 11 o'clock the same night. Act III, Scene 1: Porch of the Miller home, 1 o'clock the following afternoon. Scene 2: A strip of beach, around 9 o'clock that night. Scene 3: Nat and Essie's bedroom, around 10 o'clock that night.

The last major New York production of *Ah, Wilderness!* took place on Broadway 6/14/88 for 12 performances.

Street Corner Symphony (79). Musical conceived by Marion J. Caffey. Produced by Kenneth Waissman and Bryan Bantry at the Brooks Atkinson Theater. Opened November 24, 1997. (Closed February 1, 1998)

Clarence .... Eugene Fleming
Narrator; Mrs. Cynthia .... Carol Dennis
Jessie Lee .... Jose Llana
Sukki .... Catherine Morin

C.J. .... C.E. Smith
Debbie .... Debra Walton
Chip .... Victor Trent Cook
Susan .... Stacy Francis

Orchestra: Lon Hoyt conductor, synthesizer; Ronald Metcalfe associate conductor, synthesizer; Konrad Adderley bass; Annette Aguilar percussion; Steve Bargonetti guitar; Jimmy Cozier woodwinds; Clint de Ganon drums; Craig Johnson trumpet.

Understudies: Miss Dennis—Toni SeaWright; Misses Francis, Morin, Walton—CJay Hardy; Men—Jamie.

Directed by Marion J. Caffey; musical direction, Lon Hoyt; scenery, Neil Peter Jampolis; costumes, Jonathan Bixby; lighting, Jules Fisher, Peggy Eisenhauer; sound, Jonathan Deans; musical supervision, orchestrations and dance music arrangements, Daryl Waters; vocal arrangements, Michael McElroy; musical coordinator, Seymour Red Press; associate producer, Sharleen Cooper Cohen; casting, Peter Wise & Associates; production stage manager, Robert Mark Kalfin; stage manager, Jimmie Lee Smith; press, The Pete Sanders Group, Pete Sanders, Helene Davis.

Young people of the 1960s and 70s weaving the song hits of the era into their lives.

ACT I: Neighborhood Memories—The 1960s

"Dancing in the Street" .... Company
"Dance to the Music" .... Company
"Try to Remember"/"The Way We Were" .... Mrs. Cynthia
"The Way You Do the Things You Do" .... Clarence, Guys
"Good Old Acapella" .... C.J., Company
"I Wanna Know Your Name" .... Chip, Guys
"My Boyfriend's Back" .... Sukki, Debbie, Susan
"It's in His Kiss" (Shoop Shoop Song) .... Susan, Sukki, Debbie
"Hot Fun in the Summertime" .... Company
"Baby Workout" .... Jessie-Lee, Company
"Dance Chant" .... Company
"Baby Workout" (Reprise) .... Jessie-Lee, Company
"Grandma's Hands" .... Mrs. Cynthia, C.J., Debbie
"Dancing in the Street" (Reprise) .... Clarence, Company
"Love Is Like a Heat Wave" .... Sukki, Debbie, Susan
"Please, Please, Please" .... C.J., Company
"Unchained Melody" .... C.J.
"Good Old Acapella" (Reprise) .... C.J., Guys
"Grandma's Hands" (Reprise) .... Mrs. Cynthia
"Psychedelic Shack" .... Company
"I Want to Take You Higher" .... Company
"Cloud Nine" .... Company
"I Want to Take You Higher" (Reprise) .... Company
"Love's in Need of Love Today" .... Mrs. Cynthia
"Ohio"/"Machine Gun" .... Jessie-Lee, Company
"American Pie" .... Mrs. Cynthia
"Love's in Need of Love Today"/"American Pie" (Reprise) .... Company

ACT II: Concert Fantasies—The 1970s

"Get Ready" .... Chip, Company
"Want Ads" .... Susan, Sukki, Debbie
"Love Train" .... Clarence, Guys
"Oh Girl" .... Jessie-Lee, Guys
"Betcha By Golly Wow" .... Chip, Guys
"Heaven Must Be Missing an Angel" .... Guys
"The Tracks of My Tears" .... Susan
"Can I?" .... Chip
"Midnight Train to Georgia" .... Mrs. Cynthia, Clarence, Jessie-Lee, C.J.
"Me and Mrs. Jones" .... Guys

"Proud Mary" .... Debbie, Sukki, Susan
"Hold on I'm Coming" .... C.J., Clarence
"Soul Man" .... C.J., Clarence
"End of the Road" .... Mrs. Cynthia, Company
"Love Train" (Reprise) .... Company

*The Diary of Anne Frank (208). Revival of the play by Frances Goodrich and Albert Hackett; newly adapted by Wendy Kesselman. Produced by David Stone, Amy Nederlander-Case, Jon B. Platt, Jujamcyn Theaters and Hal Luftig in association with Harriet Newman Leve and James D. Stern at The Music Box. Opened December 4, 1997.

Anne Frank	Natalie Portman	Mr. Van Daan	Harris Yulin
Otto Frank	George Hearn	Mrs. Van Daan	Linda Lavin
Edith Frank	Sophie Hayden	Mr. Dussel	Austin Pendleton
Margot Frank	Missy Yager	lst Man	Peter Kybart
Miep Gies	Jessica Walling	2d Man	James Hallett
Peter Van Daan	Jonathan Kaplan	3d Man	Eddie Kaye Thomas
Mr. Kraler	Philip Goodwin		

Understudies: Misses Portman, Yager, Walling—Kieren van den Blink; Messrs. Hearn, Yulin—Peter Kybart; Misses Hayden, Lavin—Lori Wilner; Mr. Kaplan—Eddie Kaye Thomas; Mr. Goodwin—James Hallett; Mr. Pendleton—Philip Goodwin.

Directed by James Lapine; scenery, Adrianne Lobel; costumes, Martin Pakledinaz; lighting, Brian MacDevitt; sound, Dan Moses Schreier; casting, Ilene Starger; production stage manager, David Hyslop; stage manager, Greg Schanuel; press, The Publicity Office, Bob Fennell, Marc Thibodeau, Michael S. Borowski.

Time: During the years of World War II. Place: The top floors of the annex to an office building in Amsterdam, Holland.

This revised version of the drama based on the book *Anne Frank: The Diary of a Young Girl* includes some new material from its source and the redirection of some of its emphases. The last major New York revival of this work took place on Broadway 12/28/78 for 78 performances.

Lori Wilner replaced Sophie Hayden 1/20/98. Rachel Miner replaced Missy Yager 2/19/98. Nathalie Paulding replaced Natalie Portman 6/2/98. Sophie Hayden replaced Lori Wilner 4/7/98.

*The Sunshine Boys (191). Revival of the play by Neil Simon. Produced by National Actors Theater, Tony Randall founder and chairman, Winton M. Blount president, at the Lyceum Theater. Opened December 8, 1997.

Willie Clark	Jack Klugman	Eddie	Stephen Beach
Ben Silverman	Matthew Arkin	Sketch Nurse	Peggy Joyce Crosby
Al Lewis	Tony Randall	Registered Nurse	Ebony Jo-Ann
Patient	Jack Aaron	Voice; TV Director	Martin Rudy

Standbys: Mr. Randall—Jack Aaron; Mr. Klugman—Martin Rudy. Understudies: Mr. Arkin—Stephen Beach; Misses Crosby, Jo-Ann—Anita Dashiell.

Directed by John Tillinger; scenery, James Noone; costumes, Noel Taylor; lighting, Kirk Bookman; sound, Richard Fitzgerald; executive producer, Manny Kladitis; casting, Deborah Brown; production stage manager, Anita Ross; press, Springer/Chicoine Public Relations, Gary Springer, Susan Chicoine.

Act I, Scene 1: An apartment in an old hotel on upper Broadway in New York City, early afternoon, mid-winter. Scene 2: The following Monday, a few minutes before eleven. Act II, Scene 1: A television studio. Scene 2: Willie's apartment two weeks later, late afternoon.

The Sunshine Boys was first produced on Broadway 12/20/72 for 538 performances and was named a Best Play of its season. This is its first major New York revival.

*Roundabout Theater Company. Schedule of three revivals. *A View From the Bridge (161). By Arthur Miller. Opened December 14 , 1997. (Closed February 22, 1998). Reopened at the Neil Simon Theater April 15, 1998; see note. *Cabaret (85). Revival of the musical based on the play by John Van Druten and stories by Christopher Isherwood; book by Joe Masteroff; music by John Kander; lyrics by Fred Ebb. Opened March 19, 1998. **The Deep Blue Sea** (61). By Terence Rattigan. Opened March 26, 1998. (Closed May 17, 1998) Produced by Roundabout Theater Company, Todd Haimes artistic director, Ellen Richard general manager, *A View From the Bridge* and *The Deep Blue Sea* at Criterion Center Stage Right, *Cabaret* at Henry Miller's Theater (restyled as The Kit Kat Klub).

A VIEW FROM THE BRIDGE

Alfieri	Stephen Spinella	Mike	Mark Zeisler
Eddie	Anthony LaPaglia	Rodolpho	Gabriel Olds
Louis	Daniel Serafini-Sauli	Marco	Adam Trese
Catherine	Brittany Murphy	1st Officer	John Speredakos
Beatrice	Allison Janney	2d Officer	Christian Lincoln

Ensemble: Caren Browning, Debbie D'Amore, Gregory Esposito, Elaine Formicola, Dayna Frongillo, Nick Gisonde, James Gunn, Paul Hrisikos, Diana Marie Jensen, Gloria Kahn, Dianna Mango, Jerry Marino Jr., Tricia Paoluccio, Lou Patane, David Petrolle, Lea Pinsky, Vincent Pugliese, Jason Raftopoulos, Maria Silverman, Faith Whitehill, Glenn Zarr.

Understudies: Mr. LaPaglia—John Speredakos; Miss Janney—Caren Browning; Mr. Spinella—Mark Zeisler; Miss Murphy—Tricia Paoluccio; Mr. Olds—Crispin Freeman; Mr. Trese—Paul Hrisikos, Christian Lincoln; Messrs. Serafini-Sauli, Zeisler—Gregory Esposito; Messrs. Speredakos, Lincoln—Paul Hrisikos.

Dircted by Michael Mayer; scenery, David Gallo; costumes, Michael Krass; lighting, Kenneth Posner; sound, Mark Bennett; fight direction, J. Steven White; casting, Jim Carnahan, Julie Tucker; production stage manager, Nancy Harrington; stage manager, Shawn Senavinin; press, Boneau/Bryan-Brown, Adrian Bryan-Brown, Erin Dunn.

The last major New York revival of *A View From the Bridge* took place on Broadway 2/3/83 for 149 performances. The play was presented in two parts.

Robert LuPone replaced Stephen Spinella and Jeffrey Donovan replaced Adam Trese at the Roundabout. Gregory Esposito replaced Daniel Serafini-Sauli 4/15/98.

Note: In its extended run at the Neil Simon Theater beginning 4/15/98, the Roundabout production of *A View From the Bridge* was presented by Roger Berlind, James M. Nederlander, Nathaniel Kramer, Elizabeth Ireland McCann and Roy Gabay in association with Old Ivy Productions, with James Harker as production stage manager and Shawn Senavinin as stage manager.

CABARET

Emcee	Alan Cumming	Hans	Bill Szobody
The Kit Kat Girls:		Herman	Fred Rose
Rosie	Christina Pawl	Sally Bowles	Natasha Richardson
Lulu	Erin Hill	Clifford Bradshaw	John Benjamin Hickey
Frenchie	Joyce Chittick	Ernst Ludwig	Denis O'Hare
Texas	Leenya Rideout	Customs Official; Max	Fred Rose
Fritzie	Michele Pawk	Fraulein Schneider	Mary Louise Wilson
Helga	Kristin Olness	Fraulein Kost	Michele Pawk
The Kit Kat Boys:		Rudy	Bill Szobody
Bobby	Michael O'Donnell	Herr Schultz	Ron Rifkin
Victor	Brian Duguay	Gorilla	Joyce Chittick

Boy Soprano (recording): Alex Bowen. Others: Members of the Company.

The Kit Kat Band: Patrick Vaccariello conductor, piano; Fred Lassen assistant conductor, keyboards; Gary Tillman drums; Bill Sloat bass; Rich Raffio, Christina Pawl trumpet; Bill Szobody trombone; Denis O'Hare, Michael O'Donnell clarinet; Kristin Olness clarinet, tenor saxophone; Brian Duguay alto and tenor saxophone; Joyce Chittick alto saxophone; Erin Hill alto saxophone, flute, harp; Leenya Rideout violin; Fred Rose cello; Michele Pawk accordion. Swings: Linda Romoff trumpet, Vance Avery banjo.

Standbys: Miss Wilson—Taina Elg; Mr. Rifkin—Bruce Katzman. Understudies: Miss Richardson—Linda Romoff; Mr. Hickey—Brian Duguay; Mr. O'Hare—Fred Rose; Mr. Cumming—Vance Avery; Miss Pawk—Erin Hill.

Directed by Sam Mendes; co-direction and choreography, Rob Marshall; musical direction, Patrick Vaccariello; scenery, Robert Brill; costumes, William Ivey Long; lighting, Peggy Eisenhauer, Mike Baldassari; sound, Brian Ronan; orchestrations, Michael Gibson; dance and incidental music arrangements, David Krane; original dance music arrangements, David Baker; musical coordinator, John Monaco; associate choreographer, Cynthia Onrubia; casting, Jim Carnahan, Pat McCorkle; production stage manager, Peter Hanson; stage manager, John Krause.

Time: 1929–1930. Place: Berlin, Germany.

The last major New York revival of *Cabaret* took place on Broadway 10/22/87 for 262 performances.

ACT I

"Wilkommen"	Emcee, Kit Kat Klub
"So What"	Fraulein Schneider
"Don't Tell Mama"	Sally, Kit Kat Girls
"Mein Herr"	Sally, Kit Kat Girls
"Perfectly Marvelous"	Sally, Cliff
"Two Ladies"	Emcee, Lulu, Bobby
"It Couldn't Please Me More"	Fraulein Schneider, Herr Schultz
"Tomorrow Belongs to Me"	Emcee
"Maybe This Time"	Sally
"Money"	Emcee, Kit Kat Girls
"Married"	Herr Schultz, Fraulein Schneider, Fritzie
"Tomorrow Belongs to Me" (Reprise)	Fraulein Kost, Ernst Ludwig, Company

ACT II

Entr'acte	Kit Kat Band
"Kick Line"	Kit Kat Klub
"Married" (Reprise)	Herr Schultz
"If You Could See Her"	Emcee, Gorilla
"What Would You Do?"	Fraulein Schneider
"I Don't Care Much"	Emcee
"Cabaret"	Sally
Finale	Company

THE DEEP BLUE SEA

Hester Collyer	Blythe Danner	Mr. Miller	Olek Krupa
Mrs. Elton	Sandra Shipley	Sir William Collyer	Edward Hermann
Philip Welch	Ben Shenkman	Freddie Page	David Conrad
Ann Welch	Vivienne Benesch	Jackie Jackson	Rick Holmes

Understudies: Misses Danner, Shipley—Jennifer Harmon; Messrs. Hermann, Krupa—Doug Stender; Mr. Conrad—Rick Holmes; Messrs. Shenkman, Holmes—Bryan Umiker; Miss Benesch—Kate Hampton.

Directed by Mark Lamos; scenery, John Arnone; costumes, Jane Greenwood; lighting, Robert Wierzel; casting, Jim Carnahan; production stage manager, Jay Adler.

Time: A single day in September 1951. Place: The converted top floor flat of a Victorian mansion in a badly blitzed neighborhood of London. Act I: Morning. Act II: Afternoon. Act III: Evening. The play was presented in two parts.

The Deep Blue Sea was first produced on Broadway 11/5/52 for 132 performances. This is its first major New York revival of record.

Note: The Roundabout Theater Company's Criterion Center Stage Right also housed *Paul McKenna's Hypnotic World,* performed by hypnotist Paul McKenna with audience participation and subtitled A Comedy of the Mind, produced by Nederlander of New York, Inc., with Clare Staples as associate producer, Sunday and Monday evenings 3/8/98–4/27/98.

*Ragtime (153). Musical based on the novel by E.L. Doctorow; book by Terrence McNally; music by Stephen Flaherty; lyrics by Lynn Ahrens. Produced by Livent (U.S.) Inc., Garth H.

CABARET—Natasha Richardson *(center)* and The Kit Kat
Girls in the Roundabout's Tony-winning musical revival

Drabinsky chairman and C.E.O., Myron I. Gottlieb president, at the Ford Center for the Performing Arts. Opened January 18, 1998.

Little Boy .... Alex Strange	Harry K. Thaw; Policeman .... Colton Green
Father .... Mark Jacoby	Admiral Peary; Reporter .... Rod Campbell
Mother .... Marin Mazzie	Matthew Henson; Black Lawyer;
Mother's Younger Brother ...... Steven Sutcliffe	Gang Member .... Duane Martin Foster
Grandfather; Foreman . ... Conrad McLaren	Reporter; Fireman; Clerk .... Jeffrey Kuhn
Coalhouse Walker Jr. .... Brian Stokes Mitchell	Kathleen; 2d Bureaucrat;
Sarah .... Audra McDonald	Welfare Official .... Anne Kanengeiser
Booker T. Washington .... Tommy Hollis	Doctor; Dirty Old Man;
Tateh .... Peter Friedman	White Lawyer .... Bruce Winant
Little Girl .... Lea Michele	Sarah's Friend .... Vanessa Townsell-Crisp
Harry Houdini .... Jim Corti	Trolley Conductor; Reporter;
J.P. Morgan; Judge .... Mike O'Carroll	Charles S. Whitman .... Gordon Stanley
Henry Ford; Policeman;	Willie Conklin .... David Mucci
Town Hall Bureaucrat .... Larry Daggett	Brigit; Baron's Assistant .... Anne L. Nathan
Emma Goldman .... Judy Kaye	Conductor .... Joe Locarro
Evelyn Nesbit .... Lynnette Perry	Pas de Deux .... Monica L. Richards,
Stanford White .... Kevin Bogue	Keith LaMelle Thomas
	Little Coalhouse .. Michael Redd, Shane Rogers

Ensemble: Shaun Amyot, Darlene Bel Grayson, Kevin Bogue, Sondra M. Bonitto, Jamie Chandler-Torns, Ralph Deaton, Rodrick Dixon, Bernard Dotson, Donna Dunmire, Adam Dyer, Duane Martin Foster, Patty Goble, Colton Green, Elisa Heinsohn, Anne Kanengeiser, Jeffrey Kuhn, Joe Langworth, Joe Locarro, Anne L. Nathan, Panchali Null, Mimi Quillin, Monica L. Richards, Orgena Rose, Gordon Stanley, Angela Teek, Keith LaMelle Thomas, Allyson Tucker, Leon Williams, Bruce Winant.

Swings: Karen Andrew, John D. Baker, Mark Cassius, Dioni Michelle Collins, Mary Sharon Dziedzic, Valerie Hawkins, Kennl Hobson, Todd Thurston.

Orchestra: David Loud conductor; James Moore associate conductor; Paul Woodiel concertmaster; Blair Lawhead, Cecelia Hobbs Gardner, Chris Cardona, Lesa Terry, Ella Rutkovsky violin; Susan Follari, Richard Clark viola; Jenny Langham, Vivian Israel cello; Bob Renino bass; Brian Miller, flute, piccolo; Owen Kotler clarinet, E flat clarinet; Bill Meredith, oboe, English horn; Vinnie DellaRocca flute, alto sax, soprano sax, bass clarinet; Jeff Kievit, Chris Jaudes trumpet; Paul Riggio, Lisa Pike, French horn; Charles Gordon trombone; Dean Plank bass trombone; Earl McIntyre tuba, baritone horn; Steve Marzullo synthezizer I; James Moore synthesizer II; Marty Morell drums; Bruce Doctor percussion; Greg Utzig guitar, banjo, mandolin; Pattee Cohen harp.

Understudies: Mr. Mitchell—Duane Martin Foster; Miss Mazzie—Patty Goble, Anne Kanengeiser; Mr. Friedman—Jim Corti, Bruce Winant; Mr. Jacoby—Rod Campbell, Todd Thurston; Miss McDonald—Monica L. Richards, Orgena Rose, Angela Teek; Mr. Sutcliffe—Jeffrey Kuhn, Joe Langworth, Joe Locarro; Miss Perry—Jamie Chandler-Torns, Elisa Heinsohn; Mr. Corti—Colton Green, Jeffrey Kuhn, Joe Langworth; Miss Kaye—Valerie Hawkins, Anne L. Nathan; Mr. Strange— Pierce Cravens; Miss Michele—Nicole Dos Santos; Mr. Hollis—Leon Williams, Duane Martin Foster; Mr. Daggett— Todd Thurston, Bruce Winant; Miss Townsell-Crisp—Darlene Bel Grayson, Sondra M. Bonitto; Mr. Mucci—Bruce Winant; Messrs. O'Carroll, McLaren, Campbell—Todd Thurston; Mr. Stanley—Colton Green; Mr. Foster—Mark Cassius.

Directed by Frank Galati; musical staging, Graciela Daniele; musical direction, David Loud; scenery, Eugene Lee; costumes, Santo Loquasto; lighting, Jules Fisher, Peggy Eisenhauer; sound, Jonathan Deans; orchestrations, William David Brohn; music supervision, Jeffrey Huard; dance music arrangements, David Krane; vocal arrangements, Stephen Flaherty; projections, Wendall K. Harrington; magic illusions, Franz Harary; associate choreographer, Willie Rosario; casting, Beth Russell, Arnold J. Mungioli; production stage manager, Randall Whitescarver; stage manager, Dean Greer; press, Mary Bryant, Wayne Wolfe, Ian Rand.

The intersecting lives of white, black and immigrant families in turn-of-the-century America, focusing on the racist persecution and bold retaliation of a black ragtime pianist turned revolutionary.

ACT I

Scene 11: New Rochelle and New York City
"Justice" .... Coalhouse, Ensemble
"President" .... Sarah
"Till We Reach That Day" .... Sarah's Friend, Coalhouse, Emma Goldman,
Younger Brother, Mother, Tateh, Ensemble

ACT II

Entr'acte: "Harry Houdini, Master Escapist" .... Little Boy, Harry Houdini
Scene 1: The streets of New Rochelle/Mother's house
"Coalhouse's Soliloquy" .... Coalhouse
"Coalhouse Demands" .... Company
Scene 2: The Polo Grounds
"What a Game!" .... Father, Little Boy, Ensemble
Scene 3: Mother's house
"Atlantic City" .... Evelyn Nesbit, Harry Houdini
"New Music" (Reprise) .... Father
Scene 4: Atlantic City/Million Dollar Pier/Boardwalk
"Atlantic City, Part II" .... Ensemble
"The Crime of the Century"/"Harry Houdini, Master Escapist" (Reprise) .... Evelyn Nesbit,
Harry Houdini
"Buffalo Nickel Photoplay, Inc." .... Baron Askenazy (Tateh)
"Our Children' .... Mother, Baron Ashkenazy
Scene 5: Harlem/Coalhouse's hideout
"Sarah Brown Eyes" .... Coalhouse, Sarah
"He Wanted to Say" .... Emma Goldman, Younger Brother, Coalhouse,
Coalhouse's Men
Scene 6: The beach, Atlantic City
"Back to Before" .... Mother
Scene 7: The Morgan Library, New York City
"Look What You've Done" .... Booker T. Washington, Coalhouse,
Coalhouse's Men
"Make Them Hear You" .... Coalhouse
Epilogue: "Ragtime"/"Wheels of a Dream" (Reprise) .... Company

The Capeman (68). Musical with book and lyrics by Paul Simon and Derek Walcott; music by Paul Simon. Produced by Plenaro Productions, Dan Klores, Brad Grey, Edgar Dobie and James L. Nederlander in association with Dreamworks Records and King World Productions, Inc. at the Marquis Theater. Opened January 29, 1998. (Closed March 28, 1998)

Salvi Agron (age 7) .... Evan Jay Newman	Santero .... Ray De La Paz
Esmeralda Agron .... Ednita Nazario	Lazarus .... Nestor Sanchez
Salvador Agron (age 36–42) ..... Ruben Blades	Bernadette .... Sophia Salguero
Sal Agron (age 16–20) .... Marc Anthony	Yolanda .... Natascia A. Diaz
Carlos Apache .... Julio Monge	Cookie .... Elan
Angel Soto .... Raymond Rodriguez	Mrs. Young .... Cass Morgan
Frenchy Cordero .... Ray Rodriguez-Rosa	Mrs. Krzesinski .... Luba Mason
Babu Charlie Cruz .... Lugo	Wahzinak .... Sara Ramirez
Tony Hernandez .... Renoly Santiago	lst Inmate .... John Lathan
Rev. Gonzalez .... Philip Hernandez	Warden .... John Jellison
Aurea Agron (age17–43) .... Michelle Rios	Luis .... Jose Joaquin Garcia
Aurea Agron (age 8) ...... Tara Ann Villanueva	Virgil .... Stephen Lee Anderson

Doo-Wop Group: Milton Cardona, Ray De La Paz, Myrna Lynn Gomila, Roger Mazzeo, Frank Negron, Yassmin Alers, Kia Joy Goodwin.

Children's Choir: Evan Jay Newman, Sebastian Perez, Khalid Rivera, Amanda A. Vacharat, Tara Ann Villanueva.

People at the Asilo, Celebrants, People on New York Street, Inmates, Guards, Immigrants, Guests, Sales Clerks: Yassmin Alers, Stephen Lee Anderson, Milton Cardona, Rene Ceballos, Tony Chiroldes, Ray De La Paz, Elan, Jose Joaquin Garcia, Myrna Lynn Gomila, Kia Joy Goodwin, Elise Hernandez, John Jellison, John Lathan, Lugo, Luba Mason, Roger Mazzeo, Claudia Montiel, Marisol Morales, Frank Negron, Evan Jay Newman, Sebastian Perez, Mark Price, Sara Ramirez, Khalid Rivera, Ray Rodriguez-Rosa, Raymond Rodriguez (dance captain), Ramon Saldana, Claudette Sierra, Amanda A. Vacharat, Tara Ann Villanueva.

Orchestra: Oscar Hernandez conductor, keyboard; Oriente Lopez associate conductor, keyboard, flute, accordion; Bobby Allende, Richard Bastar, Latin percussion; Robby Ameen drums, percussion; Nelson Gonzalez tres, cuatro; Paul Livant guitar, harmonica; Bernie Minoso acoustic and upright bass; Edgardo Miranda cuatro, guitar; Vincent Nguini guitar; Gordon Titcomb pedal steel guitar, mandolin; Bobby Franceschini, Tim Ries saxophone; Barry Danielian, Jose Jerez trumpet; Ozzie Melendez trombone; Charles Pillow oboe; Jorge Marera bassoon; Peter Gordon, French horn; David Forestier mallet percussion player; Hector Falcon, Francisco Salazar violin; John R. Dexter II viola; Enrique Orenga cello.

Understudies: Mr. Blades—Jose Joaquin Garcia; Mr. Monge—Jason Martinez, Raymond Rodriguez; Messrs. Anthony, Santiago—Lugo, Jason Martinez; Messrs. Rodriguez, Rodriguez-Rosa, Lugo—Jason Martinez, Mark Price; Miss Salguero—Yassmin Alers, Kia Joy Goodwin; Miss Elan—Myrna Gomila, Kia Joy Goodwin; Misses Diaz, Rios—Yassmin Alers, Lada Boder; Mr. Hernandez—Ray De La Paz, Ramon Saldana; Miss Nazario—Rene Ceballos, Claudette Sierra; Mr. Newman—Sebastian Perez; Miss Villanueva—Amanda A. Vacharat; Mr. Sanchez—Stephen Lee Anderson, Ray De La Paz, Jose Joaquin Garcia; Mr. Lathan—Ray De La Paz; Mr. Jellison—Tony Chiroldes, Osborn Focht; Miss Morgan—Lada Boder, Rene Ceballos; Miss Mason—Lada Boder; Miss Rios—Yassmin Alers, Lada Boder; Miss Ramirez—Lada Boder, Marisol Morales; Mr. Anderson—Osborn Focht, Roger Mazzeo.

Swings: Lada Boder, Osborn Focht, Jason Martinez.

Directed and choreographed by Mark Morris; musical direction, Oscar Hernandez; scenery and costumes, Bob Crowley; lighting, Natasha Katz; sound, Peter J. Fitzgerald; projections, Wendall K. Harrington; orchestrations, Stanley Silverman; co-producer, Stephen Eich; casting, Bernard Telsey; production stage manager, Malcolm Ewen; stage managers, Fredric H. Orner, Valerie Lau-Kee Lai; press, Boneau/Bryan-Brown, Adrian Bryan-Brown, John Barlow.

Young real-life murderer known as The Capeman viewed as a victim of poverty and environment.

ACT I

New York City, 1959
"El Coqui" .... Children's Choir, Salvador
"Born in Puerto Rico" .... Salvador, Sal, Carlos, Angel, Frenchy, Babu Charlie,
Tony Hernandez, Rev Gonzalez

Puerto Rico, 1949
"In Mayaguez" .... Salvador, Esmeralda, Nuns, Children
"The Santero" .... Lazarus, Esmeralda, Santero, Celebrants
"Chimes" .... Esmeralda

New York City, 1959
"Satin Summer Nights" .... Sal, Bernadette, Cookie, Tony Hernandez, Doo-Wop Group
"Bernadette" .... Sal, Bernadette, Doo-Wop Group
"The Vampires" .... Tony Hernandez, Sal, Carlos, Angel, Frenchy,
Babu Charlie, Doo-Wop Group
"Shopliftin' Clothes" .... Sal, Tony Hernandez, Carlos, Angel, Frenchy,
Babu Charlie, Sales Clerks, Doo-Wop Group
"Dance to a Dream" .... Carlos, Yolanda, Bernadette, Sal
"Quality" .... Bernadette, Yolanda, Cookie, Sal, Salvador, Doo-Wop Group
"Manhunt" .... Salvador, Carlos, Sal, Tony Hernandez, Ensemble
"Can I Forgive Him" .... Esmeralda, Mrs. Young, Mrs. Krzesinski
"Adios Hermanos" .... Sal, Salvador, Aurea, Tony Hernandez, Bernadette,
Yolanda, Ensemble

ACT II

New York City, 1962
"Jesus Es Mi Senor" .... Congregants, Rev. Gonzalez, Esmeralda, Aurea, Bernadette,
Yolanda, Lazarus

New York City, 1963
"Sunday Afternoon" .... Esmeralda
Various prisons in New York State, 1963–76
"Time Is an Ocean" .... Sal, Salvador, Esmeralda
Fishkill Prison, 1976–77
"Wahzinak's First Letter" .... Wahzinak
"Killer Wants to Go to College" .... lst Inmate, Warden, Inmate
"Virgil" .... Virgil, Warden
"Wahzinak's Letter" (Duet) .... Salvador, Wahzinak
"My Only Defense" .... Sal
"Virgil and the Warden" .... Virgil, Salvador, Warden
The Desert, Arizona, 1977
"El Malecon" .... Salvador, Salvi, Young Aurea, Esmeralda
"You Fucked Up My Life" .... Angel, Babu Charlie, Sal, Tony Hernandez,
Frenchy, Salvador, Doo-Wop Group
"Lazarus"/"Last Drop of Blood" .... Lazarus, Salvador, Mrs. Young, Ensemble
"Wahzinak's Last Letter" .... Wahzinak
New York City, 1979
"El Coqui" (Reprise) .... Children's Choir, Salvador
"Tony Hernandez" .... Salvador, Tony Hernandez
"Carlos and Yolanda" .... Aurea, Salvador, Carlos, Yolanda, Ensemble
"Sal's Last Song" .... Salvador, Esmeralda
"Esmeralda's Dream" .... Esmeralda, Sal, Doo-Wop Group

*Freak (109). Solo performance by John Leguizamo; written by John Leguizamo; produced by Arielle Tepper and Bill Haber in the Gregory Mosher production at the Cort Theater. Opened February 12, 1998.

Directed and developed by David Bar Katz; scenery, Douglas Stein; lighting, Jan Kroeze; sound, T. Richard Fitzgerald; projection design, Wendall K. Harrington; production stage manager, Pat Sosnow; press, Bill Evans & Associates, Jim Randolph.

Self-described as a "demi-semi-quasi-autobiographical comedy" by the author-performer. Previously produced in regional theater at the Goodman Theater, Chicago, and the Theater on the Square, San Francisco, and off off Broadway at P.S. 122. The play was presented in two parts.

*Art (105). By Yasmina Reza; translated by Christopher Hampton. Produced by David Pugh, Sean Connery and Joan Cullman at the Royale Theater. Opened March 1, 1998.

Marc .... Alan Alda   Yvan .... Alfred Molina
Serge .... Victor Garber

Standbys: Messrs. Garber, Molina—Tom Hewitt; Messrs. Molina, Alda—John Procaccino.
Directed by Matthew Warchus; scenery and costumes, Mark Thompson; lighting, Hugh Vanstone; music, Gary Yershon; sound, Mic Pool; associate producers, Dafydd Rogers, Stuart Thompson; casting, Daniel Swee; production stage manager, William Joseph Barnes; stage manager, Jill Cordle; press, Boneau/Bryan-Brown, Adrian Bryan-Brown, Michael Hartman.
Place: Paris—Serge's apartment, Yvan's apartment, Marc's apartment. The play was presented without intermission.
Artistic and comedic pros and cons of a white-on-white minimalist painting. A foreign play previously produced in Paris, London and elsewhere. Winner of the 1997–98 New York Drama Critics Circle and Tony Awards for best play; see its entry in the Prizewinning Plays section of this volume.

*The Sound of Music (93). Revival of the musical suggested by *The Trapp Family Singers* by Maria Augusta Trapp; book by Howard Lindsay and Russel Crouse; music by Richard Rodgers; lyrics by Oscar Hammerstein II. Produced by Hallmark, Thomas Viertel, Steven Baruch, Richard Frankel and Jujamcyn Theaters in association with The Rodgers and Hammerstein

Organization, Charles Kelman Productions, Simone Genatt Haft, Marc Routh, Jay Binder and Robert Halmi Jr. at the Martin Beck Theater. Opened March 12, 1998.

Sister Margaretta	Jeanne Lehman	Brigitta von Trapp	Tracy Alison Walsh
Sister Berthe	Gina Ferrall	Marta von Trapp	Andrea Bowen
Mother Abbess	Patti Cohenour	Gretl von Trapp	Ashley Rose Orr
Sister Sophia	Ann Brown	Rolf Gruber	Dashiell Eaves
Maria Rainer	Rebecca Luker	Ursula	Lynn C. Pinto
Capt. Georg von Trapp	Michael Siberry	Elsa Schraeder	Jan Maxwell
Franz	John Curless	Max Detweiler	Fred Applegate
Frau Schmidt	Patricia Conolly	Herr Zeller	Timothy Landfield
Liesl von Trapp	Sara Zelle	Baron Elberfeld	Gannon McHale
Friedrich von Trapp	Ryan Hopkins	Baroness Elberfeld	Martha Hawley
Louisa von Trapp	Natalie Hall	New Postulant	Laura Benanti
Kurt von Trapp	Matthew Ballinger	Admiral von Schreiber	Reno Roop

Neighbors & Servants of Capt. von Trapp, Nuns, Novices, Postulants, Priests, Clerics, Nazis, Contestants in the Festival Concert: Anne Allgood, Joan Barber, Laura Benanti, Ann Brown, Patricia Conolly, Gina Ferrall, Natalie Hall, Martha Hawley, Kelly Cae Hogan, Siri Howard, Matt Loney, Patricia Phillips, Lynn C. Pinto, Reno Roop, Kristie Dale Sanders, Ben Sheaffer, Sara Zelle.

Orchestra: Michael Rafter conductor; Steven Tyler associate conductor, keyboard, accordion; James Baker assistant conductor, percussion; Elizabeth Lim-Dutton, Karl Kawahara, Krystof Witek, Karen Milne violin; Maxine Roach viola; Adam Grabois, Sarah J. Seiver cello; Bill Ellison bass; Helen Campo, Rick Heckman, Jon Manasse, Robert Ingliss, Don McGeen woodwinds; Carl Albach, John Dent trumpet; Dick Clark trombone; Matt Ingman bass trombone, tuba; Scott Kuney guitar, mandolin, zither, autoharp; Javier Gandara, Leise Anschuetz Paer, French horn.

Standby: Mr. Siberry—Timothy Landfield. Understudies: Miss Luker—Laura Benanti, Betsi Morrison; Mr. Siberry—Matt Loney; Miss Cohenour—Jeanne Lehman; Miss Maxwell—Kristie Dale Sanders, Kelly Cae Hogan; Mr. Applegate—Gannon McHale, Tad Ingram; Miss Zelle—Siri Howard; Messrs. Hopkins, Ballinger—Lou Taylor Pucci; Misses Hall, Walsh—Nora Blackall; Misses Bowen, Orr—Marissa Gould; Mr. Eaves— Ben Shaeffer; Miss Lehman—Anne Allgood, Margaret Shafer; Miss Ferrall—Joan Barber; Miss Brown—Lynn C. Pinto, Betsi Morrison; Mr. Curless—Reno Roop, Tad Ingram; Miss Conolly—Martha Hawley; Mr. Landfeld—Matt Loney, Tad Ingram; Messrs.McHale, Roop—Tad Ingram; Misses Pinto, Hawley, Benanti—Betsi Morrison, Margaret Shafer. Swings: Tad Ingram, Betsi Morrison, Margaret Shafer.

Directed by Susan H. Schulman; choreography, Michael Lichtefeld; musical direction, Michael Rafter; scenery, Heidi Ettinger; costumes, Catherine Zuber; lighting, Paul Gallo; sound, Tony Meola; orchestrations, Bruce Coughlin; dance and incidental music arrangements, Jeanine Tesori; original orchestrations, Robert Russell Bennett; original choral and dance arrangements, Trude Rittmann; music coordinator, John Miller; associate producers, James D. Stern, PACE Theatrical Group; production supervisor, Beverley Randolph; stage manager, Ira Mont; press, Peter Cromarty & Company.

The last major New York revival of *The Sound of Music* was by New York City Opera 3/8/90 for 54 performances.

ACT I

Preludium	Mother Abbess, Sisters Margaretta, Berthe, Sophia, Nuns, Novices, Postulants
"The Sound of Music"	Maria
"Maria"	Mother Abbess, Sisters Margaretta, Berthe, Sophia
"I Have Confidence"	Maria
(lyrics by Richard Rodgers)	
"Do-Re-Mi"	Maria, Liesl, Friedrich, Louisa, Kurt, Brigitta, Marta, Gretl
"Sixteen Going on Seventeen"	Rolf, Liesl
"My Favorite Things"	Maria, Children
"How Can Love Survive?"	Max, Elsa
"The Sound of Music" (Reprise)	Capt. von Trapp, Children, Maria
"So Long, Farewell"	Children
"Morning Hymn"	Mother Abbess, Nuns, Novices, Postulants
"Climb Ev'ry Mountain"	Mother Abbess

ACT II

Opening Act II	Max, Children
"No Way to Stop It"	Elsa, Max, Capt. von Trapp
"Something Good"	Maria, Capt. von Trapp
(lyrics by Richard Rodgers)	
"Wedding Processional"	Mother Abbess, Nuns, Novices, Postulates
"Sixteen Going on Seventeen" (Reprise)	Maria, Liesl
"The Lonely Goatherd"	Maria, Capt. von Trapp, Children
"Edelweiss"	Capt. von Trapp, Maria, Children
"So Long, Farewell" (Reprise)	Maria, Capt. von Trapp, Children
Finale Ultimo	Mother Abbess, Nuns, Novices, Postulants

*The Chairs (61). Revival of the play by Eugene Ionesco; translated by Martin Crimp. Produced by Bill Kenwright, Carole Shorenstein Hays, Scott Rudin and Stuart Thompson in the Théâtre de Complicité/Royal Court Theater production at the Golden Theater. Opened April 1, 1998.

Old Woman	Geraldine McEwan	Orator	Mick Barnfather
Old Man	Richard Briers	Others	Sarah Baxter

Understudy: Miss McEwan—Sarah Baxter.

Directed by Simon McBurney; scenery and costumes, Quay Brothers; lighting, Paul Anderson; sound, Paul Arditti; production stage managers, Cath Binks, Patrick Ballard; press, Philip Rinaldi, Barbara Carroll.

The Chairs was first produced in New York by the Phoenix Theater 1/9/58 for 22 performances. Its only previous major New York revival was in French off Broadway by Le Tréteau de Paris 5/5/70 for 8 peformances.

Golden Child (69). Revised version of the play by David Henry Hwang. Produced by Benjamin Mordecai, Dori Bernstein, John Kao and the John F. Kennedy Center for the Performing Arts in association with South Coast Repertory, The Joseph Papp Public Theater/New York Shakespeare Festival and the American Conservatory Theater at the Longacre Theater. Opened April 2, 1998. (Closed May 31, 1998)

Ma; Eng Ahn	Julyana Soelistyo	Eng Siu-Yong	Tsai Chin
Andrew Kwong;		Eng Luan	Kim Miyori
Eng Tieng-Bin	Randall Duk Kim	Rev. Anthony Baines	John Horton
Elizabeth Kwong; Eng Eling	Ming-Na Wen		

Servants, Ghosts: Julienne Hanzelka Kim, Lisa Li, James Saito. Understudies: Mr. Kim—James Saito; Misses Chin, Miyori—Lisa Li; Misses Soelistyo, Wen—Julienne Hanzelka Kim; Mr. Horton— Jonathan Bustle.

Directed by James Lapine; scenery, Tony Straiges; costumes, Martin Pakledinaz; lighting, David J. Lander; sound, Dan Moses Schreier; incidental music, Lucia Hwong; casting, Jay Binder, Jordan Thaler, Heidi Griffiths, Joanna DeNaut; production stage manager, Allison Sommers; stage manager, Brendan Smith; press, Richard Kornberg & Associates, Rick Miramontez, Don Summa, Jim Byk.

Time: Act I, the present and winter 1918; Act II, spring 1919 and the present. Place: Manhattan and Eng Tieng-Bin's home village near Amoy in Southeast China.

Successful Chinese businessman and his family come to terms, painfully, with their conflicting East-West cultural traditions. Previously produced in regional theater and off Broadway by The Joseph Papp Public Theater/New York Shakespeare Festival 10/19/96 for 24 performances.

*Wait Until Dark (65). Revival of the play by Frederick Knott. Produced by Alan N. Lichtenstein, Robert L. Young, Gregory Young, Jon B. Platt, Liz Oliver, Stewart F. Lane and Rodger Hess in association with Olympia Entertainment at the Brooks Atkinson Theater. Opened April 5, 1998.

THE JUDAS KISS—Liam Neeson as Oscar
Wilde in the play by David Hare

Lisa; Police Officer .... Diana LaMar	Susy Hendrix .... Marisa Tomei
Mike Talman .... Stephen Lang	Sam Hendrix .... James Whalen
Sgt. Carlino .... Juan Carlos Hernandez	Gloria .... Imani Parks
Harry Roat .... Quentin Tarantino	Police Officer .... Ritchie Coster

Standbys: Miss Tomei—Diana LaMar; Mr. Tarantino—Ritchie Coster. Understudies: Misses LaMar, Tomei, Mr. Coster—Natacha Roi; Mr. Hernandez—Ritchie Coster; Miss Parks—Shevonne Tucker; Messrs. Talman, Whalen—Danny Mastrogiorgio.

Directed by Leonard Foglia; scenery, Michael McGarty; costumes, David C. Woolard; lighting, Brian MacDevitt; sound, Darron L. West; fight direction, Rick Sordelet; casting, Bernard Telsey; production stage manager, Michael Brunner; press, James LL Morrison & Associates, Candi Adams, Tom D'Ambrosio.

Place: A basement apartment on New York's Lower East Side.

Wait Until Dark was first produced on Broadway 2/2/66 for 373 performances. This is its first major New York revival of record.

The Herbal Bed (13). By Peter Whelan. Produced by Alexander H. Cohen, Max Cooper, Anne Strickland Squadron and Chase Mishkin by arrangement with Duncan C. Weldon. Opened April 16, 1998. (Closed April 26, 1998)

Rafe Smith	Armand Schultz	John Hall	Tuck Milligan
Hester Fletcher	Amelia Campbell	Susanna Hall	Laila Robins
Jack Lane	Trent Dawson	Elizabeth Hall	Zena Grey, Annie Rinsky
Bishop Parry	Herb Foster	Barnabus Goche	Simon Jones

Understudies: Misses Robins, Campbell—Elizabeth Hanly Rice; Messrs. Milligan, Foster, Jones—Martin Kildare; Messrs. Dawson, Schultz—Peter Bradbury.

Directed by Michael Attenborough; scenery, David Jenkins; costumes, Alvin Colt; lighting, Beverly Emmons; sound, T. Richard Fitzgerald; music, Adrian Johnston; co-producer, Hildy Parks; associate producers, Edward Schor, Nancy Myers; casting, Bernard Telsey; production stage manager, Alan Hall; stage manager, Ruth E. Rinkin; press, David Rothenberg Associates, David J. Gersten.

Time: The summer of 1613. Place: Stratford-upon-Avon. Act I, Scene 1: An afternoon in June. Scene 2: 30 minutes later. Scene 3: Late that evening. Act II, Scene 1: Two days later. Scene 2: Five weeks later. Scene 3: Some weeks later.

Shakespeare's daughter defends herself against a public accusation of adultery. A foreign play previously produced by the Royal Shakespeare Company.

*The Beauty Queen of Leenane (45). Transfer from off Broadway of the play by Martin McDonagh. Produced by Atlantic Theater Company, Randall L. Wreghitt, Chase Mishkin, Steven M. Levy and Leonard Soloway in association with Julian Schlossberg and Norma Langworthy in the Druid Theater Company/Royal Court Theater production at the Walter Kerr Theater. Opened April 23, 1998.

Mag Folan	Anna Manahan	Ray Dooley	Tom Murphy
Maureen Folan	Marie Mullen	Pato Dooley	Brian F. O'Byrne

Directed by Garry Hynes; scenery and costumes, Francis O'Connor; lighting, Ben Ormerod; sound, David Murphy, Peter J. Fitzgerald; special effects, Gregory Meeh; original music, Paddy Cunneen; associate producer, Charles Whitehead; production stage manager, Matthew Silver; stage manager, Darcy Stephens; press, Boneau/Bryan-Brown, Andy Shearer.

Place: Leenane, a small town in Connemara, County Galway. The play was presented in two parts.

Middle-aged, neurotic daughter vs. the selfish, aged mother living in her care. A foreign play previously produced in Ireland, London and off Broadway by Atlantic Theater Company, Neil Pepe artistic director, Hilary Hinkle managing director, 2/26/98–4/5/98 for 46 performances.

*Honour (41). By Joanna Murray-Smith. Produced by Ron Kastner and Marcus Viscidi in association with New York Stage and Film at the Belasco Theater. Opened April 26, 1998.

Gus	Robert Foxworth	Honor	Jane Alexander
Claudia	Laura Linney	Sophie	Enid Graham

Understudies: Mr. Foxworth—Doug Spender; Misses Linney, Graham—Joan Buddenhagen; Miss Alexander—Jennifer Sternberg.

Directed by Gerald Gutierrez; scenery, Derek McLane; costumes, Jane Greenwood; lighting, Peter Kaczorowski; sound, Aural Fixation; associate producer, Roy Gabay; casting, Stuart Howard, Amy Schechter; production stage manager, Frank Hartenstein; stage manager, Karen Armstrong; press, Philip Rinaldi, Barbara Carroll.

Ways of love in the disruption of a marriage between a New York newspaperman and a poetess. A foreign play previously produced at the Playbox Theater Center, Melbourne, Australia. The play was presented in one act.

*High Society (40). Musical with book by Arthur Kopit based on the play *The Philadelphia Story* by Philip Barry and the motion picture *High Society;* music and lyrics by Cole Porter; additional lyrics by Susan Birkenhead. Produced by Lauren Mitchell and Robert Gailus, Hal Luftig and Richard Samson and Dodger Endemol Theatricals, in association with Bill Haber, at the St. James Theater. Opened April 27, 1998.

Polly .... Jennifer Smith
Arthur .... Glenn Turner
Chester .... Barry Finkel
Sunny .... Kisha Howard
Stanley .... Jeff Skowron
Patsy .... Betsy Joslyn
Peg .... Dorothy Stanley
Edmund .... William Ryall
Margaret Lord .... Lisa Banes

Dinah Lord .... Anna Kendrick
Tracy Samantha Lord .... Melissa Errico
Uncle Willie .... John McMartin
C.K. Dexter Haven .... Daniel McDonald
Mike Connor .... Stephen Bogardus
Liz Imbrie .... Randy Graff
George Kittredge .... Marc Kudisch
Seth Lord .... Daniel Gerroll

Orchestra: Paul Gemignani conductor; Nicholas Archer associate conductor, keyboard 1; Suzanne Ornstein concert master; Paul Ford keyboard 2; Andy Schwartz guitar, banjo; Peter Donovan string bass; Paul Pizzuti drums; Scott Shachter woodwind 1; Dennis Anderson woodwind 2; Bob Millikan solo trumpet; James Pugh solo trombone; Ronald Sell solo French horn; Martin Agee violin 2; Richard Brice viola; Clay Ruede cello; Thad Wheeler percussion, 2d assistant conductor.

Standbys: Miss Errico—Stacey Logan; Messrs. McDonald, Bogardus, Kudisch—Richard Muenz. Understudies: Misses Banes, Graff—Dorothy Stanley, Jennifer Smith; Miss Kendrick—Holiday Segal; Miss Errico—Sarah Solie Shannon; Messrs. McMartin, Gerroll—William Ryall, Barry Finkel; Mr. Bogardus—Jeff Skowron. Swings: Vince Pesce, Sarah Solie Shannon.

Directed by Christopher Renshaw; musical staging, Lar Lubovitch; musical direction, Paul Gemignani; scenery, Loy Arcenas; costumes, Jane Greenwood; lighting, Howell Binkley; sound, Tony Meola; orchestrations, William David Brohn; dance music and overture arrangements, Glen Kelly; associate producer, Kevin C. Whitman; casting, Jay Binder; production stage manager, Steven Zweigbaum; stage manager, Rolt Smith; press, Boneau/Bryan-Brown, Susanne Tighe.

Time: A glorious weekend in June 1938. Place: Oyster Bay.

As in the 1939 play and 1940 movie, played by Katharine Hepburn, and the 1956 movie musical, played by Grace Kelly, the heiress Tracy Lord tries to decide which man she prefers among the many hovering around her, glasses of champagne in hand.

ACT I

Scene 1: The Lords' estate
"High Society"* .... Household Staff
Scene 2: Tracy's Room
"Ridin' High" .... Tracy, Household Staff
Scene 3: The veranda
"Throwing a Ball Tonight"* .... Margaret Lord, Tracy, Uncle Willie, Dinah
Scene 4: The nursery
"Little One" .... Dexter, Dinah
Scene 5: The grounds
"Who Wants To Be a Millionaire" .... Liz, Mike
Scene 6: The south parlor
"I Love Paris" .... Dinah, Tracy
Scene 7: The pavilion
"She's Got That Thing" .... Uncle Willie, Dexter, Company
Scene 8: The pool
"Once Upon a Time"* .... Tracy
"True Love" .... Dexter, Tracy

ACT II

Scene 1: Uncle Willie's house, very early Sunday morning
"High Society"* .... Household Staff
Scene 2: Uncle Willie's ballroom
"Let's Misbehave"** .... Tracy, Uncle Willie, Company
"I'm Getting Myself Ready for You** .... Uncle Willie, Liz
Scene 3: Dexter's house
"Once Upon a Time"* (Reprise) .... Dexter
"Just One of Those Things" .... Dexter
Scene 4: Uncle Willie's kitchen
"Well, Did You Evah?"* .... Household Staff, Tracy, Uncle Willie, Liz

Scene 5: Uncle Willie's grounds
  "You're Sensational" .... Mike
  "Say It With Gin" .... Uncle Willie
  "Ridin' High" (Reprise) .... Margaret Lord
Scene 6: The Lords' pool
  "It's All Right With Me" .... Tracy
Scene 7: The Lords' garden
  "He's a Right Guy" .... Liz
Scene 8: The terrace, the next morning
  "Samantha" .... Dexter
  "True Love" (Reprise) .... Tracy, Dexter
*New lyrics or **additional lyrics by Susan Birkenhead

*The Judas Kiss (38). By David Hare. Produced by Robert Fox, Scott Rudin, Roger Berlind, Joan Cullman and The Shubert Organization in the Almeida Theater Company production, Ian McDiarmid and Jonathan Kent artistic directors, at the Broadhurst Theater. Opened April 29, 1998.

Phoebe Cane .... Stina Nielsen
Arthur Wellesley .... Alex Walkinshaw
Sandy Moffatt .... Richard Clarke
Robert Ross .... Peter Capaldi
Lord Alfred Douglas .... Tom Hollander
Oscar Wilde .... Liam Neeson
Galileo Masconi .... Daniel Serafini-Sauli

Understudies: Messrs. Capaldi, Clarke—Simon Brooking; Messrs. Hollander, Walkinshaw, Serafini-Sauli—Matthew Greer; Miss Nielsen—Miranda Kent.

Directed by Richard Eyre; scenery and costumes, Bob Crowley; lighting, Mark Henderson; music, George Fenton; sound, John A. Leonard; casting, Daniel Swee, Patsy Pollack; production stage manager, Susie Cordon; press, Boneau/Bryan-Brown, Adrian Bryan-Brown, John Barlow.

Act I: London, 1895. Scene 1: Early afternoon. Scene 2: Late afternoon. Act II: Italy, 1897. Scene 1: Dusk. Scene 2: Dawn.

The consequences of Wilde's ill-fated suit against Lord Alfred Douglas's father, the Marquess of Queensberry, before and after his imprisonment. A foreign play previously produced in London.

PLAYS PRODUCED
OFF BROADWAY

Some distinctions between off-Broadway and Broadway productions at one end of the scale and off-off-Broadway productions at the other end are blurred in the New York Theater of the 1990s. For the purposes of *Best Plays* listing, the term "off Broadway" signifies a show which opened for general audiences in a mid-Manhattan theater seating 499 or fewer and 1) employed an Equity cast, 2) planned a regular schedule of 8 performances a week in an open-ended run (7 a week for solo shows) and 3) offered itself to public comment by critics after a designated opening performance.

Occasional exceptions of inclusion (never of exclusion) are made to take in visiting troupes, borderline "showcase" presentations and nonqualifying productions which readers might expect to find in this list because they appear under an off-Broadway heading in other major sources of record.

Figures in parentheses following a play's title give number of performances. These numbers do not include previews or extra non-profit performances.

Plays marked with an asterisk (*) were still in a projected run on June 7, 1998. Their number of performances is figured from opening night through May 31, 1998.

Certain programs of off-Broadway companies are exceptions to our rule of counting the number of performances from the date of the press coverage. When the official opening takes place late in the run of a play's regularly-priced public or subscription performances (after previews), we sometimes count the first performance of record, not the press date, as opening night—and in any such case in the listing we note the variance and give the press date.

In a listing of a show's numbers—dances, sketches, musical scenes, etc.—the titles of songs are identified wherever possible by their appearance in quotation marks (").

HOLDOVERS FROM PREVIOUS SEASONS

Off-Broadway shows which were running on June 1, 1997 are listed below. More detailed information about them appears in previous *Best Plays* volumes of appropriate date. Important cast changes since opening night are recorded in the Cast Replacements section of this volume.

*The Fantasticks (15,744; longest continuous run of record in the American Theater). Musical suggested by the play *Les Romanesques* by Edmond Rostand; book and lyrics by Tom Jones; music by Harvey Schmidt. Opened May 3, 1960.

*Perfect Crime (4,586). By Warren Manzi. Opened October 16, 1987.

*Tony 'n' Tina's Wedding (3,587). By Artificial Intelligence. Opened February 6, 1988.

*Tubes (2,962). Performance piece by and with Blue Man Group. November 17, 1991.

*Stomp (1,791). Percussion performance piece created by Luke Cresswell and Steve Mc-Nicholas. Opened February 27, 1994.

*Grandma Sylvia's Funeral (1,345). Transfer from off off Broadway of the environmental theater piece conceived by Glenn Wein and Amy Lord Blumsack; created by Glenn Wein, Amy Lord Blumsack and the original company. Opened October 4, 1994.

Making Porn (511). By Ronnie Larsen. Opened June 12, 1996. (Closed September 14, 1997)

*I Love You, You're Perfect, Now Change (761). Musical revue with book and lyrics by Joe DiPietro; music by Jimmy Roberts. Opened August 1, 1996.

*When Pigs Fly (744). Musical revue conceived by Howard Crabtree and Mark Waldrop; sketches and lyrics by Mark Waldrop; music by Dick Gallagher. Opened August 14, 1996.

Full Gallop (392). Return engagement of the solo performance by Mary Louise Wilson; written by Mark Hampton and Mary Louise Wilson. Opened September 24, 1996. (Closed August 30, 1997)

Magic on Broadway (334). Magic revue performed by Joseph Gabriel. Opened September 29, 1996. (Closed July 13, 1997)

*Late Nite Catechism (594). By Vicki Quade and Maripat Donovan. Opened October 3, 1996.

*Forbidden Broadway Strikes Back (722). Musical revue created and written by Gerard Alessandrini. Opened October 17, 1996.

A Brief History of White Music (308). Musical revue conceived by DeeDee Thomas and David Tweedy; music and lyrics by various authors. Opened November 19, 1996. (Closed September 14, 1997)

Capitol Steps (152). Musical revue conceived and written by Bill Strauss and Elaina Newport; with contributions from the cast. Opened February 13, 1997. (Closed June 29, 1997)

Stonewall Jackson's House (128). By Jonathan Reynolds. Opened February 19, 1997. (Closed June 15, 1997)

Tap Dogs (182). Dance revue choreographed by Dein Perry; music by Andrew Wilkie. Opened March 16, 1997. (Closed August 24, 1997)

Roundabout Theater Company. All My Sons (65). Revival of the play by Arthur Miller. Opened May 4, 1997. (Closed June 29, 1997)

How I Learned to Drive (400). Transfer from off off Broadway of the play by Paula Vogel. Opened May 6, 1997. (Closed April 19, 1998)

Bermuda Avenue Triangle (177). By Renée Taylor and Joe Bologna. Opened May 11, 1997. (Closed October 12, 1997)

Men on the Verge of a His-Panic Breakdown (117). Solo performance by Felix A. Pire; written by Guillermo Reyes. Opened May 13, 1997. (Closed July 13, 1997)

As You Like It (10). Revival of the play by William Shakespeare. Opened May 18, 1997. (Closed June 4, 1997)

Manhattan Theater Club. Collected Stories (80). By Donald Margulies. Opened May 20, 1997. (Closed July 27, 1997)

PLAYS PRODUCED JUNE 1, 1997–JUNE 7, 1998

When 1997–98 production schedules overlap our seasonal cutoff date of May 31, we fully include the shows that opened in the first week of June.

*Gross Indecency: The Three Trials of Oscar Wilde (414). Transfer from off off Broadway of the play by Moisés Kaufman. Produced by Leonard Soloway and Chase Mishkin in the Tectonic Theater Project production at the Minetta Lane Theater. Opened June 5, 1997.

Oscar Wilde	Michael Emerson	Carson; Narrator	John McAdams
Lord Alfred Douglas	William D. Dawes	Narrator; Atkins; Judge	Andy Paris
Queensberry; Gill;		Narrator; Wood; Shaw	Greg Pierotti
Lockwood	Robert Blumenfeld	Narrator; Parker; Harris	Troy Sostillio
Clarke	Trevor Anthony	Narrator; Mavor; Taylor	Greg Steinbruner

Others: Trevor Anthony, John McAdams, Andy Paris, Greg Pierotti, Troy Sostillio, Greg Steinbruner.

Directed by Moisés Kaufman; scenery, Sarah Lambert; costumes, Kitty Leech; lighting, Betsy Adams; sound, Wayne Frost; dialect coach, Robert Blumenfeld; casting, Judy Henderson & Associates; production stage manager, Rachel Putnam; press, Kevin P. McAnarney.

Oscar Wilde's trials and demise, dramatized from first-hand sources such as transcripts, letters and biographies written by Wilde and his contemporaries, previously produced off off Broadway 3/18/97 in this production. The play was presented in two parts. Co-winner of the 1997–98 Lucille Lortel Award for best off-Broadway play; see the Prizewinning Plays section of this volume.

Edward Hibbert replaced Michael Emerson 11/11/97.

Playwrights Horizons. 1996–97 schedule concluded with **Baby Anger** (9). By Peter Hedges. Produced by Playwrights Horizons, Tim Sanford artistic director, Leslie Marcus managing director, Lynn Landis general manager, at Playwrights Horizons. Opened June 8, 1997. (Closed June 15, 1997)

Larry Paterson	John Pankow	Jeremy Dodge	Ben Shenkman
Mary Kay Paterson	Kristen Johnston	Shawn Paterson	Carl J. Matusovich
Man	Robert Ari	Eric	Adam Rose
Woman	Linda Emond		

Directed by Michael Mayer; scenery, Mark Wendland; costumes, Jess Goldstein; lighting, Frances Aronson; original music and sound, David Van Tieghem; production stage manager, William H. Lang; press, James LL Morrison, Tom D'Ambrosio.

Comic treatment of parents exploiting their child in an award-winning TV commercial. The play was presented in two parts.

Manhattan Theater Club. 1996–97 schedule concluded with **Seeking the Genesis** (24). By Kia Corthron. Produced by Manhattan Theater Club, Lynne Meadow artistic director, Barry Grove executive producer, Victoria Bailey general manager, at Manhattan Theater Club Stage II. Opened June 17, 1997. (Closed July 6, 1997)

Kite	Kevin Rahsaan Grant	Cheryl; Customer	Soraya Butler
Justin	Donn Swaby	Mitch	Lloyd Goodman
Teacher	Sharon Washington	Sac	Chris McKinney
C. Ana	Aunjanue Ellis	Pizza Man; Professor	Armand Schultz
Kandal	Lindsay E. Finnie		

Directed by Kaia Calhoun; scenery, Christine Jones; costumes, Tom Broecker; lighting, Scott Zielinski; sound, Fabian Obispo; fight coordinator, J. Allen Suddeth; associate artistic director, Michael Bush; production stage manager, Laurie Goldfeder; press, Boneau/Bryan-Brown, Jackie Green.

Probing for causes of violent behavior, with an inner-city 6-year-old as the principal subject. The play was presented in two parts.

The Joseph Papp Public Theater/New York Shakespeare Festival Shakespeare Marathon. Henry VIII (22). Revival of the play by William Shakespeare. Produced by The Joseph Papp Public Theater/New York Shakespeare Festival, George C. Wolfe producer, Rosemarie Tichler associate producer, Anne F. Zimmerman managing director, with the cooperation of the City of New York, Rudolph W. Giuliani Mayor, Peter F. Vallone Speaker of the City Council, Schuyler Chapin Commissioner of the Department of Cultural Affairs, Henry J. Stern Commissioner of the Department of Parks & Recreation, at the Delacorte Theater in Central Park. Opened June 13, 1997; see note. (Closed July 9, 1997)

Prologue; Epilogue .... Julia McIlvaine	Sir Henry Guildford; Page;
Duke of Buckingham .... Larry Bryggman	Garter; King of Arms .... Jason Butler Harner
Duke of Norfolk .... Adam Dannheisser	Anne Boleyn .... Marin Hinkle
Earl of Surrey .... Julio Monge	lst Gentlewoman .... Julia Gibson
Cardinal Wolsey .... Josef Sommer	2d Gentlewoman .... Sybyl Walker
Gardiner; Bishop of	Sir Nicholas Vaux; Scribe; Official
Winchester .... Peter Jay Fernandez	at the Trial .... Andrew Brooks McGinn
Brandon; Arresting Officer;	Duke of Suffolk .... Miguel Perez
Gentleman Usher; Chancellor ..... Sam Catlin	Old Lady; Anne Boleyn's
Sergeant-at-Arms; Crier; Official	Friend .... Betty Henritze
at the Trial .... Reuben Jackson	Cardinal Campeius; Porter; Gatekeeper
King Henry VIII ...... Ruben Santiago-Hudson	at the Palace .... John Ellison Conlee
Queen Katharine .... Jayne Atkinson	Queen's Gentlewoman .... Liliana Amador
Surveyor for Buckingham; Cranmer; Arch-	Patience; Queen's
bishop of Canterbury .... Michael Stuhlbarg	Waiting Woman .... Ana Reeder
Lord Chamberlain .... Herb Foster	Thomas Cromwell .... Teagle F. Bougere
Lord Sands .... Daniel Sunjata	Griffith; Queen's Usher .... Mark Hammer
Sir Thomas Lovell .... Stephen Kunken	Man; Gatekeeper's Companion .... Tom Aulino

Masquers, Priests, Ladies-in-Waiting: Tom Aulino, Emma Bowers, Angel Desai, Peter Jay Fernandez, Michael Hyatt, Julio Monge, Michael Stuhlbarg, Daniel Sunjata.

Directed by Mary Zimmerman; scenery, Riccardo Hernandez; costumes, Toni-Leslie James; lighting, Michael Chybowski; sound, JR Conklin; original music, Michael Bodeen; choreography, Sabrina Peck; senior director of external affairs, Margaret M. Lioi; associate producer, Wiley Hausam; artistic associate, Brian Kulick; associate producer, Bonnie Metzgar; casting, Jordan Thaler, Heidi Griffiths; production stage manager, James Latus; stage manager, Buzz Cohen; press, Carol R. Fineman, Tom Naro, Bill Coyle.

Time: Early 16th Century. Place: London. The play was presented in two parts.

The last major New York production of record of *Henry VIII* took place on Broadway by the Repertory Theater 11/6/46 for 40 performances, directed by Margaret Webster, with music by Lehman Engel; and a short-lived off- or off-off-Broadway presentation was mentioned in the report of the 1959–60 season.

Note: Press date for *Henry VIII* was 6/27/97.

Note: *Henry VIII* is the 36th and final production in The Joseph Papp Public Theater/New York Shakespeare Festival's 10-year Shakespeare Marathon, which has now presented all of Shakespeare's plays. The previous productions in this series have taken place as follows: 1987–88 season, *A Midsummer Night's Dream, Julius Caesar, Romeo and Juliet;* 1988–89 season, *Much Ado About Nothing, King John, Coriolanus, Love's Labour's Lost, The Winter's Tale, Cymbeline;* 1989–90 season, *Twelfth Night, Titus Andronicus, Macbeth, Hamlet;* 1990–91 season, *The Taming of the Shrew, Richard III, Henry IV, Part 1* and *Part 2;* 1991–92 season, *Othello* and *Pericles, Prince of Tyre;* 1992–93 season, *As You Like It, The Comedy of Errors;* 1993–94 season, *Measure for Measure, All's Well That Ends Well, Richard II;* 1994–95 season, *The Merry Wives of Windsor, The Two Gentlemen of Verona, The Merchant of Venice;* 1995–96 season, *The Tempest, Troilus and Cressida, King Lear;* 1996–97 season, *Henry V, Timon of Athens, Henry VI* (in two parts entitled *The Edged Sword* and *Black Storm*), *Antony and Cleopatra;* 1997–98 season, *Henry VIII.*

Second Stage. 1996–97 schedule concluded with **Something Blue** (25). Solo performance by Michaela Murphy; written by Michaela Murphy. Produced by Second Stage Theater, Carole Rothman artistic director, Suzanne Schwartz Davidson producing director, at Second Stage Theater. Opened June 22, 1997. (Closed July 13, 1997)

Directed by Tim Blake Nelson; costumes, Crystal Thompson; lighting, Jan Kroeze; production stage manager, Rebecca C. Monroe; press, Richard Kornberg.

The details of multiple characters and events of an eccentric wedding, presented without intermission.

Queens Blvd. (32). By Paul Corrigan. Produced by Joel O. Thayer at the Players Theater. Opened June 23, 1997. (Closed July 20, 1997)

Frank .... Steve Hayes   David .... Tony Meindl
Jules .... Russell Leib

Directed by Vincent J. Cardinal; scenery, Bill Clarke; costumes, Mary Myers; lighting, Brian Aldous; sound, Bernard Fox; production stage manager, J. Andrews Burgreen; press, Jeffrey Richards Associates.

Two gays trying to determine whether their handsome lodger is gay or straight. The play was presented in two parts.

Always . . . Patsy Cline (192). Musical with book by Ted Swindley; music and lyrics by various authors (see listing below). Produced by Opryland Theatricals in association with the Randy Johnson Company at the Variety Arts Theater. Opened June 24, 1997. (Closed December 7, 1997)

Patsy .... Tori Lynn Palazola
Louise .... Margo Martindale

Musicians: Gene Hicks conductor, piano; Bob Mastro fiddle, rhythm guitar; Rick Palley bass; CJ Masters guitar; John Widgren pedal steel; Shannon Ford drums.

Standby: Misses Palazola, Martindale––Becky Barta. Understudy: Misses Palazola, Martindale— Teresa Williams.

Director, Ted Swindley; musical direction, Vicky Masters; scenery, Christopher Pickart; costumes, Thom Heyer; lighting, Stephen Quandt; sound, Peter J. Fitzgerald; casting, Joseph McConnell; production stage manager, Pamela Edington; press, Empire/Sunshine Productions, Inc., Boneau/Bryan-Brown.

The life and times of Patsy Kline, country music singer who died in a 1963 plane crash, seen through the eyes of an adoring fan.

MUSICAL NUMBERS, ACT I: "Honky Tonk Merry Go Round" (by Stan Gardner and Frank Simon), "Back in Baby's Arms" (by Bob Montgomery), "Anytime" (by Herbert Happy Lawson), "Walkin' After Midnight" (by Don Hecht and Allen Block), "I Fall to Pieces" (by Hank Cochran and Harlan Howard), "It Wasn't God Who Made Honky Tonk Angels" (by J.D. Miller), "Come on In (and Sit Right Down)" (by Michael B. Clark), "Your Cheatin' Heart" (by Hank Williams Sr.), "She's Got You" (by Hank Cochran), "San Antonio Rose" (by Bob Willis), "Lovesick Blues" (by Irving Mills and C. Friend).

ACT II: "Sweet Dreams" (by Don Gibson), "Three Cigarettes in an Ashtray" (by Eddie Miller), "Crazy" (by Willie Nelson), "Seven Lonely Days" (by Earl Shuman, Alden Shuman and Marshall Brown), "If I Could See the World (Through the Eyes of a Child)" (by Sammy Masters, Richard Pope and Tex Satterwhite), "Just a Closer Walk With Thee" (traditional), "Blue Moon of Kentucky" (by Bill Monroe), "Gotta Lot of Rhythm in My Soul" (by Barbara Ann Vaughan and W.S. Stevenson), "Faded Love" (by John Wills and Bob Wills), "True Love" (by Cole Porter).

As Bees in Honey Drown (366). Transfer from off off Broadway of the play by Douglas Carter Beane. Produced by Edgar Lansbury, Everett King, Randall L. Wreghitt, Chase Mishkin, Steven M. Levy and Leonard Soloway, by special arrangement with Lucille Lortel, in The Drama Dept. production, Douglas Carter Beane artistic director, Michael S. Rosenberg managing director, at the Lucille Lortel Theater. Opened July 24, 1997. (Closed June 7, 1998)

CAST: Photographer, Swen, Kaden—Mark Nelson; Evan Wyler—Bo Foxworth; Amber, Back-Up Singer, Secretary, Bethany, Ginny—Amy Ryan; Alexa Vere de Vere—J. Smith-Cameron; Waiter, Back-Up Singer, Carla, Newsstand Woman, Denise, Illya—Sandra Daley; Ronald, Skunk, Long Hair, Mike—T. Scott Cunningham.

Directed by Mark Brokaw; scenery, Allen Moyer; costumes, Jonathan Bixby; lighting, Kenneth Posner; original music and sound, David Van Tieghem; fight direction, Rick Sordelet; associate lighting designer, Jeff Croiter; associate producer, Chloe Clovis Hatcher; casting, Pat McCorkle; production stage manager, James FitzSimmons; press, Boneau/Bryan-Brown, Chris Boneau, Miguel Tuason.

Time: The present. Place: In and around New York City. The play was presented in two parts.

Comedy in which a novelist, gay, learns to love a spirited socialite who wants him to write a movie based on her life.

The Joseph Papp Public Theater/New York Shakespeare Festival. Schedule of six programs. **On the Town** (25). Revival of the musical based on a concept of Jerome Robbins; book and lyrics by Betty Comden and Adolph Green; music by Leonard Bernstein. Opened August 1, 1997. (Closed August 31, 1997) **A Dybbuk, or Between Two Worlds** (48). Revival of the play by S. Ansky; translated by Joachim Neugroschel; adapted by Tony Kushner. Opened October 28, 1997. (Closed December 7, 1997) **Ballad of Yachiyo** (32). By Philip Kan Gotanda. Opened November 11, 1997. (Closed December 7, 1997) **Macbeth** (17). Revival of the play by William Shakespeare. Opened March 15, 1998. (Closed March 29, 1998). **Saturn Returns: A Concert** (16). Song cycle with music and lyrics by Adam Guettel. Opened March 31, 1998. (Closed April 12, 1998) **The Cripple of Inishmaan** (48). By Martin McDonagh. Opened April 7, 1998. (Closed April 17, 1998) Produced by The Joseph Papp Public Theater/New York Shakespeare Festival, George C. Wolfe producer, Rosemarie Tichler artistic producer, Anne F. Zimmerman managing director, *On the Town* at the Delacorte Theater in Central Park, other productions at The Joseph Papp Public Theater (see note).

ALL PLAYS: Senior director, external affairs, Margaret M. Lioi; associate producers, Wiley Hausam, Bonnie Metzgar; artistic associate, Brian Kulick; casting, Jordan Thaler, Heidi Griffiths; press, Carol R. Fineman, Bill Coyle, Thomas V. Naro.

ON THE TOWN

Workman; Miss Turnstiles	Policeman .... Jesse Means II
Announcer .... Luiz-Ottavio Faria	Mr. S. Uperman;
Ozzie .... Robert Montano	Master of Ceremonies .... Blake Hammond
Chip .... Jesse Tyler Ferguson	Hildy Esterhazy .... Lea DeLaria
Gabey .... Jose Llana	Waldo Figment .... Leslie Feagan
Flossie .... Linda Mugleston	Claire DeLoone .... Kate Suber
Flossie's Friend .... Chandra Wilson	Primitive Man &
Subway Bill Poster;	Woman .... Nickemil Concepcion,
Rajah Bimmy .... Glenn Turner	Margaux Zadikian
Little Old Lady;	Pas de Deux Dancers .... Patricia Tuthill,
Mme. Maude P. Dilly .... Mary Testa	Jassen Virolas
Miss Turnstiles Announcer; Diana	Pitkin W. Bridgework .... Jonathan Freeman
Dream; Dolores Dolores .... Nora Cole	Lucy Schmeeler .... Annie Golden
Ivy Smith .... Sophia Salguero	

Quartet: Leslie Feagan, Blake Hammond, Jesse Means II, Glenn Turner. Mannequins: Ivy Fox, Keri Lee, Joanne McHugh, Chandra Wilson. Women of Carnegie Hall: Nora Cole, Linda Mugleston, Chandra Wilson. Diamond Eddie's Girls: Rachel Alvarado, Ivy Fox, Keri Lee, Joanne McHugh, Patricia Tuthill, Margaux Zadikian.

Dance Ensemble: Rachel Alvarado, Andy Blankenbuehler, Nickemil Concepcion, Karl duHoffman, Ivy Fox, Darren Gibson, Clay Harper Jackson, Keri Lee, Joanne McHugh, Patricia Tuthill, Jassen Virolas, Margaux Zadikian.

The People of New York: Nora Cole, Luiz-Ottavio Faria, Leslie Feagan, Annie Golden, Blake Hammond, Jesse Means II, Linda Mugleston, Mary Testa, Glenn Turner, Chandra Wilson.

Swings: Carol Bentley, Byron Easley.

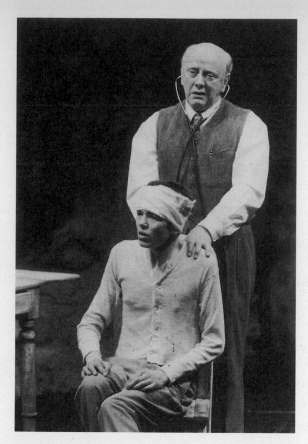

THE CRIPPLE OF INISHMAAN—Ruaidhri
Conroy *(seated)* and Peter Maloney in a scene
from the play by Martin McDonagh

On the Town Orchestra: Kevin Stites conductor; Todd Ellison standby conductor; Dennis Anderson,
William Blount, Edward Salkin, Edward Zuhlke, Kenneth Adams, Roger Rosenberg, Barry Nudelman
woodwinds; Robert Millikan, Christian Jaudes, Kamau Adilfu trumpet; Larry Farrell, Charles Gordon,
Joel Shelton trombone; Roger Wendt, Jeffrey Scott, French horn; Jeffrey Harris keyboards; Robert
Renino bass; Brian Grice drums; Eric Kivnick percussion.

Directed by George C. Wolfe; choreography, Eliot Feld; musical direction, Kevin Stites; scenery,
Adrianne Lobel; costumes, Paul Tazewell; lighting, Paul Gallo; sound, Jon Weston; orchestrations, Bruce
Coughlin; music coordination, Seymour Red Press; casting, Jordan Thaler, Heidi Griffiths; production
stage manager, Lisa Buxbaum.

The last major New York revival of *On the Town* took place on Broadway 10/31/71 for 73 performances.

ACT I

Scene 1: The Brooklyn Navy Yard
  "I Feel Like I'm Not Out of Bed Yet" .... Workman, Quartet
  "New York, New York" .... Gabey, Chip, Ozzie, Company
Scene 2: A subway train in motion
Scene 3: A New York street

"Gabey's Comin' " .... Ozzie, Chip, Gabey, Mannequins
Scene 4: Presentation of Miss Turnstiles
"Presentation of Miss Turnstiles" .... Announcers, Ivy Smith, Dance Ensemble
Scene 5: A taxicab
"Come Up to My Place" .... Hildy, Chip
Scene 6: The Museum of Natural History
"Carried Away" .... Claire, Ozzie, Primitive Man & Woman
Scene 7: A busy New York City street
"Lonely Town" .... Gabey, Dance Ensemble
Scene 8: A corridor and studio in Carnegie Hall
"Carnegie Hall Pavane" .... Ivy, Mme. Dilly, Women of Carnegie Hall
Scene 9: Central Park
"Lucky To Be Me" .... Gabey, Chorus
Scene 10: Claire's and Hildy's apartments
"I Understand" .... Pitkin
"I Can Cook Too" .... Hildy
Scene 11: Times Square
"Times Square Ballet" .... Company

ACT II

Scene 1A: Diamond Eddie's nightclub
"So Long, Baby" .... Diamond Eddie's Girls
"I Wish I Was Dead" .... Diana Dream
Scene 1B: The Congacabana
"I Wish I Was Dead" .... Dolores Dolores
"Ya Got Me" .... Hildy, Claire, Ozzie, Chip
Scene 1C: The Slam Bang Club
"I Understand" .... Pitkin, Lucy
Scene 2: The subway train to Coney Island
"Subway Ride" .... Gabey, The People of New York
Scene 3: The dream Coney Island
"Imaginary Coney Island" .... Gabey, Ivy, Dance Ensemble
Scene 4: Subway platform
"Some Other Time" .... Claire, Hildy, Ozzie, Chip
Scene 5: The Real Coney Island
"The Real Coney Island' .... Rajah Bimmy
Scene 6: The Brooklyn Navy Yard
"I Feel Like I'm Not Out of Bed Yet" (Reprise) .... Workman
"New York, New York" (Reprise) .... Company

A DYBBUK, OR BETWEEN TWO WORLDS

Khonen .... Michael Stuhlbarg
1st Batlon; 1st Passenger;
    2d Rabbinnical Judge .... David Lipman
2d Batlon; Nakhman; 2d Passenger;
    3d Hasid .... Stuart Zagnit
3d Batlon; 3d Passenger;
    2d Hasid .... Ümit Celebi
Messenger .... Ed Shea
Mayer; 1st Rabbinical Judge ..... Joshua Mostel
Channa-Esther; Mrs. Nahkman .... Joan
                                      Copeland
Henekh; 1st Hasid .... Stephen Kunken
Leah .... Marin Hinkle

Fradde .... Lola Pashalinski
Girl .... Eve Michelson
Sender .... Robert Dorfman
Beggar; Rabbi Shimshin .. Christopher McCann
Poor Woman; Holy Bride;
    Bessye .... Joyce Chittick
Poor Woman With Baby;
    Ghost of Leah's Mother .... Nina Goldman
Holy Bridegroom .... Daniel Wright
Rabbi Mendl; Mikhl .... Bernie Passeltiner
Menashe; Scribe .... Hillel Meltzer
Rabbi Azriel .... Ron Leibman

Idlers at the Synagogue, Miropol Hasids: Joyce Chittick, Stephen Kunken, Christopher McCann, Hillel Meltzer, Joshua Mostel, Bernie Passeltiner, Lorin Sklamberg, Daniel Wright.

Directed by Brian Kulick; scenery, Mark Wendland; costumes, Elizabeth Hope Clancy; lighting, Mimi Jordon Sherin; sound, Tom Morse; original music, The Klezmatics; choreography, Naomi Goldberg; production stage manager, Erica Schwartz.

The last major New York production of this tale was by New York Shakespeare Festival in the Mira Rafalowicz-Joseph Chaikin adaptation entitled *A Dybbuk* 12/6/77 for 62 performances. This Kushner adaptation was previously produced in regional theater at the Hartford, Conn. Stage Company, Mark Lamos artistic director. The play was presented in two parts.

BALLAD OF YACHIYO

Yachiyo Matsumoto .... Sala Iwamatsu	Mama (Takayo Matsumoto) ... Dian Kobayashi
Hiro Takamura .... Francois Chau	Willie Higa .... Greg Watanabe
Okusan (Sumiko Takamura) ..... Emily Kuroda	Osugi Chong .... Annie Yee
Papa (Hisao Matsumoto) .... Sab Shimono	

Koken: J.B. Barricklo, Peggy Cheng, Kim Ima.

Directed by Sharon Ott; scenery, Loy Arcenas; costumes, Lydia Tanji; lighting, Peter Maradudin; sound, Stephen LeGrand; original music, Dan Kuramoto; puppet design, Bruce Schwartz; production stage manager, Buzz Cohen.

Time: Around 1919. Place: Kauai, Hawaiian Islands. The play was presented in two parts.

Love triangle involving a 16-year-old girl with the adult married couple with whom she lives. Previously produced in regional theater at Berkeley, Calif. Repertory Theater and South Coast Repertory, Costa Mesa, Calif.

MACBETH

1st Witch; Gentlewoman ...... Midori Nakamura	Banquo; Seyton .... Liev Schreiber
2d Witch .... Latonya Borsay	Angus; Murderer .... Greg Porretta
3d Witch .... Ana Reeder	Lady Macbeth .... Angela Bassett
Duncan; Siward; Scottish Doctor ... Rocco Sisto	Servant; Murderer .... Anil Kumar
Malcolm .... Michael Hall	Fleance; Young Siward .... Zach Braff
Sergeant; Porter; Scottish Thane .... Dan Moran	Macduff .... Jeffrey Nordling
Lennox .... Adam Dannheisser	Donalbain; Murderer .... Jason Butler Harner
Ross .... Nathan Hinton	Lady Macduff .... Rene Augesen
Macbeth .... Alec Baldwin	Macduff's Son .... Adam Lamberg

Musicians: Carlos Valdez, Eric Kivnick, Anne H. Pollack.

Directed by George C. Wolfe; scenery, Riccardo Hernandez; costumes, Toni-Leslie James; lighting, Scott Zielinski; sound, Kurt Fischer; original music, Carlos Valdez; fight direction, J. Steven White; production stage manager, Erica Schwartz.

Place: Scotland and England. The play was presented in two parts.

The last major New York revival of *Macbeth* was in the Joseph Papp Public Theater's Shakespeare Marathon 5/8/90 for 24 performances.

SATURN RETURNS: A CONCERT

Vocalists: Vivian Cherry, Lawrence Clayton, Annie Golden, Jose Llana, Theresa McCarthy, Bob Stillman.

Musicians: Ted Sperling conductor, violin, keyboards; Dan Wieloszynski, Chuck Wilson, John Winder woodwinds; Larry Lunetta trumpet; Steve Bargonetti guitar; Douglas Romoff bass; Norbert Goldberg drums, percussion; Todd Ellison keyboards.

Directed by Tina Landau; musical direction, Ted Sperling; scenery and costumes, James Schuette; lighting, Blake Burba; sound, Stuart J. Allyn; projection design, Jan Hartley; orchestrations, Don Sebesky, Jamie Lawrence; music coordination, Seymour Red Press; production stage manager, Lisa Porter.

Non-narrative cycle of songs with themes of faith and longing, based on ancient myths, hymn texts and the quest for meaning. The show was presented without intermission.

MUSICAL NUMBERS: "Saturn Returns: The Flight"—Company; "Icarus"—Bob Stillman, Jose Llana, Company; "Migratory V"—Theresa McCarthy; "Jesus the Mighty Conqueror" (lyric from "The Temple Trio," hymn edition)—Lawrence Clayton, Vivian Cherry, Llana, Stillman; "Pegasus" (lyric by

Ellen Fitzhugh)—Stillman, Annie Golden, McCarthy; "Children of the Heavenly King" (lyric from "Temple Trio")—Cherry; "At the Sounding" (lyric from "Temple Trio")—Cherry, Clayton, Llana, McCarthy; "Build a Bridge"—Stillman; "Sisyphus" (lyric by Ellen Fitzhugh)—Llana, Company; "Life Is But a Dream"—Cherry; "Every Poodle"—Company; "Hero & Leander"—Llana; "Come to Jesus"—McCarthy, Stillman; "How Can I Lose You"—Golden; "The Great Highway"—McCarthy, Company; "There's a Land" (lyric from "Temple Trio")—Company; "There's a Shout" (lyric from "Temple Trio")—Cherry; "Awaiting You"—Clayton; "Saturn Returns: The Return"—Company.

THE CRIPPLE OF INISHMAAN

Kate	Elizabeth Franz	Helen	Aisling O'Neill
Eileen	Roberta Maxwell	Babbybobby	Michael Gaston
Johnnypateenmike	Donal Donnelly	Dr. McSharry	Peter Maloney
Cripple Billy	Ruaidhri Conroy	Manny	Eileen Brennan
Bartley	Christopher Fitzgerald		

Directed by Jerry Zaks; scenery, Tony Walton; costumes, Ann Roth; lighting, Brian Nason; sound, Aural Fixation; projection design, Sage Marie Carter; production stage manager, James Latus.

Time: Circa 1934. Place: The island of Inishmaan, off the western coast of Ireland. The play was presented in two parts.

Handicapped Aran islander seeks a role in the Robert Flaherty documentary *Man of Aran* in order to impress his girl friend. A foreign play previously produced at the Druid Theater in Galway and the Royal National Theater in London.

Note: In The Joseph Papp Public Theater are many auditoria. *A Dybbuk, or Between Two Worlds,* and *The Cripple of Inishmaan* played the Estelle R. Newman Theater, *Ballad of Yachiyo* and *Macbeth* played Martinson Hall, *Saturn Returns: A Concert* played LuEsther Hall.

Roundabout Theater Company. Schedule of four programs. **Misalliance**. (76). Revival of the play by George Bernard Shaw. Opened August 7, 1997. (Closed October 12, 1997) **Cyrano de Bergerac** (56). By Edmond Rostand; adapted from the Brian Hooker translation by Frank Langella. Opened December 9, 1997. (Closed January 25, 1998) **A Flea in Her Ear** (77). Revival of the play by Georges Feydeau; adapted by Jean-Marie Besset and Mark O'Donnell. Opened March 5, 1998. (Closed May 10, 1998) And *You Never Can Tell* by George Bernard Shaw, scheduled to open 6/21/98. Produced by Roundabout Theater Company, Todd Haimes artistic director, Ellen Richard general manager, Gene Feist founding director, at Criterion Center Laura Pels Theater.

MISALLIANCE

Johnny Tarleton	Don Reilly	Mr. John Tarleton	Brian Murray
Bentley Summerhays	Alan Tudyk	Lina Szczepanowska	Elizabeth Marvel
Hypatia Tarleton	Joanna Going	Joseph Percival	Sam Robards
Mrs. Tarleton	Patricia Conolly	Julius Baker ("Gunner")	Zak Orth
Lord Summerhays	Remak Ramsay		

Understudies: Miss Conolly—Jennifer Sternberg; Messrs. Murray, Ramsay—George Bartenieff; Misses Going, Marvel—Annie Parisse; Messrs. Tudyk, Orth—Haynes Thigpen; Messrs. Reilly, Robards—Stephen Kunken.

Directed by David Warren; scenery, Derek McLane; costumes, Catherine Zuber; lighting, Kenneth Posner; original music and sound, John Gromada; casting, Pat McCorkle; production stage manager, Mary Porter Hall; stage manager, Lori Lundquist; press, Boneau/Bryan-Brown, Adrian Bryan-Brown, Erin Dunn.

Time: May 31, 1909. Place: The house of John Tarleton. The play was presented in two parts.

The last major New York revival of *Misalliance* was by Roundabout Theater Company off Broadway 6/23/81 for 192 performances.

MISALLIANCE—Remak Ramsay, Brian Murray and Joanna Going in the Roundabout revival of the play by George Bernard Shaw

CYRANO DE BERGERAC

Christian	Gabriel Macht	Valvert	Armand Schultz
Rageneau	Terry Alexander	Montfleury	Adam LeFevre
Lise	Lisa Leguillou	Cyrano	Frank Langella
Le Bret	George Morfogen	Carbon	Ron McLachlan
Roxane	Allison Mackie	Priest	Marcus Chait
Marguerite	Mikel Sarah Lambert	Soldier	Jeffrey Cox
DeGuiche	Shawn Elliott		

Understudies: Mr. Langella—Ray Virta; Messrs. Morfogen, Elliott, McLachlan—Timothy Wheeler; Misses Mackie, Leguillou, Lambert—Teri Lamm; Messrs. Alexander, LeFevre, Chait—Brian Keane; Messrs. Macht, Schultz—Marcus Chait.

Directed by Frank Langella; scenery, James Noone; costumes, Carrie Robbins; lighting, Gil Wechsler; sound, Laura Grace Brown; fight director, J. Steven White; casting, Jim Carnahan; production stage manager, Jay Adler; stage manager, John Handy; press, Boneau/Bryan-Brown, Andy Shearer.

Act I, Scene 1: A hall. Scene 2: A bakery shop. Scene 3: A garden. Act II, Scene 1: A camp. Scene 2: A garden.

The last major New York revival of this Rostand play was in a musical version, *Cyrano: The Musical*, 11/21/93 on Broadway for 137 performances; and as a play by the Royal Shakespeare Company on Broadway 10/16/84 for 59 performances.

A FLEA IN HER EAR

Camille Chandebise	Shaun Powell	Lucie Hominides de Histingua	Angie Phillips
Ninette	Camilia Sanes	Constance Chandebise	Kali Rocha
Etienne	Michael Countryman	Victor Chandebise; Dodo	Mark Linn-Baker
Dr. Migraine	Richard B. Shull	Tournel	Bruce MacVittie

Carlos Homenides
de Histingua .... Mark McKinney
Justin Battalion .... James Lally
Ginette .... Virginia Louise Smith

Olympia Battalion .... Alice Playten
Baptistin .... George Hall
Rugby .... Wally Dunn

"L'Amour, L'Amour" written and performed by Alice Playten; arrangement, Tom Fay.

Understudies: Misses Rocha, Phillips, Sanes—Virginia Louise Smith; Messrs. Countryman, Shull—Wally Dunn; Misses Smith, Playten—Kate Gleason; Messrs. Linn-Baker, McKinney, Lally—Bobby Cannavale; Messrs. Hall, Dunn, MacVittie, Powell—Saxon Palmer.

Directed by Bill Irwin; scenery, Douglas Stein; costumes, Bill Kellard; lighting, Nancy Shertler; sound, Tom Morse; associate director, Nancy Harrington; casting, Julie Tucker; production stage manager, Gary Mickelson; stage manager, Becky Garrett.

Time: An earlier time. Place: Paris. Act I: The drawing room of Victor Chandebise. Act II: The Hotel Pussycat. Act III: The drawing room of Victor Chandebise. The play was presented in two parts.

The last major New York revival of *A Flea in Her Ear* took place on Broadway 10/3/69 for 11 performances.

Mere Mortals and Others (166). Transfer from off off Broadway of the program of six one-act plays by David Ives, including the premieres of *Time Flies* and *Dr. Fritz or: The Forces of Light*. Produced by Casey Childs, Richard Gross, Jeffrey Richards and Ted Snowden in the Primary Stages Company production, Casey Childs artistic director, at the John Houseman Theater. Opened August 13, 1997. (Closed January 4, 1998)

ACT I

Foreplay or: The Art of the Fugue
Amy .... Jessalyn Gilsig
Chuck I .... Willis Sparks
Annie .... Nancy Opel
Chuck II .... Arnie Burton
Alma .... Anne O'Sullivan
Chuck III .... Danton Stone
Time: Evening. Place: A miniature golf course.
Previously produced OOB in 1991 by Manhattan Punch Line.

Mere Mortals
Joe .... Willis Sparks

Charlie .... Danton Stone
Frank .... Arnie Burton
Time: Lunchtime. Place: A girder, 50 stories up.
Previously produced OOB in 1990 by Ensemble Studio Theater.

Time Flies
May .... Anne O'Sullivan
Horace .... Arnie Burton
David Attenborough .... Willis Sparks
Time: Evening. Place: A pond.
The wooing of a pair of mayflies.

ACT II

Degas, C'est Moi
CAST: Degas—Danton Stone; Doris, Homeless Woman, Twin Donuts Worker—Nancy Opel; Driver #2, Newsman, Jockey, Chorus Boy, Renoir—Arnie Burton; Driver #1, Grocery Worker, OTB Worker, Figure With Dog, Museum Guard, Top Hat Man—Willis Sparks; Drycleaner, Unemployment Worker, Librarian, Museum Goer, Parasol Lady—Anne O'Sullivan; Ballerina, Young Woman—Jessalyn Gilsig.
Place: Manhattan.
Previously produced OOB in 1996. By Ensemble Studio Theater.

Speed-The-Play
M.C. .... Nancy Opel

Donny; Gould; Bernie .... Danton Stone
Bobby; John .... Arnie Burton
Teach; Fox; Danny .... Willis Sparks
Carol; Karen; Deborah .... Jessalyn Gilsig
Joan .... Anne O'Sullivan
Place: Joliet, Ill. Men's Club.
Previously produced OOB in 1989 at a Lincoln Center benefit for Broadway Cares, honoring David Mamet.

Dr. Fritz or: The Forces of Light
Tom .... Arnie Burton
Maria .... Nancy Opel
Place: Bona Fortuna.
Tourist seeking the help of a doctor is confronted and confused by his Spanish receptionist.

ALL PLAYS: Directed by John Rando; scenery, Russell Metheny; costumes, Anita Yavich; lighting, Phil Monat; sound, Aural Fixation; associate producer, Seth Gordon; casting, Peggy Adler; stage manager, Christine Catti; press, Tony Origlio Publicity.

Note: *Mere Mortals and Others* transferred to an off-Broadway schedule at Primary Stages 6/10/97 but did not move to the John Houseman Theater until 8/13/97.

John, His Story (45). By Jeannette Clift George. Produced by A.D. Players, Jeannette Clift George artistic director, at Lamb's Theater. Opened August 29, 1997. (Closed October 5, 1997).

CAST: Stephen Baldwin, Marion Arthur Kirby, Whitney Presley, Patty Tuel Bailey.

Directed by Lee Walker; scenery, Lee Walker; costumes, Donna Southern, based on original concepts by Franklin Hollenbeck; lighting, Sissy Pulley; sound, Gerry Poland; stage manager, Lisa Lagasse.

The life of Jesus presented in the story-telling style of this Houston-based theater group. The play was presented without intermission.

Playwrights Horizons. Schedule of five programs. **Plunge** (25). By Christopher Kyle. Opened September 28, 1997. (Closed October 19, 1997) **Mud, River, Stone** (17). By Lynn Nottage. Opened December 14, 1997. (Closed December 28, 1997) **Gun-Shy** (25). By Richard Dresser. Opened February 1, 1998. (Closed February 22, 1998) **From Above** (22). By Tom Donaghy. Opened April 23, 1998. (Closed May 10, 1998) And *Lillian* by David Cale, scheduled to open 6/15/98. Produced by Playwrights Horizons, Tim Sanford artistic director, Leslie Marcus managing director, Lynn Landis general manager, at Playwrights Horizons.

PLUNGE

Clare Dunn	Ashley Crow	Matty Bonham	Bruce Norris
Harris Nyquist	Taylor Nichols	Val Nyquist	Jessica Hecht
Jim Mackey	Frederick Weller		

Directed by Ron Lagomarsino; scenery, Rob Odorisio; costumes, Jennifer Von Mayrhauser; lighting, Donald Holder; original music, Lewis Flynn; sound, Raymond D. Schilke; casting, James Calleri; production stage manager, Lloyd Davis Jr.; press, James LL Morrison & Associates.

Time: Over the week before Labor Day. Place: A New York City Hotel Room and a restored farmhouse in Western Connecticut. The play was presented in two parts.

Comedy, former college classmates get together for a house party in the country sorting out the realities of their postgraduate lives.

MUD, RIVER, STONE

Sarah Bradley	Paula Newsome	Ama Cyllah	Oni Faida Lampley
David Bradley	Michael Potts	Neibert	John McAdams
Joaquim	Maduka Steady	Simone Frick	Mirjana Jokovic
Mr. Blake	Brian Murray		

Directed by Roger Rees; scenery, Neil Patel; costumes, Kaye Voyce; lighting, Frances Aronson; sound, Red Ramona; casting, James Calleri; production stage manager, Laurie Goldfeder.

Time: The present. Place: Briefly Manhattan; South East Africa. The play was presented in two parts.

Black American couple on vacation in Africa strays off the beaten path and experiences a small village's social and political stresses.

GUN-SHY

Evie	Maryann Urbano	Caitlin	Jessalyn Gilsig
Carter	Christopher Innvar	Duncan	Jeffrey DeMunn
Waiter; Ramon; Neil;			
Nurse; Paramedic	Lee Sellars		

Directed by Gloria Muzio; scenery, Allen Moyer; costumes, Jess Goldstein; lighting, Peter Kaczorowski; sound, Martin Desjardins; stage manager, Denise Yaney.

Romantic comedy of two couples intertwined in the relationships of marriage and divorce. The play was presented in two parts. Previously produced in regional theater at the Actors Theater of Louisville.

FROM ABOVE

Evvy	Patricia Kalember	Jimmy	Neal Huff
Linny	Meg Gibson	Roz	Mary Testa
Peaches	Stephen Mendillo	Sean	Stephen Stout

Directed by David Warren; scenery, Derek McLane; costumes, Laura Bauer; lighting, Donald Holder; original music and sound, John Gromada; film, Andy Clayman/Mediaworks; production stage manager, Janet Takami.

Middle-aged widow is visited by a man who is claiming to be her dead husband.

Three-for-All (8). Comedy performance piece created and peformed by tricicle (Joan Gracia, Paco Mir and Carles Sans). Produced by Steven Baruch, Richard Frankel, Tom Viertel and Marc Routh, with Alan J. Schuster and Mitchell Maxwell, at the Union Square Theater. Opened October 13, 1997. (Closed October 19, 1997)

Scenery, Dino Ibanez, Joan Jorba; costumes, Pepe Aubia; lighting, Joan Sales, Joan Jorba; original music, Josep Bardagi, Josep Pons; associate producer, Alvaro Sarmiento; press, Boneau/Bryan-Brown.

American premiere of physically active comedy performance of skits and routines, previously produced in Barcelona and elsewhere in Europe, presented without intermission.

Tell-Tale (17). Transfer from off off Broadway of the play by Erik Jackson. Produced by Performance Associates and Sanders Productions Inc., in the Théâtre Couture production at the Cherry Lane Theater. Opened October 15, 1997. (Closed November 2, 1997)

Lenore Usher	Sherry Vine	Juan; Buddy Starcher;	
Cora Tripetta	Jackie Beat	Detective Sanders	Mario Diaz

Directed by Joshua D. Rosenzweig; scenery and lighting, Kevin Adams; costumes, Marc Happel, sound, Tim Schellenbaum; visual effects, Basil Twist; choreography, Jane Comfort; stage manager, Allison Loebel; press, The Zeisler Group, Ron Lasko.

Comedy thriller taking off from Edgar Allan Poe's *The Telltale Heart* into a tale of drag queens with murder on the mind. The play was presented in two parts. Previously produced in this production off off Broadway at P.S. 122.

10 Naked Men. (175). By Ronnie Larsen. Produced by Caryn Horwitz at the Actors' Playhouse. Opened October 16, 1997. (Closed March 1, 1998)

Photographer	John R. Petrie	Jim	Mark Leneker
Robert	Joe Bailey	Richard	Cameron Page
Kenny	Roy Scruggs	Jeffrey	Paul Waters
Steve	Anthony Albanese	Mike	Jeffrey Middleton
Allen	Adam Beckworth	Ex-Con	Joe Moretti

Directed by Ronnie Larsen; assistant director, Toni Marie Davis; scenery, Craig B. Wollam; lighting, Brian Aldous; costumes, Bosco DuChamp; press, Caryn Horwitz.

Time: The present. Place: Hollywood, Calif. The play was presented in two parts.

Purveyors and customers of prostitution in the film world.

The Last Session (154). Transfer from off off Broadway of the musical with book by Jim Brochu; music and lyrics by Steve Schalchlin; additional lyrics by John Bettis and Marie Cain. Produced by Carl D. White, Jamie Cesa, Michael Alden, Jay Cardwell, Kim and Ronda Espy/Bob-A-Lew Music and Nancy Nagel Gibbs at the 47th Street Theater. Opened October 17, 1997. (Closed March 1, 1998)

Gideon	Bob Stillman	Vicki	Amy Coleman
Jim	Dean Bradshaw	Buddy	Stephen Bienskie
Tryshia	Grace Garland		

Directed by Jim Brochu; scenery, Eric Lowell Renschler; costumes, Markas Henry; lighting, Michael Gottlieb; sound, Mike Nolan; musical direction, John Kroner; musical supervision and arrangements, Steve Schalchlin; vocal arrangements, Michael D. Gaylord; additional arrangements, Bob Stillman; associate producers, Donald L. Kirkpatrick, Jeremy Koch; casting, Charles Rosen, Annette Kurek; production stage manager, Thomas Clewell; press, Keith Sherman & Associates, Keith Sherman, Kevin Rehac.

Time: Tonight. Place: A recording studio.

A composer battling AIDS and working on his final recording session. Previously produced off off Broadway 5/8/97 by Currican/Playful Productions, Andrew Miller artistic director.

ACT I

"Save Me a Seat" .... Gideon
"The Preacher and the Nurse" .... Company
"Somebody's Friend" .... Vicki, Tryshia, Gideon
"The Group" .... Vicki, Tryshia, Gideon
"Going It Alone" .... Buddy

ACT II

"At Least I Know What's Killing Me" .... Gideon
"Friendly Fire" .... Company
"Connected" .... Gideon
"The Singer and the Song" .... Tryshia, Company
"When You Care" .... Company

*Manhattan Theater Club. Schedule of six programs (see note). Alligator Tales (56). Solo performance by Anne Galjour; written by Anne Galjour; produced in association with Seattle Repertory Theater, Daniel Sullivan artistic director. Opened October 21, 1997. (Closed December 7, 1997) Three Days of Rain (32) By Richard Greenberg. Opened November 12, 1997. (Closed January 4, 1998) Eyes for Consuela (64). By Sam Shepard; based on the story The Blue Bouquet by Octavio Paz. Opened February 10, 1998. (Closed April 5, 1998). Mizlansky/ Zilinsky or "Schmucks" (80). By Jon Robin Baitz. Opened February 17, 1998. (Closed April 26, 1998) *Power Plays (13). Program of three one-act plays: The Way of All Fish and In and Out of the Light by Elaine May and Virtual Reality by Alan Arkin. Opened May 21, 1998. *Labor Day (1). By A.R. Gurney. Opened June 1, 1998. Produced by Manhattan Theater Club, Lynne Meadow artistic director, Barry Grove executive producer, at City Center, Three Days of Rain, Mizlansky/Zilinsky and Labor Day at Stage I, Alligator Tales and Eyes for Consuela at Stage II, Power Plays at the Promenade Theater.

ALL PLAYS: Associate artistic director, Michael Bush; general manager, Victoria Bailey; press, Boneau/Bryan-Brown, Chris Boneau, Andy Shearer, Susanne Tighe, Patrick Paris.

ALLIGATOR TALES

Directed by Sharon Ott; scenery, Kate Edmunds; costumes, Laura Hazlett; lighting, Kent Dorsey; sound, Stephen LeGrand; production stage manager, Kelly Kirkpatrick.

Anne Galjour in characterizations of Cajun folk in Louisiana bayou country during the hurricane season. Previously produced in regional theater.

THREE DAYS OF RAIN

Walker; Ned .... John Slattery   Pip; Theo .... Bradley Whitford
Nan/Lina .... Patricia Clarkson

Understudy: Messrs. Slattery, Whitford—Jack Koening.

Directed by Evan Yionoulis; scenery, Chris Barreca; costumes, Candice Cain; lighting, Donald Holder; sound, Red Ramona; original music, Mike Yionoulis; special effects, Gregory Meeh; casting, Nancy Piccione; production stage manager, Roy Harris.

Time: Act I, 1995. Act II, 1960. Place: In and around an apartment in downtown Manhattan.

Above, Jose Perez and Tanya Gingerich
in *Eyes for Consuela* by Sam Shepard;
right, John Slattery and Patricia Clarkson in *Three Days of Rain* by Richard
Greenberg; *below,* Lewis J. Stadlen and
Nathan Lane in *Mizlansky/Zilinsky or
"Schmucks"* by Jon Robin Baitz

Brother and sister in search of a mysterious truth about their parents, with the actors playing the members of both generations. Previously produced in regional theater at South Coast Repertory, Costa Mesa, Calif.

EYES FOR CONSUELA

Viejo	Jose Perez	Amado	Daniel Faraldo
Consuela	Tanya Gingerich	Guitarist	Josué Perez
Henry	David Strathairn		

Directed by Terry Kinney; scenery, Santo Loquasto; costumes, Walt Spangler; lighting, Jennifer Tipton; musical direction and sound, Rob Milburn; original music, Josué Perez; choreography, Peter Pucci; fight direction, Rick Sordelet; casting, Nancy Piccione; production stage manager, Ruth Kreshka.

Place: Mexico. The play was presented in two parts.

American meets bandits in the Mexican jungle, quarreling over affairs of the heart.

MIZLANSKY/ZILINSKY OR "SCHMUCKS"

Alan Tolkin	Mark Blum	Miles Brook	Lee Wilkof
Lionel Hart	Paul Sand	Paul Trecker	Glenn Fitzgerald
Dusty Fink	Jennifer Albano	Horton De Vries	Larry Pine
Davis Mizlansky	Nathan Lane	Sam Zilinsky	Lewis J. Stadlen

On Speakerphone: Sylvia Zilinsky—Christine Baranski; Esther Arthur—Julie Kavner; Mr. Braithwait—Harry Shearer.

Understudy: Miss Albano—Elaine Bayless.

Directed by Joe Mantello; scenery, Santo Loquasto; costumes, Ann Roth; lighting, Brian MacDevitt; original music and sound, David Van Tieghem; casting, Nancy Piccione; production stage manager, Leila Knox.

Time: December 1984; last scene January 9, 1985. Place: Los Angeles. Act I, Scene 1: December 14, 1984, 12:30 p.m. Scene 2: 3:45 p.m. the same day. Scene 3: 6:15 p.m. the same day. Act II, Scene 1: 7:30 p.m. that evening. Scene 2: December 15, lunchtime. Scene 3: 5:15 p.m. the same day. Scene 4: 6:20 p.m. the same day. Scene 5: January 9, 1985, 4 p.m.

Pair of Hollywood operators working on a shady deal. Previously produced in regional theater at L.A. Theater Works.

POWER PLAYS

The Way of All Fish

Ms. Asquith	Elaine May	Lefty	Anthony Arkin
Miss Riverton	Jeannie Berlin		

In and Out of the Light

Virtual Reality

		Dr. Kesselman	Alan Arkin
		Sue	Elaine May
De Recha	Alan Arkin	Harry	Anthony Arkin
		Wanda	Jeannie Berlin

Understudies: Messrs. Alan and Anthony Arkin—Jed Diamond; Misses Berlin, May—Margo Skinner.

Directed by Alan Arkin; scenery, Michael McGarty; costumes, Michael Krass; lighting, Adam Silverman; sound, Andrew Keister; production stage manager, Doug Fogel.

Comedies, featuring two men in a warehouse in *Virtual Reality,* a highly-strung executive and her secretary in *The Way of All Fish* and a dentist's office with the doctor, his son, his assistant and a patient in *In and Out of the Light.*

LABOR DAY

John	Josef Sommer	Ginny	Veanne Cox
Dennis	Brooks Ashmanskas	Ralph	James Colby
Ellen	Joyce Van Patten		

Directed by Jack O'Brien; scenery, Ralph Funicello; costumes, Michael Krass; lighting, Kenneth Posner; sound, Jeff Ladman; production stage manager, Denise Yaney.

Time: The present, Labor Day. Place: Northwestern Connecticut. The play was presented in two parts.

John, the playwriting character of Gurney's play *The Cocktail Hour,* has another problematical script, this one about his wife and children. Previously produced in regional theater at the Old Globe Theater, San Diego.

Note: Manhattan Theater Club also presented *Manhattan Music: A Performance Festival,* three musical acts—Mary Cleere Haran in her *Pennies From Heaven,* an interpretation of 1930s movie songs, 5/19–6/7/98; James Naughton's one man show, 6/9–6/28/98; and *Hot Mouth,* an *a cappella* vocal group performance conceived by Grisha Coleman, 6/30–7/19/98.

H. Finn Esq. (22). By Peter Zablotsky. Produced by Jappen Productions, Inc. at the Martin R. Kaufman Theater. Opened October 26, 1997. (Closed November 23, 1997)

CAST: H. Finn—Michael Genet; lst Police Officer, 2d Pigeon, MHP One, Dauphin, 1st Black Demonstrator, Reverend Polly—Kent C. Jackman; Tom—Gary Lowery; lst Pigeon, 2d Judge, Boss, Auctioneer, Deputy, lst White Demonstrator, Rogers—Tim Miller; Jim Watson, George, Al Shepherdson, 3d Judge—Bill Mitchell; lst Judge, 2d Police Officer, MHP Two, Bridgewater, 2d White Demonstrator, 3d Pigeon—Paul Parente; Joanna, Emily Grangerford, Becky—Ruth Ann Phimister.

Directed by John Ahlers; scenery, Luna Hirai; costumes, Amy Carll; lighting, Lawrence H. Clayton; sound, Johnna Doty; casting, Carl Schmehl; production stage manager, Stephanie McCormick; press, Tony Origlio, Karen Greco, Michael Cullen.

Time: The present. Place: The banks of the Mississippi River. The play was presented in three parts.

A con man and his defense attorney—great-great grandsons of Tom Sawyer and Huck Finn—travel up the Mississippi from New Orleans to Hannibal, Mo. in a present-day adventure.

Momix (8). Performance piece created by the company; Moses Pendleton artistic director. Produced by ICM Artists, Ltd. and City Center at City Center. Opened October 28, 1997. (Closed November 2, 1997)

Tim Acito	Suzanne Lampl
Erin Elliott	Yasmine Lee
Claire Kaplan	Cynthia Quinn
P.I. Keohavong	Brian Simerson

Lighting, Howell Binkley, Bruce Goldstein, Moses Pendleton; production director, Bruce Goldstein; press, Jeffrey Richards.

Effects created by a group of dancer-illusionists based in Washington, Conn., previously presented elsewhere in the United States and in 21 countries around the world, and with the number entitled Sputnik (Fellow Traveler) having its premiere in this production.

ACT I

Jonas et Latude: With Tim Acito, Brian Simerson. Choreography, Sandy Chase, Brian Sanders, Moses Pendleton; prop design, Cynthia Quinn; costumes, Kitty Daly; music, Antonio Vivaldi.

The Wind-Up: With Cynthia Quinn. Choreography, Moses Pendleton, Cynthia Quinn; music, "Spirit of the Forest" by Martin Cradick.

TUU: With Tim Acito, Suzanne Lampl. Choreography, Tim Acito, Solveig Olsen, Moses Pendleton; costumes, Cynthia Quinn; music, "TUU" by TUU.

Spawning: With Suzanne Lampl, Yasmine Lee, Cynthia Quinn. Choreography, Moses Pendleton, Lisa Giobbi, Dianne Howarth, Cynthia Quinn; music, "Mercy Street" by Peter Gabriel.

Underwater Study #5: With Tim Acito. Created by Brian Sanders; music, Art of Noise.

White Widow: With Cynthia Quinn. Choreography, Moses Pendleton, Cynthia Quinn; costume, Cynthia Quinn; music, "The World Spins," music by Angelo Badalerenti, lyrics by David Lynch.

Skiva: With Tim Acito, Yasmine Lee; choreography, Moses Pendleton, Company; music, King Sunny Ade and His African Beats.

ACT II

Table Talk: With Tim Acito. Choreography, Moses Pendleton and Karl Baumann; music, "Safe From Harm" by R. Del Naja, A. Vowles, G. Marshall.

Orbit: With Erin Elliott. Choreography, Erin Elliott, Moses Pendleton; music from Feed Your Head, compiled by Michael Dog.

Sputnik (Fellow Traveler): With Tim Acito, Claire Kaplan, P.I. Keohavong, Suzanne Lampl, Yasmine Lee, Cynthia Quinn, Brian Simerson. Directed by Moses Pendleton; assisted by Tim Acito, Ezra Caldwell, Lorin Campolattaro, Claire Kaplan, P.I. Keohavong, Suzanne Lampl, Yasmine Lee, Cynthia Quinn, Brian Sanders, Brian Simerson; music, "Diamante" by Brenda Perry and Lisa Gerard.

E.C.: With the Company. Choreography, Moses Pendleton, Company; music by Laraaji, Vena, and Moses Pendleton.

*Secrets Every Smart Traveler Should Know (252). Musical revue with songs and sketches by Douglas Bernstein, Francesca Blumenthal, Michael Brown, Barry Creyton, Lesley Davison, Addy Fieger, Stan Freeman, Murray Grand, Glen Kelly, Barry Kleinbort, Jay Leonhart, Denis Markell. Produced by Scott Perrin at the Triad Theater. Opened October 30, 1997.

James Darrah   Jay Leonhart
Kathy Fitzgerald   Liz McConahay
Stan Freeman   Michael McGrath

Directed by Patrick Quinn, assistant, Matthew Lacey; musical direction and arrangements, Stan Freeman; scenery and lighting, Rui Rita, associate, Jeff Nellis; costumes, David Brooks; sound, Kurt B. Kellenberger; special material, Lesley Davison; associate producers, Peter Martin, Nancy McCall, Steve McGraw; stage manager, Alex Lyu Volckhausen; press, Media Blitz, Beck Lee.

Lampoon in songs and sketches of the pitfalls and aggravations of modern travel, inspired by the Fodor publication of the same title.

SONG NUMBERS AND SKETCHES: "Secrets Every Smart Traveler Should Know" (by Lesley Davison)—Company; "Travel Secrets" (by Barry Creyton)—Company; "Naked in Pittsburgh" (by Lesley Davison)—James Darrah; Reservations (by Barry Creyton)—Michael McGrath, Kathy Fitzgerald; "Star Search" (by Stan Freeman)—Liz McConahay; "Customs" (by and with Jay Leonhart); "Hertz" (by Lesley Davison)—McGrath, McConahay; This Is Your Captain Speaking (by and with Stan Freeman); "See It Now" (by Stan Freeman)—Company; "Acapulco" (music by Addy Fieger, lyrics by Francesca Blumenthal)—Fitzgerald; "Salzburg" (by Stan Freeman)—Company; Private Wives (by Barry Creyton)—Darrah, McConahay; "Me and Margarita" (by and with Jay Leonhart); "Red Hot Lava" (by Murray Grand)—McGrath, Darrah, Fitzgerald; "I Get Around" (by Barry Kleinbort)—McConahay; "Seeing America First" (by Lesley Davison)—McGrath, Fitzgerald; "Paradise Found" (by and with Stan Freeman); "The French Song" (by Glen Kelly)—McConahay, Fitzgerald; "She Spoke Spanish" (by Michael Brown)—McGrath; "Honey, Sweetie, Baby" (by Douglas Bernstein and Denis Markell)—McGrath, Fitzgerald, Darrah; "Home" (by Michael Brown)— Company.

Two Pianos Four Hands (231). Play with music created and performed by Ted Dykstra and Richard Greenblatt. Produced by David Mirvish, Ed Mirvish, Ben Sprecher and William P. Miller at the Promenade Theater. Opened October 30, 1997. (Closed May 10, 1998)

Alternates: Ted Dykstra—Andrew Lippa; Richard Greenblatt—Jed Rees.

Directed by Gloria Muzio; scenery and costumes, Steve Lucas; lighting, Tharon Musser; associate director, Andy McKim; executive producer, Brian Sewell; associate producer, Linda Intaschi; production stage manager, Beatrice Campbell; press, Jeffrey Richards Associates, Rebecca Ramirez, Irene Gandy, Caral Craig.

Two performers, each seated at a piano, look back on a musician's intense strivings to develop his talent to concert dimensions, in a series of scenes embellished with musical passages. A foreign play originally produced at the Tarragon Theater, Toronto.

MUSICAL NUMBERS, ACT I: D Minor Concerto–1st Movement by J.S. Bach, "Heart and Soul" by Hoagy Carmichael, "In My Little Birch Canoe" by Lelia Fletcher, "By the Stream" by Richard

Greenblatt, "Our Band Goes to Town" arranged by J.B. Duvernoy, Sonatina No. 6 in F Major by Beethoven, Sonatina Facile in C Major–lst Movement and Sonata for One Piano, Four Hands in D Major–lst Movement by Mozart, *In Der Halle des Bergkonigs–Peer Gynt* Suite I by Edvard Grieg, D Minor Concerto–lst Movement by J.S. Bach (reprise).

ACT II: Prelude in D Flat Major by Chopin, *Leyenda* by I. Albeniz, Rondo for Two Pianos, Four Hands in C Major by Chopin, *Fantasiestucke* No 2 by Schumann, *Pathetique* Sonata No 8 in C Minor–lst and 2d Movements by Beethoven, Ballade No 2 in F major by Chopin, Mephisto Waltz No 1 by Franz Liszt, Medley of Pop Tunes, A Flat Impromptu by Schubert, "My Funny Valentine" by Richard Rodgers, "Piano Man" by Billy Joel, Horowitz recording (Mephisto Waltz), D Minor Concerto–lst Movement (Reprise) and Sheep May Safely Graze by J.S. Bach.

American Place Theater. Schedule of three programs. **Fly** (30). By Joseph Edward. Opened November 2, 1997. (Closed November 30, 1997) **BAFO (Best and Final Offer)** (29). By Tom Strelich. Opened March 8, 1998. (Closed April 5, 1998) And *Sakina's Restaurant* by Aasif Mandvi, scheduled to open 6/24/98. Produced by American Place Theater, Wynn Handman artistic director, Susannah Halston executive director, at the American Place Theater.

FLY

Fly Lewis	Joseph Edward	Male Roles	Arthur French
Female Roles	Amy-Monique Waddell		

Directed by Wynn Handman; scenery, Joel Reynolds; costumes, Helen Simmons; lighting, Chad McArver; sound, David Wright; production stage manager, Dwight R.B. Cook; press, Springer/Chicoine Public Relations.

Place: A roof top in Brooklyn, N.Y. The play was presented without intermission.

Exploring the kinetic personality and tragi-comic life experiences of a prototypical young New York black man.

BAFO (BEST AND FINAL OFFER)

Willie Peet	Christopher Wynkoop	Ashe	Kent Broadhurst
Clay	Tom Ligon	Shokanje	Jill Marie Lawrence
Sayles	Beau Gravitte	P.K.	Sam Freed

Directed by Robert Kalfin; scenery, Robert Mitchell; costumes, Gail Cooper-Hecht; lighting, Robert Williams; sound, David Wright; fight direction, B.H. Barry; casting, Irene Stockton; production stage manager, D.C. Rosenberg; press, Susan Chicoine, Barry Springer, Charlie Siedenburg.

Time: The present. Place: The offices of a small defense aerospace contractor somewhere in Southern California.

Eccentric developments at a Pentagon supplier threatened with downsizing.

Previously produced in regional theater at South Coast Repertory, Costa Mesa, Calif.

Defying Gravity (41). By Jane Anderson. Produced by Daryl Roth at the American Place Theater. Opened November 2, 1997. (Closed January 4, 1998)

Monet	Jonathan Hadary	Ed	Frank Raiter
Elizabeth	Alicia Goranson	C.B.	Philip Seymour Hoffman
Teacher	Candy Buckley	Donna	Sandra Daley
Betty	Lois Smith		

Understudies: Messrs. Hadary, Raiter, Hoffman—Jeffrey Bean; Misses Goranson, Buckley, Daley—Jan Leslie Harding; Miss Smith—Sally Parrish.

Directed by Michael Wilson; scenery and projection design, Jeff Cowie; costumes, David C. Woolard; lighting, Michael Lincoln; original music and sound, John Gromada; associate producer, Mollie Zweig; casting, Bernard Telsey; production stage manager, R. Wade Jackson; stage manager, Lisa Iacucci; press, Boneau/Bryan-Brown, Andy Shearer.

Spiritual fantasy based on the space shuttle Challenger disaster. Previously produced in regional theater at the Williamstown, Mass. Theater Festival.

MindGames (237). Solo peformance piece by and with Marc Salem. Produced by Anita Waxman, David Richenthal and Jeffrey Ash at the Westside Theater Downstairs. Opened November 17, 1997. (Closed May 31, 1998)

Scenery, Ray Recht; lighting, Chris Dallos; sound, Raymond Schilke; press, Jeffrey Richards Associates.

Program of magical tricks of mindreading. The performance was presented without intermission.

Second Stage Theater. Schedule of two programs (see note). **A Madhouse in Goa**. (24). By Martin Sherman. Opened November 17, 1997. (Closed December 7, 1997) **Bad Sex With Bud Kemp** (8). Solo performance by Sandra Tsing Loh; written by Sandra Tsing Loh. Opened May 5, 1998. (Closed May 10, 1998) Produced by Second Stage Theater, Carole Rothman artistic director, Carol Fishman managing director, Alexander Fraser executive director, at the McGinn-Cazale Theater.

A MADHOUSE IN GOA

Part I: A Table for a King, summer 1966	Oliver .... Daniel Gerroll
David .... Rick Stear	Heather .... Judith Ivey
Mrs. Honey .... Judith Ivey	Dylan .... Mark Kevin Lewis
Costos .... Mark Kevin Lewis	Aliki .... Denise Faye
Nikos .... Daniel Gerroll	Barnaby Grace .... Rick Stear
Part II: Keeps Rainin' All the Time,	
summer 1986	
Daniel Hosani .... Russ Thacker	

Directed by Nicholas Martin; scenery, James Noone; costumes, Michael Krass; lighting, Frances Aronson; sound, Kurt B. Kellenberger; casting, Johnson-Liff Associates; production stage manager, Leila Knox; stage manager, Delicia Turner; press, Richard Kornberg & Associates, Don Summa, Rick Miramontez, Jim Byk.

Satire on modern moral and political standards, set on two Greek islands in a portrayal of a writer's rise and fall. An American play previously produced in London in 1989.

BAD SEX WITH BUD KEMP

Directed by David Schweitzer; scenery and lighting, Kevin Adams; costumes, Peter Cohen; sound, Robert Murphy; production stage manager, Rebecca C. Monroe; press, Richard Kornberg.

The singles life in New York City in the 1990s.

Note: Second Stage also presented a special return engagement of its 1994 presentation *Ricky Jay and His 52 Assistants,* a solo show written and performed by Ricky Jay under the direction of David Mamet, for 55 performances 1/14/98 to 3/29/98.

Clue: The Musical (29). Musical based on the Parker Brothers' Board Game; book by Peter DePietro; music by Galen Blum, Wayne Barker and Vinnie Martucci; lyrics by Tom Chiodo. Produced by Explorer Productions in association with DLR Entertaiment and Manhattan Repertory Company at the Players Theater. Opened December 3, 1997. (Closed December 28, 1997)

Mr. Boddy .... Robert Bartley	Col. Mustard .... Michael Kostroff
Mrs. Peacock .... Wysandria Woolsey	Mrs. White .... Daniel Leroy McDonald
Prof. Plum .... Ian Knauer	Mr. Green .... Marc Rubman
Miss Scarlet .... Tiffany Taylor	Detective .... Denny Dillon

Orchestra: James Followell leader, piano; Steven Machamer percussion; Victor Lawrence cello.
Understudies: Male roles—Dennis R. St. Pierre; female roles—Denise Summerford.

Directed and choreographed by Peter DePietro; musical direction, James Followell; costumes, David R. Zyla; lighting, Annmarie Duggan; arrangements and orchestrations, Wayne Barker; production stage manager, Bart Kahn; press, Keith Sherman & Associates, Kevin Rehac.

Place: Boddy Manor. The play was presented without intermission.

A murder mystery to be solved, as in the board game.

MUSICAL NUMBERS

"The Game" .... Mr. Boddy, Company
"Life Is a Bowl of Pits" .... Mrs. White
"Everyday Devices" .... Miss Scarlet, Mr. Green, Company
"Once a Widow" .... Mrs. Peacock
"Corridors and Halls" .... Boddy, Scarlet, Green, Col. Mustard, Prof. Plum, White, Peacock
"The Murder" .... Company
"The Game" (Reprise) .... Boddy, Company
"She Hasn't Got a Clue" .... Scarlet, Green, Mustard, Plum, White, Peacock
"Everyday Devices" (Reprise) .... Scarlet, Green, Company
"Seduction Deduction" .... Plum, Detective
"Foul Weather Friend" .... Scarlet, Green, Mustard, Plum, White, Peacock
"Don't Blame Me" .... Company
"The Final Clue" .... Boddy, Scarlet, Green, Mustard, Plum, White, Peacock
"The Game" (Finale) .... Boddy, Company

Lincoln Center Theater. Schedule of two programs. **Pride's Crossing** (137). By Tina Howe. Opened December 7, 1997. (Closed April 5, 1998). And *A New Brain*, musical with book by James Lapine and William Finn, music and and lyrics by William Finn, scheduled to open 6/15/98. Produced by Lincoln Center Theater under the direction of Andre Bishop and Bernard Gersten at the Mitzi E. Newhouse Theater.

PRIDE'S CROSSING

CAST: Mabel Tidings Bigelow—Cherry Jones; Vita Bright, Phineas Tidings, Pru O'Neill, Kitty Lowell—Angie Phillips; Chandler Coffin, Mary O'Neill, Dr. Peabody—Dylan Baker; West Bright, Frazier Tidings, David Bloom, Pinky Wheelock—David Lansbury; Gus Tidings, Anton Gurevitch, Porter Bigelow, Wheels Wheelock—Casey Biggs; Maud Tidings, Julia Renoir—Kandis Chappell; Minty Renoir, Emma Bigelow—Julia McIlvaine.

Understudies: Miss Jones—Linda Cook; Misses Phillips, Chappell—Jacqueline Antaramian; Mr. Baker—Martin Kildare; Mr. Lansbury— Christopher Burns; Mr. Biggs—Jack Wetherall; Miss McIlvaine—Danielle Hildreth.

Directed by Jack O'Brien; scenery, Ralph Funicello; costumes, Robert Morgan; lighting, Kenneth Posner; music and sound, Mark Bennett; projections, Jan Hartley; casting, Daniel Swee; stage manager, Julie Baldauff; press, Philip Rinaldi.

Time: This year. Place: Pride's Crossing, Mass. and *in Mabel's memory*.

Act I, Scene 1: Mabel's bedroom, the end of June, the present. Scene 2: *The Tidings dining room, summer 1917.* Scene 3: Mabel's living room, the next day, the present. Scene 4: *The Tidings kitchen, summer 1922.* Scene 5: Mabel's living room, later that afternoon, the present. Scene 6: *The Tidings living room, summer 1927.* Act II, Scene 1: Mabel's living room, four days later, the present. Scene 2: *Mabel and Porter Bigelow's living room, Boston, summer 1942.* Scene 3: The next day, the 4th of July, Mabel's bedroom, the present. Scene 4: *King's Chapel, Boston, 1967.* Scene 5: Mabel's lawn, moments later, the present. Scene 6: *The cliffs of Dover, England, 1928.*

The life of a woman Channel swimmer portrayed by Cherry Jones from childhood to age 90. Previously produced in regional theater at the Old Globe Theater, San Diego. Winner of the 1997–98 New York Drama Critics Circle Award for the best American play; see its entry in the Prizewinning Plays section of this volume.

The Show Goes On (88). Musical revue with songs by Tom Jones and Harvey Schmidt. Produced by the York Theater Company, James Morgan artistic director, Joseph V. De Michele managing director, at the Theater at St. Peter's Church. Opened December 17, 1997. (Closed March 1, 1998)

JoAnn Cunningham	J. Mark McVey
Tom Jones	Harvey Schmidt
Emma Lampert	

Direction and musical staging by Drew Scott Harris; musical staging and choreography, Janet Watson; scenery, James Morgan; costumes, Suzy Benzinger; lighting, Mary Jo Dondlinger; casting, Stephen De Angelis; production stage manager, Barnett Feingold; press, Keith Sherman & Associates, Kevin Rehac.

Per its subtitle, A Portfolio of Theater Songs by the authors of *The Fantasticks* and other shows.

MUSICAL NUMBERS, ACT I: "Come on Along"—Tom Jones, Harvey Schmidt; "Try to Remember"—Emma Lampert, J. Mark McVey, JoAnn Cunningham; "Mr. Off-Broadway"—Jones, Schmidt; "Everyone Looks Lonely"—Cunningham; "I Know Loneliness Quite Well"—McVey; "The Story of My Life"—Lampert; "The Holy Man & The New Yorker"—Jones, Schmidt; "It's Gonna Be Another Hot Day"—Cunningham, Lampert, McVey; "I Can Dance"—Lampert; "Dessau Dance Hall"—Cunningham; "Flibberty-Gibbet"—Cunningham, Lampert; "Melisande"—McVey; "Simple Little Things"—Cunningham; "I Do, I Do"—Company (from show), Lampert (Thirties), Cunningham, McVey (duet); "The Honeymoon Is Over"—Company; "My Cup Runneth Over"—Company.

ACT II: "Celebration"—Company; "Orphan in the Storm"—Lampert; "Survive"—McVey; "Under the Tree"—Cunningham, McVey; "Fifty Million Years Ago"—Cunningham, Lampert, McVey; "Decorate the Human Face"—Cunningham; "Where Did It Go?"—McVey; "Wonderful Way to Die"—Jones, Schmidt; "The Room Is Filled With You"—Cunningham; "Time Goes By"—McVey; "Goodbye, World"—Lampert; "The Show Goes On"—Company.

*Visiting Mr. Green (215). By Jeff Baron. Produced by Arnold Mittelman at the Union Square Theater. Opened December 17, 1997.

Mr. Green	Eli Wallach
Ross Gardiner	David Alan Basche

Understudies: Mr. Basche—Peter Ackerman; Mr. Wallach—Ed Setrakian.

Directed by Lonny Price; scenery, Loren Sherman; costumes, Gail Brassard; lighting, Phil Monat; original music, David Shire; sound, Aural Fixation; casting, Pat McCorkle; production stage manager, Karen Moore; press, Jeffrey Richards Associates, Irene Gandy.

Time: The present. Place: The Upper West Side of Manhattan. The play was presented in two parts.

Growing friendship between an elderly curmudgeon and an affable young man.

Joseph Gabriel Magic '98 (131). Magic show devised and performed by Joseph Gabriel. Produced by Archangel Productions, Inc. at the Lamb's Theater. Opened January 13, 1998. (Closed May 17, 1998)

Magic Assistants: Lucy Gabriel, Vincent Giordano. Juggler: Romano Frediani. Dancers: Heather Rochelle Harmon (Line Captain), Heather Shanahan, Raquel Galarza. Magic Technicians: Vincent Giordano, Thom Rubino.

Lighting, Gregory Cohen; sound, Robert Cotnoir; stage manager, Andrew Forste; press, David Rothenberg Associates, David J. Gersten.

New version of Gabriel's magic show previously produced 9/29/96 off Broadway as *Magic on Broadway* for 334 performances.

June Moon (69). Transfer from off off Broadway of the revival of the comedy by Ring Lardner and George S. Kaufman; music and lyrics by Ring Lardner. Produced in the McCarter Theater production, Emily Mann artistic director, by Edgar Lansbury, Howard Erskine, Everett King and Soloway/Levy at the Variety Arts Theater; original production by The Drama Dept., Douglas Carter Beane artistic director. Opened January 15, 1998. (Closed March 15, 1998)

VISITING MR. GREEN—David Alan Basche and
Eli Wallach in a scene from the play by Jeff Baron

Fred Stevens	Geoffrey Nauffts	Goldie; Miss Rixey	Amy Hohn
Edna Baker	Jessica Stone	Window Cleaner;	
Paul Sears	Robert Joy	Piano Player	Bruce W. Coyle
Lucille	Becky Ann Baker	Benny Fox	Lee Wilkof
Eileen	Cynthia Nixon	Mr. Hart	Robert Ari
Maxie	Albert Macklin		

Understudies: Misses Stone, Hohn—Samantha Brown; Misses Nixon, Baker—Tasha Lawrence; Messrs. Joy, Macklin, Ari, Coyle—Ken Marks; Messrs. Nauffts, Wilkof—Matthew Saldivar.

Directed by Mark Nelson; musical direction, Robert Lamont; scenery, Bill Clarke; costumes, Jonathan C. Bixby; lighting, Kirk Bookman; sound, One Dream Sound; associate producer, Sonny Everett; casting, Bernard Telsey; production stage manager, Susie Cordon; press, Boneau/Bryan-Brown, Chris Boneau.

June Moon's only previous major New York revival of record took place on Broadway 5/15/33 for 49 performances. The present revival opened off off Broadway 1/8/97.

Virtue: Senpo Sugihara (7). By Koichi Hiraishi; translated by David W. Griffith and Mariko Hori. Produced by International Cultural Production, Inc., Kazuto Ohira chief executive officer, in the Gekidan Dora Theatrical Company production at the Sylvia and Danny Kaye Playhouse. Opened January 16, 1998 (see note). Closed January 23, 1998.

Chiune Sugihara	Fumio Sato
Yukiko Sugihara	Nobuko Hiraguchi

Others: Shoichi Yamada, Hayao Senda, Saho Yatagawa, Tomoko Gungi, Yuri Hasegawa, Hidehito Morita, Hisao Yokote, Motohiko Tateno, Jun Kuriki.

Directed by Shoichi Yamada; scenery, Yoshiaki Sono; costumes, Mayumi Ryoji; lighting, Genichiro Yokota; sound, Naokatsu Nakajima; original music, Eiryu Ko; arrangements, Kouichi Iizuka; production stage manager, Taisuke Inaba; press, James LL Morrison & Associates.

True story of a heroic Japanese diplomat who managed to free thousands of Polish Jews while stationed in Lithuania at the start of World War II. A foreign play previously produced in Japan and elsewhere.

Note: Press date for *Virtue: Senpo Sugihara* was 1/18/98.

Never the Sinner (146). By John Logan. Produced by Jeffrey Richards, Richard Gross, Bud Yorkin, Steven M. Levy, Harold Reed and the American Jewish Theater, Stanley Brechner artistic director, at the John Houseman Theater. Opened January 24, 1998. (Closed May 31, 1998)

Leopold .... Jason Bowcutt	Reporter #1 .... Paul Mullins
Loeb .... Michael Solomon	Reporter #2 .... Jurian Hughes
Darrow .... Robert Hogan	Reporter #3 .... Howard W. Overshown
Crowe .... Glen Pannell	

Directed by Ethan McSweeny; scenery, Lou Stancari; costumes, Tom Broecker; lighting, Howell Binkley; sound, David Maddox; musical staging, Karma Kamp; casting, Stuart Howard Associates; production stage manager, Christine Lemme; press, Jeffrey Richards Associates, Irene Gandy.

Time: 1924. Place: Chicago, Illinois. The play was presented in two parts.

Dramatization of the Leopold and Loeb trial for murder, an infamous thrill killing. Previously produced in regional theater at the Signature Theater (Virginia) and Rep Stage (Columbia, Md.).

The New 42nd Street Inc. Schedule of three programs. **Romeo and Juliet** (10). Revival of the play by William Shakespeare in The Acting Company production, Margot Harley producing director. Opened January 29, 1998. (Closed February 8, 1998) **The Number 14** (10). By Peter Anderson, Melody Anderson, Gina Bastone, Colin Heath, David Mackay, Wayne Specht, Roy Surette, Beatrice Zeilinger; additional material developed by Darlene Brookes, Tom Jones and Allan Zinyk; in the Axis Theater Company and Touchstone Theater production. Opened March 27, 1998. (Closed April 5, 1998) **The Wind in the Willows** (18). Musical adapted by Gerardine Clark from Kenneth Grahame's novel; music, lyrics and additional text by Dianne Adams and James McDowell; additional lyrics by Gerardine Clark and Katharine Clark; the Syracuse Stage production, James A. Clark producing director, Robert Moss artistic director, in association with Syracuse University. Opened May 29, 1998. (Closed June 14, 1998) Produced by The New 42d Street Inc., Cora Cahan president, Lisa L. Post project director, at the New Victory Theater.

ROMEO AND JULIET

Chorus; Juliet .... Heather Robison	Capulet .... James Farmer
Chorus; Romeo .... Hamish Linklater	Montague; Peter; Friar John .. Stephen DeRosa
Sampson; Paris .... James Stanley	Lady Montague .... Jennifer Rohn
Gregory; Nurse .... Lisa Tharps	Escalus .... Jason Alan Carvell
Balthasar; Mercutio .... Daniel Pearce	Potpan;
Benvolio; Apothecary;	Friar Laurence ..... Robert Alexander Owens
Watchman .... Christopher Edwards	Lady Capulet .... Erika Rolfsrud
Tybalt; Watchman ...... Clark Scott Carmichael	Servants .... Company

Understudies: Misses Robison, Rolfsrud, Tharps, Messrs. Owens, Stanley—Jennifer Rohn; Messrs. Linklater, Edwards, Pearce, Miss Robinson—Clark Scott Carmichael; Miss Tharps—Erika Rolfsrud; Messrs. Pearce, DeRosa, Carmichael, Owens—Jason Alan Carvell; Mr. Carvell—Lisa Tharps; Mr. Farmer—James Stanley; Messrs. DeRosa (Montague), Stanley—Daniel Pearce; Mr. Owens—Stephen DeRosa; Mr. DeRosa (Friar John)—Christopher Edwards.

Directed by James Bundy; scenery, Ming Cho Lee; costumes, Ann Hould-Ward; lighting, Robert Wierzel; original music, Kim D. Sherman; fight direction and choreography, Felix Ivanov; voice, speech and text consultant, Elizabeth Smith; casting, Bernard Telsey; production stage manager, Linda Harris; press, Springer/Chicoine Public Relations, Gary Springer, Susan Chicoine.

Shakespeare's tragedy, presented in two parts and performed as though it took place in the late 19th century. The last major New York revival of *Romeo and Juliet* was in the New York Shakespeare Festival Shakespeare Marathon 5/24/88 for 16 performances.

THE NUMBER 14

CAST: Peter Anderson, Darlene Brookes, Colin Heath, David Mackay, Wayne Specht, Beatrice Zeilinger.

Directed by Roy Surette; scenery, Pam Johnson; costumes, Nancy Bryant; lighting, Gerald King; original music, Douglas Macaulay; mask design, Melody Anderson; assistant to the director, Mark Weatherley; additional choreography, Jennifer Faulkner; stage manager, Darren Adam; press, Lauren Daniluk.

Act I: A.M. Act II: P.M.

Comedy, six performers portraying 60 characters on a bus.

THE WIND IN THE WILLOWS

CAST: Mole—Eric Collins; Rat—Timothy A. Fitz-Gerald; Badger—Michael Poignand; Toad—Lee Zarrett; Otter, Stoat—Steven X. Ward; Squirrel, Stoat, Weasel, Portly—Lana Quintal; Horse, Old Gaoler, Great Weasel, Stoat—Stewart Gregory; Policeman, Hedgehog, Stoat Sergeant—Dee King; Chief Magistrate, Bear, Weasel, Stoat—Price Waldman; Gaoler's Daughter, Stoat, Weasel—Stacey Sargeant; Rabbit, Stoat, Weasel—Alan Souza; Rabbit, Washerwoman, Stoat, Weasel—Beth Lapierre; Stoat Weasel, Fox—Martha Thomas.

Instrumentalists: Dianne Adams conductor, piano; Henry Aronson associate conductor, piano; Chris Persad trumpet, tenor horn; Jeff Barone guitars; Don Haviland baritone saxophone, clarinet, alto saxophone, flute; Francesca Vanasco cello; John Loehrke acoustic bass; Pat O'Donnell drums, percussion.

Understudies: Mole—Alan Souza; Rat, Toad—Stewart Gregory; Badger—Price Waldman.

Directed by Gerardine Clark and Anthony Salatino; musical direction, vocal arrangements and orchestrations, Dianne Adams, James McDowell; musical staging, Anthony Salatino; scenery, Beowulf Boritt; costumes, Mirene Rada; lighting, A. Nelson Ruger IV; sound, David Schnirman; sound effects, James W. Wildman; stage manager, Megan Schneid.

Place: The pastoral countryside of Edwardian England. The play was presented in two parts.

The adventures of Mole, Rat, Badger and Toad, in a regional theater production paying New York City a visit.

MUSICAL NUMBERS: "The Wind in the Willows," "Song of the River," "Things With Wheels," "Song of the Wild Wood," "It's Time to Take Toad in Hand," "Dulce Domum," "I, Glorious Toad," "Mercy-Justice," "The End of Toad," "Joy Shall Be Yours in the Morning," "Missing Him," "The Triumph of Toad," "Weapons Underscore," "Stoats Forever," "The Battle Song," Finale.

Note: The New 42d Street Inc. also presented a number of special programs at the New Victory Theater during the season; see its entry in the Plays Produced off off Broadway section of this volume.

Brooklyn Academy of Music. Schedule of eight programs. **Three Sisters** (7). Revival of the play by Anton Chekhov; presented in the Russian language with simultaneous English translation in the Moscow Art Theater production, Oleg Efremov artistic director, Viacheslav Efimov executive director; produced with The Ministry of Culture of the Russian Federation, Natalya Dementyeva minister, and The American Theater Exchange Initiative, Benjamin Mordecai executive producer. Opened February 6, 1998. (Closed February 14, 1998). **Much Ado About Nothing** (13). Revival of the play by William Shakespeare in the Cheek by Jowl production, artistic directors Declan Donnellan and Nick Ormerod; a co-production with Théâtre National de Bretagne and Le-Maillon Théâtre de Strasbourg. Opened March 25, 1998. (Closed April 5, 1998) **Othello** (6). Revival of the play by William Shakespeare in the Royal National Theater production, Trevor Nunn director. Opened April 8, 1998. (Closed April 12, 1998) And **Hamlet, Henry VIII, Krapp's Last Tape, Everyman** and **Cymbeline** in Royal Shakespeare Company repertory May 21, 1998 to June 7, 1998; see their entries under a separate heading in this section of this volume. Produced by Brooklyn Academy of Music, Bruce C. Ratner chairman of the board, Harvey Lichtenstein president and executive producer, *Three Sisters, Hamlet* and *Cymbeline* at the Brooklyn Academy of Music Opera House, *Much Ado About Nothing, Othello, Henry VIII, Krapp's Last Tape* and *Everyman* at the Majestic Theater.

THREE SISTERS

Andrei Prozorov .... Dmitri Brusnikin
Natalya Ivanovna .... Natalia Egorova
Olga .... Olga Barnet
Masha .... Vera Sotnikova
Irina .... Polina Medvedeva
Kulygin .... Andrei Miagkov
Vershinin .... Stanislav Lubshin
Baron Tuzenbach .... Viktor Gvozditsky
Solyony .... Aleksei Jarkov

Chebutykin .... Viacheslav Nevinny
Fedotik .... Aleksandr Alekseev
Rode .... Andrey Davidov
Ferapont .... Vladlen Davydov
Anfisa .... Iya Savvina
Maid .... Diana Korzun
Musicians .... Irina Grishina,
Aleksandra Skachkova
Aide to Chebutykin .... Andrey Panin

Directed by Oleg Efremov; production design, Valery Leventhal; lighting, Damir Ismagilov; English translation by Carol Rocamora, read by Fay Greenbaum; music by Aleksandr Scriabin; assistant director, Nikolai Skorik; associate artistic director, Anatoly Smeliansky; stage manager, Olga Rosliakova; press, Susan Yung.

Time: The turn of the century. Place: In and around the Prozorovs' house in a Russian provincial town. Act I: Early May, midday. Act II: The following February, evening. Act III: Two years later, early morning. Act IV: The following autumn, midday. The play was presented in two parts with the intermission following Act II.

The most recent major New York revivals of *Three Sisters* took place last season, both on Broadway, in a Moscow Theater Sovremennik production in the Russian language 11/7/96 for 5 performances and by the Roundabout Theater Company 1/22/97 for 61 performances.

MUCH ADO ABOUT NOTHING

The Army:
Don Pedro .... Stephen Mangan
Don John .... Paul Goodwin
Claudio .... Bohdan Poraj
Benedick .... Matthew Macfadyen
Balthasar .... Andrew Price
Borachio .... Justin Salinger
Conrade .... Mark Lacey
Messenger .... Riz Abbasi
Leonato's Household:
Leonato .... Gregory Floy

Ursula .... Ann Firbank
Hero .... Sarita Choudhury
Beatrice .... Saskia Reeves
Margaret .... Zoë Aldrich
Friar Francis .... Andrew Price
The Watch:
Dogberry .... Derek Hutchinson
Verges .... Sam Beazley
1st Watchman .... Andrew Price
2d Watchman .... Riz Abbasi
Sexton .... Zoë Aldrich

Others: Members of the Company.

Directed by Declan Donnellan; design, Nick Ormerod; lighting, Judith Greenwood; composer and musical director, Paddy Cunneen; director of movement, Jane Gibson; stage managers, Simon Sturgess, Kim Beringer.

The last major New York revival of *Much Ado About Nothing* was in the New York Shakespeare Festival Shakespeare Marathon 7/14/88 for 10 performances.

OTHELLO

Roderigo .... Crispin Letts
Iago .... Simon Russell Beale
Brabantio; Gratiano .... Trevor Peacock
Othello .... David Harewood
Cassio .... Colin Tierney
Duke of Venice; Lodovico .... Clifford Rose
1st Senator; 3d Cyprus Soldier ..... Ken Oxtoby
2d Senator; Clown .... Fergus Webster

3d Senator; Montano .... James Hayes
4th Senator; 2d Cyprus Soldier .... Jamie Leene
Servant to Senate;
1st Cyprus Soldier .... Francis Maguire
Desdemona .... Claire Skinner
Emilia .... Maureen Beattie
Bianca .... Indira Varma

Others: Members of the Company

Musicians: Martin Allen music director, percussion; Terry Davies keyboards; Colin Rae trumpets, synthesizer.

Directed by Sam Mendes; scenery and costumes, Anthony Ward; lighting, Paul Pyant; music, Paddy Cunneen; sound, Simon Baker; movement direction, Jonathan Butterell; fight direction, Terry King; stage manager, Kim Beringer.

The last major New York revival of *Othello* was by the Acting Company off Broadway 5/15/95 for 6 performances.

Encores! Great American Musicals in Concert. Schedule of three musical revivals presented in limited concert engagements. **Strike Up the Band** (5). Musical with book by George S. Kaufman; music by George Gershwin; lyrics by Ira Gershwin. Opened February 12, 1998. (Closed February 15, 1998) **Li'l Abner** (5). Musical based on characters created by Al Capp; book by Norman Panama and Melvin Frank; music by Gene De Paul; lyrics by Johnny Mercer. Opened March 26, 1998. (Closed March 29, 1998) **St. Louis Woman** (5). Musical based on the novel *God Sends Sunday* by Arna Bontemps; book by Arna Bontemps and Countee Cullen; music by Harold Arlen; lyrics by Johnny Mercer. Opened April 30, 1998. (Closed May 3, 1998). Produced by City Center, Kathleen Marshall artistic director, Judith E. Daykin president and executive director, at the City Center.

STRIKE UP THE BAND

Timothy Harper	David Elder	Joan Fletcher	Judy Kuhn
C. Edgar Sloane	David Garrison	Jim Townsend	Jere Shea
Horace J. Fletcher	Philip Bosco	George Spelvin	Ross Lehman
Mrs. Draper	Lynn Redgrave	Col. Holmes	David Schramm
Anne Draper	Kristin Chenoweth	Soldier	Benjamin Brecher

Dancers: Brad Bradley, Byron Easley, Denis Jones, Kevin Mockrin.

Ensemble: Ana Maria Andricain, Rebecca Baxter, Benjamin Brecher, Tony Capone, Bryan T. Donovan, Colleen Fitzpatrick, Peter Flynn, John Halmi, Keith Byron Kirk, Damon Kirschenmann, Ann Kittredge, Bruce Moore, Linda Mugleston, Karyn Overstreet, Jennifer Laura Thompson, Katherine Valentine.

Coffee Club Orchestra: Rob Fisher, conductor; Suzanne Ornstein concert mistress; Christoph Franzgrote, Maura Giannini, Marilyn Reynolds, Belinda Whitney-Barratt, Xin Zhao violin; Tim Melosh flute, piccolo; Red Press flute, piccolo, alto saxophone; Blair Tindall oboe; Les Scott clarinet, tenor saxophone; Lawrence Feldman clarinet, alto saxophone; John Campo bassoon; Russ Rizner, Roger Wendt, French horn; John Frosk, Lowell Hershey trumpet; Jack Gale trombone; Jill Jaffe, David Cerutti, David Blinn viola; Clay Ruede, Lanny Paykin cello; John Beal acoustic bass; John Rudsecker drums; Erik Charlston percussion; Grace Paradise harp.

Directed by John Rando; musical direction, Rob Fisher; concert adaptation, David Ives; choreographer, Jeff Calhoun; scenic consultant, John Lee Beatty; lighting, Donald Holder; sound, Bruce Cameron; apparel coordinator, Jonathan Bixby; musical coordinator, Seymour Red Press; casting, Jay Binder; production stage manager, R. Wade Jackson; stage manager, Daniel S. Rosokoff; press, Philip Rinaldi.

Strike Up the Band was first produced on Broadway 1/14/30 for 191 performances. This is its first major New York revival of record.

ACT I

The Horace J. Fletcher American Cheese Company, Hurray, Connecticut
   "Fletcher's American Cheese Choral Society" .... David Elder, David Garrison,
                                                                         Philip Bosco, Ensemble
   "17 and 21" .... Elder, Kristin Chenoweth
   "Typical Self-Made American" .... Bosco, Jere Shea, Ensemble
   "The Man I Love" .... Judy Kuhn, Shea
   "The Unofficial Spokesman" .... Bosco, David Schramm, Ensemble
Fletcher's Ballroom
   "Patriotic Rally" .... Ensemble
   "Soon" .... Shea, Kuhn
   "17 and 21" (Reprise) .... Lynn Redgrave, Bosco
   "Hangin' Around With You" .... Chenoweth, Elder

1998 musical Encores! at the City Center included *(above)* George and Ira Gershwin's *Strike Up the Band*, starring Lynn Redgrave and Philip Bosco

Finaletto, Act I .... Shea, Bosco, Garrison, Schramm, Kuhn, Elder, Ensemble
"Strike Up the Band" .... Elder, Ensemble, Dancers
   (new dance music arrangement by Mark Hummel)

ACT II

Somewhere in Switzerland
  "Oh, This Is Such a Lovely War" .... Ensemble
  "Come-Look-at the-War Choral Society" .... Ladies of the Ensemble
  "Mademoiselle in New Rochelle" .... Ross Lehman, Ladies of the Ensemble
  "Military Dancing Drill" .... Elder, Chenoweth, Dancers
  "Hoping That Someday You'd Care" .... Shea, Kuhn
  "I've Got a Crush on You" .... Redgrave
  "How About a Man?" .... Bosco, Schramm, Redgrave
  Finaletto, Act II .... Company
  "The Man I Love" (Reprise) .... Kuhn
A boat
  "Homeward Bound" .... Benjamin Brecher, Gentlemen of the Ensemble
Fletcher's Ballroom
  "The War That Ended War" .... Ensemble
  Finale Ultimo: "Strike Up the Band" (Reprise) .... Company

LI'L ABNER

Moonbeam McSwine	Cady Huffman	Sen. Jack S. Phogbound	Tom Riis Farrell
Marryin' Sam	Lea DeLaria	Dr. Rasmussen T. Finsdale	Jonathan Freeman
Earthquake McGoon	Michael Mulheren	Government Man;	
Daisy Mae	Alice Ripley	Evil Eye Fleagle	John Mineo
Pappy Yokum	Dick Latessa	Available Jones; Dr. Schleifitz	Marcus Neville
Mammy Yokum	Dana Ivey	Stupefyin' Jones	Julie Newmar
Li'l Abner	Burke Moses	Gen. Bullmoose	David Ogden Stiers
Mayor Dan'l Dawgmeat;		Appassionata von Climax	Kate Finneran
Dr. Krogmeyer	Rick Crom	Dr. Smithborn	Danny Burstein

The Scraggs: Danny Burstein, Bryan T. Donovan, Jesse Means II. Beautified Husbands: Brandon G. Acevedo, H. Giovanni DeLacruz, A.J. DiCaprio, Marcus Heileman, Antonio Newman, Larry Serrahn.

Dancers: Seán Martin Hingston, Nancy Lemenager, Carol Lee Meadows, Elizabeth Mills, Cynthia Onrubia, Joey Pizzi, Alex Sanchez, Daniel Wright.

Ensemble: Luann Aronson, Danny Burstein, Rachel Coloff, Rick Crom, Bryan T. Donovan, Thursday Farrar, Cady Huffman, Sheryl McCallum, Jesse Means II, Bruce Moore, Marcus Neville, Alet Oury.

Coffee Club Orchestra: Rob Fisher, conductor; Mary Powell concert mistress; Red Press flute, piccolo, clarinet, alto saxophone; Al Regni clarinet, bass clarinet, alto saxophone; Harvey Estrin flute, clarinet, tenor saxophone; Rick Heckman oboe, English horn, clarinet, tenor saxophone; Gene Scholtens clarinet, bassoon, baritone saxophone; John Frosk, Glenn Drewes, Kamau Adilifu trumpet; Jack Gale, Randy Andos trombone; Jack Schatz trombone, bass; John Redsecker drums; Erik Charlston percussion; David Evans piano; Christoph Franzgrote, Maura Giannini, Rebekah Johnson, Jon Kass, Robert Lawrence, Belinda Whitney-Barratt, Masako Yanagita, Xin Zhao violin; Jill Jaffe, David Blinn, Crystal Garner viola; Jeanne LeBlanc, Lanny Paykin cello; Louis Bruno bass; Jay Berliner guitar, banjo.

Directed by Christopher Ashley; musical direction, Rob Fisher; concert adaptation, Christopher Durang; choreography, Kathleen Marshall; original direction and choreography, Michael Kidd; scenic consultant, John Lee Beatty; apparel coordinator, Paul Tazewell; lighting, Ken Billington; sound Scott Lehrer; musical coordinator, Seymour Red Press; original orchestration, Phillip J. Lang; casting, Jay Binder; production stage manager, R. Wade Jackson.

Li'l Abner was first produced on Broadway 11/15/56 for 693 performances. This is its first major New York revival of record.

ACT I

Overture .... Orchestra
Dogpatch, U.S.A.
  "A Typical Day" .... Company

"If I Had My Druthers" .... Burke Moses, Men of Ensemble
"If I Had My Druthers" (Reprise) .... Alice Ripley
"Jubilation T. Cornpone" .... Lea DeLaria, Ensemble
"Rag Off'n the Bush" .... Tom Riis Farrell, Ensemble
"Namely You" .... Ripley, Moses
"Unneccessary Town" .... Moses, Ripley, Ensemble
Washington, D.C.: Gen. Bullmoose's Office
"What's Good for General Bullmoose" .... Men of Ensemble
Dogpatch, U.S.A.
"The Country's in the Very Best of Hands" .... Moses, DeLaria, Ensemble
Sadie Hawkins Day Ballet .... Company

ACT II

Entr'acte .... Orchestra
Washington, D.C.: Government Testing Laboratory
"Oh Happy Day" .... Jonathan Freeman, Danny Burstein, Rick Crom,
Marcus Neville
Dogpatch, U.S.A.
"I'm Past My Prime" .... Ripley, DeLaria
Washington, D.C.: Gen. Bullmoose's Mansion
"Love in a Home" .... Ripley, Moses
"Progress Is the Root of All Evil" .... David Ogden Stiers
Washington, D.C.: Government Testing Laboratory
"Put 'Em Back the Way They Wuz" .... Ladies of the Ensemble
Dogpatch, U.S.A.
"The Matrimonial Stomp" .... DeLaria, Company
Finale: "Jubilation T. Cornpone" (Reprise) .... Company

ST. LOUIS WOMAN

Badfoot	Chuck Cooper	Leah	L. Scott Caldwell
Barney	Victor Trent Cook	Piggie	A.J. Baptiste-Cassell
Lila	Helen Goldsby	Jackie	Corey Antonio Hawkins
Mississippi	Wendell Pierce	Celestine	Tavia Riveé Jefferson
Della Green	Vanessa L. Williams	Mr. Hopkins	Wayne Pretlow
Biglow Brown	Charles S. Dutton	Joshua	Jesse Means II
Ragsdale	Roger Robinson	Preacher	David White
Butterfly	Yvette Cason	Danny Jenkins	Eric Christian
Li'l Augie	Stanley Wayne Mathis		

Ensemble: Sherrita Duran, Iris Fairfax, Thursday Farrar, Roberta Gumbel, Richard Hobson, Clinton Ingram, Elmore James, Sheryl McCallum, Jesse Means II, Kimberley Michaels, Amy Jo Phillips, Reginald Pindell, Wayne Pretlow, Joseph Webster, David White, Laurie Williamson.

Dancers: Eric Christian, Bryan Haynes, Greta Martin, Andrew Pacho, Dina Wright, Valencia Yearwood.

Coffee Club Orchestra: Rob Fisher, conductor; Suzanne Ornstein concert mistress; Red Press flute, piccolo, clarinet, alto saxophone; Al Regni clarinet, flute, alto saxophone; Lawrence Feldman flute, clarinet, tenor saxophone; Dennis Anderson oboe, English horn, clarinet, tenor saxophone; John Campo clarinet, bass clarinet, bassoon, baritone saxophone; Russ Rizner, Roger Wendt, French horn; John Frosk, Glenn Drewes, Kamau Adilifu trumpet; Jack Gale, David Bargeron trombone; John Redsecker drums; Erik Charleston percussion; Patrick Brady piano, celeste; Grace Paradise harp; Jay Berliner guitar, banjo; Mary Rowell, Maura Giannini, Rebekah Johnson, Ashley Horne, Belinda Whitney-Barratt, Christoph Franzgrote, Aloysia Friedmann, Kathryn Livolsi violin; Jill Jaffe, David Blinn, Mitsue Takayama viola; Clay Ruede, Jeanne LeBlanc cello; John Beal bass.

Directed and adapted by Jack O'Brien; musical direction, Rob Fisher; choreography, George Faison; scenery consultant, John Lee Beatty; apparel coordinator, Theoni V. Aldredge; lighting, Peter Kaczorowski; sound, Scott Lehrer; orchestrations, Ralph Burns; dance music orchestrations, Luther Henderson; musical coordinator, Seymour Red Press; casting, Jay Binder; production stage manager, Arthur Gaffin.

St. Louis Woman was first produced on Broadway 3/30/46 for 113 performances. This is its first major New York revival of record.

ACT I

Overture .... Orchestra
A stable, early afternoon of a day in August 1898
    "Li'l Augie Is a Natural Man" .... Chuck Cooper
Biglow's Bar, late afternoon the same day
    "Sweeten' Water" .... Victor Trent Cook, Cooper, Wendell Pierce,
        Vanessa L. Williams, Ensemble
    "Any Place I Hang My Hat Is Home" .... Williams, Ensemble
    "I Feel My Luck Comin' Down" .... Stanley Wayne Mathis
    "I Had Myself a True Love" .... Helen Goldsby
Outside Barney's room at twilight
    "Legalize My Name" .... Yvette Cason
A ballroom, evening of the same day
    "Cakewalk Your Lady" .... Company
Li'l Augie and Della's house, late afternoon the following week
    "Come Rain or Come Shine" .... Williams, Mathis
    "Sweeten' Water" (Reprise) .... Williams
    "Chinquapin Bush" .... A.J. Baptiste-Cassell, Corey Antonio Hawkins, Tavia Riveé Jefferson
    "Lullaby" .... Williams
    "Sleep Peaceful, Mr. Used-To-Be" .... Goldsby

ACT II

Entr'acte .... Orchestra
Funeral Parlor
    Funeral Scene: Prelude .... Company
    "Leavin' Time" .... Company
Li'l Augie and Della's house, early evening
    "Come Rain or Come Shine" (Reprise) .... Williams
    "Come Rain or Come Shine" (Reprise) .... Mathis
The alley
    "It's a Woman's Prerogative" .... Cason
Biglow's Bar
    "Ridin' on the Moon" .... Mathis, Ensemble
    "I Wonder What Became of Me" .... Goldsby
The stable
    "Least That's My Opinion" .... Cooper, Mathis
Street corner close to racetrack
    "Racin' Form" .... L. Scott Caldwell
    "Come on, L'il Augie" .... Company
    Finale: "Come Rain or Come Shine" .... Company

*Hedwig and the Angry Inch (104). Transfer from off off Broadway of the musical with book by John Cameron Mitchell; music and lyrics by Stephen Trask. Produced by Alice's Enterprises, The Westside Theater and J.B.F. Producing Corp. at the Jane Street Theater. Opened February 14, 1998.

Performed by John Cameron Mitchell; with Miriam Shor.
Cheater (orchestra): Scott Bilbrey bass, vocals; David McKinley drums; Stephen Trask keyboards, guitar, vocals; Chris Weilding guitar, vocals.
Directed by Peter Askin; musical staging, Jerry Mitchell; scenery and projections, James Youmans; costumes, Fabio Toblini; lighting, Kevin Adams; sound, Werner F; associate producers, Eric Osbun, Terry Byrne; production stage manager, Joe Witt; press, James LL Morrison & Associates, James LL Morrison, Tom D'Ambrosio.

The adventures of a sex-changed East Berlin rock singer on the lower levels of American life. The play was performed without intermission.

MUSICAL NUMBERS: "Tear Me Down," "The Origin of Love," "Sugar Daddy," "Angry Inch," "Wig in a Box," "Wicked Little Town," "The Long Grift," "Hedwig's Lament," "Exquisite Corpse," "Wicked Little Town" (Reprise), "Midnight Radio."

Theater for a New Audience. Rotating repertory of two revivals of plays by William Shakespeare: **Richard II** (23) and **Richard III** (35). Produced by Theater for a New Audience, Jeffrey Horowitz artistic director, Jaan Whitehead executive director, Chris Jennings general manager at the Playhouse at St. Clements. Repertory opened February 15, 1998. (Closed April 5, 1998)

Performer	*Richard II*	*Richard III*
Graham Brown	York; 1st Gardener	Stanley
Helmar Augustus Cooper	Northumberland	Canterbury; Lieutenant of the Tower
Patricia Dunnock	Isabel	Lady Anne
Mark Engelhardt	Hotspur; Morris Dancer	Dorset
Jonathan Fried	Ross; Westminster	Clarence; Lord Mayor
Tom Hammond	Bagot; Scroop	Catesby; Murderer
Edward Henwood	Green; Surrey; Keeper	Ratcliffe; Murderer
Brian Homer	Aumerle; Captain	Grey; Tyrrell
Laurie Kennedy	Duchess of Gloucester; Duchess of York; Queen's Attendant	Duchess of York
Seth Michael May	2d Gardener; Groom	Duke of York (Son)
Christopher McCann	Bolingbroke	Gloucester (later King Richard III)
Mark Niebuhr	Willoughby; Norfolk	Edward IV; Richmond
Pamela Payton-Wright		Margaret
Sharon Scruggs		Elizabeth
Steven Skybell	King Richard II	Buckingham
Robert Stattel	John of Gaunt; Carlisle	Hastings
Kevin Waldron	Bushy; Exton	Rivers; Lovel
Scott Wood	Salisbury; Fitzwater; York Servant; Morris Dancer	Edward

Others: Members of the Company.

Directed by Ron Daniels; scenery, Neil Patel; costumes, Constance Hoffman; lighting, Donald Holder; original music, Michael Philip Ward; fight direction, B.H. Barry; assistant director, Leland Patton; casting, Deborah Brown; production stage manager, C.A. Clark; stage manager, David A. Winitsky; press, Springer/Chicoine Public Relations, Gary Springer, Susan Chicoine.

Place: *Richard II,* England and Wales; *Richard III,* London and others parts of England.

The last major New York revival of *Richard II* was in the New York Shakespeare Festival Shakespeare Marathon 3/31/94 for 38 performances; of *Richard III* was at Brooklyn Academy of Music 6/9/92 for 14 performances.

I Will Come Back (72). Musical with book by Timothy Gray; new songs with music by Hugh Martin, lyrics by Timothy Gray. Produced by New Journeys Ahead, Ltd. at the Players Theater. Opened February 25, 1998. (Closed April 26, 1998)

Judy .... Tommy Femia
A Friend of Barbra .... Kristine Zbornik

Understudies: Mr. Femia—Chuck Sweeney; Miss Zbornik—Tracey Moore.

Directed by Timothy Gray; musical direction, arrangements and orchestrations, David K. Maiocco; scenery, Leo Meyer; costumes, Marc Bouwer; lighting, Jen Acomb; sound, Robert Kaplowitz; assistant director and associate producer, J.T. O'Connor; production stage manager and associate producer, Dyanne M. McNamara; press, Tony Origlio Publicity, David Lotz.

Celebration of the life and talents of Judy Garland. The play was presented in two parts.

MUSICAL NUMBERS, ACT I: "I Will Come Back," "La Cucaracha" (traditional); "Come on In," "They Don't Write 'Em Like That Anymore," "Two Is Company," "Optimism" (by Hugh Martin and Timothy Gray); "Smile" (by John Turner, Geoffrey Parsons and Charles Chaplin); "Zing Went the Strings of My Heart" (by John Hanley); "After You've Gone" (by Henry Creamer and Turner Layton); "Somewhere Out There" (by James Horner, Barry Mann and Cynthia Weil).

ACT II: "Meet Me in St. Louis" (by Andrew Sterling, Kerry Mills and Timothy Gray); "The Boy Next Door," "The Trolley Song" (by Hugh Martin and Ralph Blane); "Rock-a-Bye Your Baby With a Dixie Melody" (by Sam Lewis, Joe Young and Jean Schwartz); "Just in Time" (by Betty Comden, Adolph Green and Jule Styne); "Happy Days Are Here Again" (by Jack Yellen and Milton Ager); "Get Happy" (by Ted Koehler and Harold Arlen); "Over the Rainbow" (by E.Y. Harburg and Harold Arlen); "I Will Come Back" (Reprise).

The Beauty Queen of Leenane (46). By Martin McDonagh. Produced by Atlantic Theater Company, Neil Pepe artistic director, Hilary Hinkle managing director, in the Druid Theater Company/Royal Court Theater production at the Atlantic Theater. Opened February 26, 1998. (Closed April 5, 1998 and transferred to Broadway; see its entry in the Plays Produced on Broadway section of this volume)

Mag Folan	Anna Manahan	Ray Dooley	Tom Murphy
Maureen Folan	Marie Mullen	Pato Dooley	Brian F. O'Byrne

Directed by Garry Hynes; scenery and costumes, Francis O'Connor; lighting, Ben Ormerod; original music, Paddy Cunneen; production stage manager, Matthew Silver; stage manager, Darcy Stephens; press, Boneau/Bryan-Brown.

Place: Leenane, a small town in Connemara, County Galway. The play was presented in two parts.

Middle-aged, neurotic daughter vs. the selfish, aged mother living in her care. A foreign play previously produced in Ireland and London. Co-winner of the 1997–98 Lucille Lortel Award for best off-Broadway play; see the Prizewinning Plays section of this volume.

*R & J (104). Transfer from off off Broadway of the Joe Calarco adaptation of *Romeo and Juliet* by William Shakespeare. Produced by Frederic B. Vogel, Bruce Lazarus and Roger Allen Gindi at the John Houseman Studio Theater. Opened March 3, 1998 (see note).

Cast: Mercutio, Friar Lawrence, Lady Capulet, Others—Sean Dugan; Nurse, Tybalt, Balthazar, Others—Danny Gurwin; Romeo, Others—Greg Shamie; Juliet, Benvolio, Friar John, Others—Daniel J. Shore.

Understudies: Caesar Samayoa, Rob A. Wilson.

Directed by Joe Calarco; lighting, Jeffrey T. Lowney; associate producers, Jack Dalgleish, Fern Kershon, Libby Ann Russler, Kevin J. Fay; production stage manager, Joshua Goldstein; press, Tony Origlio Publicity, Michael Cullen, Karen Greco, David Lotz.

Four prep school students act all the roles of Shakespeare's play. The last major New York revival of *Romeo and Juliet* was the Acting Company's this season, 1/29/98, for 10 off-Broadway performances.

Note: *R & J* opened 1/22/98 as a regular 7-performances-a-week off off Broadway production whose status was raised to full off Broadway in the course of its run.

Mystery School (50). Solo performance by Tyne Daly; written by Paul Selig. Produced by En Garde Arts, Anne Hamburger executive producer, and the Long Wharf Theater, Doug Hughes artistic director, at the Angel Orensanz Foundation Center for the Arts. Opened March 11, 1998. (Closed April 19, 1998)

Directed by Doug Hughes; scenery, Neil Patel; costumes, Linda Fisher; lighting, Michael Chybowski; original music and sound, David Van Tieghem; projection design consultant, Jan Hartley; associate producer, Carol Bixler; casting, Meg Simon; production stage manager, Charles Means; press, James LL Morrison & Associates, Candi Adams, Tom D'Ambrosio.

Miss Daly as five different women in search of spiritual fulfillment.

Shopping etc. (see note) (30). Transfer from off off Broadway of the play by Mark Ravenhill. Produced by New York Theater Workshop, James C. Nicola artistic director, based on the original Out of Joint/Royal Court Theater production, at New York Theater Workshop. Opened March 17, 1998 (see note). (Closed April 11, 1998)

Lulu .... Jennifer Dundas Lowe
Robbie .... Justin Theroux
Mark .... Philip Seymour Hoffman
Brian .... Matthew Sussman
Gary .... Torquil Campbell

Directed by Gemma Bodinetz and Max Stafford-Clark; scenery and costumes, Julian McGowan; lighting, Lap-Chi Chu, Julian McGowan; sound, Paul Arditti; casting, Bernard Telsey; production stage manager, Kate Broderick; press, Richard Kornberg & Associates, Don Summa.

The dehumanizing effects of our dysfunctional society on its sex life, its economic life and other major activities. A foreign play previously produced in London at the Royal Court Theater Upstairs.

Note: This play's full title, *Shopping and Fucking,* uses a word which has appeared in *Best Plays* volumes, including elsewhere in this one, when it has occurred as an appropriate element of naturalistic dialogue or reportage. Its use in a title, however, appears to us an act of exhibitionism in which we will not participate except, for the record, in this note and in the index.

Note: This play opened February 3, 1998 as a 7-performances-a- week, off off Broadway production whose status was raised to full off-Broadway in the course of its run.

Hot Klezmer (8). Klezmer musical revue with compositions by Harold Seletsky and Mary Feinsinger. Produced by The American Jewish Theater, Stanley Brechner artistic director, in association with Carol Ostrow at the Greenwald Theater. Opened March 31, 1998. (Closed April 5, 1998)

With Harold Seletsky (clarinet), Hal Jeffrin (vocal), Mary Feinsinger (synthesizer, vocal), Ellis Berger (drums), Avram Pengas (guitar, oud, bouzouki, vocal), Zohar Fresco (percussion, drum), Peter Stan (accordion), Julie Signitzer Krajicek (violin), Shoshanna (dancer).

Directed by Michael Leeds; choreography, Arte Phillips; scenery and costumes, Bruce Goodrich; lighting, Jeff Croiter; sound, Raymond Schilke; production stage manager, Nick Oredson; press, Jeffrey Richards Associates.

Varieties of Klezmer music, past and present. The show was presented without intermission.

Anadarko (20). By Tim Blake Nelson. Produced by MCC Theater, Robert LuPone and Bernard Telsey executive directors, at MCC Theater. Opened April 1, 1998. (Closed April 18, 1998)

Ray .... David Patrick Kelly
Guard .... J.R. Horne
Bobby Boy .... Paul Romeo
Officer .... John Griesemer
Jimmy .... Myk Watford
American Indian .... Lurch Pagan
Night Man .... Lanny Flaherty

Directed by Doug Hughes; scenery, Neil Patel; costumes, Catherine Zuber; lighting, Christopher Akerlind; original music and sound, David Van Tieghem; fight direction, Rick Sordelet; production stage manager, Katherine Lee Boyer; press, Boneau/Bryan-Brown.

Mistreatment of prisoners in a midwestern small-town jail.

*Savion Glover/Downtown (23). Performance piece by the cast. Produced by Dodger Endemol Theatricals and Maniactin Productions in association with KISS FM at the Variety Arts Theater. Opened May 19, 1998; see note.

Ayodele Casel
Abron Glover

Savion Glover
Chance Taylor

Musicians: Eli Fountain, Tommy James, Gregory Jones, Patience Higgins.

Impromptu-style musical performances known as "jams," no two shows alike, starring Savion Glover.

Note: Press date for *Savion Glover/Downtown* was 5/28/98.

Royal Shakespeare Company Visits Brooklyn

The Royal Shakespeare Company's spring visit with a repertory of five plays, under the sponsorship of the Brooklyn Academy of Music, included *(above)* the anonymous morality play *Everyman,* with Paul Hamilton (Strength), Joseph Mydell (Everyman) and Edward Woodall (Five Wits), its first New York production of record in this version; and *Hamlet* (pictured *at left* in the prayer scene with Paul Freeman in the role of King Claudius)

Royal Shakespeare Company. Repertory of five revivals. **Hamlet** (10). By William Shakespeare. Opened May 21, 1998. (Closed May 24, 1998) **Henry VIII, or All Is True** (7). By William Shakespeare. Opened May 26, 1998. (Closed May 31, 1998) **Krapp's Last Tape** (3). Solo performance by Edward Petherbridge; written by by Samuel Beckett. Opened May 27, 1998. (Closed May 29, 1998) **Everyman** (7). Anonymous. Opened June 2, 1998. (Closed June 7, 1998) **Cymbeline** (5). By William Shakespeare. Opened June 3, 1998. (Closed June 6, 1998) Produced by Brooklyn Academy of Music, Bruce C. Ratner chairman of the board, Harvey Lichtenstein president and executive producer, in the Royal Shakespeare Company productions, Adrian Noble artistic director, *Hamlet* and *Cymbeline* at the BAM Opera House, *Henry VIII, Krapp's Last Tape* and *Everyman* at the Majestic Theater.

HAMLET

Hamlet	Alex Jennings	Guildenstern	Rhashan Stone
King Claudius	Paul Freeman	Rosencrantz	Richard Cant
Laertes	William Houston	Player Queen	Syreeta Kumar
Polonius	David Ryall	Gravedigger	Alan David
Queen Gertrude	Susannah York	Priest	John Killoran
Ophelia	Derbhle Crotty	Osric	Toby Longworth
Children	Evan Couch, Rachel London	Ophelia's Lady	Jenifer Armitage
Horatio	Colin Hurley		
Ghost of Hamlet's Father;			
Player King	Edward Petherbridge		

Players: Jenifer Armitage, John Killoran, Toby Longworth, Derek Exenagu. Party Guests: Alexandra Brodsky, Laura Caparrotti, Joseph Coleman, Ivan Espeche, Joe Farrell, Jarod Gibson, Kate Hamilton, George Hannah, Gail London, Elise Long, Chris Lucey, Deborah Marcano, Francessca Napoletano, Rafael Weil.

Musicians: Christopher Lacey flutes, piccolo, recorder; Victor Slaymark clarinets, saxophone; Peter Wright trumpet; Richard Sandland tuba, euphonium; David Carroll, guitar, mandolin; Alyn Ross bass guitar; Tony McVey percussion; Jonathan Rutherford, Richard Brown keyboards.

Understudies: Misses York, Kumar—Jenifer Armitage; Messrs. Longworth, Killoran—Richard Cant; Mr. Jennings—William Houston; Mr. Freeman—Colin Hurley; Messrs. Houston, Petherbridge (Player King)—John Killoran; Misses Crotty, Armitage—Syreeta Kumar; Messrs. Ryall, Petherbridge (Ghost), David—Toby Longworth; Messrs. Cant, Stone—Rex Obano; Mr. Hurley—Rhashan Stone.

Directed by Matthew Warchus; design, Mark Thompson; lighting, Hugh Vanstone; lighting design re-creation, Geraint Pughe; sound, Paul Arditti; music, Gary Yershon; movement, Quinny Sacks; fight direction, Terry King; film sequence director, Rik Statman; music direction, Richard Brown; assistant director, David Hunt; stage manager, Jane Pole; press, Susan Yung.

The last major New York revival of *Hamlet* was Ralph Fiennes's 5/2/95 for 91 performances.

HENRY VIII, OR ALL IS TRUE

King Henry VIII	Paul Jesson	Lady Ann Bullen	Claire Marchionne
Queen Katharine	Jane Lapotaire	Old Lady	Cherry Morris
Cardinal Wolsey	Ian Hogg	Sir Thomas Lovell	Orlando Seale
Cardinal Campeius; Lord Sands;		Caputius	Rex Obano
Porter's Man	Barry Aird	Thomas Cromwell	Robert Whitelock
Thomas Cranmer, Archbishop		Gardiner; Buckingham's	
of Canterbury	David Collings	Surveyor	Paul Bentall
Duke of Norfolk	John Kane	Griffith	David Hobbs
Duke of Buckingham	Paul Greenwood	Ladies-in Waiting:	
Duke of Suffolk	David Beames	Patience	Eileen Battye
Earl of Surrey	Jo Stone-Fewings	Inez	Nadine Marshall
Lord Chamberlain	Guy Henry		

Musicians: Edward Watson bass clarinet, saxophones, recorder, percussion; Andrew Stone-Fewings, Roderick Tearle trumpet; David Hissey trombone; Ruth Holden harp, percussion; James Jones percussion; Roger Hellyer keyboards.

Understudies: Messrs. Whitelock, Seale, Obano—Barry Aird; Misses Lapotaire, Morris—Eileen Battye; Mr. Jesson—David Beames; Mr. Hogg—David Hobbs; Mr. Aird—Vincent Leigh, Rex Obano; Misses Marchionne, Battye—Nadine Marshall; Messrs. Henry, Stone-Fewings, Bentall, Hobbs—Orlando Seale; Messrs. Greenwood, Beames—Jo Stone-Fewings; Messrs. Collings, Kane—Robert Whitelock.

Directed by Gregory Doran; design, Robert Jones; lighting, Howard Harrison; sound, Martin Slavin; music, Jason Carr; music direction, Roger Hellyer; movement, Terry John Bates; assistant director, Kate Raper; stage manager, Laura Deards.

The last major New York production of *Henry VIII* was in the Joseph Papp Public Theater/New York Shakespeare Festival's Shakespeare Marathon 5/13/97 for 22 performances—the first play and the second-to-last play of the 1997–98 off-Broadway season.

KRAPP'S LAST TAPE

Krapp .... Edward Petherbridge

Directed by Edward Petherbridge and David Hunt; design, Anthony Rowe; lighting, Stephen Brady; lighting design re-creation, Wayne Dowdeswell; sound, Martin Slavin; stage manager, Laura Deards; American stage manager, Judith Binus.

The last major New York revival of record of *Krapp's Last Tape* took place off Broadway 8/27/86 for 104 performaces.

EVERYMAN

CAST: Death, Kindred, Knowledge, Charlatan Priest—Josette Bushell-Mingo; God, Goods, Strength, Charlatan Priest—Paul Hamilton; Spinster, Bride, Confession, Cousin, Beauty, Charlatan Priest, Christ—Johnny Lodi; Nin, Good Deeds, Charlatan Priest—Myra McFadyen; Everyman—Joseph Mydell; Fellowship, Five Wits, Angel, Charlatan Priest—Edward Woodall.

Musicians: Jude Springate violin, percussion; Richard Adey accordion.

Directed by Kathryn Hunter and Marcello Magnani; design, Rosa Maggiora; lighting, Chris Davey; sound, Tim Oliver; music direction, Ben Livingstone; movement, Toby Sedgwick; sound re-creation, Martin Slavin; stage manager, Jane Pole; American stage manager, Judith Binus.

The first New York production of record of this 15th century morality play *Everyman* (author unknown) took place at Mendelsson Hall 10/12/02 for 75 performances. It was revived in 1907, 1910, 1913, 1918 and 1927; and in the Hugo von Hofmannstahl adaptation 12/7/27 for 14 performances, revived in 1941 and 1953.

CYMBELINE

Prologue .... John Kane
Britain:
  Cymbeline .... Edward Petherbridge
  Queen .... Joanna McCallum
  Imogen .... Joanne Pearce
  Posthumus Leonatus .... Damian Lewis
  Cloten .... Guy Henry
  Pisanio .... Paul Bentall
  Helen .... Shuna Snow
  1st Gentleman .... John Killoran
  2d Gentleman .... Nicholas Hutchinson
  Cornelius .... David Hobbs
  Captain .... Vincent Leigh
  Gaoler .... Rod Arthur
  Attendants ...... Rex Obano, Paul Swinnerton

Rome:
  Iachimo .... Paul Freeman
  Philario .... David Glover
  Frenchman .... Rod Arthur
  Dutchman .... Vincent Leigh
  Spaniard .... Rex Obano
  Caius Lucius .... Ewart James Walters
  Soothsayer .... John Kane
Wales:
  Belarius .... Ian Hogg
  Guiderius .... Jo Stone-Fewings
  Aviragus .... Richard Cant
  Ghost of Sicilius Leonatus ...... David Glover
  Ghost of Posthumus's
    Mother .... Jenifer Armitage
  Jupiter .... Ewart James Walters

Musicians: Christopher Lacey flute, piccolo, recorder; Claire Philpot oboe, cor anglais; Gareth Brady clarinet, bass clarinet, saxophone; Roger Hellyer bassoon, contrabassoon; Roderick Tearle trumpet; Brian Newman, Philip Thorne horn; David Hissey trombone, sackbut; James Jones, Tony McVey percussion; Richard Brown harp, percussion.

Understudies: Misses McCallum, Snow—Jenifer Armitage; Messrs, Hogg, Kane—Rod Arthur; Messrs. Killoran, Hutchinson—Richard Cant; Mr. Petherbridge—David Hobbs; Messrs. Bentall, Arthur, Glover—Nicholas Hutchinson, Rex Obano; Messrs. Henry, Cant, Stone-Fewings—John Killoran; Messrs. Lewis, Hobbs—Vincent Leigh; Misses Pearce, Armitage—Shuna Snow; Mr. Freeman—Ewart James Walters.

Directed by Adrian Noble; design, Anthony Ward; lighting, Hugh Vanstone; lighting design re-creation, Geraint Pughe; music, Stephen Warbeck; music direction, Richard Brown; sound, Paul Slocombe; sound re-creation, Rebecca Watts; movement, Sue Lefton; fights, Terry King; assistant director, Kate Raper; stage manager, Eric Lumsden; American stage manager, Dianne Trulock.

The last major New York revival of record of *Cymbeline* took place in The Joseph Papp Public Theater/New York Shakespeare Festival's Shakespeare Marathon 5/31/89 for 55 performances.

*****Dinah Was** (5). Transfer from off off Broadway of the musical by Oliver Goldstick. Produced by Jean Doumanian in the WPA Theater production, Kyle Renick artistic director, at the Gramercy Theater. Opened May 28, 1998.

Maye; Waitress;
  Violet .... Adriane Lenox
Frick; Rollie .... Bud Leslie
Dinah Washington .... Yvette Freeman

Joe Spinelli;
  Sam Greenblatt .... Vince Viverito
Mama Jones;
  Chase Adams .... Darryl Alan Reed

Musicians: Lanny Hartley piano, Emanuel Chulo Gatewood bass, Brian Grice drums, Bobby Eldridge woodwinds, Winston Byrd trumpet.

Directed by David Petrarca; musical direction, additional arrangements and orchestrations, Lanny Hartley; choreography, George Faison; scenery, Michael Yeargan; costumes, Paul Tazewell; lighting, Stephen Strawbridge; sound, Laura Grace Brown; musical supervision, orchestrations and arrangements, Jason Robert Brown; casting, James Calleri; production stage manager, Paul J. Smith; stage manager, Thomas Borchard; press, Jeffrey Richards Associates, Irene Gandy, Caral Craig, Brett Kristofferson, Robert Shuter.

Time: 1959 and stops along the way. Place: The lobby of the Sahara Hotel, Las Vegas.

The life and career of Dinah Washington, previously produced at Williamstown Theater Festival, Peter Hunt artistic director, and off off Broadway by the WPA Theater 3/24/98.

MUSICAL NUMBERS (all sung by Dinah), ACT I: "Bad Luck," "Showtime," "Baby, You Got What It Takes" (Boss, Dinah), "Slick Chick (On the Mellow Side)" (Dinah, Ensemble), "What a Difference a Day Makes," "I Wanna Be Loved."

ACT II: "Long John Blues," "I Won't Cry Anymore," "Come Rain or Come Shine," "This Bitter Earth," "Sometimes I'm Happy," "A Rockin' Good Way" (Dinah, Violet), "I Don't Hurt Anymore."

CAST REPLACEMENTS AND TOURING COMPANIES

Compiled by Jeffrey A. Finn

The following is a list of the major cast replacements of record in productions which opened in previous years, but were still playing in New York during a substantial part of the 1997–98 season; and other New York shows which were on a first-class tour in 1997–98.

The name of each major role is listed in *italics* beneath the title of the play in the first column. In the second column directly opposite appears the name of the actor who created the role in the original New York production (whose opening date appears in *italics* at the top of the column). In shows of the past five years, indented immediately beneath the original actor's name are the names of subsequent New York replacements, together with the date of replacement when available. In shows that have run longer than five years, only this season's or the most recent cast replacements are listed under the names of the original cast members.

The third column gives information about first-class touring companies. When there is more than one roadshow company, #1, #2, etc., appear before the name of the performer who created the role in each company (and the city and date of each company's first performance appears in *italics* at the top of the column). Their subsequent replacements are also listed beneath their names in the same manner as the New York companies, with dates when available.

ANNIE

	New York 3/26/97	*Houston 11/29/96*
Annie	Brittny Kissinger	Joanna Pacitti Brittny Kissinger 2/25/97
Miss Hannigan	Nell Carter	Roz Ryan Nell Carter 1/3/97 Sally Struthers
Grace Farrell	Colleen Dunn	Colleen Dunn Lisa Gunn
Oliver Warbucks	John Schuck	John Schuck
Rooster Hannigan	Jim Ryan	Jim Ryan Laurent Girouy
Lily	Karen Byers Blackwell	Karen Byers Blackwell

BEAUTY AND THE BEAST

	New York 4/18/94	*Minneapolis 11/7/95*
Beast	Terrence Mann Jeff McCarthy Chuck Wagner	Frederick C. Inkley

261

Belle	Susan Egan Sarah Uriarte Christianne Tisdale Kerry Butler Deborah Gibson 9/24/97	Kim Huber Erin Dilly 2/11/98
Lefou	Kenny Raskin Harrison Beal	Dan Sklar
Gaston	Burke Moses Marc Kudisch Steve Blanchard	Tony Lawson
Maurice	Tom Bosley MacIntyre Dixon Tom Bosley Kurt Knudson Tim Jerome	Grant Cowan
Cogsworth	Heath Lamberts Peter Bartlett Gibby Brand	Jeff Brooks
Lumiere	Gary Beach Lee Roy Reams Patrick Quinn Gary Beach	Patrick Page David DeVries
Babette	Stacey Logan Pamela Winslow Leslie Castay	Leslie Castay Mindy Paige Davis 2/15/97 Heather Lee
Mrs. Potts	Beth Fowler Cass Morgan Beth Fowler Leslie Castay	Betsy Joslyn Barbara Marineu 7/2/97

BRING IN 'DA NOISE BRING IN 'DA FUNK

	New York 4/25/96	*Detroit 9/30/97*
'Da Beat	Savion Glover Baakari Wilder 6/27/97	Derick K. Grant
Performer	Baakari Wilder Dulé Hill 7/1/97	Jimmy Tate
Performer	Jimmy Tate Jason Samuels 7/1/97	Christopher A. Scott
Performer	Vincent Binghamon Omar A. Edwards 2/4/97	Dominique Kelley
'Da Voice	Jeffrey Wright Curtis McClarin 8/5/97	Thomas Silcott
'Da Singer	Ann Duquesnay Lynette G. DuPre 8/5/97	Vickilyn Reynolds
Drummer	Jared Crawford	David Peter Chapman
Drummer	Raymond King	Dennis J. Dove
The Kid	Dulé Hill Jason Samuels 7/1/97 Marshall L. Davis Jr. 9/16/97	B. Jason Young

CATS

	New York 10/7/82	National tour 1/94
Alonzo	Hector Jaime Mercado Hans Kriefall 4/24/95	William Patrick Dunne Rudd Anderson 6/6/95
Bustopher	Stephan Hanan Michael Brian	Richard Poole William R. Park Andy Gale 7/11/95 Bart Shatto 3/12/96 Brian Noonan 10/1/96 Daniel Eli Friedman 4/14/97
Bombalurina	Donna King Marlene Danielle 1/9/84	Helen Frank Courtney Young 10/1/97
Cassandra	Rene Ceballos Meg Gillentine	Laura Quinn Izabela Lekic 5/16
Coricopat	Rene Clemente Billy Johnstone	(not in tour)
Demeter	Wendy Edmead Amanda Watkins	N. Elaine Wiggins Jeanine Meyers 6/18/96
Grizabella	Betty Buckley Liz Callaway 9/22/97	Mary Gutzi Natalie Toro 3/24/97
Jellylorum	Bonnie Simmons Jean Arbeiter	Patty Goble Kris Koop 12/26/95
Jennyanydots	Anna McNeely Carol Dilley 8/22/94	Alice C. DeChant
Mistoffeles	Timothy Scott Jacob Brent	Christopher Gattelli Randy André Davis 3/12/96
Mungojerrie	Rene Clemente Roger Kachel 5/11/92	Gavan Palmer Gavan Palmer 5/28/96
Munkustrap	Harry Groener Michael Gruber Abe Sylvia	Robert Amirante James Patterson 12/17/96
Old Deuteronomy	Ken Page Jimmy Lockett	John Treacy Egan Doug Eskew
Plato/Macavity	Kenneth Ard Steve Geary	Steve Bertles Taylor Wicker
Pouncival	Herman W. Sebek Christopher Gattelli	Joey Gyondla Michael Barriskill 4/19/96
Rum Tum Tugger	Terrence Mann Dave Hibbard	Ron Seykell David Villella 12/17/97
Rumpleteazer	Christine Langner Maria Jo Ralabate 4/1/96	Jennifer Cody Amy Shure 4/28/97
Sillabub	Whitney Kershaw Bethany Samuelson	Lanene Charters Carolyn J. Ockert 10/28/96
Skimbleshanks	Reed Jones Owen Taylor	Carmen Yurich Josh Prince 12/31/96
Tantomile	Janet L. Hubert Silvia Aruj	(not in tour)
Tumblebrutus	Robert Hoshour Andrew Hubbard	Joseph Favolora Mark R. Moreau 10/28/96

Victoria	Cynthia Onrubia	Tricia Mitchell
	Missy Lay Zimmer	

Note: Only this season's or the most recent cast replacements are listed above under the names of the original cast members. For previous replacements, see previous volumes of *Best Plays*.

CHICAGO

	New York 11/14/96	*#1 Cincinatti 3/25/97* *#2 Ft. Myers, FL 12/12/97*
Velma Kelly	Bebe Neuwirth	#1 Jasmine Guy Janine LaManna Jasmine Guy Donna Marie Asbury Stephanie Pope #2 Stephanie Pope Jasmine Guy
Roxie Hart	Ann Reinking Marilu Henner Karen Ziemba	#1 Charlotte d'Amboise Belle Calaway #2 Karen Ziemba Nancy Hess Charlotte d'Amboise
Amos Hart	Joel Grey Ernie Sabella	#1 Ron Orbach Michael Tucci #2 Ernie Sabella Tom McGowan Ron Orbach Tom McGowan Ron Orbach
Matron "Mama" Morton	Marcia Lewis	#1 Carol Woods Lea DeLaria #2 Avery Sommers
Billy Flynn	James Naughton Gregory Jbara Hinton Battle	#1 Obba Babatunde Alan Thicke #2 Brent Barrett
Mary Sunshine	David Sabella	#1 M.E. Spencer D.C. Levine #2 D.C. Levine M.E. Spencer

DEFENDING THE CAVEMAN

	New York 3/26/95	*Miami 1/14/97*
(No character name)	Rob Becker	Rob Becker

THE FANTASTICKS

	New York 5/3/60
El Gallo	Jerry Orbach John Savarese 10/7/97
Luisa	Rita Gardner Gina Schuh-Turner 10/7/97

BEAUTY AND THE BEAST—Beast and Belle were played by Chuck Wagner and Deborah Gibson in this season's cast of the long-running Disney musical

Matt	Kenneth Nelson
	Eric Meyersfield

Note: Only this season's or the most recent replacements are listed above under the names of the original cast members. For previous replacements, see previous volumes of *Best Plays*.

A FUNNY THING HAPPENED ON THE WAY TO THE FORUM

New York 4/18/96

Pseudolus	Nathan Lane
	Whoopi Goldberg 2/11/97
	David Alan Grier

Hysterium	Mark Linn-Baker
	Ross Lehman
Senex	Lewis J. Stadlen
	Dick Latessa
	Robert Fitch
Philia	Jessica Boevers
Hero	Jim Stanek
Domina	Mary Testa

GREASE

	New York 5/11/94	*Syracuse 9/19/94*
Vince Fontaine	Brian Bradley	Davy Jones
	Jeff Conaway	Brian Bradley 1/9/97
	Brian Bradley	Nick Santa Maria
		Brian Bradley
Miss Lynch	Marcia Lewis	Sally Struthers
	Marilyn Cooper	Sally Struthers 8/20/96
Betty Rizzo	Rosie O'Donnell	Angela Pupello
	Angela Pupello	Mackenzie Phillips
	Lucy Lawless	Tracy Nelson
	Linda Blair	Mackenzie Phillips
	Angela Pupello	
Doody	Sam Harris	Scott Beck
	Ric Ryder	Roy Chicas 4/96
Kenickie	Jason Opsahl	Douglas Crawford
	Steve Geyer	Christopher Carothers
Frenchy	Jessica Stone	Beth Lipari
	Alisa Klein	Beth Lipari 10/8/96
	Beth Lipari	
	Alisa Klein	
Danny Zuko	Ricky Paull Goldin	Rex Smith
	Sean McDermott	Adrian Zmed 9/20/96
Sandy Dumbrowski	Susan Wood	Trisha M. Gorman
	Melissa Dye	Kelli Bond Severson 4/29/97
	Lacey Hornkohl	
	Melissa Dye	
Patty Simcox	Michelle Blakely	Melissa Papp
	Dominique Dawes	Stephanie Seely 9/5/96
	Melissa Papp	
Teen Angel	Billy Porter	Kevin-Anthony
	Darlene Love	Kevin-Anthony 10/15/96
	Kevin-Anthony	
	Billy Porter	
	André Garner	

HOW I LEARNED TO DRIVE

New York 5/6/97

Li'l Bit
Mary-Louise Parker
Jayne Atkinson 7/29/97
Molly Ringwald 10/7/97
Deirdre Lovejoy 2/26/98

Peck
David Morse
Joel Colodner 7/29/97
Bruce Davison 8/19/97
Cotter Smith 1/98

THE KING AND I

	New York 4/11/96	*Minneapolis 4/1/97*
Anna Leonowens	Donna Murphy Faith Prince 3/17/97 Kay McClelland Marie Osmond 12/19/97	Hayley Mills Marie Osmond 4/15/98
Royal Dance Soloists	Camille M. Brown/ Lainie Sakakura Kristine Bendul 8/5/96	Hsin-Ping Chang Youn Kim
The King of Siam	Lou Diamond Phillips Kevin Gray 6/10/97	Victor Talmadge
Lun Tha	Jose Llana Benjamin Bryant 6/30/97	Timothy Ford Murphy
Tuptim	Joohee Choi Cornilla Luna 3/24/97	Luzviminda Lor
Lady Thiang	Taewon Kim	Naomi Itami Helen Yu 5/27/97

THE LAST NIGHT OF BALLYHOO

New York 2/27/97

Lala Levy
Jessica Hecht
Cynthia Nixon 8/26/97
Ilana Levine 1/29/98

Reba Freitag
Celia Weston
Joanne Camp 1/29/98

Boo Levy
Dana Ivey
Carole Shelley 8/26/97
Kelly Bishop 2/17/98

Adolph Freitag
Terry Beaver
Peter Michael Goetz 1/6/98

Joe Farkas
Paul Rudd
Mark Feuerstein 6/2/97
Paul Rudd 8/12/97
Christopher Gartin 1/6/98

Sunny Freitag	Arija Bareikis	
	Kimberly Williams 8/26/97	
	Arija Bareikis 10/9/97	
	Amy Wilson 1/6/98	
Peachy Weil	Stephen Largay	
	Todd Weeks 1/6/98	

LATE NITE CATECHISM

	New York 10/3/96
Sister	Maripat Donovan
	Patti Hannon 10/97

THE LIFE

	New York 4/26/97
Jojo	Sam Harris
	Michael Brian
	Brian Lane Green
Memphis	Chuck Cooper
Queen	Pamela Isaacs
Sonja	Lillias White
Fleetwood	Kevin Ramsey
Mary	Bellamy Young

LES MISERABLES

	New York 3/12/87	*Tampa 11/18/88*
Jean Valjean	Colm Wilkinson	Gary Barker
	Robert Marien 3/12/97	Gregory Calvin Stone 3/3/97
	Ivan Rutherford 9/9/97	
	Robert Marien 12/12/97	
	Craig Schulman 3/3/98	
Javert	Terrence Mann	Peter Samuel
	Christopher Innvar 10/15/96	Todd Alan Johnson 3/31/97
	Robert Gallagher 12/6/97	
Fantine	Randy Graff	Hollis Resnik
	Juliet Lambert 3/12/97	Lisa Capps 3/24/97
	Lisa Capps 4/15/98	Holly Jo Crane
Enjolras	Michael Maguire	Greg Zerkle
	Stephen R. Buntrock 3/12/97	Brian Herriott
		Kurt Kovalenko
		Michael Todd Cressman
Marius	David Bryant	Matthew Porretta
	Peter Lockyer 3/12/97	Rich Affannato 8/12/96
		Steve Scott Springer
		Tim Howar
Cosette	Judy Kuhn	Jacquelyn Piro
	Christeena Michelle Riggs	Kate Fisher 9/9/96
	3/12/97	Regan Thiel

Eponine	Frances Ruffelle	Michele Maika
	Sarah Uriarte Berry 3/12/97	Rona Figueroa 3/31/97
		Jessica-Snow Wilson

Note: Only this season's or the most recent cast replacements are listed above under the names of the original cast members. For previous replacements, see previous volumes of *Best Plays*.

MISS SAIGON

	New York 4/11/91	*Seattle 3/16/95*
The Engineer	Jonathan Pryce	Thom Sesma
	Luoyong Wang 10/2/95	Joseph Anthony Foronda
		4/22/97
Kim	Lea Salonga	Deedee Lynn Magno
	Joan Almedilla	Elizabeth Paw
	Deedee Lynn Magno	Kristine Remigio
Chris	Willy Falk	Matt Bogart
	Matt Bogart 1/12/98	Will Chase 4/16/96
		Steve Pasquale

Note: Only this season's or the most recent cast replacements are listed above under the names of the original cast members. For previous replacements, see previous volumes of *Best Plays*.

THE PHANTOM OF THE OPERA

		#1 Los Angeles 5/31/90
		#2 Chicago 5/24/90
	New York 1/26/88	*#3 Seattle 12/13/92*
The Phantom	Michael Crawford	#1 Michael Crawford
	Thomas James O'Leary	Frank D'Ambrosio 3/28/94
	10/11/96	#2 Mark Jacoby
		Ron Bohmer 9/97
		#3 Frank D'Ambrosio
		Brad Little 9/28/96
Christine Daae	Sarah Brightman	#1 Dale Kristien
	Tracy Shayne	Lisa Vroman 12/2/93
	Sandra Joseph 1/27/98	Karen Culliver (alt.) 6/3/97
	Adrienne McEwan (alt.)	#2 Karen Culliver
	4/21/97	Marie Danvers 1/13/98
	Kimilee Bryant (alt.) 3/12/98	Teri Bibb 4/98
		Rita Harvey (alt.) 3/98
		#3 Tracy Shayne
		Amy Jo Arrington
		Megan Starr-Levitt (alt.)
		1/21/98
Raoul	Steve Barton	#1 Reece Holland
	Gary Mauer 10/7/96	Christopher Carl 7/2/96
		#2 Keith Buterbaugh
		Lawrence Anderson
		Jason Pebworth 1/13/98
		#3 Ciaran Sheehan
		Jim Weitzer

Note: Only this season's or the most recent cast replacements are listed above under the names of the original cast members. For previous replacements, see previous volumes of *Best Plays*.

CATS—Among the 1997–98 felines in this longest-running musical in Broadway history are Rumpleteazer (Maria Jo Ralabate) and Mungojerrie (Roger Kachel)

RENT

	New York 4/29/96	#1 Boston 11/18/96 #2 La Jolla 7/1/97
Roger Davis	Adam Pascal Norbert Leo Butz (alt.) Richard H. Blake (alt.) 11/97 Norbert Leo Butz 11/97	#1 Sean Keller Manley Pope 3/14/97 Christian Anderson #2 Christian Mena Cary Shields
Mark Cohen	Anthony Rapp Jim Poulos	#1 Luther Creek Christian Anderson Trey Ellet #2 Neil Patrick Harris Kirk McDonald
Tom Collins	Jesse L. Martin Michael McElroy 7/15/97	#1 C.C. Brown #2 Mark Leroy Jackson
Benjamin Coffin III	Taye Diggs Jacques C. Smith 9/12/97	#1 James Rich Dwayne Clark #2 D'Monroe
Joanne Jefferson	Fredi Walker Gwen Stewart	#1 Sylvia MacCalla Kamilah Martin #2 Kenna Ramsey Monique Daniels

Angel Schunard	Wilson Jermaine Heredia
	Wilson Cruz 12/2/97
	Shaun Earl
		#1 Stephan Alexander
		  Shaun Earl
		  Evan D'Angeles
		#2 Wilson Cruz
		  Andy Senor

Mimi Marquez	Daphne Rubin-Vega Marcy Harriell 4/5/97	#1 Simone Laura Dias #2 Julia Santana

Maureen Johnson	Idina Menzel
	Sherrie Scott 7/2/97
	Kristen Lee Kelly
		#1 Carrie Hamilton
		  Amy Spanger 6/5/97
		  Erin Keaney
		#2 Leigh Hetherington
		  Carla Bianco
		  Leigh Hetherington

SMOKEY JOE'S CAFE

	New York 3/2/95	Minneapolis 8/16/96
Ken	Ken Ard	Eugene Fleming Michael-Demby Cain 10/7/97
Adrian	Adrian Bailey	Trent Kendall Dwayne Clark 4/17/97
Brenda	Brenda Braxton	Reva Rice
Victor	Victor Trent Cook James Beeks 6/8/97	Darrian C. Ford Jeffrey Polk 8/26/97
B.J.	B.J. Crosby D'Atra Hicks 1/3/98	Alltrinna Grayson
Pattie	Pattie Darcy Jones	Kim Cea
DeLee	DeLee Lively	Mary Ann Hermansen Rachelle Rak 10/14/97
Michael	Michael Park Jerry Tellier 9/9/97	Jerry Tellier Scott Beck 9/9/97
Fred	Frederick B. Owens	Ashley Howard Wilkinson Stephonne Smith 8/26/97

TITANIC

	New York 4/23/97
Capt. E.J. Smith	John Cunningham
1st Officer William Murdoch	David Costabile
Frederick Barrett	Brian d'Arcy James
Harold Bride	Martin Moran
Henry Etches	Allan Corduner Henry Stram
Thomas Andrews	Michael Cerveris
Isidor Straus	Larry Keith

Ida Straus	Alma Cuervo
Edgar Beane	Bill Buell
Alice Beane	Victoria Clark
Kate McGowen	Jennifer Piech
Jim Farrell	Clarke Thorell

OTHER NEW YORK SHOWS
ON FIRST CLASS TOURS IN 1997–98

BIG

Wilmington, Del. 9/26/97

Josh Baskin	Jim Newman
Susan	Jacquelyn Piro
MacMillan	Ron Holgate
Mrs. Baskin	Judy McLane
Paul	Nick Cokas
Billy	Brett Tabisel Alex Brumel 3/3/98
Young Josh	Joseph Medeiros Travis Greisler 4/14/98
Cynthia Benson	Demaree Alexander

DREAMGIRLS

Providence 9/30/97

Curtis Taylor, Jr.	Brian Evaret Chandler
Deena Jones	LaTanya Hall
Lorrell Robinson	Tonya Dixon
C.C. White	Gary E. Vincent
Effie Melody White	Roz White B.J. Crosby
James Thunder Early	Kevin-Anthony
Marty	Darrin Lamont Byrd
Michelle Morris	Kimberly JuJuan

JOSEPH AND THE AMAZING TECHNICOLOR DREAMCOAT

Toronto 5/31/95

Joseph	Donny Osmond
	David Burnham 6/97
	Donny Osmond 1/98
Narrator	Kelli James Chase
	Donna Kane 11/12/95
	Kelli James Chase 3/97
	Sarah Litsinger 1/98
Jacob/Potiphar/Guru	James Harms
	Gary Krawford 11/29/95
	James Harms 3/31/96
Pharoah	Johnny Seaton
	Abe Reybold
Butler	J.C. Montgomery
	Martin Murphy
Baker	Erich McMillan-McCall
	Paul J. Gallagher
Mrs. Potiphar	Carole Mackereth
	Julia Alicia Fowler 3/31/96
	Carole Mackereth

MASTER CLASS

Boston 11/96

Maria Callas	Faye Dunaway
Manny	Gary Green
	Daniel Faitus 10/7/97
Sharon	Suzan Hanson
Sophie	Melinda Klump
Tony	Kevin Paul Anderson
Stagehand	Scott Davidson

PETER PAN

Seattle 11/28/97

Wendy Darling	Elisa Sagardia
John Darling	Michael LaVolpe
	Chase Kniffen 4/20/98
Mrs. Darling	Barbara McCulloh
Michael Darling	Paul Tiesler
	Drake English 2/2/98
Peter Pan	Cathy Rigby
Captain Hook	Paul Schoeffler

PICASSO AT THE LAPIN AGILE

	Stamford, Conn. 10/6/97
Pablo Picasso	Paul Provenza
Albert Einstein	Mark Nelson
Freddy	Ian Barford
Gaston	Jim Mohr
Sagot	Ken Grantham

RAGTIME

		#1 Los Angeles 6/15/97 *#2 Washington, D.C. 4/29/98*
	New York 1/18/98	
Father	(see *Ragtime* entry in the Plays Produced on Broadway section of this volume)	#1 John Dossett Joseph Delger 5/98 #2 Chris Groenendahl
Mother		#1 Marcia Mitzman Gaven Donna Bullock 5/98 #2 Rebecca Eichenberger
Younger Brother		#1 Scott Carollo Tom Daugherty 5/98 #2 Aloysius Gigl
Coalhouse Walker Jr.		#1 Brian Stokes Mitchell Kingsley Leggs 11/97 #2 Alton Fitzgerald White
Sarah		#1 LaChanze #2 Darlesia Cearcy
Tateh		#1 John Rubinstein #2 Michael Rupert
Harry Houdini		#1 Jason Graae William Akey 5/98 #2 Bernie Yvon
Henry Ford		#1 Bill Carmichael #2 Larry Cahn
Emma Goldman		#1 Judy Kaye Mary Gutzi 11/97 #2 Theresa Tova
Evelyn Nesbit		#1 Susan Wood Jamie Chandler-Torns #2 Melissa Dye

SHOW BOAT

	#1 Los Angeles 11/12/96
	#2 Detroit 3/11/97
	#3 Chicago 3/24/96
Cap'n Andy	#1 George Grizzard
	Tom Bosley 2/97
	Len Cariou 4/97
	Dean Jones 9/30/97
	#2 Tom Bosley
	#3 John McMartin
	Pat Harrington 5/12/97
Parthy	#1 Cloris Leachman
	Karen Morrow 2/97
	Cloris Leachman 4/97
	#2 Karen Morrow
	#3 Dorothy Loudon
	Anita Gillette 6/97
Magnolia	#1 Teri Hansen
	Gay Willis 1/13/98
	#2 Sarah Pfisterer
	#3 Gay Willis
Gaylord Ravenal	#1 J. Mark McVey
	Hugh Panaro 4/97
	Stephen Bogardus 6/22/97
	Keith Buterbaugh 1/13/98
	#2 John Ruess
	#3 Mark Jacoby
	Keith Buterbaugh 5/12/97
Julie	#1 Valarie Pettiford
	Karen-Angela Bishop 5/97
	#2 Debbie DeCoudreaux
	#3 Marilyn McCoo
	Terry Burrell 2/97
Frank	#1 Keith Savage
	#2 Kirby Ward
	#3 Eddie Korbich
Ellie	#1 Jacquey Maltby
	Kerri Clarke
	#2 Beverly Ward
	#3 Clare Leach
	Ann Van Cleave 5/12/97
Queenie	#1 Anita Berry
	Jo Ann Hawkins White
	#2 Gretha Boston
	Janelle Robinson 2/23/98
	#3 Jo Ann Hawkins White
Steve	#1 Todd Noel
	Kip Wilborn 3/29/96
	Ross Neill 5/97
	#2 John Clonts
	Craig Ashton 3/6/98
	#3 Todd Noel

Joe	#1 Dan Tullis Jr.
	Michel Bell
	#2 Andre Solomon-Glover
	#3 Michel Bell
	Kenneth Nichols 2/97

STATE FAIR

	University Park, Pa. 9/7/97
Abel Frake	John Davidson
Melissa Frake	Carol Swarbrick
	SuEllen Estey 10/21/97
	Carol Swarbrick 11/17/97
Margy Frake	Valerie A. Accetta
Emily Arden	Deborah Foley
Pat Gilbert	Mark Martino
Wayne Frake	John Simeone

THE SEASON
OFF OFF BROADWAY

OFF OFF BROADWAY

By Mel Gussow

WHILE Broadway musicals have become larger and larger, making each venture an event intended to draw the widest possible audience, off off Broadway continues to experiment in subject as well as style of presentation. In the 1997–98 season, three of the five citations for outstanding OOB productions were for musicals, and the other two had strong musical elements.

Certainly one of the oddest shows of this or any year—and an outstanding OOB production—was *Hedwig and the Angry Inch,* the impossibly intricate story of a German transsexual (Hedwig) who becomes a rock star but is haunted by questions of identity (political as well as sexual), originally produced at Westbeth and later brought up to off Broadway. Emigrating to middle America, the glittering Hedwig soon finds him/herself out of place and out of time. She becomes the mentor of Tommy Gnosis, who is the next and greater singing sensation. Acting as author, actor and singer, John Cameron Mitchell dreamed up *Hedwig,* wrote the book and played the title role within an angry inch of her life. This hard-driving show had a curiously wistful appeal. Stephen Trask's score, music and lyrics, was raucous but impressive. As with *Cabaret* on Broadway, *Hedwig* (staged by Peter Askin) was performed within a mockup of a cabaret in the newly renovated (and historic) Jane Street Theater.

In *A Harlot's Progress* at the Performing Garage, the inventive puppeteer Theodora Skipitares turned her keen eye on William Hogarth. Her show, based on Hogarth's series of drawings, had the effect of placing the audience inside the pictures. With exquisite attention to detail, she animated those drawings into an Hogarthian environment. The designs extended from the lifesize puppets to the puppeteers, who manipulated the characters Bunraku style but were themselves clothed in a tapestry of Hogarth. The effect was to make it difficult to distinguish puppet from puppeteer, mover from movement. Towering over the tale were larger-than-life totemic creatures. The story followed the descent of Moll Hackabout, a 15 year old who comes to London from the provinces and in quick order is seduced, corrupted and discarded. The score sung by three live performers gave the show the underpinning of an oratorio. With *A Harlot's Progress,* Skipitares moved into a sinister world of sex and sinfulness, a fascinating sidestep for someone whose pre-

279

vious shows had dealt with science, history and nutrition. The score and the libretto were by Barry Greenhut, the design and direction by Skipitares; as with the puppets, the creativity was irrevocably intertwined.

In contrast, Dan Hurlin's *The Shoulder* at Dance Theater Workshop, a chamber opera written in collaboration with the composer Dan Moses Schreier, was upbeat, though not without its melancholic moments. Along with *Hedwig* and *Harlot,* this was a most unlikely subject for a musical, which should not have been surprising since Hurlin was also the creator of *Quintland,* a one man show about the Dionne Quintuplets, and *NO(thing so powerful as TRUTH),* a musical about William Loeb, the reactionary publisher of the Manchester Union Leader in New Hampshire. With *The Shoulder,* Hurlin borrowed another public event, in this case the obscure tale of an aged farmer who drove across the state of Iowa to visit his ill brother. What made the story so unusual was the farmer's vehicle of choice: a power lawn mower. Driving at seven miles per hour, the slowest possible speed, it took him a month and a half to finish his journey. The show was a breezy 90 minutes, enlivened by Hurlin's presence as all the minor characters, and his artfulness as scenic designer. The Grant Wood-like landscape was populated by toy cars, models and dolls. This was a vest-pocket musical that would fit in a trunk. Or strap it to a lawnmower and take it on tour.

All three musicals were ideally suited to off off Broadway, but each demonstrated an expansiveness of talent, as did Richard Foreman's *Benita Canova (Gnostic Eroticism),* the fourth outstanding OOB production. This swift, jagged dream at the Ontological-Hysteric Theater was as mysterious as the author's other work. The setting was a girls' school (or was it a madhouse?), in which a covey of schoolgirls is bedeviled by a demonic headmistress called Madame (played by David Greenspan). The show was written, directed and designed by Foreman. He may be the only one who fully understands what he wrought, though as major domo he keeps the audience captivated with alternating currents of power: threat and counterthreat, innocence and corruption. As always, his deaign was an exhibition by itself. Just as Skipitares was inspired by Hogarth, Foreman's muse was Balthus, with his erotic images of seemingly pliant young women. Joanna P. Adler played the nubile title character. This was one of two Foreman plays this year. The other was *Pearls for Pigs,* a plotless piece about a maestro (Daniel Patrick Kelly) and a doctor (Tom Nelis), which was at least partly a clown show.

The fifth citation goes to Warren Leight's *Side Man,* an engrossing family play about the public and private lives of a small group of jazzmen. Undaunted about their own lack of success, they play for the love of jazz, and the camaraderie of their close-knit combo. Together, the musicians get through the day—and their gigs—as the play tracks them over a period of four decades. The playwright brings the audience up close to their music and to their interrupted family life, poignantly personalized (and apparently drawn from Leight's own background). The play, produced by Weissberger Theater Group, would have benefited if the actors also played instruments, but there is one very evocative moment when they simply sit and listen to recorded sound—and are transported by it. Under Michael Mayer's direction, the actors are an ensemble, with especially vivid work by Kevin Geer as a drugged-out musician.

After its OOB success, *Side Man* moved to Broadway. The upward route that was followed this year by a number of ventures. *The Beauty Queen of Leenane,* a piercingly truthful drama by Martin McDonagh, made its New York debut at the Atlantic Theater with the original Irish production from the Druid Theater and then moved to Broadway via off Broadway. *Side Man* and *Beauty Queen* are examples of the advantage of trying out a play far off the mainstream. Each was given an excellent production and, on the wave of critical and audience appreciation, moved to a wider venue. Similarly, *Dinah Was,* a musical about Dinah Washington, began at the WPA and then shifted into an extended off-Broadway engagement. As demonstrated by these plays and *Never the Sinner,* a drama about Leopold and Loeb, and *R & J,* in which a group of schoolboys act out an all male *Romeo and Juliet,* more and more works move from showcases into commercial engagements.

Robert Wilson briefly visited the Brooklyn Academy of Music with *Time Rocker,* a rock opera written by Darryl Pinckney in collaboration with Lou Reed. In the story, inspired by *The Time Machine,* characters flee through history, from ancient Egypt to contemporary rural America and dance to the music of time. Wilson's imagery was stunning: an Edward Hopper house on the prairie; a landscape out of Dali that suddenly shifts to Magritte, a blood red background mixed with stark white. Wilson himself as a major experimentalist, is important enough to spoof. *Bob* by Anne Bogart at New York Theater Workshop pastiched dialogue from published interviews. Aside from the fact that Will Bond, the actor playing Wilson, did not look or sound anything like his role model, and the point of view wavered from putdown to sendup, the show had sparks of interest. Will Wilson respond with a show called *Anne*? Unlikely.

One of the season's disappointments was *Elsinore,* Robert Lepage's reworking of *Hamlet.* The production (at BAM) had some of the visual imagination that one associates with Lepage, but not the daring of plays like *The Seven Streams of the River Ota.* One element that it lacked—and needed—was the director's presence as a performer. Peter Darling, who acted the one-man *Hamlet,* was woefully inadequate to this most demanding task. If not a Lepage, the role demanded a Kevin Kline, or if it were to be a spoof, Everett Quinton.

70 Hill Lane was one of the weirder shows of the season. In essence it was a play about tape, as in Scotch and sticky. Brought to Performance Space 122 by the Improbable Theater, an English company, this was a bizarre ghost story. Phelim McDermott, the evening's author and lead actor, once lived in a house in Manchester, England that was thought to be inhabited by a poltergeist. Through a bit of magic (and a lot of that tape), he brought that experience to life onstage. What Richard Foreman does with string, McDermott did with tape, using it to define rooms and spaces. In performance, this was esoteric, to say the least. It was also overlong (too much tape!) but strange and interesting. McDermott's artfulness in

On these pages are photos of the OOB offerings cited as outstanding 1997–98 productions: *above,* the Hogarthian ambiance of Theodora Skipitares's puppet chamber opera *A Harlot's Progress*—"moved into a sinister world of sex and sinfulness;" *at right,* Christina Campanella and David Greenspan in Richard Foreman's *Benita Canova*—a "swift, jagged dream;" *below,* Michael Mastro, Frank Wood and Joseph Lyle Taylor in Warren Leight's *Side Man*—"an engrossing family play about . . . . . a small group of jazzmen"

Above, Dan Hurlin, Doug Marcks and Don Chastain in the Hurlin-Dan Moses Schreier chamber opera *The Shoulder*—"a breezy 90 minutes;" *at right,* John Cameron Mitchell in his and Steven Trask's *Hedwig and the Angry Inch*—"the impossibly intricate story of a German transsexual . . . . . a curiously wistful appeal"

folding a newspaper and turning its pages into an assortment of puppets was an origami number in itself.

While *Titanic* was king of the movie world and *Titanic,* the musical, continued DiCaprio-less on Broadway, there was a small quirky retelling of the tragedy in *Scotland Road* by Jeffrey Hatcher (at Primary Stages). In this version, a "survivor" is discovered today holding to an iceberg. Unharmed and not aged, she seems to have passed the decades in a kind of enforced oblivion. Of course, this is a hoax. Or is it? The character seems to have all the authenticity (and history) on her side, asking her investigators and the audience to suspend disbelief. A mystery play with twist upon twist, it was sharply acted by a cast headed by Daniel Gerroll. In *The Water Children* at Playwrights Horizons, Wendy MacLeod wrote a many-sided play about the subject of abortion. The issues were provocative, although the play proved to be manipulative, forcing opposites into a romantic alliance.

Increasingly, name actors signed up for limited engagements OOB, with Primary Stages staging a coup by drawing Brian Cox, a leading English actor, to replay *St. Nicholas,* a monodrama by Conor McPherson, one of England's more promising young playwrights. The play was really a two-parter, with the first (and far more effective) half dealing sardonically with a malicious theater critic, who—in Part II—is caught up in a family of vampires. Cox easily held the stage by himself and was superb throughout. *Shopping etc.*'s title (see Index) dared not speak its name in print, but it sold the show at New York Theater Workshop to a curious public. Here we go again with London lowlife (money and sex), except that the play has diminishing dramatic returns. Slightly higher lowlife was exemplified by *Goose-Pimples* at The New Group, the long delayed arrival of an early play by Mike Leigh, in which humor is based on the fact that an Arab character cannot speak English.

The Signature Theater Company, which began its estimable career by devoting full seasons to the work of Romulus Linney, Lee Blessing and others, decided to focus this year on Arthur Miller. In contrast to past Signature choices, Miller was less in need of rediscovery; his plays are often revived (as with the Broadway production of *A View From the Bridge*). His Signature series began with a revival of *The American Clock,* a collage of Depression America, with the production placing emphasis on the songs of the period. That was followed by a double bill of one-acts, *The Last Yankee* and *I Can't Remember Anything,* concluding with the world premiere of *Mr. Peters' Connections.* Although this could be considered a coup for off off Broadway, the play proved to be a dispiriting contemplation of death. As Mr. Peters (a very dour Peter Falk) muses in a metaphorical bar, figures from his past appear, including his brother and a Marilyn Monroe-lookalike. Anne Jackson momentarily brightened the play as Mrs. Peters, but then the evening dimmed again.

The Signature idea may be catching on. There was a Mac Wellman festival with 11 plays by this daringly inventive playwright appearing all over the OOB map: revivals of Wellman classics like *Terminal Hip* and *Sincerity Forever,* as well as premieres of new and older works (*Bodacious Flapdoodle*). Kicking off the series was *Fnu Lnu,* a devious yarn about Ybor City, Florida, which raised the question of who put the Y in Ybor. There were no answers but, as always with Wellman, tantalizing clues. Stephen Mellor was his usual masterly self tracking the author's wordbending dialogue. The festival was a salute to an archetypal downtown artist.

Following up Joanne Woodward's rediscovery of plays by Clifford Odets, Richard Caliban revivified *Clash by Night.* Though a cut below other Odets, this melodrama about working class violence was given an understated production, with Jodie Markell fine in the central role and strong support from Geneva Carr and Dominic Comperatore. Under the auspices of the Blue Light Theater, James Naughton directed a colorful revival of Eduardo de Filippo's *Filumena,* with Maria Tucci delivering a zestful performance in the title role. Andrei Serban returned to La Mama with his engaging version of *The Caucasian Chalk Circle,* and the Irish Repertory

Theater revived *Long Day's Journey Into Night,* starring Frances Sternhagen and Brian Murray (the busiest and one of the most versatile of actors).

The Ensemble Studio Theater's 21st annual Marathon of one-act plays was highlighted by Leslie Ayvazian's monodrama *Plan Day* (a mother's obsessions through the years), Ari Roth's *Prelude to a Crisis* (an unfulfilled affair between a professor and a student), and Paul Rudnick's *Mr. Charles, Currently of Palm Beach,* a very funny and malicious monologue by a gay cable channel talker given a flamboyant performance by Peter Bartlett. On other stages, monologuists abounded: Danny Hoch, Sandra Bernhard, Tim Miller. One of the most popular (and overrated) was Eddie Izzard in *Dress to Kill,* a curiously rambling tour of the actor's life and ideas, with little sense of pace and only an occasional smile. In September, Karen Finley brought her one woman play, *The American Chestnut,* to New York, with her outrageously outspoken comments on the abuse of women (and others).

There was, of course, another side: entertainment, in this case provided by The Drama Dept., which along with Blue Light and the New Group continue to enrich the theatrical landscape. Early on, The Drama Dept. deconstructed *Uncle Tom's Cabin* (on other stages, two O'Neills were also deconstructed: *The Emperor Jones* and *More Stately Mansions*). As with The Drama Dept.'s revival of *June Moon* the previous year, and *Once in a Lifetime* this year at the Atlantic Theater, there is even room for nostalgia off off Broadway.

PLAYS PRODUCED
OFF OFF BROADWAY

AND ADDITIONAL N.Y.C. PRODUCTIONS

Compiled by Camille Dee

Here is a comprehensive sampling of off-off-Broadway and other experimental or peripheral 1997–98 productions in New York. There is no definitive "off-off-Broadway" area or qualification. To try to define or regiment it would be untrue to its fluid, exploratory purpose. The listing below of hundreds of works produced by more than 100 OOB groups and others is as inclusive as reliable sources will allow, however, and takes in all leading Manhattan-based, new-play producing, English-language organizations.

The more active and established producing groups are identified in **bold face** type, in alphabetical order, with artistic policies and the names of the managing directors given whenever these are a matter of record. Each group's 1997–98 schedule, with emphasis on new plays and with revivals of classics usually omitted, is listed with play titles in CAPITAL LETTERS. Often these are works-in-progress with changing scripts, casts and directors, sometimes without an engagement of record (but an opening or early performance date is included when available).

Many of these off-off-Broadway groups have long since outgrown a merely experimental status and are offering programs which are the equal in professionalism and quality (and in some cases the superior) of anything in the New York theater, with special contractual arrangements like the showcase code, letters of agreement (allowing for longer runs and higher admission prices than usual) and, closer to the edge of the commercial theater, a so-called "mini-contract." In the list below, all available data on opening dates, performance numbers and major production and acting credits (almost all for Equity members) is included in the entries of these special-arrangement offerings.

A large selection of lesser-known groups and other shows that made appearances off off Broadway during the season appears under the "Miscellaneous" heading at the end of this listing.

American Jewish Theater. Produces plays reflecting the Jewish experience. Stanley Brechner artistic director.

SAM AND ITKEH. By Jack LaZebnik. October 28, 1997. Director, Richard Harden; scenery and costumes, William Schroder; lighting, Jason Boyd; sound, Laura Brown. With Marilyn Sokol, David Little.

NEVER THE SINNER. By John Logan. November 30, 1997. See its entry in the Plays Produced Off Broadway section of this volume.

HOT KLEZMER. Music, Harold Seletsky and Mary Feinsinger. March 31, 1998. See its entry in the Plays Produced Off Broadway section of this volume.

UNCLE PHILIP'S COAT (one-man show). By Matty Selman, based on a story by Matty Selman and Larry Block. May 5, 1998. Director, Marcia Jean Kurtz; scenery, Ray Recht; lighting, Chris Dallos; costumes, Chris Fields. With Larry Block.

American Theater of Actors. Dedicated to providing a creative atmosphere for new American playwrights, actors and directors. James Jennings artistic director.

Schedule included:

BITTER HERBS. By I.W. Fellner. June 11, 1997. Director, Robin Carson. With Jewel Donohue, Mort Forrest, James Kloiber, Selma Oshen, Baz Snider.

BALLOONS. By Eric Beall. June 25, 1997. Director, Peter Marinos. With William Greville, J.C. Islander, Matthew Klein, Mario Macaluso, Robert Mack, Christi Spain.

COYOTES. By Lee Patton. July 16, 1997. Director, Kristina McFadden. With Alexandra Cremer, Daniel Martin, Sarah Hubbard, Greg Morvillo, Mark Schmetterer, Christine Syron, Stephen Tollafield.

ALFRED. By Tom LaBar. July 23, 1997. Director, James Jennings. With Tom Bruce.

HELEN. By Euripides. July 30, 1997. Director, James Jennings. With Sheila Willis, Derrick Begin, Will Buchanan, Paul Stafford, Lesley Malin, Wanda O'Connell.

BOOMERANG. By Michael Wallerstein. August 6, 1997. Director, Andrew M. Segal. With Nona Pipes, Timothy Patrick, Lamis Faris, Greggory Milano.

MARIE. By Donnally Miller. August 13, 1997. Director, Teresa Fischer. With Risa Glenn, Sarah Hubbard, Ginger Masoud, Kathrine Lyn Neuman, Allan Pollack, Noel O'Neill.

HEARTS' SOUNDS. By Alex Menza. August 20, 1997. Director, Barbara Pitcher. With Judith Caporale, Ken Coughlin, Joe Iacona.

A MATTER OF HONOR. By Irving Leitner. September 10, 1997. Director, Courtney Everette. With Cherita Armstrong, Sarah Hubbard, Christi Spain, Derrick Begin, Michael Moran, Hugh Brennan.

MOZART AT McDONALD'S. Written and directed by James Jennings. September 24, 1997. With Peter Coriaty, Wanda O'Connell, Jay Cavanaugh.

AFTERTHOUGHTS. By Thomas Pasquenza. October 15, 1997. Director, Sharon Kellogg. With Christina Bauer, Troy Hall, Mark Joe Lawrence, Susan Spano, Justin Yoo.

THE BURDEN OF LIGHT. By Errol Selkirk. November 5, 1997. Director, Dan Tedlie. With William Greville, Debra Conn, Sara Kay Rinde, J. Richey Nash, Jack Garrity, Marie Thomas.

THE CLUB MED ACCOUNT. By Judith Keller. November 12, 1997. Director, Elysabeth Kleinhans. With Antoinette Gallo, Joe Iacona, Joe Leone, Kimberly Nickerson, Mark Schmetterer, Debra Smock.

NIJINSKY'S LAST DANCE. Written and directed by James Jennings. November 19, 1997. With Rhett Dennis, Jane Culley, Charlie Lee, Aaron Angello, Michael Midori.

GOD BLESS MY DYING BOYS. By Ben Wilensky. November 19, 1997. Director, Alex Lippert. With Nicole Poole, Ken Coughlin.

JUDITH'S STORY. By Betty Jane Isquith. December 3, 1997. Director, Barbara Pitcher. With Laura LeBlanc, David Tillestrand, Antoinette Gallo, Ginny Paynter, Sheila Willis, Robert Hess.

WHISPERS OF THE KOSHARES. Written and directed by James Jennings. December 10, 1997. With Adam Brown, Don Carlson, Melanie Stites.

PAINTING LESSONS. By Leslie D. McGriff. December 17, 1997. Director, Mark Anthony Thomas. With Marianne Mueller, Maureen Campbell, Roxanna Young.

CONVERSATIONS WITH A ROPE. Written and directed by James Jennings. January 14, 1998. With Tom Bruce, Greg Pekar, Tori Agresti.

ATLANTIC THEATER COMPANY—Matthew Ross and
Patrick Fitzgerald in a scene from *Mojo* by Jez Butterworth

SPIDERS ACROSS THE STARS. By Meny Berrio. January 21, 1998. Director, Minander K. Saini.
With Melanie Bean, Wanda O'Connell, Tori Agresti.

DUB. By Henry Slesar. February 11, 1998. Director, Mark Neveldine. With J.P. Lavin, Nick Rose,
Ronit Feinglass, Chad Damiani, Petra Dielewicz.

THE REAL STUFF. By Carol Anne Ryan. February 18, 1998. Director, Christopher Bellis. With
Dean Negri, Eric Axen, Mary Emily Beal, Kara Engeldahl.

THE HUNGER WALTZ. By Sheila Gallaghan. February 25, 1998. Director, Paul Angelo. With
Don Carlson, Jennifer Leigh Jones, Greg Pekar, Tori Agresti.

REQUIEM FOR ANDRE. By Frank Barth. March 18, 1998. Director, Richard Bach. With Hugh
Brennan, Lynne Valley, Jim Hazard, Elysabeth Kleinhans.

GROSSMAN'S URN. By John E. Shea. March 25, 1998. Director, Bart Lovins. With Tom Bruce,
Eric Friedman, Leonard Gibbs, Brian Herzer, Joe Iacona, J.C. Islander, Mark Ransom.

RUBICON. Written and directed by Ron Weissenberger. April 1, 1998. With Robert Crafford, Rich
Guerreiro, Bill Quinlan.

THIS ONE'S FOR YOU, DADDY. By Pauline Smolin. April 22, 1998. Director, Elysabeth Kleinhans. With Eve Austin, John Murray, Erin Pederson, Vincent Yannone.

DREAMS OF A WINTER NIGHT. Written and directed by James Jennings. April 29, 1998. With
Jane Culley, Jennifer Shaw, Gary Swanson.

JUST ANOTHER DAY ON DEATH ROW. By Joan Forster. May 13, 1998. Director, Shira Kline.
With Peter Coriaty, Mark Neveldine, Ken Coughlin, Adam Brown, Todd Fredericks, Alex Johnson,
Allen Cove.

Atlantic Theater Company. Produces new plays or reinterpretations of classics that speak to
audiences in a contemporary voice on issues reflecting today's society. Neil Pepe artistic director, Hilary Hinckle managing director.

MOJO (68). By Jez Butterworth. November 10, 1997. Director, Neil Pepe; scenery, Walter Spangler; lighting, Tyler Micoleau; costumes, Laura Bauer; music, David Yazbek. With Joseph Kern, Patrick Fitzgerald, Matthew Ross, Clark Gregg, Chris Bauer, Jordan Lage.

THE BEAUTY QUEEN OF LEENANE. By Martin McDonagh. February 26, 1998. See its entry in the Plays Produced Off and On Broadway sections of this volume.

ONCE IN A LIFETIME. By George S. Kaufman and Moss Hart. May 31, 1998. Director, David Pittu; scenery, James Noone; lighting, Howard Werner; costumes, Meg Neville; sound, David Margolin Lawson. With Kate Blumberg, Larry Bryggman, David Pittu, Ron Butler, Tony Carlin, John Ellison Conlee, Cynthia Darlow, Johanna Day, Peter Jacobson, Susan Knight, Amelia White.

Blue Light Theater Company. Produces a wide range of plays and strives to give young working actors the opportunity to grow by working with established theater artists. Greg Naughton actor-manager, William S. Doble general manager.

FILUMENA: A MARRIAGE ITALIAN STYLE (55). By Eduardo De Filippo, translated by Maria Tucci. November 6, 1997. Director, James Naughton; scenery, Hugh Landwehr; lighting, Rui Rita; costumes, Marion Williams; sound, Kurt Kellenberger. With Maria Tucci, Tony Amendola, Joe Grifasi, Mary Fogarty, Melissa Bowen, Greg Naughton, Lenny Venito, Matt Saldivar, Dana Bledsoe, Rik Colitti.

AMAZING GRACE (33). By Michael Cristofer. March 15, 1998. Director, Edward Gilbert; scenery, Michael Schweikardt; lighting, Tom Sturge; costumes, Laurie Churba; sound, Scott Silvian. With Marsha Mason, Bethel Leslie, Carlin Glynn, Adina Porter, Marsha Dietlein, Anthony Lamont, Stephen Bradbury, Jerry Mayer.

THE SEAGULL (20+). By Anton Chekhov, translated by Tom Stoppard. May 27, 1998. Director, Austin Pendleton; scenery, Michael Schweikardt; lighting, John Lasiter; costumes, Laurie Churba; sound, Jerry M. Yager. With Angie Phillips, Maria Tucci, Mark Blum, Greg Naughton, Molly Regan, Alex Draper, Francesca DiMauro, Bill Striglos, Joe Ponazecki, Tom Brennan.

Brooklyn Academy of Music Next Wave Festival. Since 1981, this annual three-month festival has presented over 200 events, including more than 50 world premieres. Featuring leading international artists, it is one of the world's largest festivals of contemporary performing arts. Harvey Lichtenstein president and executive producer.

ELSINORE (7). Based on *Hamlet* by William Shakespeare; created and directed by Robert Lepage. October 7, 1997. Scenery, Carl Fillion; lighting, Alain Lortie, Nancy Mongrain; costumes, Yvan Gaudin; music, Robert Caux. With Peter Darling.

ANTONY AND CLEOPATRA (6). By William Shakespeare. October 28, 1997. Director, Barrie Rutter; scenery and costumes, Jessica Worrall; lighting, Brian Harris; music, Conrad Nelson. With Northern Broadside (Ishia Bennison, Barrie Rutter, Conrad Nelson, Michelle Hardwick, Julie Livesey, Sally Ann Matthews, Matthew Booth, Roy North, Dennis Conlon, John Elkington, Paul Gabriel, Richard Hollick, Geoffrey Leesley, John Gully, Andy Wear, Andrew Whitehead).

MISSIONARIES (5). Conceived, composed and directed by Elizabeth Swados. November 4, 1997. Lighting, Beverly Emmons; costumes, Kaye Voyce; musical direction, David Gaines. With Josie de Guzman, Dorothy Abrahams, Vanessa Aspillaga, Carrie Crow, Pierre Diennet, Marisa Echeverria, Abby Freeman, Peter Kim, Gretchen Lee Krich, Fabio Polanco, Nick Petrone, Heather Ramey, Nina Shreiber, Tina Stafford, Rachel Stern, Amy White.

TIME ROCKER (pop opera) (10). Text, Darryl Pinckney; translation into German, Wolfgang Wiens; music and lyrics, Lou Reed. November 12, 1997. Direction and scenery, Robert Wilson; lighting, Heinrich Brunke, Robert Wilson; costumes, Frida Parmeggiani; sound, Stefan Wulff; musical direction, Mike Rathke. With Stephan Benson, Sona Cervena, Samuel Fintzi, Sandra Flubacher, Hannes Hellmann, Jorg Holm, Hans Kremer, Stefan Kurt, Annette Paulmann, Cornelia Schirmer, Nicki von Tempelhoff, Victoria Trauttmansdorff.

YOU A.N.C. NOTHING YET! (one-man show) (12). By and with Pieter-Dirk Uys. November 13, 1997.

Classic Stage Company. Reinventing and revitalizing the classics for contemporary audiences. David Esbjornson artistic director, Mary Esbjornson executive director.

THERESE RAQUIN (32). Adapted by Neal Bell from Emile Zola's novel. October 29, 1997. Director, David Esbjornson; scenery, Narelle Sissons; lighting, Christopher Akerlind; costumes, Kaye Voyce; music and sound, Rinde Eckert, Gina Leishman. With Elizabeth Marvel, Beth Dixon, Todd Weeks, Sean Haberle, Ed Hodson, Angela Reed, Clement Fowler, Steven Rattazzi.

CHRISTMAS AT THE IVANOVS' (28). By Aleksander Vvedensky, translated by Karin Coonrod and Julia Listengarten. December 14, 1997. Director, Karin Coonrod; scenery, Sarah Edkins; lighting, Kevin Adams; costumes, P.K. Wish; puppets, Joseph Brajcki; music and sound, Tony Geballe. With Ledlie Borgerhoff, Mary Christopher, Paula Murray Cole, Michael Escamilla, DJ Mendel, Thomas Jay Ryan, Steven Rattazzi. Co-produced by Arden Party.

PHAEDRA IN DELIRIUM (28). By Susan Yankowitz. January 28, 1998. Co-produced by the Women's Project and Productions; see its entry in that listing in this section.

En Garde Arts. Dedicated to developing the concept of "site-specific theater" in the streets, parks and buildings of the city. Anne Hamburger founder and producer.

MYSTERY SCHOOL (50). By Paul Selig. March 11, 1998. See its entry in the Plays Produced Off Broadway section of this volume.

Ensemble Studio Theater. Membership organization of playwrights, actors, directors and designers dedicated to supporting individual theater artists and developing new works for the stage. Over 200 projects each season, ranging from readings to fully-mounted productions. Curt Dempster artistic director.

OCTOBERFEST. Festival of over 60 new works by members. September 26-October 26, 1997.

FLIGHT (17). By Arthur Giron. November 16, 1997. Director, Jamie Richards; scenery, Kert Lundell; lighting, Greg MacPherson; costumes, Amela Baksic; sound, Laura Brown. With Daniel Ahearn, Brad Bellamy, Suzanna Hay, Thomas McHugh, Michael Louis Wells.

THICKER THAN WATER (one-act plays by the Youngblood playwrights group): WOODWIND HYPOTHESES by Sharon Eberhardt, directed by Peg Denithorne; SOCKDOLAGER by Christopher Shinn, directed by Jimmy Bohr; A LITANY OF SORROWS by David Zellnik, directed by Gus Rogerson; KNOT STEW by John Belluso, directed by Chris Smith. December 7, 1997. With Kyra Sedgwick, Jack Gilpin, Jon-Michael Hernandez, Matt Servitto, David Arrow, Andrea Maulella, Susan Pilar, Grant Varjas, Susan Bruce, Rainn Wilson.

MARATHON '98 (festival of one-act plays). MR. CHARLES, CURRENTLY OF PALM BEACH by Paul Rudnick, directed by Christopher Ashley; DREAM by Billy Aronson, directed by Jamie Richards; THE HUNDRED PENNY BOX by Barbara Sundstrom, from Sharon Bell Mathis's book, directed by Woodie King Jr.; KILLING HAND by David Zellnik, directed by Chris Smith; THE TRIO by Shel Silverstein, directed by Art Wolff; HOW TO PLANT A ROSE by Elizabeth Diggs, directed by Mark Roberts; DONUT HOLES IN ORBIT by Prince Gomolvilas, directed by Charles Karchmer; SCRAPPLE by Jennifer Mattern, directed by Susann Brinkley; THE JADE MOUNTAIN by David Mamet, directed by Curt Dempster; PLAN DAY by Leslie Ayvazian, directed by Curt Dempster; MARY MACGREGOR by Keith Alan Benjamin, directed by Joe White; THE EARTHQUAKE by Elinor Renfield and Joyce Carol Oates, directed by Elinor Renfield; PRELUDE TO A CRISIS by Ari Roth, directed by Mark Nelson. May 6–June 14, 1998.

INTAR. Mission is to identify, develop and present the talents of gifted Hispanic American theater artists and multicultural visual artists. Max Ferra artistic director.

THE ALAMO (work-in-progress) (3). Conceived and performed by Sigfrido Aguilar and Jim Calder. September 25, 1997.

THE NEXT STOP (13). By Carmen Rivera. December 5, 1997. Director, Michael John Garces; scenery, Jim Larkin; lighting, Ken Allaire; costumes, Mimi O'Donnell. With Amarylis Perez, Joselin Reyes, Felix Solis, Jeannette Torruella de Plaza, David Zayas.

MYSTERY OF THE ROSE BOUQUET (42). By Manuel Puig; translated by Allan King. March 19, 1998. Director, Max Ferra; scenery, Van Santvoord; lighting, Robert Williams; costumes, Ricardo Morin; sound, Johnna Doti. With Virginia Rambal, Doris DiFarnecio.

Irish Repertory Theater. Aims to bring works by Irish and Irish American masters and contemporary playwrights to a wider audience and to develop new works focusing on a wide range of cultural experiences. Charlotte Moore artistic director, Ciaran O'Reilly producing director.

MASS APPEAL (42). By Bill C. Davis. July 9, 1997. Director, Charlotte Moore; scenery, David Raphel; lighting, Gregory Cohen; costumes, David Toser. With Tony Coleman, Paul McGrane.

THE IRISH . . . AND HOW THEY GOT THAT WAY (98). By Frank McCourt. October 2, 1997. Director, Charlotte Moore; choreography, Alexia Hess Sheehan; scenery, Shawn Lewis; lighting, Dan Walker; costumes, David Toser; musical direction, Rusty Magee. With Terry Donnelly, Bob Green, Marian Tomas Griffin, Ciaran O'Reilly, Ciaran Sheehan.

MAJOR BARBARA (32). By George Bernard Shaw. November 24, 1997. Direction, scenery and costumes, Tony Walton; lighting, Kirk Bookman; sound, Randy Freed. With Scott Beehner, Thomas Carson, Terry Donnelly, Melissa Errico, Boyd Gaines, Schuyler Grant, Paul McGrane, Charlotte Moore, Jack Ryland, Rob Sedgwick.

SONG AT SUNSET (one-man show) (29). Conceived and directed by Shivaun O'Casey. January 22, 1998. Lighting, Gregory Cohen; sound, Ruben Kenig. With Niall Buggy.

LONG DAY'S JOURNEY INTO NIGHT (46). By Eugene O'Neill. March 22, 1998. Director, Charlotte Moore; scenery, Akira Yoshimura; lighting, Gregory Cohen; costumes, Linda Fisher; music, Jason Robert Brown. With Brian Murray, Frances Sternhagen, Paul Carlin, Paul McGrane, Rosemary Fine.

Jewish Repertory Theater. Presents plays in English relating to the Jewish experience. Ran Avni artistic director, Michael Lichtenstein managing director.

JEST A SECOND! (36). By James Sherman. June 15, 1997. Director, Dennis Zacek; scenery and costumes, Bruce Goodrich; lighting, Deborah Constantine. With Linnea Todd, Paul Urcioli, Michael Perreca, Roslyn Alexander, Stan Lachow, Jordan Leeds.

THE ADJUSTMENT (15). By Michael T. Folie. November 9, 1997. Director, Pamela Berlin; scenery, Narelle Sissons; lighting, Matthew Frey; costumes, David C. Woolard; sound, Raymond Schilke. With Liz Larsen, Matte Osian, Glenn Fleshler.

TOO JEWISH TWO! (one-man show) (21). Written, directed and performed by Avi Hoffman. April 28, 1998. Scenery and lighting, Paul S. Morrill; sound, Michael Pistone; musical direction, Phil Hinton.

The Joseph Papp Public Theater/New York Shakespeare Festival. Schedule of special projects, in addition to its regular off-Broadway productions. George C. Wolfe producer, Rosemarie Tichler artistic producer, Mark Litvin managing director, Michael Hurst general manager, Margaret M. Lioi senior director of external affairs.

First Stages (works-in-progress); 12 performances each

SANTA CONCEPCION. By Anne Garcia-Romero. April 9, 1998. Director, Susana Tubert; scenery and costumes, Clint Ramos; lighting, David Higham; sound, Don Dinicola. With Maria Cellario, Divina Cook, Al Espinosa, Mateo Gomez, Zabryna Guevara, Maricela Ochoa.

NEW WORK NOW! (festival of staged readings). Schedule included STOP KISS by Diana Son, directed by Jo Bonney; A BICYCLE COUNTRY by Nilo Cruz, directed by Karin Coonrod; CIVIL SEX written and directed by Brian Freeman; AMERICAN DREAMS adapted from the novel by Sapphire and directed by Jaye Austin-Williams; SILENCE written and directed by Moira Buffini; LOBSTER ALICE by Kira Obolensky, directed by David Esbjornson; CARRIAGE by Jerome Hairston, directed by Robert O'Hara; BIRDSEED BUNDLES by Ain Gordon, directed by Michael Sexton; THIRST by Neena Beber, directed by Bartlett Sher; GUANABANA by Elizabeth Ruiz, directed by Loretta Greco; SMOKE, LILIES AND JADE by Carl Hancock Rux, directed by Leah C. Gardiner; ROMEO SIERRA TANGO by Rinde Eckert; FIRE EATER by Brighde Mullins, directed by Maria Mileaf. April 20–May 3, 1998.

EVERYBODY'S RUBY: STORY OF A MURDER IN FLORIDA. By Thulani Davis. May 7, 1998. Director, Roberta Levitow; scenery, Michael McGarty; lighting, D.M. Wood; costumes, Alvin Perry. With Terry Alexander, Rosalyn Coleman, Sheila Kay Davis, Dwight Ewell, Ron Faber, Fanni Green, Ron C. Jones, Darrie Lawrence, Chuck Patterson, Raynor Scheine, James Shanklin, Robert Stanton, Evan Thompson, Jonathan Walker.

La Mama (a.k.a. LaMama) Experimental Theater Club (ETC). A busy workshop for experimental theater of all kinds. Ellen Stewart founder and artistic director.

Schedule included:

FAUST IN VITRO. Written and directed by Michael D'Antonio. June 12, 1997.

YOU'RE JUST LIKE MY FATHER. By and with Peggy Shaw. June 15, 1997. Director, James-Neal Kennerly; sound, Lacka Daisical.

THE SEVEN BEGGARS. By Rabbi Nachman, adapted and directed by Victor Attar and Geula Jeffet Attar. June 26, 1997. Music, Tamar Muskal.

LOVE, IN THE EYES OF HOPE, DIES LAST (eight short plays). By Sofia Murashkovsky. October 9, 1997. Director, Leslie Lee; music, Alexander Zhurbin.

GUYS DREAMIN'. By and with Jean Claude van Itallie, Court Dorsey and Kermit Dunkelberg. November 6, 1997. Direction, Kim Mancuso, Joel Gluck. With the Pilgrim Theater of Ashland.

LA TROTA (THE TROUT). Written and directed by Dario D'Ambrosi. November 6, 1997.

THE LOVE SUICIDES AT AMIJIMA. By Monzaemon Chikamatsu, translated by Donald Keene. November 27, 1997. Director, Kazuki Takase; music, Genji Ito.

WATERSHED. By Tom Soper. December 4, 1997. Director, Zishan Ugurlu.

SQUEAL LIKE A PIG. By and with Slant (Richard Ebihara, Wayland Quintero, Perry Yung). January 1, 1998.

THE BLACK MILK QUARTET (mini operas): ACTAEON by Gina Leishman; BLACK MILK by Ellen Maddow; PRICE SLASHER by Harry Mann; COLORED GLASSES by Dan Froot; libretto and direction, Paul Zimet. January 22, 1998. With the Talking Band (William Badgett, Dina Emerson, Kimberly Gambino, Marcy Jellison, Ellen Maddow, Larry Marshall, Forrest McClendon, Eric Meyersfield, Tom Nelis).

ONE/UNO (multimedia performance). By Stefano Zazzera and Aldo Milea. January 29, 1998. With Teatro a Benzina.

CALLBACKS (one-act play). Written and directed by Harold Dean James. February 12, 1998. Scenery, Harold Dean James; lighting, Harold Mulanix; costumes, Barbara Gallimore. With Robin Cornett, Frank Damico, Christine O'Neil, Tracy Podell, Mar Riehl, Patrick Tully, Thomas F. Walsh.

AT THE END OF THE CENTURY. Written and directed by Aminta De Lara, translated by Francine Jacome. February 12, 1998. With Aminta De Lara, Daniel Bort.

THE SANDLEWOOD BOX and THE DAMNED THING. By Mac Wellman. February 26, 1998. Director, Bob McGrath; music, Jim Farmer. With the Ridge Theater.

FIESTA WARE. Written and directed by Milton Diaz. February 26, 1998.

DEVOTION. By Mary Fulham. March 12, 1998. Director, Eureka.

THE ADVENTURES OF KAT WOMAN. Written and directed by Arnold Ruhlman. March 12, 1998.

SOLID PEACH. Written and directed by Lisette Merenciana. March 23, 1998.

FESTA PRIMAVERA: A NIGHT AT OLDE TURNE HALL. Written and directed by Emelise Aleandri. March 26, 1998.

IRISH REPERTORY THEATER—Bob Green, Ciaran O'Reilly, Marian Tomas Griffin *(with guitar),* Terry Donnelly, Ciaran Sheehan and Rusty Magee in *The Irish . . . And How They Got That Way* by Frank McCourt

POSITIVE WOMEN (one-act plays). By L.E.F.T. (Latino Experimental Fantastic Theater). April 2, 1998. (Includes works by Candido Tirado, Carmen Rivera, Migdalia Cruz, Michael John Garces.)

WHITE NIGHTS. By Fyodor Dostoyevsky, adapted and directed by Andrea Paciotto. April 9, 1998. Music, John Sullivan.

JEWS & JESUS. Book, Oren Safdie; music and lyrics, Ronnie Cohen. April 16, 1998. Director, Tom Patellis.

FLIGHT. By and with the Yara Arts Group and Buryat National Theater of Siberia. April 24, 1998. Direction, Virlana Tkacz, Erzhena Zhambalov; music, Genji Ito.

EXILE IN JERUSALEM. By Motti Lerner, translated by Hillel Halkin. May 7, 1998. Direction, Victor Attar, Geula Jeffet Attar. With Victor Attar, Tim Shepard.

THE CAUCASIAN CHALK CIRCLE. By Bertolt Brecht, translated by John Willett. May 15, 1998. Direction, Andrei Serban, Niky Wolcz; music, Elizabeth Swados; scenery, Jun Maeda; lighting, Howard Thies; costumes, Vicki R. Davis. With Elizabeth Mutton, Angela Fie, Mia Yoo, Andrew Garman, Jimmie Woody, George Drance Jr., David Wilson Barnes, Gabriel Portoundo.

The Club
PULP NELLIE. By Nora Burns and Terrence Michael. June 14, 1997. Director, Peg Healey. With The Nellie Olesons (Nora Burns, John Cantwell, Marissa Copeland, Terrence Michael).

I AM A COFFIN. By Edgar Oliver. October 30, 1997.

THE SCREAMING TARGET THEATER VARIETY SHOW. By and with Slant (Richard Ebihara, Wayland Quintero, Perry Yung). November 10, 1997.

WAS THAT MY 15 MINUTES? By and with Susan Jeremy. November 10, 1997. Director, Mary Fulham.

FULL MOON BACKLASH. By and with Thom Fogarty. December 4, 1997.

THE TEMPEST. By William Shakespeare, adapted and performed by Thaddeus Phillips. January 1, 1998.

SECOND ANNUAL TELETHON. By and with David Ilku and Ken Bullock. January 15, 1998.

BROADWAY '68 (musical revue). February 12, 1998. Director, Scott Wittman; choreography, Joey Pizzi. With Debbie Gravitte, Annie Golden, Maggie Moore, Laura Kenyon, Tracey Berg, Matthew Soursourian.

RADICAL MENSCHES AND MANIACS (Jewish comedy festival). March 12, 1998. Director, Judith Sloan.

NATASHA FEARLESS LIEDER. Music, lyrics and performed by Natasha Shulman. April 2, 1998. Director, Robert Molossi; scenery, Gary Hayes.

FULL FRONTAL NELLIE. By and with The Nellie Olesons. April 23, 1998.

Lincoln Center Festival. An annual international summer arts festival offering classic and contemporary works. For Lincoln Center for the Performing Arts, Beverly Sills Chairman, Nathan Leventhal President, John Rockwell festival director.

Schedule included:

LES DANAIDES (12). A reconstruction of Aeschylus's lost tetralogy, adapted and directed by Silviu Purcarete. July 8, 1997. Scenery and costumes, Stefania Cenean; lighting, Silviu Purcarete, Vadim Levinschi. With Coca Bloos, Mariana Buruiana, Micaela Caracas, Mihai Dinvale, Jean-Jacques Dulon, Victor Rebengiuc, Alexandru Repan.

Woza Africa: After Apartheid (four programs):

THE SUIT (7). By Can Themba, adapted by Mothobi Mutloatse. July 8, 1997. Director, John Matshikiza; lighting, Denis Hutchinson. With Stella Khumalo, Sello Maake ka Ncube.
MA-DLADLA'S BEAT (monologue) written and directed by Magi Nonzini Williams, with Delly Malinga; BERGVILLE STORIES written and directed by Duma Ndlovu, with Thami Cele, Bheki Sibiya, Siyabonga Twala (7). July 15, 1997. Lighting, Denis Hutchinson.
ON MY BIRTHDAY (7). Written and directed by Aubrey Sekhabi. July 22, 1997. Scenery, Roslyn Wood; lighting, Denis Hutchinson. With Kgomotso Ntulwana, John Nhlanhla Lata, Don Eric Mlangeni, Silindile Nodangala, Kholofelo Kola.
ONCE A PIRATE by Paul Slabolepszy, directed by Lara Foot Newton, with Seputla Sebogodi; WHITE MEN WITH WEAPONS by and with Greig Coetzee, directed by Garth Anderson (monologues) (6). July 22, 1997. Lighting, Denis Hutchinson.

INCIDENT AT COBBLER'S KNOB (4). By the Talent Family (Amy and David Sedaris). July 8, 1997. Direction and scenery, Hugh Hamrick; choreography, Drew Geraci; lighting, Howard Thies; costumes, Mitchell Bloom; music and lyrics, Jackie Hoffman, Mark Levinson. With Chuck Coggins, Jackie Hoffman, Jodi Lennon, Andy Richter, Amy Sedaris, Sarah Thyre, Toby Wherry.

UMABATHA: THE ZULU MACBETH (7). Written, directed and composed by Welcome Msomi. July 21, 1997. See its entry in the Plays Produced Off Broadway section of this volume.

Mabou Mines. Theater collaborative whose work is a synthesis of motivational acting, narrative acting and mixed-media performance. Collective artistic leadership. Frederick Neumann, Terry O'Reilly, Ruth Maleczech, Lee Breuer artistic directors.

RESIDENT ARTIST SERIES. Schedule included THE SOCIALITE by James F. Murphy; MUTATIONS by Sally Sussman; THE "OR" BIT by Monique Holt; THE BRIDGE DOVE by Bill Tivenan; THE FLEA by Polina Klimovitskaya and Mirra Ginsburg, translated from Yevgeny Zamyatin's play, *The Flea.* THE INFERNO MACHINE by Osiris Hertz, based on Dante Alighieri's *The Inferno.* June 5–29, 1997.

HAPPY DAYS (24). By Samuel Beckett. March 13, 1998. Director, Robert Woodruff; scenery, Doug Stein; lighting, John Martin; costumes, Jack Taggart. With Ruth Maleczech, Tom Fitzpatrick. Co-produced by the La Jolla Playhouse.

MCC Theater. Dedicated to the promotion of emerging writers, actors, directors and theatrical designers. Robert LuPone and Bernard Telsey executive directors.

ANADARKO (17). By Tim Blake Nelson. April 1, 1998. See its entry in the Plays Produced Off Broadway section of this volume.

Music-Theater Group. Pioneering in the development of new music-theater. Lyn Austin producing director, Diane Wondisford general director.

Schedule included:

RUNNING MAN (7). By Cornelius Eady; music, Diedre Murray. June 25, 1997. Director, Diane Paulus; costumes, Christianne Myers; musical direction, Curtis McKonly. With De'Adre Avery, Ronnell Bey, Darius de Haas, Romain Fruge.

Negro Ensemble Company. Provides quality productions of material written, performed by, and relevant to the needs and interests of black people around the world. Susan Watson Turner producing director, Carole Khan-White executive producer.

AND BABY MAKES TWO (39). By and with Kim Tooks. February 14, 1998. Director, Florante Galvez; scenery, Rona Ballasteros Taylor; lighting, Antoinette Tynes; costumes, Anne M. Skeete; sound, David Wright.

TROUBLE IN MIND (37). By Alice Childress. March 27, 1998. Director, Carole Khan-White; scenery, Michael Odell Green; lighting, Christopher Pierre; costumes, Anne M. Skeete; sound, Richard V. Turner. With Jackie Miller, Paul Franklin, Vincent Lacey, Sherri Sinclair, Ron Lee Jones, Liz Maccie, Bob Manus, Tom Vergason, J. Stephen Hall.

New Dramatists. An organization devoted to playwrights; member writers may use the facilities for anything from private cold readings of their material to public script-in-hand readings. Todd London artistic director, Jana Jevnikar director of administration and finance, Paul A. Slee executive director.

Readings:

LOVE IN THE AFTERNOON. Book and lyrics, Barry Jay Kaplan; music, Lewis Flinn. August 14, 1997. Director, Anne D'Zmura.
KNIFE IN THE HEART. By Susan Yankowitz. September 8, 1997. Director, Liz Diamond.
THE POSSUM PLAY. By Benji Aerenson. September 15, 1997. Director, Bill Hart.
WHEN IT'S COCKTAIL TIME IN CUBA. By Rogelio Martinez. September 17, 1997. Director, Eduardo Machado.
IT COMES AROUND. By Y York. September 24, 1997.
TAKE FIVE (graduating playwrights festival): THE HOLE by Wendy Hammond, directed by Seth Gordon; THE LOST BOY by Liz Egloff, directed by Lisa Peterson; COLLECTED STORIES by Donald Margulies; AMERICAN SIDDHARTHA by Darrah Cloud, directed by Stephen Haff. October 17–24, 1997.
SIXTEEN ROUTINES. By Murray Mednick. November 24, 1997. Director, Darrell Larson.
SEALOVE, MANAGER. By Sander Hicks. December 1, 1997. Director, Richard Eion Nash-Sielecki.
VORTEX DU PLAISIR. By Gordon Dahlquist. December 15, 1997. Director, Beth Schachter.
THE BRIEF BUT EXEMPLARY LIFE OF THE LIVING GODDESS. By Neena Beber. January 16, 1998. Director, Jean Randich.
IDEAS OF GOOD AND EVIL. Written and directed by Erik Ehn. January 22, 1998.
RECENT SAINT PLAYS/EROTIC CURTSIES. By Erik Ehn. January 27, 1998. Director, Maria Mileaf.
KING ISLAND CHRISTMAS. By Deborah Baley Brevoort. February 9, 1998.

ACAPULCO. By Jacquelyn Reingold. February 23, 1998.
FAR SEA PHARISEE. By Stephanie Fleischmann. February 25, 1998. Director, David Herskovits.
WRECKERS. By Jonathan Ceniceroz. March 12, 1998.
GOLDHAWK ROAD. By Simon Bent. March 13, 1998. Director, Jean Randich.
BIG TIM AND MAGGIE. By Jack Gilhooley. March 16, 1998. Director, Julie Boyd.
STIGMATA AND OTHER SYMPTOMS. By Kate Robin. March 25, 1998. Director, Tim Cunningham.
GETCO. By Eve Sawyer. March 30, 1998. Director, Jean Randich.
HOW UNCONSCIOUS IS SHE. By August Baker. April 6, 1998. Director, Damien Gray.
WONDERLAND. By Chay Yew. April 21, 1998. Director, Ron Daniels.
TIME AND THIS NIGHT FOREVER. By Louise M. Schwarz. April 24, 1998. Director, Lou Jacob.
TO MANDELA. By Herman Daniel Farrell III. April 28, 1998. Director, Marion McClinton.
FALL. By Bridget Carpenter. May 4, 1998. Director, Maria Mileaf.
THE MYOPIA. Written and directed by David Greenspan. May 7, 1998.
7.26.96. By Rogelio Martinez. May 8, 1998. Director, Eduardo Machado.
AGELESS. By Silvia Gonzalez S. May 15, 1998.
THE MIGRANT FARMWORKER'S SON. By Silvia Gonzalez S. May 19, 1998. Director, Bill DeLuca.
THE GOVERNOR'S FAMILY. By Beatrix Christian. May 26, 1998. Director, Ron Daniels.

New Federal Theater. Dedicated to integrating minorities and women into the mainstream of American theater by training artists and by presenting plays by minorities and women to integrated, multicultural audiences. Woodie King Jr. producing director.

INCOMMUNICADO (12). Written and directed by Lee Gundersheimer. November 13, 1997. Scenery, Si Joong Yoon; lighting, Michael Hairston; costumes and masks, Melanie Guzman. With Charmain Falode, Denice J. Sealy.

MY ONE GOOD NERVE: A VISIT WITH RUBY DEE (one-woman show) (27). By and with Ruby Dee. February 5, 1998. Director, Charles Nelson Reilly; scenery, James Noone; lighting, Kirk Bookman; costumes, Robert Macintosh; sound, Tim Schellenbaum.

CHRISTOPHER COLUMBUS (30). By Nikos Kazantzakis. February 18, 1998. Director, Lloyd Richards; scenery and costumes, G.W. Mercier; lighting, Shirley Prendergast; music, Scott Richards. With David Wolos-Fonteno, Paul Campbell, Dennis Parlato, Kim Yancey Moore, Mary Alice, Roger Robinson.

The New Victory Theater. Purpose is to introduce young people and families, reflective of New York City's diverse communities, to live performances. Cora Cahan president.

Schedule included:

THE JUNGLE BOOK (33). Book and lyrics, David Schechter and Barry Keating, adapted from Rudyard Kipling's book; music, Barry Keating. July 14, 1997. Director, David Schechter; choreography, Dominick DeFranco; scenery, Rob Odorisio; lighting, Vivien Leone; costumes, Martha Bromelmeier; musical direction, Greg Pliska. With Joseph Edward, Michael Messer, Larry Purifory, Terri White.

THE MAESTRO INVADES MANHATTAN (10). By and with Tomas Kubinek. October 24, 1997.

DARK COWGIRLS AND PRAIRIE QUEENS (10). Written and directed by Linda Parris-Bailey. November 7, 1997. With Linda Parris-Bailey, Margaret Ann Miller, Sylvia Rupert, Vida Werner, Victor Kelly, Jeffrey L. Cody, Julia Boulette.

CIRCUS OZ (45). November 20, 1997.

ROMEO AND JULIET. By William Shakespeare. January 29, 1998. With The Acting Company. See its entry in the Plays Produced Off Broadway section of this volume.

S.W.A.R.M. (THE SYMPHONIC WORK ASSEMBLY OF RHYTHM AND MOVEMENT) (percussion band) (14). Music and musical direction, Gregory Kuzak. February 11, 1998. With Scott Bishop, David Hatfield, Gregory Kozak, Robin Reid, Bill Wallace.

AIR TIME: FRED GARBO INFLATABLE THEATER COMPANY (9). March 7, 1998. With Fred Garbo, Daielma Santos.

THE NUMBER 14 (11). By Peter Anderson, Melody Anderson, Gina Bastone, Colin Heath, David Mackay, Wayne Specht, Roy Surette and Beatrice Zeilinger; additional material, Darlene Brooks, Tom Jones and Allan Zinyk. March 27, 1998. See its entry in the Plays Produced Off Broadway section of this volume.

THE GREAT GILLY HOPKINS (12). Book, music and lyrics, David Paterson and Steve Liebman, based on Katherine Paterson's book. April 15, 1998. Director, J. Daniel Herring; scenery, Stage One production staff; lighting, Kathleen Kronauer; costumes, Donna E. Lawrence; musical direction, Scott Kasbaum. With Katie Blackerby, Debra Macut, Jack Wallen Jr., Omar Morris, William Groth, Shammen McCune, Karen Sabo, Breton Frazier, Michelle Ludwig. Co-produced by Stage One Professional Theater for Young Audiences, Louisville.

NICKY, SOMEWHERE ELSE (10). By Saskia Janse; concept, Marijke Meijer. May 8, 1998. Director, Onny Huisink; scenery, Vincent Sturkenboom. With Speeltheater Holland (Marc-Marie Huybregts, Saskia Janse, Michel Marang, Jitka Lejdarova).

THE WIND IN THE WILLOWS (19). By Kenneth Grahame. See its entry in the Plays Produced Off Broadway section of this volume.

New York Theater Workshop. Produces new theater by American and international artists and encourages risk and stimulates experimentation in theatrical form. James C. Nicola artistic director, Jo Beddoe managing director.

MORE STATELY MANSIONS (32). By Eugene O'Neill, adapted by Karl Ragnar Gierow. September 25, 1997. Director, Ivo van Hove; scenery, lighting and costumes, Jan Versweyveld; sound, Red Ramona. With Tim Hopper, Jenny Bacon, Joan MacIntosh, Robert Petkoff, Joel M. Rooks, Ben Hammer.

BRIDES OF THE MOON (43). By and with the Five Lesbian Brothers (Maureen Angelos, Babs Davy, Dominique Dibbell, Peg Healey, Lisa Kron). December 2, 1997. Director, Molly D. Smith; scenery, Neil Patel; lighting, Nancy Schertler; costumes, Gabriel Berry; sound, Carmen Borgia; music, Tom Judson.

SHOPPING ETC. By Mark Ravenhill. February 2, 1998. See its entry in the Plays Produced Off Broadway section of this volume.

BOB (one-man show) (24 +). Conceived by Anne Bogart and Will Bond; text arrangement, Jocelyn Clarke. May 5, 1998. Director, Anne Bogart; scenery, Neil Patel; lighting, Mimi Jordan Sherin; costumes, James Schuette; sound, Darron L. West. With Will Bond.

Pan Asian Repertory Theater. Celebrates and provides opportunities for Asian American artists to perform under the highest professional standards and to create and promote plays by and about Asians and Asian Americans. Tisa Chang artistic/producing director.

SHANGHAI LIL'S. Book and lyrics, Lilah Kan; music, Louis Stewart. Reopened October 15, 1997.

OUT OF THE WHEELCHAIR AND INTO THE FIRE (7). By Esther Goodhart and Stewart M. Schulman. November 12, 1997. Director, Stewart M. Schulman; scenery and costumes, Tema Levine; lighting, Gerard P. McCarthy; music, Gary Guttman. With Esther Goodhart.

ALOHA LAS VEGAS (24). By Edward Sakamoto. April 17, 1998. Director, Ron Nakahara; scenery, Cornell Riggs; lighting, Victor En Yu Tan; costumes, Hugh Hanson; sound, Peter Griggs. With Kati Kuroda, Ron Nakahara, Les J.N. Mau, Dawn Akiyama, Paul Keoni Chun, Katsumi Nobori, Millie Chow.

Staged Reading

CARRY THE TIGER TO THE MOUNTAIN. By Cherylene Lee. December 15, 1997. Director Ed Herendeen.

Performance Space 122. Exists to give artists of a wide range of experience a chance to develop their work and find an audience. Mark Russell executive/artistic director.

TELL-TALE. By Erik Jackson. June 13, 1997. Director, Joshua D. Rosensweig; choreography, Jane Comfort; scenery and lighting, Kevin Adams; costumes, Marc Happel; visual effects, Basil Twist. With Sherry Vine (Keith Levy), Mario Diaz, Jackie Beat. (Produced by Theater Couture.)

FREAK (work-in-progress) (7). By and with John Leguizamo. August 16, 1997.

THE AMERICAN CHESTNUT (12). By and with Karen Finley. September 11, 1997. Lighting, Christopher Fleming.

CAB LEGS (12). By and with Elevator Repair Service (Steve Bodow, John Collins, Jon Feinberg, Rinne Groff, James Hannaham, Blake Koh, Carson Kreitzer, Leo Marks, Katherine Profeta, Zoe Rotter, Scott Shepherd, Clay Shirky, Susie Sokol, Tory Vasquez, Colleen Werthmann). September 11, 1997. Director, John Collins; choreography, Katherine Profeta; lighting, Clay Shirky; costumes, Colleen Werthmann, Carson Kreitzer; sound, Blake Koh. Reopened May 14, 1998 for 6 performances.

GLORIOUS (18). Written, directed and performed by Eddie Izzard. September 22, 1997.

COME TO LIFE (JEAN SEBERG, AND WHAT SHE SAID) (8). By and with Kyle deCamp. October 9, 1997.

SKETCHES ON MORNING, NOON & NIGHT (work-in-progress) (7). November 3, 1997. By and with Spalding Gray.

THE TRANNY CHASE (12). By and with Linda Simpson. November 19, 1997. Director, Eureka; scenery, Steven Hammel.

SHIRTS AND SKIN (11). By and with Tim Miller, based on his book. December 5, 1997. Music, Doug Sadownick.

THE MAN WHO WAS THURSDAY: A NIGHTMARE (8). By and with Great Small Works (John Bell and Jenny Romaine), adapted from G.K. Chesterton's novel. December 26, 1997. Director, Mark Sussman; choreography, Clarinda Mac Low.

70 HILL LANE (13). By Phelim McDermott; additional material by Guy Dartnell and Steve Tiplady. January 1, 1998. Director, Lee Simpson; lighting, Colin Grenfell; music, Ben Park. With Guy Dartnell, Steve Tiplady, Phelim McDermott. (Produced by Improbable Theater.)

NEVER BEEN ANYWHERE (4). Conceived and directed by Eric Bass, adapted from stories by Castle Freeman Jr. January 8, 1998. Lighting, Finn Campman; costumes, Kiki Smith, Ines Zeller Bass; puppet design, Eric Bass, Finn Campman. With Sandglass Theater (Eric Bass, Ines Zeller Bass, Finn Campman, Tom Howe, Susan Myers, Barbara Whitney).

CLONE SQUAD (puppetry) (16). By and with The Elementals (John Pavlik, James Nichols, James Godwin, Gina Nelson). January 22, 1998.

NAILGUN (2). By and with Eric Bogosian. February 20, 1998.

FIRE IN THE HOLE (work-in-progress). By and with Colleen Werthmann, adapted from Oskar Werthmann's *Kriegsgefangenschaft in der Sowjetunion,* translated by Carina Liebeknecht. February 26, 1998. Lighting, Aimee Schneider.

WRECKAGE (8). By Aaron Landsman. March 19, 1998. Director, Christopher Bayes; lighting, David Herrigel; sound, Todd Griffin. With Aaron Landsman, Todd Griffin.

JAILS, HOSPITALS AND HIP-HOP (30+). By and with Danny Hoch. March 30, 1998. Director, Jo Bonney.

TERMINAL JUNCTURE (12). By Kelly Copper. April 2, 1998. Direction and scenery, Pavol Liska; lighting, Stephen Brady; costumes, Jocelyn Worrall; sound, Scott Mascena. With Marc Dale, Priscilla Holbrook, Julie Atlas Muz, Zachary Oberzan.

TOTAL FICTIONAL LIE (work-in-progress). By and with Elevator Repair Service. May 7, 1998.

CHICAS 2000 (39). By Carmelita Tropicana. May 20, 1998. Director, Uzi Parnes. With Carmelita Tropicana, Uzi Parnes, Rebecca Summer Burgos, Ana Margaret Sanchez.

PERFORMANCE SPACE 122—John Bell and
Jenny Romaine in a scene from *The Man Who Was
Thursday: A Nightmare*

Playwrights Horizons New Theater Wing. Full productions of new works, in addition to the
regular off-Broadway productions. Tim Sanford artistic director.

> THE WATER CHILDREN (21). By Wendy MacLeod. November 2, 1997. Director, David Petrarca;
> scenery and lighting, Michael Philippi; costumes, Therese Bruck; sound, Edward Cosla. With Eliz-
> abeth Bunch, Kevin Isola, Deirdre Lovejoy, Wendy Makkena, Michael Mastro, Joyce Reehling,
> Robert Sella, Jonathan Walker. Co-produced by the Women's Project and Productions.

Primary Stages. Dedicated to new American plays by new American playwrights. Casey Childs
artistic director, Margaret Chandler general manager, Janet Reed associate artistic director,
Seth Gordon associate producer.

> BRUTALITY OF FACT (20). By Keith Reddin. November 5, 1997. Director, Casey Childs; scenery,
> B.T. Whitehill; lighting, Chris Dallos; costumes, Debra Stein; music and sound, David Van Tieghem.
> With Rebecca Nelson, Leslie Lyles, Scotty Bloch, Greg Stuhr, Ken Marks, Robin Morse, Samantha
> Brown.

> SCOTLAND ROAD (21). By Jeffrey Hatcher. January 27, 1998. Director, Melia Bensussen; scen-
> ery, James Noone; lighting, Dan Kotlowitz; costumes, Claudia Stephens; music and sound, David
> Van Tieghem. With Katy Selverstone, Daniel Gerroll, Leslie Lyles, Scotty Bloch.

ST. NICHOLAS (42). Written and directed by Conor McPherson. March 17, 1998. Lighting, Deborah Constantine. With Brian Cox.

NASTY LITTLE SECRETS (20). By Lanie Robertson. May 20, 1998. Director, Casey Childs; scenery, William Barclay; lighting, Phil Monat; costumes, Debra Stein; music and sound, David Van Tieghem. With Matthew Mabe, Craig Fols, David McCallum, Bryan Clark.

Puerto Rican Traveling Theater. Professional company presenting bilingual productions primarily of Puerto Rican and Hispanic playwrights, emphasizing subjects of relevance today. Miriam Colon-Valle founder and producer.

Schedule included:

THE EVIL SPELL OF THE BUTTERFLY. By Federico Garcia Lorca. July 9, 1997. Director, Tony Mata; costumes, Katherine L. Rodman; music, Samuel J. Hamm Jr. With Amelia Branyon.

CHECKING OUT (Morir Sonando). By Candido Tirado, translated by Raul Davila. March 19, 1998. Director, Michael John Garces; scenery, Troy Hourie; lighting, Philip Widmer; costumes, Mimi O'Donnell; sound, David Margolin Lawson. With Lourdes Martin, Carlos Orizondo.

THE EMPTY BEACH (La Playa Vacia). By Jaime Salom, translated by Jack Agueros. May 6, 1998. Director, Alba Oms; scenery, Troy Hourie; lighting, Philip Widmer. With Fulvia Vergel, Virginia Rambal, Jaime Sanchez, Louis Moreno, Gilberto Ramon Arribas.

Signature Theater Company. Dedicated to the exploration of a playwright's body of work. James Houghton artistic director, Thomas C. Proehl managing director.

THE AMERICAN CLOCK (35). By Arthur Miller. October 19, 1997. Director, James Houghton; choreography, Annie Loui; scenery, E. David Cosier; lighting, Jeffrey S. Koger; costumes, Gail Brassard; sound, Red Ramona; musical direction, Loren Toolajian. With Kale Browne, Laura Esterman, Jason Fisher, Patrick Husted, David Kener, Melissa King, Chris Messina, Keira Naughton, Paul Niebanck, Stephen Pearlman, Lewis J. Stadlen, Myra Lucretia Taylor, Isiah Whitlock Jr., Mary Catherine Wright, Christopher Wynkoop.

I CAN'T REMEMBER ANYTHING and THE LAST YANKEE (one-act plays) (35). By Arthur Miller. January 11, 1998. Director, Joseph Chaikin; scenery, E. David Cosier; lighting, Kevin J. Lawson; costumes, Teresa Snider-Stein; music and sound, David Van Tieghem. With Joseph Wiseman, Rebecca Schull, Kevin Conroy, Peter Maloney, Kate Myre, Shami Chaikin, Betty H. Neals.

MR. PETERS' CONNECTIONS (49). By Arthur Miller. May 17, 1998. Director, Garry Hynes; scenery, Francis O'Connor; lighting, Beverly Emmons; costumes, Teresa Snider-Stein; sound, Red Ramona. With Peter Falk, Erica Bradshaw, Kris Carr, Anne Jackson, Alan Mozes, Daniel Oreskes, Tari Signor, Jeff Weiss.

Soho Rep. Dedicated to new and avant-garde American playwrights. Julian Webber artistic director, Lisa Portes associate director.

SUMMER CAMP 3: REFUGE by Jessica Goldberg, directed by Christopher McCann; HELP! POLICE! by Madeleine Olnek, directed by Gina Kaufman; MIDDLE-CLASS GIRLS LOVE OASIS by Michael Weiner, directed by Mary Brezovich. July 9–26, 1997.

A COMMON VISION (5). By Neena Beber. August 20, 1997. Director, Lisa Portes; scenery, Michael Schweikardt; lighting, John Lasiter. With Marc Ardito, Yusef Bulos, Joe Goodrich, Leslie Lyles, Alison Tatlock, Melinda Wade.

FNU LNU (19). By Mac Wellman; music, David Van Tieghem. October 9, 1997. Director, Julian Webber; scenery and costumes, Anthony MacIlwaine; lighting, Adam Silverman; sound, Jill Duboff, David Van Tieghem; musical direction, Randall Schloss. With Steve Mellor, Zivia Flomenhaft, Sarah Abramson, Welker White.

FRIDA K (19). By Gloria Montero. November 6, 1997. Director, Peter Hinton; scenery, Glenn Davidson, adapted from Ken Garnhum's original design; lighting, Bonnie Beecher. With Allegra Fulton.

NATURAL CHILD (4). By Michael Duff McClung. March 4, 1998. Director, Matthew Wilder. With Todd Cerveris, Dennis Fox, Aimee McCormick, Bruce McKenzie, Alison Tatlock, Rachel Tomlinson, Laurie Williams.

HOW TO WRITE WHILE YOU SLEEP (19). By Madeleine Olnek. May 1, 1998. Director, Lisa Portes; scenery, James Youmans; lighting, Paul Bartlett; costumes, Michael Allen Stein. With Mary Shultz, Joanne Bayes, Josie de Guzman, Jake-ann Jones, Cynthia Kaplan, Tom Myler, Kevin Seal.

ILLUSTRATED RADIO SHOWS (4). By Valda Setterfield, David Gordon and Ain Gordon. May 28, 1998. Lighting, Karen Spahn. With Tadej Brdnik, Tine Byrsted, Norma Fire, Karen Graham, Jule Ramirez, Valda Setterfield, David Gordon, Ain Gordon. Co-produced by the Pick Up Performance Company.

Theater for the New City. Developmental theater and new American experimental works. Crystal Field executive director.

Schedule included:

SPRINGTIME written and directed by Maria Irene Fornes; COUNTING THE WAYS by Edward Albee, directed by Joseph Chaikin. June 7, 1997. With The Other Theater.

EVENTS: LIFE WORLD DREAM DEATH (11). Conceived and directed by Tom Walker. June 12, 1997. Lighting, Paul Ferri. With The Living Theater (Amber, Johnson Anthony, Robert Hieger, Marlene Lortev, Lois Kagan Mingus, Craig Peritz, Rob Schmidt, Tom Walker, Joanie Fritz Zosike). Reopened September 11, 1997 for 4 performances.

PIRATES, OR GO FOR THE GOLD (13). Book, lyrics and direction, Crystal Field; music, Christopher Cherney. August 2, 1997. Scenery, Walter Gurbo, Pamela Mayo, Mary Blanchard, Tony Angel; costumes, Julienne Schubert; musical direction, Cynthia Hilts. With Joseph C. Davies, Crystal Field, Cheryl Gadsden, Michael-David Gordon, Jerry Jaffe, Mark Marcante, Craig Meade, Michael Vazquez.

VIRGIL (8). By Victoria Linchon. August 14, 1997. Director, Mark Hammond; lighting, Zdenek Kriz; costumes, Jocelyn Worrall; sound, J.D. Adams. With Eric Christie, Victoria Linchon, Ron Moreno.

HOURS OF DANGER: WHEN WE SLEEP by Luke Landric Leonard, Michael LoPorto and Anthony Salerno, directed by Michael LoPorto; HOOKER GREEN LIGHT by Luke Landric Leonard, directed by Ian L. Gordon (one-act plays). August 21, 1997. Scenery, Si Joong Yoon; lighting, Ian L. Gordon. With the Hawk Moon Ensemble (Lionel "Bruce" Campbell, Luke Landric Leonard, Michangelo Noto, Si Joong Yoon, Michael LoPorto, Nikki Potter, Natalie Cook).

SISTER. By Mario Fratti. September 4, 1997. Director, Michael Hillyer; scenery and lighting, Jason Sturm; sound, Gerard Drazba. With Annette Hunt, Julia Levo, Wayne Maugans, Mark Ellmore.

HIDE MOTHER IN MY HEART. Written and directed by Ralph Pezzullo. September 18, 1997. Scenery, John Paino; lighting and sound, Mark Marcante. With Doug Barron, Xan Replogle, Nick Daddazio.

MICKEY'S HOME. By Stephen Fife. September 25, 1997. Director, Thomas Caruso; lighting, Rebecca Smithmeyer. With Sylvia Gassel, Joel Friedman, Ron Bagden.

HIROSHIMA (20). Written and directed by Ron Destro; music, Yoko Ono. October 2, 1997. Scenery, Mark Marcante; lighting, Jon D. Andreadakis; costumes, Siching Song. With Pamela Hurt, Vanessa David, Angela Tom, Ariel Estrada, Siching Song, Joe Sorge, Eric Rasmussen, Toru Ohno.

THE LIFE OF JUANITA CASTRO and LINE/BIRTH, PLAY/BIRTH (one-act plays). By Ronald Tavel. October 2, 1997. Direction, Harvey Tavel, Donald L. Brooks. With Agosto Machado, Deborah Auer, Deborah Huber, Marlyn Matias, Harvey Tavel, Clio Young.

SEX INDUSTRY: A DECENT JOB and CLOSETS FULL OF JUICY PLUMS (one-act plays) (8). Written and directed by Bina Sharif. October 16, 1998. With Kevin Mitchell Martin, Amy Minty, Jes see Sutherland, Michelle Wright, Helene Johnson, David Aronson, Standing Bear, Jerry Jaffe, Bina Sharif.

PLAY GENET (12). Written and directed by Jimmy Camicia. November 6, 1997. Lighting, Jiri Schubert; music, Steve Kaufman, Joe Longo. With Hot Peaches (Jimmy Camicia, Mark Hannay, Lavinia Co-op).

BACK WHEN—BACK THEN. By Raymond J. Barry. November 6, 1997. Director, Martha Gehman; scenery, lighting and costumes, Markus Maurette. With Thomas Draper, Raymond J. Barry.

THE MOTHER. By Bertolt Brecht, translated by Lee Baxandall. November 26, 1997. Director, Jim Niesen; scenery, Kennon Rothchild; lighting, Herrick Goldman; costumes, Christianne Myers; music, Hans Eisler; musical direction, Walter Thompson. With the Irondale Ensemble Project (Sarah Dacey Charles, Michael Goodfriend, Michael-David Gordon, Terry Greiss, Amy Elizabeth McKenna, Patrena Murray, Damen Scranton, John Silvers).

THE JET LAG SHOW. Written and directed by Ayelet Ron. November 28, 1997. Lighting, Bridget Welty; costumes, Iris Cavallero. With the I Yell At Theater Group (Stacey Ference, Karin Amano, Michal Chen, Maja Wampuszyc, Heather Gillespie, Michael S. Waelter).

THE BURNING OUT OF '82 (11). By Arthur Sainer. December 4, 1997. Direction and lighting, David Vining; choreography, Tanya Kane-Parry; scenery, Michael Anderson; costumes, Margradel Hicks; music, Sarah Snider. With Ralph Carideo, Maurice Edwards, Nancy Franklin, Kelly Rogers.

LINCOLN PLAZA. Book and lyrics, Tom Attea; music, Arthur Abrams. January 21, 1998. Director, Mark Marcante; choreography, Craig Meade; scenery, Markus Maurette; lighting, Jon D. Andreadakis; costumes, Lolly Alejandro. With Ray Cullom, Christine Rea, Lisa Roxanne Walters, Ralph Pezzullo, Jerry Coyle, Craig Meade, Steven DeLorenzo.

JOHN GRACE RANTER (opera). Book, Michael Sahl and Margaret Yard; music, Michael Sahl; lyrics, Margaret Yard. January 22, 1998. Director, Tom O'Horgan; scenery, Tom Lee; lighting, Stephen Petrilli; musical direction, Richard Cordova. With Jeffrey Stackhouse, Carole Schaffer, Thomas Jirayut Meglioranza, Michael Messer.

CROSSINGS (12). By Barbara Kahn. February 5, 1998. Direction, Lisa Marjorie Barnes, Barbara Kahn; scenery, Andrea Lauryn Singer; lighting, Todd Reemtsma; costumes, Laurita E. Shields. With Barbara Kahn, Alyss Henderson, Kimberly Wright, Karen Klebbe, Catherine Dowling, Lisa Gluckin, Nikki Walker, Jennifer DeMartino.

GINT. Written and directed by Romulus Linney, based on Ibsen's *Peer Gynt.* February 12, 1998. Scenery, Mark Marcante; lighting, Jon D. Andreadakis; costumes, Jonathan Green. With David Van Pelt, Christine Parks, Susan Ericksen, Christopher Capiello, Bill Cwikowski, Rebecca Harris, T. Cat Ford, Heather Melton, Christopher Roberts.

NON-VIOLENT EXECUTIONS (one-man show) (12). By and with Steve Ben Israel. February 19, 1998.

CUBA AND THE NIGHT. By Eduardo Machado. March 15, 1998. Direction, Rogelio Martinez, Eduardo Machado; choreography, Robert Maiorano; scenery and lighting, Lucy Thurber; costumes, Katherine Roth. With Heather Simms, Tatyana Yassukovich, Yul Vazquez, Jaime Sanchez, Ed Vassallo, Clark Jackson.

UPSTATE (16). Written and directed by Crystal Field. March 21, 1998. Scenery, Donald L. Brooks; lighting, Jon D. Andreadakis; costumes, Carol Tauser; music, David Tice. With Jonathan Slaff, Alexander Bartenieff, Don Arrington, Ruby Lynn Reyner, Kevin Mitchell Martin, Craig Meade.

CLONING AROUND (short plays). By Walter Corwin. April 16, 1998. Direction, Yuji Takematsu, Jason LaRosa; scenery, Rich Crooks; lighting, Jon D. Andreadakis. With Gianni Baratta, Paige Jennifer Barr, Jerry Jaffe, Frank Marzullo, J B Riemer, Marian Sarach, Jack Tynan.

A SLOW BOAT HOME. By William Melvin Kelley, adapted by Marie Giorda. April 23, 1998. Director, Rich Crooks; lighting, Jon D. Andreadakis; costumes, Samantha Ryan. With Paris Campbell, Kira Madallo Sesay, Matt Ritchey, Linda Pia Ignazi, Rick Schneider, Cherita Armstrong.

BLOO REVIEW: A BLOOLIPS RETROSPECTACLE. Sketches and lyrics, Neil Bartlett, Jimmy Camicia, Ray Dobbins, Paul Shaw and Oscar Wilde. April 30, 1998. Director, David Willis; scenery and lighting, Cecile Thunder; musical direction, Simon Deacon. With Bette Bourne, Precious Pearl (Paul Shaw), Simon Deacon.

DEGENERATE ART (20). By and with the Irondale Ensemble Project (Sarah Dacey Charles, Heidi K. Eklund, Michael Goodfriend, Michael-David Gordon, Terry Greiss, Patrena Murray, John Silvers, Damen Scranton). May 2, 1998. Director, Jim Niesen; scenery, Kennon Rothchild; lighting, Herrick Goldman; costumes, Christianne Meyers; music, Walter Thompson.

IT'S ONLY PLAY, IT DOESN'T HURT (4). By Max Gad, translated by Wilfried Prantner and Kathrin Kerkhoff-Saxon. May 21, 1998. Director, Burkhard Stulecker; scenery and costumes, Edgar Sorgo. With Roberta Wallach, Stuart Burney.

Ubu Repertory Theater. Committed to acquainting American audiences with new works by contemporary French-speaking playwrights from around the world in English translations, as well as modern classics in the original French. Francoise Kourilsky artistic director.

THE MISUNDERSTANDING (Le Malentendu) (20). By Albert Camus, translated by Stuart Gilbert. October 8, 1997. Director, Francoise Kourilsky; scenery, Watoku Ueno; lighting, Greg MacPherson; costumes, Carol Ann Pelletier; sound, Genji Ito. With Michael Moinot, Jacqueline Bertrand, Tracy Bryce, Flo Cabre-Andrews, Simon Jutras, Tatiana Abbey. Reopened February 4, 1998 for 21 performances with Jacqueline Bertrand, Michael Moinot, Tatiana Abbey, Myriam Cyr, Lee Godart.

JEWISH STORIES PARIS BRUSSELS: MAMA'LL BE BACK POOR ORPHAN by Jean-Claude Grumberg and BORIS SPIELMAN'S BIG COMEBACK by Serge Kribus, translated by Suzanne Quittner (one-act plays) (14). November 12, 1997. Director, Jonas Jurasas; scenery, Watoku Ueno; lighting, Greg MacPherson; costumes, Carol Ann Pelletier; music and sound, Brian Hallas. With Jerry Matz, Denise Luti, Nick Plakas.

THE JUST (Les Justes) (21). by Albert Camus, translated by Richard Miller. March 11, 1998. Director, Francoise Kourilsky; scenery, Watoku Ueno; lighting, Greg MacPherson; costumes, Carol Ann Pelletier; music and sound, Genji Ito. With Simon Fortin, Tatiana Abbey, Marc Forget, John Livingstone, Richard Thompson, Michael Moinot, Louise-Marie Mennier.

The Vineyard Theater. Multi-art chamber theater dedicated to the development of new plays and musicals, music-theater collaborations and innovative revivals. Douglas Aibel artistic director, Barbara Zinn Krieger executive director, Jon Nakagawa managing director.

THE BATTING CAGE (40). By Joan Ackermann. November 9, 1997. Director, Lisa Peterson; scenery, Robert Brill; lighting, Anne Militello; costumes, Candice Donnelly; sound, Janet Kalas. With Veanne Cox, Babo Harrison, Justin Hagan, Anne Pitoniak.

THE MAIDEN'S PRAYER (38). By Nicky Silver. February 22, 1998. Direction, sound and music, Evan Yionoulis; scenery, Derek McLane; lighting, Donald Holder; costumes, Jess Goldstein. With Geoffrey Nauffts, Patricia Clarkson, Joanna Going, Christopher C. Fuller, Daniel Jenkins.

THE DYING GAUL (40). By Craig Lucas. May 31, 1998. Director, Mark Brokaw; scenery, Allen Moyer; lighting, Christopher Akerlind; costumes, Jess Goldstein; sound, David Van Tieghem. With Tony Goldwyn, Linda Emond, Tim Hopper, Robert Emmet Lunney.

The Women's Project and Productions. Nurtures, develops and produces plays written and directed by women. Julia Miles artistic director, Patricia Taylor managing director.

THE WATER CHILDREN (21). By Wendy MacLeod. November 2, 1997. Co-produced by Playwrights Horizons New Theater Wing; see its entry in that listing in this section.

PHAEDRA IN DELIRIUM (28). By Susan Yankowitz. January 28, 1998. Director, Alison Summers; scenery, Christine Jones; lighting, Beverly Emmons; costumes, Teresa Snider-Stein; sound, Fabian Obispo. With Kathleen Chalfant, Peter Jay Fernandez, Sandra Shipley. Co-produced by Classic Stage Company.

THE SUMMER IN GOSSENSASS (27). Written and directed by Maria Irene Fornes. April 7, 1998. Scenery, Donald Eastman; lighting, Philip Widmer; costumes, Gabriel Berry. With Daniel Blinkoff, Joseph Goodrich, Molly Powell, Clea Rivera, Valda Setterfield.

WPA THEATER—Marcus Giamatti and Ellen
Parker in a scene from *Century City* by Mark Lee

WPA Theater. Produces new American plays and neglected American classics in the realistic idiom. Kyle Renick artistic director, Lori Sherman managing director.

QUEEN AMARANTHA (35). By Charles Busch. October 23, 1997. Direction, Charles Busch, Carl Andress; scenery and costumes, Eduardo Sicangco; lighting, Michael Lincoln; music and sound, Aural Fixation. With Carl Andress, Charles Busch, Ruth Williamson, Marcus Lovett.

CENTURY CITY (28). By Mark Lee. January 14, 1998. Director, Constance Grappo; scenery, Rob Odorisio; lighting, Matt Frey; costumes, Tom Broecker; sound, Robert C. Cotnoir. With Ellen Parker, Marcus Giamatti.

DINAH WAS (53). By Oliver Goldstick. March 24, 1998. See its entry in the Plays Produced Off Broadway section of this volume.

York Theater Company. Specializing in producing new musicals, as well as in reviving unusual, forgotten or avant-garde musicals. Janet Hayes Walker founding artistic director, James Morgan artistic director.

THE SHOW GOES ON (musical revue) (88). Music and lyrics, Tom Jones, Harvey Schmidt. December 17, 1997. See its entry in the Plays Produced Off Broadway section of this volume.

Miscellaneous

In the additional listing of 1997–98 off-off-Broadway productions below, the names of the producing groups or theaters appear in CAPITAL LETTERS and the titles of the works in *italics*. This list consists largely of new or reconstituted works. It includes a few productions staged by groups which rented space from the more established organizations listed previously.

ACTING COMPANY. Staged readings: *The Orchestra* by Jean Anouilh. February 2, 1998. Directed by Mary Lou Rosato; with Lisa Banes, Frances Conroy, Patricia Elliot, Dana Ivey, Laura Linney, Dakin Matthews, Henry Stram. *The Chinese Prime Minister* by Enid Bagnold. February 23, 1998. Directed by Dana Ivey; with Marian Seldes. *Dickens's Women* by and with Miriam Margolyes; March 16, 1998. Directed by Sonia Fraser. *The Complaisant Lover* by Graham Greene. April 6, 1998. Directed by John Miller-Stephany; with Christian Camargo, Laura Linney, Dakin Matthews. *Somebody in My I* by Florence Ercolano. April 27, 1998. Directed by Eve Shapiro.

THE ACTORS COMPANY THEATER. *The Play's the Thing* by Ferenc Molnar. September 29, 1997. Directed by Scott Alan Evans; with Bradford Cover, Maia Danziger, Simon Jones, Greg McFadden, James Murtaugh, Gregory Salata, Scott Schafer, Tom Stewart. *Light Up the Sky* by Moss Hart. November 17, 1997. Directed by Scott Alan Evans; with Peter Bisgaier, Ivar Brogger, Nora Chester, Susan Greenhill, Delphi Harrington, David Edward Jones, John Christopher Jones, Tom Kiesche, Larry Pine, John Plumpis, Lyn Wright. *Mademoiselle Colombe* by Jean Anouilh. January 24, 1998. Directed by Scott Alan Evans; with Daryl Boling, Arnie Burton, Cynthia Darlow, Francesca Di Mauro, Rick Hammerly, Delphi Harrington, David Edward Jones, Simon Jones, Tom Stewart, Evan Thompson. *Trelawny of the Wells* by Arthur Wing Pinero. March 9, 1998. Directed by Richard Sabellico; with Sean Arbuckle, Ryan Atrzberger, Nora Chester, Julia Dion, Burt Edwards, Rick Hammerly, Patricia O'Connell, Shawnee Rowe, Gregory Salata, Scott Schafer, Joan Shepard, Tari Signor, Christine Siracusa, David Staller, Tom Toner, Lyn Wright. *The Torch-Bearers* by George Kelly. May 4, 1998. Directed by Scott Alan Evans; with Susan Cover, Delphi Harrington, Cynthia Harris, Jack Koening, Elizabeth Martin, Greg McFadden, Nancy Opel, Scott Schafer, Tom Stewart, Dan Tedlie, Lynn Vogt.

ACTORS' PLAYHOUSE. *Ronnie Larsen's Peep Show* written and directed by Ronnie Larsen. March 31, 1998. Scenery, Gerard MacMillan; costumes, Bosco DuChamp; lighting, Brian Aldous. With Deborah Berman, Justin Christopher, Michael A. Fox, Laura Frenzer, Pia Glenn, Steve Hunneshagen, Joanna Keylock, Mark T. Leneker, Josh Aaron McCabe, Cloud Michaels, Jeffrey Middleton, Eliza Pryor Nagel.

ACTORS STUDIO. 50th Anniversary Festival of Group Theater plays (staged readings). Schedule included *1931* by Paul and Claire Sifton; *Night Over Taos* by Maxwell Anderson; *Big Night* by Dawn Powell and *Success Story* by John Howard Lawson; *Casey Jones* by Robert Ardrey; *The Gentle People* by Irwin Shaw; *Weep for the Virgins* by Nelisse Child; *Gentlewoman* by John Howard Lawson and *Gold Eagle Guy* by Melvin Levy. April 27–May 18, 1998. With Eli Wallach, Anne Jackson, Shelley Winters, Ben Gazzara, Harvey Keitel, Rip Torn, Estelle Parsons, Cliff Robertson, Lee Grant, Arthur Storch, Gene Saks, Miriam Colon, Daniel Selznick, Earle Hyman, Ruben Blades, Stephen Lang.

ADOBE THEATER COMPANY. *Notions in Motion* written and directed by Jeremy Dobrish. July 16, 1997. *Duet! A Romantic Fable* by Gregory Jackson and Erin Quinn Purcell. October 15, 1997. Directed by Gregory Jackson, Erin Quinn Purcell and Jeremy Dobrish; with Erin Quinn Purcell, Gregory Jackson, Derin Basden, Frank Eisenberger. *The Handless Maiden* by Jeremy Dobrish. February 25, 1998. Directed by Damon Kiely; with Molly Renfroe, Lia Yang, Vin Knight, Janice O'Rourke, Arthur Aulisi, Christopher Marobella.

ALCHEMY THEATER COMPANY. *The Normal Heart* by Larry Kramer. January 19, 1998. Directed by Robert Saxner; with Tom Paitson Kelly, Kate Levy, Richard Lear, Scott Galbraith, Chet Carlin.

ANGEL ORENSANZ FOUNDATION CENTER FOR THE ARTS. *Cigarettes and Chocolate* by Anthony Minghella. July 29, 1997. Directed by Gabriele Jakobi; with Kimberly Jardin, David Jacob Ryder, Paris Kiely, David Usner, Sid Williams, Sally Willig, Heidi Modr.

ATLANTIC THEATER. *Freak* (work-in-progress) by and with John Leguizamo. September 16, 1997.

THE BARROW GROUP. *Women of Manhattan* by John Patrick Shanley. June 6, 1997. Directed by Paul Rice; with Katie Davis, Fiona Gallagher, Patrick F. Kline, Scott Lawrence, Elizabeth Hanly Rice.

BEACON THEATER. *Thank God! The Beat Goes On* book by Barry Singer and Loren Dean Harper; music, lyrics and direction, Loren Dean Harper. October 20, 1997. With Alyson Williams, Tony Terry, Gertrude E. Bailey, Gerald Atkins, Shiro, Ricke Howell.

CHAIN LIGHTNING THEATER. *Women of Paris* by Henry Bacque, translated by Jacques Barzun. June 15, 1997. Directed by Kricker James and Devon Schwartz; with Munro Bonnell, Brandee Graff, Constance Kane, William Lainey, Lyle Walford. *Two by Synge: Riders to the Sea* and *In the Shadow of the Glen* by J.M. Synge. September 5, 1997. Directed by Tony Torn; with Angelica Torn, Frank Nastasi, Kricker James, Danae Torn, Holly Bush Wilkinson, Jill Larson, Conn Horgan. Co-produced by the Sanctuary Theater. *Acts of Faith* by Stephen Mantin. April 26, 1998. Directed by Martha Pinson; with Anthony Spina, Rik Francis, Shela Evans.

CHERNUCHIN THEATER. *You Shouldn't Have Told* by O.L. Duke. December 10, 1997. Directed by Anne L. Thompson-Stretching. *Thanksgiving* by James McLure. February 17, 1998. Directed by Owen Thompson; with Jadah Carroll, Trent Dawson, Scott Galbraith, Abbe Levin, James Reynolds, Jaimi B. Williams.

CHERRY LANE THEATER. *Tell-Tale* by Erik Jackson. October 8, 1997. Directed by Joshua D. Rosenzweig; with Sherry Vine (Keith Levy), Jackie Beat, Mario Diaz. *Black Humor* (one-man show) by and with Lewis Black. January 10, 1998.

CHRYSLER THEATER COMPANY. *Three White Horses* by Gary Swanson and Jennifer Shaw. September 10, 1997. Directed by Gary Swanson; with Jennifer Shaw, Jane Culley.

CLARK STUDIO THEATER. *4 Views With a Room: The Lonely Room* by Charles Watson; *Duet* by Linda Faigao-Hall; *The Last Chair* by Gail Noppe-Brandon; *Papa* by Frank de Las Mercedes; *Wounded Heart* by Stacey Robinson (one-act plays). May 7, 1998. Directed by Gail Noppe-Brandon.

CURRICAN THEATER. *Lone Star Grace* by Suzanne Bradbeer. November 3, 1997. Directed by Linda Ames Key; with Julie Flanders, Gay Isaacs, Ellen Barker, Rob Skolits. *Fixing Frank* by Ken Hanes. November 20, 1997. Directed by Mike Wills; with Andrew Miller, Curt May, Steven Ogg. *The Chairs* by Eugene Ionesco. January 15, 1998. Directed by Andrew Dallmeyer; with Bart Vanlaere, Louise Seyffert.

DANCE THEATER WORKSHOP. *Wonder of the World* by David Lindsay-Abaire (staged reading). September 27, 1997. With Molly Powell, Pamela Nyberg, Kirk Jackson, John McAdams. *The Shoulder* (chamber opera) libretto, lyrics and direction by Dan Hurlin; music by Dan Moses Schreier. January 1, 1988. With Don Chastain, Doug Marcks, Dan Hurlin.

THE DIRECTORS COMPANY. *Those Left Behind* by Ben Bettenbender. July 7, 1997. Directed by Judy Minor; with Rob Sedgwick, Janis Dardaris, Michael Ornstein. *Good Will* by Joan Rater and Tony Phelan, adapted from Jane Smiley's novella. March 16, 1998. Directed by Tony Phelan; with John Bedford Lloyd, Dana Reeve, Michael Phelan, Brenda Pressley, Phoebe Jonas, Marj Dusay.

DO GOODER PRODUCTIONS. *The Lunch Anxieties* by Larry Kunofsky. December 3, 1997. Directed by Michael Rupert; with Brian Quirk, Tracey Stroock, Jeffrey Yates, Gabra Zackman.

DOUGLAS FAIRBANKS THEATER. *Bashevis: Tales of Isaac Bashevis Singer* (one-man show). Adapted from stories by Isaac Bashevis Singer. December 9, 1997. Directed by Eric Krebs; with David Margulies.

THE DRAMA DEPT. *Uncle Tom's Cabin, or Life Among the Lowly* adapted by Randolph Curtis Rand and Floraine Kay, based on Harriet Beecher Stowe's novel. December 11, 1997. Directed by Randolph Curtis Rand; with K. Todd Freedman, Stacy Highsmith, Gretchen Krich, Noel Robichaux, David Wheir.

DUALITY PLAYHOUSE. *Mother Son* by and with Jeffrey Solomon. March 4, 1998. Directed by David L. Carson.

EXPANDED ARTS. *Romeo and Juliet* by William Shakespeare. September 11, 1997. Directed by Joe Calarco; with Greg Shamie, Daniel J. Shore, Sean Dugan, Robertson Carroll.

FLEA THEATER. *Bedfellows* by Herman Daniel Farrell III. October 16, 1997. Directed by Jim Simpson; with Peter Jay Fernandez, Gerry Bamman, Bryan Clark, Peggy Schoditsch, Lazaro Perez, Reed Birney, Phyllis Somerville.

FOOLS COMPANY SPACE. *Frankenstein's Wake* by Theater Labyrinth. September 16, 1997. Directed by Raymond Bobgan; with Holly Holsinger. *Balm in Gilead* by Lanford Wilson. November 5, 1997. Directed by Kaipo Schwab; with the Imua Theater Company.

42ND STREET WORKSHOP. *Slouching Toward the Millennium: The Consequences of Goosing; The Cowboy, the Indian and the Fervent Feminist; Sexaholics* (one-act plays) by Murray Schisgal. June 5, 1997. *The Man Who Was Peter Pan* by Allan Knee. March 4, 1998. Directed by Bennett Windheim; with Bruce Barney, Joe Barrett, Holly Hawkins, Nicholas Joy, Jordan Roth, Tommy Walsh.

GALATEA THEATER COLLECTIVE. *Dead and Gone to Granny's* by Jussi Wahlgren. February 19, 1998.

GENE FRANKEL THEATER. *Jodie's Body* (one-woman show) by and with Aviva Jane Carlin. May 4, 1998. Directed by Kenneth Elliott.

GREENWICH HOUSE THEATER. *Skyscraper* by David Auburn. September 28, 1997. Directed by Michael Rego.

GROVE STREET PLAYHOUSE. *Private Life.* By Craig Archibald. February 8, 1998. Directed by Jim Frangione; with Craig Archibald, Matthew Del Negro, Carolyn Baeumier. *Freestyle Repertory Theater* (improvisation): *Emilio Buckett's Traveling Tarot Revue, Chameleons, Spontaneous Broadway, Theatersports* and *Innovations.* March 5-May 9, 1998. With Kenn Adams, Ross Aseron, Dan Diggles, Michael Durkin, Laura Livingston, Debora Rabbai, Christine Turner, Alyssa Weiss.

HAROLD CLURMAN THEATER. *A Lullaby for Murder* by Le Wilhelm. August 5, 1997. Directed by Sharon Fallon; with Carey Cromelin, Cecelia Frontero, Sarah Halstead, Joe Heffernan, Sharman Howe, Charles Kelly. *Cursing Macbeth: Tales and Superstitions* written and directed by Craig George. March 24, 1998.

HERE. *Homework* by Kim Coles and Charles Randolph-Wright. June 12, 1997. Directed by Charles Randolph-Wright; with Kim Coles, Shaun Baker, Wolfgang Bodison, Scotch Ellis Loring, Gustavo Rex. *Caught in the Act: The Executioners* by Fernando Arrabal; *Rocking Back and Forth* by Gunter Grass; *Steinway Grand* by Ferenc Karinthy; *Nights in the Tour de Nesle* by Pierre-Henri Cami; *The Gas Heart* by Tristan Tzara (one-act plays). September 11, 1997. *Work-Pain-Success* by Harry Pritchett. September 17, 1997. Directed by Anna Ivara. *Mad Shadows* by Kristin Marting, based on Marie-Claire Blais's novel. October 19, 1997. With Susan Hightower, Mark Gerow. *A Tattle Tale: Eyewitness in Mississippi* (one-woman show) by Judith Sloan and Warren Lehrer. November 13, 1997. Directed by Maxine Kern; with Judith Sloan. *Tuesday* by Paul Mullins. January 15, 1998. Directed by Randy Rollison; with Chuck Montgomery, Celia Botet, Tonya Canada, Ed Cannan, Melissa Hurst, Jesse McKinley, Alison White. *Blithedale: A Virtual Utopia* conceived and directed by Tim Maner, written and adapted from Nathaniel Hawthorne's novel, *The Blithedale Romance.* March 29, 1998. With David Anzuelo, Kimberly Gambino, Jan-Peter Pedross, T. Ryder Smith, Erica Stuart, Alison White. *These Women* book by Freda Rosen; music and lyrics by Lewis Finn, Freda Rosen and Amy Pivar. April 29, 1998. *Symphonie Fantastique* (puppetry) conceived by Basil Twist; music by Hector Berlioz. May 28, 1998. Puppeteers: Basil Twist, Sam Hack, Chris Hymas, Brian Selznick.

HUDSON GUILD THEATER. *The Mandala* by Waldemar Hansen. February 17, 1998. Directed by Cyndy Marion; with Martha Thimmesch, John Griffith, Vivien Landau, Chris Gunn, Mimi Stuart.

IMPACT THEATER. *The Incubus* by John Chatterton. March 19, 1998. Directed by John Cable.

INTAR THEATER. *Chuppah* by Lance Crowfoot-Suede. June 15, 1997. Directed by Frank Pisco; with Wendell Laurent, Susan Wallack, Matthew Wexler. *The Quick Change Room (Scenes From a Revolution)* by Nagle Jackson. October 12, 1997. Directed by Orson Bean; with Alley Mills, Sydney Bennett, Lisa Barnes, Marilyn Fox, Simon Jones, Susan Dexter.

IRISH ARTS CENTER. *A Night in November* (one-man show) by Marie Jones. February 21, 1998. Directed by Pam Brighton; with Dan Gordon. *Ghost on Fire* by Michael Weller. March 14, 1998. Directed by Amy Feinberg; with Lee Sellars, Betsy Aidem, Nelson Avidon, Dannah Chaifetz, Aasne Vigesaa.

J.E.T. THEATER. *Rachel* by Carl Stillitano. June 21, 1997. With Molly Culver, Peter J. Coriaty, Ed Hardesty, Lawrence Winslow.

JEAN COCTEAU REPERTORY. *Rough Crossing* by Tom Stoppard. August 9, 1997. Directed by Scott Shattuck; with Craig Smith, Harris Berlinsky, Elise Stone, Christopher Black, Charles Parnell, Tim Deak. *Hedda Gabler* by Henrik Ibsen, translated by Rolf Fjelde. September 28, 1997. Directed by Eve Adamson; with Elise Stone, Harris Berlinsky, Craig Smith, Marilyn Bernard, Patrick Hall. *The Cure at Troy* by Seamus Heaney, based on Sophocles's play *Philoctetes.* November 21, 1997. Directed by Robert Hupp; with Craig Smith, Elise Stone, Tracey Atkins, Tim Deak, Charles Parnell. *The Man in the Glass Booth* by Robert Shaw. January 18, 1998. Directed by Eve Adamson; with Harris Berlinsky, Christopher Black, Marilyn Bernard. *The Imaginary Invalid* by Molière, translated by Martin Sorrell. March 13, 1998. Directed by Scott Shattuck; with Craig Smith, Elise Stone, Tim Deak, Harris Berlinsky, Christopher Black, Charles Parnell, Mary Ellen Taylor. *Talley and Son* by Lanford Wilson. May 24, 1998. Directed by Scott Shattuck; with Tracey Atkins, Harris Berlinsky, Christopher Black, Tim Deak, Christine Hall, Patrick Hall, Sidney Marcus, Charles Parnell, Elise Stone, Mary Ellen Taylor, Sabrina Veroczi.

JEWISH THEATER OF NEW YORK. *Father of the Angels* adapted and directed by Tuvia Tenenbom, from the writings of Jacob Israel de Haan, Avraham Tehomi, David Ben-Gurion and others. October 18, 1997. With Ben Lipitz, Wayne Scherzer, Matt Meyer, Kelly Roden, Tom Flynn, Kimberly Reiss.

JOHN HOUSEMAN STUDIO THEATER. *The American Plan* by Richard Greenberg. October 12, 1997. Directed by Mark Roberts; with Kim Bey, Nick Gregory, Missy Hargraves, Daniel Vespa, Catherine Wolf. *The Broadway Kids Sing Broadway* (song revue) by Bruce J. Robinson. January 10, 1998. Directed by Christopher Scott. *R & J* adapted and directed by Joe Calarco, from William Shakespeare's *Romeo and Juliet.* January 22, 1998. See its entry in the Plays Produced Off Broadway section of this volume.

JOHN MONTGOMERY THEATER. *Encore: They Eat Their Young* by Liz Bartucci, directed by Peggie Lee Brennan; *Jump Start* by Suzanne Bachner, directed by Patricia Minskoff; *Danny Boy* by Robert L. Bachner (one-act plays). July 19, 1997. With Claudine Alfano, Steve Mize, Stan Carp, Bill Mullen. *Alice Through the Looking Glass* by Suzanne Bachner, adapted from Lewis Carroll's book, *Through the Looking Glass.* October 25, 1997. Directed by Thom Fudal; with Patricia Minskoff, Patrick Hillan. *On the Verge, or The Geography of Learning* by Eric Overmyer. December 6, 1997. Directed by David Leidholdt; with Renee Flemings, Bruce Katlin, Alex McCord, Mary Alice McGuire. *Patient 23* by Peter B. Sonenstein. January 24, 1998. Directed by Patricia Minskoff; with Patrick Hillan, Barbara Hentschel. *Icons and Outcasts* written and directed by Suzanne Bachner. April 29, 1998.

JUDITH ANDERSON THEATER. *Bea's Nest* by John DiGiacomo. September 17, 1997. Directed by Paul Andrew Perez. *Pledge of Allegiance* written and directed by Mark R. Giesser. October 14, 1997. With Dana White, Christopher Flockton, Steven Ditmyer, Michael Pemberton, Ivanna Cullinan. *O'Casey's Knock* book, music and lyrics by Paul Dick, based on Sean O'Casey's novel, *I Knock at the Door.* Directed by Ron Nash; with Valerie Fagan, Kate McCauley, Chad Hudson, Stephen Lloyd Webber. *Black Snow* adapted by Keith Reddin, from Mikhail Bulgakov's novel; music by Alexander Zhurbin. February 4, 1998. Directed by Ralph Buckley; with Christopher Duva, Sal Mistretta, Margaret Reed.

KRAINE THEATER. *Desire Under the Elms* by Eugene O'Neill. July 10, 1997. Directed by Dan Wackerman; with George Bartenieff, Devora Millman.

LA TEA THEATER. *Moe Green Gets It in the Eye* by Tony DiMurro. February 22, 1998. Directed by Joseph Summa; with Anthony Patellis, Patrick Michael Buckley, Matthew Bonifacio, Anthony Barile, Lynellen Kagen, Louis Tucci.

LINHART THEATER. *Savior of the Universe* by Gip Hoppe. February 23, 1998. Directed by David Strohmeyer; with Edward Burke, Evan Thompson, Dan Conroy, Jamie Heinlein, Rob Skolits.

MA-YI THEATER ENSEMBLE. *A Portrait of the Artist as Filipino* by Nick Joaquin. July 29, 1997. Directed by Jorge V. Ledesma; with Ruth Henry, Catol de Mesa. *You Can't Take It With You* by Moss Hart and George S. Kaufman. Co-produced by the National Asian American Theater Company; see its listing in this section.

MARTIN R. KAUFMAN THEATER. *About Time* (cabaret) by and with Paulette Attie. September 11, 1997. Directed by Justin Ross. *H. Finn, Esq.* by Peter Zablotsky. October 21, 1997. Directed by John Ahlers. See its entry in the Plays Produced Off Broadway section of this volume. *Tallulah's Party* book by Bob Griffiths, Latifah Taormina and J.D. Maria; music by Arthur Siegel; lyrics by Mae Richard. March 19, 1998. Directed by Latifah Taormina; with Tovah Feldshuh, Robert Cary, Bobby Clark, Alan Gilbert.

HAROLD CLURMAN THEATER—Cecelia Frontero, Charles Kelly, Joe Heffernan and Carey Cromelin in *A Lullaby for Murder* by Le Wilhelm

MELTING POT THEATER COMPANY. *Home* by Samm-Art Williams. June 4, 1997. Directed by Kent Gash; with Saidah Arrika Ekulona, E. Phillip McGlaston, Tamilla Woodard. *Cotton Patch Gospel* book by Tom Key and Russell Treyz, based on Clarence Jordan's book, *The Cotton Patch Version of Matthew and John;* music and lyrics by Harry Chapin. November 14, 1997. Directed by Danny Peak; with Mimi Bessette, Samuel D. Cohen, Kevin Fox, John C. Havens, Emily Mikesell, Ken Triwush. *The Good Doctor* by Neil Simon. February 6, 1998. Directed by Howard Rossen; with Andre DeShields, Jane Connell, Gordon Connell, Sybyl Walker, Stuart Zagnit.

METROPOLITAN PLAYHOUSE. *The Return of Peter Grimm* by David Belasco; music by John Fritz. November 1, 1997. Directed by David Zarko; with David Carson, Duane Noch, Fernando Arze, Christian Kaufmann, Mari-Esther Magaloni, Sandra Drakes. *Washington Irving's Sketchbook* adapted by Frank Higgins and Rebecca Taylor. March 8, 1998. Directed by Rebecca Taylor; with Margaret Burnham, Ben Busch, Ed Chemaly, Todd Alexander Kovner, Robert Ruffin, Mary Wadkins.

MINT THEATER COMPANY. *Oroonoko, or The Royal Slave* by Thomas Southerne. June 6, 1997. Directed by Jonathan Bank; with Randy Aramondo, Lisa M. Bostnar, Cassandra Johnson, Billy Miller, M.W. Reid, Timothy Joseph Ryan, Ron Sanborn, Carol Schultz, John D. Thompson. *Uncle Tom's Cabin* by George L. Aiken, adapted from Harriet Beecher Stowe's novel. September 5, 1997. Directed by Charles Dumas; with Bo Rucker, John L. Damon, Peter William Dunn, Peter Giles, Thomas Gilpin, Karen Lynn Gorney, Sandra P. Grant, Clark Jackson, George Spaventa, Cordell Stahl, Sally Stewart, Lynne Workinger. *Mr. Pim Passes By* by A.A. Milne. December 4, 1997. Directed by Jonathan Bank; with Ken Kliban, Lisa Bostnar, Bill Roulet, Kim Wimmer. *Human Resources* by and with Richard Hoehler. March 5, 1998. Directed by Chuck Brown. *The House of Mirth* by Edith Wharton and Clyde Fitch. May 22, 1998. Directed by Jonathan Bank; with Lisa M. Bostnar, Michael Stebbins, Donald Warfield, Gus Kaikkonen, Mike Hodge.

MIRANDA THEATER COMPANY. *Lebensraum* by Israel Horovitz. October 15, 1997. Directed by Richard McElvain; with Jeremy Silver, Scott Richards, Emme Shaw. *Sex in Advertising* by Margaret Elman. November 6, 1997. Directed by Matt Lenz; with Lisa Roberts Gillan, Johnny Fido, Jessica Lynn. *Innocent Thoughts* by William Missouri Downs. May 17, 1998. With Daniel Whitner, Patrick Fredrick.

NATIONAL ASIAN AMERICAN THEATER COMPANY. *Ah, Wilderness!* by Eugene O'Neill. July 22, 1997. Directed by Stephen Stout; with Ron Nakahara, Wai Ching Ho, Mel Duane Gionson, Jennifer Kato. *Long Day's Journey Into Night* by Eugene O'Neill. November 9, 1997. Directed by Stephen Stout; with Ernest Abuba, Mia Katigbak, Andy Pang, Paul Nakauchi, Midori Nakamura. *You Can't Take It-*

with You by George S. Kaufman and Moss Hart. February 17, 1998. Directed by Stephen Stout; with Henry Yuk, Boni Alvarez, Jodi Lin, Nicky Paraiso, Ralph Pena, Virginia Wing. Co-produced by Ma-Yi Theater Ensemble.

NEIGHBORHOOD PLAYHOUSE. *Sun Flower* by and with Elizabeth Perry. January 10, 1998.

NEW GEORGES. *Fishes* by Diana Son. June 13, 1997. Directed by Judy Minor; with William Badgett, Ken Barnett, Amy Povich, Camilia Sanes, Connie Winston. *Stepping Out With Mr. Markham* by Jeanne Dorsey. December 10, 1997. Directed by Martha Banta; with Marissa Copeland, Paul Dawson, Jeanne Dorsey, Michael Ornstein, Timothy Britten Parker.

THE NEW GROUP. *Goose-Pimples* by Mike Leigh. December 18, 1997. Directed by Scott Elliott; with Caroline Seymour, Adam Alexi-Malle, Gillian Foss, Max Baker. *Hazelwood Junior High* by Rob Urbinati. March 5, 1998. Directed by Scott Elliott; with Chloe Sevigny, Amy Whitehouse, Stephanie Gatschet, Heather Gottlieb, Brooke Sunny Moriber, Margaret Burkwit. *The Fastest Clock in the Universe* by Philip Ridley. May 7, 1998. Directed by Jo Bonney; with David Cale, Jeanette Landis, Bray Poor, Joey Kern, Ellie Mae McNulty.

NEW MYSTERY THEATER COMPANY. *Stonykill Lookout* by Linda Segal Crawley. March 7, 1998. Directed by Bill Coyle; with John Frey, Meg Kelly, Peggy Pope, Manuel Rivera, David Rosenbaum.

NEW PERSPECTIVES THEATER COMPANY. *Love Bites Again: Quick and Dirty* by Dave Riedy; *The Virgin* by Cheryl Davis; *Second Estimate* by Rick Balian; *Dutch Treat* by Melody Brooks; *We Gotta Talk* by India Cooper; *The Dick Dailey Show* by Erica Silberman (one-act plays). June 17–27, 1997. *Kolonists* by Steven Dykes. September 18, 1997. Directed by Julia Carey; with Frank Morgan.

NEW YORK GILBERT AND SULLIVAN PLAYERS. *The Yeoman of the Guard.* December 26, 1997. Directed by Albert Bergeret and Jan Holland; with Brandon Jovanovich, Tyler Bunch, Katie Geissinger, Charlotte Detrick, Stephen O'Brien, Amy Ellen Anderson, Duane McDevitt, Michael Collins. *The Mikado.* January 8, 1998. Directed by Albert Bergeret and Jan Holland; with Andrew McPhail, Stephen O'Brien, Philip Reilly, Heide Holcomb, Jana Carlson, Edward Prostak, Michael Collins. *Iolanthe.* January 15, 1998. Directed by Albert Bergeret.

NEW YORK INTERNATIONAL FRINGE FESTIVAL. Schedule included *Americana Absurdum* by Brian Parks, directed by John Clancy; *Baby Redboots' Revenge* by Philip-Dimitri Galas, directed by Lynne Griffin; *Charlatan* written, directed and performed by Tony Tanner; *Louis and Dave* by Norm Foster, directed by John Verhaeven; *Make My Doris Day: Confessions From Suburbia* by Libba Bray, directed by Ed Roland; *Mortal Coil—Voices From the Hospice* by Lester Thomas Shane, directed by Jared Hammond; *Witches' Macbeth* adapted from William Shakespeare's play and directed by Richard Kimmel. August 13–24, 1997.

NEW YORK PUBLIC LIBRARY FOR THE PERFORMING ARTS READING ROOM READINGS. *The Dark Kalamazoo* by Oni Faida Lampley. October 20, 1997. Directed by Lynn Thompson; with Oni Faida Lampley, Darci Picoult. *Buying Time* by Michael Weller. November 10, 1997. Directed by Douglas Hughes; with Larry Block, Robert Joy, Gerry Bamman, Ned Eisenberg, Sharon Scruggs. *Yankee Diva* by Albert Innaurato. December 15, 1997. Directed by Michael Sexton; with Elizabeth Franz, Daniel Gerroll, Alexandra Gersten, Reed Birney. *Lillian Yuralia* by Barbara Eda-Young. January 12, 1998. Directed by Josephine Abady; with Barbara Eda-Young, Joseph Wiseman, Evan Macosko. *Supple in Combat* by Alexandra Gersten. February 23, 1998. Directed by Max Mayer; with John Slattery, Alexandra Gersten, Tom Mardirosian. *Event Horizon* by Christopher Kyle. March 16, 1998. Directed by Randolph Curtis Rand; with Jim Jacobson, Ralph Pena, Larry Block. *Adam Baum and the Jew Movie* by Daniel Goldfarb. April 20, 1998. Directed by Daniel Sullivan; with Ron Leibman, Boyd Gaines, Adam Lamberg. *The Elektra Fugues* by Ruth Margraff. May 18, 1998. Directed by Liz Diamond; with David Greenspan, Jonathan Fried, Kimberly Gambino.

NEW YORK THEATER EXCHANGE. *Bloody Poetry* by Howard Brenton. April 16, 1998. Directed by Chris Hayes.

NUYORICAN POETS CAFE. *Julius Caesar Set in Africa* adapted from William Shakespeare's play and directed by Rome Neal. May 7, 1998. With Marc McTizic, Renauld White, Robert Turner, Chet Anekwe.

OHIO THEATER. *The Marital Bliss of Francis and Maxine* book, music and lyrics by Fay Simpson and Bill Torres. September 5, 1997.

ONTOLOGICAL-HYSTERIC THEATER. *Benita Canova (Gnostic Eroticism)* written, directed and designed by Richard Foreman. January 16, 1998. With Joanna P. Adler, Christina Campanella, Susan Tierney, David Greenspan. *The 7 Minute Series* (festival of short performance pieces). April 16–26, 1998. *Yield* by Jill Szuchmacher. May 2, 1998. Directed by Mike Taylor; with 3-Legged Dog. *Gold Russian Finger Love* written and directed by Whit MacLaughlin. May 21, 1998. With Matt Saunders, Lee Ann Etzold, Aaron Mumaw, Mary Katherine McCool, Rene Ligon Hartl, Jeb Kreager, Elizabeth A. Roberts.

OTHER THEATER. *Women. War. Comedy (Frauen. Krieg. Lustspiel)* by Thomas Brasch, translated by Norbert Ruebsaat. December 4, 1997. Directed by Richard Armstrong.

PARADISE THEATER. *Wang Dang* written and directed by Tom Noonan. February 5, 1998. With Missi Pyle, Tristine Skyler, Tom Noonan, Keith Uhlich.

PEARL THEATER COMPANY. *Hard Times* by Charles Dickens, adapted by Stephen Jeffreys. August 26, 1997. Directed by Lou Jacob; with Richard Thompson, Joel Leffert, Robin Leslie Brown, Carol Schultz. *The Forest* by Alexander Ostrovsky. October 21, 1997. Directed by Shepard Sobel; with Richard Thompson, Bradford Cover, Carol Schultz, Joe Palmieri. *The School for Scandal* by Richard Brinsley Sheridan. December 16, 1997. Directed by John Morrison. *Richard II* by William Shakespeare. February 10, 1998. Directed by Shepard Sobel; with Bradford Cover. *Miss Julie* by August Strindberg. April 7, 1998. Directed by Christopher Martin; with Tom Spackman, Hope Chernov.

PERFORMING GARAGE. *A Harlot's Progress* (chamber opera) written by Barry Greenhut and Theodora Skipitares; music and lyrics by Barry Greenhut. May 14, 1998. Directed by Theodora Skipitares; with Christina Campanella, Felicity La Fortune, Lee Winston.

PHIL BOSAKOWSKI THEATER. *Sex, Drugs, Rock & Roll* by Eric Bogosian. October 27, 1997. Directed by Chris Marcantel; with Oscar Riba. *Wild Echinacea* by Jonathan Reuning. December 3, 1997. Directed by Eva Saks; with Scott Hudson, Sharon Nordlinger, Missi Pyle.

PRODUCERS' CLUB. *Find Me a Voice* by SuzAnne Barabas and Gabor Barabas; music by Merek Royce Press. September 11, 1997. Directed by SuzAnne Barabas; with Marian Akana, Christopher Casoria, Elisah Joy Gordon, Dorothy Kerr, Harlan Tuckman. *The Official Show: Now With Blimp!* by Rob Keefe. October 8, 1997. Directed by Ted Sluberski. *Murder Mayhem* by Ron Wilson. October 27, 1997. Directed by Doug Hall; with Daniel Brennan, Paul Drinan, Jeremy Guskin, Jennifer Howard, Bill Mullen. *Help!!Desk* book by Elizabeth Edwards; music by Keith Edwards; lyrics by Elizabeth Edwards and Keith Edwards. November 22, 1997. Directed by Robyn Cronulla Lee; with Mike Finesilver, Thierry Laurence, Chev Rodgers, Stephanie Sweeney, Robert Wagner. *Some of My Best Friends* (one-woman show). With T'Keyah Crystal Kaymah. February 6, 1998. Directed by Jeffrey V. Thompson. *Jim Beckwourth* by Mark Weston. April 21, 1998.

PULSE ENSEMBLE THEATER. *The Seagull* by Anton Chekhov, adapted and directed by Alexa Kelly. June 25, 1997. With Christine Jones, Sandy York, Don Scime, Nelson Avidon, Sam Stewart. *Kamchik, the Singing Cowboy* (one-man show). By and with Avner Kam. September 5, 1997. Directed by Brian Richardson. *The Good Woman of Setzuan* by Bertolt Brecht, translated by Eric Bentley; music and lyrics by Michael Rice. March 18, 1998. Directed by Alexa Kelly; with Brian Richardson, Hazel Anne Raymundo, Noel Johansen, Angelina Fiordellisi, Kwang Sung, Paula Roth.

QUEENS THEATER IN THE PARK. *Princess Grace and the Fazzaris* (one-woman show). By Marc Alan Zagoren. February 11, 1998. Directed by Peter Bennett; with Lois Nettleton.

RATTLESTICK PRODUCTIONS. *Hello and Goodbye* by Athol Fugard. September 9, 1997. Directed by Howard Meyer; with Pamela Bel Anu, Brian Quirk. *A Pirate's Lullaby* by Jessica Litwak. October 19, 1997. Directed by Melanie Sutherland; with Louise Favier, Delphi Harrington, Jessica Litwak, Sharon Round, Jeff Woodman. *And the Pursuit of Happiness* by James Edwin Parker. December 7, 1997. Directed by Julian Woolford; with Michael Curry, Charlie Schroeder. *Whale Music* by Anthony Minghella. March 12, 1998. Directed by Alison Summers; with Francie Swift, Chandler Vinton, Kristin DiSpaltro, Melinda Wade, Amanda Peet. *Ascendancy* by Gary Bonasorte. May 13, 1998. Directed by Rob Bundy; with Bryan Batt, Rob Bogue, Dominick Cuskern, Kenneth Favre, Tasha Lawrence, Michael Malone, Linda Powell.

RAYMOND J. GREENWALD THEATER. *Only You* by Timothy Mason. September 11, 1997. Directed by Harry Carnahan; with Jeremy Scott Johnson, Julianne Zinkewicz, Cynthia King, David Palmieri, P.J. Sosko, Robert Johnson.

SALON THEATER. *The Tragedie of Othello* by William Shakespeare. March 19, 1998. Directed by Randolph Curtis Rand; with Joshua Spafford, Robyn Hussa, Al Benditt, Bill Coelius.

SAMUEL BECKETT THEATER. *Hell's Cuisinart* by David Caudle. July 27, 1997. Directed by Andrew Volkoff; with Kerry O. Burns, Sally Fairman, Michael Linstroth, Jay Potter, Vincent Rutherford, Nicole Wells. *Adjoining Trances* by Randy Buck. September 28, 1997. Directed by Marc Geller; with Sally Frontman, Marc Geller. *Hermione: Tales of Sexual Frustration: Cute Lonely Guys Looking for You* and *Hermione* (one-act plays) by John Attanas. October 22, 1997. Directed by Eliza Beckwith and Charles Loffredo. *Anapest* by Lee Wochner. January 22, 1998. Directed by Eliza Beckwith; with Courtney Rohler, Jed Krascella, Jamie Heinlein, Glen Williamson, James Raymond Sutton.

SANFORD MEISNER THEATER. *Mercury: The Afterlife and Times of a Rock God* written and directed by Charles Messina. February 14, 1998. With Paul Goncalves. *Love Soup* by Julie Rottenberg. May 30, 1998. Directed by Christie Wagner Lee; with Torben Brooks, Wendy Hoopes, Cady Huffman, Josh Lewis, Ivan Martin, Andrea Rosen, Nathan Smith.

78TH STREET THEATER LAB. *The Rose and the Knife* by Marc Pascal; music by Alex Wurman. December 8, 1997. Directed by Tobias Heilmann; with Christopher Flockton, Maria Galante, John Marino, Sven Miller, Wallace Norman. *With and Without* by Jeffrey Sweet. February 21, 1998. Directed by Michael Montel; with Reed Birney, Mia Dillon, Kit Flanagan, Erol K.C. Landis.

THE STUDIO. *White Noise* by Gino DiIorio. May 13, 1998. Directed by Frank Licato; with Brendan Patrick Burke, George Macaluso, Stephanie Martini, Passion, Brocton Pierce, Joel Rooks.

SYLVIA AND DANNY KAYE PLAYHOUSE. *Puttin' on the Ritz—The Irving Berlin Songbook* (musical revue). January 29, 1998. Directed by Karen Azenberg; with Carol Lawrence.

SYMPHONY SPACE. *Sarah Bernhardt Comes to Town* (short stories and works) by Anton Chekhov, translated by Peter Constantine, adapted and directed by Vanessa Redgrave. May 13, 1998. With Rachel Kempson, Vanessa Redgrave.

SYNCHRONICITY SPACE. *Talk Show* by Fred Rosenberg, directed by Colette Duvall; *The Old Block* by Robert Remington Wood, directed by Stephanie Rosenblum. September 11, 1997. With Ray Luetters, Aysha Quinn, Charles Chessler, Matthew Brown, Kristianne Kurner, Nikoye Banks, Mark Gorman, Ed Franklin. *On the Open Road* by Steve Tesich. February 1, 1998. Directed by Mark Roberts; with William Hill, John Slagle, Ivan Dirkx, Eric Scott, Matthew Staniec. *The Twilight of the Golds* by Jonathan Tolins. March 11, 1998. Directed by James Knopf; with Christopher Scott, Michael Oberlander, Jane Ross, Len Stanger, Karin Sibrava. *The Death of Frank* by Stephen Belber. April 22, 1998. Directed by Lucie Tiberghien.

TARGET MARGIN THEATER. *Strictly Dishonorable* by Preston Sturges. September 3, 1997. Directed by David Herskovits; with Andrew Dolan, Patricia Dunnock, Mary Neufeld, Steven Rattazzi, David Letwin. *Mamba's Daughters* by Dorothy and DuBose Heyward. February 24, 1998. Directed by David Herskovits; with William Badgett, Melody Cooper, David Eye, Heather Gillespie, Billie James, Greig Sargeant.

THEATER AT ST. CLEMENT'S. *Church of Billy* by Bill Talen. June 12, 1997. Directed by Andrew O'Hehir; with Gary Bass, P.J. Nelson, Vanessa Klimek, Bill Talen.

THEATER AT ST. PETER'S CHURCH. *Sugar Down Bille Hoak* by Brian Silberman. July 28, 1997. Directed by Guy Stroman; with Jon A. Abrahams, Michael Cambden Richards, Brian Vincent. *The Top of the Bottom Half (The Keeper of All Knowledge: Take Two)* (one-woman show) by Liza Vann and Katherine Griffith. March 4, 1998. Directed by Andrew McBean; with Liza Vann.

THEATER ROW THEATER. *A Flower of Water* by Yuko Hamada and Yukihiro Saji. June 15, 1997. Directed by Yuko Hamada; with Miki Kosugi, Katie Takahashi, Masahiko Furutachi, Mariko Fusillo, Akiko Miyama, Tomo Omori, Mika Saburi, Humiko Tanaka, Naomi Watanabe. *Two Divas and the Dog* by Kira Arne. July 9, 1997. Directed by Kenneth Richardson. *Miracle Mile* (one-man show) by Clark Middleton and Robert Knopf. September 7, 1997. Directed by Michael Warren Powell; with Clark Middleton. *Fictitious History* (one-act plays) by George Bernard Shaw. December 8, 1997. Directed by Lisa Ann Goldsmith and Owen Thompson. *The Libertine* by Stephen Jeffreys. January 11, 1998. Directed by Stephen Hollis; with Carrie Preston, Mark Vietor, Ritchie Coster, Aideen O'Kelly, Carole Healey, Karl Kenzler, Doug Stender. *Subtle Bodies* by Clive Barker. February 6, 1998. Directed by Thomas Caruso; with Anthony Gelsomino, Jo Anne Glover, Joel Friedman, George Hahn. *Dance With*

Me by Jean Reynolds. March 13, 1998. Directed by Alan Wynroth; with Peter Michael Brouwer, Lillo Way, Kara V. Sekuler.

THEATER 3. *Clash by Night* by Clifford Odets. February 12, 1998. Directed by Richard Caliban; with Jodie Markell, Michael DellaFemina, Dominic Comperatore, Geneva Carr.

THEATER 22. *Killing Time in 3-D* by Mark Mensher and Heath Mensher. July 11, 1997. Directed by Mark Mensher; with Joshua Cary, Patrick Gallo, Heath Mensher, Julie Ellis, Martin Gura.

TOWN HALL. *Fyvush Finkel—From Second Avenue to Broadway: A Musical Comedy Gift.* December 25, 1997. With Fyvush Finkel, Ian Finkel, Elliot Finkel, Byron Stripling.

TRIAD. *The Porker Sisters* by Mark York. September 14, 1997.

TRIANGLE THEATER COMPANY. *White Panther* by Dan Seymour, Ariane Brandt, Isiah Whitlock Jr. and Yanna Kroyt Brandt. April 24, 1998. Directed by Kenneth Johnson; with Isiah Whitlock Jr., Ariane Brandt.

TRIBECA PERFORMING ARTS CENTER. *Tony and Son* by Louis Delgado. June 18, 1997. Directed by Max Daniels; with David Vayas, Mtume Gant, Stacie Linardos, AJ Lopez, Delilah Picart, Robert Rodriguez. *Tibet Does Not Exist* by Don Thompson. September 21, 1997. Directed by Brian Clay Luedloff; with Dominic Cuskern, Les J.N. Mau, Tiffany Marshall, Wynn Harmon, Katie Atcheson, L. Trey Wilson, Stephanie Kovacs, Johann Helf. *Pearls for Pigs* written and directed by Richard Foreman. December 3, 1997. With David Patrick Kelly, Tom Nelis, Peter Jacobs, Stephanie Cannon, Scott Blumenthal, David Cote, Yehuda Duenyas, John Oglevee.

TRILOGY THEATER. *Dotted Line* and *Even Steven* by Anthony Giunta. October 19, 1997. Directed by Mark Harborth; with Daniel Sherman, Jason Roth, Kathleen McInerney, Dennis Keely, Jay Scully, Alisa Klein, Melissa Rayworth, David Duffield. *Butterflies and Tigers* written and directed by John Glines. February 5, 1998. With Gene Chen, Darcy Chin, Ann Hu, Douglas Kim, Frances Lee, Keong Sim, Edward Wong.

TWEED. *Lypsinka Is Harriet Craig!* by S.P. Ellbound. February 8, 1998. Directed by Kevin Malony; with John Epperson, Varla Jean Merman, Jay Rogers, Colleen O'Neill, Stephen Pell, Russell Scott Lewis.

28TH STREET THEATER. *Fixin' to Die* (one-man show). By Robert Myers. September 11, 1997. Directed by George Furth; with Bruce McIntosh.

29TH STREET REPERTORY THEATER. *Tracers* conceived by John DiFusco, written by Vincent Caristi, Richard Chaves, John DiFusco, Eric E. Emerson, Rick Gallavan, Merlin Marston, Harry Stephens, Sheldon Lettich. September 11, 1997. Directed by Leo Farley; with Tony DeVito, Neil Necastro, Walker Richards, William Francis Smith, David Mogentale, Jonathan D. Powers, Vincent Rotolo, Thomas Wehrle. *Bobby Supreme* by J.B. Miller. May 1, 1998. Directed by Tim Corcoran; with David Mogentale, Paula Ewin, Charles Willey, Leo Farley, Elizabeth Elkins, Moira McDonald.

URBAN STAGES. *Asian Women Speak: I See My Bones* by Kitty Chen, directed by Ben Harney; *Details/Cannot/Body/Wants* by and with Chin Woon Ping, directed by Alan Kuharski. November 30– December 21, 1997 (in repertory). With Blanche Cholet, Sylvia Gassel, Will H'Ao, Susan Willis. *Pieces of the Sky* by David L. Paterson. April 22, 1998. Directed by T.L. Reilly; with Robert Ari, Jamie Bennett, George Cavey, Diane Grotke, Mick Weber. *Legal Alien* (one-man show) by and with Kevin Fisher. April 26, 1998. Directed by Jamie Richards.

VEGAS ROOM. *Aunt Chooch's Birthday* written and directed by Larry Pellegrini. May 11, 1998. With Dana Lorge, Michael Saia, Susan Varon, Kathleen Bergman, Vincent Gerard.

VINEYARD THEATER. *Hamlet: A Puppet Tragedy* adapted from William Shakespeare's play and a Czech puppet version, and directed by Vit Horejs. October 4, 1997. With Deborah Beshaw, Charley Hayward, Vit Horejs, Theresa Linnihan.

WEISSBERGER THEATER GROUP. *Side Man* by Warren Leight. March 11, 1998. Directed by Michael Mayer; with Edie Falco, Kevin Geer, Michael Mastro, Robert Sella, Joseph Lyle Taylor, Angelica Torn, Frank Wood.

WEST END THEATER. *Stalking the Nightmare* adapted from Harlan Ellison's writings and directed by Robert Armin. March 6, 1998. With Femi Emiola, Johnny Kitt, Kristine Nevins, David Sitler, Ronald Venable, David Vogel. *Side by Side by Seymour Glick* book, music and lyrics by Steve Allen. May 15,

WEST END THEATER—Amy Soucy, Tom Schmid, Kristine Nevins and Tracy Rosten in *Side by Side by Seymour Glick,* a program of Steve Allen's comedy songs

1998. Directed by Robert Armin; with Robert Armin, Steve Liebman, Kristine Nevins, Tracy Rosten, Tom Schmid, Amy Soucy.

WESTBETH THEATER CENTER. *Sing Low Sweet Love: John Kelly in Concert.* November 9, 1997. *I'm Still Here . . . Damn It!* (one-woman show) by and with Sandra Bernhard. November 11, 1997. *Dress to Kill* (one-man show) by and with Eddie Izzard. March 26, 1998.

WILLOW CABIN THEATER. *Rootless Beauties: Confessional* and *The Mutilated* (one-act plays) by Tennessee Williams. March 2, 1998. Directed by Edward Berkeley; with John Billeci, Lee Coleman, Fiona Davis, Kenneth Favre, Ken Forman, Joshua Harto, Ryan S. Hull, Larry Gleason, Angela Nevard. *Bus Riley and Company: Bus Riley's Back in Town, The Boy in the Basement, The Tiny Closet, Memory of Summer* and *The Mall* (one-act plays) by William Inge. May 4, 1998. Directed by Larry Gleason; with Cynthia Besteman, Joel Van Liew, Jed Sexton, Robert Harte.

THE WOOSTER GROUP. *The Emperor Jones* by Eugene O'Neill. March 9, 1998. Directed by Elizabeth LeCompte; with Kate Valk, Willem Dafoe, Dave Shelley, Ari Fliakos.

WORKING THEATER. *City Water Tunnel #3* (one-woman show) by and with Marty Pottenger. May 26, 1998. Directed by Jaye Austin-Williams.

THE SEASON
AROUND
THE UNITED STATES

OUTSTANDING NEW PLAYS
CITED BY
AMERICAN THEATER CRITICS
ASSOCIATION
and
A DIRECTORY OF NEW-PLAY
PRODUCTIONS

○
○
○

THE American Theater Critics Association (ATCA) is the organization of more than 280 leading drama critics in all media in all sections of the United States. One of this group's stated purposes is "To increase public awareness of the theater as a *national* resource" (italics ours). To this end, beginning in 1977 ATCA has annually cited outstanding new plays produced around the U.S., to be represented in our coverage by excerpts from each of their scripts demonstrating literary style and quality. This year, one of these—*The Cider House Rules, Part II,* adapted by Peter Parnell from the John Irving novel and first presented by Seattle Repertory Theater—has been designated ATCA's 22d annual principal citation and its 13th annual New Play Award winner of $1,000.

Two other 1998 ATCA new play citations for plays first produced in the calendar year 1997 went to August Wilson's full-length version of his one-acter *Jitney,* which premiered at the Pittsburgh Public Theater, and *The Old Settler* by John Henry Redwood, which had a dual premiere at Princeton's McCarter Theater Center and New Haven's Long Wharf Theater.

ATCA's fourth annual Elizabeth Osborn Award for an emerging playwright was voted to Rebecca Gilman for her *The Glory of Living* at the Circle Theater, Chicago. Richard Strand was the runner-up for his *My Simple City* at Rivendell Powertap Productions, Chicago.

Of the 25 new scripts (a record number) nominated by ATCA members for the New Play and Osborn Awards, six were selected as New Play finalists by the 1998 awards committee before making their final citations. In addition to the three winners, the finalists and the organizations which premiered them were *The Darker Face of the Earth* by Rita Dove at Oregon Shakespeare Festival, *Black Russian* by Thomas Gibbons at Philadelphia's InterAct Theater and *My Simple City* by Richard Strand, also eligible for the Osborn Award and its runner-up.

Other New Play category nominees and the groups which produced them were *Ambition Facing West* by Anthony Clarvoe (Trinity Repertory Theater); *Private Eyes* (Arizona Theater Company and Louisville Humana Festival) and *Still Life With Iris* (Seattle Children's Theater), both by Steven Dietz; *The Guy Upstairs* by Mark Elman (Charlotte Repertory Theater); *Sidney Bechet Killed a Man* by Mark Eisman (Victory Gardens Theater); *Freedomland* by Amy Freed (South Coast Repertory); *Magic Fire* by Lillian Garrett-Groag (Oregon Shakespeare Festival); *Polaroid Stories* by Naomi Lizuka (Humana Festival); *Last Lists of My Mad Mother* by Julie Jensen (Salt Lake Acting Company); *Fakes* by Lynne Kauffman (Florida Studio Theater); *Tongue of a Bird* by Ellen McLaughlin (Intiman Theater); *The Singing Weatherman* by Jim McGinn and Keith Herrmann (Seven Angels Theater); *Escher's Hands* by Dawson Nichols (AHA Theater); *Ralph Nader Is Missing* by Charlie Varon (Marsh Theater); *The Mineola Twins* by Paula Vogel (Trinity Repertory Theater); *Euphoria* by Tracy Young (Actors' Gang Theater).

The process of selection of these outstanding plays is as follows: any ATCA member may nominate the first full professional production of a finished play (not a reading or an airing as a play-in-progress) during the calendar year under consideration. Nominated scripts were studied and discussed by the 1998 ATCA playreading committee chaired by Michael Grossberg of the Columbus *Dispatch* and comprising Misha Berson of the Seattle *Times,* Lawrence Bommer of the Chicago *Reader* and *Tribune,* Marianne Evett of the Cleveland *Plain Dealer,* Robert Hurwitt of the San Francisco *Examiner,* Beatrice MacLeod of the Ithaca *Journal,* Ed Siegel of the Boston *Globe* and alternates Alec Harvey of the Birmingham *News* and Herb Simpson of Rochester's *City Newspaper.*

These committee members made their choices on the basis of script rather than production. If the timing of nominations and openings prevents some works from being considered in any given year, they will be eligible for consideration the following year if they haven't since moved to New York. We offer our sincerest thanks and admiration to the ATCA members and their committee for the valuable insights into the 1997 theater year around the United States which their selections provide for this *Best Plays* record, in the form of excerpts from the outstanding scripts, and most particularly in the introductory reviews by Misha Berson (*The Cider House Rules, Part II*), Christopher Rawson of the Pittsburgh *Post-Gazette* (*Jitney*) and Michael Grossberg (*The Old Settler*).

1997 ATCA New Play Award

○○○
○○○
○○○
○○○
○○○
○○○ # THE CIDER HOUSE RULES, PART II

A Play in Two Acts

ADAPTED BY **PETER PARNELL**
FROM THE NOVEL BY **JOHN IRVING**

CONCEIVED FOR THE STAGE BY **TOM HULCE,
JANE JONES** AND **PETER PARNELL**

Cast and credits appear on pages 409–10 of
The Best Plays of 1996–97

PETER PARNELL has been a working and produced playwright for almost two decades. He first came to the attention of New York audiences with Sorrows of Stephen, *which New York Shakespeare Festival first workshopped and then produced for 167 performances on December 11, 1979. Parnell soon found a longer lasting home at Playwrights Horizons which put on a succession of his plays:* Romance Language *(1984),* Hyde in Hollywood *(1989),* Flaubert's Latest *(1992) and* An Imaginary Life *(1993). He is also the author of* The Rise and Rise of Daniel Rocket *and has seen his works performed all over the regional theater in Los Angeles, San Diego, Baltimore and Denver venues. The first part of his stage adaptation of John Irving's novel* The Cider House Rules *was first produced March 2, 1996 by Seattle Repertory Theater, which premiered the ATCA New Play Award-winning second part of the work a season later. He has been the recipient of grants and fellowships from NEA, Guggenheim, Ingram Merrill, Lecomte de Nouey and Fund for New American Plays (for* An Imaginary Life *and* The Cider House Rules, Part I*).*

INTRODUCTION: The kind of pleasures gained in leisurely reading an ample novel, and the rewards of spending an evening watching an absorbing stage play, are usually quite different in nature. Every blue moon, however, these two distinct

319

literary genres meet and mesh in felicitous ways, offering an audience both the breadth and depth of a great read and the vital immediacy of live theater.

Such a bonding occurred in 1981, when the Royal Shakespeare Company brought David Edgar's much-celebrated dramatization of Charles Dickens's *Nicholas Nickleby* to Broadway. And in 1997 a similarly happy hybrid was introduced at the Seattle Repertory Theater, when playwright Peter Parnell and his collaborators, co-directors Tom Hulce and Jane Jones, successfully premiered their version of the modern John Irving novel, *The Cider House Rules.*

While David Edgar's RSC adaptation of *Nicholas Nickleby* had a total running time of eight and a half hours, featured a cast of 42 actors and was British to the core, the stage edition of *The Cider House Rules* (unveiled at the Mark Taper Forum in Los Angeles in 1998) unfolds in six hours, requires 20 actors (give or take a few) and conveys a thoroughly American view of three generations of New Englanders, circa 1880s to the 1950s.

There are crucial elements that bind these two engrossing stage epics and help account for their riveting effect on theatergoers in an age of ever-shrinking attention spans. For one thing, both scripts lovingly preserve much of a skilled novelist's original prose. Both works also employ bare-stage, ensemble-driven, story-theater techniques (the kind pioneered by Peter Brook, Paul Sills and others) to alternately narrate a fictional saga and embody it. And both prosper by hewing close to the spirit of Charles Dickens—whose oeuvre directly inspired the narrative sweep, richness of incident and character and moral amplitude of Irving's 1985 novel.

In fact, *Cider House Rules* is something of an homage to Dickens. It refers frequently to two of the Victorian-era author's most beloved novels, *Great Expectations* and *David Copperfield,* and like them it is a *Bildungsroman* chronicling the fortunes of an orphan-protagonist—one Homer Wells, who, echoing young Copperfield, earnestly ponders "whether I shall turn out to be the hero of my own life."

Yet despite the 19th century conventions and Dickensian flavor, *Cider House Rules* views heroism very much in contemporary terms. Both the play and novel consider unflinchingly one of the most divisive issues of our own time: whether American women should have access to legal abortions. By weaving the abortion question inextricably through the braided plot, and considering it in medical, historical and personal terms over a period of some 80 years and among several dozen characters, *Cider House Rules* never becomes schematic or preachy. Abortion is not seen as an isolated phenomenon or an abstract legal and moral conundrum, but as a running motif in the experiences of very specific poor and affluent, black and white, immigrant and native, parent and child, male and female individuals. And the charged clash of deeply-felt views on abortion comes not in the form of rhetorical debate or contrived conflicts, but in the complex responses of flawed, endearing human beings to ever-changing life circumstances.

Part I of Parnell's drama reaches back to the 1880s, to illuminate the suffering and deaths caused by illegal abortions of that period and the lasting effect of that suffering on Dr. Wilbur Larch, a Harvard medical student who becomes a dedicated orphanage director—and illicit abortionist. Entwining this narrative is a humorous and touching account of how, in the 1920s, Homer Wells comes to spend his entire childhood at the St. Cloud's, Maine home for orphans, as the surrogate son and medical protégé of the childless bachelor, Larch.

In *The Cider House Rules, Part II* (which can be performed immediately following Part I or on a separate evening), the teenaged Homer Wells rejects his mentor's values and plans for him and moves out into the world beyond the safe but troubling haven of St. Cloud's. Over time, the unexpected encounters and complications the adult Homer experiences ultimately alter his idea of what the proper "rules" of conduct are, revise his understanding of Larch and reshape his concept of heroism.

It is rare in the modern theater that a play has the elbow room to do what a serialized Dickens novel could—trace the gradual transformation of a person's values and attitudes on a canvas large enough to accommodate it. The challenging process of bringing this kind of wide-spanning fiction to the stage began with noted film and stage actor Tom Hulce obtaining Irving's blessing to adapt the best-selling novel. Co-directors Hulce and Jones, and playwright Parnell, then spent several years sculpting a comprehensive but workable stage text from a book of nearly 600 pages. Readings and workshops at the Julliard School, Lincoln Center Theater, Trinity Repertory Company, the Atlantic Theater and other institutions helped nurture the demanding piece along, as did a dedicated core group of actors (several from Jones's Seattle-based literary drama troupe, Book-It Theater) who stayed with the process over the long haul.

Cider House Rules also benefitted from the ongoing commitment of the nonprofit Seattle Repertory Theater and from Seattle theater patrons who responded wholeheartedly to the generous, moving, funny, disturbing yarn in its various incarnations. Even many of those subscribers who swore they could not sit happily through a play that exceeded seven hours (as it did in its early phases) found themselves not only caught up in the experience but regretful to see it end.

Will *The Cider House Rules* someday regale audiences on Broadway, as *Nicholas Nickleby* did? Perhaps—and maybe not, given its large cast, touchy subject and sometimes graphic subject matter and extraordinary time demands. But if there is any justice at all, the play will certainly have a continued life in the American theater and serve as a shining example of what can happen when a gripping yarn is respectfully, creatively transferred from the page to the living, breathing stage.

—MISHA BERSON

Excerpts From *The Cider House Rules, Part II*

As *The Cider House Rules, Part II* opens in the late 1930s, the teenaged Homer is about to leave home for the first time, to visit a Maine apple farm with two new friends, Wally and Candy. But first, there is a choral synopsis of *The Cider House Rules* plot so far.

ENTIRE COMPANY: Here in St. Cloud's,
OLIVE: In St. Cloud's, Maine in the 1920s . . .

LARCH: Dr. Wilbur Larch, founder of the St. Cloud's hospital and orphanage ..... was an obstetrician. He delivered babies into the world. His colleagues called this ...

ENTIRE COMPANY: "The Lord's work."

LARCH: And he was an abortionist. He delivered mothers, too. His colleagues called this ...

ENTIRE COMPANY: "The Devil's work."

SNOWY: But it was ALL the Lord's work to Wilbur Larch.

LARCH: Everything we do, we do FOR the orphans. We deliver THEM!

NURSE EDNA: It was not until the 1930s that they encountered their first problem.

HOMER: His name was

ENTIRE COMPANY: Homer Wells.

NURSE ANGELA: Homer Wells came back to St. Cloud's so many times, after so many failed foster families, that he began to think of St. Cloud's as his home.

HOMER: I'd like to stay, Dr. Larch. I'd like—I want to stay.

LARCH: Well, then, Homer, I expect you to be of use.

HOMER: For Homer Wells, this was easy. Of use, he felt, was all that an orphan was born to be.

CURLY DAY: One day, walking back from the incinerator, Homer saw something on the ground.

WILBUR WALSH: He ran with it, straight to Dr. Larch.

HOMER: I found something.

LARCH: It was about three months—at the most, four. Not quite quick, but almost.

HOMER: What is it?

LARCH: The Lord's work.

HOMER: The Lord's work?

LARCH: Yes, Homer. The Lord's work.

NURSE ANGELA: And so his education began.

LARCH: I'm going to teach you surgery, my boy. You're going to be my assistant .....

NURSE ANGELA: With his discovery that a fetus—as early as eight weeks—has an expression, Homer Wells felt in the presence of what some call a soul.

HOMER: I won't perform an abortion. Not ever.

LARCH: Perhaps you're having second thoughts about becoming a doctor.

HOMER: I never really had a first thought about it. Never said I wanted to be.

CANDY: Hi. I'm Candy Kendall.

HOMER: Homer Wells.

WALLY: I'm Wally Worthington. I've got an idea. Why not come back with us? We can pick up some trees and bring them back here to plant. Apples. An orchard.

HOMER (to Larch): He's a real Prince of Maine, Dr. Larch! He's a real King of New England!

LARCH: Of course you should go, Homer. It's—a great opportunity ...

Engrossed in the world of apple farming and infatuated with Candy, Homer stays on at Heart's Haven. He writes a letter to Dr. Larch:

HOMER: "Dear Dr. Larch . . . Tonight I realized something, and I don't know what to do about it . . . " *(Pause.)* Wonder if I should tell him. Maybe not . . . *(Writes.)* "The folks here at the apple mart are strange. There's a man, Herb Fowler, who hands everybody prophylactics . . . " *(Scratches this out.)* Don't think I should tell him about Herb, either. *(Writes.)* "I miss you." No, he'll think that'll mean I want to come back . . . *(Pause.)* "The swimming lessons with Candy are going well. Candy is so beautiful when she swims. Also, when she plays tennis. And she drives her own car—and knows how to use jumper cables! . . . " *(Stops writing.)* Candy . . . At night, when I'm in Wally's room, I try not to think about Candy . . .

At the cider mill, Homer also gets to know the black migrant laborers led by their tough but friendly crew boss, Mr. Rose.

HOMER: So this is where you all live?

MR. ROSE: Yes, Homer. This is crew quarters. Mrs. Worthington always makes it nice for us. She puts fresh flowers everywhere.

HOMER: What are these?

MR. ROSE: Those are the rules.

HOMER: The rules?

MUDDY: The cider house rules.

HOMER *(reads):*   One. Please don't operate the grinder or the press if you've been drinking. Two. Please don't smoke in bed or use candles. Three. Please don't go up on the roof if you've been drinking—especially at night. Four. Please don't take bottles with you when you go up on the roof. What's all this about the roof?

PEACHES: You can see the ocean from the roof.

MR. ROSE: At night, you can see the Ferris wheel and the carnival lights in Cape Kenneth.

MUDDY: We sit up on the roof all night, some nights.

PEACHES: We get drunk up there and fall off, some nights.

MUDDY: One night, last year, Peaches got so drunk and sweaty, running the press, that he passed out in the cold storage and woke up with pneumonia.

HOMER: You don't exactly wake up with pneumonia, Muddy. It's more complicated than that.

MUDDY: Really?

MR. ROSE: You can listen to Homer. He's a smart man.

MUDDY: Anyway, nobody pays no attention to them rules. Every year, Mrs. Worthington writes them up, and every year, nobody pays no attention.

Back in St. Cloud's, the aging Dr. Larch is hatching a plot to make Homer his successor at the orphanage. Larch invents a heart condition for Homer, to excuse him from hard labor and Army service. And he "borrows" the identity of a dead orphan, Fuzzy Stone, to concoct a "Dr. Stone," complete with medical credentials.

Part of the ruse is a two-way correspondence Larch invents with the imaginary Fuzzy.

FUZZY *(curtly):* Dear Dr. Larch. I just received your last letter. I feel it my duty to search my soul regarding my personal debt to you, as opposed to the perhaps larger debt to society, and to all the murdered unborn of the future . . .

LARCH: Good one!

FUZZY: It is, frankly, hard for me to listen to my conscience and not turn you in to the authorities . . . I suggest we cease all present communications . . .

LARCH *(at typewriter):* Sincerely . . .

FUZZY and LARCH: Dr. F. Stone . . .
          Pause.

LARCH: Thank you, Fuzzy. You will be my perfect replacement. One who is acceptable to the authorities. You will also be my perfect lie. You will be on record as claiming to be against the very thing you shall continue to perform. You will play a role in life that is more strenuous than you ever could have been capable of.
          Fuzzy disappears.

The fact that you died when you were eight years old is beside the point. *(Pause.)* Now. The only question is . . . How will I get Homer Wells to play the part?

Homer is now passionately in love with Candy, Wally's fiancee. One night, Homer blurts out his feelings to Candy.

HOMER: No doubt, Homer Wells misunderstood the unfamiliar weight he felt upon his heart. What he felt was only love. But what he thought he felt was his pulmonary valve stenosis. (*Homer puts his hands to his chest. He has trouble breathing.*) I . . . I . . .

CANDY *(looks at him, suddenly upset):* Is it your heart? Oh God, you don't have to say anything—please don't even think about it!

HOMER: My heart. You know about my heart?

CANDY: YOU know?!

HOMER: I . . . I . . .

CANDY: Don't worry!

HOMER: I love you . . .

CANDY: Yes, I know. Don't think about it. Don't worry about anything. I love you, too.

HOMER: What? You DO . . . ?

CANDY: Yes. Yes. And Wally, too. I love you AND I love Wally. But don't worry about it . . .

HOMER: What defined. . . . ?

CANDY: Don't even think about it.

In 1941, when the U.S. enters World War II, Wally enlists in the Army Air Corps, while Homer stays behind to help Candy and her mother run the apple orchard.

One day, they receive news that Wally was shot down over Burma and is missing in action. Homer and Candy comfort one another.

    Night. Homer and Candy walk to the cider house.
    COMPANY MEMBER: That night in August, the trees were full, the boughs bent and heavy
    COMPANY MEMBER: And the apples—all but the bright, waxy-green Gravensteins—
    COMPANY MEMBER: Were a pale green-going-to-pink.
    COMPANY MEMBER: The grass in the rows between the trees was knee-high.
    COMPANY MEMBER: There would be one more mowing before the harvest.
    COMPANY MEMBER: That night, there was an owl hooting from the orchard called Cock Hill.
    COMPANY MEMBER: Candy and Homer also heard a fox bark from the orchard called Frying Pan.
    HOMER: Foxes can climb trees.
    CANDY: No, they can't.
    HOMER: Apple trees, anyway. Wally told me. What is it?
    CANDY: The rain. Do you think it sounds as loud as that? Over there?
    HOMER: I don't know.
    CANDY: And the smell of the cider apples. It smells like the floor of the jungle . . .
    Homer enters the cider house, holding Candy.

Candy is soon pregnant with Homer's child and trying to miscarry. Homer urges Candy to marry him; out of loyalty to Wally, she refuses. But she agrees to go with him to St. Cloud's, give birth at Larch's orphanage and pretend the baby is an orphan she's adopted. Larch welcomes them and one night gives Homer hints about his "Dr. Stone" plan.

    HOMER: What IS all this about Fuzzy Stone? Fuzzy Stone died years ago . . .
    LARCH: The way you carved the turkey tonight. You haven't lost your touch.
    HOMER: My touch?
    LARCH: Your knife work. Very fine. *(Pause.)* How's the missionary work been going, Fuzzy? In India?
    HOMER: Missionary work? India? I don't know what . . .
    LARCH: How's your reading? Have you been studying the Greenhill? And the *New England Journal of Medicine.* And *JAMA.*
    HOMER: Listen to me. I'm not Fuzzy. And I'm not going to get taken in by you, either.
    LARCH: Taken in?
    HOMER: I know what you're doing by bringing up all this doctor business. And it won't work.
    LARCH: Homer, don't you see what is going on? Since you two have come back, you're making a home for yourselves—and Candy is happy here . . .

HOMER: We're not staying. We're only here until the baby comes.

LARCH: If you stay, you can be a real married couple here.

HOMER: And have to live by your rules?

LARCH: Rules? What rules?

HOMER: The rules you make everybody here live by! And stop talking to Candy behind my back! Telling her that I have a gift—

LARCH: You DO have a gift! A great one! And you are throwing it away!

HOMER: By becoming a father? And an apple farmer! And maybe a lobsterman?!

LARCH: You don't know the first thing about—

HOMER: I'm learning, goddammit! I learned obstetrical procedure, right?! And the far easier procedure—the one that is against MY rules!

LARCH: Selfish you are! When you won't even try and help the women who have nowhere else to go!

HOMER: They come to YOU!

LARCH: And for how long?! Look at me, Homer. Look. Do you really think I can keep going on like this forever? *(Pause.)* Listen to me. You know who the doctor is!

HOMER: It's you! You're the doctor!

After bringing their new son, Angel, home to Heart's Haven, Candy and Homer learn that Wally is alive but paralyzed and wheelchair-bound. The couple make a pact.

CANDY: Let's agree to something.

HOMER: Okay.

CANDY: Whatever happens, we share Angel.

HOMER: Of course.

CANDY: We both get to be his parents. Regardless of what happens. We both get to live with him. We get to be his family. Nobody ever moves out.

HOMER: In the same house? Even if you go with Wally?

CANDY: Like a family.

HOMER: Like a family.

> *Candy picks up a baby and holds it in her arms. Wally appears and sits in a wheelchair.*

WALLY: Candy and Wally had been married less than a month after Wally returned to Ocean View. Wally weighed one hundred and forty-seven pounds.

HOMER: And Homer pushed the wheelchair down the church aisle.

As time passes, Candy and Homer continue their clandestine affair. Wally remains innocent of it (or pretends to), and Angel grows into adolescence without knowing who his real parents are. Now very elderly, Larch is still running the orphanage at St. Cloud's but doubting his medical competence.

NURSE EDNA: Wilbur? Listen to me, please. You're NOT too old. You're NOT incompetent. You're NOT too old . . .

THE CIDER HOUSE RULES—A scene from the 1997 Seattle Repertory Theater production of the play adapted by Peter Parnell from the novel by John Irving

LARCH: But Wilbur Larch couldn't hear her. He was too busy writing a letter. He told Homer everything. He told him about Fuzzy Stone. He did not beg. He said he was sure Angel would accept his father's sacrifice. He'll value your need to be of use . . .

. . . Here is the trap you are in, Homer. And it's not my trap—I haven't trapped you. Because abortions are illegal, women who need and want them have no choice in the matter, and you—because you know how to perform them—have no choice, either. What has been violated here is your freedom of choice, and every woman's freedom of choice, too. If abortion was legal, a woman would have a choice—and so would you. You would feel free not to do it because someone else would. But the way it is, you're trapped. Women are trapped, and so are you. You are my work of art. Everything else has just been a job . . . I don't know if you've got a work of art in you, but I know what your job is, and you know what it is, too. You're the doctor.

One day soon after, Larch returns home from a short trip and accidentally overdoses on ether. At Heart's Haven, Homer is rocked by the news of Larch's death. And then he learns that his son Angel's girl friend, Rose Rose, is locked in an incestuous relationship with her migrant-worker father, Mr. Rose.

> *Jack calls, rushing in.*

JACK: Mr. Wells! Mr. Wells! You gotta come quickly!

HOMER: What . . . ?

JACK: It's Candy and Angel! They're at the cider house . . .

> *Candy and Angel approach the cider house.*

ANGEL: Rose!

MUDDY: You can't go in there. Mr. Rose, he make his own rules.

ANGEL: What do you mean . . . ? Where is Rose . . . ?

MUDDY: They in there.

ANGEL: You mean . . . ?

> *A scream from inside.*

CANDY: My God. Oh, my God . . .

> *Another cry. Mr. Rose emerges from the cider house.*

MR. ROSE: I don't hurt her. I just love her is all.

ANGEL: Love her?!

CANDY: Angel—go away!

MR. ROSE: I been protecting her. My own flesh and blood. Protecting her, you understand? The first man she with, he no good. Not good enough for her.

ANGEL: And you're the only one good enough for her?!

MR. ROSE: Things ain't always easy to explain, son.

ANGEL: ROSE!

> *He starts to go in. Homer appears.*

HOMER: Angel! No!

> *Mr. Rose turns him round lightly, twisting his arm. He lets Angel go. Angel starts back at him, but Mr. Rose falters slightly.*

MR. ROSE: Good, son. You defend her. But, she . . . she good. She already take care of herself.

> *Mr. Rose buckles. He has already been knifed.*

Where she get the knife, Muddy?

MUDDY: What knife?

MR. ROSE: It look like your knife—what I seen of it. *(Pause.)*

MUDDY: I gave it to her.

MR. ROSE: Thank you for doin' that, Muddy. She good with that knife. She almost the best. And who taught her?

> *Rose Rose emerges from the cider house.*

ROSE ROSE: You did.

MR. ROSE: That right. That why you almost as good as me. Where's Homer?

HOMER: Right here, Mr. Rose.

MR. ROSE: You got a good boy there. A good kid. You take care of him.

HOMER: I will.

MR. ROSE *(whispers):* You breakin' them rules, too, Homer. Say you know how I feel.

HOMER: I know how you feel.

MR. ROSE *(grinning):*   Right. You tell them I stabbed myself. I mean to kill myself. My daughter run away. And I so sorry that I stuck myself. You hearin' this right, Homer?

HOMER: Yes, Mr. Rose, I'm hearing it.

MR. ROSE: That how you report it . . . According to the rules . . .

HOMER: According to the rules . . .

>   *Mr. Rose collapses, dies.*

Homer decides to return to St. Cloud's and assume the false "Dr. Fuzzy Stone" identity Dr. Larch had prepared for him. He takes over the orphanage (and abortion practice) and finds a new relationship with a sympathetic young nurse, Caroline. But the spirit of Dr. Larch lingers on.

The Cider House Rules, Part II *was first produced at the Seattle Repertory Theater, on the same program with* The Cider House Rules, Part I, *January 15, 1997 under the direction of Tom Hulce and Jane Jones.*

ATCA New Play Citation

OOO
OOO
OOO
OOO
OOO
OOO **JITNEY**

A Play in Two Acts

BY AUGUST WILSON

Cast and credits appear on page 404 of *The Best Plays of 1996–97*

AUGUST WILSON was born in 1945 in the Hill District of Pittsburgh, where his father worked as a baker and his mother determinedly introduced her son to the written word and had him reading at 4 years old. Despite his early acquaintance and continuing fascination with words, he didn't pursue a formal education, leaving Central Catholic High School before graduating. He can clearly remember when he began to approach writing as a profession: it was April 1, 1965. He had just earned $20 writing a term paper for his sister, and he bought a typewriter which, he remembers, "represented my total commitment" because it took every penny he had. Lacking bus fare, he carried it home.

Wilson started with poetry. By 1972 he was writing one-acts. His first production was Jitney, *staged in 1978 by Black Horizons Theater, a group which he himself had founded in 1968. This play, rewritten as a full-length and produced last season at Pittsburgh Public Theater, now wins him an ATCA citation. Set in the Hill District in 1971, it takes a chronological place representing the 1970s in the subsequent parade of Wilson plays about black Americans.*

The one-act version of Jitney *was repeated in 1982 by Allegheny Repertory Theater and in 1985 by Penumbra Theater in St. Paul; meanwhile Wilson's* Black Bart and the Sacred Hill *was produced in 1981 by Penumbra. Then came* Ma Rainey's Black Bottom. *After a staged reading at the O'Neill Theater Center in 1982 and production by Yale Repertory Theater April 3, 1984 (both organizations and the play itself directed by Lloyd Richards),* Ma Rainey *was brought to Broadway October 11, 1984 for 275 performances, its author's first full New York production, first Best Play, first Tony nominee and the winner of the New York Drama Critics Circle citation as the season's best play.*

All six of Wilson's New York productions have been named Best Plays, all figured prominently in the Critics citations, and all have been directed by Richards. Wilson's Fences *was also developed at the O'Neill and premiered at Yale Rep April 25, 1985, receiving the first annual American Theater Critics Association New Play Award, as recorded in* The Best Plays of 1985–86. *It was produced on Broadway March 26, 1987 for 526 performances and carried off the Critics best-of-bests citation, the Pulitzer Prize and the Tony Awards for both play and direction. A year later,* Fences *was still running when Wilson's* Joe Turner's Come and Gone *opened on Broadway March 27, 1988 after previous stagings at Yale Rep and the Huntington Theater Company, Boston.* Joe Turner *won its author his third Best Play and third Critics Award for best-of-bests, playing 105 performances.*

During the 1987–88 season, Wilson's The Piano Lesson *received an O'Neill tryout, followed by a Goodman Theater, Chicago production cited by ATCA for its fourth New Play Award. It came to Broadway April 16, 1990 for a run of 329 performances, and in the course of its career it received its author's fourth Best Play citation, fourth Critics best-of-bests Award and second Pulitzer Prize. Wilson's* Two Trains Running *had already received the ATCA New Play Award after four regional theater productions when it arrived on Broadway April 13, 1992 for 160 performances, its author's fifth straight Best Play and Critics Award winner (for best American play).*

About the same time as its opening on Broadway March 28, 1996, Wilson's Seven Guitars *received an ATCA 1995 New Play Citation.* Seven Guitars *played 187 Broadway performances, made it an even half dozen Best Plays for Wilson and won his sixth Critics Award (for best-of-bests). It is one of the seven full-length plays in its author's cycle about the life of black Americans through the decades:* Joe Turner *(the Teens),* Ma Rainey *(1920s),* Piano Lesson *(1930s),* Seven Guitars *(1940s),* Fences *(1950s),* Two Trains *(1960s) and now* Jitney *(1970s).*

Wilson is an alumnus of New Dramatists (which presented his The Mill Hand's Lunch Bucket *in staged readings in 1983 and 1984) and the Playwrights Center in Minneapolis. He is a Whiting Writers Award winner, a recipient of Bush, McKnight, Rockefeller and Guggenheim Fellowships and is a member of the American Academy of Arts and Sciences and the American Academy of Arts and Letters. He is married to the costume designer Constanza Romero, has one daughter and makes his home in Seattle.*

INTRODUCTION: As August Wilson built his extraordinary African-American dramatic epic, moving briskly toward his goal of a play set in each decade of the 20th century, he always said his 1970s play was already in place. But as the Wilson rocket ignited with the 1982 workshop of *Ma Rainey's Black Bottom* at the O'Neill Theater Center, and as six plays were staged on Broadway and at regional theaters, *Jitney* remained quietly left behind.

Jitney had been written soon after Wilson moved to St. Paul, leaving his native Pittsburgh—which remains the setting of all his major plays except *Ma Rainey*. He had just been back to Pittsburgh on a visit, and the idea came to him on the drive back to St. Paul. "I wrote it in ten days," he says. It played a key role in his career.

Dealing realistically with life as he had known it in Pittsburgh's Hill District, it is the first surviving play in what turned out to be his mature style.

After a 1978 premiere in Pittsburgh, *Jitney* went on to a 1980 reading at the Playwrights Center in Minneapolis, which awarded Wilson a Jerome Fellowship— "manna from heaven"—which made it possible for him to persevere as a playwright. After stagings at Pittsburgh's Allegheny Repertory Theater in 1982 and St. Paul's Penumbra Theater (1985), *Jitney* was left untouched until Edward Gilbert, artistic director of the Pittsburgh Public Theater, asked to give it professional rebirth in June 1996. Working with director Marion McClinton, Wilson added a new scene and expanded an uncharacteristically terse text from 90 minutes to two hours—an unusual process for a playwright who usually has to pare.

Skillfully staged, it revealed itself as a comic, heart-tugging drama of generational struggle. Wilson has always been a poet of expressive street language heightened into a supple instrument of conflict and revelation, but *Jitney* reminds us he is also a poet of the heart. As always, his characters are instinctive story tellers, and he still finds rich humor in both aspiration and defeat. But *Jitney* transcends cultural specificity with its vivid depiction of the casual ambush of the heart amid the drone of daily life in a scruffy jitney (unlicensed taxi) station in Pittsburgh's Hill District. A father-son relationship is the spine of the play, but we discover this slowly and late. Becker, a fair, strong man, runs the station; his son, Booster, is about to be released from the penitentiary after 20 years without a single visit from his father. But Wilson focuses first on the interactions among the other men and the reflection they provide of life outside. They play checkers, joke, argue, reminisce, fight—Wilson's characteristically vivid mix of comedy and passion, backed by a solid sociology of men struggling to survive. "That's my business," they say. But where does business stop? We feel the crackle of emotion under taut skin.

An explosive meeting between father and son is the Act I climax. A terse meeting in Act II leaves Booster still bottled up. Wilson lets the mood brighten while holding the main conflict smoldering in the distance. When Booster learns of Becker's sudden death, he erupts in a violent wail. The final scene is elegiac, the village gathering to mourn and sustain. At the last moment, Booster seems to accept the mantle of his dead father with a gesture that allows the audience tentative closure. Wilson has written of fathers and sons before, most emphatically in *Fences*. But he has never written of it more movingly. If it takes a wise father to know his own son, the reverse is just as true.

In April, 1997, *Jitney* was re-staged at the Crossroads Theater in New Brunswick, N.J., one of the country's leading black theaters. Wilson's first pre-New York staging by a black company was a timely pendant to his much-discussed public debate with Robert Brustein about the balance between black theaters and white.

For Crossroads, working with a new director, Walter Dallas, Wilson added a five-page scene to Act II, pointed the dialogue and changed the time from 1971 to 1977. The cast was mainly the same as in Pittsburgh, except for Youngblood and Booster—but since Booster is central, that mattered a lot. On balance, the Pittsburgh staging had greater intensity, a more seamless magic than at Crossroads, where Dallas set a sunnier tone. Jerome Preston Bates was a rangy, charismatic Booster, but in Pittsburgh, Leland Gantt's controlled anger made the confrontations more telling and his release into grief more heart-rending. Paul Butler's Becker remained a powerful presence at Crossroads, but softer. To some degree, he is. A sensitive speech about marriage was added, and the new scene in which Becker decides to fight city hall, however preachy, is an important development for Becker, who had spent his life accommodating to "the man." This feeds into the argument between Becker and Booster about integrity. Becker has grown.

Jitney is still evolving. As we go to press, the next production is targeted for Boston's Huntington Theater in October 1998, once again directed by McClinton (also a playwright who, incidentally, played Becker in St. Paul in 1985). "We're going to scrap everything else, the set and the costumes and the actors," Wilson told the *Pittsburgh Post-Gazette* in March. "We may use some of the same actors, but we're going to start over, and I'm going to do rewrites, particularly the Becker-Booster scenes. I want to rethink the whole character of Booster and their relationship; I wrote that eighteen, nineteen years ago, and I think maybe if I re-imagine it, now that I'm more mature, they'll say different things."

—CHRISTOPHER RAWSON

Excerpts From *Jitney*

The two following excerpts are presented out of order. The play's vivid interaction among the jitney drivers is well represented by the first excerpt, taken from the start of Act II. That interaction in general forms the background for the conflict between father and son, seen here in the final scene of Act I.

> *The time is early fall, 1977. The setting is a gypsy cab station in Pittsburgh, Pennsylvania. The paint is peeling off the walls, and the floor is covered with linoleum that is worn through in several areas. In the middle of the wall stage left sits an old-fashioned pot-bellied stove that dominates the room. Upstage of it is a blackboard on which is written the rates to different parts of the city—and the daily, marginally illegal policy numbers. Downstage on the wall is a pay telephone. The entire right wall is made up of the entrance down right and a huge picture window. Along the upstage wall is a sofa, with several chairs of various styles and ages scattered about to complete the setting . . . . .*
>
> *Doub sits in one of the chairs reading a newspaper . . . . .*

TURNBO: Now here's another something I don't understand. Lena Horne. How come everybody say she pretty? I even hear some people say she's the prettiest woman in the world.

DOUB: I ain't gonna say all that. But if she ain't, she right up there.

TURNBO: She ain't as pretty as Sarah Vaughn.

DOUB: Naw. Naw. We talking about Lena Horne. Some things just ain't open to debate. Lena Horne being pretty is one of them.

TURNBO: Sarah Vaughn got more nature than Lena Horne.

DOUB: What's that supposed to mean? Even if she do . . . how you gonna measure it? It ain't like saying she got more hair or something.

TURNBO: She got a prettier smile, too. A lot of people sleeping on Sarah Vaughn.

DOUB: How you know how many people sleeping with her?

TURNBO: I said sleeping on her, not with her. Everybody talking about Lena Horne and people sleeping on Sarah Vaughn. People don't know Sarah Vaughn got more of everything than Lena Horne. They just believe what they hear. But Sarah Vaughn got more nature . . . got a prettier smile . . . got more personality . . . and she can sing better.

DOUB: We ain't said nothing about that. We ain't said nothing about singing. You said Lena Horne wasn't pretty.

TURNBO: She ain't. She ain't pretty as people think. People just think she pretty.

DOUB: Oh, I see . . . people just think dogs bite. People just think if you cut yourself, you'll bleed.

Fielding enters.

Hey, Fielding . . . Turnbo say Lena Horne ain't pretty.

FIELDING: Some people say shit don't stink. Sooner or later, they gonna find out otherwise. It's them pretty women like Lena Horne get a man killed.

TURNBO: You ain't got to be pretty to get a man killed. Any woman will get any man killed if he ain't careful. Am I right, Doub? I seen it happen.

DOUB: You right. That's why I don't talk about women. I don't talk about money either. Them is the two things you never hear me talk about too much. Them is the two things that get most people killed.

FIELDING: Women and money will get a preacher killed.

TURNBO: I seen it happen. You go and ask one of them fellows, say "Why you do that?" You have to catch him after he cooled down. You have to get him down there in the jail after about six or nine months and you ask him why he killed so and so. And he'll tell you. He'll say Geraldine, or Betty Sue, or whoever stayed on my mind so I couldn't think right. Then when I seen . . . Rufus . . . or Leroy . . . or John D talking to her, it seem like he was the cause of all my trouble. See . . . first thing a man do when he get a woman, he don't want nobody else to have her. He say this is mine. I'm gonna hold on to this. I'm gonna go over and see Betty Jean . . . but I'm gonna hold on to this. If I see anybody sneaking around her sniffing . . . I'm gonna bust his nose and break both of his legs . . . if I don't shoot him with my 44. He say that, and then he go on over to Betty Jean. He don't know some fellow done said the same thing about catching somebody around Betty Jean. That fellow . . . he go over to see Betty Sue, while this other fellow sniffing around his Betty Jean. Sooner or later . . . somebody gonna get their wires crossed. Somebody gonna see Betty Sue when he should have been seeing Betty Jean, and that'll be all she wrote for him. The only thing left to do is to write it on his tombstone. "Here lie Bubba Boo. Was caught with Betty Jean instead of Betty Sue." Yeah, now Betty Jean and Betty Sue, they gonna meet up at the undertaker's, and what you think they gonna talk about? "Oh, you use Dixie Peach? I never did like that. I use Royal

Crown. It keeps my hair looking nice. Where you buy you stocking at? Is that Midnight in Paris you wearing? That smell good." You think I'm lying. Go ask Foster. The man laying there cold and stiff as a board, and they talking about perfume and hair grease. You hear what I'm saying?

DOUB: I wouldn't doubt it.

TURNBO: You go ask Foster. See if I ain't right.

> *The phone rings. Fielding answers it.*

FIELDING: Car service. *(Pause.)* Yeah, sure I'll tell him. Turnbo, that was Aunt Lil. She say you supposed to pick her up at the doctor's.

TURNBO: You know she done joined the Jehovah Witness. When I come back, I'll be able to tell you everything you wanna know about the Bible.

> *Turnbo exits reluctantly. Fielding starts to lie down on the couch as the phone rings. He goes to answer it.*

FIELDING: Car service. *(Pause.)* Yeah, I'll be right there. Green car.

DOUB: No, wait a minute. I thought Becker put you out.

FIELDING: Aw, me and Becker straight.

> *Fielding exits as Youngblood enters carrying a cup of coffee.*

YOUNGBLOOD: Hey, Doub, what's this I hear about the station closing?

DOUB: You just now finding out? They fixing to board up the whole block. Tear it down and build some houses.

YOUNGBLOOD: Damn! What they wanna do that for?

DOUB: I'm glad to see them do it. It's about time they done something around here. They been talking for years about how they was gonna fix it up.

YOUNGBLOOD: White folks ain't got no sense of timing. They wait till I get in the position to buy me a house, and then they pull the rug out from under me!

DOUB: That white man ain't paying you no mind. You ought to stop thinking like that. They been planning to tear these shacks down before you was born. You keep thinking everybody's against you and you ain't never gonna get nothing. I seen a hundred niggers too lazy to get up out bed in the morning, talking about the white man is against them. That's just an excuse. You want to make something of your life, then the opportunity is there. You just have to shake off that "White folks is against me" attitude. Hell, they don't even know you alive . . . . .

> *The lights come up on the jitney station . . . . . Turnbo and Fielding have been joined by Booster who sits upstage on the sofa. He is dressed in his prison-issued suit and wears a white shirt without a tie.*

FIELDING: Yeah, I know your Daddy real good.

> *He drinks from the bottle and offers it to Booster, who declines.*

I've been driving jitneys with him for eight years now. And I used to know him when he was down at the mill, too. That's when I was younger. Here, get yourself a nip.

BOOSTER: Naw, that's all right. You say he should be back in a minute?

TURNBO: He went out on a trip. He'll be back directly. Things done changed since the last time you seen them, I reckon.

BOOSTER: Yeah, pretty much.

JITNEY—Russell Andrews (Youngblood), Paul Butler (Becker) and Stephen McKinley Henderson (Turnbo) in a scene from the Pittsburgh Public Theater production of the play by August Wilson

TURNBO: They're tearing everything down around here. They done tore down part of the Irene Kaufman Settlement House, and all along Wylie there. You see they done tore down and they say they gonna build up.

FIELDING: You got to have somebody you can count on, you know. Now, my wife . . . we've been separated for twenty-two years now . . . but I ain't never loved nobody the way I loved that woman. You know what I mean?

BOOSTER: Yeah, I know.

FIELDING: She the only thing in the world that I got. I had a dream once. It just touched me so. I was climbing this ladder. It was a solid gold ladder, and I was climbing up into heaven. I get to the top of the ladder, and I can see all the saints sitting around . . . and I could see her, too . . . sitting there in her place in glory. Just as I reached the top, my hand started to slip and I called out for help. All them saints and angels . . . St. Peter and everybody . . . they just sat there and looked at me. She was the only one who left her seat in glory and tried to help me to keep from falling back down that ladder. I ain't never forgot that. When I woke up . . . tears was all over my face, just running all down in my ears, and I laid there and cried like a baby . . . 'cause that meant so much to me. To find out after all these years that she still loved me.

BOOSTER: That's some heavy drama, my man.

FIELDING: Oh, she love me all right. I know she do. I ain't seen that woman in twenty-two years . . . but I know she loves me.

> *Fielding takes another drink as Becker enters and stands in the doorway glaring at Fielding.*

FIELDING: Hey, Becker. I was just talking to your son.

BECKER: I thought I told you not to be here when I got back.

> *Fielding staggers to his feet.*

FIELDING: All right, Becker. You win. I'm going.

> *Fielding starts toward the door. Becker crosses to the stove and picks up the money.*

BECKER: Take your money with you.

FIELDING: They're gonna board it up, Becker. Turnbo told me. Let me work the two weeks. I'll be sober in the morning. It's almost over, Becker. It's almost over.

BECKER: Go on home, Fielding. I'll see you in the morning.

> *Fielding exits. Becker turns to face Booster.*

BOOSTER: How you doing, Pop.

> *Booster holds out his hand. Becker takes it awkwardly.*

BECKER: Fine. Fine. How you doing, Clarence? You look good.

BOOSTER: I feel pretty good. Lucille told me you'd be down here. I just stopped by to see you. See how you doing.

BECKER: Turnbo, go next door and tell Clifford to see me one of those fish sandwiches, will you?

> *Turnbo exits reluctantly.*

So? What you gonna do now with the rest of your life? The part that you ain't ruined?

BOOSTER: Live it. Like everybody else.

BECKER: That ain't what I mean, boy, and you know it. What you gonna do about a job?

BOOSTER: I don't know. I ain't thought about it.

BECKER: I know some people down at the mill. I could get you on. You can make a decent living.

BOOSTER: No thanks, Pop. That's not for me. That's why I didn't accept that parole five years ago. I figured after all that time, five more years wouldn't make that much difference, and when I got out, I would be free. Would have no parole officer telling me to get a job and watching over me to see what I do. Naw, I didn't want that. Now, I'm my own man. I don't owe nobody nothing.

BECKER: You don't want to work, huh? Want to be your own man? You don't owe nobody nothing? Well, who in the hell's gonna take care of you? How you gonna live? What you gonna eat?

BOOSTER: I can take care of myself. I'm not eighteen years old anymore. I don't expect nobody to take care of me. I'll make some money some kind of way.

BECKER: Some kind of way, huh? You done went down there to the penitentiary and found a new way to make money other than working?

BOOSTER: Pop, I don't want this between us. I just wanted to stop and say Hi and see how you was doing.

BECKER: I'm doing fine. I ain't spent twenty years of my life locked up behind bars like an animal. I'm doing just fine. I got me a wife . . . a little house. It ain't much . . . but it's mine. I can come and go when I want to. I can go downtown, go to a movie. Go to a club. Hear some music. I'm doing just fine. What about you? Mr. I Don't Want To Work. Mr. I Got A New Way To Make Money. Mr. Walk In Here To Say Hi To Pop After Twenty Years Like You Been On Vacation. Mr. I Don't Owe Nobody Nothing.

BOOSTER: You can't change me, Pop. I'm a grown man.

BECKER: You ain't nothing! After twenty years, I'm looking at you and I can see you ain't nothing. You less than the day you was born.

BOOSTER: What is you? You a big man? You a deacon at the church. Boss of the jitney station. A man with responsibility. You work thirty years in the mill and ain't got a union card. Why? Because you got to work six months straight to get one. They work you five and a half months and lay you off for two weeks. Then you got to start all over. Did you ever tell them bastards to go to hell? Did you ever knock the foreman on his ass when he said you were laid off? Did you ever even ask them why they was keeping you out of the union? No, Pop. You accepted whatever kind of shit they threw your way. And now you want to hold that up as some kind of example for me. I ain't blaming you, Pop. You made your choice. You took your road. You done what was right for you. I can't blame you for that. I'm just saying that's not my way. You can't live through my flesh 'cause I won't let you.

BECKER: What is you way? You talk like a fool.

BOOSTER: I'm a warrior, Pop. Any way they come at me, I'm gonna fight them. They got it all picked out for me. They got a mold they want to put me in. But I ain't gonna let them. Because it's not me. It don't say anything to what I feel kicking in my gut. It don't say anything to my rhythm.

BECKER: Boy, you ain't making no sense. If you wasn't such a hot-headed fool, you never would have been down there in the first place.

BOOSTER: It was a matter of principle. A matter of someone betraying me. I wasn't going to the penitentiary for nothing. I done what I had to do, and it's over and done with now.

BECKER: You want to know why I never came to see you?

BOOSTER: No, I don't want to know. That's your business.

BECKER: I kept seeing your face at your mother's funeral. How you just stood there and never shed a tear. Stood there with a scowl on your face. And now you want to come in here and ridicule me. "Why didn't you knock the foreman on his ass?" You wanna know why? I'll tell you why. Because I had your black ass at home crying to be fed. Crying to have a roof over your head. To have clothes to wear to school and lunch money in your pocket. That's why! Because I had a family. I had responsibility. If I had knocked him on his ass, you would have went hungry. You wouldn't have had clothes on your back or a roof over your head. I done what I had to do. I swallowed my pride and let them mess over me, all the time saying, "You bastards got it coming. Look out! Becker's Boy's coming to straighten this shit out! You're not gonna fuck over him! He's gonna grow big and strong! Watch out for Becker's Boy! Becker's taking this ass-whipping so his boy can stride through this shit like Daniel in the lion's den! Watch out for Becker's Boy! He's coming through. Watch out for Becker's Boy." (*Becker has worked himself into a frenzy and is now near tears.*) And what I get, huh? You tell me. What I get? Tell me what I get! Tell me what I get! Tell me, huh? Tell me! What I Get?

BOOSTER (*moves toward him*): Pop . . .

BECKER: Stay away from me! What I get, huh? What I get? Tell me?
    Booster is silent.
I get a murderer, that's what. A murderer.

BOOSTER: Pop, look . . .

BECKER: And the way your mama loved you. You killed her! You know that? You a double murderer!

BOOSTER: I ain't killed her, Pop. You know that.

BECKER: What you call it? That woman took sick the day that judge sentenced you, and she ain't never walked or said another word or ate another thing for twenty-three days. She just laid up in that room until she died. Now you tell me that ain't killing her! Tell me that ain't killing her! You are my son. I helped to bring you into this world. But from this moment on . . . I'm calling the deal off. You ain't nothing to me. Boy. You just another nigger on the street.
    Becker exits. Booster stands looking down at the floor. The phone rings.
    The lights go down to black.

The full-length version of Jitney *was first produced at the Pittsburgh Public The-ater, June 14, 1996 under the direction of Marion Isaac McClinton.*

ATCA New Play Citation

OOO
OOO
OOO
OOO
OOO
OOO

THE OLD SETTLER

A Play in Two Acts

By JOHN HENRY REDWOOD

Cast and credits appear on page 404 of *The Best Plays of 1996–97*

JOHN HENRY REDWOOD is a stage and screen actor who has appeared in most of August Wilson's plays in regional theater and in The Piano Lesson *on Broadway and now takes a place side by side with Wilson as an ATCA-cited playwright for the 1997 productions of* The Old Settler. *It is by no means Redwood's first play or first award. His past works include* MarkVIII:xxxvi *(1986 AUDELCO Award) and* A Sunbeam *(McDonald's Literary Achievement Award). The Old Settler was previously honored with the 1995 Beverly Hills Theater Guild/Julie Harris and Virginia Duvall Mann Playwrighting Awards. It is to be produced in Russia via a joint arrangement between the Russian Theater Union and the O'Neill Theater Center. Redwood is also the author of the full length* Acted Within Proper Departmental Procedure *and a number of one acts including* What if You're the One? *An ex-Marine, he has also served as Honorary Co-Chairman of the "Race for the Cure" of breast cancer (in 1984), as a Literacy Volunteer and as a board member of Pittsburgh's Dr. Martin Luther King Jr. Cultural and Performing Arts Center. He holds master's degrees in both history and religion and has completed his classwork for a doctorate in the latter. His biographical sketch in* The Old Settler *playbill ends by wishing "God's love and blessings to all."*

INTRODUCTION: Call a play "old-fashioned," and that could be interpreted as dismissive. In the charmingly old-fashioned case of *The Old Settler,* it's a compliment. Here is a well-written, well-constructed play with an interesting beginning, suspenseful middle and satisfying end. Here is a two-act comedy, simply staged with four appealing characters on one set, that respects the traditional Aristotelian unities of plot, character and theme.

It's easy to imagine a Broadway audience of the 1940s or 1950s enjoying *The Old Settler*—except that the commercial theater of that era did not include black playwrights or such full-bodied black characters at center stage. Playwright John Henry Redwood makes the characters and culture of 1940s Harlem live again by blending a sibling rivalry between two aging sisters with a situation that couldn't be more old-fashioned—a hesitant May–October romance between a younger man and an aging black spinster or "old settler."

Yet the two rich female roles are at the core of this observant period piece. Quilly, 53, has just moved into the modest Harlem tenement apartment of her high-minded sister, Bessie, 55. They bicker and fuss one minute, laugh and make up the next. Their stormy history—they were estranged for years after Quilly married the man Bessie loved—colors their relationship, but their arguments are limited by the unspoken mutual understanding that all they really have is each other.

Both are struggling domestic workers. To cover the rent, Bessie has taken in a nice but naive 28-year-old man as a boarder. Husband (an amusingly pointed name) has migrated from the South to find his girlfriend Lou Bessie (the smallest and broadest role), unaware that she has changed her name to Charmaine to fulfill her immature fantasies of big-city sophistication.

Gradually, Bessie's kindness and Husband's respect deepen into a wistful mutual affection—but is it strong enough to withstand Charmaine's manipulative charms and Quilly's jealous cynicism? Is Husband a mamma's boy attracted to Bessie as a mother substitute, or true husband material—and her last best hope for happiness?

The first act sets up the situation with rueful comedy and colorful dialogue; the second act deepens the characters with bittersweet drama. Balancing Redwood's strong sense of character is an equally strong sense of place. *Old Settler* evokes a Harlem in decline from its former glamorous Cotton Club era, but still enough at the center of black America to inspire dreams of dancing at the Savoy Ballroom.

Redwood has a feeling for the period and compassionate understanding for his characters and era. *Old Settler* aptly reflects the social change and conflicts as migrating blacks reconsider their identity, and the homespun values of the rural South give way to the faster pace of the urban North. Yet, much change still lies ahead, for blacks still must give up seats to whites on segregated 1940s trains.

In themes that resonate with today's black culture, *Old Settler* underlines the importance of family, the role of the church and the resilience of black women. More subtly, Redwood explores the lingering effects of slavery on self-image and social expectations. In the end, bowing to the constraints imposed by sex, race, class and history, *Old Settler* affirms a quiet realism over romanticism.

An actor-playwright, Redwood has been compared to James Earl Jones and August Wilson. Significantly, Redwood played Doaker and Avery in Broadway's *The Piano Lesson*. Like Wilson, who clearly has inspired and influenced him, Redwood brings to his work an underlying spirituality and a positive view of black Americans. Above all, *Old Settler* offers an affectionate, understanding and compassionate tribute to black women. In a *Best Plays* interview, Redwood said the play was inspired by his boyhood recollections of Harlem and his upbringing by three women—his late mother and her sister, who lived together for two years before his mother died, and their mother. In fact, Bess was his mother's name; Quilly, a cousin; and Husband, a boy he used to play with. With *Old Settler,* Redwood truly honors his past—but also suggests hope for the future.

Coincidentally, Wilson sparked a recent debate about whether black theater has a future, and whether that future will be separatist. Redwood's *The Old Settler* helps answer that question. With emerging playwrights as talented as Redwood, black theater has a bright future. And with the play being staged across the country—at black and white theaters—it should be clear that the future of black theater will not and should not be separatist. Like all good theater, *Old Settler* brims with a humanity that transcends categories.

—MICHAEL GROSSBERG

Excerpt From *The Old Settler*

QUILLY: Oh, Lord have mercy! Whew! Them stairs. Shoot!

ELIZABETH: You forgot to turn the radio off again, Quilly.

QUILLY: I left it on so these robbers and rapists would think somebody's home. That's the way I did it in Brooklyn.

ELIZABETH: You ain't living in Brooklyn no more. I've got to pay the electric here.

QUILLY: Shoot!

> *Quilly crosses to a chair and sits. She picks up a hand fan from under an end table and begins to fan herself.*

Jesus, it's hot. *(Calling offstage.)* What we got to eat, Bess?

ELIZABETH: You're supposed to be cooking this week. What you asking me for?

QUILLY: If you cook tonight, I'll take two of your nights next week.

ELIZABETH: No you won't. You'll scheme and connive to get out of it just like you're doing now. Cooking all that food on Saturday and then we eat the same old leftovers all week long.

QUILLY: Shoot, Bess, I'm tired. That's the God's honest truth.

ELIZABETH: I don't understand it. You're two years younger than I am and you act like you're five years older.

> *Elizabeth exits to the bedroom taking off her hat.*

QUILLY *(calling offstage):* Age ain't got nothing to do with it, shoot.

ELIZABETH *(from offstage):* You should be tired. Running around like a chicken with his head cut off trying to get to that funeral.

QUILLY: And you still made us late.

ELIZABETH: I'm in no rush to get to no funeral—mine or nobody else's.

QUILLY: I wanted to get a good seat.

ELIZABETH: There's no such thing as a good seat at a funeral, Quilly.

QUILLY: I wanted to get where I could see.

ELIZABETH: I'm surprised you didn't get one of them folding chairs and sit right up front next to the casket.

QUILLY *(ignoring Elizabeth):* Did you see that dress they put on her? That was one ugly dress.

Elizabeth re-enters from the bedroom buttoning her house dress.

ELIZABETH: Her sister said that was her favorite dress. Said her husband wanted to put her away in something she liked and wore when she was living . . .

QUILLY: It was ugly then too, shoot.

ELIZABETH: . . . so her sister picked out that dress.

QUILLY: Quiet as it's kept, that dress probably killed her. Then they put her in all that bright red lipstick. Now they know she was too dark for all that bright red lipstick. Shoot, she looked better when she was living.

ELIZABETH: You're supposed to, Quilly.

QUILLY: That sure is some way to spend eternity: in an ugly dress and bright red lipstick.

ELIZABETH: Quilly, will you please be quiet about that woman.

QUILLY: All I'm saying is, we're sisters, and I hope whichever one of us goes first, the other one does better by her than that poor woman was done by her husband and sister. That's all I'm saying. Shoot. You think he's going to get married again?

ELIZABETH: That woman's not in the ground good, Quilly. He's got to let a decent amount of time pass.

QUILLY: What for? She ain't going to get no deader. *(Quilly stands and begins pulling on her girdle.)* I sure hope they didn't put no girdle on her. She'll be pulling on that thing forever, shoot. *(Pause.)* You getting ready to cook?

ELIZABETH: I told you I wasn't cooking. I'm going to eat that dinner I brought back from the church.

Elizabeth exits to the kitchen and begins to eat. Quilly follows her.

QUILLY: See now, that ain't right. You went down there and got you a dinner and didn't get me one.

ELIZABETH: They ran out of food. I told you, I said, "Quilly, come on now, let's get us a dinner." But no, you wanted to sit there until the last minute waiting for them to close that coffin.

QUILLY: It wasn't no such thing. I didn't want all them little snotty-nosed kids, running around down there with their greasy hands, to touch my dress. I don't have no money to be buying another white dress, shoot.

ELIZABETH: You didn't have to wear that dress today, Quilly. You were just showing off.

QUILLY: The Ladies of the Golden Scepter were . . .

ELIZABETH: Don't nobody in that church know nothing about no Ladies of the Golden Scepter . . . except you and Sister Wallace. You haven't been to a meeting since you moved back here from Brooklyn a month ago. Over fifty and you and her running around the church in some old ugly uniform looking like the Gold Dust Twins.

QUILLY: Oh, you just jealous.

ELIZABETH: All right, I'm jealous. But I tell you this, you opened your mouth about frying chicken for Sister Wallace and her children to take on the train when they go back down to Georgia for Mother's Day. Now, don't you fix it in your head to try and connive me into frying that chicken because that's my week to cook. She's your lodge sister.

QUILLY: I ain't going to ask you nothing.

ELIZABETH: I'm just saying. I know you, Quilly.

QUILLY: I ain't studying you. *(Pause.)* I sure wish I had somebody to go to Singleton's restaurant and get me something to eat. I can't climb them stairs no more today . . . not with this girdle, shoot.

ELIZABETH: Then take it off and stop complaining. *(Pause.)* Ain't no use you looking, Quilly, you ain't getting none of my pig feet. Now you go on and eat them leftovers you cooked for the whole week.

> *The doorbell rings.*

Look and see who that is.

QUILLY: Shoot.

> *Quilly crosses to the window and looks out.*

(Calling.) Who is it? *(Pause.)* Oh, it's you . . . When you ring the bell, come out and stand on the sidewalk so we can see who . . .

> *Elizabeth enters from the kitchen.*

ELIZABETH: Who are you talking to like that?

QUILLY: Your "roomer."

ELIZABETH: Husband?

QUILLY: Yeah, "Husband."

ELIZABETH: Did you throw the key down to him?

QUILLY: I had to find out who it was first. I keep telling him after he rings the bell to come out and stand where we can see him. He rings the bell, then stands in the hallway. Now how am I supposed to know who I'm throwing the key to if he stands in the hallway where nobody can see him? Shoot! What happened to the keys you gave him?

ELIZABETH: I don't know. Just throw him the key, Quilly.

QUILLY *(looking for the key):* I don't know why you want to take in some strange man anyway . . . *(Quilly finds the key tied to a handkerchief.)* You don't know nothing about him . . .

> *Quilly crosses to the window and throws the key out.*

(Out the window.) Here! *(To Elizabeth.)* You don't know who you're letting into our house . . . He could be a rapist or something.

ELIZABETH: Well, unless something is wrong with him, you and me don't have nothing to worry about.

QUILLY: I don't know what you're talking about. You better talk for yourself, shoot.

> *Elizabeth stands in the doorway and talks as she eats.*

THE OLD SETTLER—Brenda Pressley (Elizabeth) and
Myra Lucretia Taylor (Quilly) in the McCarter Theater,
Princeton, staging of John Henry Redwood's play

ELIZABETH: He wrote to me a couple of times after we agreed about him renting the room . . . and I wrote him back. He's a very nice, polite young man. Now, I want you to try and be nice to him. We need the money.

QUILLY: Where's he going to get money from? He ain't got no job.

ELIZABETH: How's he going to get a job when he's only been up here for three days, Quilly?

QUILLY: Well, if he'd stop running all over Harlem looking for that woman every day, he might be able to find him a job. And why ain't he in the Army like a lot of young men his age? There's a war going on. You ever ask yourself that . . . or him?

ELIZABETH: No, I never asked myself that . . . or him. If he wants me . . . or you to know, he'll tell us. And as far as his money goes, as long as he gets it honest, it's none of our business where he gets it from.

QUILLY: Well, if it's none of our business where he gets it from, then we don't know where he gets it from, so we don't know if he gets it honest or not.

ELIZABETH: The man ain't going to be up here forever, Quilly. Just as soon as he finds his girl friend, he's going back down home.

QUILLY: Yeah, that's what they all say, until they get up here and it starts getting good to them. What's taking him so long to come upstairs?

ELIZABETH: Deacon Slater said that Husband came into some money from selling some of the land left to him after his Mama passed on. Now, he's paid a month's rent in advance, and Deacon Slater has spoken for him, and that's enough for me.

QUILLY: Well, Deacon Slater don't have to live with him. That's all I've got to say, shoot. And you can't trust no gator-tail eating geechees no ways. And both of them from the same home town, too. And one geechee is up here looking for another geechee who ran away from . . . What's the name of that place he comes from?

There is a knock at the door.

ELIZABETH: You just remember that his rent is helping us keep this apartment.

QUILLY: I don't want to have nothing to do with him. All I want him to do is stay out of my way.

There is another knock at the door.

We're coming! *(To Elizabeth.)* Well . . . Open the door for your "roomer."

Elizabeth puts her plate down on the kitchen table and crosses to the door, opening it. A young black man, Husband Witherspoon, 28, enters carrying two cardboard suitcases. One has a rope around it.

HUSBAND: Afternoon, Miss Elizabeth . . . Afternoon, Mrs. McGrath.

QUILLY: What's the name of that place you come from down in South Carolina?

ELIZABETH: Quilly!

HUSBAND: You mean Frogmore?

QUILLY: Yeah! Frogmore! That's just what I mean! Frogmore, South Carolina!

ELIZABETH: Quilly! . . . How did you make out, Husband?

HUSBAND: You mean with Lou Bessie?

QUILLY *(to herself):* Lou Bessie. Lord have mercy.

ELIZABETH: Yes.

HUSBAND: I went by that restaurant again where Lou Bessie had been working. The lady there, that I had been asking about Lou Bessie . . . I guess she felt sorry for me . . .

QUILLY: I don't blame her.

HUSBAND: Well, she finally told me that Lou Bessie was cleaning house out in some place called . . .

Putting down his suitcases, he takes a piece of paper from his pocket.

Some place called Great Neck. You know where that's at, Miss Elizabeth?

ELIZABETH: Yeah. That's out there on Long Island somewhere.

HUSBAND: I figure maybe I'll try and go out there and see if I can find her. The woman gave me the address. *(Proudly.)* She said she had heard of me and that Lou Bessie used to talk about me all the time when she first got up here.

QUILLY: You ain't down there in big foot country. You better not go out there messing around in them white folks' neighborhood unless you wearing a dress and carrying a shopping bag.

ELIZABETH: Did the lady in the restaurant give you a telephone number so you might call Lou Bessie?

HUSBAND: No, Ma'am.

ELIZABETH: Well, see, you just can't go out walking around in these white folks' neighborhoods, because if the police don't get you, a bunch of white men might. Now, don't you go thinking that because you're up here in the north, it's any different than it is in the south. In some ways, it's worse.

HUSBAND: Maybe you're right. I think I'll go back to that restaurant and see if that lady has a telephone number for where Lou Bessie works.

QUILLY: Before you go, where's the set of keys Miss Elizabeth gave you?

HUSBAND: Oh ... I'm sorry, Mrs. McGrath ... Miss Elizabeth ... but I kind of lost them.

QUILLY: Oh, Lord. You can't go around losing keys. They cost money. And what if a rapist found ...

ELIZABETH: That's okay, Husband. I got another set you can have.

HUSBAND: Thank you very kindly, Miss Elizabeth. I'll pay for them. It's just that I ain't used to no keys. We never lock our doors down home. When I got to the front door with my bags, I went in my pocket looking for the keys, and they were gone ... Oh, I forgot ...

ELIZABETH: What's the matter?

HUSBAND: I left my other two bags with a man in the hallway to watch for me while I brought these suitcases up.

QUILLY: Are you crazy?

ELIZABETH: Go on back down there and get your bags, man.

HUSBAND: Yes, Ma'am.

Husband rushes out the door.

QUILLY *(calling after him):* If he's still there. *(To Elizabeth.)* How stupid can one man be? I bet if he takes off his shoes, he still has chicken doody between his toes ... with his old country self.

ELIZABETH: Leave him be, Quilly. You forgot what you looked like when you first got up here.

Elizabeth crosses to the window and looks out.

QUILLY: I didn't look like that, shoot!

ELIZABETH: He's not there. The poor man is running up and down the street.

Quilly crosses to the window and looks out.

QUILLY: Serves him right. Look at him. If he keeps it up, he's going to get hit by one of those cars.

ELIZABETH: Why are you so mean to him?

QUILLY: What are you getting all upset about?

ELIZABETH: There's no reason for you to treat him like you're doing. He hasn't done nothing to warrant that.

QUILLY: It ain't right, that's why. You never even talked to me about taking in no roomer.

ELIZABETH: When I tried to talk to you about him, you wouldn't listen!

QUILLY: He was already here then!

ELIZABETH: Truth be known, I didn't have to talk to you about him at all. You wasn't even living here when I promised to rent the room to the man.

QUILLY: What's gotten into you, Bess? You were going to be living in this place all by yourself with some strange man?

ELIZABETH: People take in roomers to help with rent all over Harlem and you know it.

QUILLY: But what Christian woman do you know living alone in the same apartment with a man that's not her husband?

ELIZABETH: Annie Mae Oxford who works down in . . .

QUILLY: I said "Christian" woman! People down there at the church are talking about . . .

    The doorbell rings. Elizabeth looks out of the window.

I bet he ran out of here without the key.

ELIZABETH *(out the window):* Who is it? *(Pause.)* After you ring the bell, Husband, don't stand in the hallway. Come out and stand where we can see who it is.

QUILLY: I told you.

ELIZABETH: Oh, shut up. *(Out the window.)* Just a minute, Husband.

    Elizabeth looks around for the key. She crosses to Husband's suitcase and gets the key. She throws it out of the window.

The Old Settler *was produced at the McCarter Theater, Princeton, February 7, 1997, under the direction of Walter Dallas, in a dual premiere with Long Wharf Theater, New Haven, February 4, 1997.*

A DIRECTORY
OF NEW-PLAY PRODUCTIONS

Professional productions June 1, 1997–May 31, 1998 (plus a very few that opened too late in the spring of 1997 to be included in last year's *Best Plays* volume) of new plays by leading resident companies around the United States, who supplied information on casts and credits at Camille Dee's request, are listed here in alphabetical order of the locations of more than 60 producing organizations. Date given is opening date. Most League of Resident Theaters (LORT) and other regularly-producing Equity groups were queried for this comprehensive Directory. Active cross-country theater companies not included in this list either did not offer new or newly-revised scripts during the period under review or had not responded to our query by press time. Most productions listed below are world premieres; a few are American premieres, new revisions, noteworthy second looks or scripts not previously reported in *Best Plays*.

Ashland, Ore.: Oregon Shakespeare Festival

(Libby Appel artistic director; Paul Nicholson executive director)

THE MAGIC FIRE. By Lillian Garrett-Groag. July 30, 1997. Director, Libby Appel; scenery, Richard L. Hay; costumes, Deborah M. Dryden; lighting, Ann G. Wrightson; sound, Sara Jane Schmeltzer; composer, Todd Burton; voice and text director, Nancy Benjamin; movement director, John Sipes; choreographer, Xedex.

Lise .... Vilma Silva
Young Lise .... Alyn McKenna Bartell
Giovanni Guarneri;
   Gianni "Juan" Guarneri .... Ken Albers
Otto Berg .... Anthony Heald
Amalia Berg .... Demetra Pittman
Elena Guarneri;
   Blasina Guarneri .... Judith-Marie Bergan
Young Gianni .... Dylan Heald
Paula Guarneri .... Dee Maaske
Maddalena Guarneri .... Eileen DeSandre
Clara Stepanek .... Catherine E. Coulson
Henri Fontannes .... Richard Howard
Alberto Barcos .... Michael J. Hume
Rosa Arrua .... Robynn Rodriguez
   Time: The winter of 1952. Place: Buenos Aires. Two intermissions.

Unstaged Reading

EL PASO BLUE. By Octavio Solis. July 18, 1997. Director, Tim Bond.

Baltimore: Center Stage

(Irene Lewis artistic director; Peter W. Culman managing director)

SPLASH HATCH ON THE E GOING DOWN. By Kia Corthron. November 13, 1997. Director, Marion McClinton; scenery, Michael Yeargan; costumes, Katherine Beatrice Roth; lighting, Stephen Strawbridge; sound, Janet Kalas; fight choreographer, J. Allen Suddeth; presented in cooperation with the Yale Repertory Theater, Stan Wojewodski Jr. artistic director.

Thyme .... Margaret Kemp
Erry .... Akili Prince
Marjorie .... Ami Brabson
Shaneequa .... Cherita A. Armstrong
Ollie .... David Toney
   Time: The present day. Place: Harlem. One intermission.

Berkeley, Calif: Berkeley Repertory Theater

(Tony Taccone artistic director; Susan Medak managing director)

EVOLUTION OF A HOMEBOY: JAILS, HOSPITALS & HIPHOP. Solo performance by Danny Hoch; written by Danny Hoch. October 22, 1997. Director, Jo Bonney; lighting, Steevon Summers. No intermission.

THE BIRDS. By Aristophanes; newly adapted by John Glore and Culture Clash. March 8, 1998. Co-produced with South Coast Repertory, Costa Mesa, David Emmes producing artistic director, Martin Benson artistic director (see its entry in the Costa Mesa section of this listing).

Boca Raton, Fla.: Caldwell Theater Company

(Michael Hall artistic and managing director)

HIMSELF! Musical with book by Sheila Walsh, lyrics by Sheila Walsh and Jonathan Brielle; music by Jonathan Brielle. January 9, 1998. Director, George Rondo; musical direction, Jonathan Brielle; scenery, Tim Bennett; costumes, David Toser; lighting, Thomas Salzman; sound, Steve Shapiro, M. Anthony Reimer.
 CAST: James Joyce, Stephen Dedalus—Len Cariou; John Joyce, Judge, Darantiere, Bloom—John Felix; Joyce's Mother, Whore, Nora, Sylvia Beach, Joyce's Daughter Lucia, Girl on Rock, Molly—Jacqueline Knapp; Priest, Publisher—Brian Mallon.
 Time: 1882–1941. Place: Dublin, Trieste, Paris, Zurich. One intermission.

THE GARDENS OF FRAU HESS. By Milton Frederick Marcus. February 22, 1998. Director, John Henry Davis; scenery, Narelle Sissons; costumes, Christianne Myers; lighting, Thomas Salzman; sound, Steve Shapiro.

Frau Hess .... Patricia Hodges
Isaac Baum .... Ken Kliban
Franz .... Sam Kitchin
 Time: Late spring, 1944. Place: Germany, the Hess home. Act I, Scene l: Morning. Scene 2: Half hour later. Scene 3: Three weeks later. Act II, Scene l: One week later. Scene 2: Three weeks later. Scene 3: Four weeks later.

Playsearch: Readings

HANDSHAKE. by Julie Gilbert and Robert A. Brodner. December 15, 1997.
DON'T TELL THE TSAR. By Michael McKeever. March 9, 1998.
THE NORMALS. By Chris Widney. March 30, 1998.
FANNY & WALT. By Jewel Seehaus. April 20, 1998.
THE KING'S MARE. By Oscar E. Moore. May 11, 1998.

Cambridge, Mass.: American Repertory Theater

(Robert Brustein artistic director)

PETER PAN & WENDY. By Elizabeth Egloff; conceived by Marcus Stern and Elizabeth Egloff; based on the novel *Peter and Wendy* by J.M. Barrie. December 17, 1997. Director, Marcus Stern; scenery, Allison Koturbash; costumes, Catherine Zuber; lighting, Scott Zielinski; sound, Marcus Stern, Christopher Walker.
Wendy Darling .... Emma Roberts
Peter Pan .... Justin Campbell
John Darling .... Jason Weinberg
Michael Darling .... William Dunn
Mrs. Darling .... Karen McDonald
Mr. Darling .... Jeremy Geidt
Nana; Tootles .... Remo Airaldi
Tinkerbell .... Nora Zimmett

Captain Hook .... Will LeBow
Smee .... Stephen Rowe
Skylight .... Robert Kropf
Slightly .... Jeremy Rabb
 No intermission.

ALBEE'S MEN. Solo performance by Stephen Rowe; excerpted from the works of Edward Albee; created by Glyn O'Malley and Stephen Rowe. March 25, 1998. Director, Glyn O'Malley; lighting, Glyn O'Malley, Kimberly Scott. One intermission.

NOBODY DIES ON FRIDAY. By Robert Brustein; inspired by the memoirs of Susan and John Strasberg. April 16, 1998. Director, David

ASHLAND—Ken Albers, Alyn McKenna Bartell and Vilma Silva in a scene from *The Magic Fire* by Lillian Garrett-Groag at the Oregon Shakespeare Festival

Wheeler; scenery, Michael Griggs; costumes, Catherine Zuber; lighting, John Ambrosone; sound, Christopher Walker.

Lee Strasberg .... Alvin Epstein
Paula Strasberg .... Annette Miller
Susan Strasberg .... Emma Roberts
John Strasberg .... Robert Kropf

Marilyn Monroe .... Rachael Warren
Time: 1960. Place: The Strasberg apartment on Central Park West.

Act I: New Year's Day at 11 a.m. Act II, Scene 1: 5 p.m. that afternoon. Scene 2: 8 p.m. that evening.

Cedar City, Utah: Utah Shakespearean Festival

(Douglas Cook producing artistic director)

New-Plays-in-Progress Readings

WHO LOVES YOU, JIMMIE ORRIO. By Cheryldee Huddleston. July 31, 1997. Director, George Judy. With Heather Landry, Jan Roggé, Ty Burrell, Raphael Peacock, Camille Diamond.

OUR LADY GUINEVERE. By Ace G. Pilkington. August 7, 1997. Director, Barbara Bosch. With David Ivers, Don Burroughs, Carol Johnson, Karen K. Wegner, Allan Neal, George Judy, Tessa Auberjonois, Susanna Morrow, Paul Hope, Scott

Janes, Patrick Placzkowski, Chris DuVal, Brian Vaughn.
WHAT IN THE WORLD'S COME OVER YOU? By Red Shuttleworth. August 14, 1997. Director, Rod Ceballos. With Todd Denning, Heidi Ewart, Annie Wersching, Ross Dippel, John Oswald, Aaron Serotsky.

THE SPIRIT SEEKERS. By William Lang. August 21, 1997. Director, George Judy. With George Judy, P.J. Rockwell, Jan Roggé, Heidi Stricker, Michael Harding, Wayne Pyle, Carine Montbertrand, Kelly King Simpson, Dawn Youngs.

Chicago: Court Theater

(Charles Newell artistic director)

THE IPHIGENIA CYCLE: *Iphigenia at Aulis* and *Iphigenia in Tauris*. By Euripides; newly translated and adapted by Nicholas Rudall. September 5, 1997. Director, JoAnne Akalaitis; scenery, Paul Steinberg; costumes, Doey Luthi; lighting, Jennifer Tipton; composer and sound, Bruce Odland; choreographer, Ginger Farley.

Iphigenia at Aulis
Agamemnon .... Jack Willis
Old Man .... Nathan Davis
Menelaos .... Eddy Saad
Messenger .... Wilson Cain III
Clytemnestra .... Ora Jones
Iphigenia .... Anne Dudek
Achilles .... Taylor Price
    Women of Chalkis: Genevra Gallo, Michele Graff, Lynn M. House, Carmen Roman, Genevieve VenJohnson, Marie-Francoise Theodore.

Place: Outside Agamemnon's encampment at Aulis.

Iphigenia in Tauris
Iphigenia .... Anne Dudek
Orestes .... Taylor Price
Pylades .... Eddy Saad
Herdsman; Messenger .... Wilson Cain III
Herdsman .... Nathan Davis
Thoas .... Jack Willis
Athena .... Ora Jones
    Greek Women, Captive Slaves of Thoas: Genevra Gallo, Michele Graff, Lynn M. House, Carmen Roman, Genevieve VenJohnson, Marie-Francoise Theodore.
    Place: The Temple of Artemis on the north coast of the Black Sea.

Chicago: Goodman Theater

(Robert Falls artistic director; Roche Edward Schulfe executive director)

HOUSE ARREST: FIRST EDITION. By Anna Deavere Smith. November 7, 1997. Produced in collaboration with Arena Stage, Washington, D.C., Douglas C. Wager artistic director, Mark Taper Forum, Los Angeles, Gordon Davidson artistic director and Intiman Theater, Seattle, Warner Shook artistic director (see its entry in the Washington, D.C. section of this listing).

GRILLER. By Eric Bogosian. January 19, 1998. Director, Robert Falls; scenery, Derek McLane; costumes, Mara Blumenfeld; lighting, Kenneth Posner; sound Richard Woodbury; fight choreographer, Robin McFarquhar.
Gussie .... Robert Klein
Jeremy .... Alex Kirsch
Roz .... Nahanni Johnstone
Uncle Tony .... Howard Witt
Michelle .... Karen Valentine

Gloria .... Caroline Aaron
Granma Betty .... Irma Ste. Paule
Dylan .... Mark Ruffalo
Terence .... Marc Grapey
    Time: Fourth of July, 1997. Place: Suburban New Jersey. One intermission.

LET ME LIVE. By Oyamo. April 20, 1998. Director, Ron O.J. Parson; scenery, Lori Fong; costumes, Christine Pascual; lighting, Kathy Perkins; sound, Matt Kozlowski; produced in association with Onyx Theater Ensemble.
Shonuff .... Clifton Williams
Jenkins .... Earnest Perry Jr.
Clancy .... Ellis Foster
Kennedy .... Freeman Coffey
Bracey .... Mississippi Charles Bevel
Smiley .... Leonard Roberts
Dupree .... Trent Harrison Smith

Angelo .... Craig Boyd
Allen .... Gene Cordon

One intermission.

Chicago: Steppenwolf Theater Company

(Martha Lavey artistic director; Michael Gennaro managing director)

SPACE. By Tina Landau. December 7, 1997. Director, Tina Landau; scenery, James Schuette; costumes, Mara Blumenfeld; lighting, Scott Zielinski; sound and musical composition, Michael Bodeen, Rob Milburn; projection design, John Boesche.
Dr. Allan Saunders .... Tom Irwin
Dr. Bernadette Jump Cannon .... Amy Morton
Devin Gee .... Craig Zimmerman
Dr. Jim Lacey .... Robert Breuler
Joan Bailey .... Mariann Mayberry
Taj Mahal .... Morocco Omari
Carl Himayo .... Daniel Smith
Lorna Shipley .... Alexandra Billings
     Time: December, the present. Place: A university and its surroundings. One intermission.

GOODBYE STRANGER. By Carrie Luft. January 25, 1998. Director, Polly Noonan; scenery, Dan Ostling; costumes, Janice Pytel; lighting, Christine Solger-Binder; original music and sound, David P. Earle.
Glad .... Paul Adelstein
Passerby; Screaming Man;
     Passenger .... Pat Healy
Louise .... Marilyn Dodds Frank
Desperate Woman; Customer;
     Kim; Sharon .... Greta Oglesby
Shade .... Denise Odom
April .... Jill Kraft
Todd .... Dale Ray Rivera
     Place: New York City. Act I, Scene l: A vacant lot. Scene 2: Louise's apartment. Scene 3: The

street. Scene 4: A coffee house. Scene 5: A bar. Scene 6: A clinic. Scene 7: Louise's apartment. Act II, Scene 8: The street. Scene 9: Java Hut. Scene 10: Louise's apartment. Scene 11: A clinic. Scene 12: The stoop. Scene 13: Louise's apartment. Scene 14: The road.

THE MEMORY OF WATER. By Shelagh Stephenson. February 15, 1998. Director, Les Waters; scenery, Annie Smart; costumes, Allison Reeds; lighting, Christine Solger-Binder; sound, Richard Woodbury.
Mary .... Amy Morton
Vi .... Mary Beth Fisher
Teresa .... Martha Lavey
Catherine .... Heather Ehlers
Mike .... Tim Grimm
Frank .... Rick Snyder
     Time: The present. Place: Northern England. One intermission.

The New Plays Lab: Ensemble Readings

SIC. By Melissa James Gibson. March 9, 1998. Director, Anna D. Shapiro.
MINE EYES HAVE SEEN. By Nambi Kelley. March 23, 1998. Director, Leslie Holland.
THE TRAIL OF HER INNER THIGH. By Erin Cressida Wilson. April 13, 1998. Director, Anna D. Shapiro.
THE BLUEBONNET STATE. By Bruce Norris. June 1, 1998. Director, Anna D. Shapiro.

Chicago: Victory Gardens Theater

(Dennis Zacek artistic director; John Walker managing director; Marcelle McVay managing director 11/97)

THE SUTHERLAND. By Charles Smith. September 18, 1997. Director, Dennis Zacek; scenery, Mary Griswold; costumes, Claudia Boddy; lighting, Todd Hensley; sound, Lindsay Jones.
Eugene Taylor .... Dexter Zollicoffer
Annette .... Velma Austin
Lucas Taylor; Redd Fox .. John Steven Crowley
Fiona .... Kelley Hazen
Musician; George Hunter;
     Wiggler .... Kenn E. Head
Trumpet Solos .... Malachi Thompson
     Time: 1955 to 1980. Place: The Sutherland Hotel; the play takes place in 1980 in Chicago and in

the mind of Eugene Taylor from 1955 to 1980 in Chicago and Vienna.

ROMANCE IN D. By James Sherman. November 13, 1997. Director, Dennis Zacek; scenery, Bill Bartelt; costumes, Claudia Boddy; lighting, Bob Shook; sound, Andre Pluess, Ben Sussman.
Charles Norton .... James Leaming
Isabel Fox .... Linnea Todd
Sam Fox .... Howard Witt
Helen Norton .... Henrietta Hermeli
     Time: The present, December. Place: Two efficiency apartments in the Old Town area of Chicago.

BEFORE MY EYES. By Joel Drake Johnson. January 23, 1998. Director, Sandy Shinner; scenery, costumes and lighting, Sam Ball; sound, Andre Pluess, Ben Sussman.

John Garrison .... Timothy Hendrickson
Ann Garrison .... Annabel Armour
Ross Garrison .... Rob Riley
Aunt Ruth; Mrs. Cartwright; Pastor Bowman;
  Barbra Streisand .... Marc Silvia
Monte; A.J.; Rich; Philip .... Jeff Parker
    Time: 1962–1988. Place: Various places. One intermission.

FLYOVERS. By Jeffrey Sweet. May 21, 1998. Director, Dennis Zacek; scenery, Mary Griswold; costumes, Jeff Bauer; lighting, Todd Hensley; sound, Andre Pluess, Ben Sussman.

Ted .... William Petersen
Iris .... Amy Morton
Oliver .... Marc Vann
Lianne .... Linda Reiter
    One intermission.

Cincinnati: Cincinnati Playhouse in the Park

(Edward Stern producing artistic director; Buzz Ward executive director)

COYOTE ON A FENCE. By Bruce Graham. January 27, 1998. Director, Edward Stern; scenery, Paul Shortt; costumes, Gordon DeVinney; lighting, Dan Kotlowitz; sound, David B. Smith.

Shawna DuChamps .... Connie Nelson
John Brennan .... Christopher McHale

Sam Fried .... Anderson Matthews
Bobby Reyburn .... Jordan Matter
    Time: The present and recent past. Place: In and around a prison in the southern United States. No intermission.

Cleveland: The Cleveland Play House

(Peter Hackett artistic director; Dean R. Gladden managing director)

A RUSSIAN ROMANCE. By Murphy Guyer. December 30, 1997. Director, Peter Hackett; scenery, Vicki Smith; costumes, Lindsay W. Davis; lighting, Don Darnutzer; sound, Robin Heath.

Svetlana Verminitsky .... Nina Landey
Ivan Ilyitch Veminitsky .... Murphy Guyer
Brad Bradley .... Brad Bellamy
Katherine Cavendish .... Monica Koskey
Kitty Cavendish .... Tandy Cronyn
Bunny Cavendish .... David Wasson
Michael Nasjagai .... Edward Vassallo
Policeman .... David A. Tyson

    Time: Late Autumn, 1992. Place: A Manhattan hotel room and the Skywater Estate, Saratoga Springs. One intermission.

The Next Stage: Staged Readings

THE WORK OF WATER. By John Orlock. January 4, 1998. Director, Scott Kanoff.

STRANGERS' GROUND. By Erik Brogger. January 11, 1998. Director, Mary B. Robinson.

THE SMELL OF THE KILL. By Michele Lowe. January 18, 1998. Director, Scott Kanoff.

LOUIE, LOUIE! By William Hoffman and Ken Kacmar. January 25, 1998. Director, William Hoffman.

Costa Mesa, Calif: South Coast Repertory

(David Emmes producing artistic director; Martin Benson artistic director)

FREEDOMLAND. By Amy Freed. October 10, 1997. Director, David Emmes; scenery, Michael C. Smith; costumes, Susan Denison Geller; lighting, Peter Maradudin; sound, B.C. Keller.

Sig .... Heather Ehlers
Polly .... Annie LaRussa
Seth .... Simon Billig
Noah .... Peter Michael Goetz
Claude .... Karen Kondazian
Titus .... Maury Ginsberg
Lori .... Erin J. O'Brien

Place: An old house somewhere in upstate New York. One intermission.

THE BIRDS. By Aristophanes; newly adapted by John Glore and Culture Clash. January 24, 1998. Director, Mark Rucker; music and musical direction, Michael Roth; scenery, Christopher Barreca; costumes, Shigeru Yaji; lighting, Lonnie Rafael Alcaraz; choreography, Sylvia C. Turner; sound, B.C. Keller; co-produced by Berkeley Repertory Theater, Tony Taccone artistic director.

On Chicago Stages

Above, Robert Klein and Howard Witt in Eric Bogosian's *Griller* at the Goodman Theater; *left,* Anne Dudek as Iphigenia in Nicholas Rudall's translation of Euripides's *Iphigenia in Tauris,* directed by JoAnne Akalaitis, at the Court Theater; *below,* Daniel Smith, Tom Irwin and Amy Morton in Tina Landau's *Space* at Steppenwolf

Gato; Others .... Richard Montoya
Booby; Others .... Ric Salinas
Hoopoe; Others .... Herbert Siguenza
Foxx .... Victor Mack
    Others: Gunnar Madsen, Vincent Montoya,
Amy X. Neuberg, Susan Zelinsky.
    No intermission.

HURRAH AT LAST. By Richard Greenberg.
May 30, 1998. Director, David Warren; scenery,
Neil Patel; costumes, Candice Donnelly; lighting,

Peter Maradudin; music and sound, John Gromada.
Laurie .... Peter Frechette
Thea .... Ileen Getz
Eamon .... Gareth Williams
Oliver .... Frederick Weller
Gia .... Judith Blazer
Sumner .... George Coe
Reva .... Dori Brenner
    One intermission.

Denver: The Changing Scene

(Al Brooks and Maxine Munt executive producers)

FLO & MAX. By Toby Armour. October 30,
1997. Director, Dennis Bontems; design, Dennis
Bontems; choreography, Marta Barnard.
Flo .... Nancy Thomas
Max .... Brian M. Hughes
Daisie .... Eileen L. Sherrill
Sammy .... Bill Zabel
Florian; Rev. Billy Joe
    Gates .... Darren Schroader
Woman Dancing .... Taylor Smith
Florette .... Monica Schuster
    One intermission.

LIVING DOLLS. By Frank Higgins. February 12,
1998. Director, Pavlina Emily Morris; scenery,
Roni Muniz; cotumes, Pavlina Emily Morris; lighting, Scott Hasbrouck; sound, Stephen Remund.
Lois; Lois Doll .... Bonnie Brodsky
Herb .... Darren Schroader
Adam .... David Zaffore
Evie; Friend .... Anna Hadzi
Keith; Lonnie Guy .... Brian Folkins
    Time: This year. Place: Your town. Act I,
Scene 1: A restaurant. Scene 2: Lois's house. Scene
3: A supermarket. Scene 4: Herb's apartment. Act
II, Scene 1: A restaurant; Scene 2: A ranch in
Santa Fe, N.M. Scene 3: Herb's apartment. Scene
4: A mountain top in Santa Fe, N.M. Scene 5: A
funeral home.

Summerplay XI
July 17-August 3

INSTAGROW, INC. By Thomas Owen Meinen.
Director, Trace Oakley.
Jarred J. Eilig .... David Zaffore
TV Announcer .... Randy Elliot
Jelly Eilig .... Megan Wallace
Pressira Rennen Eilig .... Ingred Downs
Q. Nick Sofort .... Nelson Embleton
Christy .... Amy Michelle Smith

WIDOW. By Vida Tobi Kanter. Director, Faylee
Favara.

Minnie .... Miranda Tilp
Donnie .... Nick Webb
THE SAME RIVER TWICE. By Sam DeLeo.
Director, Therese Pickard.
Man .... Dan Horsey
Woman .... Marion Berry

GROUP. By Dave Johnson. Director, Pavlina
Emily Morris.
Ben Rogers .... Mark Donnachaidh
Bill Palmaloid .... Darren Schroader
Brad Bettroy .... Russ Cannon
Barbara Stevenson .... Betsy Grisard
Brett Danson .... Matthew Schultz
Bob Jamison .... Steven Divide
Dr. Janice Richley .... Louniece SanFilippo

Colorado Quickies V, April 16-May 3
Directed by the playwrights

BE MY GUEST. By Tyler Smith.
Frank .... Steven Divide
Charley .... Ed Halloran

SOAP, EGGPLANT. By Olivia Laney Edwards.
Left .... Pavlina Emily Morris
Right .... Daniel Horsey

FISHER CEMETERY. By Kathleen O'Neill
Hopkins.
John .... Ken Witt
Anne .... Mary Ann Amari
Orrin .... Robert Smith
Willard .... Terry Wood

THAT FOGGY NIGHT. By Mark Ogle.
David .... Damon Lindenberger
Joanna .... Amy Rome
Alien .... Sarah Ogle
    Alien costume designed and created by Agnes
Sonnenfeld.

NOSTOI. By Kimberly Savage.
Sandra .... Lisa Rosenhagen
Steven .... Robert Mason Ham
Roger .... Karl deMarrais

Renee .... Tracy Clifton
THE HUNDRED STEPS. By Jeannene Bybee.
Sarah .... Bevin Antea
Reverend .... Ed Halloran
Witness .... Dan Horsey
THE FRONT SEAT. By Robert Sheely.

Ed .... Steve Jordan
Helen .... Ruth Crowley
NOT THE DOG'S BABY THIS TIME. By Steve Hunter.
Carol .... Mary Ann Amari
Ted .... Steven Divide

Denver: Denver Center Theater Company

(Donovan Marley artistic director; Barbara E. Sellers producing director)

FABLES. Conceived and written by Pavel Dobrusky and Per-Olav Sorensen. May 15, 1998. Directors and designers, Pavel Dobrusky, Per-Olav Sorensen; music, music direction and arrangements, Larry Delinger; movement coordinator, Luan Schooler; sound, David R. White.

With Arthur T. Acuña, Taro Alexander, Russ Appleyard, Yolande Bavan, Kathleen M. Brady, Leandro Cano, Peter Daniel, Sheetal Gandhi, Jahneen, Christine Toy Johnson, Soomi Kim, Luan Schooler, Bruce Turk, Chris Vasquez.

Children's Choir: Chandi Aldena, Lauren Dandurand, Tamoi Elliott, Nicole Harris, Risa Jiron, Monica Ly, Jillian Mackey, Nova Schneider, Aaron Terriquez, Ruby Valles.

Time: Once upon a time. Place: India, Persia, Greece, Turkey, China, Japan, Korea, Indonesia, Greenland, Canada, West Indies, Nigeria, Zambia, Zaire, Mexico, Guatemala, Vietnam. No intermission.

THE SERVANT OF TWO MASTERS. By Carlo Goldoni; newly translated and adapted by Sylvie Drake. September 24, 1997. Director, James Dunn; scenery, Andrew V. Yelusich; costume and mask design, Kevin Copenhaver; lighting, Charles R. MacLeod; sound, Gary Grundei.
Pantalone .... Randy Moore
Clarice .... Rachel K. Taylor
Dr. Lombardi .... William Denis
Silvio .... Michael Rahhal
Beatrice Rasponi .... Annette Helde
Florindo Aretusi .... Robert Westenberg
Brighella .... Keith L. Hatten
Smeraldina .... Leslie O'Carroll
Truffaldino .... Mark Rubald
lst Waiter; lst Porter .... Peter Daniel
2d Waiter; 2d Porter .... Tina Anderson
Musician .... Russ Appleyard
    Time: The early 1700s. Place: Venice, Italy. One intermission.

ELIOT NESS ... IN CLEVELAND. Musical with book by Peter Ullian based on his play In the Shadow of the Terminal Tower; music and lyrics by Robert Lindsey Nassif; co-adaptation and additional material by Nick Corley. January 15, 1998.

Director, Nick Corley; choreography, Vera Huff; musical direction, Joshua Rosenblum; scenery, Mark Wendland; costumes, David Kay Mickelsen; lighting, Allen Lee Hughes; sound, Tony Meola; orchestrations, Michael Starobin; vocal and dance arrangements, Robert Lindsey Nassif.
Eliot Ness .... Peter Samuel
Capone .... Terence Goodman
Newsboys .... Austin Teobalt, Alex Wyatt
Seeley .... Timothy Gulan
Marlo .... Peter Van Wagner
Stoneham .... William Parry
Hildy .... Alice M. Vienneau
Hobo Woman .... Janine Morick
Woman 1 .... Karen Burlingame
Woman 2 .... Suzanne Hevner
Wife .... Kate Coffman
Mayor .... Bernie Sheredy
Saloon Singer .... Capathia Jenkins
Sidney .... David Gunderman
Karpis .... Mark Lotito
Frank .... James Bohanek
    Ensemble: Jamie Bishton, James Bohanek, Karen Burlingame, David Gunderman, Suzanne Hevner, Vera Huff, Capathia Jenkins, Mark Lotito, Hiromi Naruse, Alan Osburn, Tom Pardoe, Mercedes Perez, Bernie Sheredy.
    Time: The Great Depression. Place: Cleveland, Ohio. One intermission.

TREASURE ISLAND. Newly adapted by Nagle Jackson from the novel by Robert Louis Stevenson. January 29, 1998. Director, Nagle Jackson; scenery, Michael Ganio; costumes, David Kay Mickelsen; lighting, Don Darnutzer; sound, Jason F. Roberts; music, Lee Stametz; fight direction, J. Allen Suddeth.
Jim Hawkins, Esq. .... Douglas Harmsen
Jim as a Boy .... Jeremy Palmer
Bill Bones;
    Thomas Redruth .... William Whitehead
Dr. Livesy .... William Denis
Margaret Hawkins .... Kathleen M. Brady
Blind Pew; John Hunter .... Michael Rahhal
Squire Trelawney .... Randy Moore
Long John Silver .... John Hutton
Black Dog; Sam Carter .... Erik Tieze

Capt. Smollett .... Bob Burrus
Ben Gunn .... Robertson Carricart
Job Anderson .... Kenneth Martines
Israel Hands .... Mark Rubald
George Merry .... Michael Scarsella
Tom Morgan .... Chad Henry
Dick Johnson .... Keith L. Hatten
Solomon .... Charlee Chiv
Richard Joyce .... Patrick Goss
    Time: 1740 and 1725. Place: England, the Caribbean, an island. One intermission.

TAKING LEAVE. By Nagle Jackson. April 15, 1998. Director, Nagle Jackson; scenery, Bill Curley; costumes, David Kay Mickelsen; lighting, Charles R. MacLeod; sound, Gary Grundei.
Eliot Pryne .... Tony Church
Eliot, Once Removed .... Michael Santo
Mrs. Fleming .... Kathleen M. Brady
Alma .... Jeanne Paulsen
Liz .... Susan Cella
Cordelia .... Jennifer Schelter
    Time: The present. Place: Suburban Seattle. One intermission.

LIFE IS A DREAM. By Pedro Calderon de la Barca; newly adapted by Laird Williamson; based on a literal translation by Jennifer McCray Rincón. May 15, 1998. Director, Laird Williamson; scenery and costumes, Andrew V. Yelusich; lighting, Don Darnutzer; sound, David R. White.
Rosaura .... Jacqueline Antaramian
Bocazas .... Leslie O'Carroll
Segismundo .... John Hutton
Clotaldo .... William Denis
Violante .... Mercedes Perez
Astolfo .... Robert Westenberg
Estrella .... Gloria Biegler
Basilio .... Jamie Horton
Deceased Queen .... Kate Harwood
    Guards to Segismundo: Paul J. Curran, Keith L. Hatten, Richard J. Nelson, Alan Osburn. Royal Counsellors to King Basilio: Robertson Carricart,

Kenneth Martines, Mark Rubald. Ladies of the Court: Christine Jugueta, Mercedes Perez, Gabriella Cavallero. Court Singers: Gabriella Cavallero, Kate Harwood, Ingrid Shea. Attending Gentlemen: Robertson Carricart, Gregory Brent Johnson, Kenneth Martines. Rebel Leaders: Keith L. Hatten, Alan Osburn, Mark Rubald.
    Place: The mountains at the frontier of Polonia; the royal palace of Polonia; a battlefield outside the capital. One intermission.

DON QUIXOTE. Based on the character created by Miguel de Cervantes; conceived by Pavel Dobrusky; written by Pavel Dobrusky and Luan Schooler. May 21, 1998. Directors, Pavel Dobrusky, Luan Schooler; design, Pavel Dobrusky, Milan David; lighting, Pavel Dobrusky; music, Larry Delinger; choreography, Gary Abbott.
Cervantes .... Archie Smith, Randy Moore
Don Quixote .... Shawn Elliott
Sancho Panza .... Anthony Powell
Niece .... Jennifer Regan
Padre .... Clark Middleton
Teresa .... Brenda Cummings
Andres .... Martin Marion
Basque .... Erik Tieze
Altisidora .... Susan Spencer
Maritornes .... Kate Gleason
Innkeeper; Duke .... Bruce Turk
Puppeteer; Cook .... Chad Henry
Duchess .... Ken Jennings
Bishop .... Randy Moore
Girlie .... Luan Schooler
Musicians .... Russ Appleyard, Daniel Flick
    Ensemble: Ted Bettridge, Paul Cosentino, Brenda Cummings, Lee Eskey, Mark Evans, Kate Gleason, Chad Henry, Leslie Henson, Ken Jennings, Martin Marion, Clark Middleton, Randy Moore, Jennifer Regan, Luan Schooler, Susan Spencer, Laurie Strickland, Erik Tieze, Bruce Turk.
    One intermission.

Dorset, Vt.: Dorset Theater Festival

(Jill Charles artistic director; John Nassivera producing director)

THE COLOR OF LOVE. By John Nassivera. September 18, 1997. Director, Mark Ramont; scenery, William John Aupperlee; costumes, Angela Brande; lighting and sound, Matthew Richards.
Moz Washington .... Adrian Roberts
Sally Bruno .... Jurian Hughes

Robert Bruno .... Kelly AuCoin
Grace Lopez .... Robin Miles
    Time: The present, over a period of two weeks. Place: The two apartments of Moz and the Brunos in a high rise apartment building on midtown Manhattan's West Side. One intermission.

East Farmingdale, N.Y.: Arena Players Repertory Company

(Frederic De Feis producer/director)

REFLECTIONS OF A MURDER. By Jerome Coopersmith and Lucy Freeman. February 12, 1998. Director, Frederic De Feis; design, Fred Sprauer; costumes, Lois Lockwood; lighting, Al Davis.

Dr. Eve Lane .... Linda Rameizl
Dr. John Benton .... Michael Lang
Robert .... Seth Vaughn
Susan .... Sue Anne Dennehy
Officer Plotkin .... Jack Maloney

Emma .... Sheila Gaeckler
Mr. Cordero .... Vincent Platania
    Place: A study in the home of Dr. John Benton on the grounds of a state psychiatric hospital. Act I, Scene 1: The present. Scene 2: Several minutes later. Scene 3: 15 minutes later. Scene 4: Two days later. Act II, Scene 1: Two days later. Scene 2: The next day. Scene 3: Several hours later. Scene 4: The next day, afternoon. Scene 5: A few hours later.

East Haddam and Chester, Conn.: Goodspeed Opera House.

(Michael P. Price executive director)

LUCKY IN THE RAIN. Musical conceived and written by Sherman Yellen; music by Jimmy McHugh; lyrics by Harold Adamson and Dorothy Fields; additional music and lyrics by Hoagy Carmichael, Walter Donaldson, Al Dubin, Ted Koehler, Jan Savitt and Johnny Watson. July 9, 1997. Director, Christopher Ashley; choreography, Randy Skinner; musical direction, Michael O'Flaherty; scenery, Eduardo Sicangco; costumes, Gail Brassard; lighting, Frances Aronson; orchestrations, Peter Matz; dance arrangements, Wally Harper; vocal arrangements, Wally Harper, Michael O'Flaherty.

Elder Henderson Booth;
    Gen. Maclean .... Ryan Hilliard
Henderson Booth .... Patrick Wilson
Jane Wiley .... Maria Schaffel
Gertrude Stein .... Susan Browning
Alice B. Toklas .... Patti Mariano
Josephine Baker .... Cheryl Howard
Isadora Duncan .... Luba Mason
Mike Malone .... David Brummel
Robert Leary .... Marcus Neville
Regine Duvalier .... Jennifer Smith
Zach Monroe .... Scott Wise
Momma McLean;
    Elder Jane Wiley .... Rita Gardner
    Others: Kelli Barclay, Ronald Brooks, Will Gartshore, Peter Gregus, Jessica Kostival, Rebecca Kupka, Michael McCoy, Courtney Morris, Bill Szobody, Erika Vaughn.
    One intermission.
    MUSICAL NUMBERS, ACT I: "Montmartre," "I'm Shooting High," "Exactly Like You," "Rendezvous Time in Paree," "On the Sunny Side of the Street," "Comin' in on a Wing and a Prayer," "It's a Wonderful World," "Doin' the New Low Down," "A Lovely Way to Spend an Evening," "I Walked In," "Where Are You?", "Love Me as Though There Were No Tomorrow," "When Love Goes Wrong (Nothin' Goes Right)," Finale.
    ACT II: "You," "I Must Have That Man!", "I Couldn't Sleep a Wink Last Night," "Don't Blame Me," "South American Way," "You're a Sweetheart," "I Can't Give You Anything but Love," "Doin' the New Low Down" (Reprise), "The Music Stopped," "It's a Most Unusual Day," "I Got Lucky in the Rain."

HOUDINI. Musical with book by James Racheff; music by William Scott Duffield; lyrics by William Scott Duffield and James Racheff. September 25, 1997. Director and choreographer, Gabriel Barre; musical direction and arrangements, Michael O'Flaherty; scenery, Loren Sherman; costumes, Pamela Scofield; lighting, Phil Monat; magic, Peter Samelson; orchestrations, Michael Gibson; produced by special permission of Jane Bergere Productions.

Mme. Tolka; Wilma .... Natalie Blalock
Bess .... Barbara Walsh
Theo .... Lewis Cleale
Casey; Carnival Boss; Theater Manager;
    German Official .... Bob Freschi
Martin Beck .... P.J. Benjamin
Mr. Maxwell; J.R. Paul;
    Florenz Ziegfeld; British Official;
    Stage Manager .... Warren Kelley
Harry .... Timothy Gulan
Mrs. Weiss .... Barbara Andres
Rabbi Weiss; P.T. Barnum; P.J. Spaulding;
    Dr. Ames; Doctor .... Steve Pudenz
Strongman; Policeman;
    Gordon Whitehead .... Jody Ashworth
Juggler; French Official .... Eric Olson

EAST HADDAM—Jennifer Smith and Marcus Neville in
the musical *Lucky in the Rain* at Goodspeed Opera House

Rosabelle Girl .... Becky Rosenbluth
Rosabelle Girl;
   Annie Oakley .... Stephanie Lynge
Mrs. Kelly; Mrs. Wilkinson .... Judith Jarosz
Buffalo Bill .... Philip A. Chaffin
Margery .... Suzan Postel
Jenny .... Antonia Carlotta Shaw
   Booking Agents: Philip A. Chaffin, Steve Pud-
enz, Warren Kelley; Fortune Tellers: Natalie Blal-
ock, Judith Jarosz, Krissy Johnson; Assistants:
Paul Lincoln, Brian Yashenko, Heath Hamilton,
Andrew McPhail.
   MUSICAL NUMBERS, ACT I: "The Se-
ance," "Whatever the Challenge," "Smart Fly,"
"Doctor Lynn's Circus and Medicine Show,"
"Wonder," "Coney Island Midway," "Rosa-
belle," "Doors Sequence," "To See an Open
Door," "With You," "You Know It When You
See It," "The Letter," "I Must Be Crazy," "What-
ever the Challenge" (Reprise), "Houdini Will Ac-
cept the Dare," "I Need These Wonders, Too,"
Finale/"Pain."
   ACT II: "Man in the Air," "Stars," "Tell 'Em
What They Want to Hear," "If You Were My
Wife," "There Has To Be a Way," "Smart Fly"
(Reprise), "Think About How Far We've Come,"
"The Magic That I Need," "The Chinese Water
Torture Cell," "I Did It for You," "Music Box
Sequence," "With You" (Reprise), "There Will
Never Be Another Night," "The Seance" (Re-
prise).

Goodspeed-at-Chester Productions

(Michael P. Price executive director; Sue Frost associate producer; Warren Pincus casting director; Michael O'Flaherty music director)

KUDZU THE SOUTHERN MUSICAL. Musical by Jack Herrick, Doug Marlette and Bland Simpson; adapted from the comic strip *Kudzu* by Doug Marlette. May 15, 1998. Director and choreographer, Marcia Milgrom Dodge; musical direction, Jack Herrick; scenery, David Gallo; costumes, Michael Krass; lighting, Kenneth Posner; puppets, Martin P. Robinson; sound, Jay Hilton.

Kudzu	Jeff Edgerton
Mike	Kelli Rabke
Mazee	Aisha De Haas
Mama	Michele Pawk
Nasal	Kevin Carolan
Maurice	Ryan Toby
Big Bubba	Roger Howell
Veranda	Ali McLennan
Will B. Dunn	Ray DeMattis

The Red Clay Ramblers:

Peabo	Clay Buckner
Purvis; Masuki Kabuki	Ed Butler
Hiram; Mystic Pilgrim	Chris Frank
Little Precious;	
Yamamoto Kabuki	Jack Herrick
Booger	Mark D. Roberts
Uncle Dub	Bland Simpson

Time: Now. Place: Bypass, N.C.

MUSICAL NUMBERS, ACT I: "Dixie Kind of Life," "Why Pass Bypass By," "Mine," "Fatherless," "The Lord Works in Mysterious Ways," "Live at Lunch & Traffic Ballet," "I Play It by Ear," "Duet for One," "Jesus Was Not an Alien," "Master Plan," "Kudzu."

ACT II: "The Cat Came Back," "City on a Hill," "Hey, Earl," "Air Nasal," "No More Sauce," "Mine" (Reprise), "Home," "Karaoke Saturday Night," "Letter From a Faraway Place," "We're Your Mamas," "National Recognition," "Home" (Reprise).

GOTHAM! Musical by Douglas Bernstein and Denis Markell. August 7, 1997. Director and choreographer, Ted Pappas; musical direction and vocal arrangements, David Evans; scenery, James Noone; costumes, Martha Bromelmeier; lighting, Kirk Bookman; sound, Jay Hilton.

Tinker	Jay Aubrey Jones
Stephen the Balladeer	Ed Romanoff
Ale-Wife	Jane Smulyan
Baker's Wife	Kelly Ebsary
Cowherd; Herald;	
Executioner	David Jachin Kelley
Jane	Adriana Rowe
Alice	Kathleen Harris
Trudy	Alli Steinberg
Carpenter	Erik Stein
Farmer	Bruce Montgomery
Father Dennis	Tim Salamandyk
Hugh the Drover	Robert Bartley
Mayor	Paul Stolarsky
Annie	Morgan Firestone
Sherman	Ray Wills
Lord Morris	Ron Wisniski
Randolph	James E. Kampf
Samantha	Michelle Blakely
Lucy	Melanie Farrow
Nurse	Ellen Foley
King John	Sam Tsoutsouvas

Time: April 1209. Place: Gotham Town Common.

MUSICAL NUMBERS, ACT I: "Almost," "Sherman the What," "Dover Beach," "I've Never Done That," "Pray With Me," "Homeward," "Dover Beach" (Reprise), "I've Never Done That" (Reprise), "On the Map."

ACT II: "Mistress May," "Progress," "Homeward" (Reprise), "The Stupid Men of Gotham," "Pray With Me" (Reprise), "Anyday," "Gotham," "I Never Know," "Mistress May" (Reprise), "Almost" (Reprise).

THE TIN PAN ALLEY RAG. Musical by Mark Saltzman; music by Scott Joplin and Irving Berlin. October 30, 1997. Director, Alan Bailey; choreographer, Larry Sousa; musical direction and arrangements, Brad Ellis; scenery, Peter Harrison; costumes, Zoe DuFour; lighting, Mary Jo Dondlinger.

Cast: Treemonisha, Hattie, Freddie Alexander—Kimla Beasley; Hopeful Songwriter, Jimmy Kelly, Valet—Hunter Bell; Montgomery Cook, Scott Joplin—Damon Evans; Miss Esther Lee, Monisha—Cheryl Howard; Salon Singer, Dorothy Goetz, Lula—Kim Lindsay; Irving Berlin—Danny Strauss; Williams, Ned, Freddie's Father—Glenn Turner; Ted Snyder, John Stark, Alfred Ernst—Richard Vida; Gitlo, Payton—Sean P. Waters.

Time: April 1915. Place: The office of Berlin and Snyder, music publishers, New York City. No intermission.

MUSICAL NUMBERS: "Pluggers on Parade," "I Love a Piano," "A Real Slow Drag," "Oh, Promise Me," "The Maple Leaf Rag," "Sweet Italian Love," "Moishe Sings an Irish Song," "Yiddishe Nightingale," "When the Midnight Choo-Choo Leaves for Alabam'," "The Ragtime Dance," "You'd Be Surpised," "Ev'rybody's Doin' It," "Solace," "When I Lost

You," "A Simple Melody," "The Entertainer," "I Want to See My Child Tonight," "American Rhapsody," "Alexander's Ragtime Band," "A Real Slow Drag" (Finale).

BMI-Lehman Engel
Musical Theater Workshop

A VISIT FROM THE FOOTBINDER. Musical with book and lyrics by David Dreyfus; music by

Jeffrey Hardy. December 21, 1997. Director, Elizabeth Margid; musical direction, Bob Goldstone.

DORIAN. Musical based on the novel by Oscar Wilde; book, music and lyrics by Richard Gleaves. December 21, 1997. Director, Gabriel Barre; musical direction, Michael O'Flaherty.

Evanston, Ill.: Next Theater Company

(Steve Pickering artistic director through 3/11/98; Kate Buckley artistic director; Peter Rybolt managing director)

SNOW. By Tom Szentgyorgyi. November 14, 1997. Director, Sarah Tucker; scenery, Scott Cooper; costumes, Kristine Benzschawel Knanishu; lighting, Shannon McKinney; sound, Teff Uchima, Barry G. Funderburg; original music, Barry G. Funderburg.
Billie .... Mary Ann Thebus
Hal .... James Deuter
The Pilot .... Chris Kipiniak
Voice of Sally .... Robin Shorr
    Time: Autumn. Place: A mountain road. No intermission.

BURNING CHROME. By William Gibson; newly adapted by Steve Pickering and Charley Sherman. February 6, 1998. Director, Steve Pickering; scenery, Scott Cooper; costumes, Kristine Benzschawel Knanishu; original music and sound, Barry G. Funderburg.
The Finn .... David Silvis
Automatic Jack .... Ted Koch
Crow Jane .... Susannah Kavanaugh
Black Myron .... Brian Jude Leahy
Tiger .... Wendy Evans
Bobby Quine .... Michael Park Ingram
Miles .... Guy Massey
Chrome; Snag .... Mia Livas
Rikki "Wildside" .... Stephanie Ferrell

Time: 2021. Place: Various locations in The Sprawl—an urban environment that stretches from what used to be Boston to what used to be Atlanta. No intermission.

CARDENIO, OR THE SECOND MAIDEN'S TRAGEDY. Authorship uncertain; attributable to William Shakespeare and John Fletcher. April 3, 1998. Director, Kate Buckley; scenery, Joseph P. Tilford; costumes, Kristine Benzschawel Knanishu; lighting, Charles Jolls; sound, Barry G. Funderburg; fight choreography, Steve Pickering.
The Court:
The Tyrant .... Steve Pickering
Govianus .... Kevin Theis
The Lady .... Michele Graff
Helvetius .... Jeffrey Bunn
Memphonius .... Ron Rains
Sophonius .... Robert Chaviano
Guard .... Benjamin Shields
Soldier #1 .... Ed Smaron
Soldier #2 .... Robert Schleifer
Soldier #3 .... Chris Kipiniak
The Household:
The Wife .... Karen Raymore
Anselmus .... Nathan Vogt
Votarius .... Joseph Wycoff
Leonella .... Meredith Mapel
Bellarius .... William Sidney Parker

Gainesville, Fla.: Hippodrome State Theater

(Mary Hausch producing director; Lauren Caldwell artistic director; Mark Sexton general manager)

COOKIN' AT THE COOKERY. By Marion J. Caffey. June 6, 1997. Director, Marilyn J. Caffey; musical direction, Darryl Ivey; scenery, James Morgan; costumes, Marilyn Wall-Asse; lighting and sound, Robert P. Robins; musical supervision and arrangements, Danny Holgate.
Alberta .... Ernestine Jackson
Narrator .... Debra Walton

MUSICAL NUMBERS, ACT I: "My Castle's Rockin'," "My Castle's Rockin'" (Reprise), "Rough and Ready Man," "I'm Having a Good Time," "I've Got a Mind to Ramble," "Two Cigarettes in the Dark," "Darktown Strutters' Ball," "Down Hearted Blues," "I've Got a Mind to Ramble" (Reprise), "I'm Having a Good Time" (Reprise), "Nobody," "Two Cigarettes in the

EVANSTON—Mary Ann Thebus, Chris Kipiniak and James Deuter in a scene from *Snow* by Tom Szentgyorgi at Next Theater Company

Dark" (Reprise), "Black Shadows," "I've Got a Mind to Ramble" (Reprise).

ACT II: "Nobody Knows You When You're Down and Out," "St. Louis Blues," "I'm Having a Good Time" (Reprise), "My Handy Man," "Amtrak Blues," "Mack the Knife," "Always," "Sweet Georgia Brown," "The Love I Have for You."

In Repertory

JUST SO STORIES. By Rudyard Kipling; newly adapted for the stage by Lauren Caldwell. July 25, 1997. Director, Lauren Caldwell; scenery, James Morgan; costumes, Marilyn Wall-Asse; lighting, Kristie Griffith; sound, Douglas Maxwell; choreography, Ric Rose.

Musicians .. Daniel J. DeVito, Keith Krutchkoff
O' Eldest Magician .... Bonnie Harrison
Olivier .... Carl McNulty
Teshumai (Taffy) .... Tamerin Corn
　Animal Ensemble: Rochelle Douris, Ric Rose, Isa Garcia-Rose.
　No intermission.

AN ENCHANTED LAND. Solo performance by Sara Morsey; written by Mary Hausch. July 25, 1997. Director, Mary Hausch; scenery, James Morgan, costumes, Marilyn Wall-Asse; lighting, Kristie Griffith; sound, Rocky Draud.
Marjorie Kinnan Rawlings .... Sara Morsey
　No intermission.

Gloucester, Mass.: Gloucester Stage

(Israel Horovitz artistic director)

ONE UNDER. By Israel Horovitz. August 24, 1997. Director, Paul Dervis; scenery and costumes, Lisa Pegnato; lighting, Ian McColl.
Bennie Foss .... Peter Berkrot

Randolf .... Joseph Garland
"X"avier .... Ricardo P. Engerman
Women .... Katrina Stevens
　No intermission.

Hartford, Conn.: Hartford Stage

(Mark Lamos artistic director; Michael Wilson artistic director 4/1/98; Stephen J. Albert managing director)

... LOVE, LANGSTON. Musical by Loni Berry; based on the poems and short stories of Langston Hughes. January 9, 1998. Director, Reggie Montgomery; musical direction, Alva Nelson; choreography, Hope Clarke; scenery, Donald Eastman; costumes, Felix E. Cochren; lighting, Donald Holder; sound, Frank Pavlich.

With Nora Cole, Sheila Kay Davis, Bobby Daye, Cedric Turner, Emily Yancy.

One intermission.

SUENO. Newly adapted from Pedro Calderon de la Barca's *Life Is a Dream* by Jose Rivera. February 14, 1998. Director, Lisa Peterson; scenery,

Michael Yeargan; costumes, Meg Neville; lighting, Christopher Akerlind; sound, David Budries; fight direction, David Leong.

Rosaura .... Michi Barall
Clotaldo .... Yusef Bulos
Estrella .... Alene Dawson
Clarin .... Jan Leslie Harding
Segismundo .... John Ortiz
Servant .... Ken Parker
Basilio .... Geno Silva
lst Soldier .... Sam Wellington
Astolfo .... Damian Young
    Soldiers, Guards, Servants: Darin Dunston, John Socas.

Houston: The A.D. Players

(Jeannette Clift George founder and artistic director)

THROUGH THE LOOKING GLASS. Adapted from Lewis Carroll by Jeannette Clift George. April 16, 1998. Director, Jeannette Clift George; musical direction and arrangements, Patricia Wells Morris; choreography, Cyndi Crittenden; scenery and lighting, Mark A. Lewis; costumes, Donna Southern; sound, Lawrence Rife.

CAST: Hazel, Larkspur, Red Queen—Rebekah Dahl; Al, Tiger Lily, Tweedle Dee, White Knight—Marion Arthur Kirby; Joe, Snap Dragon, Conductor, Humpty Dumpty, White Rabbit—David Morris; Georgia, Rose, White Queen—Whitney Presley; Eloise, Alice—Jenney Sanchez; Tom, Dandelion, Tweedle Dum, Red Knight—Russell R. Swanson III.

KING OF PROVERBS. By James Masters. May 8, 1998. Director, William D. Shryock; scenery, Mark A. Lewis; costumes, Donna Southern; lighting, Sissy Pulley; sound, Lawrence Rife.
King Ulister .... Lee Walker
Demas .... Jeffrey D. Querin

Talbot .... Ted Doolittle
Malchin .... Douglas Taurel
Rachel .... Jessica L. Kell
John .... Lawrence V. Rife
Snit .... Danny Seibert
    Petitioners, etc.: Patty Tuel Bailey, Todd Boring, Adam Estes, Shondra Marie, Erin Rambo.

Time: Sometime between 975 and 1100 A.D. Place: A Kingdom in Northumbria. Act I, Scene 1: A place far away from the palace, and the palace courtroom three months later. Scene 2: The palace prison, 15 minutes later. Scene 3: The King's bedchamber, the next night. Scene 4: The palace courtroom, the next morning. Scene: 5: The King's bedchamber, that night. Scene 6: The palace courtroom, a few days later. Scene 7: The palace chapel and a city street, a few days later. Act II, Scene 1: Outside the palace, nighttime, one week later. Scene 2: Outside the castle, twilight, a few days later. Scene 3: The palace courtroom, three days later. Scene 4: The palace courtroom, early the next morning.

Key West, Fla.: Key West Theater Festival

(Joan McGillis artistic director; Phil Lindsay event coordinator)

6th Annual Key West Theater Festival
October 2–12, 1997

WHERE THERE'S SMOKE. Solo performance by Lesley Abrams; written by Lesley Abrams and Tim Ferrell. Director, Tim Ferrell; scenery and lighting, Tim Ferrell.

THIS BLOOD'S FOR YOU. By Dave Christner. Director, John Papais; scenery, Michelle von Gary; lighting, Barry Fitzgerald.
Father John .... John Papais
Surgeon .... Kathleen Balsemo
Charlie .... C. Michael Johnson
Sherry .... Chris Stone

Hanna .... Mary Falconer
Verlene .... Sinead Mylalsingh
Beatrice .... Vanessa McCaffrey
Peter Rudman .... Steve Baylis
Father James .... Eric Hastreiter
Mack .... George Gugleotti
Warden .... Bryant Lanier
Patrick Jr. .... Scott Genn
    Time: The present. Place: Florida state correctional facility. One intermission.

NEW ORLEANS STORY. By Michael McKeever. Director, Barry Steinman; scenery, Michelle von Garyostumes, Ellis Tillman; lighting, Barry Fitzgerald.
Kevin .... Tom Wahl
Jackie .... Nell Gwynn
Colin .... Michael McKeever
Thing 1 .... Todd Behrend
Thing 2 .... Karen Gordon
Thing 3 .... Hugh Murphy
    Time: The present. Place: The French Quarter. No intermission.

LIFE, LIBERTY AND THE PURSUIT OF ....
By Frank J. Adler. Director, Morgan Kostival.
Emmett Bell .... Joe DeLuca
David Harris .... David Baird
Joe Walker .... Jerry Campbell
Bailiff .... Haig Jacobs
Judge .... Sandra Taylor
    Time: The present. Place: A courtroom. One intermission.

GIGI, THE MERRY-GO-ROUND HORSE. By Zouanne LeRoy; director, Daniel Bonnett; scenery, Rick Worth; costumes, Courtney Kimball, Betty Rubenstein; lighting, Armando Lodigiani.
Gigi .... Sean Morey
Joseph .... Michael Wirsching
Victorine .... Nicole DiNicola
Apollo .... Nicholas Kersch
Fritz .... Ralph Garcia
Isobel .... Holly Hopkins
Lili .... Victoria Phillips
Adolf .... Matthew Ciavolino
Mariana .... Erin Elkins
Kathleen .... Mac Skiver
Collette .... Zahara Zahav
Rita .... Kristin Walterson
Tommy .... Spencer Gates
Polly .... Samantha Steele
Patricia .... Mysha Browning
Franz .... Alexander Freer
Mr. Wagner .... Jim Somma
Mr. Leroy .... Steve Baylis
Charlie .... Haig Jacobs
Myrtle .... Gerri Louise Gates
Elsie .... Elizabeth Watts

Bertha .... Joanie Sullivan
Nurse .... Barbara Gilreath
Painter .... Johnny Larkin
Papa .... David Harlow
Lady .... Jesse Brown
Rat .... Emily Bender
Rabbit .... Gregory Garcia
    Child Chorus: Janell Garcia, Emily Bender, Gregory Garcia, Jenna Regelmann, Zev Zahav, Mysha Browning, Senora Tillman. Adult Chorus: Judy Gorman, David Harlow, Blake Wilk, Steve Baylis, Johnny Larkin.
    Scene 1: Time, late 1930s; place, Wurstelprater, Vienna, Austria. Scene 2: Time, late 1930s; place, shed and stables where horses live. Scene 3: Time, 1939; place, Caldonian Market. Scene 4: Time, 1940; place, hold of a ship. Scene 5: Time, some years later; place, front lawn of Elsie's house.

SIX IN THE GARDEN—ONE ACTS. By David Fleisher. Director, Ann Boese; scenery, David Laughlin; costumes, Nadja Hansen; lighting and sound, Sir Sammy the Sound Man, Graff Kelly.

Out of the Clear Blue
Adam .... Tom Luna
Eve .... Conni Atkins

Silent Partners
Robert .... Tom Luna
Pamela .... Conni Atkins

The Delivery
Douglas .... Tom Luna
Darlene .... Conni Atkins
UPS Man .... Mark Hayes

By My Side
Steve .... Tom Luna
Jennifer .... Conni Atkins

Flat Tire
Dexter .... Tom Luna
AAAWoman .... Conni Atkins

Weekend
Gilbert Schnapps .... Tom Luna
Gloria Schnapps .... Conni Atkins
    No intermission.

Play Readings
October 6–10, 1997

CURSE OF THE ANGELS. By Janyce Lapore.

DELERIUM. By Daniel O'Brien.

BIRTHDAY PIE. By Arthur Wooten.

MARLA'S DEVOTION. By Linda Eisenstein.

BURDEN. By Robert E. Williams.

TABLE NO. 3. By Alexandre Olivier Philippe.

Indianapolis: Indiana Repertory Theater

(Janet Allen artistic director)

LES TROIS DUMAS. By Charles Smith. April 24, 1998. Directed by Tazewell Thompson; scenery, Donald Eastman; costumes, Merrily Murray-Walsh; lighting, Robert Wierzel; music, Fabian Obispo.

Dumas fils .... Ryan Artzberger
Victor Hugo .... Peter Aylward
General; Alexis .... Leon Addison Brown
Napoleon .... Jay K. DuVal
Harel; Governor .... Wynn Harmon
Marie Louise; Mlle. Mars .... Kelley Hazen
Dumas pere .... Keith Randolph Smith
Ida Ferrier .... Kim Wimmer
George Sand .... Pilar Witherspoon
One intermission.

La Jolla, Calif: La Jolla Playhouse

(Michael Greif artistic director; Terrence Dwyer managing director)

HARMONY. Musical with book and lyrics by Bruce Sussman; music by Barry Manilow. October 19, 1997. Director, David Warren; choreography, Charles Moulton; musical direction, Joseph Thalken; scenery, Derek McLane; costumes, Mark Wendland; lighting, Kenneth Posner; sound, Steve Canyon Kennedy; orchestration, Ralph Burns; incidental music and dance arrangements, Joseph Thalken; vocal arrangements, Randy Crenshaw; additional vocal arrangement, Seth Rudetsky.

"Rabbi" .... Danny Burstein
Harry .... Thom Christopher Warren
Bobby .... James Clow
Lesh .... Mark Chmiel
Erich .... Steven Goldstein
"Chopin" .... Patrick Wilson
Mary .... Rebecca Luker
Ruth .... Janet Metz
Rally Leader .... Tom Titone
Marlene .... Jodi Stevens
Felix; Einstein; Aaronson ...... Scott Robertson
Dirk .... Scott Robinson
Ezra .... Casey Nicholaw
Madame .... Jessica Sheridan
Standartenfuhrer .... Kurt Zizkie
Josephine .... Thursday Farrar
Obersturmfuhrer .... Trent DeLong

Young Women on a Train: Jodi Stevens, Lisa Mayer, Jennifer Morris, Kiersten Van Horne.

Ensemble: Trent DeLong, Thursday Farrar, Christiane Farr-Wersinger, Pascale Faye, Sean Grant, Lisa Mayer, Jennifer Morris, Casey Nicholaw, Arte Phillips, Scott Robertson, Scott Robinson, Jessica Sheridan, Jodi Stevens, Tom Titone, Kiersten Van Horne, Kurt Ziskie.

One intermission.

MUSICAL NUMBERS, ACT I: Overture, "Harmony," "There's Something About That Girl," "This Is Our Time," "Your Son Is Becoming a Singer!", "Lost in the Shadows," "In This World," "How Can I Serve You, Madame?", "Every Single Day," "Harmony" (Reprise), "Home."

ACT II: "Something Like Paradise," "Follow the Wind," "Crystal Ball," "Come to the Fatherland," "Where You Go," "We've Gone Bananas!", "Little Men," "Threnody," "Stars in the Night."

Lansing, Mich: BoarsHead Theater

(John L. Peakes founding artistic director; Judith Gentry Peakes managing director)

Staged readings

OTHER WORLD LOVERS. By Shepsu Aahku. December 3, 1997. With Charlotte Nelson, Roosevelt Johnson, Brendesha Tynes, Monrico Ward, Charlie Smith.

ALICE IN IRELAND. By Judy Sheehan. March 11, 1998.

LA JOLLA—Barry Manilow *(seated)*, composer of the music for *Harmony*, and Bruce Sussman *(center)*, author of its book and lyrics, with the six actors who played The Comedian Harmonists in the musical at La Jolla Playhouse

Little Rock: Arkansas Repertory Theater

(Cliff Fannin Baker producing artistic director)

IDOLS OF THE KING. Musical with book by Ronnie Claire Edwards and Allen Crowe. September 12, 1997. Director, Cliff Fannin Baker; musical direction and arrangements, Jonathan Joyner; scenery, Mike Nichols; costumes, Margaret L. Whedon; lighting, Michael Reese; sound, Ryan C. Mansfield.

The Man .... Kevin Bartlett
The Woman .... Dale Dickey
The King .... Lance Zitron
   MUSICAL NUMBERS, ACT I: "Blue Suede Shoes," "Burning Love," "Love Me Tender,"

"Shake, Rattle and Roll," "Jail House Rock," "Hard Headed Woman."
   ACT II: "Return to Sender," "Where Do You Come From?", "I Can't Stop Loving You," "Are You Lonesome Tonight," "Rock-a-Hula Baby," "Softly and Tenderly," "America Medley."

THE THREE MUSKETEERS. By Alexandre Dumas; newly adapted by Brad Mooy. January 29, 1998. Director, Brad Mooy; scenery, Mike Nichols; costumes, Margaret L. Whedon; lighting, Michael A. Reese; sound and arrangements, Ryan C.

Mansfield; fight direction, Dan O'Driscoll; movement choreographer, Tonya Dugger.

D'Artagnan .... John Houfe
Athos .... Vincent Lamberti
Porthos .... Eddie Weiss
Aramis; Duke of Buckingham ... Michael Janes
Constance .... Margo White
Cardinal Richelieu .... Ronald J. Aulgur
Anne of Austria .... Barbara Brandt
Louis XIII .... Carl Palmer
Milady de Winter .... Casey Stewart-Lindley
Rochefort .... Leraldo Anzaldua
Bonacieux .... Rick Kinkaid
Planchet .... Michael Vines
Jussac;
    Golden Lily Innkeeper ...... Patrick McClusky
Cardinal's Page .... Jordy Neill
King's Attendant;
    Red Dovecote Innkeeper .... F. Alan Lee
King's Attendant .... Daniel J. Kronzer
Lady of Chantilly .... Paula Isbell
Port Captain; Executioner ..... Shannon Farmer

Patrick .... James Harris
Felton .... Jason Plumb
Abbess .... Cindy Neill

Workshop Production

FORT CHAFFEE. By Cliff Fannin Baker; contributing composers, Michael Rice, Nick Anselmo, Wally Valenti, Albert Menendez. June 5, 1997. Director, Cliff Fannin Baker; choreography, Mia Michaels; scenery, Mike Nichols; costumes, Lori Gann-Smith; lighting, Michael A. Reese, sound, Ryan C. Mansfield.

With Nick Anselmo, Rob Anthony, Don Bryant Bailey, Juan Betancur, Don Bolinger, Theodora Castellanos, Mark Whitman Johnson, Seth Wyatt Kinney, Francisco Martinez, Jason Manuel Olazabal, Jessica K. Peterson, Amber Ryan, Wally Valenti, Steve Wilkerson.

Second Stage

LAUGHTOUR. Conceived by Brad Mooy. October 2, 1997. Director, Brad Mooy. With Paula Isbell, Daniel J. Kronzer, Michael Vines.

Los Angeles: Center Theater Group/Mark Taper Forum

(Gordon Davidson artistic director)

MULES. By Winsome Pinnock. June 17, 1997. Director, Lisa Peterson; scenery, Christopher Barreca; costumes, Candice Cain; lighting, Geoff Korf; sound, Mitchell Greenhill.

Cast: Lyla, Rog, Allie—Gail Grate; Bridie, Piglet, Rose, Bad Girl—Saundra Quarterman; Lou, Sammie, Pepper, Olu, Bad Girl—Bahni Turpin.

One intermission.

HOUSE ARREST: FIRST EDITION. By Anna Deavere Smith. November 7, 1997. Produced in collaboration with Arena Stage, Washington, D.C., Douglas C. Wager artistic director, Goodman Theater, Chicago, Robert Falls artistic director and Intiman Theater, Seattle, Warner Shook artistic director (see its entry in the Washington, D.C. section of this listing).

Los Angeles: L.A. Theater Works

(Susan Albert Loewenberg producing director; Stephen Gutwillig managing director)

Live Radio Theater Series

WILD AMERIKA. By Erika Schickel. July 9, 1997. Director, JoBeth Williams; music, Casey Cohen.

Host; Others .... Shannon Cochran
Male Roles .... Paul Mercier
Erika .... Erika Schickel

MIZLANSKY/ZILINSKY OR "SCHMUCKS." Revised version of the play by Jon Robin Baitz. October 22, 1997. Director, Ron West; incidental music, Laura Hall and the Expatriates.

Wendi Fink .... Samantha Bennett
Esther Arthur .... Julie Kavner
Davis Mizlansky .... Nathan Lane
Alan Tolkin .... Richard Masur

Paul Trecker .... Rob Morrow
Sam Zilinsky .... Paul Sand
Miles Brook .... Grant Shaud
Arthur Firnbach;
    Mr. Braithwait .... Harry Shearer
Horton De Vries .... Kurtwood Smith
Lionel Hart .... Robert Walden
    One intermission.

SHEINDELE. By Rami Danon and Amnon Levi. March 4, 1998. Director, Jon Matthews.

Admor .... Theodore Bikel, Al Ruscio
Itta .... Estelle Getty
Rochel .... Joy Gregory
Itzel .... David Groh
Sheindele .... Kaitlin Hopkins
Feige .... Lainie Kazan

Yossl .... Daniel Passer
Avrum Steinitz .... Raphael Sbarge

One intermission.

Louisville, Ky.: Actors Theater of Louisville

(Jon Jory producing director)

WILDER REDISCOVERED. World premieres of four one-act plays by Thornton Wilder: *Youth, A Ringing of Doorbells, In Shakespeare and the Bible* and *The Rivers Under the Earth.* October 29, 1997. Director, Tazewell Thompson; scenery, Paul Owen; costumes, Marcia Dixcy Jory; lighting, John Lasiter; sound, Martin R. Desjardins.

Youth
Lemuel Gulliver .... Malachy Cleary
Mistress Belinda Jenkins .... Kim Awon
Dame Sibyl Ponsonby .... Kate Rigg
Duke of Cornwall .... Michael Janes
Simpson .... Christopher Keene Kelly
Boys .... Adam Hefferman, Craig Michael Bollard
    Time: The 18th century. Place: A tropical island.

A Ringing of Doorbells
Mrs. Beattie .... Adale O'Brien
Mrs. McCullum .... Jan Neuberger
Mrs. Kinkaid .... Maia Danziger
Daphne .... Kate Rigg
    Place: The front room of Mrs. Beattie's small house in Mt. Hope, Fla.

In Shakespeare and the Bible
John Lubbock .... Michael Janes
Marget .... Jan Neuberger
Mrs. Mowbrey .... Adale O'Brien
Katy Buckingham .... Kim Awon
    Time: 1898. Place: An over-sumptuous parlor, New York.

The Rivers Under the Earth
Mrs. Carter .... Maia Danziger
Tom .... Christopher Keene Kelly
Francesca .... Kim Awon
Mr. Carter .... Malachy Cleary
    Time: Sometime in mid-20th century. Place: A point of land on a lake in southern Wisconsin.

22d Humana Festival
Of New American Plays
February 24–March 29, 1998

RESIDENT ALIEN. By Stuart Spencer. February 24, 1998. Director, Judy Minor; scenery, Paul Owen; costumes, Nanzi Adzima; lighting, Amy Appleyard; sound, Martin R. Desjardins.
Michael .... William McNulty
Priscilla .... Carolyn Swift
Ray .... Brad Bellamy
Alien .... V Craig Heidenreich

Hank .... Brian Keeler
Billy .... Corey Thomas Logsdon
    Time: The present. Place: Various locations in and around a small town in Wisconsin. One intermission.

MR. BUNDY. By Jane Martin. February 28, 1998. Director, Jon Jory; scenery, Paul Owen; costumes, Nanzi Adzima; lighting, Amy Appleyard; sound, Martin R. Desjardins; fight director, Steve Rankin.
Cassidy Ferreby .... Margaret Streeter
Robert Ferreby .... Mark Schulte
Catherine Ferreby .... Stephanie Zimbalist
Jimmy Ray Bosun ....:.... Normal Maxwell
Mr. Bundy .... William Cain
Tianna Bosun .... Peggity Price
Mrs. McGuigan .... Adale O'Brien
    Time: The present. Place: Various locations in the middle of the country. No intermission.

DINNER WITH FRIENDS. By Donald Margulies. March 4, 1998. Director, Michael Bloom5; scenery, Paul Owen; costumes, Jeanette deJong; lighting, Greg Sullivan; sound, Michael Rasbury; fight direction, Steve Rankin.
Gabe .... Adam Grupper
Karen .... Linda Purl
Beth .... Devora Millman
Tom .... David Byron
    Act I, Scene 1: Karen and Gabe's kitchen in Connecticut, evening, winter. Scene 2: Tom and Beth's bedroom, later that night. Scene 3: Karen and Gabe's living room, later still. Act II, Scene 1: A house on Martha's Vineyard, summer, twelve and a half years later. Scene 2: Karen and Gabe's patio, six months after the events in Act I, spring. Scene 3: A restaurant in New York, the same day. Scene 4: Karen and Gabe's bedroom, that night.

LIKE TOTALLY WEIRD. By William Mastrosimone. March 10, 1998. Director, Mladen Kiselov; scenery, Paul Owen; costumes, Nanzi Adzima; lighting, Greg Sullivan; sound, Michael Rasbury; fight direction, Steve Rankin.
Kenny .... Kevin Blake
Jimmy .... Chris Stafford
Russ Rigel .... V Craig Heidenreich
Jennifer Barton .... Kim Rhodes
    Time: Now. Place: Los Angeles. No intermission.

THE TRESTLE AT POPE LICK CREEK. By Naomi Wallace. March 13, 1998. Director, Adrian

LOUISVILLE—*Above,* Malachy Cleary, Kim Awon and Kate Rigg in *Youth,* one of the Thornton Wilder one-acts in their world premieres on the program *Wilder Rediscovered* on the Actors Theater mainstage; *below,* Stephanie Zimbalist, Margaret Streeter and Mark Schulte in Jane Martin's *Mr. Bundy* under Jon Jory's direction in Actors Theater's Humana Festival

Hall; scenery, Paul Owen; costumes, Jeanette deJong; lighting, Greg Sullivan; sound, Martin R. Desjardins; fight direction, Steve Rankin.

Dalton Chance .... Michael Linstroth
Pace Creagan .... Tami Dixon
Chas Weaver .... Jonathan Bolt
Gin Chance .... Marion McCorry
Dray Chance .... Michael Medeiros
    Time: 1936. Place: A town outside a city, somewhere in the United States. One intermission.

TI JEAN BLUES. By JoAnne Akalaitis. March 19, 1998. Director, JoAnne Akalaitis; scenery, Paul Owen; costumes, Jeanette deJong; lighting, Greg Sullivan; sound, Martin R. Desjardins.
    With Spencer S. Barros, Christopher Michael Bauer, Gretchen Lee Krich, Lisa Louise Langford, Jesse Sinclair Lenat.
    Place: America. One intermission.

Humana Festival

Of 10-Minute Plays
March 28 & 29, 1998

MEOW. By Val Smith. Director, Frank Deal.
Pat .... Stephanie Zimbalist
Linda .... Peggity Price
Waitress .... Sara Sommervold

ACORN. By David Graziano. Director, Sandra Grand.
Bags .... Matthew Damico
Catherine .... Catherine Papafotis

LET THE BIG DOG EAT. By Elizabeth Wong. Director, Frank Deal.
Ted .... William McNulty
Bill .... Brian Keeler
Michael .... Fred Major
Warren .... William Cain

    Ten-Minute Play Designers: Scenery, Paul Owen; costumes, Kevin R. McLeod; lighting, Greg Sullivan; sound, Mark Huang.

Madison, N.J.: New Jersey Shakespeare Festival

(Bonnie J. Monte artistic director; Michael Stotts managing director)

THE THREEPENNY OPERA. By Bertolt Brecht; newly translated by Robert David Mac-Donald; music by Kurt Weill. July 12, 1997 (American premiere). Director, Paul Mullins; musical direction, Rick Knutsen; choreography, John Evans; scenery, P.K. Wish; costumes, Amela Baksic; lighting, Michael Giannitti; tango choreography, Joshua Finkel.

Street Singer; Rev. Kimball .... Joshua Finkel
Mack the Knife .... Stephen Lee Anderson
Jenny Diver .... Gayton Scott
Jonathan Peachum .... Ron Lee Savin
Charles Filch; Jimmy .... Clark S. Carmichael
Celia Peachum .... Debbie Lee Jones
Matt .... Joe Roseto
Polly Peachum .... Kristie Dale Sanders
Jake .... Jeff Applegate
Bob; Constable .... Don Meehan
Ned .... Michael Criscuolo
Walt; Smith .... Bret Mosley
Tiger Brown .... Kurt Ziskie
Nelly .... Kate Ward
Vixen .... Kathleen Connolly

Dolly .... Kim Barron
Betty .... Danielle Duvall
Kitty .... Dee Billia
Lucy Brown .... Kimberly Kay
Messenger .... Todd Ross
    Beggars: Jeff Applegate, Kim Barron, Michael Criscuolo, Danielle Duvall, Joe Roseto.
    Time: The time of the King's Coronation. Place: London.
    MUSICAL NUMBERS, ACT I: "The Lay of Mack the Knife," "Mr. Peachum's Morning Chorale," "Rather Than," "Wedding Anthem for the Less Well-Off," "Pirate Jenny," "The Cannon Song," "Love Duet," "Barbara Song," 1st Threepenny Finale.
    ACT II: "Melodrama," "Polly's Lied," "The Ballad of Sexual Slavery," "Tango for a Pimp," "The Ballad of the Easy Life," "Jealousy Duet," 2d Threepenny Finale.
    ACT III: "The Ballad of Sexual Dependency," "The Song of Inadequacy," "The Song of Solomon," "A Call From the Grave," "Ballad in Which Macheath Begs All Men's Forgiveness," 3d Threepenny Finale.

Miami, Fla: Coconut Grove Playhouse

(Arnold Mittelman producing artistic director)

GOODBYE, MY FRIDUCHITA. By Dolores Sendler. November 11, 1997. Director, Barbara Lowery; choreography, Damaris Ferrer; original music and underscoring, Greg Sendler; scenery,

Stephen M. Lambert; costumes, Ellis Tillman; lighting, M. Todd Williams; sound, Steve Shapiro.
Frida Kahlo .... Judith Delgado
Young Frida .... Delma Miranda

The Fridos .... Alejandro Bahia, Juana Escobar
The Voice .... Stephen G. Anthony
Time: The first half of the 20th century. Place:

Coyoacan, a suburb of Mexico City. One intermission.

Millburn, N.J.: Paper Mill Playhouse

(Angelo Del Rossi executive producer; Robert Johanson artistic director)

CHILDREN OF EDEN. Revised version of the musical based on a concept by Charles Lisanby; book by John Caird; music and lyrics by Stephen Schwartz. November 5, 1997. Director, Robert Johanson; choreography, Dawn DiPasquale; musical director, Danny Kosarin; scenery, Michael Anania; costumes, Gregg Barnes; lighting, Jack Mehler; sound, David R. Paterson.

Father .... William Solo
Adam; Noah .... Adrian Zmed
Eve; Mama Noah .... Stephanie Mills
Cain; Japheth .... Darius de Haas
Abel; Ham .... Hunter Foster
Seth; Shem .... Vincent D'Elia
Yonah .... Kelli Rabke
Aysha .... Emy Baysic
Aphra .... Sheetal Gandhi
Seth's Wife .... Susan Pfau
Young Cain .... James Anthony Johnson
Young Abel .... Barry Cavanagh
Dance Captain .... Gary Kilmer
    Snake: Emy Baysic, Vincent D'Elia, Sheetal Gandhi, Angela Garrison, Jim Weaver. "Wasteland" Soloists: Cheryl Allison, Charles Bergell, LaTonya Holmes, Capathia Jenkins, Trent Armand Kendall, Bart Shatto. "Generations" Soloists: Capathia Jenkins, Trent Armand Kendall.
    Adult Storytellers: Cheryl Allison, Damron R. Armstrong; Yu Asuka, Emy Baysic, Charles Bergell, J. Jon Briones, David Burtka, Donna L. Clark, Darius de Haas, Vincent D'Elia, Rebecca

Dolan, Shawn Emamjomeh, Diane Foster, Hunter Foster, Sheetal Gandhi, Angela Garrison, Enders Groff, Steve Hogle, LaTonya Holmes, Michael Hunsaker, Capathia Jenkins, Trent Armand Kendall, Gary Kilmer, Robyn Lee, Lynnette E. Marrero, Therese Panicali, Susan Pfau, Kelli Rabke, Dena Risha, Beth Roe, Bart Shatto, Jimmy Smagula, Frank Donovan Tamez, Jim Weaver, Christopher Windom.
    Children Storytellers: Barry Cavanagh, Erica L. Cenci, Crystal-Eve, Russell Aaron Fischer, Matthew Francisco, Kassandra Marie Hazard, Kristopher Michael Hazard, Paul S. Iacono, James Anthony Johnson, Jason Daniel Kus, Shawn Frederick Leggett, Carla Martinez, Siena A. Nuzzi, Alexa Petronaci, Camila J. Proffitt, Casey Lee Ross, Dina Jo Sison, Jeffrey Songco, Jessica Waxman, Rori Brooke Wolfe.
    MUSICAL NUMBERS, ACT I: "Let There Be," "The Naming," "Grateful Children," "Father's Day," "The Spark of Creation," "In Pursuit of Excellence," "A World Without You," "The Expulsion," "The Wasteland," "Close to Home," "A Ring of Stones," "The Mark of Cain," "Children of Eden."
    ACT II: "Generations," "A Piece of Eight," "The Return of the Animals," "Stranger to the Rain," "In Whatever Time We Have," "The Flood," "What Is He Waiting For?", "Sailor of the Skies," "The Hardest Part of Love," "Ain't It Good?", "In the Beginning."

Minneapolis: Théâtre de la Jeune Lune

(Barbra Berlovitz Desbois, Vincent Gracieux, Robert Rosen, Dominique Serrand artistic directors)

THE PURSUIT OF HAPPINESS: CINEMA-MERICA and LIFELIBERTY. Created and written collaboratively by the company. Cinemamerica October 11, 1997; Lifeliberty November 12, 1997. Director, Dominique Serrand; scenery and scenography, Dominique Serrand, Elizabeth Mead, Daniel Lori; costumes, Sonya Berlovitz; lighting, Dominique Serrand; original music—Cinemamerica Eric Jensen, Lifeliberty Michael Koerner; sound, Joel Spence; sculptures, Elizabeth Mead.

Cinemamerica
Writer; Ginny Starr .... Luverne Seifert

Mom; The Statue ..... Barbra Berlovitz Desbois
Producer; Philosopher .... Vincent Gracieux
Director .... Steven Epp
Abe; Dealer .... Robert Rosen
Lovers .... Sarah Agnew, Joel Spence
Visitor; Cab Driver .... Dominique Serrand
    Stage hand, juggler, Dan Schultz; wiggist, Jacque Bilyeu; music director, keyboardist, Eric Jensen.

Lifeliberty
Switcher .... Luverne Seifert
Alice .... Barbra Berlovitz Desbois

Philosopher .... Vincent Gracieux
Visitor .... Dominique Serrand
Dealer .... Robert Rosen
Scavengers:
   Alligator .... Steven Epp
   Fool .... Sarah Agnew
   Middle Man .... Joel Spence
   Child .... Cynthia Lohman
   Singer .... Bradley Greenwald
   Music director, keyboardist, Michael Koerner;
violin, Elizabeth Decker; cello, Michael Severens.

RED HARVEST. Adapted from Dashiell Hammett's novel by Steven Epp, Vincent Gracieux, Sarah Agnew and Joel Spence. May 6, 1998. Director, Vincent Gracieux; choreography, Barbra

Berlovitz; scenery, Dominique Serrand, Daniel Lori; lighting, Dominique Serrand, Sonya Berlovitz; sound, Joel Spence, Sarah Agnew.
Detective .... Robert Rosen
Mickey; Bob MacSwain .... Joel Spence
Chief of Police;
   Charles Proctor Dawn .... Luverne Seifert
Wife of Donald Willsson; Don Rolff;
   Ella Willsson .... Barbra Berlovitz
Reno Starkey; Albury .... Steven Epp
Lew Yard; Dupont .... Vincent Gracieux
Max Thaler; Ted Wright ... Dominique Serrand
Dinah Brand .... Sarah Agnew
Jerry Hooper .... Jeff Ehren
Helen Albury .... Kate Behm
One intermission.

Nashville: Tennessee Repertory Theater

(Mac Pirkle artistic director; Brian J. Laczko managing director)

THE HUNCHBACK OF NOTRE DAME. Musical based on the novel by Victor Hugo; book, music and lyrics by Dennis DeYoung. September 3, 1997. Director, Mac Pirkle; musical direction, James Vukovich; choreography, Danny Herman; scenery and lighting, Dale F. Jordan; costumes, David Kay Mickelsen; sound, Gary Loizzo; orchestrations, Michael Morris; fight direction, Troy Gillette.
Quasimodo .... Mike Eldred
Father Frollo .... James Barbour
Esmerelda .... Ana Maria Andricain
Mahiette .... Naz Edwards
Capt. Phoebus .... Joseph Mahowald
Gudule .... Robert Frisch
Clopin .... Travis Harmon
Legless Beggar .... Christopher Harrod
Blind Beggar; Duke of Egypt ..... Brian K. Hull
King's Torturer .... Brian Mathis
Quasimodo's Mother .... Missy Maxwell
Beggar Boy .... Frank Rains Jr.

Ensemble: Brian Best, Caroline Bridges, Brooke Bryant, Matthew Carlton, Julie Partin Cox, Rick Cox, David Ford, Timothy Orr Fudge, Christopher Harrod, Brian K. Hull, Brian Mathis, Missy Maxwell, Ginger Newman, Shelean Newman, Frank Rains Jr., Bill Whitefield, Martha Wilkinson.

MUSICAL NUMBERS, ACT I: "Who Will Love This Child", "King of Fools," "Hail Quasimodo," "By the Grace of God," "Lovers of Music," "When I Dance for You," "Did You See That Priest," "Alms for the Beggar Man," "Come Behold," "Ave Maria," "When I Dance" (Reprise), "A Votre Service," "Paradise," "Bless Me Father," "With Every Heartbeat."

ACT II: "Beneath the Moon," "Ave Maria" (Reprise), "Swords of the King," "While There's Still Time," "If I Die," "This I Pray," "This I Pray" (Reprise), "Esmerelda," "Gypsy Victory Dance," "Sanctuary," "The Confrontation," "With Every Heartbeat" (Reprise).

New Brunswick, N.J.: Crossroads Theater

(Ricardo Khan artistic director)

THE DARKER FACE OF THE EARTH. By Rita Dove. October 4, 1997. Director, Ricardo Khan; scenery, Richard L. Hay; costumes, Michael Allen Stein; lighting, Jim Sale; fight choreographer, Rick Sordelet.
Louis .... David Atkins
Scylla .... Trazana Beverley
Jones .... Mike Danner
Narrator .... Saidah Ekulona
Ben; Conspirator .... Stephon Fuller
Phebe .... BW Gonzalez

Henry; Conspirator .... Marcis Harris
Diana; Dancer .... Jacquelyne R. Hodges
Scipio .... Marc Damon Johnson
Augustus .... Ezra Knight
Amalia .... Felicity La Fortune
Ticey .... Dionne Lea
Alexander .... Jasper McGruder
Hector .... Ramon Moses
Doctor .... William Perley
Leader .... Brian Weddington
Psyche; Dancer .... Tiffany Williams

Time: Prologue, 1820; Acts I and II, 1840s. Place: On a South Carolina plantation.

SPIRIT NORTH. By Leslie Lee. January 17, 1998. Director, Harold Scott; scenery, John Ezell; costumes, Alvin B. Perry; lighting, Mitchell F. Dana; original music, Odetta Gordon.

Ben .... Ray Aranha
Leila .... Joy DeMichelle Moore
Paul .... Victor Love
Shelby .... Moné Walton
Time: Now. Place: Harlem, New York. One intermission.

New Brunswick, N.J.: George Street Playhouse

(David Saint artistic director)

VOICES IN THE DARK. By John Pielmeier. March 7, 1998. Director, Christopher Ashley; scenery, David Gallo; costumes, David C. Woolard; lighting, Donald Holder; sound, Raymond D. Schilke; music, Albert Ahronheim; produced in association with Ben Sprecher, Aaron Levy, William P. Miller and The Shubert Organization.
Caller .... Nicole Fonarow

Lil .... Gates McFadden
Hack .... Peter Bartlett
Bill .... Larkin Malloy
Owen .... Robert Petkoff
Red .... Charles F. Wagner IV
Blue .... John Ahlin
Egan .... Jonathan Hogan
One intermission.

New Haven, Conn.: Long Wharf Theater

(Doug Hughes artistic director)

MYSTERY SCHOOL. Program of five monologues by Paul Selig: *Tongues, Amelia's Second Step, Francie's Benevolent Universe, Slide Show* and *Dr. Edie Gives a Commencement Speech.* December 19, 1997. Director, Doug Hughes; scenery, Neil Patel; costume, Linda Fisher; lighting, Michael Chybowski; sound, David Van Tieghem; coproduced with En Garde Arts, Anne Hamburger artistic director.
With Tyne Daly.
No intermission.

WIT. By Margaret Edson. November 5, 1997. Director, Derek Anson Jones; scenery, Myung Hee Cho; costumes, Ilona Somogyi; lighting, Michael Chybowski; sound, David Van Tieghem.

Vivian Bearing .... Kathleen Chalfant
Harvey Kelekian; Mr. Bearing .. Walter Charles
Jason Posner .... Alec Phoenix
Susie Monahan .... Paula Pizzi
E.M. Ashford .... Helen Stenborg
No intermission.

LOVE AND UNDERSTANDING. By Joe Penhall. March 18, 1998. Director, Mike Bradwell; scenery and costumes, Es Devlin; lighting, Rick Fisher; sound, Simon Whitehorn.
Neal .... Nicholas Tennant
Richie .... Paul Bettany
Rachel .... Celia Robertson
One intermission.

New Haven, Conn.: Yale Repertory Theater

(Stan Wojewodski Jr. artistic director; Victoria Nolan managing director)

GEOGRAPHY. Performance piece conceived by Ralph Lemon; text by Tracie Morris; soundscores by Francisco Lopez and Paul D. Miller. October 23, 1997. Director and choreographer, Ralph Lemon; sensors, Paul D. Miller realized with Ralph Lemon; visual art, Nari Ward; costumes, Liz Prince; lighting, Stan Pressner; sound, Rob Gorton.
Performers: From Guinea/U.S.—Djeli Moussa Diabate. From Groupe Ki-Yi M'bock, Côte d'Ivoire (Werewere Liking artistic director)—Djédjé Djédjé, Nai Zou, Goulei Tchépoho, Zaoli Mabo Tapé. From Ensemble Koteba, Côte

d'Ivoire (Souleymane Koly artistic director)—Akpa Yves Didier ("James"), Kouakou Yao ("Angelo"). From U.S.—Carlos Funn, Ralph Lemon.
Live percussive music: Zaoli Mabo Tapé, Goulei Tchepoho, Djeli Moussa Diabate, Carlos Funn.
Traditional African Songs: "Nagboko" (rhythm), "Kongo," "Golibonoulo," "Soungourougnigbai," "Iya Kolon," "NToronke," Contemporary song: "Nounou" by Boni Gnahoke (Ki-Yi M'bock).

SPLASH HATCH ON THE E GOING DOWN. By Kia Corthron. November 13, 1997. Presented

Above, Athol Fugard and Owen Sejake *(seated)* in the American premiere of Fugard's *The Captain's Tiger* at the McCarter Theater in Princeton; *left,* Saidah Ekulona, Ron McBee and Jacquelyne R. Hodges in a scene from *The Darker Face of the Earth* by Rita Dove at the Crossroads Theater in New Brunswick

in cooperation with Center Stage, Baltimore, Irene Lewis artistic director (see its entry in the Baltimore section of this listing).

PETERSBURG. By C.B. Coleman. April 30, 1998. Director, Evan Yionoulis; scenery, Andrew Cavanaugh Holland; costumes, Linda Cho; lighting, Donald Holder; sound, Malcolm Nicholls.

Apollon Apollonovich Ableukhov;
  Spirit of Bakunin .... John Wylie

Nikolai Apollonovich
  Ableukhov .... Jason Butler Harner
Semyon Semyononych .... William Preston
Alexander Dudkin .... Richard Topol
Morkovin .... Michael Potts
Lippanchenko .... Christopher McHale
Varvara Elgrafovna .... Teri Lamm
Sofia Petrovna Likhutina .... Sevanne Martin
  Time: 1905. Place: St. Petersburg, various locations. No intermission.

Philadelphia: Walnut Street Theater

(Bernard Havard producing artistic director)

Independence Studio on 3

SHYLOCK. Solo performance by William Leach; written by Mark Leiren-Young. February 24, 1998. Director, Deborah Block; scenery, Thom Bum-

blauskas; costumes, Ashlynn Billingsley; lighting, Troy A. Martin-O'Shia.

Shylock; Jon Davies .... William Leach
  Time: Tomorrow. Place: A stage. No intermission.

THE GIFT. By Will Stutts. April 21, 1998. Director, Will Stutts; scenery, Cindy Felice, Conrad Maust; costumes, Colleen McMillan; lighting, Joe Levy; sound, Scott Smith.

Nelle .... E. Ashley Izard
Buddy .... Warren Kelley
    Time: 1959, early spring, around noontime until just before dawn the next morning. Place: The porch and immediate vicinity of Nelle's home in Alabama. One intermission.

BY GEORGE. Solo performance by Frank Ferrante; written by Frank Ferrante. May 19, 1998. Director, Amanda Rogers; scenery, Steven D. Lowe, adapted by Erika Morris; costumes, Scott Westervelt; lighting, Russell Hodgson; sound, Ann Marie Elder; produced in association with American Stage, St Petersburg, Fla.

George S. Kaufman .... Frank Ferrante
    Time: November 1953. Place: Broadway's Belasco Theater and Kaufman's study. One intermission.

Portland, Me.: Portland Stage Company

(Christopher Akerlind and Anita Stewart artistic directors)

CULTURE OF DESIRE. Conceived by Anne Bogart; created and performed by the Saratoga International Theater Institute (SITI). March 19, 1998. Director, Anne Bogart; scenery, Neil Patel; costumes, James Schuette; lighting, Mimi Jordan Sherin; sound, Darron L. West; produced in association with Pittsburgh City Theater and SITI and in cooperation with the Andy Warhol Museum, Pittsburgh.
    With Will Bond, Jeffrey Frace, Akiko Aizawa, Ellen Lauren, Barney O'Hanlon, Karenjune Sanchez, Stephen Webber.
    No intermission.

Princeton, N.J.: McCarter Theater

(Emily Mann artistic director; Jeffrey Woodward managing director)

THE HOUSE OF BERNARDA ALBA. By Federico Garcia Lorca; newly adapted by Emily Mann. October 21, 1997. Director, Emily Mann; scenery, Thomas Lynch; costumes, Jennifer von Mayrhauser; lighting, Nancy Schertler; composer, Baikida Carroll.

Bernarda Alba .... Helen Carey
Maria Josefa .... Lucille Patton
Angustias .... Molly Regan
Magdalena .... Tracy Sallows
Amelia .... Annika Peterson
Martirio .... Natacha Roi
Adela .... Gretchen Cleevely
Maid .... Pamela Wiggins
La Poncia .... Isa Thomas
Prudencia .... Giulia Pagano
    Time: 1936. Place: Spain. No intermission.

THE GIMMICK. Solo performance by Dael Orlandersmith; conceived by Peter Askin; written by Dael Orlandersmith. February 19, 1998. Director, Peter Askin; scenery, Donald Eastman with Jessica Falstein; costumes, Anita Yavich; lighting, Matthew Frey; sound, Red Ramona.
    Time: Late 1970s, early 1980s. Place: Harlem, New York City. No intermission.

SAFE AS HOUSES. By Richard Greenberg. March 17, 1998. Director, Emily Mann; scenery,

Thomas Lynch; costumes, Jennifer von Mayrhauser; lighting, Peter Kaczorowski; music, Baikida Carroll.

Ken Landis .... David Margulies
Tina von Hagen .... Barbara Garrick
Rob Siegal .... Gus Rogerson
Timmy Landis .... Sam Blackman Boyles
Irene Landis .... Michael Learned
Scott Landis; Tim Landis .... Fredrick Weller
Elise .... Leslie Ayvazian
    Others: Jim Connerton, June Connerton.
    Place: A large house in Connecticut. Act I: 1980, summer. Act II: 1987, fall. Act III: 1995, winter.

THE CAPTAIN'S TIGER. By Athol Fugard. May 5, 1998 (American premiere). Directors, Athol Fugard and Susan Hilferty; scenery and costumes, Susan Hilferty; lighting, Dennis Parichy; music composer and arranger, Lulu van der Walt; produced in association with Mannie Manim Productions, the Civic Theater, Johannesburg and the State Theater, Pretoria.

The Tiger .... Athol Fugard
Donkeyman .... Owen Sejake
Betty .... Jennifer Steyn
    Time: 1952. Place: Number 4 Hatch of the S/S Graigaur. No intermission.

Providence, R.I.: Trinity Repertory Company

(Artistic director, Oskar Eustis)

PEER GYNT. Newly adapted by David Henry Hwang from the play by Henrik Ibsen; conceived by David Henry Hwang and Stephan Müller. January 30, 1998. Director, Stephan Müller; scenery, Eugene Lee; costumes, William Lane; lighting, Roger Morgan; choreography, Paula Hunter; music, Kevin Fallon.

Older Peer Gynt; Solveig's Father;
  Invisible Hand .... Timothy Crowe
Peer Gynt .... Fred Sullivan Jr.
Ase; Psychiatrist .... Cynthia Strickland
Aslak; Herr Trumpeterstrale .... Bob Grady
Mads Moen; Ugly Boy; M. Ballon;
  Fellah; Cook .... Mauro Hantman
Father Moen; Troll King; Ship's Captain;
  Coin Inspector .... Robert J. Colonna
Mother Moen; Kari .... Barbara Orson
Solveig .... Melinda Pinto
Ingrid; Anitra .... Rebecca Poole
Ingrid's Father; Troll Courtier; Mr. Cotton;
  Cancer; Psychiatrist .... Brian McEleney
Woman in Green; Old Hag .... Liesl Tommy
Anitra .... Rebecca Poole
Violinist .... Kevin Fallon
  One intermission.

A GIRL'S LIFE. By Kathleen Tolan. February 27, 1998. Director, Barry Edelstein; scenery, Narelle Sissons; costumes, Marcia Zammarelli; lighting, Jeff Nellis; sound, Kurt Kellenberger; original music, Mark Humble.
Bev .... Ellen McLaughlin
Ken; Pasteur .... William Damkoehler
Jen .... Rebecca Hart
Jesse .... Bianca DiSarro
Lernoux .... Nigel Gore
Sheila; St Catherine .... Sharon Ambielli
Terry .... Chris Roblee
  Additional Convention Voices: Neal Baron, Barbara Orson, Cynthia Strickland. Conference Participants: Company.

THE CHEMISTRY OF CHANGE. By Marlane Meyer. April 3, 1998. Director, Constance Grappo; scenery, Narelle Sissons; costumes, William Lane; lighting, Jeff Nellis; sound, Peter Sasha Hurowitz.
Dixon .... Cynthia Strickland
Corlis .... Janice Duclos
Lee .... Judith Roberts
Farley .... Eric Tucker
Shep .... Mauro Hantman
Baron .... Jamison Selby
Smokey .... Paul O'Brien
  One intermission.

St. Louis: Repertory Theater of St. Louis

(Steve Woolf artistic director; Mark D. Bernstein managing director)

THE SKINFLINT. Musical with book and lyrics by Barbara Field; music by Hiram Titus. December 3, 1997. Director, Susan Gregg; choreography, Williamichael Badolato; musical direction and additional arrangements, Jeffrey Buchsbaum; scenery, John Ezell; costumes, James Scott; lighting, Phil Monat; orchestrations, Larry Hochman.
Barker .... Don Richard
Vinny .... John Cudia
Harry K. Pomander .... Paul Boesing
Chip Pomander .... Max Perlman
Elsie Pomander .... Yvette Lawrence
Mary Ann .... Nancy Anderson
Flora Sweeney .... Adinah Alexander
Radio Announcer;
  Mr. Anselmo .... David Heuvelman
Nathan Filberg .... Christopher Bloch
Bolivia .... Ann Harada
Simple Simon; Officer O'Malley ... Don Richard

Time: October 1929. Place: Coney Island, Brooklyn. One intermission.
MUSICAL NUMBERS, ACT I: "Coney Island," "Follow Me," "Money Waltz," "Mary Ann," "Marriage," "Mary Ann" (Reprise), "What's a Hat?", "Maturity," "Skinflint!".
ACT II: "Company's Expected," "Maturity" (Reprise), "Mary Ann" (Reprise), "Quiet," "The Trap," "Love's a Funny Business," "Stolen!", "Love's a Funny Business" (Reprise), Finale.

Imaginary Theater Company

JOHNNY APPLESEED. Musical with book, lyrics and music by Jack Herrick. October 20, 1997 (tour), April 4, 1998 (mainstage). Director, Kathleen Singleton; scenery and costumes, J. Bruce Summers.
  With Steve Broadnax, Eric J. Conners, Alexandra Aufderheide, Denise Roemerman.

ST. LOUIS—John Cudia, Ann Harada, Christopher Bloch, Yvette Lawrence and Max Perlman as Chip in a scene from the Barbara Field-Hiram Titus musical *The Skinflint* at the Repertory Theater

St. Louis: St. Louis Municipal Theater

(Paul Blake executive producer)

THREE COINS IN THE FOUNTAIN. Musical based on the novel *Coins in the Fountain* by John H. Secondari; book by Paul Blake and Doris Baizley; music by Jule Styne; lyrics by Sammy Cahn. July 7, 1997. Director, Paul Blake; choreography, Gemze de Lappe, Mike Phillips; musical direction, Lynn Crigler; scenery, William Eckart; costumes, Robert Fletcher; lighting, Martin Aronstein; sound, Erik von Ranson.

Fred Shadwell .... Joel Higgins
Frances Bertin .... Leslie Denniston
Ginny .... Michele Pawk
Phil .... Lara Teeter
Anita .... Maureen Brennan
Giorgio .... James Clow
Wayne Arnold .... Wayne Salomon
Rodolfo .... Ray Fournie

Others: Robert Earl Gleason, Michael Kaer Miller, Rich Pisarkiewicz.

Time: 1954. Place: Rome. One intermission.

MUSICAL NUMBERS: "I've Heard That Song Before," "I'll Walk Alone," "It's Been a Long, Long Time," "Saturday Night (Is the Loneliest Night of the Week," "It's Magic," "Time After Time," "Guess I'll Hang My Tears Out to Dry," "I Fall in Love Too Easily," "The Brooklyn Bridge," "Put 'Em in a Box," "The Song's Gotta Come From the Heart," "Give Me Five Minutes More."

San Diego: Old Globe Theater

(Jack O'Brien artistic director)

THE LEGACY. By Mark Harelik. July 19, 1997. Director, Laird Williamson; scenery and costumes, Andrew Yelusich; lighting, Michael Gilliam; sound, Jeff Ladman.

Nathan Estanitsky .... Joey Zimmermann
Aunt Sarah .... Ann Guilbert
Dave Estanitsky .... Mark Harelik
Rachel Estanitsky .... Jacqueline Antaramian
Rabbi Jacob Bindler .... Len Lesser
    Time: 1962. Place: A small town in West Texas. One intermission.

LABOR DAY. By A.R. Gurney. February 12, 1998. Director, Jack O'Brien; scenery, Ralph Funicello; costumes, Michael Krass; lighting, Kenneth Posner; sound, Jeff Ladman; co-produced with the Roundabout Theater Company, New York City.

John .... Josef Sommer
Dennis .... Brooks Ashmanskas
Ellen............................ Joyce Van Patten
Ginny .... Veanne Cox
Ralph .... James Colby
    Time: Labor Day, today. Place: Northwestern Connecticut. One intermission.

WHAT THE WORLD NEEDS NOW . . . A MUSICAL FABLE. Musical with book by Kenny Solms; music by Burt Bacharach; lyrics by Hal David; conceived by Gillian Lynne and Kenny Solms based on the songs by Burt Bacharach and Hal David. April 2, 1998. Director, Gillian Lynne; musical direction, Alex Rybeck; scenery, Bob Crowley; costumes, Gregg Barnes; lighting, Kenneth Posner; sound, Jeff Ladman; orchestrations, Harold Wheeler; dance arrangements, David Krane.

Alfie .... Lewis Cleale
Jennifer .... Sutton Foster
Arnie .... John Bolton
Liz ....'...... Paula Newsome
The Other Woman .... Alicia Irving
    Trio: Misty Cotton, Alicia Irving, Monica Pége.
    Ensemble: Roxane Barlow, Brendan Byrnes, Jack Donahue, Christiane Farr-Wersinger, Amy Heggins, Jenny Hill, Joanne Manning, Adam Matalon, Rod McCune, Jonathan Sharp, Mark Anthony Taylor, Courtney Young. Swings: Lindsay Chambers, Pamela Gold.
    Time: Today. Place: New York City. One intermission.
    MUSICAL NUMBERS: "What the World Needs Now," "Always Something There to Remind Me," "The Guy's in Love With You," "Knowing When to Leave," "I'll Never Fall in Love Again," "Raindrops Keep Falling on My Head," "She Likes Basketball," "Walk on By," "The World Is a Circle," "Cotillion," "Close to You," "The Look of Love," "You'll Think of Someone," "I Say a Little Prayer," "I Just Have to Breathe," "Alfie," "Paper Mache," "The Balance of Nature," "Don't Make Me Over," "Trains and Boats and Planes," "Wives and Lovers,"· "Any Old Time of the Day," "Make It Easy on Yourself," "Denial Ballet," "A House Is Not a Home," "What's New Pussycat?"/"Wishin' & Hopin'," "One Less Bell to Answer," "Blue on Blue," "Here Where There Is Love," "Anyone Who Had a Heart."

San Francisco: American Conservatory Theater

(Carey Perloff artistic director)

HIGH SOCIETY. Musical based on the play *The Philadelphia Story* by Philip Barry and the motion picture *High Society;* book by Arthur Kopit; music and lyrics by Cole Porter; additional lyrics by Susan Birkenhead. September 10, 1997. Director, Christopher Renshaw; choreography, Christopher d'Amboise; musical direction, Paul Gemignani; scenery, Loy Arcenas; costumes, Judith Anne Dolan; lighting, Christopher Akerlind; sound, Tony Meola; orchestrations, William David Brohn.

Tracy Lord .... Melissa Errico
Dinah Lord .... Lisbeth Zelle
Mother Lord .... Lisa Banes
Uncle Willie .... John McMartin
C.K. Dexter Haven .... Daniel McDonald

Mike Connor .... Jere Shea
Liz Imbrie .... Randy Graff
Seth Lord .... Michael Goodwin
George Kittredge .... Marc Kudisch
    Others: Bryan T. Donovan, Christopher Fitzgerald, George Maguire, Donna Lee Marshall, Anna McNeely, Jennifer Laura Thompson, Clif Thorn, Kirsten Wyatt.
    One intermission.
    MUSICAL NUMBERS: "High Society," "I Am Loved," "Ridin' High," "Little One," "Who Wants To Be a Millionaire?", "I Love Paris," "She's Got That Thing," "Once Upon a Time," "I Worship You," "True Love," "I'm Getting Myself Ready for You," "Just One of Those Things,"

"Let's Misbehave," "You're Sensational," "Well, Did You Evah?"/"Say It With Gin!"/"Nobody's Chasing Me"/"Why Don't We Try Staying at Home?", "It's All Right With Me," "He's a Right Guy," "Samantha."

MARY STUART. By Friedrich Schiller; newly translated by Michael Feingold. April 1, 1998. Director, Carey Perloff; scenery, Ralph Funicello; costumes, Deborah Dryden; lighting, Peter Maradudin; original music, David Lang, performed by Chanticleer; sound, Garth Hemphill; fight direction, Gregory Hoffman.

Sir Amyas Paulet .... James Carpenter

Drudgeon Drury .... Bryan Close
Hannah Kennedy .... Penelope Kreitzer
Mary Stuart .... Susan Gibney
Mortimer .... Johnny Moreno
Baron of Burleigh .... Scott Wentworth
William Davison .... Tommy A. Gomez
Elizabeth I .... Caroline Lagerfelt
Earl of Leicester .... Marco Barricelli
Count Bellievre; Melvil ... Warren David Keith
Count Aubespine; Burgoyne ...... Luis Oropeza
George Talbot .... William Paterson
Margaret Curie .... Emilie Talbot
Guard; Sherriff .... Tim Redmond
One intermission.

San Franciso: Magic Theater

(Mame Hunt artistic director)

THE PHARMACIST'S DAUGHTER. By Monika Monika. November 12, 1997. Director, Jonathan Moscone; scenery, Tom Langguth; costumes, Meg Neville; lighting, David Cuthbert; sound, Garth Hemphill.

John Gorajick .... Charles Shaw Robinson
Becky Mancuso .... Lisa Ann Porter
Harry Mancuso;
  Bill Clinton .... Brian Keith Russell
Joan Mancuso;
  Hillary Clinton .... Kimberly Richards

Cootie Richardson .... Soren Oliver
Detective Reid .... Niki Botelho
Child With Emphysema .... Miles Sauter,
                                  Nicholas Walker
Jaundiced Girl .... Juliet Tanner
  Time: From President Clinton's inaugural day, January, 1993, forward. Place: Fruitport, Mich., Washington, D.C. and Brooklyn, N.Y. One intermission.

San Franciso: Theater Rhinoceros

(Adele Prandini, artistic director; Doug Holsclaw associate artistic director)

ROUTE 80: CARS, COWS & CAFFEINE. By Erin-Kate Whitcomb. September 11, 1997. Director, Amy Resnick; scenery, Andrea Bechert; costumes, Jess Daniel Amoroso; lighting, Christina L. Hulen; sound, John F. Karr.

Lisa; Others .... Elaine Tse
Etheleen; Others .... Erin-Kate Whitcomb
Voice of Nick .... Brian Thorstenson

THE LAST HAIRDRESSER. By Doug Holsclaw. November 6, 1997. Director, Danny Scheie; scenery, Iva Walton; costumes, Lori Oldham; lighting, Christina L. Hulen; music, Don Seaver.
  CAST: Guy Voss—Danny Scheie; Foley—P.A. Cooley; Pere—Brian Yates; Drunken Queen, Waiter, Mr. Toad, Shrink, Pissy Clerk, Dr. Weinhard, Huey, Steward—Kim Larsen; Principal, Shana, Gin Blossom, Miss Renata, Karen O'Quinn, Winnie, Doctor #2— Alexis Lezin; Scoutmaster, Junior Foley, Hippy Rick, Customer, Rory Palmyra, Hock Foley, Gabby, Prisoner—Robert Mackey; Billy, Trip Floy, Sloan, Manny, Doctor #1, Brutus—Paul Sardi; Miss Rasmussen, Audrey, Janelle, Norma, Dog Owner, Mrs. Gabor,

Mrs. Geneva Wally, Doctor #3, Marshall—Sandy Schlecter.
  One intermission.

EX-LOVERS. Musical by Scott O'Hara and Tom Phillips. January 15, 1998. Director, Russell Blackwood; musical direction, Tom Phillips; scenery, Donyale Werle; costumes, Dara Gabrielle Barber; lighting, Heather Basarab; sound, Gretchen Hildebran.

Piano Player .... Tom Phillips
Carp .... Paul Tena
Harry .... Phil Dunn
Leuko .... Bradley Merle Smith
Cavil .... Craig Souza
Pooh .... Russell Pachman
Vim .... M Shane
Plakia .... Mark Farrell
Myrna .... Cec Levinson
Anton .... Len Moors
Vigor .... Yawar Charlie
  MUSICAL NUMBERS, ACT I: "The Stage of Memory," "With Friends Like These ... ", "Between Dog and Wolf," "He Doesn't Pay At-

SAN FRANCISCO—Elaine Tse and Erin-Kate Whitcomb in the latter's *Route 80: Cars, Cows and Caffeine* at Theater Rhinoceros

tention," "A Diagnosis," "Invocation and Reprise," "The Law."

ACT II: "There Was a Time," "Break My Heart," "Break My Heart" (Reprise), "Love Is Like a Business," "An Actuary," "Time Passes," "Benediction."

Work-in-Progress

UP JUMPED SPRINGTIME. Conceived by Col-man Domingo; based on selections from Joseph Beam and Essex Hemphill's anthology *Brother to Brother;* adapted by Colman Domingo and Maurice Lee; additional material by Maurice Lee. June 1, 1997. Director, Maurice Lee; co-produced with Afrobluesoulpower.

San Jose, Calif: San Jose Repertory Theater

(Timothy Near artistic director)

ICARUS. By Edwin Sanchez. April 24, 1998. Director, Melia Bensussen; scenery, Yael Pardess; costumes, Beaver Bauer; lighting, Derek Duarte; sound, Jeff Mockus.

Altagracia .... Denise Casano
The Gloria .... Lorri Holt
Mr. Ellis .... Douglas Markkanen
Primitivo .... Sean San Jose
Beau .... Daniel Travis
No intermission.

Sarasota: Golden Apple Dinner Theater

(Robert Turoff artistic director)

GREENWILLOW. Musical based on the novel by B.J. Chute; original book by Lesser Samuels and Frank Loesser; new book by Douglas Holmes and Walter Willison; music and lyrics by Frank Loesser. June 12, 1997. Director, Walter Willison; choreography, Brad Wages; musical direction, Michael Sebastian; scenery, Benjamin M. Turoff; costumes, B.G. FitzGerald.

Gideon Briggs .... Andrew Driscoll
Dorrie .... Maxine Wood
Martha Briggs .... Marianne Carson Rhodes
Amos Briggs .... Walter Willison
Granny Briggs .... Helen Blount
Little Fox Jones .... Douglas Holmes
Mrs. Hasty .... Cynthia Heininger
Mrs. Aggie Likewise .... Jacquiline Rohrbacker
Mr. Lunny .... Richard Bigelow
Mr. Preeb; The Boggle .... Brad Wages
Jack Fink .... Roy Johns
Rev. Lapp .... Jeffrey Atherton

Miss Emma .... Lorraine M. Sheeler
Miss Maidy .... Chrystal Lee
Micah Briggs .... Ben Caswell
Shadrach Briggs .... Olli Haaskivi
Shelby Briggs .... Ashley Rose Orr
Obediah Briggs .... Josh Cash
Jabez Briggs .... Zachary D. Yowarski
Rev. Birdsong .... Sam Reni
Thomas Clegg .... James Pritchett
Clara Clegg .... Maggi Taylor
   One intermission.
   MUSICAL NUMBERS: "A Day Borrowed From Heaven," "Riddleweed," "Summertime Love," "Dorrie's Wish"/"House and Garden," "My Beauty," "Gideon Briggs, I Love You," "Walkin' Away Whistlin'," "The Sermon," "Knit Pretty," "Could've Been a Ring!", "Truly Loved," "Never Will I Marry," "Greenwillow Christmas Carol," "Clang Dang the Bell," "What a Blessing," "Faraway Boy," "He Died Good," "Micah Hunts the Devil," "The Music of Home."

Seattle: Intiman Theater

(Warner Shook artistic director)

TONGUE OF A BIRD. By Ellen McLaughlin. September 17, 1997. Director, Lisa Peterson; scenery, Rachel Hauk; costumes, Candice Cain; lighting, Mary Lousie Greiger; music and sound, Gina Leishman.

Charlotte .... Alison Bacich
Evie .... Gina Nagy
Zofia .... Judith Roberts
Dessa .... Sheila Tousey
Maxine .... Jennifer Van Dyck
   One intermission.

HOUSE ARREST: FIRST EDITION. By Anna Deavere Smith. November 7, 1997. Produced in collaboration with Arena Stage, Washington, D.C., Douglas C. Wager artistic director, Goodman Theater, Chicago, Robert Falls artistic director and Mark Taper Forum, Los Angeles, Gordon Davidson artistic director (see its entry in the Washington, D.C. section of this listing).

Skokie, Ill: Northlight Theater

(Russell Vandenbroucke artistic director; Richard Friedman managing director)

THE GLASS HOUSE. Musical with book, music and lyrics by Ellen Gould. December 10, 1997. Director, Russell Vandenbroucke; musical direction, Jeff Lewis; choreography, Marla Lampert; scenery, Scott Cooper; costumes, Shifra Werch; lighting, Robert Christen; sound, Bruce Holland; musical arrangements and orchestrations, Ilya Levinson.

Isa Kremer .... Ellen Gould
The Chassid .... David Studwell
   Time: Kristallnacht, November 9, 1938. Place: Isa Kremer's dressing room and stage. One intermission.

MUSICAL NUMBERS: "The Teller and the Tale," "The Mirror," "Sparks, Glass," "I Am Not a Lithuanian," "Two Prophets on a Train," "A Yingele Fun Poilen" ("A Young Boy From Poland," folk song), "She Talked About the Light," "The Glass House Rehearsal," "When I Stand in Front of You," "The Glass House," "Yearn for Me," "Set Me as a Seal Upon Your Heart," "In the Beginning," "The Mirror," "Yearn for Me"/ "Set Me as a Seal" duet, "You," "Oy, Avram" (folk song), "I Am the Shattered Vessel," "When I Stand in Front of You" (Reprise).

THE LAST SURVIVOR. By Eleanor Reissa. March 25, 1998. Director, J.R. Sullivan; scenery and lighting, Michael Philippi; costumes, Karin Kopischke; sound, Joe Cerqua; produced by arrangement with WM Productions.

CAST: Helen Schlusselberg—Jackie Katzman; Chaskel Schlusselberg—David Darlow; Harry Goodson, Johnny, Titus—Guy Adkins; Sarable, Claire, Carla, Visitor 2, Grandmother—Mary Ernster; Mr. Ian Goodson, Office Man, Hershel, Visitor 1, Grandfather—Tony Dobrowolski; Translator, Harry—Si Osborne.

Time: Out of time, travelling throughout the 20th century. One intermission.

THE WOUND & THE BOW. By Amlin Gray; English version of *Philoctetes* by Sophocles; prologue and epilogue by Russell Vandenbroucke. May 13, 1998. Director, Russell Vandenbroucke; scenery and lighting, Michael Philippi; costumes, Nan Zabriskie; composer and musical direction, Whayne Braswell; movement, Marianne Kim.

Odysseus	David Darlow
Neoptolemus	Jon Mozes
Philoctetes	David Studwell
Voice	David Hadinger
Attendant	Rodney R. To

Musicians ..... Whayne Braswell, Rodney R. To

Chorus: Ted Koch, Robert Barnett, John Harrell.

Time: The tenth and final year of the Trojan War, the beginning of summer. Place: A barren island in an unforgiving sea. No intermission.

Stockbridge, Mass.: Berkshire Theater Festival

(Arthur Storch artistic director; Kate Maguire managing director)

GOOD COMPANY: SONGS THAT MADE IT FROM SHOWS THAT DIDN'T. Musical revue with book by Sheldon Harnick; music and lyrics by various authors. July 9, 1997. Director, Michael Montel; choreography, Karen Azenberg; musical direction and arrangements, Fred Wells; scenery, Gary English; set illustrations, Al Hirschfeld; costumes, Laura Crow; lighting, Phil Monat; sound, James Wildman.

With Lewis Cleale, Patti Cohenour, Kathy Fitzgerald, Sheryl McCallum, Michael McGrath. One intermission.

MUSICAL NUMBERS, ACT I: "Good Company" by Sheldon Harnick and Fred Wells, "On the Sunny Side of the Street" and "I Can't Give You Anything But Love" by Dorothy Fields and Jimmy McHugh, "All the Things You Are" and "Don't Ever Leave Me" by Oscar Hammerstein II and Jerome Kern, "Isn't It a Pity" and "Strike Up the Band" by George and Ira Gershwin, "Blue Skies" by Irving Berlin, "With a Song in My Heart" and "Ten Cents a Dance" by Richard Rodgers and Lorenz Hart, "It's Only a Paper Moon" by E.Y. Harburg, Billy Rose and Harold Arlen, "Get Happy" by Ted Koehler and Harold Arlen, "Any Place I Hang My Hat Is Home," "I Had Myself a True Love" and "Come Rain or Come Shine" by Johnny Mercer and Harold Arlen.

ACT II: "From This Moment On" and "At Long Last Love" by Cole Porter, "Take Love Easy" by John Latouche and Duke Ellington, "Here's That Rainy Day" by Johnny Burke and James Van Heusen, "Triplets" by Howard Dietz and Arthur Schwartz, "Time Heals Everything" by Jerry Herman, "Love Changes Everything" by Don Black, Charles Hart and Andrew Lloyd Webber, "A Quiet Thing" by John Kander and Fred Ebb, "The Picture of Happiness" by Sheldon Harnick and Jerry Bock, "Sweet Bye & Bye" by Ogden Nash and Vernon Duke, "Old Friends" and "Not a Day Goes By" by Stephen Sondheim. "Sometimes I'm Happy" by Irving Caesar and Vincent Youmans, "More Than You Know" and "Great Day" by Billy Rose, Edward Eliscu and Vincent Youmans, "Time on My Hands" by Harold Adamson, Mack Gordon and Vincent Youmans.

OVER THE RIVER AND THROUGH THE WOODS. By Joe DiPietro. August 13, 1997. Director, Joel Bishoff; associate director, Laura Josepher; scenery, Neil Peter Jampolis; costumes, Pamela Scofield; lighting, Jane Reisman; sound, James Wildman; incidental music, Jimmy Roberts.

Nick Cristano	Jim Bracchitta
Frank Gianelli	Herbert Rubens
Aida Gianelli	Shirl Bernheim
Nunzio Cristano	Allen Swift
Emma Cristano	Marie Lillo
Caitlin O'Hare	Amy Cronise

One intermission.

ASCAP Staged Reading Series

90 NORTH. Musical with book and lyrics by Patti McKenny and Doug Frew; music by Dan Sticco. August 3, 1997. Director, Scott Schwartz.

JOSIE AND THE WOMEN OF TOMBSTONE. Musical with book by Thomas Edward West; music by Michele Brourman; lyrics by Sheliah Rae. August 17, 1997. Director, Josephine Abady.

TUCSON and PHOENIX—Carol Roscoe and Michael Winters *(in background)* in Arizona Theater Company's *Rocket Man* by Steven Dietz

Tucson and Phoenix: Arizona Theater Company

(David Ira Goldstein artistic director; Jessica L. Andrews managing director)

ROCKET MAN. By Steven Dietz. Tucson March 6, 1998; Phoenix April 4, 1998. Director, David Ira Goldstein; scenery, Scott Weldin; costumes, Carolyn Keim; lighting, Rick Paulsen; sound, Brian Jerome Peterson.

Donny .... Kurt Rhoads

Trisha .... Carol Roscoe
Rita .... Pamela Stewart
Louise .... Lauren Tewes
Buck .... Michael Winters
Time: The present. And another one. Place: The attic of an American home. One intermission.

Washington, D.C.: Arena Stage

(Douglas C. Wager artistic director; Stephen Richard executive director)

HOUSE ARREST: FIRST EDITION. By Anna Deavere Smith. November 7, 1997. Director, Mark Rucker; scenery, Douglas Stein; costumes, Candice Donnelly; lighting, Scott Zielinski; original music, Michael Gordon, Julia Wolfe; sound, Timothy M. Thompson; choreography, Jawole Willa Jo Zollar; produced in collaboration with Goodman Theater, Chicago, Robert Falls artistic

director, Mark Taper Forum, Los Angeles, Gordon Davidson artistic director, and Intiman Theater, Seattle, Warner Shook artistic director.

Izumi .... Michi Barall
Betty .... Lynette DuPre
PW .... Gail Grate
Dee .... Pamela J. Gray
Genet .... Ron Cephas Jones

Peaches .... Karen Kandel,
Nicole Ari Parker (alternating)
Peter .... Reese Madigan
Eddie .... Alec Mapa
Todd .... Frankie Muniz
Samantha .... Deirdre O'Connell
Oscar .... John Ortiz
Liz .... Judy Reyes
Mihai .... Ivan Stamenov
Boy .... Lee Thompson Young
Act I: Rehearsal. Quotations from real people:
Panoptic—Lucia (Cinder) Stanton; At All at All
at All at All—R.W. Apple; Herd Mentality, Battle
for Who Runs the Country—James Carville; On
Behalf of My Audience—Sam Donaldson; The
Gary Hart Question—Gary Hart; Click Click—
Peggy Noonan; Welfare as We Know It—Paulette
Jenkins; Wolf by the Ears—Penny Kiser; Body
Watch, Rubber Chicken, Film in Camera— Brian
Palmer; A Troubling Time—Mike McCurry; San
Francisco Jail #7—Rebecca Benoit, Sunny
Schwartz; What's Love Got to Do With It—Pa-
tricia Williams; Presidential Peach—Alice Wa-
ters; President's Haircut—Stanley Sheinbaum,
DeeDee Myers, Homi Bhabha, Jill Abramson; Ca-

nary Bird—Liz McDuffie; Daddys' Asses—Studs
Terkel; One Third of a Nation—Franklin Delano
Roosevelt; Perceived Racial Identity—Annette
Gordon-Reed.
Act II: Performance. That's It—Andre Houle;
Daniel and the Lion's Den, It's Gonna Rain—
Rev. Elijah Weaver; To Fight, Chipping Away,
Lie Detector #2, Hat Box, Reading the Bible, Just
Use Words, Been There, Done That— Maggie
Williams; Feeding Frenzy, Washington Political
Insider, Silver Pistol With a Pearl Handle, Just
Sounds, Can't Say That on Tape—Alexis Her-
man; Speaking Truth to Power, Lie Detector #1,
Daniel in the Lion's Den, The Press, House Ar-
rest—Anita Hill; Cricket, We on Tape, My Fa-
ther's House—Sherri Rideout; Maggie Wil-
liams—James Carville; What Do They Want You
For—Mark Fabiani; Peach Orchard—Laura
Smalley; Cool—Ann Richards, Jane Hickie;
Watching—Nell Painter; Mirror to Her Mouth—
Paulette Jenkins; Captives—Ed Bradley; The
Deal, Spinning—George Stephanopoulos; A Crit-
ically Injured Princess—Judith Butler; They Vote
With You, but They Think Like Us—William Jef-
ferson Clinton.

Waterbury, Conn.: Seven Angels Theater

(Semina De Laurentis artistic director)

MY FATHER'S HOUSE. By Jerry Mazza. No-
vember 15, 1997. Director, Michael Clark Haney;
scenery and lighting, Richard Meyer; costumes,
Jeffrey Schoenberg; sound, Johnna Doty; pro-
duced in association with James Farentino.
Joey Politano Jr. .... James Farentino
Joe Politano Sr. .... Len Lesser
Mrs. Rivers .... Melinda Peterson
One intermission.

HAVE I GOT A GIRL FOR YOU! Musical with
book by Joel Greenhouse and Penny Rockwell;
music and lyrics by Dick Gallagher. October 18,
1997. Director and choreographer, Richard Sabellico; scenery, Barry Axtell; costumes, Gail Bal-
doni; lighting, Peter Petrino; sound, Eric Talorico.
Dr. Pretorius .... Michael Danek
Nurse Mary Phillips .... Semina De Laurentis

Elke .... Susan Flynn
Igor .... Hans Friedrichs
Monster .... Paul Liberti
Dr. John Frankenstein .... Gary Lynch
Bavarian Peasants, Others: Debbie Rubin,
Nikki Sanders, Anthony Santelmo Jr.
Time: 1948. Place: Bavaria, the castle of Baron
von Frankenstein and the laboratory of Dr. Pre-
torius, mad scientist. One intermission.

EXPECTATIONS. By Susan Barsky. March 14,
1998. Director, Scott Alan Evans; scenery, Eric
Renschler; costume coordinator, Erin Kienan;
lighting, Amy Appleyard; sound, Matt Lapierre.
Edith .... Mary Fogarty
Karen .... Sioux Madden
Doris .... Lenka Peterson
Time: The present. Place: A small Northeast-
ern city.

Waterford, Conn.: Eugene O'Neill Theater Center

(George C. White founder and chairman of the board; Steve Wood president; Lloyd Richards artistic director, National Playwrights Conference; Paulette Haupt artistic director, National Music Theater Conference)

National Playwrights Conference
June 29–July 26, 1997
Staged Readings

THE EYE OF THE STORM ... A SHIP-WRECK TRILOGY program of three one-act plays: *Wreckage, The Bog Queen* and *Tom and Eva.* By Hilary Bell.

STRANGERS' GROUND. By Erik Brogger.

DISGRUNTLED EMPLOYEES. By Kevin Crowley.

LOVE AND DROWNING. By Will Dunne.

MEAN CREEK. By Jacob Estes.

LA LLORONA ... AND OTHER TALES OF THE AMERICAN SOUTHWEST. By Elise Forier.

THE END OF THE ROAD. By Robert Kerr.

THE FEAST OF THE FLYING COW ... AND OTHER STORIES OF WAR. By Jeni Mahoney.

THE SECOND GENERATION. By Joshua Metzger.

DREAMS THE SILENT DEAD. By Jeffrey Alan Miiller.

NO COMMENTS by Ilya Ognev, translated by Ellen Pinchuk.

TRUEBLINKA. By Adam Rapp.

ANGEL ON MY SHOULDER. By Michele Raper Rittenhouse.

MONDAY? DON'T TELL ME IT'S MONDAY! By Karl Sundby; translated by Ingrid Haug.

THE NUT HOUSE. By Nina Bunche Pierce.

Directors: Casey Childs, Israel Hicks, Karen Nersisyan, William Partlan, Amy Salz, Oz Scott.

National Music Theater Conference
July 28–August 9, 1997
Staged Concert Readings

THE WILD PARTY. Musical-in-progress based on the work by Joseph Moncure March; book, music and lyrics by Andrew Lippa. Director, Gabriel Barre; music director, David Loud.

RICHARD CORY. Musical-in-progress adapted from the play by A.R. Gurney; based on the poem by Edwin Arlington Robinson; book, music and lyrics by Ed Dixon. Director, Kent Gash; music director, Jeff Halpern.

Westport, Conn.: Westport Country Playhouse

(James B. McKenzie executive producer; Eric Friedheim associate producer)

JACKIE O'S GLASSES. By Tracey Jackson. June 23, 1997. Director, Dennis Erdman; scenery, Richard Ellis; costumes, Ingrid Maurer; lighting, Susan Roth; sound, Peter Freedman.
Calley .... Alison Fraser
Kaplan .... Tim Donoghue
Bentley .... John Hickok

Act I, Scene 1: Limbo, the present. Scene 2: Calley's apartment, June 1975. Scenes 3,4,5,6: Calley and Bentley's apartment, July 1975, June 1977, December 1981, October 1987. Act II, Scene 1: Limbo, the present. Scene 2: Kaplan's apartmnent, 1990. Scenes 3,4,5: Calley's apartment, evening 1992, 1994, 1995.

Williamstown, Mass.: Williamstown Theater Festival

(Michael Ritchie producer; Deborah Fehr general manager; Jenny C. Gersten associate producer)

MISHA'S PARTY. By Richard Nelson and Alexander Gelman. August 20, 1997 (American premiere). Director, Lawrence Sacharow; scenery, Douglas Stein; costumes, Martin Pakledinaz; lighting, Rui Rita; sound, Kurt B. Kellenberger; commissioned by the Royal Shakespeare Company and the Moscow Art Theater.
The Russians:
  Misha .... Harris Yulin

Katia .... Laurie Kennedy
Fiodor .... Gerry Bamman
Natasha .... Kate Burton
Valeriy .... Tom Irwin
Masha .... Jennifer Dundas
Lydia .... Melissa Bowen
Singer .... Rachael Warren
Old Waiter .... Ad Wienert
Young Waiter .... Michael Rubinstein

Onstage
In Massachusetts

Left, Emma Roberts, Alvin Epstein, Robert Kropf and Annette Miller in *Nobody Dies on Friday* by Robert Brustein in Cambridge at American Repertory Theater

At right, Julie White and Alexandra Gersten in Albert Innaurato's *Dreading Thekla* at the Williamstown Theater Festival; *below,* James Michael Reilly as Mephistopheles in a scene from *The Story of Dr. Faust,* adapted by Marc P. Smith, at Worcester Foothills Theater Company

The Americans:

Mary .... Penny Fuller
Susan .... Tertia Lynch
Fred .... Greg Naughton
Timothy Rodgers .... P.J. Brown
Keyboardist .... Trevor Exter,
                            Charles Alterman
    Time: The night of August 20, 1991 and early the following morning. Place: The Ukraine Hotel, Moscow, overlooking the Russian White House. One intermission.

The Other Stage

STEVIE WANTS TO PLAY THE BLUES. By Eduardo Machado; songs by Geri Allen; lyrics by Eduardo Machado; additional music by Rodney Kendrick, John Ore, Charles Davis and Jim Simpson. July 2, 1997. Director, Jim Simpson; scenery, Michael Brown; costumes, Marion Williams; lighting, Jeffrey Nellis; sound, Kurt Kellenberger; musical direction, Rodney Kendrick.

Stevie .... Christy Baron
Peter .... Jeremy Blynn
Ruth .... Yvette Cason
Saxophone Player .... Charles Davis
Harry .... Robert LuPone
Mary Ann .... Terumi Matthews
Al .... John Ore
Ernest .... Thom Christopher
Janitor .... Aaron Shipp
Waiter .... Chime Day Serra
    One intermission.

DREADING THEKLA. By Albert Innaurato. July 30, 1997. Director, Nicholas Martin; scenery, Alexander Dodge; costumes, Marion Williams; lighting, Rui Rita; sound, Kurt Kellenberger.

Panna .... Julie White
Michael .... John Benjamin Hickey
Thekla .... Alexandra Gersten
Jody .... Christian Lincoln
Annette .... Kate Gleason
Matthew; Wilfred .... Dion Graham
Woman #1 .... Lisa Benavides
Woman #2 .... Suzi Takahashi
    Washington Square People: Christopher Keslar, Michael Laurino, Joshua Grant Lewis, Ezekiel Morgan, Alexis Ryan, Mary Unruh.
    Act I, Prologue: Panna's dream. Scene 1: The present, Panna's co-op. Scene 2: The present, the terrace upstairs. Scene 3: Fall 1974, Harvard. Scene 4: The present, NYU laundry room. Scene 5: The present, St. Vincent's mental ward. Scene 6: Spring 1975, Harvard. Act II, Scene 1: 1994, Panna's old apartment. Scene 2: The present, Panna's co-op. Scene 3: The present, CNN. Scene 4: The present, Washington Square Park.

LA RONDE. By Arthur Schnitzler; new translation/adaptation by Steve Lawson. August 13, 1997. Director, Joanne Woodward; scenery, Troy Hourie; costumes, Mattie Ullrich; lighting, Russell H. Champa; sound, Jerry Yager; musical coordinator, Deborah R. Lapidus.

The Hustler .... Thomas McCarthy
The Soldier .... Gabriel Macht
The Maid .... Lisa Renee Pitts
The Young Gentleman .... Alex Draper
The Wife .... Allison Mackie
The Husband .... Edmond Genest
The Young Girl .... Gretchen Cleevely
The Playwright .... Scott Cohen
The Actress .... Angie Phillips
The Count .... Steven Barker Turner
'Tweenies .... Sara Barnett, Jennifer Klein
    Time: 1897. Place: In and around Vienna. One intermission.

The Free Theater

PRINCESS TURANDOT. By Carlo Gozzi; newly adapted by Darko Tresnjak. July 24, 1997. Director, Darko Tresnjak; choreographer, Debra Fernandez; scenery, Laurie Powell; costumes, Linda Cho; lighting, Kathleen Kronauer; sound, Corey Harrison; masks and puppets, Daniel Weissbrodt; original music, Antonio Carlos DeFeo.

Turandot .... Rachael Warren
Imperial Judge .... Pete Simpson
Imperial Executioner .... William Brock
Barach .... Matthew Yeoman
Calaf .... James Stanley
Dorma .... Rachel Parness
Nessun .... Trevor Exter
Ishmael .... Gregory Esposito
Altoum .... Crispin Freeman
Brighella .... Jim Hart
Pantalone .... Liam Craig
Truffaldino, Favorite Eunuch .... J.W. Ferver
2d Eunuch .... Charles Day
3d Eunuch .... Sara Barnett
Adelma .... Judith Annozine
Zelina .... Tertia Lynch
    Imperial Guards: David Hornsby, James Marvel, Shane Taylor. Altoum's Men: Cy Carter, Ebon Moss-Bachrach. Turandot's Women: Cheryl Bowers, Kerrin Cuffe, Meg Higgins, Jennifer Klein, Sheryl Ann Ochs, Jessica Smith, Sarah Tucker. Puppeteers: Brian Morreale, Jessica Smith, Daniel Weissbrodt.
    Time and Place: Mythical China.

New Play Readings

HIS MAJESTY, MR. KEAN. By Charles Higham. July 5, 1997. Director, Maria Mileaf.

ONE SLIGHT HITCH. By Lewis Black. July 26, 1997. Director, Bill Foeller.

THE RACES. By Ferdinand Bruckner. August 2, 1997. Director, Barry Edelstein.

THE WORGELT STUDY. By Kate Moira Ryan. August 9, 1997. Director, Bartlett Sher.

THE KILLING ACT: A VAUDEVILLIAN TRAGEDY. By Trevor Anthony and Thomas McCarthy. August 16, 1997. Director, Thomas McCarthy.

Worcester, Mass.: Worcester Foothills Theater Company

(Marc P. Smith executive producer and artistic director)

THE STORY OF DR. FAUST. Adapted from various sources by Marc P. Smith. March 8, 1998. Director, Marc P. Smith; scenery, Crystal Tiala; costumes, Ted Giammona; lighting, Mark O'Maley; sound, TJ Bandla.

Father Lucien .... John Adair
Father Dieter .... Dorian Ross
Wagner .... Joe Smith
Johann Faust .... Scott Kealey
Mephistopheles .... James Michael Reilly
Barnard; Rolf; Alexander .... Doug Shapiro
Ernst; Charles; Otto; Old Man ... Neil Gustafson
Margaret; Helen .... Annie Mosher

Time: The mid-16th century. Place: Wittenberg, Germany. One intermission.

FACTS AND
FIGURES

LONG RUNS ON BROADWAY

The following shows have run 500 or more continuous performances in a single production, usually the first, not including previews or extra non-profit performances, allowing for vacation layoffs and special one-booking engagements, but not including return engagements after a show has gone on tour. In all cases, the numbers were obtained directly from the show's production offices. Where there are title similarities, the production is identified as follows: (p) straight play version, (m) musical version, (r) revival, (tr) transfer.

THROUGH MAY 31, 1998

(PLAYS MARKED WITH ASTERISK WERE STILL PLAYING JUNE 1, 1998)

Plays	Number Performances	Plays	Number Performances
†*Cats	6,533	Crazy for You	1,622
A Chorus Line	6,137	Ain't Misbehavin'	1,604
Oh! Calcutta! (r)	5,959	Mary, Mary	1,572
*Les Misérables	4,615	Evita	1,567
*The Phantom of the Opera	4,345	The Voice of the Turtle	1,557
42nd Street	3,486	Barefoot in the Park	1,530
Grease	3,388	Brighton Beach Memoirs	1,530
Fiddler on the Roof	3,242	Dreamgirls	1,522
Life With Father	3,224	Mame (m)	1,508
Tobacco Road	3,182	Grease (r)	1,503
*Miss Saigon	2,956	Same Time, Next Year	1,453
Hello, Dolly!	2,844	Arsenic and Old Lace	1,444
My Fair Lady	2,717	The Sound of Music	1,443
Annie	2,377	Me and My Girl	1,420
Man of La Mancha	2,328	How to Succeed in Business Without	
Abie's Irish Rose	2,327	Really Trying	1,417
Oklahoma!	2,212	Hellzapoppin	1,404
Pippin	1,944	The Music Man	1,375
South Pacific	1,925	*Smokey Joe's Cafe	1,349
The Magic Show	1,920	Funny Girl	1,348
Deathtrap	1,793	Mummenschanz	1,326
Gemini	1,788	Angel Street	1,295
Harvey	1,775	Lightnin'	1,291
Dancin'	1,774	Promises, Promises	1,281
La Cage aux Folles	1,761	The King and I	1,246
Hair	1,750	Cactus Flower	1,234
*Beauty and the Beast	1,722	Sleuth	1,222
The Wiz	1,672	Torch Song Trilogy	1,222
Born Yesterday	1,642	1776	1,217
The Best Little Whorehouse in		Equus	1,209
Texas	1,639	Sugar Babies	1,208
		Guys and Dolls	1,200
		Amadeus	1,181
		Cabaret	1,165
		Mister Roberts	1,157

† On 6/19/97 *Cats* became the longest running show in Broadway history with 6,138 performances

Plays	Number Performances	Plays	Number Performances
Annie Get Your Gun	1,147	My Sister Eileen	864
Guys and Dolls (r)	1,144	No, No, Nanette (r)	861
The Seven Year Itch	1,141	Song of Norway	860
Butterflies Are Free	1,128	Chapter Two	857
Pins and Needles	1,108	A Streetcar Named Desire	855
Plaza Suite	1,097	Barnum	854
They're Playing Our Song	1,082	Comedy in Music	849
Grand Hotel (m)	1,077	Raisin	847
Kiss Me, Kate	1,070	Blood Brothers	839
Don't Bother Me, I Can't Cope	1,065	You Can't Take It With You	837
The Pajama Game	1,063	La Plume de Ma Tante	835
Shenandoah	1,050	Three Men on a Horse	835
The Teahouse of the August		The Subject Was Roses	832
Moon	1,027	Black and Blue	824
Damn Yankees	1,019	The King and I (r)	807
Never Too Late	1,007	Inherit the Wind	806
Big River	1,005	Anything Goes (r)	804
The Will Rogers Follies	983	No Time for Sergeants	796
Any Wednesday	982	Fiorello!	795
Sunset Boulevard	977	Where's Charley?	792
A Funny Thing Happened on the Way		The Ladder	789
to the Forum	964	Forty Carats	780
The Odd Couple	964	Lost in Yonkers	780
Anna Lucasta	957	The Prisoner of Second Avenue	780
Kiss and Tell	956	M. Butterfly	777
Show Boat (r)	949	Oliver!	774
Dracula (r)	925	The Pirates of Penzance (1980 r)	772
Bells Are Ringing	924	Woman of the Year	770
The Moon Is Blue	924	My One and Only	767
Beatlemania	920	Sophisticated Ladies	767
The Elephant Man	916	Bubbling Brown Sugar	766
Kiss of the Spider Woman	906	Into the Woods	765
Luv	901	State of the Union	765
The Who's Tommy	900	Starlight Express	761
Chicago (m)	898	The First Year	760
Applause	896	Broadway Bound	756
Can-Can	892	You Know I Can't Hear You When the	
Carousel	890	Water's Running	755
I'm Not Rappaport	890	Two for the Seesaw	750
Hats Off to Ice	889	Joseph and the Amazing Technicolor	
Fanny	888	Dreamcoat (r)	747
Children of a Lesser God	887	Death of a Salesman	742
Follow the Girls	882	For Colored Girls, etc.	742
City of Angels	878	Sons o' Fun	742
*Bring in 'da Noise Bring in 'da		Candide (m, r)	740
Funk	875	Gentlemen Prefer Blondes	740
Camelot	873	The Man Who Came to Dinner	739
*Rent	873	Nine	739
I Love My Wife	872	Call Me Mister	734
The Bat	867	Victor/Victoria	734

Plays	Number Performances	Plays	Number Performances
West Side Story	732	The Green Pastures	640
High Button Shoes	727	Auntie Mame (p)	639
Finian's Rainbow	725	A Man for All Seasons	637
Claudia	722	Jerome Robbins' Broadway	634
The Gold Diggers	720	The Fourposter	632
Jesus Christ Superstar	720	The Music Master	627
Carnival	719	Two Gentlemen of Verona (m)	627
The Diary of Anne Frank	717	The Tenth Man	623
A Funny Thing Happened on the Way to the Forum (r)	715	The Heidi Chronicles	621
I Remember Mama	714	Is Zat So?	618
Tea and Sympathy	712	Anniversary Waltz	615
Junior Miss	710	The Happy Time (p)	614
Last of the Red Hot Lovers	706	Separate Rooms	613
The Secret Garden	706	Affairs of State	610
Company	705	Oh! Calcutta! (tr)	610
Seventh Heaven	704	Star and Garter	609
Gypsy (m)	702	The Mystery of Edwin Drood	608
The Miracle Worker	700	The Student Prince	608
That Championship Season	700	Sweet Charity	608
Da	697	Bye Bye Birdie	607
Cat on a Hot Tin Roof	694	Irene (r)	604
Li'l Abner	693	Sunday in the Park With George	604
The Children's Hour	691	Adonis	603
Purlie	688	Broadway	603
Dead End	687	Peg o' My Heart	603
The Lion and the Mouse	686	Master Class	601
White Cargo	686	Street Scene (p)	601
Dear Ruth	683	Flower Drum Song	600
East Is West	680	Kiki	600
Come Blow Your Horn	677	A Little Night Music	600
The Most Happy Fella	676	Agnes of God	599
Defending the Caveman	671	Don't Drink the Water	598
The Doughgirls	671	Wish You Were Here	598
The Impossible Years	670	Sarafina!	597
Irene	670	A Society Circus	596
Boy Meets Girl	669	Absurd Person Singular	592
The Tap Dance Kid	669	A Day in Hollywood/A Night in the Ukraine	588
Beyond the Fringe	667	The Me Nobody Knows	586
Who's Afraid of Virginia Woolf?	664	The Two Mrs. Carrolls	585
Blithe Spirit	657	Kismet (m)	583
A Trip to Chinatown	657	Gypsy (m, r)	582
The Women	657	Brigadoon	581
Bloomer Girl	654	Detective Story	581
The Fifth Season	654	No Strings	580
Rain	648	Brother Rat	577
Witness for the Prosecution	645	Blossom Time	576
Call Me Madam	644	Pump Boys and Dinettes	573
*Chicago (m) (r)	643	Show Boat	572
Janie	642	The Show-Off	571

Plays	Number Performances	Plays	Number Performances
Sally	570	Damn Yankees (r)	533
Jelly's Last Jam	569	The Unsinkable Molly Brown	532
Golden Boy (m)	568	The Red Mill (r)	531
One Touch of Venus	567	Rumors	531
The Real Thing	566	A Raisin in the Sun	530
Happy Birthday	564	Godspell (tr)	527
Look Homeward, Angel	564	Fences	526
Morning's at Seven (r)	564	The Solid Gold Cadillac	526
The Glass Menagerie	561	*The Last Night of Ballyhoo	525
I Do! I Do!	560	Biloxi Blues	524
Wonderful Town	559	Irma La Douce	524
Rose Marie	557	The Boomerang	522
Strictly Dishonorable	557	Follies	521
Sweeney Todd, the Demon Barber of Fleet Street	557	Rosalinda	521
The Great White Hope	556	The Best Man	520
A Majority of One	556	Chauve-Souris	520
The Sisters Rosensweig	556	Blackbirds of 1928	518
Sunrise at Campobello	556	The Gin Game	517
Toys in the Attic	556	Sunny	517
Jamaica	555	Victoria Regina	517
Stop the World—I Want to Get Off	555	Fifth of July	511
Florodora	553	Half a Sixpence	511
Noises Off	553	The Vagabond King	511
Ziegfeld Follies (1943)	553	The New Moon	509
Dial "M" for Murder	552	The World of Suzie Wong	508
Good News	551	The Rothschilds	507
Peter Pan (r)	551	On Your Toes (r)	505
How to Succeed in Business Without Really Trying (r)	548	Sugar	505
Let's Face It	547	Shuffle Along	504
Milk and Honey	543	Up in Central Park	504
Within the Law	541	Carmen Jones	503
Pal Joey (r)	540	The Member of the Wedding	501
What Makes Sammy Run?	540	Panama Hattie	501
The Sunshine Boys	538	Personal Appearance	501
What a Life	538	Bird in Hand	500
Crimes of the Heart	535	Room Service	500
		Sailor, Beware!	500
		Tomorrow the World	500

LONG RUNS OFF BROADWAY

Plays	Number Performances	Plays	Number Performances
*The Fantasticks	15,744	*Tony 'n' Tina's Wedding	3,587
*Perfect Crime	4,586	*Tubes	2,962
Nunsense	3,672	The Threepenny Opera	2,611

Plays	Number Performances	Plays	Number Performances
Forbidden Broadway 1982–87	2,332	*When Pigs Fly	744
Little Shop of Horrors	2,209	Isn't It Romantic	733
Godspell	2,124	Dime a Dozen	728
Vampire Lesbians of Sodom	2,024	The Pocket Watch	725
Jacques Brel	1,847	The Connection	722
Forever Plaid	1,811	*Forbidden Broadway Strikes Back	722
*Stomp	1,791	The Passion of Dracula	714
Vanities	1,785	Adaptation & Next	707
You're a Good Man Charlie Brown	1,597	Oh! Calcutta!	704
The Blacks	1,408	Scuba Duba	692
One Mo' Time	1,372	The Foreigner	686
*Grandma Sylvia's Funeral	1,345	The Knack	685
Let My People Come	1,327	The Club	674
Driving Miss Daisy	1,195	The Balcony	672
The Hot l Baltimore	1,166	Penn & Teller	666
I'm Getting My Act Together and Taking It on the Road	1,165	America Hurrah	634
Little Mary Sunshine	1,143	Oil City Symphony	626
Steel Magnolias	1,126	Hogan's Goat	607
El Grande de Coca-Cola	1,114	Beehive	600
The Proposition	1,109	The Trojan Women	600
Beau Jest	1,069	*Late Nite Catechism	594
Tamara	1,036	The Dining Room	583
One Flew Over the Cuckoo's Nest (r)	1,025	Krapp's Last Tape & The Zoo Story	582
The Boys in the Band	1,000	Three Tall Women	582
Fool for Love	1,000	The Dumbwaiter & The Collection	578
Other People's Money	990	Forbidden Broadway 1990	576
Cloud 9	971	Dames at Sea	575
Sister Mary Ignatius Explains It All for You & The Actor's Nightmare	947	The Crucible (r)	571
Your Own Thing	933	The Iceman Cometh (r)	565
Curley McDimple	931	The Hostage (r)	545
Leave It to Jane (r)	928	What's a Nice Country Like You Doing in a State Like This?	543
The Mad Show	871	Forbidden Broadway 1988	534
Scrambled Feet	831	Frankie and Johnny in the Clair de Lune	533
The Effect of Gamma Rays on Man-in-the-Moon Marigolds	819	Six Characters in Search of an Author (r)	529
A View From the Bridge (r)	780	All in the Timing	526
The Boy Friend (r)	763	Oleanna	513
True West	762	Making Porn	511
*I Love You, You're Perfect, Now Change	761	The Dirtiest Show in Town	509
		Happy Ending & Day of Absence	504
		Greater Tuna	501
		A Shayna Maidel	501
		The Boys From Syracuse (r)	500

NEW YORK DRAMA CRITICS CIRCLE AWARDS, 1935–36 TO 1997–98

Listed below are the New York Drama Critics Circle Awards from 1935–36 through 1997–98 classified as follows: (1) Best American Play, (2) Best Foreign Play, (3) Best Musical, (4) Best, regardless of category (this category was established by new voting rules in 1962–63 and did not exist prior to that year).

1935–36—(1) Winterset
1936–37—(1) High Tor
1937–38—(1) Of Mice and Men, (2) Shadow and Substance
1938–39—(1) No award, (2) The White Steed
1939–40—(1) The Time of Your Life
1940–41—(1) Watch on the Rhine, (2) The Corn Is Green
1941–42—(1) No award, (2) Blithe Spirit
1942–43—(1) The Patriots
1943–44—(2) Jacobowsky and the Colonel
1944–45—(1) The Glass Menagerie
1945–46—(3) Carousel
1946–47—(1) All My Sons, (2) No Exit, (3) Brigadoon
1947–48—(1) A Streetcar Named Desire, (2) The Winslow Boy
1948–49—(1) Death of a Salesman, (2) The Madwoman of Chaillot, (3) South Pacific
1949–50—(1) The Member of the Wedding, (2) The Cocktail Party, (3) The Consul
1950–51—(1) Darkness at Noon, (2) The Lady's Not for Burning, (3) Guys and Dolls
1951–52—(1) I Am a Camera, (2) Venus Observed, (3) Pal Joey (Special citation to Don Juan in Hell)
1952–53—(1) Picnic, (2) The Love of Four Colonels, (3) Wonderful Town
1953–54—(1) The Teahouse of the August Moon, (2) Ondine, (3) The Golden Apple
1954–55—(1) Cat on a Hot Tin Roof, (2) Witness for the Prosecution, (3) The Saint of Bleecker Street
1955–56—(1) The Diary of Anne Frank, (2) Tiger at the Gates, (3) My Fair Lady
1956–57—(1) Long Day's Journey Into Night, (2) The Waltz of the Toreadors, (3) The Most Happy Fella
1957–58—(1) Look Homeward, Angel, (2) Look Back in Anger, (3) The Music Man
1958–59—(1) A Raisin in the Sun, (2) The Visit, (3) La Plume de Ma Tante
1959–60—(1) Toys in the Attic, (2) Five Finger Exercise, (3) Fiorello!
1960–61—(1) All the Way Home, (2) A Taste of Honey, (3) Carnival
1961–62—(1) The Night of the Iguana, (2) A Man for All Seasons, (3) How to Succeed in Business Without Really Trying

1962–63—(4) Who's Afraid of Virginia Woolf? (Special citation to Beyond the Fringe)
1963–64—(4) Luther, (3) Hello, Dolly! (Special citation to The Trojan Women)
1964–65—(4) The Subject Was Roses, (3) Fiddler on the Roof
1965–66—(4) The Persecution and Assassination of Marat as Performed by the Inmates of the Asylum of Charenton Under the Direction of the Marquis de Sade, (3) Man of La Mancha
1966–67—(4) The Homecoming, (3) Cabaret
1967–68—(4) Rosencrantz and Guildenstern Are Dead, (3) Your Own Thing
1968–69—(4) The Great White Hope, (3) 1776
1969–70—(4) Borstal Boy, (1) The Effect of Gamma Rays on Man-in-the-Moon Marigolds, (3) Company
1970–71—(4) Home, (1) The House of Blue Leaves, (3) Follies
1971–72—(4) That Championship Season, (2) The Screens (3) Two Gentlemen of Verona (Special citations to Sticks and Bones and Old Times)
1972–73—(4) The Changing Room, (1) The Hot l Baltimore, (3) A Little Night Music
1973–74—(4) The Contractor, (1) Short Eyes, (3) Candide
1974–75—(4) Equus (1) The Taking of Miss Janie, (3) A Chorus Line
1975–76—(4) Travesties, (1) Streamers, (3) Pacific Overtures
1976–77—(4) Otherwise Engaged, (1) American Buffalo, (3) Annie
1977–78—(4) Da, (3) Ain't Misbehavin'
1978–79—(4) The Elephant Man, (3) Sweeney Todd, the Demon Barber of Fleet Street
1979–80—(4) Talley's Folly, (2) Betrayal, (3) Evita (Special citation to Peter Brook's Le Centre International de Créations Théâtrales for its repertory)
1980–81—(4) A Lesson From Aloes, (1) Crimes of the Heart (Special citations to Lena Horne: The Lady and Her Music and the New York Shakespeare Festival production of The Pirates of Penzance)

1981–82—(4) The Life & Adventures of Nicholas Nickleby, (1) A Soldier's Play

1982–83—(4) Brighton Beach Memoirs, (2) Plenty, (3) Little Shop of Horrors (Special citation to Young Playwrights Festival)

1983–84—(4) The Real Thing, (1) Glengarry Glen Ross, (3) Sunday in the Park With George (Special citation to Samuel Beckett for the body of his work)

1984–85—(4) Ma Rainey's Black Bottom

1985–86—(4) A Lie of the Mind, (2) Benefactors (Special citation to The Search for Signs of Intelligent Life in the Universe)

1986–87—(4) Fences, (2) Les Liaisons Dangereuses, (3) Les Misérables

1987–88—(4) Joe Turner's Come and Gone, (2) The Road to Mecca, (3) Into the Woods

1988–89—(4) The Heidi Chronicles, (2) Aristocrats (Special citation to Bill Irwin for Largely New York)

1989–90—(4) The Piano Lesson, (2) Privates on Parade, (3) City of Angels

1990–91—(4) Six Degrees of Separation, (2) Our Country's Good, (3) The Will Rogers Follies (Special citation to Eileen Atkins for her portrayal of Virginia Woolf in A Room of One's Own)

1991–92—(4) Dancing at Lughnasa, (1) Two Trains Running

1992–93—(4) Angels in America: Millennium Approaches, (2) Someone Who'll Watch Over Me, (3) Kiss of the Spider Woman

1993–94—(4) Three Tall Women (Special citation to Anna Deavere Smith for her unique contribution to theatrical form)

1994–95—(4) Arcadia, (1) Love! Valour! Compassion! (Special citation to Signature Theater Company for outstanding artistic achievement)

1995–96—(4) Seven Guitars, (2) Molly Sweeney, (3) Rent

1996–97—(4) How I Learned to Drive, (2) Skylight, (3) Violet (Special citation to Chicago)

1997–98—(4) Art, (1) Pride's Crossing, (3) The Lion King (Special citation to the revival production of Cabaret)

NEW YORK DRAMA CRITICS CIRCLE VOTING 1997–98

In a spirited session of voting for the bests of this season, the New York Drama Critics Circle members went to four ballots for bests of bests, three for best American play and two for best musical.

Voting on the first ballot for the best play of the year regardless of category (foreign or American), registering the first choices of the 22 voting critics (6 by proxy), went as follows: *The Beauty Queen of Leenane* 11 (Ben Brantley, Mary Campbell, Robert Feldberg, Michael Kuchwara, Donald Lyons, Ken Mandelbaum, Peter Marks, David Sheward, Michael Sommers, David Patrick Stearns, Richard Zoglin), *Art* 6 (John Heilpern, Aileen Jacobson, Jack Kroll, James le Sourd, Frank Scheck, John Simon), *Three Days of Rain* 2 (Alexis Greene, Linda Winer) and 1 each for *Pride's Crossing* (Clive Barnes), *Pearls for Pigs* (Michael Feingold) and *The Cripple of Inishmaan* (Jan Stuart).

The Beauty Queen of Leenane was also the first choice of Fintan O'Toole, who joined the group in voting on subsequent ballots. But on this first ballot it fell just short of a majority, receiving only 11 of the 22 opening votes, so that the critics proceeded to a subsequent, point-weighted ballot (first choice 3 points, second choice 2 points, third choice 1 point). On point-weighted ballots, to win, an entry must collect a number of points equal to or higher than three times the number of Circle members voting, divided by two, plus one. On the second ballot, with each critic naming three plays, *Gross Indecency: The Three Trials of Oscar Wilde, From Above, Goose-Pimples, Side Man, The Forest, The Batting Cage, Mojo, Defying Gravity, Collected Stories*, and *Mizlansky/Zilinsky or "Schmucks,"* also figured in the voting.

No play having collected a winning point total, the critics proceeded to a third ballot with only the top three second-ballot plays—*Art, The Beauty Queen of Leenane* and *Three Days of Rain*—now eligible for one-choice voting. Two plays tied at 7 apiece at the top of this third ballot—*Art* and *Beauty Queen*—so these two went head-to-head on a fourth ballot. The 17 voters gave *Art* a victory over *Beauty Queen* for the best-of-bests award by 9 votes to 8.

Having selected a foreign play as their best for 1997–98 regardless of category, the critics proceeded to vote their first choices, some proxies included, for a best American play, as follows: *Pride's Crossing* 7 (Barnes, Jacobson, Kuchwara, le Sourd, Lyons, Simon, Sommers), *Three Days of Rain* 7 (Campbell, Feingold, Feldberg, Greene, Kroll, Mandelbaum, Winer), *Side Man* 3 (Heilpern, Marks, Scheck) and 1 each for *Mizlansky/Zilinsky* (Sheward), *Golden Child* (Stearns) and *The Handless Maiden* (Stuart). The second, point-weighted ballot was also inconclusive, with *The Old Neighborhood, Pearls for Pigs, From Above, As Bees in Honey Drown, The Batting Cage, Defying Gravity, Freak, Collected Stories* and *Scotland Road* also entering the lists. On the third ballot limited to the three second-ballot leaders, *Pride's Crossing* was named best American play with a plurality of 8 votes against 7 for *Three Days of Rain* and 2 for *Side Man*.

The critics found it easier to select a best musical, though not on the first ballot. Again, the front-runner fell one vote short of a majority, as follows: *Ragtime* 11 (Barnes, Campbell, Feingold, Kuchwara, Mandelbaum, O'Toole, Scheck, Simon, Sommers, Stearns, Zoglin), *The Lion King* 6 (Feldberg, Greene, Kroll, le Sourd, Sheward, Winer), *Hedwig and the Angry Inch* 3 (Jacobson, Lyons, Marks) and 1 each for *Side Show* (Brantley) and *Triumph of Love* (Stuart). But on the second, point-weighted ballot, with proxies eliminated and with *The Scarlet Pimpernel, Saturn Returns, Time Rocker, The Capeman* and *The Last Session* brought into play among 18 voters, *The Lion King* collected 32 points (see below), 4 more than the 28 needed to win it the award for the best musical of the season.

The critics then voted a special citation to the Roundabout Theater revival production of *Cabaret*.

SECOND BALLOT FOR BEST MUSICAL

Critic	1st Choice (3 pts.)	2d Choice (2 pts.)	3d Choice (1 pt.)
Clive Barnes *Post*	Ragtime	Side Show	Lion King
Mary Campbell *AP*	Ragtime	Side Show	Scarlet Pimpernel
Michael Feingold *Village Voice*	Ragtime	Hedwig	Saturn Returns
Robert Feldberg *Bergen Record*	Lion King	Triumph of Love	Side Show
Alexis Greene *InTheater*	Lion King	Hedwig	Scarlet Pimpernel
Aileen Jacobson *Newsday*	Hedwig	Lion King	Ragtime

Jack Kroll *Newsweek*	Lion King	Side Show	Triumph of Love
Michael Kuchwara *AP*	Ragtime	Lion King	Triumph of Love
Jacques le Sourd Gannett Newspapers	Lion King	Hedwig	Ragtime
Donald Lyons *Wall Street Journal*	Hedwig	Time Rocker	The Capeman
Ken Mandelbaum *InTheater*	Ragtime	Lion King	Side Show
Peter Marks *Times*	Hedwig	Side Show	Lion King
Fintan O'Toole *Daily News*	Ragtime	Lion King	Triumph of Love
Frank Scheck *Christian Science Monitor*	Ragtime	Lion King	Triumph of Love
David Sheward *Backstage*	Lion King	Hedwig	The Last Session
John Simon *New York*	Ragtime	Lion King	Side Show
Michael Sommers Newhouse Group	Ragtime	Side Show	Hedwig
Linda Winer *Newsday*	Lion King	Triumph of Love	Hedwig

CHOICES OF SOME OTHER CRITICS

Critic	Best Play	Best Musical
Joy Browne WOR	Art	The Lion King
Sherry Eaker *Backstage*	The Beauty Queen of Leenane	Ragtime
Martin Gottfried *N.Y. Law Journal*	Art	Side Show
Ralph Howard WINS Radio	The Cripple of Inishmaan	Ragtime
Roma Torre NY1 News	The Beauty Queen of Leenane	The Lion King
John Willis *Theater World*	The Beauty Queen of Leenane	Ragtime

PULITZER PRIZE WINNERS 1916–17 TO 1997–98

1916–17—No award
1917–18—Why Marry?, by Jesse Lynch Williams
1918–19—No award
1919–20—Beyond the Horizon, by Eugene O'Neill
1920–21—Miss Lulu Bett, by Zona Gale
1921–22—Anna Christie, by Eugene O'Neill
1922–23—Icebound, by Owen Davis
1923–24—Hell-Bent fer Heaven, by Hatcher Hughes
1924–25—They Knew What They Wanted, by Sidney Howard
1925–26—Craig's Wife, by George Kelly
1926–27—In Abraham's Bosom, by Paul Green
1927–28—Strange Interlude, by Eugene O'Neill
1928–29—Street Scene, by Elmer Rice
1929–30—The Green Pastures, by Marc Connelly
1930–31—Alison's House, by Susan Glaspell
1931–32—Of Thee I Sing, by George S. Kaufman, Morrie Ryskind, Ira and George Gershwin
1932–33—Both Your Houses, by Maxwell Anderson
1933–34—Men in White, by Sidney Kingsley
1934–35—The Old Maid, by Zoe Akins
1935–36—Idiot's Delight, by Robert E. Sherwood
1936–37—You Can't Take It With You, by Moss Hart and George S. Kaufman
1937–38—Our Town, by Thornton Wilder
1938–39—Abe Lincoln in Illinois, by Robert E. Sherwood
1939–40—The Time of Your Life, by William Saroyan
1940–41—There Shall Be No Night, by Robert E. Sherwood
1941–42—No award
1942–43—The Skin of Our Teeth, by Thornton Wilder
1943–44—No award
1944–45—Harvey, by Mary Chase
1945–46—State of the Union, by Howard Lindsay and Russel Crouse
1946–47—No award
1947–48—A Streetcar Named Desire, by Tennessee Williams
1948–49—Death of a Salesman, by Arthur Miller
1949–50—South Pacific, by Richard Rodgers, Oscar Hammerstein II and Joshua Logan
1950–51—No award
1951–52—The Shrike, by Joseph Kramm
1952–53—Picnic, by William Inge
1953–54—The Teahouse of the August Moon, by John Patrick
1954–55—Cat on a Hot Tin Roof, by Tennessee Williams

1955–56—The Diary of Anne Frank, by Frances Goodrich and Albert Hackett
1956–57—Long Day's Journey Into Night, by Eugene O'Neill
1957–58—Look Homeward, Angel, by Ketti Frings
1958–59—J.B., by Archibald MacLeish
1959–60—Fiorello!, by Jerome Weidman, George Abbott, Sheldon Harnick and Jerry Bock
1960–61—All the Way Home, by Tad Mosel
1961–62—How to Succeed in Business Without Really Trying, by Abe Burrows, Willie Gilbert, Jack Weinstock and Frank Loesser
1962–63—No award
1963–64—No award
1964–65—The Subject Was Roses, by Frank D. Gilroy
1965–66—No award
1966–67—A Delicate Balance, by Edward Albee
1967–68—No award
1968–69—The Great White Hope, by Howard Sackler
1969–70—No Place To Be Somebody, by Charles Gordone
1970–71—The Effect of Gamma Rays on Man-in-the-Moon Marigolds, by Paul Zindel
1971–72—No award
1972–73—That Championship Season, by Jason Miller
1973–74—No award
1974–75—Seascape, by Edward Albee
1975–76—A Chorus Line, by Michael Bennett, James Kirkwood, Nicholas Dante, Marvin Hamlisch and Edward Kleban
1976–77—The Shadow Box, by Michael Cristofer
1977–78—The Gin Game, by D.L. Coburn
1978–79—Buried Child, by Sam Shepard
1979–80—Talley's Folly, by Lanford Wilson
1980–81—Crimes of the Heart, by Beth Henley
1981–82—A Soldier's Play, by Charles Fuller
1982–83—'night, Mother, by Marsha Norman
1983–84—Glengarry Glen Ross, by David Mamet
1984–85—Sunday in the Park With George, by James Lapine and Stephen Sondheim
1985–86—No award
1986–87—Fences, by August Wilson
1987–88—Driving Miss Daisy, by Alfred Uhry
1988–89—The Heidi Chronicles, by Wendy Wasserstein
1989–90—The Piano Lesson, by August Wilson
1990–91—Lost in Yonkers, by Neil Simon
1991–92—The Kentucky Cycle, by Robert Schenkkan

TONY AWARDS

The American Theater Wing's 52d annual Tony (Antoinette Perry) Awards are presented in recognition of distinguished achievement in the Broadway Theater. The League of American Theaters and Producers and the American Theater Wing present these awards, founded by the Wing in 1947. Legitimate theater productions opening in 37 eligible Broadway theaters during the present Tony season—May 1, 1997 to April 29, 1998—were considered by the Tony Awards Nominating Committee (appointed by the Tony Awards Administration Committee) for the awards in 21 categories. The 1997–98 Nominating Committee comprised Billie Allen, actress and director; Maureen Anderman, actress; Price Berkley, publisher; Donald Brooks, costume designer; Mary Schmidt Campbell, educator; Marge Champion, choreographer; Betty L. Corwin, theater archivist; Gretchen Cryer, composer; Tom Dillon, administrator; Mallory Factor, entrepreneur; Robert Fitzpatrick, educator; Morton Gottlieb, producer; Sheldon Harnick, lyricist; Geoffrey Holder, director; Charles Hollerith, producer; Allen Lee Hughes, lighting designer; Barnard Hughes, actor; Betty Jacobs, script consultant; Robert Kamlot, general manager; Jack Lee, musical director; Jon Nakagawa, managing director; Peter Neufeld, administrator; Polly Pen, author and composer; David Richards, writer; Franklin E. Weissberg, judge; and Lanford Wilson, playwright.

The Tony Awards are voted from the list of nominees, usually four in each category, by members of the theater and journalism professions: the governing boards of the five theater artists' organizations—Actors' Equity Association, the Dramatists Guild, the Society of Stage Directors and Choreographers, the United Scenic Artists and the Casting Society of America—the members of the designated first night theater press, the board of directors of the American Theater Wing and the membership of the League of American Theaters and Producers. Because of fluctuation in these groups, the size of the Tony electorate varies from year to year. For the 1997–98 season there were 782 qualified Tony voters.

The list of 1997–98 nominees follows, with winners in each category listed in **bold face type**.

BEST PLAY (award goes to both author and producer). *Art* by **Yasmina Reza**, produced by **David Pugh**, **Sean Connery** and **Joan Cullman**; *Freak* by John Leguizamo, produced by Arielle Tepper, Bill Haber and Gregory Mosher; *Golden Child* by David Henry Hwang, produced by Benjamin Mordecai, Dori Berinstein, John Kao, Talia Shire, John F. Kennedy Center for the Performing Arts, South Coast Repertory, The Joseph Papp Public Theater/New York Shakespeare Festival and American Conservatory Theater; *The Beauty Queen of Leenane* by Martin McDonagh, produced by Atlantic Theater Company,

Randall L. Wreghitt, Chase Mishkin, Steven M. Levy, Leonard Soloway, Julian Schlossberg, Norma Langworthy and The Druid Theater Company/Royal Court Theater.

BEST MUSICAL (award goes to the producer). *Ragtime* produced by Livent (U.S.) Inc.; *Side Show* produced by Emanuel Azenberg, Joseph Nederlander, Herschel Waxman, Janice McKenna and Scott Nederlander; *The Lion King* produced by **Disney**; *The Scarlet Pimpernel* produced by Pierre Cossette, Bill Haber, Hallmark Entertainment, Ted Forstmann and Kathleen Raitt.

BEST BOOK OF A MUSICAL. *Ragtime* by **Terrence McNally**; *Side Show* by Bill Russell; *The Lion King* by Roger Allers and Irene Mecchi; *The Scarlet Pimpernel* by Nan Knighton.

BEST ORIGINAL SCORE (music & lyrics) WRITTEN FOR THE THEATER. *Ragtime*, music by **Stephen Flaherty**, lyrics by **Lynn Ahrens**; *Side Show*, music by Henry Krieger, lyrics by Bill Russell; *The Capeman*, music by Paul Simon, lyrics by Paul Simon and Derek Walcott; *The Lion King*, music and lyrics by Elton John, Tim Rice, Lebo M, Mark Mancina, Jay Rifkin, Julie Taymor and Hans Zimmer.

BEST REVIVAL OF A PLAY (award goes to the producer). *A View From the Bridge* produced by **Roundabout Theater Company, Todd Haimes, Ellen Richard, Roger Berlind, James M. Nederlander, Nathaniel Kramer, Elizabeth Ireland McCann, Roy Gabay** and **Old Ivy Productions**; *Ah, Wilderness!* produced by Lincoln Center Theater, Andre Bishop and Bernard Gersten; *The Chairs* produced by Bill Kenwright, Carole Shorenstein Hays, Scott Rudin, Stuart Thompson and Théâtre de Complicité/Royal Court Theater; *The Diary of Anne Frank* (adapted by Wendy Kesselman) produced by David Stone, Amy Nederlander-Case, Jon B. Platt, Jujamcyn Theaters, Hal Luftig, Harriet Newman Leve, James D. Stern.

BEST REVIVAL OF A MUSICAL (award goes to the producer). *Cabaret* produced by **Roundabout Theater Company, Todd Haimes** and **Ellen Richard**; *1776* produced by Roundabout Theater Company, Todd Haimes, Ellen Richard, James M. Nederlander, Stewart F. Lane, Rodger Hess, Bill Haber, Robert Halmi Jr., Dodger Endemol Theatricals and Hallmark Entertainment; *The Sound of Music* produced by Thomas Viertel, Steven Baruch, Richard Frankel, Jujamcyn Theaters, The Rodgers and Hammerstein Organization, Charles Kelman Productions, Simone Genatt Haft, Marc Routh, Jay Binder and Robert Halmi Jr.

BEST PERFORMANCE BY A LEADING ACTOR IN A PLAY. Richard Briers in *The Chairs*; **Anthony LaPaglia** in *A View From the Bridge*; John Leguizamo in *Freak*; Alfred Molina in *Art*.

BEST PERFORMANCE BY A LEADING ACTRESS IN A PLAY. Jane Alexander in *Honour*; Allison Janney in *A View From the Bridge*; Geraldine McEwan in *The Chairs*; **Marie Mullen** in *The Beauty Queen of Leenane*.

BEST PERFORMANCE BY A LEADING ACTOR IN A MUSICAL. **Alan Cumming** in *Cabaret*; Peter Friedman in *Ragtime*; Brian Stokes Mitchell in *Ragtime*; Douglas Sills in *The Scarlet Pimpernel*.

BEST PERFORMANCE BY A LEADING ACTRESS IN A MUSICAL. Betty Buckley in *Triumph of Love*; Marin Mazzie in *Ragtime*; **Natasha Richardson** in *Cabaret*; Alice Ripley and Emily Skinner in *Side Show*.

BEST PERFORMANCE BY A FEATURED ACTOR IN A PLAY. **Tom Murphy** in *The Beauty Queen of Leenane*; Brian F. O'Byrne in *The Beauty Queen of Leenane*; Sam Trammell in *Ah, Wilderness!*; Max Wright in *Ivanov*.

BEST PERFORMANCE BY A FEATURED ACTRESS IN A PLAY. Enid Graham in *Honour*; Linda Lavin in *The Diary of Anne Frank*; **Anna Manahan** in *The Beauty Queen of Leenane*; Julyana Soelistyo in *Golden Child*.

BEST PERFORMANCE BY A FEATURED ACTOR IN A MUSICAL. Gregg Edelman in *1776*; John McMartin in *High Society*; **Ron Rifkin** in *Cabaret*; Samuel E. Wright in *The Lion King*.

BEST PERFORMANCE BY A FEATURED ACTRESS IN A MUSICAL. Anna

Kendrick in *High Society*; Tsidii Le Loka in *The Lion King*; **Audra McDonald** in *Ragtime*; Mary Louise Wilson in *Cabaret*.

BEST SCENIC DESIGN. Bob Crowley for *The Capeman*; **Richard Hudson** for *The Lion King*; Eugene Lee for *Ragtime*; Quay Brothers for *The Chairs*.

BEST COSTUME DESIGN. William Ivey Long for *Cabaret*; Santo Loquasto for *Ragtime*; Martin Pakledinaz for *Golden Child*; **Julie Taymor** for *The Lion King*.

BEST LIGHTING DESIGN. Paul Anderson for *The Chairs*; Peggy Eisenhauer and Mike Baldassari for *Cabaret*; Jules Fisher and Peggy Eisenhauer for *Ragtime*; **Donald Holder** for *The Lion King*.

BEST CHOREOGRAPHY. Graciela Daniele for *Ragtime*; **Garth Fagan** for *The Lion King*; Forever Tango Dancers for *Forever Tango*; Rob Marshall for *Cabaret*.

BEST DIRECTION OF A PLAY. Garry Hynes for *The Beauty Queen of Leenane*; Michael Mayer for *A View From the Bridge*; Simon McBurney for *The Chairs*; Matthew Warchus for *Art*.

BEST DIRECTION OF A MUSICAL. Scott Ellis for *1776*; Frank Galati for *Ragtime*; Sam Mendes with Rob Marshall for *Cabaret*; **Julie Taymor** for *The Lion King*.

BEST ORCHESTRATIONS. William David Brohn for *Ragtime*; Robert Elhai, David Metzger and Bruce Fowler for *The Lion King*; Michael Gibson for *Cabaret*; Stanley Silverman for *The Capeman*.

SPECIAL TONY AWARDS. To a regional theater company that has displayed a continuous level of artistic achievement contributing to the growth of the theater nationally, recommended by the American Theater Critics Association—**Denver Center Theater Company.** For lifetime achievement in the theater—**Edward E. Colton** and **Ben Edwards.** Tony Honor for excellence in the theater—**International Theater Institute of the United States (ITI).**

TONY AWARD WINNERS, 1947–1998

Listed below are the Antoinette Perry (Tony) Award winners in the categories of Best Play and Best Musical from the time these awards were established until the present.

1947—No play or musical award
1948—Mister Roberts; no musical award
1949—Death of a Salesman; Kiss Me, Kate
1950—The Cocktail Party; South Pacific
1951—The Rose Tattoo; Guys and Dolls
1952—The Fourposter; The King and I
1953—The Crucible; Wonderful Town
1954—The Teahouse of the August Moon; Kismet
1955—The Desperate Hours; The Pajama Game
1956—The Diary of Anne Frank; Damn Yankees
1957—Long Day's Journey Into Night; My Fair Lady
1958—Sunrise at Campobello; The Music Man
1959—J.B.; Redhead
1960—The Miracle Worker; Fiorello! and The Sound of Music (tie)
1961—Becket; Bye Bye Birdie
1962—A Man for All Seasons; How to Succeed in Business Without Really Trying
1963—Who's Afraid of Virginia Woolf?; A Funny Thing Happened on the Way to the Forum

1964—Luther; Hello, Dolly!
1965—The Subject Was Roses; Fiddler on the Roof
1966—The Persecution and Assassination of Marat as Performed by the Inmates of the Asylum of Charenton Under the Direction of the Marquis de Sade; Man of La Mancha
1967—The Homecoming; Cabaret
1968—Rosencrantz and Guildenstern Are Dead; Hallelujah, Baby!
1969—The Great White Hope; 1776
1970—Borstal Boy; Applause
1971—Sleuth; Company
1972—Sticks and Bones; Two Gentlemen of Verona
1973—That Championship Season; A Little Night Music
1974—The River Niger; Raisin
1975—Equus; The Wiz
1976—Travesties; A Chorus Line
1977—The Shadow Box; Annie

1978—Da; Ain't Misbehavin'
1979—The Elephant Man; Sweeney Todd, the Demon Barber of Fleet Street
1980—Children of a Lesser God; Evita
1981—Amadeus; 42nd Street
1982—The Life & Adventures of Nicholas Nickleby; Nine
1983—Torch Song Trilogy; Cats
1984—The Real Thing; La Cage aux Folles
1985—Biloxi Blues; Big River
1986—I'm Not Rappaport; The Mystery of Edwin Drood
1987—Fences; Les Misérables
1988—M. Butterfly; The Phantom of the Opera

1989—The Heidi Chronicles; Jerome Robbins' Broadway
1990—The Grapes of Wrath; City of Angels
1991—Lost in Yonkers; The Will Rogers Follies
1992—Dancing at Lughnasa; Crazy for You
1993—Angels in America, Part I: Millennium Approaches; Kiss of the Spider Woman
1994—Angels in America, Part II: Perestroika; Passion
1995—Love! Valour! Compassion!; Sunset Boulevard
1996—Master Class; Rent
1997—The Last Night of Ballyhoo; Titanic
1998—Art; The Lion King

LUCILLE LORTEL AWARDS

The Lucille Lortel Awards were established in 1985 by a resolution of the League of Off-Broadway Theaters and Producers, which administers them and has presented them annually since 1986 for outstanding off-Broadway achievement. Eligible for the 13th annual awards in 1998 were all off-Broadway productions which opened between March 1, 1997 and March 31, 1998 except any which had moved from an off-Broadway to a Broadway theater. The 1997–98 selection committee comprised Clive Barnes, Greg Evans, Peter Filichia, Joan Hamburg, John Heilpern, Alvin Klein, Michael Kuchwara, Emily Nunn, John Simon, Linda Winer and Miss Lortel.

PLAY. *Gross Indecency: The Three Trials of Oscar Wilde* by Moisés Kaufman and *The Beauty Queen of Leenane* by Martin McDonagh (tie).

REVIVAL. *All My Sons* produced by Roundabout Theater Company.

ACTOR. **Brian Cox** in *St. Nicholas*.

ACTRESS. **Cherry Jones** in *Pride's Crossing*.

DIRECTION. **Garry Hynes** for *The Beauty Queen of Leenane*.

SCENERY. **Adrianne Lobel** for *On the Town*.

COSTUMES. **Paul Tazewell** for *On the Town*.

LIGHTING. **Kenneth Posner** for *Pride's Crossing* and *Side Man*.

BODY OF WORK. **Brian Murray**.

LIFETIME ACHIEVEMENT. **Arthur Miller**.

SPECIAL AWARD. *R & J*.

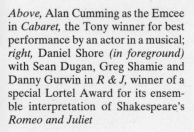

Above, Alan Cumming as the Emcee in *Cabaret,* the Tony winner for best performance by an actor in a musical; *right,* Daniel Shore *(in foreground)* with Sean Dugan, Greg Shamie and Danny Gurwin in *R & J,* winner of a special Lortel Award for its ensemble interpretation of Shakespeare's *Romeo and Juliet*

LORTEL AWARD WINNERS, 1986–98

Listed below are the Lucille Lortel Award winners in the categories of Outstanding Play and Outstanding Musical from the time these awards were established until the present.

1986—Woza Africa!; no musical award
1987—The Common Pursuit; no musical award
1988—No play or musical award
1989—The Cocktail Hour; no musical award

1990—No play or musical award
1991—Aristocrats; Falsettoland
1992—Lips Together, Teeth Apart; And the World Goes 'Round

1993—The Destiny of Me; Forbidden Broadway
1994—Three Tall Women; Wings
1995—Camping With Henry & Tom; Jelly Roll!
1996—Molly Sweeney; Floyd Collins

1997—How I Learned to Drive; Violet
1998—Gross Indecency, and The Beauty Queen
of Leenane (tie); no musical award

ATCA PRINCIPAL CITATIONS AND NEW PLAY AWARD WINNERS, 1976–1997

Beginning with the season of 1976–77, the American Theater Critics Association (ATCA) has cited one or more outstanding new plays in cross-country theater, the principal ones, listed below, to be presented in script excerpts in *Best Plays* and—since 1985—to receive the ATCA New Play Award (see the complete 1997 ATCA citations in The Season Around the United States section of this volume).

1976—And the Soul Shall Dance, by Wakako Ya-
mauchi
1977—Getting Out, by Marsha Norman
1978—Loose Ends, by Michael Weller
1979—Custer, by Robert E. Ingham
1980—Chekhov in Yalta, by John Driver and Jeffrey Haddow
1981—Talking With, by Jane Martin
1982—Closely Related, by Bruce MacDonald
1983—Wasted, by Fred Gamel
1984—Scheherazade, by Marisha Chamberlain
1985—Fences, by August Wilson
1986—A Walk in the Woods, by Lee Blessing
1987—Heathen Valley, by Romulus Linney
1988—The Piano Lesson, by August Wilson

1989—2, by Romulus Linney
1990—Two Trains Running, by August Wilson
1991—Could I Have This Dance?, by Doug Hav-
erty
1992—Children of Paradise: Shooting a Dream,
by Steven Epp, Felicity Jones, Dominique
Serrand and Paul Walsh
1993—Keely and Du, by Jane Martin
1994—The Nanjing Race, by Reggie Cheong-
Leen
1995—Amazing Grace, by Michael Cristofer
1996—Jack and Jill, by Jane Martin
1997—The Cider House Rules, Part II, by Peter
Parnell

ADDITIONAL PRIZES AND AWARDS, 1997–98

The following is a list of major prizes and awards for achievement in the theater this season. In all cases the names of winners appear in **bold face type** and the titles of winners in ***bold face italics***.

17th ANNUAL WILLIAM INGE FESTIVAL AWARD. For distinguished achievement in American theater. **Stephen Sondheim.** New voice: **David Ives**.

20th ANNUAL KENNEDY CENTER HONORS. For distinguished achievement by individuals who have made significant contributions to American culture through the arts. **Lauren Bacall, Bob Dylan, Charlton Heston, Jessye Norman, Edward Villella.**

NATIONAL MEDAL OF THE ARTS. Presented by President Clinton to those who have

made significant contributions in their fields, recommended by the National Council on the Arts. **James Levine, Jason Robards, Angela Lansbury, Edward Villella.**

20th ANNUAL SUSAN SMITH BLACKBURN PRIZES. For women who deserve recognition for having written works of outstanding quality for the English-speaking theater, selected by a committee of judges comprising Sebastian Barry, Eric Bentley, Kate Duchene, Simon Reade, Marian Seldes and Daniel Sullivan. First prizes: **Moira Buffini** (U.K) for *Silence;* **Paula Vogel** (U.S.) for *How I Learned to Drive.* Second prize: **Shelagh Steven-**

son (U.K.) for *An Experiment With an Air Pump.* Finalists: **Judith Adams** (U.K.) for *Burdalane,* **Kia Corthron** (U.S.) for *Splash Hatch on the E Going Down,* **Tina Howe** (U.S.) for *Pride's Crossing,* **Noelle Janaczewska** (Australia) for *Cold Harvest,* **Barbara Lebow** (U.S.) for *The Left Hand Singing,* **Nicola McCartney** (U.K.) for *The Hanging Tree,* **Lynn Nottage** (U.S.) for *Mud, River, Stone,* **Kathleen Tolan** (U.S.) for *A Girl's Life.*

1997 ELIZABETH HULL–KATE WARRINER AWARD. To the playwright whose work dealt with controversial subjects involving the fields of political, religious or social mores of the time, selected by the Dramatists Guild Council. **Paula Vogel** for *How I Learned to Drive.* Other finalists: Donald Margulies for *Collected Stories,* Alfred Uhry for *The Last Night of Ballyhoo,* Tina Howe for *Pride's Crossing,* Richard Greenberg for *Three Days of Rain.*

1998 RICHARD RODGERS AWARDS. For staged readings, administered by the American Academy of Arts and Letters and selected by a committee of its musical theater members comprising Stephen Sondheim, Lynn Ahrens, Jack Beeson, John Guare, John Kander, R.W.B. Lewis, Richard Maltby Jr., Terrence McNally, Francis Thorne and Robert Ward. *Little Women* by Allan Knee, Kim Oler and Alison Hubbard; *Summer* by Erik Haagensen and Paul Schwartz.

13th ANNUAL MR. ABBOTT AWARD. For lifetime achievement, presented by the Stage Directors and Choreographers Foundation. **Garson Kanin.** President's Awards for outstanding contribution to the theater: **Jerry Herman; Chase Manhattan Bank.** 1997 Joe A. Callaway Award for excellence in the craft of direction and choreography: **Moisés Kaufman.**

1998 AMERICAN THEATER WING DESIGN AWARDS. For design originating in the U.S., selected by a committee comprising Tish Dace (chairman), Mario Fratti, Alexis Greene, Mel Gussow, Henry Hewes, Jeffrey Eric Jenkins and Joan Ugaro. Scenic design: **Eugene Lee** for *Ragtime.* Costume design: **Julie Taymor** for *The Lion King.* Lighting design (tie): **Jules Fisher** and **Peggy Eisenhauer** for *Ragtime;* **Donald Holder** for *The Lion King.* Noteworthy unusual effects: **Julie Taymor** and **Michael Curry** for the mask and puppet design of *The Lion King.*

lst ANNUAL PEN/LAURA PELS AWARDS. For playwriting, selected by a committee comprising Laura Pels, Lanford Wilson and Wendy Wasserstein. To a master American dramatist for a life's work: **Arthur Miller.** To an American playwright in mid-career: **Richard Greenberg.**

64th ANNUAL DRAMA LEAGUE AWARDS. For distinguished achievement in the American theater. Musical theater: **Julie Taymor** for *The Lion King.* Revival of a play or musical: *Cabaret.* Production of a play: *The Beauty Queen of Leenane.* Production of a musical: *Ragtime.* Performance: **Brian Stokes Mitchell** in *Ragtime.* Unique contribution: **Harvey Lichtenstein** and the **Brooklyn Academy of Music.**

53d ANNUAL CLARENCE DERWENT AWARDS. For the most promising male and female actors on the metropolitan scene during the 1997-98 season. **Sam Trammell** in *Ah, Wilderness!;* **Julyana Soelistyo** in *Golden Child.*

GEORGE JEAN NATHAN AWARD. For dramatic criticism, administered by the Cornell University English Department. **Ben Brantley, Elinor Fuchs** and **Todd London.**

AMERICAN ACADEMY OF ARTS AND LETTERS GOLD MEDAL. Horton Foote.

17th ANNUAL ASTAIRE AWARDS. For excellence in dance and choreography, administered by the Theater Development Fund. Choreography: **Graciela Daniele** for *Ragtime;* **Garth Fagan** for *The Lion King.* Performance: **Kit Kat Klub Dancers** in *Cabaret.*

ELIZABETH CHAPIN AWARD FOR VOLUNTEERS IN THE ARTS. Presented by the Citizens Committee for New York City. **Isabelle Stevenson,** president of the American Theater Wing.

EDITH OLIVER AWARD. For excellence off Broadway. **Eli Wallach.**

54th ANNUAL *THEATER WORLD* AWARDS. For outstanding new talent in Broadway and off-Broadway productions during the 1997-98 season, selected by a committee comprising Clive Barnes, Peter Filichia, Alexis Greene, Harry Haun, Frank Scheck, Michael Sommers, Douglas Watt and John Willis. **Max Casella** in *The Lion King,* **Margaret Colin** in *Jackie,* **Ruaidhri Conroy** in *The Cripple of Inishmaan,* **Alan Cumming** in *Cabaret,* **Lea DeLaria** in *On the Town,* **Edie Falco** in *Side Man,* **Enid Graham** in *Honour,* **Anna Kendrick** in *High Society,* **Ednita Nazario** in *The Capeman,* **Douglas Sills** in *The Scarlet Pimpernel,* **Steven Sutcliffe** in *Ragtime,* **Sam Trammell** in *Ah, Wilderness!*

Special award: **Eddie Izzard** in *Dress to Kill.* Outstanding ensemble: **Anna Manahan, Marie Mullen, Tom Murphy, Brian F. O'Byrne** in *The Beauty Queen of Leenane.*

43d ANNUAL DRAMA DESK AWARDS. For outstanding achievement in the 1997-98 season, voted by an association of New York drama reporters, editors and critics from nominations made by a committee comprising David Sheward, Alexis Greene, Randy Gener, Barbara Siegel, Frank Scheck (chairman), Sam Whitehead and David Lefkowitz. New play: *The Beauty Queen of Leenane*. New Musical: *Ragtime*. Revival of a play: *A View From the Bridge*. Revival of a musical: *Cabaret*. Book of a musical: *Ragtime* by **Terrence McNally**. Music: *Ragtime* by **Stephen Flaherty**. Lyrics: *Ragtime* by **Lynn Ahrens**. Actor in a play: **Anthony LaPaglia** in *A View From the Bridge*. Actress in a play: **Cherry Jones** in *Pride's Crossing*. Featured actor in a play: **Alfred Molina** in *Art*. Featured actress in a play: **Allison Janney** in *A View From the Bridge*. Actor in a musical: **Alan Cumming** in *Cabaret*. Actress in a musical: **Natasha Richardson** in *Cabaret*. Featured actor in a musical: **Gregg Edelman** in *1776*. Featured actress in a musical: **Tsidii Le Loka** in *The Lion King*. Director of a play: **Michael Mayer** for *A View From the Bridge* and *Side Man*. Director of a musical: **Julie Taymor** for *The Lion King*. Choreography: **Garth Fagan** for *The Lion King*. Orchestrations: **William David Brohn** for *Ragtime*. Set design of a play: **The Quay Brothers** for *The Chairs*. Set design of a musical: **Richard Hudson** for *The Lion King*. Costume design: **Julie Taymor** for *The Lion King*. Lighting: **Donald Holder** for *The Lion King*. Sound design: **Tony Meola** for *The Lion King*. Puppets: **Julie Taymor** and **Michael Curry** for *The Lion King*. Solo performance: **John Leguizamo** in *Freak*. Unique theatrical experience: Cirque du Soleil's *Quidam*.

Special Awards: **The Vineyard Theater**; **Arthur Miller** for lifetime achievement.

48th ANNUAL OUTER CRITICS CIRCLE AWARDS. For outstanding achievement in the 1997-98 season, voted by critics on out-of-town periodicals and media from nominations voted by a committee comprising Marjorie Gunner, Mario Fratti, Glenn Loney, Patrick Hoffman, Louis A. Rachow, Ros Lipps, John T. Nourse, Aubrey Reuben and Simon Saltzman. Broadway play: *The Beauty Queen of Leenane*. Off-Broadway play: *Gross Indecency: The Three Trials of Oscar Wilde* and *Never the Sinner* (tie). Revival of a play: *A View From the Bridge*. Actor in a play: **Anthony LaPaglia** in *A View From the Bridge*. Actress in a play: **Cherry Jones** in *Pride's Crossing*. Featured actor in a play: **Robert Hogan** in *Never the Sinner*. Featured actress in a play: **Allison Janney** in *A View From the Bridge*. Director of a play: Michael Mayer for *A View From the Bridge* and *Side Man*. Broadway musical: *Ragtime*. Off-Broadway musical: *Hedwig and the Angry Inch*. Actor in a musical: **Alan Cumming** in *Cabaret*. Actress in a mu-

sical: **Natasha Richardson** in *Cabaret*. Featured actor in a musical: **Peter Friedman** in *Ragtime*. Featured actress in a musical: **Tsidii Le Loka** in *The Lion King*. Director of a musical: **Julie Taymor** for *The Lion King*. Choreography: **Garth Fagan** for *The Lion King*. Scenic design: **Richard Hudson** for *The Lion King*. Costume design: **Julie Taymor** for *The Lion King*. Lighting design: **Donald Holder** for *The Lion King*. Solo performance: **John Leguizamo** in *Freak*.

John Gassner Playwriting Award: **Douglas Carter Beane** for *As Bees in Honey Drown*. Special Achievement Award: **Alan Alda, Victor Garber** and **Alfred Molina** for ensemble performance in *Art*.

43d ANNUAL *VILLAGE VOICE* OBIE AWARDS. For outstanding achievement in off- and off-off-Broadway theater, selected by a committee comprising Michael Feingold and Alisa Solomon (co-chairmen), James Hannaham, Suzan Lori Parks, Polly Pen, Steven Samuels and Marian Seldes. Best plays: *Pearls for Pigs* and *Benita Canova* by **Richard Foreman**. Performance: **Lea DeLaria** for *On the Town*, **Mary Testa** for *On the Town* and *From Above*, **Tim Hopper** and **Joan MacIntosh** for *More Stately Mansions*, **David Patrick Kelly** for sustained excellence of performance, **Joseph Wiseman** for *I Can't Remember Anything*, **Heather Gillespie** for *Mamba's Daughters*, **Kate Valk** for sustained excellence of performance, **Marie Mullen** for *The Beauty Queen of Leenane*, **Matthew Maguire** for *I Don't Know Who He Was and I Don't Know What He Said*, **Yvette Freeman** and **Adriane Lenox** for *Dinah Was*, **Elizabeth Marvel** for *Therese Raquin* and *Misalliance*, **J. Smith-Cameron** for *As Bees in Honey Drown*, **Brian Murray** for sustained excellence of performance. Direction: **Ivo van Hove** for *More Stately Mansions*, **David Esbjornson** for *Therese Raquin*, **Jo Bonney** for sustained excellence of direction. Design: **Darron L. West** for his *Bob* soundscape design, **Mimi Jordan Sherin** for her *Bob* lighting design. Sustained achievement: **Jennifer Tipton**. Ross Wetzsteon Award: **Doug Aibel** and the **Vineyard Theater** for sustained support of artists and creativity in the theater.

Special citations: **Target Margin Theater**, *Mamba's Daughters*— **David Herskovits, Thomas Cabaniss, Lenore Doxsee, Erika Belsey, David Zinn, Tim Schellenbaum**; **John Cameron Mitchell** and **Stephen Trask** for *Hedwig and the Angry Inch*; **Mark Bennett** for sustained excellence of sound design. Special grants: **Housing Works Theater** directed by Victoria McElwaine; **Threshold Theater Company** for their *Caught in the Act* annual festival of one-acts.

8th ANNUAL CONNECTICUT CRITICS CIRCLE AWARDS. For outstanding achievement in

Connecticut theater during the 1997-98 season. Production of a play: **Long Wharf Theater** for *Wit*. Production of a musical: **Connecticut Repertory Theater** for *Man of La Mancha*. Actress in a play: **Kathleen Chalfant** in *Wit*. Actor in a play: **James McDonnell** in *Candida*. Actress in a musical: **Gina Philistine** in *A Chorus Line*. Actor in a musical: **Scott Wise** in *Lucky in the Rain*. Direction of a play: **Derek Anson Jones** for *Wit*. Direction of a musical: **Christopher Ashley** for *Lucky in the Rain*. Choreography: **Randy Skinner** for *Lucky in the Rain*. Set design: **Tony Andrea** for *The Miser*. Lighting design: **Donald Holder** for *Tiny Alice*. Costume design: **Linda Fisher** for *She Stoops to Conquer*. Sound design: **Simon Matthews** and **John Sibley** for *Dracula*. Ensemble performance: **David Beach, Michael Laswell, Deirdre Madigan, Samuel Maupin, Dee Pellitier** and **Katie S. Sparer** in *The Dining Room*.

Tom Killen Memorial Award: **Michael P. Price** of Goodspeed Opera House.

3d ANNUAL BARRYMORE AWARDS. For excellence in indigenous Philadelphia-area productions, selected by 40 nominators of the Theater Alliance of Greater Philadelphia. New play: *Black Russian* by Thomas Gibbons. Production of a play: *Quills* by the Wilma Theater. Musical: *Avenue X* by the Wilma Theater. Direction of a play: **James J. Christie** and **Harriet Power** for *Angels in America, Part II: Perestroika*. Direction of a musical: **Blanka Zizka** for *Avenue X*. Actress in a play: **Sally Mercer** in *The Glass Menagerie*. Actor in a play: **Tom McCarthy** in *Death of a Salesman*. Actress in a musical: **Carol Murphy** in *Sweeney Todd*. Actor in a musical: **James Brennan** in *1776*. Supporting actress in a play: **Maureen Torsney-Weir** in *Angels in America, Part II: Perestroika*. Supporting actor in a play: **Greg Wood** in *Death of a Salesman*. Supporting actress in a musical: **Michelle Nagy** in *Avenue X*. Supporting actor in a musical: **Charles Analosky** in *1776*. Ensemble performance: *Angels in America, Part II: Perestroika*. Choreography: **Patricia Scott Hobbes** for *Black Nativity*. Set design: **David P. Gordon** for *The Ruling Class*. Costume design: **Neil Bierbower** for *The Servant of Two Masters*. Lighting design: **Russell H. Champa** for *Quills*. Original music: **Elizabeth Fuller** for *The Chimes*.

CoreStates Community Service Award: **Interact Theater Company's Interaction**. Philadelphia *Inquirer & Daily News* Award for excellence in theater education: **Philadelphia Young Playwrights Festival**. F. Otto Haas Award for an emerging Philadelphia theater artist: **Adam Wernick**. Lifetime Achievement Award: **Doug Wing**. Special Recognition Award: **Adrienne Neye**.

16th ANNUAL ELLIOT NORTON AWARDS. For outstanding contribution to the theater in Boston, voted by a Boston Theater Critics Association Selections Committee comprising Skip Ascheim, Terry Byrne, Carolyn Clay, Iris Fanger, Arthur Friedman, Joyce Kulhawik, Jon Lehman, Bill Marx, Ed Siegel and Caldwell Titcomb. Productions—Visiting company: *Cabaret* by Barrington Stage Company and *Chicago* by Weissler. Large resident company: *The Game of Love and Chance* by Huntington Theater Company and *Man and Superman* by American Repertory Theater. Small resident company: *Faith Healer* by Gloucester Stage Company. Local fringe company: *Plum Pudding/Freaks* by Raven Theatrical. Script in its local premiere: **Anthony Clarvoe** for *Ambition Facing West*. Actor—Large company: **Don Reilly** in *Man and Superman*. Small company: **Jonathan Hammond** in *Cabaret*. Actress—Large Company: **Kristin Flanders** in *The Taming of the Shrew*. Small company: **Lizbeth Mackay** in *'Night, Mother*. Director—Large resident company: **Robert Woodruff** for *In the Jungle of Cities*. Small resident company: **Scott Edmiston** for *Molly Sweeney*. Designer—Large company: **Thomas Lynch** (scenery), **Martin Pakledinaz** (costumes) and **Peter Kaczorowski** (lighting) for *The Game of Love and Chance*. Small company: **Eric Levinson** (scenery) for *Old Wicked Songs* and *Balm in Gilead*.

Lifetime Achievement Award: **Richard Thomas**, who, though still young, has for 40 years tackled a host of daunting roles and triumphed. Norton Prize for Sustained Excellence: **Julie Taymor**, an inspired director and designer who has enriched stages here and elsewhere with unforgettable artistry. Special citation: **Paul Schmidt** for his dedicated decades of sterling stage translations from Ancient Greek, French, German and Russian.

14th ANNUAL HELEN HAYES AWARDS. In recognition of excellence in Washington, D.C. theater, presented by the Washington Theater Awards Society. Resident productions—Play: *Mourning Becomes Electra* by **The Shakespeare Theater**. Musical: *Hair* by **The Studio Theater Secondstage**. Lead actress, musical: **Liz Larsen** in *Sunday in the Park With George*. Lead actor, musical: **Lawrence Redmond** in *No Way to Treat a Lady*. Lead actress, play: **Holly Twyford** in *Romeo and Juliet*. Lead actor, play: **Edward Gero** in *Skylight*. Supporting performer, musical: **David James** in *The Wizard of Oz*. Supporting actress, play: **Franchelle Stewart Dorn** in *Mourning Becomes Electra*. Supporting actor, play: **Robert Sella** in *Mourning Becomes Electra*. Costume design, play or musical: **Jane Greenwood** for *Mourning Becomes Electra*. Sound design, play or musical: **Scott Burgess** for *Romeo and Juliet*. Lighting design: **Howell Binkley** for *The Tempest*. Set design, play or musical: **Tony Cisek** for *Things That Break*. Director, musical: **Keith Alan Baker** for *Hair*. Director, play: **Joe Banno** for *Romeo and Juliet.* Musical direction, play or musical: **John Kalbfleisch** for *Sunday in the Park With George.*

Non-resident productions—Production: **The National Theater's** *Chicago.* Lead actress: **Anna Deavere Smith** in *Twilight Los Angeles, 1992.* Lead actor: **Derick K. Grant** in *Bring in 'da Noise Bring in 'da Funk.* Supporting performer: **L. Scott Caldwell** in *Proposals.*

KMPG Pete Marwick Award for distinguished service to the Washington theater community: **Bell Atlantic Washington.** Washington *Post* Award for distinguished community service: **Signature in the Schools** project of Signature Theater and Wakefield High School. Charles MacArthur Award for outstanding new play: *Sherlock Holmes and the Case of the Purloined Patience, or The Scandal at the D'Oyly Carte* by Nick Olcutt. American Express Tribute: **Robert Prosky.**

29th ANNUAL JOSEPH JEFFERSON AWARDS. For achievement in Chicago theater during the 1996-97 season, selected by a 40-member Jefferson Awards Committee from 107 Equity productions offered by 47 producing organizations. Resident productions—New work: **Keith Reddin** for *All the Rage.* New adaptation: **Mary Zimmerman** for *Mirror of the Invisible World.* Production of a play: **Apple Tree Theater's** *Blade to the Heat,* **Shakespeare Repertory Theater's** *Hamlet,* **Famous Door Theater Co.'s** *The Living.* Production of a musical: **Apple Tree Theater's** *Assassins.* Production of a revue: **The Second City's** *Paradigm Lost.* Director of a play: **Calvin MacLean** for *The Living.* Director of a musical: **Gary Griffin** for *Assassins.* Director of a revue: **Mick Napier** for *Paradigm Lost.* Actor in a principal role, play: **Tim Decker** in *Toys in the Attic,* **Harry J. Lennix** in *Ma Rainey's Black Bottom,* **Mike Nussbaum** in *Racing Demon,* **Chris O'Neill** in *Frankly Brendan.* Actress in a principal role, play: **Laila Robins** in *A Streetcar Named Desire.* Actor in a supporting role, play: **Rick Boynton** in *A Flea in Her Ear,* **Stef Tovar** in *Blade to the Heat,* **Greg Vinkler** in *Hamlet.* Actress in a supporting role, play: **Greta Oglesby** in *Do Lord Remember Me.* Actor in a cameo role, play: **Thomas Carroll** in *Light Up the Sky.* Actress in a cameo role, play: **Beatrice Winde** in *The Young Man From Atlanta.* Actor in principal role, musical: **Tom Mula** in *Hot Mikado.* Actress in a principal role, musical: **Pamela Harden** in *Phantom,* **Alene Robertson** in *Kismet.* Actor in a supporting role, musical: **Kevin Earley** in *Assassins,* **James Fitzgerald** in *Assassins* and *Kismet,* **David Girolmo** in *Phantom.* Actress in a supporting role, musical: **Susan Moniz** in *Kismet.* Actor in a revue: **Scott Adsit** in *Paradigm Lost.* Actress in a supporting role, revue: **Rachel Dratch** in *Paradigm Lost.* Ensemble: *Do Lord Re-*

member Me, Time to Burn. Scenic design: **John Stark** for *The Living.* Costume design: **Nancy Missimi** for *Kismet,* **Kaye Voyce** for *Tartuffe.* Lighting design: **Pat Collins** for *All the Rage,* **Anne Militello** for *Hamlet* and *Timon of Athens,* **Kevin Rigdon** for *A Streetcar Named Desire,* **Scott Zielinski** for *Time to Burn.* Sound design: **Michael Bodeen** and **Rob Milburn** for *All the Rage,* **Matt Kozlowski** and **John Ridenour** for *Hamlet,* **Robert Neuhaus** for *Timon of Athens.* Choreography: **Marc Robin** for *Hot Mikado.* Original music: **Andy Jones** for *Blade to the Heat.* Musical direction: **Thomas Murray** for *Assassins,* **Jimmy Tillman** for *The Otis Redding Story.*

Touring productions—Production: **Barry & Fran Weissler's** in association with **Kardana/Hart Sharp Entertainment's** *Chicago.* Actor in a principal role: **Christopher Plummer** in *Barrymore.* Actress in a principal role: **Uta Hagen** in *Mrs. Klein.* Actor in a supporting role: **Ron Orbach** in *Chicago.* Actress in a supporting role: **Laila Robins** in *Mrs. Klein.*

25th ANNUAL JOSEPH JEFFERSON CITATIONS. For achievement by non-Equity productions in Chicago theater during the 1997-98 season. Production: *All My Sons* by **Shattered Globe Theater.** Ensemble: *You Can't Take It With You.* Director: **Louis Contey** for *All My Sons,* **Alena Murguia** for *Who's Afraid of Virginia Woolf?* Actress in a principal role: **Marguerite Hammersley** in *Out of Spite,* **Linda Reiter** in *All My Sons.* Actor in a principal role: **Wellesley Chapman** in *Equus,* **Darrell W. Cox** in *Eye of God,* **Steve Key** in *All My Sons.* Actress in a supporting role: **Bethanny Alexander** in *Who's Afraid of Virginia Woolf?,* **Maggie Carney** in *Smash,* **Cynthia Jackson** in *Four Queens—No Trump,* **Sara Rene Martin** in *Company.* Actor in a supporting role: **Rich Baker** in *All My Sons,* **Nathan Rankin** in *In the Heart of America,* **John Simmons** in *Grand Hotel,* **Ian Vogt** in *Long Day's Journey Into Night.* Scenic design: **Michael Menendian** for *You Can't Take It With You,* **Blair Thomas** for *The Ballad of Frankie and Johnny.* Costume design: **Carol Cox, Jen Keller, Sarah Laleman, Beth Nowak** and **Chris Thometz** for *The Skriker,* **Zelda Lin** for *The Ballad of Frankie and Johnny.* Lighting design: **Christine A. Solger** for *The Ballad of Frankie and Johnny.* Sound design: **Andre Pluess** and **Ben Sussman** for *In the Heart of America.* Choreography: **Kevin Bellie** for *Grand Hotel,* **Marc Robin** for *Company.* Musical direction: **Tom Murray** for *Company,* **Jon Steinhagen** for *Grand Hotel.* Original music: **Michael Zerang** for *The Ballad of Frankie and Johnny.* New work: **Jim Lasko** and **Blair Thomas** for *The Ballad of Frankie and Johnny,* **G. Riley Mills** and **Ralph Covert** for *Sawdust & Spangles.*

Special citation: **Chicago Dramatists** for its almost two decades of developing plays and playwrights in a manner that has enhanced Chicago's reputation for being a cradle for new theater works.

1996-97 LOS ANGELES OVATIONS. Year's best, peer-judged by Theater LA, an association of more than 130 theater companies and producers. All theaters—Writing of a world premiere play or musical: **Kathy Buckley** for *Don't Buck With Me!* New translation/adaptation: **Robert Cornthwaite** for *So It Is . . . If So It Seems to You.* Lead actor in a musical: **Ned Beatty** in *Show Boat.* Lead actor in a play: **Bill Campbell** in *Fortinbras.* Lead actress in a musical: **Marcia Mitzman Gaven** in *Ragtime.* Lead actress in a play: **Suanne Spoke** in *David's Mother.* Featured actor in a musical: **Michel Bell** in *Show Boat.* Featured actor in a play: **Derek Smith** in *Sylvia.* Featured actress in a musical: **Judy Kaye** in *Ragtime.* Featured ac-

tress in a play: **Bonita Friedericy** in *Our Country's Good.* Ensemble performance: Cast of *Forever Plaid.* Director of a musical: **Frank Galati** for *Ragtime.* Director of a play: **Michael Michetti** for *A Midsummer Night's Dream.* Choreography: **Graciela Daniele** for *Ragtime.*

In a larger theater—Musical: *Ragtime* at the Shubert Theater. Play: *The Heiress* at the Ahmanson Theater. Scenery: **Eugene Lee** for *Ragtime.* Costumes: **Florence Klotz** for *Show Boat.* Lighting: **Jules Fisher/Peggy Eisenhauer** for *Ragtime.* Sound: **Jonathan Deans** for *Ragtime.*

In a smaller theater—Musical: *Euphoria* at The Actor's Gang. Play: *A Midsummer Night's Dream* at the Stella Adler Theater. Scenery: **Scott Storey** for *Steaming.* Costumes: **Sherri Grider** for *A Midsummer Night's Dream.* Lighting: **Kathi O'Donohue** for *A Midsummer Night's Dream.* Sound: **Laurence O'Keefe** for *Euphoria.*

THE THEATER HALL OF FAME

The Theater Hall of Fame was created in 1971 to honor those who have made outstanding contributions to the American theater in a career spanning at least 25 years, with at least five major credits. Members are elected annually by the nation's drama critics and editors (names of those so elected in 1997 and inducted February 2, 1998 appear in **bold face italics**).

GEORGE ABBOTT
MAUDE ADAMS
VIOLA ADAMS
STELLA ADLER
EDWARD ALBEE
THEONI V. ALDREDGE
IRA ALDRIDGE
JANE ALEXANDER
WINTHROP AMES
JUDITH ANDERSON
MAXWELL ANDERSON
ROBERT ANDERSON
JULIE ANDREWS
MARGARET ANGLIN
JEAN ANOUILH
HAROLD ARLEN
GEORGE ARLISS
BORIS ARONSON
ADELE ASTAIRE
FRED ASTAIRE
EILEEN ATKINS
BROOKS ATKINSON
LAUREN BACALL
PEARL BAILEY
GEORGE BALANCHINE
WILLIAM BALL
ANNE BANCROFT
TALLULAH BANKHEAD
RICHARD BARR
PHILIP BARRY
ETHEL BARRYMORE
JOHN BARRYMORE
LIONEL BARRYMORE
NORA BAYES
BRIAN BEDFORD
S.N. BEHRMAN
NORMAN BEL GEDDES
DAVID BELASCO
MICHAEL BENNETT
RICHARD BENNETT
ERIC BENTLEY
IRVING BERLIN
SARAH BERNHARDT

LEONARD BERNSTEIN
EARL BLACKWELL
KERMIT BLOOMGARDEN
JERRY BOCK
RAY BOLGER
EDWIN BOOTH
JUNIUS BRUTUS BOOTH
SHIRLEY BOOTH
PHILIP BOSCO
ALICE BRADY
BERTOLT BRECHT
FANNIE BRICE
PETER BROOK
JOHN MASON BROWN
BILLIE BURKE
ABE BURROWS
RICHARD BURTON
MRS. PATRICK CAMPBELL
ZOE CALDWELL
EDDIE CANTOR
MORRIS CARNOVSKY
MRS. LESLIE CARTER
GOWER CHAMPION
FRANK CHANFRAU
CAROL CHANNING
RUTH CHATTERTON
PADDY CHAYEFSKY
ANTON CHEKHOV
INA CLAIRE
BOBBY CLARK
HAROLD CLURMAN
LEE J. COBB
RICHARD L. COE
GEORGE M. COHAN
JACK COLE
CY COLEMAN
CONSTANCE COLLIER
BETTY COMDEN
MARC CONNELLY
BARBARA COOK
KATHARINE CORNELL
NOEL COWARD
JANE COWL

LOTTA CRABTREE
CHERYL CRAWFORD
HUME CRONYN
RUSSEL CROUSE
CHARLOTTE CUSHMAN
JEAN DALRYMPLE
AUGUSTIN DALY
E.L. DAVENPORT
OSSIE DAVIS
RUBY DEE
ALFRED DE LIAGRE JR.
AGNES DEMILLE
COLLEEN DEWHURST
HOWARD DIETZ
DUDLEY DIGGES
MELVYN DOUGLAS
ALFRED DRAKE
MARIE DRESSLER
JOHN DREW
MRS. JOHN DREW
WILLIAM DUNLAP
MILDRED DUNNOCK
ELEANORA DUSE
JEANNE EAGELS
FRED EBB
FLORENCE ELDRIDGE
LEHMAN ENGEL
MAURICE EVANS
ABE FEDER
JOSE FERRER
CY FEUER
DOROTHY FIELDS
HERBERT FIELDS
LEWIS FIELDS
W.C. FIELDS
JULES FISHER
MINNIE MADDERN FISKE
CLYDE FITCH
GERALDINE FITZGERALD
HENRY FONDA
LYNN FONTANNE
HORTON FOOTE
EDWIN FORREST

414

Bob Fosse
Rudolf Friml
Charles Frohman
Grace George
George Gershwin
Ira Gershwin
John Gielgud
W.S. Gilbert
Jack Gilford
William Gillette
Charles Gilpin
Lillian Gish
John Golden
Max Gordon
Ruth Gordon
Adolph Green
Paul Green
Charlotte Greenwood
Joel Grey
John Guare
Tyrone Guthrie
Uta Hagen
Lewis Hallam
Oscar Hammerstein II
Walter Hampden
Otto Harbach
E.Y. Harburg
Sheldon Harnick
Edward Harrigan
Jed Harris
Julie Harris
Rosemary Harris
Sam H. Harris
Rex Harrison
Lorenz Hart
Moss Hart
Tony Hart
Helen Hayes
Leland Hayward
Ben Hecht
Eileen Heckart
Theresa Helburn
Lillian Hellman
Katharine Hepburn
Victor Herbert
Jerry Herman
James A. Herne
Al Hirschfeld
Raymond Hitchcock
Celeste Holm
Hanya Holm
Arthur Hopkins
De Wolf Hopper

John Houseman
Eugene Howard
Leslie Howard
Sidney Howard
Willie Howard
Barnard Hughes
Henry Hull
Josephine Hull
Walter Huston
Earle Hyman
Henrik Ibsen
William Inge
Bernard B. Jacobs
Elsie Janis
Joseph Jefferson
Al Jolson
James Earl Jones
Robert Edmond Jones
Raul Julia
John Kander
Garson Kanin
George S. Kaufman
Danny Kaye
Elia Kazan
Gene Kelly
George Kelly
Fanny Kemble
Jerome Kern
Walter Kerr
Michael Kidd
Sidney Kingsley
Florence Klotz
Joseph Wood Krutch
Bert Lahr
Burton Lane
Lawrence Langner
Lillie Langtry
Angela Lansbury
Charles Laughton
Arthur Laurents
Gertrude Lawrence
Jerome Lawrence
Eva Le Gallienne
Ming Cho Lee
Robert E. Lee
Lotte Lenya
Alan Jay Lerner
Sam Levene
Robert Lewis
Beatrice Lillie
Howard Lindsay
Frank Loesser
Frederick Loewe

Joshua Logan
Pauline Lord
Lucille Lortel
Alfred Lunt
Charles MacArthur
Steele MacKaye
Rouben Mamoulian
Richard Mansfield
Robert B. Mantell
Fredric March
Julia Marlowe
Ernest H. Martin
Mary Martin
Raymond Massey
Siobhan McKenna
Terrence McNally
Helen Menken
Burgess Meredith
Ethel Merman
David Merrick
Jo Mielziner
Arthur Miller
Marilyn Miller
Helena Modjeska
Ferenc Molnar
Lola Montez
Victor Moore
Zero Mostel
Anna Cora Mowatt
Paul Muni
Tharon Musser
George Jean Nathan
Mildred Natwick
Nazimova
James M. Nederlander
Mike Nichols
Elliot Norton
Sean O'Casey
Clifford Odets
Donald Oenslager
Laurence Olivier
Eugene O'Neill
Geraldine Page
Joseph Papp
Osgood Perkins
Bernadette Peters
Molly Picon
Harold Pinter
Christopher Plummer
Cole Porter
Robert Preston
Harold Prince
Jose Quintero

JOHN RAITT
TONY RANDALL
MICHAEL REDGRAVE
ADA REHAN
ELMER RICE
LLOYD RICHARDS
RALPH RICHARDSON
CHITA RIVERA
JASON ROBARDS
JEROME ROBBINS
PAUL ROBESON
RICHARD RODGERS
WILL ROGERS
SIGMUND ROMBERG
HAROLD ROME
LILLIAN RUSSELL
DONALD SADDLER
GENE SAKS
WILLIAM SAROYAN
JOSEPH SCHILDKRAUT
ALAN SCHNEIDER
GERALD SCHOENFELD
ARTHUR SCHWARTZ
GEORGE C. SCOTT
MARIAN SELDES
IRENE SHARAFF
GEORGE BERNARD SHAW
SAM SHEPARD

ROBERT E. SHERWOOD
J.J. SHUBERT
LEE SHUBERT
HERMAN SHUMLIN
NEIL SIMON
LEE SIMONSON
EDMUND SIMPSON
OTIS SKINNER
MAGGIE SMITH
OLIVER SMITH
STEPHEN SONDHEIM
E.H. SOTHERN
KIM STANLEY
MAUREEN STAPLETON
ROGER L. STEVENS
ELLEN STEWART
DOROTHY STICKNEY
FRED STONE
LEE STRASBERG
AUGUST STRINDBERG
ELAINE STRITCH
JULE STYNE
MARGARET SULLAVAN
ARTHUR SULLIVAN
JESSICA TANDY
LAURETTE TAYLOR
ELLEN TERRY
TOMMY TUNE

GWEN VERDON
NANCY WALKER
ELI WALLACH
JAMES WALLACK
LESTER WALLACK
TONY WALTON
DOUGLAS TURNER WARD
DAVID WARFIELD
ETHEL WATERS
CLIFTON WEBB
JOSEPH WEBER
MARGARET WEBSTER
KURT WEILL
ORSON WELLES
MAE WEST
ROBERT WHITEHEAD
THORNTON WILDER
BERT WILLIAMS
TENNESSEE WILLIAMS
LANFORD WILSON
P.G. WODEHOUSE
PEGGY WOOD
IRENE WORTH
ED WYNN
VINCENT YOUMANS
STARK YOUNG
FLORENZ ZIEGFELD

THE THEATER HALL OF FAME
FOUNDERS AWARD

Established in 1993 in honor of Earl Blackwell, James M. Nederlander, Gerard Oestreicher and Arnold Weissberger, The Theater Hall of Fame Founders Award is voted annually by the Hall's board of directors to an individual for his or her outstanding contribution to the theater.

1993 JAMES M. NEDERLANDER
1994 KITTY CARLISLE HART
1995 HARVEY SABINSON

1996 HENRY HEWES
1997 OTIS L. GUERNSEY JR.

MARGO JONES
CITIZEN OF THE THEATER
MEDAL

Presented annually to a citizen of the theater who has made a lifetime commitment to the encouragement of the living theater in the United States and has demonstrated an understanding and affirmation of the craft of playwriting.

1961 LUCILLE LORTEL
1962 MICHAEL ELLIS
1963 JUDITH RUTHERFORD
     MARECHAL
     GEORGE SAVAGE
     (University Award)
1964 RICHARD BARR,
     EDWARD ALBEE &
     CLINTON WILDER
     RICHARD A. DUPREY
     (University Award)
1965 WYNN HANDMAN
     MARSTON BALCH
     (University Award)
1966 JON JORY
     ARTHUR BALLET
     (University Award)
1967 PAUL BAKER
     GEORGE C. WHITE
     (Workshop Award)

1968 DAVEY MARLIN-JONES
     ELLEN STEWART
     (Workshop Award)
1969 ADRIAN HALL
     EDWARD PARONE &
     GORDON DAVIDSON
     (Workshop Award)
1970 JOSEPH PAPP
1971 ZELDA FICHANDLER
1972 JULES IRVING
1973 DOUGLAS TURNER
     WARD
1974 PAUL WEIDNER
1975 ROBERT KALFIN
1976 GORDON DAVIDSON
1977 MARSHALL W. MASON
1978 JON JORY
1979 ELLEN STEWART
1980 JOHN CLARK DONAHUE
1981 LYNNE MEADOW

1982 ANDRE BISHOP
1983 BILL BUSHNELL
1984 GREGORY MOSHER
1985 JOHN LION
1986 LLOYD RICHARDS
1987 GERALD CHAPMAN
1988 NO AWARD
1989 MARGARET GOHEEN
1990 RICHARD COE
1991 OTIS L. GUERNSEY JR.
1992 ABBOT VAN NOSTRAND
1993 HENRY HEWES
1994 JANE ALEXANDER
1995 ROBERT WHITEHEAD
1996 AL HIRSCHFELD
1997 GEORGE C. WHITE

1997-98 PUBLICATION
OF RECENTLY-PRODUCED NEW PLAYS
AND NEW TRANSLATIONS/ADAPTATIONS

American Daughter. Wendy Wasserstein. Harcourt Brace.
Amy's Views. David Hare. Faber & Faber (paperback).
Chairs, The. Eugene Ionesco, translated by Martin Crimp. Faber & Faber (paperback).
Collected Stories. Donald Margulies. TCG (paperback).
Complete Works of William Shakespeare (Abridged). Adam Long, Daniel Singer and Jess Winfield. Applause (paperback).
Crimson Thread, The. Mary Hanes. Samuel French (paperback).
Dybbuk and Other Tales of the Supernatural, A. S. Ansky, adapted by Tony Kushner. TCG (paperback).
Electra. Sophocles, adapted by Frank McGuinness. Faber & Faber (paperback).
Enemy of the People, An. Henrik Ibsen, adapted by Christopher Hampton. Faber & Faber (paperback).
Freak: A Semi-Demi-Quasi-Pseudo Autobiography. John Leguizamo with David Bar Katz. Putnam.
Getting Away With Murder. Stephen Sondheim and George Furth. TCG (paperback).
Ghost on Fire. Michael Weller. Samuel French (paperback).
Goodnight Children Everywhere. Richard Nelson. Faber & Faber (paperback).
Gross Indecency: The Three Trials of Oscar Wilde. Moisés Kaufman. Random House (paperback).
Honour. Joanna Murray-Smith. Currency Press (paperback).
Invention of Love, The. Tom Stoppard. Faber & Faber (paperback).
Jackie: An American Life. Gip Hoppe. Samuel French (acting edition).
Judas Kiss, The. David Hare. Grove (paperback).
Last Night of Ballyhoo, The. Alfred Uhry. TCG (paperback).
Life Support. Simon Gray. Faber & Faber (paperback).
Love's Fire: Seven New Plays Inspired by Seven Shakespearean Sonnets, introduced by Mark Lamos. William Morrow (paperback).
Mammary Plays, The. Paula Vogel. TCG (paperback).
Mere Mortals: Six One-Act Comedies. David Ives. Dramatists.
Not About Nightingales. Tennessee Williams. New Directions (paperback).
Notebook of Trigorin, The. Tennessee Williams. New Directions (also paperback).
Old Neighborhood, The. David Mamet. Random House (paperback).
One Flea Spare. Naomi Wallace. Broadway Play Publishers (paperback).
Question of Mercy, A. David Rabe. Grove Press (paperback).
Scapin. Molière, adapted by Bill Irwin and Mark O'Donnell. Dramatists (paperback).
Six Characters in Search of an Author. Luigi Pirandello, adapted by Robert Brustein. Ivan R. Dee (paperback).
Skull in Connemara, A. Martin McDonagh. Methuen (paperback).
Stonewall Jackson's House. Jonathan Reynolds. Broadway Play Publishing (paperback).
Things We Do for Love. Alan Ayckbourn. Faber & Faber (paperback).
Vagina Monologues, The. Eve Ensler. Random House (paperback).
Venus. Suzan-Lori Parks. TCG (paperback).
Walking on the Moon. Jason Milligan. Samuel French (paperback).

A SELECTED LIST OF OTHER PLAYS
PUBLISHED IN 1997-98

A.R. Gurney: Collected Plays: Volume II. Smith & Kraus (paperback).
Act One Wales: Thirteen One Act Plays. Phil Clark, editor. Dufour (paperback).
Aeschylus, I. The Oresteia. University of Pennsylvania (paperback).
Alan Ayckbourn: Plays 2. Faber & Faber (paperback).

418

Best American Short Plays 1996–1997, The. Glenn Young, editor. Applause (paperback).

Chekhov—The Vaudevilles and Other Short Works. Smith & Kraus (paperback).

Christopher Durang: Volume 2—Complete Full-Length Plays 1975–1995. Smith & Kraus.

Collected Plays of Neil Simon: Volume IV, The. Simon & Schuster (paperback).

Collected Short Plays of Thornton Wilder: Volume I. TCG (also paperback).

Collected Works of Oscar Wilde. Wordsworth (paperback).

Dozen French Farces: Medieval to Modern, A. Albert Bermel. Limelight (paperback).

Euripides: Volumes I, II, III. David R. Slavitt and Palmer Bovie, editors. University of Pennsylvania (paperback).

Five Plays by Michael Weller. TCG (paperbacks).

Humana Festival '97: The Complete Plays. Michael Bigelow Dixon and Liz Engelman, editors. Smith & Kraus (paperback).

John Osborne: Plays 2 and Plays 3. Faber & Faber. (paperbacks).

Molloy, Malone Dies, The Unnamable. Samuel Beckett. Random House.

Oxford Anthology of Contemporary Chinese Drama. Martha P.Y. Cheung and Jane C.C. Lai, editors and translators. Oxford.

Perfectionist and Other Plays, The. Joyce Carol Oates. Ecco Press.

Plays 2: David Hare. Faber & Faber (paperback).

Selected Plays of Michael MacLiammoir. Catholic University Press (paperback).

Six Renaissance Tragedies. Colin Gibson, editor. St. Martin's Press (paperback).

Sophocles 1. David R. Slavitt and Palmer Bovie, editors. University of Pennsylvania (paperback).

Strange Fruit: Plays on Lynching, by American Women. Kathy A. Perkins and Judith L. Stephens. Indiana University Press (paperback).

Tom Stoppard: Plays 3. Faber & Faber (paperback).

Ubu Plays, The. Alfred Jarry. Nick Hern (paperback).

NECROLOGY
MAY 1997–MAY 1998

PERFORMERS

Abbott, Philip (73)—February 23, 1998
Abrams, Ben Ford (86)—July 18, 1997
Adams, Philip Guest (85)—January 3, 1998
Aguilar, Luis (79)—October 24, 1997
Alton, Bill (73)—March 23, 1998
Anderson, Clinton G. (79)—December 5, 1997
Ashley, John (62)—October 4, 1997
Averback, Hy (76)—October 14, 1997
Babbs, Dorothy (71)—May 13, 1998
Beechman, Laurie (43)—March 8, 1998
Bell, Bob (75)—December 8, 1997
Bell, Marion (78)—December 14, 1997
Blane, Sally (87)—August 27, 1997
Bono, Sonny (62)—January 5, 1998
Bram, Rose (92)—May 14, 1997
Bridges, Lloyd (85)—March 10, 1998
Bruner, Wally (66)—November 3, 1997
Carlson, Violet (97)—December 3, 1997
Carpenter, Thelma (75)—May 14, 1997
Cassilly, Richard (70)—January 30, 1998
Chamberlain, Jennifer Holt (76)—September 21, 1997
Christopher, Keith (40)—February 23, 1998
Cisyk, Kasey (44)—March 29, 1998
Davis, Donald (69)—January 23, 1998
Denver, John (Henry John Deutschendorf Jr.) (53)—October 12, 1997
Derek, John (71)—May 22, 1998
Dove, Billie (96)—December 31, 1997
Duncan, Todd (95)—February 28, 1998
Easton, Ruth—March 16, 1998
Ebert, Joyce (64)—August 28, 1997
Evans, Gene (75)—April 1, 1998
Falco (Johann Holzel) (40)—February 6, 1998
Farley, Chris (33)—December 18, 1997
Farrah, Ibrahim (58)—February 7, 1998
Faye, Alice (83)—May 9, 1998
Fenneman, George (77)—May 29, 1997
Foster, Frances (73)—June 17, 1997
Freeman, Charles J. (83)—November 13, 1997
Gary, John (65)—January 4, 1998
Greene, Marty (69)—October 31, 1997
Griffis, William (81)—April 13, 1998
Guetary, Georges (82)—September 13, 1997
Gurney, John R. (95)—August 6, 1997
Hallahan, Charles (54)—November 25, 1997
Hare, Will (81)—August 28, 1997
Hartman, Phil (49)—May 28, 1998
Hayes, Peter Lind (82)—April 21, 1998
Haynes, Joy Hatton (64)—January 10, 1998

Hickey, William (69)—June 29, 1997
Jaeckel, Richard (70)—June 14, 1997
Jaffe, Pearl (89)—June 6, 1997
James, Dennis (79)—June 3, 1997
Jepson, Helen (92)—September 16, 1997
Kaskas, Anna (91)—March 19, 1998
Kaye, Stubby (79)—December 14, 1997
Keith, Brian (75)—June 24, 1997
Kennedy, Adam (75)—October 16, 1997
Kimbrough, David (67)—January 17, 1998
Kinley, Edwin (82)—March 31, 1998
Kuney, Francine (75)—May 9, 1997
Larson, Nicolette (45)—December 16, 1997
Lawrence, Rosina (84)—June 23, 1997
Leopold, Ethelreda (80)—January 26, 1998
Lewis, Abby (87)—November 27, 1997
Lindley, Audra (79)—October 16, 1997
Lord, Jack (77)—January 21, 1998
Maddox, Rose (72)—April 15, 1998
Manning, Bob (71)—October 23, 1997
Maslow, Florence (86)—July 3, 1997
Massey, Daniel (64)—March 25, 1998
Mather, George E. (77)—June 4, 1997
Mattingly, Hedley (83)—March 3, 1998
Meredith, Burgess (88)—September 9, 1997
Mifune, Toshiro (77)—December 24, 1997
Miller, Paco (88)—December 9, 1997
Mitchum, Robert (79)—July 1, 1997
Morris, Edmund (85)—January 6, 1998
Norden, Joseph (84)—March 30, 1998
Oyster, Jim (67)—February 23, 1998
Payton, Lawrence (59)—June 20, 1997
Petrie, George O. (85)—November 16, 1997
Phillips, Miriam (98)—October 24, 1997
Pyle, Denver (77)—December 23, 1997
Raymond, Gene (89)—May 3, 1998
Romoff, Woody (79)—January 20, 1998
Roux, Michel (73)—February 4, 1998
Russell, Bob (90)—January 24, 1998
Rysanek, Leonie (71)—March 7, 1998
Shaw, Burt (88)—May 18, 1997
Shaw, Ray (71)—March 24, 1998
Shelton, Reid (72)—June 8, 1997
Sitka, Emil (82)—January 16, 1998
Skelton, Red (Richard B.) (84)—September 17, 1997
Squires, Dorothy (83)—April 14, 1998
Stanley, Harry (100)—February 15, 1998
Stewart, James (89)—July 2, 1997
Stickney, Dorothy (101)—June 2, 1998
Symonette, Randolph (88)—January 1, 1998
Tapps, Georgie (85)—November 1, 1997
Tracy, Arthur (98)—October 5, 1997

Ulanova, Galina (88)—March 21, 1998
Vanselow, Robert A. (79)—March 30, 1998
Walsh, J.T. (54)—February 27, 1998
Warbeck, David (55)—July 23, 1997
Ward, Helen (82)—April 21, 1998
Wayne, Gus (77)—January 23, 1998
Wayne, Olive Brasno (80)—January 25, 1998
Wendelken, George T. (81)—January 3, 1998
Westcott, Helen (70)—March 17, 1998
Williams, Wendy O. (48)—April 6, 1998
Winship, Joanne Tree (73)—August 20, 1997
Witherspoon, Jimmy (74)—September 18, 1997
Wynette, Tammy (55)—April 6, 1998
Youngman, Henny (92)—February 23, 1998

PLAYWRIGHTS

Burnett, Murray (86)—September 23, 1997
Cross, Beverley (66)—March 20, 1998
Jarrico, Paul (82)—October 28, 1997
Lampell, Millard (78)—October 3, 1997
Laxness, Halldor (95)—February 8, 1998
Mankowitz, Wolf (73)—May 20, 1998
McEnroe, Robert E. (82)—February 6, 1998
Peterson, Louis (76)—April 27, 1998

COMPOSERS, LYRICISTS, SONGWRITERS

Chaplin, Saul (85)—November 15, 1997
Cora, Tom (44)—April 9, 1998
Daniel, Eliot (89)—December 6, 1997
Gregory, James (77)—February 4, 1998
Hedges, Michael (43)—December, 1997
Lane, Ronnie (51)—June 4, 1997
Lavelli, Tony (71)—January 8, 1998
Liben, Ned (44)—February 19, 1998
Merrill, Bob (78)—February 17, 1998
Perkins, Carl (65)—January 19, 1998
Powell, Mel (75)—April 24, 1998
Rabbitt, Eddie (56)—May 7, 1998
Robinson, Fenton (62)—November 25, 1997
Spina, Harold (91)—July 18, 1997
Sviridov, Georgy V. (82)—January, 1998
Tippett, Michael (93)—January 9, 1998
Williams, Rozz (34)—April 1, 1998

MUSICIANS

Allison, Luther (57)—August 12, 1997
Bishop, Walter Jr. (70)—January 24, 1998
Charles, Denis (64)—March 29, 1998

Cheatham, Adolphus (91)—June 2, 1997
Copeland, Johnny (60)—July 3, 1997
Dunbar, Ted (61)—May 29, 1998
Grappelli, Stephane (89)—December 1, 1997
Helms, Bobby (61)—June 19, 1997
Howard, George (41)—March 22, 1998
Jones, Louis Marshall (84)—February 19, 1998
Levine, Ruby (81)—April 4, 1998
Powell, Cozy (50)—April 7, 1998
Ruvinska, Paulina (85)—January 17, 1998
Tedesco, Tommy (67)—November 10, 1997
Trampler, Walter—September 27, 1997
Vestine, Henry (52)—October 20, 1997
Webb, Nick (43)—February 6, 1998
Wells, Junior (63)—January 15, 1998
White, Clifton (77)—April 2, 1998
Wilson, Carl Dean (51)—February 6, 1998
Wright, George (77)—May 10, 1998

CONDUCTORS

Blum, David (62)—April 17, 1998
Chapin, Thomas (40)—February 13, 1998
Cohn, Arthur (87)—February 8, 1998
Hillis, Margaret (76)—February 5, 1998
Johnson, Dean X. (42)—January 4, 1998
Kramer, Alex J. (94)—February 10, 1998
Novack, Saul (79)—March 4, 1998
Solti, Georg (84)—September 5, 1997
Tennstedt, Klaus (71)—January 11, 1998

PRODUCERS, DIRECTORS, CHOREOGRAPHERS

Bagley, Ben (64)—March 21, 1998
Barry, Philip Jr. (74)—May 16, 1998
Bing, Rudolf Franz Joseph (95)—September 2, 1997
Canby, Edward T. (85)—February 21, 1998
Coleman, Shepard (74)—May 12, 1998
DeWindt, Hall (72)—June 16, 1997
Elliott, Barbara (63)—April 18, 1998
Farren, Jack (75)—June 25, 1997
Feller, Peter L. (78)—March 13, 1998
Flamm, Donald (98)—February 15, 1998
Frankel, Kenneth (56)—February 12, 1998
Heller, Franklin (86)—July 8, 1997
Kormendi, Joan M. (81)—May 18, 1998
Mancebo, Niki Minter (55)—June 13, 1997
Rabb, Ellis (67)—January 11, 1998
Reid-Petty, Jane (70)—April 23, 1998
Rost, Leo (76)—August 26, 1997
Schaefer, George (76)—September 10, 1997
Sherman, Lee (84)—February 12, 1998

Stein, Barbie (40)—February 6, 1998
Stevens, Roger L. (87)—February 2, 1998
Strehler, Giorgio (76)—December 25, 1997
Thane, Adele (94)—January 25, 1998
Wilcox-Smith, Tamara (57)—January 30, 1998
Worth, Marvin (72)—April 22, 1998

CRITICS

Cohen, Joseph A. (86)—July 6, 1997
Oliver, Edith (84)—February 23, 1998
Palmer, Robert (52)—November 20, 1997
Shepard, Richard F. (75)—March 5, 1998
Taylor, Derek (65)—September 7, 1997
Van Horne, Harriet (77)—February 12, 1998
Wechsler, Bert (64)—November 30, 1997
Wetszteon, Ross (65)—February 20, 1998

DESIGNERS

Best, Marjorie O. (94)—June 14, 1997
Cranham, Tom (63)—November 19, 1997
DeVerna, Francis P. (70)—May 27, 1998
Greenfield, William E. (68)—January 24, 1998
Mackintosh, Robert (72)—February 13, 1998
McBride, Elizabeth (42)—June 16, 1997
Mintzer, William Land (52)—July 23, 1997
O'Herlihy, Michael (69)—June 14, 1997
Tilton, James (60)—April 19, 1998
Versace, Gianni (50)—July 15, 1997

OTHERS

Abner, Ewart G. Jr. (74)—December 27, 1997
    Motown Records
Barnathan, Julius (70)—December 2, 1997
    ABC
Burroughs, William S. (82)—August 2, 1997
    Author
Chandler, Dorothy Buffum (96)—July 6, 1997
    Dorothy Chandler Pavilion
Cousteau, Jacques-Yves (87)—June 25, 1997
    Oceanographer
Disney, Lillian (98)—December 16, 1997
    Widow of Walt
Doff, Aaron (76)—June 13, 1997
    Press agent

Elliott, Cheryle (54)—September 21, 1997
    Press agent
Ellner, Richard (69)—March 31, 1998
    Broadway Dance Center
Eyssell, Gustav S. (96)—January 26, 1998
    Radio City Music Hall
Fayed, Dodi (42)—August 31, 1997
    Chariots of Fire
Friendly, Fred (82)—March 3, 1998
    CBS
Gensel, Rev. John G. (80)—February 6, 1998
    St. Peter's Lutheran Church
Harvey, Helen (81)—December 22, 1997
    Agent
Jaffe, Leo (88)—August 20, 1997
    Columbia Pictures
Kampen, Irene (75)—February 1, 1998
    Lecturer
Kendall, George (86)—April 17, 1998
    MacDowell Colony
Krawetz, Richard Paul (45)—March 6, 1998
    Agent
Kuralt, Charles (62)—July 4, 1997
    CBS News
Langley, Dr. Stephen (58)—June 7, 1997
    Theater manager
Lewis, Robert (88)—November 23, 1997
    Acting teacher
Magro, John L. (90)—April 19, 1998
    Patron of arts
Mason, Richard (78)—October 13, 1997
    Novelist
McCartney, Linda (56)—April 17, 1998
    Wife of Paul
Merrill, Helen (79)—August 18, 1997
    Agent
Michener, James Albert (90)—October 16, 1997
    Author
Newi, George H. (62)—July 22, 1997
    ABC
Pirrotta, Nino (89)—January 15, 1998
    Musicologist
Riordan, Brian (45)—September 5, 1997
    Agent
Robbins, Harold (82)—October 14, 1997
    Novelist
Robinson, Sheila A. (50)—June 17, 1997
    Agent
Sanders, Lawrence (78)—February 14, 1998
    Author
Selinger, Dennis (77)—February 2, 1998
    Agent
Svetlichny, Andrei (41)—April 12, 1998
    Piano tuner
Troup, Stuart (63)—June 4, 1997
    Editor

THE BEST PLAYS, 1894–1996;
THE MAJOR PRIZEWINNERS, 1997

Listed in alphabetical order below are all those works selected as Best Plays in previous volumes of the *Best Plays* series through 1995–96, and the major prizewinners and special *Best Plays* citation in 1996–97. Opposite each title is given the volume in which the play appears, its opening date and its total number of performances. Two separate opening-date and performance-number entries signify two separate engagements off Broadway and on Broadway when the original production was transferred from one area to the other, usually in an off-to-on direction. Those plays marked with an asterisk (*) were still playing on June 1, 1998 and their number of performances was figured through May 31, 1998. Adaptors and translators are indicated by (ad) and (tr), the symbols (b), (m) and (l) stand for the author of the book, music and lyrics in the case of musicals and (c) signifies the credit for the show's conception, (i) for its inspiration. Entries identified as 94–99 are 19th century plays from one of the retrospective volumes. 94–95, 95–96 and 96–97 are 20th century plays.

PLAY	VOLUME	OPENED	PERFS
ABE LINCOLN IN ILLINOIS—Robert E. Sherwood	38–39	Oct. 15, 1938	472
ABRAHAM LINCOLN—John Drinkwater	19–20	Dec. 15, 1919	193
ACCENT ON YOUTH—Samson Raphaelson	34–35	Dec. 25, 1934	229
ADAM AND EVA—Guy Bolton, George Middleton	19–20	Sept. 13, 1919	312
ADAPTATION—Elaine May; and NEXT—Terrence McNally	68–69	Feb. 10, 1969	707
AFFAIRS OF STATE—Louis Verneuil	50–51	Sept. 25, 1950	610
AFTER THE FALL—Arthur Miller	63–64	Jan. 23, 1964	208
AFTER THE RAIN—John Bowen	67–68	Oct. 9, 1967	64
AFTER-PLAY—Anne Meara	94–95	Jan. 31, 1995	400
AGNES OF GOD—John Pielmeier	81–82	Mar. 30, 1982	599
AH, WILDERNESS!—Eugene O'Neill	33–34	Oct. 2, 1933	289
AIN'T SUPPOSED TO DIE A NATURAL DEATH—(b, m, l) Melvin Van Peebles	71–72	Oct. 20, 1971	325
ALIEN CORN—Sidney Howard	32–33	Feb. 20, 1933	98
ALISON'S HOUSE—Susan Glaspell	30–31	Dec. 1, 1930	41
ALL MY SONS—Arthur Miller	46–47	Jan. 29, 1947	328
ALL IN THE TIMING—David Ives	93–94	Feb. 17, 1994	526
ALL OVER TOWN—Murray Schisgal	74–75	Dec. 29, 1974	233
ALL THE WAY HOME—Tad Mosel, based on James Agee's novel *A Death in the Family*	60–61	Nov. 30, 1960	333
ALLEGRO—(b, l) Oscar Hammerstein II, (m) Richard Rodgers	47–48	Oct. 10, 1947	315
AMADEUS—Peter Shaffer	80–81	Dec. 17, 1980	1,181
AMBUSH—Arthur Richman	21–22	Oct. 10, 1921	98
AMERICA HURRAH—Jean-Claude van Itallie	66–67	Nov. 6, 1966	634
AMERICAN BUFFALO—David Mamet	76–77	Feb. 16, 1977	135
AMERICAN ENTERPRISE—Jeffrey Sweet (special citation)	93–94	Apr. 13, 1994	15
AMERICAN PLAN, THE—Richard Greenberg	90–91	Dec. 16, 1990	37

PLAY	VOLUME	OPENED	PERFS
GREEN BAY TREE, THE—Mordaunt Shairp	33–34 ..	Oct. 20, 1933 ..	166
GREEN GODDESS, THE—William Archer	20–21 ..	Jan. 18, 1921 ..	440
GREEN GROW THE LILACS—Lynn Riggs	30–31 ..	Jan. 26, 1931 ..	64
GREEN HAT, THE—Michael Arlen	25–26 ..	Sept. 15, 1925 ..	231
GREEN JULIA—Paul Abelman	72–73 ..	Nov. 16, 1972 ..	147
GREEN PASTURES, THE—Marc Connelly, based on Roark Bradford's *Ol' Man Adam and His Chillun*	29–30 ..	Feb. 26, 1930 ..	640
GUS AND AL—Albert Innaurato	88–89 ..	Feb. 27, 1989 ..	25
GUYS AND DOLLS—(b) Jo Swerling, Abe Burrows, based on a story and characters by Damon Runyon, (m, l) Frank Loesser	50–51 ..	Nov. 24, 1950 ..	1,200
GYPSY—Maxwell Anderson	28–29 ..	Jan. 14, 1929 ..	64
HADRIAN VII—Peter Luke, based on works by Fr. Rolfe	68–69 .:	Jan. 8, 1969 ..	359
HAMP—John Wilson, based on an episode from a novel by J.L. Hodson	66–67 ..	Mar. 9, 1967 ..	101
HAPGOOD—Tom Stoppard	94–95 ..	Dec. 4, 1994 ..	129
HAPPY TIME, THE—Samuel Taylor, based on Robert Fontaine's book	49–50 ..	Jan. 24, 1950 ..	614
HARRIET—Florence Ryerson, Colin Clements	42–43 ..	Mar. 3, 1943 ..	377
HARVEY—Mary Chase	44–45 ..	Nov. 1, 1944 ..	1,775
HASTY HEART, THE—John Patrick	44–45 ..	Jan. 3, 1945 ..	207
HE WHO GETS SLAPPED—Leonid Andreyev, (ad) Gregory Zilboorg	21–22 ..	Jan. 9, 1922 ..	308
HEART OF MARYLAND, THE—David Belasco	94–99 ..	Oct. 22, 1895 ..	240
HEIDI CHRONICLES, THE—Wendy Wasserstein	88–89 ..	Dec. 11, 1988 ..	81
	88–89 ..	Mar. 9, 1989 ..	621
HEIRESS, THE—Ruth and Augustus Goetz, suggested by Henry James's novel *Washington Square*	47–48 ..	Sept. 29, 1947 ..	410
HELL-BENT FER HEAVEN—Hatcher Hughes	23–24 ..	Jan. 4, 1924 ..	122
HELLO, DOLLY!—(b) Michael Stewart, (m, l) Jerry Herman, based on Thornton Wilder's *The Matchmaker*	63–64 ..	Jan. 16, 1964 ..	2,844
HER MASTER'S VOICE—Clare Kummer	33–34 ..	Oct. 23, 1933 ..	224
HERE COME THE CLOWNS—Philip Barry	38–39 ..	Dec. 7, 1938 ..	88
HERO, THE—Gilbert Emery	21–22 ..	Sept. 5, 1921 ..	80
HIGH TOR—Maxwell Anderson	36–37 ..	Jan. 9, 1937 ..	171
HOGAN'S GOAT—William Alfred	65–66 ..	Nov. 11, 1965 ..	607
HOLIDAY—Philip Barry	28–29 ..	Nov. 26, 1928 ..	229
HOME—David Storey	70–71 ..	Nov. 17, 1970 ..	110
HOME—Samm-Art Williams	79–80 ..	Dec. 14, 1979 ..	82
	79–80 ..	May 7, 1980 ..	279
HOMECOMING, THE—Harold Pinter	66–67 ..	Jan. 5, 1967 ..	324
HOME OF THE BRAVE—Arthur Laurents	45–46 ..	Dec. 27, 1945 ..	69
HOPE FOR A HARVEST—Sophie Treadwell	41–42 ..	Nov. 26, 1941 ..	38
HOSTAGE, THE—Brendan Behan	60–61 ..	Sept. 20, 1960 ..	127
HOT L BALTIMORE, THE—Lanford Wilson	72–73 ..	Mar. 22, 1973 ..	1,166
HOUSE OF BLUE LEAVES, THE—John Guare	70–71 ..	Feb. 10, 1971 ..	337
HOUSE OF CONNELLY, THE—Paul Green	31–32 ..	Sept. 28, 1931 ..	91
HOW I LEARNED TO DRIVE—Paula Vogel	96–97 ..	May 4, 1997 ..	400
HOW TO SUCCEED IN BUSINESS WITHOUT REALLY TRYING—(b) Abe Burrows, Jack Weinstock, Willie Gilbert, based on Shepherd Mead's novel, (m, l) Frank Loesser	61–62 ..	Oct. 14, 1961 ..	1,417

PLAY	VOLUME	OPENED	PERFS
JEST, THE—Sem Benelli, (ad) Edward Sheldon	19–20	Sept. 19, 1919	197
JOAN OF LORRAINE—Maxwell Anderson	46–47	Nov. 18, 1946	199
JOE EGG—(see *A Day in the Death of Joe Egg*)			
JOE TURNER'S COME AND GONE—August Wilson	87–88	Mar. 27, 1988	105
JOHN FERGUSON—St. John Ervine	09–19	May 13, 1919	177
JOHN LOVES MARY—Norman Krasna	46–47	Feb. 4, 1947	423
JOHNNY JOHNSON—(b, l) Paul Green, (m) Kurt Weill	36–37	Nov. 19, 1936	68
JOINED AT THE HEAD—Catherine Butterfield	92–93	Nov. 15, 1992	41
JOURNEY'S END—R.C. Sherriff	28–29	Mar. 22, 1929	485
JUMPERS—Tom Stoppard	73–74	Apr. 22, 1974	48
JUNE MOON—Ring W. Lardner, George S. Kaufman	29–30	Oct. 9, 1929	273
JUNIOR MISS—Jerome Chodorov, Joseph Fields	41–42	Nov. 18, 1941	710
K2—Patrick Meyers	82–83	Mar. 30, 1983	85
KATAKI—Shimon Wincelberg	58–59	Apr. 9, 1959	20
KENTUCKY CYCLE, THE—Robert Schenkkan	93–94	Nov. 14, 1993	34
KEY LARGO—Maxwell Anderson	39–40	Nov. 27, 1939	105
KILLING OF SISTER GEORGE, THE—Frank Marcus	66–67	Oct. 5, 1966	205
KINGDOM OF GOD, THE—G. Martinez Sierra, (ad) Helen and Harley Granville Barker	28–29	Dec. 20, 1928	92
KISS AND TELL—F. Hugh Herbert	42–43	Mar. 17, 1943	956
KISS OF THE SPIDER WOMAN, THE—(b) Terrence McNally, (m) John Kander, (l) Fred Ebb, based on the novel by Manuel Puig	92–93	May 3, 1993	906
KISS THE BOYS GOODBYE—Clare Boothe	38–39	Sept. 28, 1938	286
KNOCK KNOCK—Jules Feiffer	75–76	Jan. 18, 1976	41
	75–76	Feb. 24, 1976	152
KVETCH—Steven Berkoff	86–87	Feb. 18, 1987	31
LA BETE—David Hirson (special citation)	90–91	Feb. 10, 1991	25
LA CAGE AUX FOLLES—(b) Harvey Fierstein, (m, l) Jerry Herman, based on the play by Jean Poiret	83–84	Aug. 21, 1983	1,761
LA TRAGEDIE DE CARMEN—(ad) Peter Brook, Jean-Claude Carrière, Marius Constant from Georges Bizet's opera *Carmen* (special citation)	83–84	Nov. 17, 1983	187
LADY FROM DUBUQUE, THE—Edward Albee	79–80	Jan. 31, 1980	12
LADY IN THE DARK—(b) Moss Hart, (l) Ira Gershwin, (m) Kurt Weill	40–41	Jan. 23, 1941	162
LARGO DESOLATO—Vaclav Havel, (tr) Marie Winn	85–86	Mar. 25, 1986	40
LARK, THE—Jean Anouilh, (ad) Lillian Hellman	55–56	Nov. 17, 1955	229
LAST MEETING OF THE KNIGHTS OF THE WHITE MAGNOLIA, THE—Preston Jones	76–77	Sept. 22, 1976	22
LAST MILE, THE—John Wexley	29–30	Feb. 13, 1930	289
*LAST NIGHT OF BALLYHOO, THE—Alfred Uhry	96–97	Feb. 27, 1997	525
LAST OF MRS. CHEYNEY, THE—Frederick Lonsdale	25–26	Nov. 9, 1925	385
LAST OF THE RED HOT LOVERS—Neil Simon	69–70	Dec. 28, 1969	706
LATE CHRISTOPHER BEAN, THE—(ad) Sidney Howard from the French of Rene Fauchois	32–33	Oct. 31, 1932	224
LATE GEORGE APLEY, THE—John P. Marquand, George S. Kaufman, based on John P. Marquand's novel	44–45	Nov. 23, 1944	385
LATER LIFE—A.R. Gurney	92–93	May 23, 1993	126
LAUGHTER ON THE 23RD FLOOR—Neil Simon	93–94	Nov. 22, 1993	320

PLAY	VOLUME	OPENED	PERFS
LUTHER—John Osborne	63–64	Sept. 25, 1963	211
LUV—Murray Schisgal	64–65	Nov. 11, 1964	901
M. BUTTERFLY—David Henry Hwang	87–88	Mar. 20, 1988	777
MA RAINEY'S BLACK BOTTOM—August Wilson	84–85	Oct. 11, 1984	275
MACHINAL—Sophie Treadwell	28–29	Sept. 7, 1928	91
MAD FOREST—Caryl Churchill	91–92	Dec. 4, 1991	54
MADNESS OF GEORGE III, THE—Alan Bennett	93–94	Sept. 28, 1993	17
MADWOMAN OF CHAILLOT, THE—Jean Giraudoux, (ad) Maurice Valency	48–49	Dec. 27, 1948	368
MAGIC AND THE LOSS, THE—Julian Funt	53–54	Apr. 9, 1954	27
MAGNIFICENT YANKEE, THE—Emmet Lavery	45–46	Jan. 22, 1946	160
MAHABHARATA, THE—Jean-Claude Carrière, (ad) Peter Brook	87–88	Oct. 13, 1987	25
MALE ANIMAL, THE—James Thurber, Elliott Nugent	39–40	Jan. 9, 1940	243
MAMMA'S AFFAIR—Rachel Barton Butler	19–20	Jan. 29, 1920	98
MAN FOR ALL SEASONS, A—Robert Bolt	61–62	Nov. 22, 1961	637
MAN FROM HOME, THE—Booth Tarkington, Harry Leon Wilson	99–09	Aug. 17, 1908	406
MAN IN THE GLASS BOOTH, THE—Robert Shaw	68–69	Sept. 26, 1968	268
MAN OF LA MANCHA—(b) Dale Wasserman, suggested by the life and works of Miguel de Cervantes y Saavedra, (l) Joe Darion, (m) Mitch Leigh	65–66	Nov. 22, 1965	2,328
MAN WHO CAME TO DINNER, THE—George S. Kaufman, Moss Hart	39–40	Oct. 16, 1939	739
MARAT/SADE—(see *The Persecution and Assassination of Marat,* etc.)			
MARGIN FOR ERROR—Clare Boothe	39–40	Nov. 3, 1939	264
MARRIAGE OF BETTE AND BOO, THE—Christopher Durang	84–85	May 16, 1985	86
MARVIN'S ROOM—Scott McPherson	91–92	Dec. 5, 1991	214
MARY, MARY—Jean Kerr	60–61	Mar. 8, 1961	1,572
MARY OF SCOTLAND—Maxwell Anderson	33–34	Nov. 27, 1933	248
MARY ROSE—James M. Barrie	20–21	Dec. 22, 1920	127
MARY THE 3RD—Rachel Crothers	22–23	Feb. 5, 1923	162
MASS APPEAL—Bill C. Davis	81–82	Nov. 12, 1981	214
MASTER CLASS—Terrence McNally	95–96	Nov. 5, 1995	601
MASTER HAROLD . . . AND THE BOYS—Athol Fugard	81–82	May 4, 1982	344
MATCHMAKER, THE—Thornton Wilder, based on Johann Nestroy's *Einen Jux Will Er Sich Machen,* based on John Oxenford's *A Day Well Spent*	55–56	Dec. 5, 1955	486
ME AND MOLLY—Gertrude Berg	47–48	Feb. 26, 1948	156
MEMBER OF THE WEDDING, THE—(ad) Carson McCullers, from her novel	49–50	Jan. 5, 1950	501
MEN IN WHITE—Sidney Kingsley	33–34	Sept. 26, 1933	351
MERRILY WE ROLL ALONG—George S. Kaufman, Moss Hart	34–35	Sept. 29, 1934	155
MERTON OF THE MOVIES—George S. Kaufman, Marc Connelly, based on Harry Leon Wilson's novel	22–23	Nov. 13, 1922	381
MICHAEL AND MARY—A.A. Milne	29–30	Dec. 13, 1929	246
MILK TRAIN DOESN'T STOP HERE ANYMORE, THE— Tennessee Williams	62–63	Jan. 16, 1963	69
MINICK—George S. Kaufman, Edna Ferber	24–25	Sept. 24, 1924	141

PLAY	VOLUME	OPENED	PERFS

NINE—(b) Arthur L. Kopit, (m, l) Maury Yeston, (ad) Mario
Fratti from the Italian .... 81–82 .. May 9,   1982 .. 739
NO MORE LADIES—A.E. Thomas .... 33–34 .. Jan. 23,   1934 .. 162
NO PLACE TO BE SOMEBODY—Charles Gordone .... 68–69 .. May 4,   1969 .. 250
NO TIME FOR COMEDY—S.N. Behrman .... 38–39 .. Apr. 17, 1939 .. 185
NO TIME FOR SERGEANTS—Ira Levin, based on Mac
Hyman's novel .... 55–56 .. Oct. 20, 1955 .. 796
NOEL COWARD IN TWO KEYS—Noel Coward (*Come Into the
Garden Maud* and *A Song at Twilight*) .... 73–74 .. Feb. 28, 1974 .. 140
NOISES OFF—Michael Frayn .... 83–84 .. Dec. 11, 1983 .. 553
NORMAN CONQUESTS, THE—(see *Living Together, Round
and Round the Garden* and *Table Manners*)
NUTS—Tom Topor... 79–80 .. Apr. 28, 1980 ..   96

O MISTRESS MINE—Terence Rattigan .... 45–46 .. Jan. 23, 1946 .. 452
ODD COUPLE, THE—Neil Simon.................................. 64–65 .. Mar. 10, 1965 .. 964
OF MICE AND MEN—John Steinbeck .... 37–38 .. Nov. 23, 1937 .. 207
OF THEE I SING—(b) George S. Kaufman, (m) George
Gershwin, Morrie Ryskind, (l) Ira Gershwin .... 31–32 .. Dec. 26, 1931 .. 441
OH DAD, POOR DAD, MAMA'S HUNG YOU IN THE CLOSET
AND I'M FEELIN' SO SAD—Arthur L. Kopit .... 61–62 .. Feb. 26, 1962 .. 454
OHIO IMPROMPTU, CATASTROPHE AND WHAT WHERE—
Samuel Beckett .... 83–84 .. June 15, 1983 .. 350
OKLAHOMA!—(b, l) Oscar Hammerstein II, based on Lynn
Riggs's play *Green Grow the Lilacs,* (m) Richard Rodgers ... 42–43 .. Mar. 31, 1943 .. 2,212
OLD MAID, THE—Zoe Akins, based on Edith Wharton's
novel .... 34–35 .. Jan. 7,   1935 .. 305
OLD SOAK, THE—Don Marquis.................................... 22–23 .. Aug. 22, 1922 .. 423
OLD TIMES—Harold Pinter.. 71–72 .. Nov. 16, 1971 .. 119
OLD WICKED SONGS—Jon Marans .... 96–97 .. Sept. 5, 1996 .. 210
OLDEST LIVING GRADUATE, THE—Preston Jones .... 76–77 .. Sept. 23, 1976 .. 20
OLEANNA—David Mamet .... 92–93 .. Oct. 25, 1992 .. 513
ON BORROWED TIME—Paul Osborn, based on Lawrence
Edward Watkin's novel .... 37–38 .. Feb. 3,   1938 .. 321
ON GOLDEN POND—Ernest Thompson .... 78–79 .. Sept. 13, 1978 .. 30
                                                                       78–79 .. Feb. 28, 1979 .. 126
ON TRIAL—Elmer Rice.. 09–19 .. Aug. 19, 1914 .. 365
ONCE IN A LIFETIME—Moss Hart, George S. Kaufman......... 30–31 .. Sept. 24, 1930 .. 406
ONCE ON THIS ISLAND—(b, l) Lynn Ahrens, (m) Stephen
Flaherty, based on the novel *My Love My Love* by Rosa
Guy... 89–90 .. May 6,   1990 .. 24
                                                                       90–91 .. Oct. 18, 1990 .. 469
ONE SUNDAY AFTERNOON—James Hagan...................... 32–33 .. Feb. 15, 1933 .. 322
ORPHEUS DESCENDING—Tennessee Williams .... 56–57 .. Mar. 21, 1957 .. 68
OTHER PEOPLE'S MONEY—Jerry Sterner...................... 88–89 .. Feb. 16, 1989 .. 990
OTHERWISE ENGAGED—Simon Gray .... 76–77 .. Feb. 2,   1977 .. 309
OUR COUNTRY'S GOOD—Timberlake Wertenbaker .... 90–91 .. Apr. 29, 1991 .. 48
OUTRAGEOUS FORTUNE—Rose Franken .... 43–44 .. Nov. 3,   1943 .. 77
OUR TOWN—Thornton Wilder...................................... 37–38 .. Feb. 4,   1938 .. 336
OUTWARD BOUND—Sutton Vane .... 23–24 .. Jan. 7,   1924 .. 144
OVER 21—Ruth Gordon .... 43–44 .. Jan. 3,   1944 .. 221
OVERTURE—William Bolitho .... 30–31 .. Dec. 5,   1930 .. 41

PLAY	VOLUME	OPENED	PERFS
PRIDE AND PREJUDICE—Helen Jerome, based on Jane Austen's novel	35–36	Nov. 5, 1935	219
PRISONER OF SECOND AVENUE, THE—Neil Simon	71–72	Nov. 11, 1971	780
PROLOGUE TO GLORY—E.P. Conkle	37–38	Mar. 17, 1938	70
QUARTERMAINE'S TERMS—Simon Gray	82–83	Feb. 24, 1983	375
R.U.R.—Karel Capek	22–23	Oct. 9, 1922	184
RACKET, THE—Bartlett Cormack	27–28	Nov. 22, 1927	119
RAIN—John Colton, Clemence Randolph, based on the story by W. Somerset Maugham	22–23	Nov. 7, 1922	648
RAISIN IN THE SUN, A—Lorraine Hansberry	58–59	Mar. 11, 1959	530
RATTLE OF A SIMPLE MAN—Charles Dyer	62–63	Apr. 17, 1963	94
REAL ESTATE—Louise Page	87–88	Dec. 1, 1987	55
REAL THING, THE—Tom Stoppard	83–84	Jan. 5, 1984	566
REBEL WOMEN—Thomas Babe	75–76	May 6, 1976	40
REBOUND—Donald Ogden Stewart	29–30	Feb. 3, 1930	114
RED DIAPER BABY—Josh Kornbluth	92–93	June 12, 1992	59
REHEARSAL, THE—Jean Anouilh, (ad) Pamela Hansford Johnson, Kitty Black	63–64	Sept. 23, 1963	110
REMAINS TO BE SEEN—Howard Lindsay, Russel Crouse	51–52	Oct. 3, 1951	199
*RENT—(b,m,l) Jonathan Larson	95–96	Feb. 13, 1996	56
	95–96	Apr. 29, 1996	873
REQUIEM FOR A NUN—Ruth Ford, William Faulkner, adapted from William Faulkner's novel	58–59	Jan. 30, 1959	43
REUNION IN VIENNA—Robert E. Sherwood	31–32	Nov. 16, 1931	264
RHINOCEROS—Eugene Ionesco, (tr) Derek Prouse	60–61	Jan. 9, 1961	240
RITZ, THE—Terrence McNally	74–75	Jan. 20, 1975	400
RIVER NIGER, THE—Joseph A. Walker	72–73	Dec. 5, 1972	120
	72–73	Mar. 27, 1973	280
ROAD—Jim Cartwright	88–89	July 28, 1988	62
ROAD TO MECCA, THE—Athol Fugard	87–88	Apr. 12, 1988	172
ROAD TO ROME, THE—Robert E. Sherwood	26–27	Jan. 31, 1927	392
ROCKABY—(see Enough, Footfalls and Rockaby)			
ROCKET TO THE MOON—Clifford Odets	38–39	Nov. 24, 1938	131
ROMANCE—Edward Sheldon	09–19	Feb. 10, 1913	160
ROPE DANCERS, THE—Morton Wishengrad	57–58	Nov. 20, 1957	189
ROSE TATTOO, THE—Tennessee Williams	50–51	Feb. 3, 1951	306
ROSENCRANTZ AND GUILDENSTERN ARE DEAD—Tom Stoppard	67–68	Oct. 16, 1967	420
ROUND AND ROUND THE GARDEN—Alan Ayckbourn	75–76	Dec. 7, 1975	76
ROYAL FAMILY, THE—George S. Kaufman, Edna Ferber	27–28	Dec. 28, 1927	345
ROYAL HUNT OF THE SUN—Peter Shaffer	65–66	Oct. 26, 1965	261
RUGGED PATH, THE—Robert E. Sherwood	45–46	Nov. 10, 1945	81
RUNNER STUMBLES, THE—Milan Stitt	75–76	May 18, 1976	191
ST. HELENA—R.C. Sheriff, Jeanne de Casalis	36–37	Oct. 6, 1936	63
SAME TIME, NEXT YEAR—Bernard Slade	74–75	Mar. 13, 1975	1,453
SATURDAY'S CHILDREN—Maxwell Anderson	26–27	Jan. 26, 1927	310
SCREENS, THE—Jean Genet, (tr) Minos Volanakis	71–72	Nov. 30, 1971	28

PLAY	VOLUME	OPENED	PERFS
SPEED-THE-PLOW—David Mamet	87–88	May 3, 1988	278
SPIC-O-RAMA—John Leguizamo	92–93	Oct. 27, 1992	86
SPLIT SECOND—Dennis McIntyre	84–85	June 7, 1984	147
SQUAW MAN, THE—Edward Milton Royle	99–09	Oct. 23, 1905	222
STAGE DOOR—George S. Kaufman, Edna Ferber	36–37	Oct. 22, 1936	169
STAIRCASE—Charles Dyer	67–68	Jan. 10, 1968	61
STAR-WAGON, THE—Maxwell Anderson	37–38	Sept. 29, 1937	223
STATE OF THE UNION—Howard Lindsay, Russel Crouse	45–46	Nov. 14, 1945	765
STEAMBATH—Bruce Jay Friedman	70–71	June 30, 1970	128
STEEL MAGNOLIAS—Robert Harling	87–88	June 19, 1987	1,126
STICKS AND BONES—David Rabe	71–72	Nov. 7, 1971	121
	71–72	Mar. 1, 1972	245
STONE AND STAR—Robert Ardrey (also called *Shadow of Heroes*)	61–62	Dec. 5, 1961	20
STOP THE WORLD—I WANT TO GET OFF—(b, m, l) Leslie Bricusse, Anthony Newley	62–63	Oct. 3, 1962	555
STORM OPERATION—Maxwell Anderson	43–44	Jan. 11, 1944	23
STORY OF MARY SURRATT, THE—John Patrick	46–47	Feb. 8, 1947	11
STRANGE INTERLUDE—Eugene O'Neill	27–28	Jan. 30, 1928	426
STREAMERS—David Rabe	75–76	Apr. 21, 1976	478
STREET SCENE—Elmer Rice	28–29	Jan. 10, 1929	601
STREETCAR NAMED DESIRE, A—Tennessee Williams	47–48	Dec. 3, 1947	855
STRICTLY DISHONORABLE—Preston Sturges	29–30	Sept. 18, 1929	557
SUBJECT WAS ROSES, THE—Frank D. Gilroy	64–65	May 25, 1964	832
SUBSTANCE OF FIRE, THE—Jon Robin Baitz	90–91	Mar. 17, 1991	120
SUBURBIA—Eric Bogosian	93–94	May 22, 1994	113
SUGAR BABIES—(ad) Ralph G. Allen from traditional material (special citation)	79–80	Oct. 8, 1979	1,208
SUM OF US, THE—David Stevens	90–91	Oct. 16, 1990	335
SUMMER OF THE 17TH DOLL—Ray Lawler	57–58	Jan. 22, 1958	29
SUNDAY IN THE PARK WITH GEORGE—(b) James Lapine, (m, l) Stephen Sondheim	83–84	May 2, 1984	604
SUNRISE AT CAMPOBELLO—Dore Schary	57–58	Jan. 30, 1958	556
SUNSET BOULEVARD—(b, l) Don Black, Christopher Hampton, (m) Andrew Lloyd Webber, based on the film by Billy Wilder	94–95	Nov. 17, 1994	977
SUNSHINE BOYS, THE—Neil Simon	72–73	Dec. 20, 1972	538
SUN-UP—Lula Vollmer	22–23	May 25, 1923	356
SUSAN AND GOD—Rachel Crothers	37–38	Oct. 7, 1937	288
SWAN, THE—Ferenc Molnar, (tr) Melville Baker	23–24	Oct. 23, 1923	255
SWEENEY TODD, THE DEMON BARBER OF FLEET STREET—(b) Hugh Wheeler, (m, l) Stephen Sondheim, based on a version of *Sweeney Todd* by Christopher Bond	78–79	Mar. 1, 1979	557
SWEET BIRD OF YOUTH—Tennessee Williams	58–59	Mar. 10, 1959	375
TABLE MANNERS—Alan Ayckbourn	75–76	Dec. 7, 1975	76
TABLE SETTINGS—James Lapine	79–80	Jan. 14, 1980	264
TAKE A GIANT STEP—Louis Peterson	53–54	Sept. 24, 1953	76
TAKING OF MISS JANIE, THE—Ed Bullins	74–75	May 4, 1975	42
TALLEY'S FOLLEY—Lanford Wilson	78–79	May 1, 1979	44
	79–80	Feb. 20, 1980	277

PLAY	VOLUME	OPENED	PERFS
TARNISH—Gilbert Emery	23–24 ..	Oct. 1, 1923 ..	248
TASTE OF HONEY, A—Shelagh Delaney	60–61 ..	Oct. 4, 1960 ..	376
TCHIN-TCHIN—Sidney Michaels, based on François			
Billetdoux's play	62–63 ..	Oct. 25, 1962 ..	222
TEA AND SYMPATHY—Robert Anderson	53–54 ..	Sept. 30, 1953 ..	712
TEAHOUSE OF THE AUGUST MOON, THE—John Patrick,			
based on Vern Sneider's novel	53–54 ..	Oct. 15, 1953 ..	1,027
TENTH MAN, THE—Paddy Chayefsky	59–60 ..	Nov. 5, 1959 ..	623
THAT CHAMPIONSHIP SEASON—Jason Miller	71–72 ..	May 2, 1972 ..	144
	72–73 ..	Sept. 14, 1972 ..	700
THERE SHALL BE NO NIGHT—Robert E. Sherwood	39–40 ..	Apr. 29, 1940 ..	181
THEY KNEW WHAT THEY WANTED—Sidney Howard	24–25 ..	Nov. 24, 1924 ..	414
THEY SHALL NOT DIE—John Wexley	33–34 ..	Feb. 21, 1934 ..	62
THOUSAND CLOWNS, A—Herb Gardner	61–62 ..	Apr. 5, 1962 ..	428
THREE POSTCARDS—(b) Craig Lucas, (m, l) Craig Carnelia	86–87 ..	May 14, 1987 ..	22
THREE TALL WOMEN—Edward Albee	93–94 ..	Apr. 5, 1994 ..	582
THREEPENNY OPERA—(b, l) Bertolt Brecht, (m) Kurt Weill,			
(tr) Ralph Manheim, John Willett	75–76 ..	Mar. 1, 1976 ..	307
THURBER CARNIVAL, A—James Thurber	59–60 ..	Feb. 26, 1960 ..	127
TIGER AT THE GATES—Jean Giraudoux's *La Guerre de Troie*			
n'Aura Pas Lieu, (tr) Christopher Fry	55–56 ..	Oct. 3, 1955 ..	217
TIME OF THE CUCKOO, THE—Arthur Laurents	52–53 ..	Oct. 15, 1952 ..	263
TIME OF YOUR LIFE, THE—William Saroyan	39–40 ..	Oct. 25, 1939 ..	185
TIME REMEMBERED—Jean Anouilh's *Léocadia,* (ad) Patricia			
Moyes	57–58 ..	Nov. 12, 1957 ..	248
TINY ALICE—Edward Albee	64–65 ..	Dec. 29, 1964 ..	167
*TITANIC—(b) Peter Stone, (m, l) Maury Yeston	96–97 ..	Apr. 23, 1997 ..	460
TOILET, THE—LeRoi Jones (a.k.a. Amiri Baraka)	64–65 ..	Dec. 16, 1964 ..	151
TOMORROW AND TOMORROW—Philip Barry	30–31 ..	Jan. 13, 1931 ..	206
TOMORROW THE WORLD—James Gow, Arnaud d'Usseau	42–43 ..	Apr. 14, 1943 ..	500
TORCH SONG TRILOGY—Harvey Fierstein (*The International*			
Stud, Fugue in a Nursery, Widows and Children First)	81–82 ..	Jan. 15, 1982 ..	117
	82–83 ..	June 10, 1982 ..	1,222
TOUCH OF THE POET, A—Eugene O'Neill	58–59 ..	Oct. 2, 1958 ..	284
TOVARICH—Jacques Deval, (tr) Robert E. Sherwood	36–37 ..	Oct. 15, 1936 ..	356
TOYS IN THE ATTIC—Lillian Hellman	59–60 ..	Feb. 25, 1960 ..	556
TRACERS—John DiFusco (c); Vincent Caristi, Richard			
Chaves, John DiFusco, Eric E. Emerson, Rick Gallavan,			
Merlin Marston, Harry Stephens with Sheldon Lettich	84–85 ..	Jan. 21, 1985 ..	186
TRAGEDIE DE CARMEN, LA—(see *La Tragédie de Carmen*)			
TRANSLATIONS—Brian Friel	80–81 ..	Apr. 7, 1981 ..	48
TRAVESTIES—Tom Stoppard	75–76 ..	Oct. 30, 1975 ..	155
TRELAWNY OF THE WELLS—Arthur Wing Pinero	94–99 ..	Nov. 22, 1898 ..	131
TRIAL OF THE CATONSVILLE NINE, THE—Daniel Berrigan,			
Saul Levitt	70–71 ..	Feb. 7, 1971 ..	159
TRIBUTE—Bernard Slade	77–78 ..	June 1, 1978 ..	212
TUNA CHRISTMAS, A—Jaston Williams, Joe Sears, Ed			
Howard	94–95 ..	Dec. 15, 1994 ..	20
TWILIGHT: LOS ANGELES, 1992—Anna Deavere Smith	93–94 ..	Mar. 23, 1994 ..	13
	93–94 ..	Apr. 17, 1994 ..	72
TWO BLIND MICE—Samuel Spewack	48–49 ..	Mar. 2, 1949 ..	157

PLAY	VOLUME	OPENED	PERFS
WINGS—Arthur L. Kopit	78–79	June 21, 1978	15
	78–79	Jan. 28, 1979	113
WINGS—(b, l) Arthur Perlman, (m) Jeffrey Lunden, based on the play by Arthur L. Kopit	92–93	Mar. 9, 1993	47
WINGS OVER EUROPE—Robert Nichols, Maurice Browne	28–29	Dec. 10, 1928	90
WINSLOW BOY, THE—Terence Rattigan	47–48	Oct. 29, 1947	215
WINTER SOLDIERS—Daniel Lewis James	42–43	Nov. 29, 1942	25
WINTERSET—Maxwell Anderson	35–36	Sept. 25, 1935	195
WISDOM TOOTH, THE—Marc Connelly	25–26	Feb. 15, 1926	160
WISTERIA TREES, THE—Joshua Logan, based on Anton Chekhov's *The Cherry Orchard*	49–50	Mar. 29, 1950	165
WITCHING HOUR, THE—Augustus Thomas	99–09	Nov. 18, 1907	212
WITNESS FOR THE PROSECUTION—Agatha Christie	54–55	Dec. 16, 1954	645
WOMEN, THE—Clare Boothe	36–37	Dec. 26, 1936	657
WONDERFUL TOWN—(b) Joseph Fields, Jerome Chodorov, based on their play *My Sister Eileen* and Ruth McKenney's stories, (l) Betty Comden, Adolph Green, (m) Leonard Bernstein	52–53	Feb. 25, 1953	559
WORLD WE MAKE, THE—Sidney Kingsley, based on Millen Brand's novel *The Outward Room*	39–40	Nov. 20, 1939	80
YEARS AGO—Ruth Gordon	46–47	Dec. 3, 1946	206
YES, MY DARLING DAUGHTER—Mark Reed	36–37	Feb. 9, 1937	405
YOU AND I—Philip Barry	22–23	Feb. 19, 1923	178
YOU CAN'T TAKE IT WITH YOU—Moss Hart, George S. Kaufman	36–37	Dec. 14, 1936	837
YOU KNOW I CAN'T HEAR YOU WHEN THE WATER'S RUNNING—Robert Anderson	66–67	Mar. 13, 1967	755
YOUNG MAN FROM ATLANTA, THE—Horton Foote	94–95	Jan. 27, 1995	24
YOUNG WOODLEY—John van Druten	25–26	Nov. 2, 1925	260
YOUNGEST, THE—Philip Barry	24–25	Dec. 22, 1924	104
YOUR OWN THING—(b) Donald Driver, (m, l) Hal Hester and Danny Apolinar, suggested by William Shakespeare's *Twelfth Night*	67–68	Jan. 13, 1968	933
YOU'RE A GOOD MAN CHARLIE BROWN—(b, m, l) Clark Gesner, based on the comic strip *Peanuts* by Charles M. Schulz	66–67	Mar. 7, 1967	1,597
ZOOMAN AND THE SIGN—Charles Fuller	80–81	Dec. 7, 1980	33

INDEX

INDEX

Play titles appear in **bold face.** *Bold face italic* page numbers refer to those pages where cast and credit listings may be found.

447